Movement in Early Childhood and Primary Education

Robert P. Pangrazi

Arizona State University
Tempe, Arizona

Victor P. Dauer

Washington State University
Pullman, Washington

Macmillan Publishing Company
New York
Collier Macmillan Publishers
London

Cover design: Cherie Wyman, Wyman Graphics

Copyright © 1981 by Macmillan Publishing Company,
    a division of Macmillan Inc.
Printed in the United States of America
Library of Congress Catalog Number 80-69535
ISBN 0-02-390673-1

Macmillan Publishing Company
866 Third Avenue
New York, N.Y. 10022
Collier Macmillan Canada, Inc.

Printing   5 6 7 8   Year   7 8 9 0

Table of Contents

Preface

Young children are beginning to receive the attention they have long deserved. Many educators are placing emphasis on the physical development of youngsters, and universities and colleges are offering courses designed to train teachers of preschool and primary grade children.

If children do not receive instruction and help to reach their physical potential during the preschool years, it may be too late. The authors have often found that the physical development of youngsters has been totally ignored in preschool. We hope this text will help remedy this serious omission.

The purpose of this book is to aid professionals and lay people who work with and teach young children. For institutions in which professional preparation classes for elementary physical education majors are split into two sections—one for teaching intermediate-age youngsters and another for teaching preschool children and the primary grades—this text should be of value in the latter section. It offers activities and ideas developed specifically for preschool and primary grade children, rather than a watered-down elementary school program. It can be used for practicum classes, in which college students work in preschools under the guidance of a professor or master teacher. It is also suitable for courses at the graduate level.

The text can also be used by parents to foster the physical growth and development of their children. It is practical and easy to interpret. Many preschools could use this book as a curriculum guide for teachers who have not been through teacher-training institutions or who need an easy-to-read guide that describes functional activities.

The activities presented here are grouped by age and grade. This classification is for the convenience of teachers. Since youngsters mature at widely varying rates, the grouping of activities should serve as a guide and starting point rather than as a fixed program. The activities are presented in a progression based on their degree of difficulty. Youngsters need to be taught with a sequence of activity that builds on success. Teachers can start them according to their maturity and progress to more demanding and complex skills. The activities described here have been field tested by the authors in an attempt to analyze how children learn. No activity has been included without the benefit of "action research."

We have emphasized a broad approach to physical development, as young children need exposure to many skills and movement patterns. A large amount of material in the text deals with motor learning, guiding the learning process, and organizing for effective teaching, so that activities can be taught in a meaningful and educationally sound manner. Programs should offer a wide range of activities, to enable all youngsters a chance to find success and meaning in activity.

One area of concern for teachers is students with special needs. An in-depth chapter about this population has been included, out of the conviction that these children have been largely ignored in many preschool and primary school programs. Emphasis is given to developing a learning environment that will enhance the motor skills and physical health of children with special needs. Instructional strategies for dealing with a wide range of handicaps and impairments are included.

Other curriculum areas covered here include aquatics and perceptual-motor activities. Relaxation activities are discussed, so that children can be taught to deal with this important phase of healthful living.

The focus of the curricular approach is the child. Many strategies are offered to personalize and individualize children's experiences. The authors firmly believe that teachers should guide and encourage children through learning experiences. Much material is offered on the importance of play and creative approaches in learning motor skills. Chapters on creative play, developing creative play environments, and play and learning are offered to convince teachers of the importance of this approach.

Fitness activities must be included in a preschool or primary school program. It is becoming increasingly evident that children do not become fit on their own. Patterns of activity must be established at an early age, or else patterns of inactivity will develop—sitting in front of a television, being entertained by others, and moving as little as possible. Teachers and parents should instill positive attitudes toward activity and an understanding of its effects on fitness. The text offers a wide range of activities, designed specifically for young children, that encourage the teacher to focus on the joy of movement for the sake of fitness and health.

In addition, young children learn through movement, and many concepts can be clearly illustrated with physical activities. A chapter on movement themes concentrates on the exploration of concepts through physical activity. The basis of movement themes is divergent movement, which emphasizes experimentation, repetition, and creativity while pointing toward the refinement of selected movement patterns.

Credits for many of the drawings go to Dr. Julia Kiyoguchi and the staff artists at Burgess Publishing Company. Special acknowledgement is due to Wayne Schotanus, for his constant encouragement and interest in this project. The authors are indebted to many teachers and children for allowing them to learn from and about them.

Robert P. Pangrazi
Victor P. Dauer

Chapter 1

Directions and Influences

Whatever you cannot understand, you cannot possess.
Johann Wolfgang von Goethe

The directions taken by the newer approaches in physical education have been determined by cultural forces in society, and current philosophy of education, as well as by forces from within physical education itself. The goals of general education and physical education, however, are the same: (1) the greatest possible development of each person as an individual and (2) the effective preparation of the individual to participate as a responsible citizen in our democratic society. The emphasis rests on the development of the whole person, physically, intellectually, morally, and emotionally. Since physical education can make significant contributions to the goals of education through the medium of movement experiences, it has achieved general acceptance as a full partner in the educational picture for youngsters. This is true in particular for young children, since movement is centrally important in their living and learning. An educationally sound physical education program not only must be a part of overall elementary programs, but also must function as an important element of preschool and nursery school developmental schema.

Movement is a very personal experience for a child. It can help the child to think, to understand, and to use ideas. With guidance, movement experiences can be channeled to make contributions to the child's total development. This is the mission of physical education. While physical education should not be regarded as a substitute for learning, it has excellent educational potential, which should be put to use to serve the child's best interests.

WHAT IS PHYSICAL EDUCATION?

Physical education may be defined as learning to move, moving to learn, and learning above movement. There should be balance among these directions. There has been a tendency in some preschool and nursery school programs to concentrate rather heavily on cognitive and affective (humanistic) learning, while neglecting the development of reasonable competence in movement. Such development can begin with the child's own spontaneous play. While such play is a necessary ingredient in the young child's life, however, there must also be directed play if there is to be learning.

Some programs have overemphasized movement exploration (in which children show how many different ways they can move). While movement exploration is an important part of movement education, it is also necessary to direct or guide the child toward a target goal, so that this exploration may move into experimentation. The element of quality in movement—performing the skill better, improving the skill pattern, or making a choice as to which movement patterns are the most desirable—must enter the picture if there is to be optimum learning.

An examination of various definitions of movement education in the professional literature will lead one to conclude that the term is nearly synonymous with physical education. Certainly, the present-day physical education program, to be sound educationally, must embrace the concepts of movement education. In some programs, this emphasis on movement has caused a corresponding swing away from physical fitness goals, because of the mistaken idea that fitness development demands the command type of presentation (teacher-dominated instruction) and is therefore unrealistic for young children. This is probably a good illustration of "throwing out the baby with the bath water." Fitness goals over the years have remained unchanged, irrespective of the movement approach. Every child has the right, *within his or her maturity level and according to individual characteristics*, to possess a sturdy, strong, and well-proportioned body that provides health, vigor, and vitality for full living. Physical education must furnish the leadership to give proper attention to the physical welfare of children by providing appropriate movement experiences that stimulate and develop pertinent physical fitness qualities. From a cognitive viewpoint, a beginning should be made with young children to provide them with the incentive and knowledge to accept responsibility for their own physical fitness and to continue this physical care throughout life. It is postulated that an active child is more likely to be an active adult. A caution: if physical education does not provide the child with the experiences and the incentive to develop physically, no other area in the school curriculum will compensate to make up for the child's loss of physical development.

Important, too, are fundamental skills and perceptual-motor competencies, which may have a bearing on academic progress in the lower grades. Studies by Kephart[1] and others have revealed that these competencies are of importance for young children, particularly with respect to their reading readiness and achievement. It is reasoned that as children learn to move effectively, handle their bodies in a variety of situations and in response to various challenges, and react favorably to their physical environment, they develop a competency base upon which academic learning can develop effectively.

MOVEMENT AND COGNITIVE DEVELOPMENT

Movement can contribute to and help cognitive development in several areas. A proliferation of learning games, movement activities, and movement-related learning procedures have appeared in the literature relating to cognitive development. The danger is that needed development of coordination, movement competence, and consideration of individual physical traits are given less attention when teachers zero in heavily on cognitive target behaviors. A

quality program, then, will consider both psychomotor and cognitive development. On the other side of the coin, when movement competence is the goal, allied cognitive development should also be encouraged. For these reasons, a balanced program will best meet the needs of the child's total development.

There is a reciprocal relationship between the fields of music and physical education. Many movement activities rely on rhythm to provide a learning base and give breadth to the movement sequences. The theme of these activities is moving to rhythm.

Certain music education approaches feature the learning of music and rhythm fundamentals through movement. Movement is an important ingredient of the music education systems of (1) the Orff-Schulwerk approach, which stresses teaching music with the help of creative rhythm; and (2) the methods of Kodaly and others, who weave reproduction and sequencing of physical rhythms into the music learning patterns.

EARLY CHILDHOOD EDUCATION

Early childhood education, as defined in this discussion, takes place in the nursery school and the kindergarten. Roughly, the kindergarten includes those children who are one year away from entering the first grade, and the nursery school is designed for prekindergarten children (from about age three). Since the kindergarten was organized first, in historical terms, a discussion of its origin precedes that of the nursery school.

The Kindergarten

Contemporary European educational thinkers laid the philosophical basis for the kindergarten, which culminated in perhaps the first formalized preschool learning environment, established by Friedrich Froebel in the early nineteenth century. The word "kindergarten" literally means "garden of children," and suggests the idea that children, like garden plants, must be carefully nurtured.

Froebel stressed the value of play and sensory experience with objects as the basis of child learning. His principles included provision for self-expression, the development of personality, and social participation.

The kindergarten was adopted as part of the American educational system in the late 1800s, and by 1900 it was well established. In the United States, the kindergarten generally enrolls children at about five years of age, who

[1]Newell C. Kephart, *The Slow Learner in the Classroom* (Columbus, Ohio: Charles E. Merrill Co., 1960).

spend eight to ten months in a learning environment that precedes academic work (first grade). Most youngsters attend kindergarten for half a day.

Historically, experiences in the kindergarten were mostly sensory-social, and little attention was given to the development of fundamental motor skills or physical qualities, a concept which is now changing. Recognition of the importance of motor skills and coordination in preparing the child for academic work in the first grade has focused attention on traits that can be developed through movement programs.

Countless program variations appear in the kindergarten format, with teachers having great flexibility in their choice of what is to be taught. In recent years, certification of personnel has provided more teachers of at least minimum quality and increased the probability that the children will have a reasonable educational environment. Some kindergarten programs, responding to parental pressures, have begun teaching reading skills, and this remains a controversial practice today.

The Nursery School

The nursery school is of more recent origin than the kindergarten, with the first such school having been established in this country in about 1920. Nursery schools appear in a variety of forms and settings. They may be either public or private. They may be housed in schools, on college campuses, and in churches, homes, community buildings, and stores. Some are commercial; some are nonprofit.

The majority meet daily, and others meet on various days. Most have full-day programs, and others last one-half day. Licensing requirements vary among the states, with personnel requirements ranging from some certification to none. Increasingly, however, the burden to operate nursery school programs is being shifted to the public schools.

Many nursery programs are admittedly custodial in nature, with emphasis on safety, happy surroundings through play, and socialization with other children. Others attempt to foster some child development, encouraging fantasy play for sensory-motor and emotional growth. Through organized play, children have a chance to know themselves and their capabilities. Many of the physical experiences for children are carried out through vicarious and creative play. Much of the effectiveness of the nursery school depends upon the teacher and the social climate of the setting. In some nursery schools,

there has been a sharp swing toward cognitive-based elements, many of them developed around movement. Sociodramatic play (play-acting) is another activity that has received increased emphasis.

Project Head Start is a federally supported preschool program that is designed to help impoverished children by preparing them to cope with the challenges of entering kindergarten. The program resembles that of a nursery school, except that it has stricter guidelines of what is to be accomplished.

Children are encouraged to (1) adjust to rules necessary for group living, (2) develop responsiveness to new authority figures, and (3) achieve constructive social interaction through organized and free play. Also emphasized are preacademic skills, particularly simple speech skills. The success of these programs has varied from little or none to moderate in some learning areas, depending upon the program.

EVENTS, PEOPLE, AND MOVEMENTS THAT HAVE INFLUENCED PHYSICAL EDUCATION

That physical education has changed over the years is obvious. How and why these changes have occurred is not quite so apparent. An examination of the impact of selected individuals, educational ideas, and events on the field of physical education should provide a better understanding and appreciation of present-day physical education.

The Great Educators

The contribution of Froebel has been mentioned with respect to the establishment of the kindergarten. He did much to raise the concept of play to its present status as an important educational method.

In the early 1900s, John Dewey, noted American educator, proposed the revolutionary concept that the aim of education is to teach children to think—not what to think.[2] Physical educators did not integrate this concept into their programs until after the middle of the twentieth century.

Dewey's influence on physical education can also be seen in his Seven Cardinal Aims of Education, three of which are of particular relevance to physical education—citizenship, worthy use of leisure, and health. The aims provided status for physical education and gave it a permanent place in the education of children.

At about the same time, Marie Montessori, an Italian doctor of medicine and educator, became interested in adapting educational methods for

[2]John Dewey, *Democracy and Education* (New York: Macmillan Co., 1946).

treating mentally retarded children for use in a program for slum children in Rome. She was convinced that the critical period of learning for children occurred during the first six years of life, and that a prepared environment, together with an organized and coordinated set of materials, could promote significant learning experiences.

In motor education, freedom of movement was the key, with the children observing and interacting with one another. Motor activities were taught initially by precise demonstration, but the children were mostly on their own from this point, with subtle direction. Montessori believed that a sensory-motor base was the foundation of all motor learning. She also stressed sensory education and language training, including visual, tactile, and auditory sense education. After the initial developmental period, the child's attention was turned to academic pursuits—reading, writing, and arithmetic. In contrast to the usual nursery school program, social games and dramatic play were not originally part of the Montessori program.[3]

Because of the definitive nature of the program, successful execution of the Montessori type of nursery school curriculum required specially trained personnel. Montessori-based schools are still in vogue in various parts of the United States, and are usually operated on a private basis.

Much of what we know and believe today about cognitive development can be attributed to the work of Jean Piaget, a Swiss epistemologist. He began with studies of his own children and gradually extended his efforts to others. His developmental theory created some interest in the United States during the years around 1930, but it was not until the 1950s that his viewpoints made a significant impact on American education.

Piaget divided normal cognitive development into four stages, with the child proceeding from one stage to the next when predisposing factors are favorable. His theory is too voluminous to give adequate coverage here. It is related to movement education in that it stresses the importance of perceptual-motor maturity as a prerequisite to orderly cognitive functioning. While his views on play and motor development have met some criticism in physical education circles, his model of the developmental levels of cognitive growth provides a basis for understanding how children learn.[4]

Jean Piaget's approach to learning is one of the most thought-provoking and influential theories related to the cognitive development of children. It directs careful attention to active, discovery-oriented learning experiences, preparing the child for logical causal thinking. His sequence of cognitive developmental acquisition provides useful guidelines for physical education programs.

The Didactic Approach—Games, Health, Social Integration, and Skill Competency

From about 1900 through the 1950s, physical education could well be described by the question: "What games are we going to play today?" Lip service was given to the development of skills; since skills were needed to play games well, it was agreed that they should be taught. But it was much easier just to choose up sides and play.

The health goal directed that some attempt be made to develop physical fitness, which was primarily attuned to strength development. All students got the same dosage, mostly exercises.

A basic premise of social development was that children developed desirable social qualities in the give-and-take of the game situation. Relays, some stunts and tumbling, and a few dances were supposed to provide a "rounded" program. By playing games, one was thought to develop significant social attitudes and a variety of activities for worthy use of leisure.

During the Depression of the 1930s, physical education for children was practically eliminated for economic reasons, suffering a blow from which it has recovered with difficulty.

The Idea of Physical Fitness

Physical fitness had always been an important stated goal for children. In 1954, however, studies appeared that jolted educators, focusing their attention on demonstrated physical deficiencies in American children. The work of Dr. Hans Kraus, a Doctor of Physical Medicine, revealed disturbing fitness deficiencies in American children as compared with their European counterparts.[5] The figures, which included primary children, were supported by those of other investigators.

Fitness-oriented programs soon appeared in various parts of the country in large numbers, some lacking scientific validation and others lacking in common sense. As wiser heads pre-

---

[3]R. C. Orem, *Montessori, Her Method and the Movement* (New York: G. P. Putnam's Sons, 1974).

[4]Hans G. Furth, *Piaget for Teachers* (Englewood Cliffs, N.J.: Prentice-Hall, 1970).

[5]Hans Kraus and Ruth P. Hirschland, "Minimum Muscular Fitness Tests in School Children," *Research Quarterly of the American Association for Health and Physical Education* 25(2) (1954): 178.

vailed, the programs were modified toward more educationally sound approaches, which did develop physical fitness.

In 1954, President Eisenhower set up the President's Council for Physical Fitness, which was expanded later on to include sports and renamed the President's Council for Physical Fitness and Sports. The Council acts as a stabilizing influence, disseminating information and sponsoring clinics in various parts of the country. Unfortunately for preschool and primary children, however, most of the emphasis was originally on older children. The Council now gives more attention to the needs of younger children.

When American movement education programs began to develop in the 1960s, the pendulum started to swing away from fitness development. Educators felt that fitness activities, which featured the command approach, were unsuitable activities for children. The authors have always taken a different position, however, believing that physical fitness activities as well as movement education programs can be successfully integrated into a program that meets the needs of the whole child.

Movement Education—1960 to the Present

Movement education brought a fresh new approach, a new methodology, and a new way of providing learning experiences for children. With its emphasis on the needs of the individual child, it features the task, problem-solving, and exploratory styles of teaching.

Movement education, which had its origins in England after World War II, reached this country either directly or through Canadian programs. At present it is an indispensable and fully accepted part of American physical education. Movement education centers on the indirect method of teaching as opposed to the direct (command) approach. In practice, the degree to which indirect teaching is employed varies, giving rise to many choices of methodology.

The basis of movement education may be seen in the work of Rudolph Laban, an Austrian, who emigrated to England in the 1930s. His concepts of space, time, effort (force), and flow have given new meaning and definition to the study of human movement. These concepts have provided physical education with themes for development and a means of broadening the movement experiences of children.

Perceptual-Motor Competency—1960 to the Present

The theories of Montessori, Luria, Piaget, and others helped educators recognize the importance of motor experiences in the normal learning process of children. In the 1960s, Delacato and Kephart were among the leaders in developing a practical school approach based on the theory that children deficient in certain competencies could be helped with a structured perceptual-motor program, so they might perform better in academic pursuits.

Perceptual-motor theory holds that each child normally must pass successively through several stages of neuromuscular development during childhood. If one or more of these stages is omitted or underdeveloped, then the child will have trouble with appropriate motor responses, which can cause difficulty in normal academic progress, specifically with reading, speech, spelling, and writing. The theory holds that a program of selected perceptual-motor activities can help develop the missed stages, thus providing a better basis for normal academic achievement.

While perceptual-motor programs appear to help children with motor problems, there is no evidence that these programs help children without problems or those with high academic ability. If a well-balanced program of physical education gives proper attention to the development of visual-tactile coordination, the teaching of perceptual skills, and physical fitness, perceptual-motor programs should be reserved for children with demonstrated motor problems. Further discussion of perceptual-motor competency and programs is found in Chapter 18, pp. 287–99.

The American Medical Association

The American Medical Association has consistently reaffirmed its support for regular physical programs for all students. In 1960 the Association adopted this resolution:

Resolved: That the American Medical Association through its various divisions and departments and its constituent and component medical societies do everything feasible to encourage effective instruction in physical education for all students in our schools and colleges.[6]

This proposal was reaffirmed without change in 1969. It is in effect at this writing.

[6]American Medical Association, *Proceedings. 1960 Annual Convention* (Chicago: American Medical Association, 1960).

The Athletic Emphasis

Americans place strong emphasis on the importance of the nation's sports programs, and this has contributed to what many educators feel is an unsound trend for children. Sports programs are being designed for younger and younger children, to the point that even some three- and four-year-olds are participating in competitive athletics.

There is serious question as to whether the youngsters can handle the social and emotional pressures accompanying such competition. Although programs of interschool athletic competition for kindergarten and primary children sponsored by schools are practically nonexistent, a number of privately sponsored programs exist, organized by national groups or parents. Preparation, coaching, and the handling of young children in these programs are usually under the direction of well-meaning, if, in many cases, untrained persons.

Critics of these programs urge that parents should let children be children and not rob them of their childhood. There is no evidence that the "start-'em-early" approach produces a more highly skilled athlete. On the contrary, there is evidence to show that some youngsters drop out of secondary school sports and physical education programs because they have had negative experiences at a young age. The problem is difficult to solve, and involves the schools, because these groups seek the use of school facilities.

Public Law 94-142

A significant piece of federal legislation, Public Law 94-142 is designed to end the practice of treating persons with disabilities as second-class citizens. It mandates and provides funds so that all handicapped children will be given educational opportunities according to their needs. This process, known as "mainstreaming," will see many handicapped children participating in regular classes with nonhandicapped children.

The law also calls for making what is now termed "preschool" education a standard part of services for the handicapped, providing free public education to all handicapped children, starting at age three. Resources will be provided to help implement this program.

The law is a follow-up to Public Law 93-390, which provides that every handicapped youngster who requires "special education and related services" shall have them. The impact of these laws will be tremendous. The challenge to physical educators to provide appropriate remedial services is almost overwhelming.

One can visualize important changes in kindergarten and elementary physical education programs to include handicapped children within the normal pattern of class activity. It is not clear at this time, however, how the needs of younger handicapped children (ages three to five) are to be met. This poses important challenges to nursery school educators with respect to how the provisions of the law can be implemented for the young handicapped child.

SUMMARY

Physical education is learning to move and moving to learn. There should be a balance in the program to include movement exploration, physical fitness, fundamental motor skills, and perceptual-motor competencies. *Physical education* and *movement education* are used interchangeably to describe a total, balanced program of movement experiences.

The area of physical education for children has been influenced by many events that have changed the direction and focus of the profession. For example, the Kraus-Weber testing of children led to the formation of the President's Council on Physical Fitness which led, in turn, to a heavy emphasis on fitness in public school programs. In the 1960s, the importance of motor experiences in the normal learning process of children was emphasized. Delecato and Kephart were leaders in developing a practical school approach based on the theory that a structured perceptual-motor program could help children deficient in certain competencies to perform better academically.

Public Law 94-142 mandates funds to allow handicapped children educational opportunities based on their needs. It is increasing the practice of "mainstreaming," which offers handicapped children the opportunity to participate in physical education classes with nonhandicapped children.

ADDITIONAL REFERENCES

American Association for Health, Physical Education, Recreation, and Dance. *Desirable Athletic Competition for Children of Elementary School Age.* Reston, Va.: AAHPERD, 1970.

Bilbrough, A., and Jones, P., *Physical Education in the Primary School.* London: University of London Press, 1966.

Bloom, Benjamin S., ed. *Taxonomy of Educational Objectives: Cognitive Domain.* New York: David McKay Co., 1963.

Clein, Marvin I., and Stone, William J. "Physical Education and the Classification of Educa-

tional Objectives: Psychomotor Domain."
Physical Educator 27 (1970): 34–35.

Furth, Hans G., and Wachs, Harry. *Thinking Goes to School: Piaget's Theory in Practice.* New York: Oxford University Press, 1974.

Krathwohl, David R., Bloom, Benjamin S., and Masia, Bertram B. *Taxonomy of Educational Objectives: Affective Domain.* New York: David McKay Co., 1968.

Orlick, Terry, and Botterill, Cal. *Every Kid Can Win.* Chicago: Nelson Hall, 1975.

Tanner, Patricia, and Barrett, Kate. "Movement Education: What Does It Mean?" *Journal of Health, Physical Education and Recreation* 46 (1975): 4–19.

Tutko, Thomas, and Bruns, William. *Winning Is Everything and Other American Myths.* New York: Macmillan Co., 1976.

Chapter 2

The Basis of Movement for Children

Movement is a vital element in the development and growth of young children. It is apparent that a sound program of movement and physical activity can have long-term effects on children, enhancing their health and fitness in later years. It is necessary to insure that each child experiences an adequate amount of quality movement in order to derive such lasting benefits. To understand why such a program is important, let us examine the impact of exercise on the child's growth.

PHYSIOLOGICAL EFFECTS OF MOVEMENT

A cardiologist from California State University, Dr. Boyer, has demonstrated the importance of exercise at a young age as a factor in preventing the onset of coronary heart disease. In a study[1] conducted throughout public schools in Iowa, more than 5,000 children between the ages of six and eighteen were examined over a two-year period. Of these children, 70 percent showed some evidence of coronary heart disease, 7 percent had extremely high cholesterol levels, a large percentage had developed hypertension and high blood pressure, and at least 12 percent were overweight by at least 20 percent. It is apparent that these children needed exercise.

Any change in a child's life style must be made rather early in life in order for it to have significant effects on physical development. Studies have shown that dietary and exercise patterns are relatively easy to change prior to the child's eighth birthday, but become increasingly difficult to change as the child grows older. In a study of the developmental history of arteriosclerotic disease in man, Dr. Kenneth Rose of the University of Nebraska notes: "The first signs appear around age two, and the disease process is reversible until the age of 19. At about 19, the process of the disease becomes essentially irreversible, and from then on, it inexorably progresses until it becomes clinically manifest, usually in the 40's."[2]

Dr. John Kimball, a noted cardiologist from the University of Colorado, has stated: "Evidence is growing stronger that the earliest bodily changes leading to heart disease begin early in life."[3] He points out that more and more autopsy reports on children show that blood vessels have already begun to clog with fatty deposits that can eventually lead to cardiac difficulty. It is apparent that a child cannot be encouraged to start exercising too early in life. In fact, if a child is born into a family that shows a predisposition to heart disease, his salvation may be a carefully controlled diet coupled with exercise and movement.

At this point, it might be well to address the question, "Can a child's heart be damaged by too much or too vigorous activity?" Evidence to date shows that a healthy heart cannot be damaged in this manner. This does not mean that a child is capable of the same physical work load as an adult; however, it does mean that a child can withstand a work load similar to an adult's when it is adjusted for the child's size (height and weight). Probably, in most cases, teachers and parents have expected too little of children

---

[1]Walter Glass, "Coronary Heart Disease Proves Vitally Interesting," *California Association for Health, Physical Education and Recreation Journal*, May/June 1973, p. 7.

[2]Kenneth Rose, "To Keep the People in Health," *Journal of the American College Health Association* 22 (1973): 80.

[3]J. G. Albinson and G. M. Andrews, eds., *Child in Sport and Physical Activity* (Baltimore, Md.: University Park Press, 1976), p. 83.

for fear overactivity might permanently injure them. Physical educators involved in programs with young children are of the opinion that the capacities of children have consistently been underestimated; consequently, they have not been challenged to reach their own highest levels of development. By gradually increasing the physical demands placed on children, researchers have found that youngsters are capable of high output and outstanding physical performance.

Activity has an effect on skeletal growth as well. Vigorous activity can bring about a change in the honeycomb structure at the ends of the bones, increasing their resistance to tension and pressure. The bones also show an increase in diameter and in mineralization in response to activity. Inactivity for prolonged periods brings about demineralization of the bones, rendering them more susceptible to fractures.

Stronger bones are a response to an increase in musculature and increased strength. Muscles respond to overload and stress by increasing in strength, while bones respond to the increased work load the muscles are applying to them. Thus, the work load a child is asked to assume must be gradually increased in order to develop the child's strength.

How important is strength in enhancing motor development patterns in children? In a study by Rarick and Dobbins,[4] the investigators attempted to identify and rank in order of importance the factors that contribute to motor development in young children. The factor identified as being most important was strength and/or power in relationship to body size. From this study it was found that those youngsters who demonstrated high levels of strength in relationship to body size were more capable of performing motor skills. It appears that movement and activity designed to place demands on the child must do two things: (1) the activity must place an overload on the child's cardiovascular system, and (2) it must develop the child's strength through increasing the work load on the musculature. The earlier a child is involved in a program of such activity, the earlier he or she may be able to begin reaping the benefits of a healthy and vigorous life.

The second and third most important factors identified in this study were gross limb-eye coordination and fine visual-motor coordination.

Large and varied amounts of activity are necessary to ensure the child enough opportunity to develop and practice activities requiring coordination. Two factors that aid in the development of coordination are: (1) large play spaces and many opportunities to take part in gross motor activities such as skipping, running, and hopping; and (2) ample chances to practice fine visual-motor activities with a minimum of corrective advice. In other words, the child must be able to practice and fail and perform this cycle an unrestricted number of times without embarrassment and fear of failure.

Dead weight, or obesity, was found to be the fourth most important factor affecting motor performance in children, and it is a hindering or negative factor. Obesity is a condition characterized by excessive bodily fat. Clearly, obesity will have a restrictive influence on motor performance in young children. In many obese people, there is a tendency toward decreased muscular activity, and it appears that, as weight increases, the desire for physical exertion seems to decrease. Thus, as the child grows more obese, he or she will become locked into a difficult cycle that he or she may feel unable to control.

Interestingly enough, movement and/or activity may be the crucial factor in weight control. When one compares the food intake of obese and nonobese children, one finds that there is usually no substantial difference in their caloric consumption. In fact, in some cases, the obese and very heavy consumed less than children of normal weight. In a study of high school age girls, it was found that girls who were obese ate less, but also exercised two-thirds less (in total time) than girls of normal weight. In the same study, an examination of children in an elementary school in Massachusetts showed that they gained more weight in winter when they were less active.[5] In studies of children in a summer camp situation, movies taken of normal and overweight children demonstrated a wide difference in the activity levels of the two groups.[6] In volleyball and tennis, for example, lean youngsters tend to be in motion constantly; overweight children may be motionless much of the time.

We have often been told that we should not worry about excessive weight: that it will come off as the child matures. In fact, the opposite is

[4]Lawrence G. Rarick and D. Alan Dobbins, "Basic Components in the Motor Performances of Children Six to Nine Years of Age," *Medicine and Science in Sports* 7(2) (1975): 2.

[5]Mary L. Johnson, Bertha S. Burke, and Jean Mayer, "The Prevalence and Incidence of Obesity in a Cross Section of Elementary and Secondary School Children, *American Journal of Clinical Nutrition* 4 (1956): 231.

[6]Charles B. Corbin and Philip Fletcher, "Diet and Physical Activity Patterns of Obese and Non-obese Elementary School Children" *Research Quarterly* 39 (1968): 922.

usually true: the fat stays and continues to accumulate into adulthood, at which point it is difficult to lose. An overweight individual not only pays a tremendous psychological price for being overweight (as will be discussed later in this chapter), but is also threatened by increased risk of disease and premature death. Many experts now believe that there are two critical periods during which fat cells multiply. One is during the span of the third trimester of pregnancy through the fourth month of life, and the other is during preadolescence. Certainly, if fat cells multiply during these times, the result may be an increased tendency toward obesity. The primary way to prevent the multiplication of fat cells is to keep the child from gaining excess weight at any stage of growth and development.

It appears that childhood obesity must be challenged at an early age, and this challenge must come in the form of increased movement and activity. Children must be made aware of their activity levels. That is, obese children are aware that they are inactive, but have no conception of their degree of inactivity. The primary challenge for people who deal with children having weight problems is to increase their awareness of personal activity habits and encourage them to choose more demanding activity patterns.

A learning environment that offers a wide variety of movement and activity for the young child is crucial from another point of view. In one study, eight- and nine-year-old children were interviewed about their interests. It was found that these children had selected and made decisions about the sport and physical activities in which they were willing to participate that were based upon their present competencies.[7] If a child has had a successful and positive experience in some motor skill activity, he or she probably will feel competent and want to participate in the activity in the future. However, the reverse was also true; if a child's experiences proved unsuccessful, there was a tendency to avoid the activity in the future. Another study showed that 78 percent of all hobby interests are established before the age of twelve, and many are developed before the age of eight.[8]

A child's competence may be limited by the muscle fiber type predominant in his or her body. Muscle tissue is made up of two different types of fibers: slow-twitch fibers, which contract at a relatively slow rate, and fast-twitch fibers, which have a faster contraction rate. While most individuals possess about as much of one type as of the other, this composition can vary widely, with some individuals having as much as 80 percent fast- or slow-twitch fibers. The percentage of slow- to fast-twitch fibers may represent a biological limitation, depending on the activity selected for participation. For example, slow-twitch fibers are best suited for endurance-type activities, such as distance running; fast-twitch fibers tend to be beneficial for activities requiring speed and power, such as sprinting, basketball, and football.

A child should be allowed to discover his or her own competencies through trial and error. This experimentation must take place in a nonthreatening atmosphere where many choices are encouraged. In this type of environment, the child can find and take part in activities that are suited to his or her biological endowment.

If a child waits until he is older to try an activity, certain obstacles can appear in the path to success. The emphasis put on instant success is much greater for older children; in addition, older children are much less tolerant of each other's failures. As older children become more involved in outside interests, they find less and less time available to practice an activity to the point of overlearning, which is so necessary to establish skill patterns. It is probable that the earlier a child can participate in a wide variety of activities, the better chance he or she has of making a choice that will allow a minimum of social, emotional, and physical restrictions.

Before leaving the physiological effects of activity and movement, it might be of interest to examine the question of long-term effects. A well-known researcher, Dr. Saltin, carried out a study to see if any of the benefits of childhood activity carried over into adult life.[9] He compared the adjustability to effort of three groups of subjects in the age group 50 to 59 years. One group consisted of former athletes who had not participated in activity for over 20 years and worked at sedentary jobs. The second group consisted of former athletes who had kept up their regular training during adult years, and the third group consisted of individuals who were nonathletes during their youthful years and inactive as adults. As might be expected, he

---

[7]T. D. Orlick, "Children's Sports—A Revolution Is Coming," *Journal of the Canadian Association of Health, Physical Education and Recreation* 39 (1970).

[8]American Association for Health, Physical Eduction, Recreation, and Dance, *Children in Focus* (Washington, D.C.: AAHPERD, 1954), p. 66.

[9]B. Saltin and G. Grimby, "Physiological Analysis of Middle-aged and Old Former Athletes: Comparison with Still Active Athletes of the Same Ages," *Circulation* 38 (1968): 1104.

found the nonathlete group capable of the least adaptability to effort. The individuals who were active during their youth, yet were presently involved only in sedentary activities, scored significantly higher than the nonathletes. Of course, the group that had maintained training scored a great deal higher than the other two groups. The conclusion was that, generally speaking, functional capacity as an adult appeared to be partially a function of activity during the growing years. The need for activity and movement in the formative years of life appears to be obvious.

SOCIAL AND EMOTIONAL EFFECTS OF MOVEMENT

It is relevant to examine the beneficial effects of activity and movement on the social and emotional life of the child. One should not assume that these benefits will automatically occur as a result of activity, however, regardless of teacher involvement. Whenever social and emotional benefits are claimed for any area of the school curriculum, it should be understood that the teacher is the crucial variable. As will be discussed in the following paragraphs, self-concepts can be built and made stronger, values clarified, and feelings expressed, to an extent that depends on the environment established by the teacher.

The self-concept is usually learned. Youngsters learn who they are and what their capabilities are from the ways in which they have been treated by those around them while they are growing up. The child's self-concept is affected by the kinds of experiences he has had in life. Children develop feelings that they are liked, wanted, acceptable, and able from having had experiences in which they are liked, wanted, accepted, and successful. Certainly, a goal of teachers of young children should be to assure them many positive experiences.

Children sometimes enter a failure cycle, in which there is little opportunity for them to change and break the cycle. Let us imagine that a child's performance in the area of stunts and tumbling has been inadequate. This youngster is physically healthy and, in the teacher's eyes, is capable of much more progress. Because of his past experiences, the child believes that he cannot do a forward roll; because he doesn't try it, he doesn't get any practice; because he does not practice, he continues to do poorly. Because of his inadequate performance, his peers will tease him; and the teacher may remark that the stunt was poorly done. All this will only prove what the youngster knew in the first place, and thus his self-concept is lowered. A negative comment

or poor grade may be sent home to his parents, and this documents and emphasizes the child's failure. To finish the cycle, the parents may express to the child their concern about his evident weakness in this area. The youngster soon finds himself convinced that he is incapable, and believes that stunts and tumbling activities are something to be avoided in order to protect his self-esteem.

The school-age child should be able to experiment with activities without having to compare his performance with that of others, and without feeling that he is in competition with others. This will help him develop a positive attitude toward movement and activity in general. The urge to create can be encouraged without the risk of his falling into a failure cycle. The teacher who values experimentation and challenges rather than task conformity will help develop attitudes and values in children that will aid them in future years.

Physical attractiveness and competence in motor activities are extremely important to young children. To be capable of meeting many physical challenges is to have a great deal of status in the eyes of one's peers. Some believe that physical ability is a major key to success in the early years of school. Imagine the humiliation felt by a child who is crippled, obese, or inept at motor skills, differing from the peer group's "norm" in almost any way. One needs little insight to sense the tremendous handicap such children endure daily. There is evidence to demonstrate that students who are physically fit are usually much better adjusted to the school situation. Children learn at a very early age that society pays off for physical attractiveness and ability.

Along the same lines, some research suggests that when two children do an equal amount of work and receive a grade for their efforts, the child who is the more attractive will receive a higher grade. In similar fashion, when two children carry out an act of deviant behavior of equal intensity, the child who is less attractive may be punished more severely. This is another example of the many payoffs available for the attractive and physically capable child.

Some educators feel that, as the school curriculum becomes filled with more and more required subjects, the child finds less time to relax and take part in physical activity. It is not uncommon to find only 40 to 60 minutes of the school week, or less, devoted to physical education. For a child of five or six who thrives on activity and movement, school must often seem like an environment where one must constantly live without moving his body. An important obligation teachers have is to provide adequate opportunity for children to move, explore with their bodies, and release their inner tensions. No other area of the school curriculum can meet the child's need or urge to move and be active. Time should also be allowed for relaxation activities to help the child learn to handle tension in a productive fashion.

In summary, it appears that for children to develop a positive self-concept and a warm regard for physical activity, they will need the support of adults and peers who can "reach out" in an atmosphere of understanding and love. The child must have the opportunity for trial and error without fear of failure hanging over his head. Success breeds more success.

MOTIVATING DRIVES OF CHILDREN

Motivating drives will vary somewhat among children, but for most they are important reasons for deriving enjoyment from each day. It is difficult to rank them in order of importance, and no attempt is made to do so here, as each child will evaluate and order them from a personal standpoint.

In selecting the purposes and content of the curriculum for children, their motivating drives, characteristics, interests, and needs should be given strong consideration.

The teacher of young children should consider all these factors, especially the motivating drives, and should provide opportunity to ensure that these drives are satisfied.

The Drive for Success and Approval

Young children not only delight in success and accomplishment, but they seek approval for its own sake. They are crushed and heartbroken by frequent criticism and disapproval, whereas encouragement and warm support promote growth and personal development. Certainly, no child will ever find an environment of positive support without having to absorb some criticism, but youngsters encounter enough negative feedback in the normal course of their lives; they do not need a teacher or other important adult to arrange additional failure for them. Failure over a long period of time can lead to frustration, lack of interest, and inefficient learning. This is especially true in the area of physical activity.

The Drive for Creative Satisfaction

The curriculum should offer children the opportunity to experiment with different ways of performing activities and a chance to work with different materials, while providing an environment in which children are rewarded for creative efforts. An authority in the area of creativity, E. P. Torrence, states that "creative imagination during early childhood seems to reach a peak between four and four-and-one-half years, and is followed by a drop at about age five when the child enters school for the first time." He believes there are indications that this drop appears to be manmade rather than a natural phenomenon.[10] In light of this fact, the teacher will do well to examine the environment and background of the child so that creativity might be stimulated within the school setting.

The Drive for Adventure

One of the best ways to maintain interest among young children is to possess a large repertoire of ideas for new and different activities. Children like to play with something unique or different, climb to new heights, and explore a new environment. Adults pay much money and risk life and limb to find and maintain some adventure in their lives. Certainly a comparable attempt should be made for children by rearranging play spaces, adding new and exciting pieces of equipment, and permitting them, in the spirit of adventure, to assume certain calculated risks.

The Drive to Explore

Children are motivated by the unknown. They love to explore, to find out where something is hidden, how something works, and how to put things together. Exploration takes time, and children must be encouraged to take that time. To let the child gain maximum benefits from exploratory behavior, an atmosphere must be created that allows the child to feel secure and capable of finding success. The child needs such a supportive environment in which he can make mistakes and adjust his goals, to think of new alternatives, and to imagine new possibilities.

The Drive to Move

Most children are constantly on the move and show little desire or inclination to sit still for extended periods of time. Activity is essential, as a large share of the child's learning takes place through physical means. Joy and pleasure in movement and physical performance are found in all youngsters. The program must allow ample opportunity for satisfying this drive.

---

[10]E. Paul Torrence, *Creativity* (Washington, D.C.: National Education Association of the United States, 1963), p. 10.

The Drive for Personal Accomplishment and Recognition

Children love to please adults and other interested bystanders. Successful physical expression is a tangible product for all to see and share. Coupled with the drive for physical accomplishment is the necessity of recognition for deeds performed. Children are constantly saying, "Look at me, see what I can do, watch me," and they need much adult approval if maximum participation is to be gained.

The Drive for Rhythmic Expression

All children love rhythmic activity. They will argue over who will play with the tom-tom first or who gets to crash the cymbals. At the sound of a marching band, children begin to march in place. The program should offer much in the way of physical activities to rhythm, including action songs, dances, finger plays, and assorted ditties. Polished performers know that most physical skills are rhythmic in nature; witness the fact that when a seasoned athlete does poorly, we say that he has "lost his rhythm." The program should offer a wide variety of rhythmic activities so that all children can find something that brings them satisfaction and joy.

The Drive for Individual Identity

Children are individuals; therefore, most of their activities should be organized on an individual basis. Although they begin to play in small groups from about age six to eight, complicated team games and relays are not suitable for children of this age group. The program should be organized so that allowance can be made for individual preferences and differences. Finally, each child should be made to feel important and worthwhile in the activity setting.

CHARACTERISTICS OF CHILDREN— PROGRAM IMPLICATIONS

The following tables include characteristics of youngsters at various age levels, grouped under the cognitive, affective, and psychomotor domains. Program needs and implications are suggested for each characteristic. The tables of characteristics of youngsters will offer important guidelines to educators who are developing a program and curriculum for children. If a proposed activity is not in line with the characteristics of children in a certain age group, the activity should be considered inappropriate or may be modified to better meet their needs.

Program implications can take the form of suggested movement experiences appropriate for the age group, pertinent approaches, and relevant instructional methodology.

THE OBJECTIVES OF PHYSICAL EDUCATION

The general and overriding goal of physical education, and, for that matter, all education, is the well-rounded development of children and youth as responsible, contributing citizens. In line with this goal, children should be able to acquire personal and educational values that will endure throughout life. Developing the

TABLE 1.   CHARACTERISTICS, INTERESTS, AND NEEDS—PRESCHOOL (NURSERY SCHOOL)

Characteristics	Program Needs and Implications
Cognitive Domain	
Is unable to sit still for more than a brief period.	Utilize movement experiences for learning activities.
Constantly explores environment.	Allow for creative effort, exploratory opportunity.
Shows little differentiation of fantasy from reality.	Offer activities that include elements of reality and fantasy so that they can learn to identify both.
Uses numbers without understanding concept of quantity.	Play active games that require simple counting.
Can make a choice between two alternatives.	Provide opportunities for children to make appropriate decisions.
Is capable of following directions if not more than two ideas are given.	Keep directions simple and straightforward, with one or two points of emphasis.
Begins to use words to express feelings.	Emphasize dramatic play.
Affective Domain	
Has fear of heights, of falling.	Provide successful experiences in climbing and jumping off boxes (moderate height).
Can have strong fear of failure.	Allow to progress at own rate, but encourage experimentation.
Likes rhythmic activities.	Gross motor activities to rhythm. Simple rhythms. Marching. Action songs.
Is self-conscious.	Avoid sarcasm, ridicule, laughing at children. Seek emotional satisfaction.

TABLE 1—Continued

Characteristics	Program Needs and Implications
May be shy.	Bring out through participation and acceptance. Encourage to "show."
Has great desire to imitate.	Offer opportunities to imitate animals, machines, professional personnel, and parental figures.
Needs constant encouragement.	Place emphasis on effort rather than reward for quality performance only.
Likes to play individually or in small groups of two or three.	Allow time for individual play and aid children in learning to play with others.
Shows great imagination.	Offer play opportunities where imagination is valued. New ways of playing games or creating make-believe characters that move are excellent.
Psychomotor Domain	
Is awkward; shows inefficient movement.	Keep activity within the maturity level.
Binocular vision is slowly developing.	Provide hand-eye, object-handling experiences.
May walk well, but have difficulty with other locomotor skills.	Provide wide variety of motor challenges. Stress hopping, skipping, galloping, etc.
Climbing skills need development.	Offer experiences of climbing over low, inclined planks, packing boxes, on jungle gyms, stairs.
Balance skills are developing.	Offer activities involving simple balancing.
Begins to develop throwing patterns.	Allow for hand-eye experiences with appropriate balls, beanbags, etc.
Is learning to use the hands.	Offer experiences of handling and guiding objects such as scooters, little cars, building blocks, etc.
May have trouble with eye control.	Provide low-level hand-eye experiences.
Toilet routines may need control.	Get children to accept this responsibility.
Physical growth slows down comparatively.	As physical growth slows, the child's readiness to learn motor skills increases. Allow many opportunities for the child to practice gross and fine motor skills.
Starts to develop agility in movement.	Offer hurdles to jump and mini-obstacle courses as challenges. Offer practice in starting, stopping, dodging, and changing direction.
Begins to enjoy low-organization games.	Offer game activities that require few rules and offer activity for all children.
Catching skills begin to mature.	Practice catching skills with objects that move slowly (balloons, beachballs) and will not cause fear.
Many motor learning patterns become ingrained.	Show children the proper way to perform various skills.

TABLE 2.   CHARACTERISTICS, INTERESTS, AND NEEDS—KINDERGARTEN AND FIRST GRADE

Characteristics	Program Needs and Implications
Cognitive Domain	
Has short attention span.	Change activity often. Offer short explanations.
Is interested in what his body can do. Is curious.	Offer movement experiences. Give attention to basic movement.
Wants to know. Asks "why" often about movements.	Explain reasons for various activities and movements.
Expresses individual views and ideas.	Allow children time to do their own thing. Expect problems when children are lined up and asked to perform the same task.
Begins to understand the idea of teamwork.	Allow some opportunity for situations that require group cooperation. Discuss the importance of such.
Sense of humor is expanding.	Insert some humor into the teaching process.
Is highly creative.	Allow opportunity for students to try new and different ways of performing activities. Sharing ideas with friends will encourage them to create.

TABLE 2—Continued

Characteristics	Program Needs and Implications
Affective Domain	
Shows no sex differences regarding interests.	Offer same activities for both boys and girls.
Is sensitive and individualistic. The "I" concept is very important. Accepts defeat poorly.	Encourage taking turns; sharing with others; and winning, losing, or being caught gracefully.
Likes small group activity.	Use entire class grouping sparingly. Break into small groups.
Is sensitive to feelings of adults. Likes to please teacher.	Offer needed praise and encouragement.
Can be reckless.	Stress sane approaches.
Enjoys rough-and-tumble activity.	Include rolling, dropping to the floor, etc., in both introductory and program activities. Stress simple stunts and tumbling.
Seeks personal attention.	Recognize children through both verbal and nonverbal means. See that all have a chance to be the center of attention.
Loves to climb and explore play environments.	Provide play materials, games, and apparatus for strengthening large muscles. Examples are climbing towers, wagons, tricycles, jump ropes, mini-obstacle courses, and turning bars, to name only a few.
Psychomotor Domain	
Is noisy, constantly active, egocentric, exhibitionist. Is imitative and imaginative. Wants attention.	Offer vigorous games and stunts; games with individual roles—hunting, dramatic activities, story plays; few team games or relays.
Large muscles are more developed; game skills are not developed.	Stress basic movement and fundamental skills of throwing, catching, bouncing balls.
Is naturally rhythmical.	Provide music and rhythm with skills: creative rhythms, folk dances, singing games.
May become suddenly tired, but soon recovers.	Use activities of brief duration. Provide short rest periods or include moderately vigorous activities.
Eye-hand coordination is developing.	Offer opportunity to handle objects such as balls, beanbags, hoops, etc.
Perceptual-motor areas are important.	Offer practice in balance, unilateral, bilateral, and cross-lateral movements.
Pelvic tilt can be pronounced.	Give attention to posture problems. Provide abdominal strengthening activities.

TABLE 3.   CHARACTERISTICS, INTERESTS, AND NEEDS—SECOND GRADE

Characteristics	Program Needs and Implications
Cognitive Domain	
Is still active but has longer attention span. Shows more interest in group play.	Provide active large muscle program, including more group activity. Begin using team concept in activity and relays.
Is curious to see what he can do. Loves to be challenged.	Offer challenge in movement problems. More critical demands in stunts, tumbling, and apparatus work can be made.
Interest begins in group activities; the ability to plan with and for others is developing.	Offer group games and simple dances that involve cooperation with a partner or in a team.
Enjoys challenges and will try anything.	Offer new activities in the form of challenges. Also place emphasis on teaching safety and good judgment in these matters.
Affective Domain	
Likes physical contact and belligerent games.	Offer dodgeball games and other active games. Offer rolling stunts.
Is developing more skills and interest in skills. Wants to excel.	Organize practice in a variety of throwing, catching, moving, and other skills. Stress fundamental movement work.
Is becoming more socially conscious.	Encourage abiding by rules and playing fair. Stress social customs and courtesy in rhythmic areas.
Likes to do things well and be admired for it.	Begin to stress quality to some extent. Provide opportunity to achieve.

TABLE 3—Continued

Characteristics	Program Needs and Implications
Is essentially honest and truthful.	Accept their word. Give opportunity for trust in game and relay situations.
Does not lose willingly.	Provide opportunity for children to learn to accept defeat gracefully and win with humility.
Sex differences are still of little importance.	Do not introduce different activities for boys and girls.
Psychomotor Domain	
Is capable of rhythmic movement.	Continue creative rhythms, action songs, and folk dances.
Shows improved hand-eye and perceptual-motor coordination.	Provide opportunity for handling hand apparatus. Provide movement experiences. Offer practice in perceptual-motor skills—right and left, unilateral, bilateral, and cross-lateral movements.
Is becoming more interested in sports.	Introduce simple sports skills and lead-up activities.
Sport-related skill patterns are mature in some cases.	Emphasize practice in these skill areas through simple ball games, stunts, and rhythmic patterns.
Reaction time is slow.	Avoid highly organized ball games, which require and place a great premium on quickness and accuracy.

powers of creativity and imagination should be an outgrowth of the program. Children are said to peak in creative power at an early age, which emphasizes the need to allow them time and rewards for creating. The desire to create and explore seems to be a key factor in becoming productive at any stage of life. If the child is challenged with movement problems requiring a satisfactory and adequate solution, his reasoning powers can be developed. Such qualities as self-confidence, initiative, and perseverance can be given opportunity for development through problem-solving experiences.

Physical development and well-being are essential if the child is to enjoy full living and achieve in a learning environment. Recent evidence suggests that, in general, the learning potential of school children increases or decreases according to their personal degree of physical fitness.[11] The extent to which this is true for preschool children has not yet been determined.

Certain physical fitness qualities contribute to the learning and performance of skills. Basic strength necessary to perform a skill is certainly an essential, together with power and flexibility to perform reasonably well.

Integrating the child into the social situation is a direction to which physical education can make a contribution. Channeling play habits into desirable courses, so that the child plays well with peers, is also an attainable objective. A warm and stable atmosphere can provide a sense of security.

There can be many occasions for personal satisfaction when one participates in varied movement experiences. The ability to have fun, play hard, and take part enthusiastically in physical activity may be the high spot for the child in the total school curriculum. More academic demands are being placed on children each year as the complexity of the world increases. Unquestionably, children need an opportunity to seek relief from tension and anxiety, to maintain their well-being. Providing a situation where children can find the opportunity to relax and "let off steam" appears to be a strong justification for a sound movement program.

The program should also aid in developing the child's level of conceptualization. Good teaching predicates that the child be aided in seeing how various concepts are related and linked together, not only in relation to the physical education program, but as they fit into his or her total life style. The child should be able to do more than just move; a basic understanding of the how and why of movement should be established.

Not much has been said about the development of play. One does not really develop play, but rather guides the natural play instincts of the child toward target behaviors. In a sense, attainment of all the objectives has a hand in helping the child toward better play.

Finally, physical education should provide the young child with a stimulating environment in which he will be encouraged to increase his experience both in and through movement. The environment must provide the

[11]*Physical Fitness Research Digest* (Washington, D.C.: President's Council on Physical Fitness and Sports, 1976), ser. 6, no. 4, p. 3.

child with a direction for the release of physical energies and a challenge for her adventurous spirit. It is hoped that the program will excite the child's natural curiosity and be enjoyable.

The objectives of the movement program should be designed to enhance total development of the child. All domains of learning should be touched by the objectives to provide a rounded, well-balanced program. Teaching motor skills alone, without providing knowledge of how to implement them and without giving attention to proper attitudes and feelings, represents mere teaching for the moment without concern for the future of the child.

The objectives have been classified under separate domains, which are not meant to be exclusive. It is recognized that all three domains apply to most objectives, but the objective has been classified under the domain in which it makes the heaviest impact. For example, the physical fitness objective is primarily psychomotor, but without pertinent knowledge and the will to achieve, it functions at a low level of attainment.

The Psychomotor Domain

Program objectives in the psychomotor domain include the development of movement competency, developing and maintaining a personalized level of physical fitness and well-being, and the acquisition of needed safety and survival skills.

DEVELOP MOVEMENT COMPETENCY

The program should help the child develop competence in movement. Children who can move well and are successful in physical skills are more likely to be accepted by peers. For some children, physical activity is the area at school where they find most fulfillment and a sense of achievement. The effect of movement activities on attitudes and responses of these children to other phases of school life is often quite positive. Children enjoy being challenged to achieve various physical skills, and this enjoyment is the direct result of a teacher's skillful guidance, which utilizes their natural enthusiasm for activity and play.

Movement competency may be divided into the areas of body management skills, visual-tactile coordination, rhythmic movement proficiency, and competency in fundamental movements and other simple motor skills.

Competency in Body Management. The term "body management" refers to physical control of the body in a variety of movement situations in relation to environmental demands. Basically, proper management of the body is needed to counteract the force of gravity in normal activity. This is the maintenance of good posture. The child should understand, appreciate, and employ simple postural skills.

Other concerns in body management are control and balance of the body in different positions, agility, coordination, and efficient movement. A child should be able to manage his body effectively on the floor (as in balance or flexibility stunts), moving across the floor, in the air (off the floor), and suspended on apparatus. Also, body management includes efficient use of force in such tasks as pushing and pulling, as well as weight-support tasks.

Perceptual-motor competency is an important body management goal. Included is the concept of laterality, which in children has a correlation with learning difficulties. The ability to control the two sides of the body, separately and simultaneously, must be developed. Good body management implies that the child can make unilateral, bilateral, and cross-lateral movements with ease and in good balance.

Visual-Tactile Coordination. Visual-tactile coordination is coordination among the senses for effective movement. It is most relevant in manipulative activity, but has some application to other skills as well. Four areas in manipulative activity seem pertinent to the development of this coordination:

1. *Eye-hand coordination,* as in catching or hitting objects.
2. *Eye-foot coordination,* exemplified by kicking or trapping a ball.
3. *Eye-hand-foot coordination,* as illustrated by the punt, in which the ball is dropped from the hands to a point where it can be kicked.
4. *Kinesthetic sensing,* which involves controlling the movement of objects with selected parts of the body. Illustrations are hula-hooping, balancing an object on various parts of the body, and the simple act of holding an object. Kinesthesis has wide application to other movement patterns, but its importance for visual-tactile coordination is largely in the area of object-handling skills.

The discussions and activities pertaining to manipulative activity (Chapter 13) provide instructional procedures and learning experiences designed to develop and enhance this objective. The recommendation is to employ experiences with many kinds of manipulative objects, together with sufficient repetition so that the four areas of coordination, which make up generalized visual-tactile coordination, can be developed to the degree that the child can enjoy activity and play with peers. Visual-tactile coordination is vitally important in game skills, success in which is influential in building the child's self-esteem.

Rhythmic Movement Proficiency. Most movement has a rhythmic quality, and in some the quality of movement is a critical ingredient. Simple locomotor skills have rhythmic qualities, even and uneven, depending upon the movement. Performing fundamental movements to rhythm opens up another avenue of movement for the child, giving him greater versatility. Action songs and simple folk dances promote varied actions to the accompaniment of music.

Fundamental Movement Patterns and Other Simple Motor Skills. The young child should increase his proficiency in walking and running. Other fundamental locomotor skills and a number of selected nonlocomotor skills are targeted for development as the child moves along the path of movement ability.

Manipulative skills (throwing, catching, rebounding, striking, kicking) are also considered a part of fundamental movement skills. Proficiency in such skills lays the needed foundation for successful participation in play activity with peers.

Selected special and sports skills may be given some attention in the late second grade, as interest seems to begin to blossom at this time. However, introductory sports skills instruction is usually begun in the third grade, with progressive development throughout the middle grades. The focus of skill development for young children should be on the fundamental skills.

The figure below illustrates the entire continuum of skills that youngsters can be expected to follow. It makes sense to expect children to establish a solid foundation of competency in fundamental skills before they can be expected to meet the challenge of the more complex and more precise game and sports skills.

Continuum of Skill Development and Goals Based on Progressive Attainment

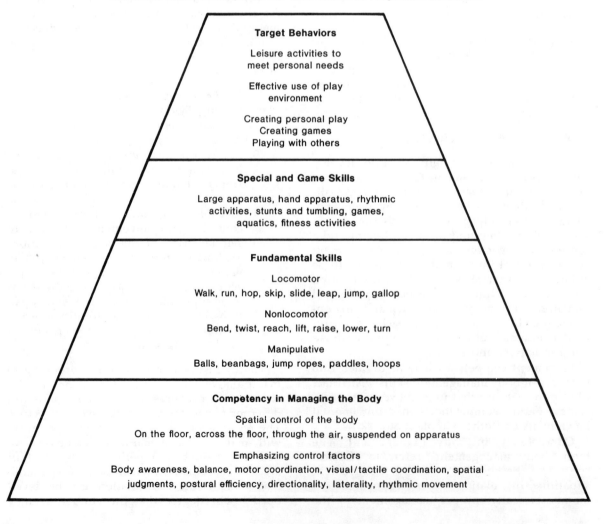

Target Behaviors

Leisure activities to meet personal needs

Effective use of play environment

Creating personal play
Creating games
Playing with others

Special and Game Skills

Large apparatus, hand apparatus, rhythmic activities, stunts and tumbling, games, aquatics, fitness activities

Fundamental Skills

Locomotor
Walk, run, hop, skip, slide, leap, jump, gallop

Nonlocomotor
Bend, twist, reach, lift, raise, lower, turn

Manipulative
Balls, beanbags, jump ropes, paddles, hoops

Competency in Managing the Body

Spatial control of the body
On the floor, across the floor, through the air, suspended on apparatus

Emphasizing control factors
Body awareness, balance, motor coordination, visual/tactile coordination, spatial judgments, postural efficiency, directionality, laterality, rhythmic movement

DEVELOP AND MAINTAIN PHYSICAL FITNESS AND WELL-BEING

The movement program should be so structured that the child can develop a personalized level of fitness. For young children, this means sufficient gross motor activity on a regular basis to challenge growth. Varied activity should be sufficiently challenging to provide stimulation for the cardiorespiratory system.

Since an appropriate level of fitness is essential to the needs of both the individual and society, such fitness should be a goal of education. The many benefits of fitness and its contributions to physical development have been mentioned earlier in this chapter. One value should be stressed. A good state of physical well-being helps the child to integrate and make the best of his potentiality in the overall learning situation.

For young children the approach to fitness development lies in a full range of activity challenges, much of it promoted in the play environment. This should be a positive, planned approach. Each lesson must give attention to broad activity challenges.

Physical fitness transcends simple muscular fitness. Some generalized goals like vim, vigor, and vitality are inferred. In addition, concern for postural efficiency and general health status is a necessary inclusion.

The fitness emphasis should be in keeping with the maturity and capacity of the children. No attempt should be made to impose the more structured developmental programs of the middle school and high school.

ACQUIRE SAFETY AND SURVIVAL SKILLS

The program should leave the child equipped with needed safety and survival skills. Movement, safety, and survival go hand in hand. Movement is often protection against various types of bodily harm. It can be a defense against unforeseen dangers. The child may be able to avoid some moving body or dodge a thrown object.

Instruction in any activity must include the safety factors in order that children may know and comprehend safe procedures. Teachers cannot escape the legal responsibility of providing a safe learning environment for children. Good supervision is needed to guide children in safe participation. Stress should be placed on safety for oneself and safety for others. Children need to understand that, because of the nature of physical education activities, rules are needed and safe procedures must be followed. Sheer recklessness must be avoided, but on the other hand, care must be taken not to create fear and overcautiousness in activity.

No child is as vulnerable to accidental death as the one under six years of age. The physical education or movement education specialist should teach an understanding of safety and attempt to develop transfer to situations at home, on the playground, and around the streets. Developing understanding and an involvement of the child's conscience so that he may live safely should be a desired outcome. Self-discipline, through a comprehension of safety rules, rather than a thoughtless acceptance of such rules, could be a major addition to a child's life.

Highly important in terms of survival skills is the area of water safety. In some areas where schools provide little opportunity for aquatic instruction, students should be encouraged to seek swimming instruction. Communities should look for cooperation among the various agencies to see that a swimming and water safety program is a part of the total educational opportunity for the child.

The Cognitive Domain

Program objectives in the cognitive domain include establishing for the child an awareness of the body, teaching the child the cognitive elements of movement patterns, helping the child to enjoy wholesome and lifelong recreation, and enhancing the child's creativity.

To be truly educational, the program must include consideration for cognitive learning. A good deal of learning can come about in response to the children's own questions. Opportunity must be provided for discussion, which gleans answers from the children, rather than from the teacher-authority. Through subtle questioning, direction, and problem-solving techniques, the students can be stimulated to think and make value judgments. Directing the focus onto "how" and "why" distinguishes this procedure.

Cognitive information is also drawn from the movement environment, of course, and teachers should recognize that both verbal and nonverbal communication will have an influence. Cognitive learning should be a full partner with motor learning in helping children develop a vocabulary of skills.

Those cognitive items that should be imparted to the children should be listed in the lesson plan. When it is suggested that an activity or skill be done a certain way, the teacher can say, "We are doing it this way because . . . ." If there is an appropriate or recommended way to perform, this information should be a part of the instruction.

ESTABLISH BODY IMAGE

Body image, or body awareness, is truly an awareness by the individual of his or her body, its parts, and how they function. It involves the identification, location, shape, size, and function of various body segments and parts. To know what movements can be made by the various body parts, either singly or in combination, and what functions they can perform contributes to body awareness and provides a measure of self-evaluation.

With young children, first approaches to understanding the body entail learning the names of the various body parts—shoulder, arm, foot, knee, etc.—and experimenting to ascertain respective functions. Stabilization of internal directions—front, side, back, right side, left side—follows, with appropriate movement reinforcement. Later development is in the relation of self to environment.

The child must also manage the body in relation to the external environment. Action words should be translated into movement language. He or she should respond with appropriate movement to such commands as "over," "under," "through," "up," "down," "around," etc. There are a multitude of these action words governing movement direction. The child should also react to force terms, such as "light," "heavy," "sudden," or "smooth." Movement actions should be appropriate for such verbs as "bend," "shake," and "roll," for example. While the movement vocabulary is developed and enlarged, understanding of movement terminology should also be acquired.

DEVELOP UNDERSTANDING OF COGNITIVE ELEMENTS OF MOVEMENT PATTERNS

This component part of the cognitive domain may be regarded as an extension of body awareness, which is a more generalized pattern of knowledge. While a child may know where his foot is and how the foot functions, the components of proper walking entail some additional knowledge, which will help him walk more efficiently. He or she should acquire the knowledge that the foot should be pointed reasonably ahead on the step, and that the transfer of weight goes from the heel to the toes.

This goal can be approached directly through discussions and perhaps observation of walking patterns illustrative of the points in question. With respect to foot direction, tiles or blocks providing stepping patterns can be placed so that the child achieves the desired effect in performance. Instructional aids, such as pictures, diagrams, and motion pictures, may also be of help.

The informational output should be established so that the child can garner knowledge of the "how" and the reinforcing "why," giving him or her the basis for a value judgment about his or her own motor pattern.

DEVELOP APPRECIATION FOR WHOLESOME AND LIFELONG RECREATION

Since children will play for many hours beyond the opportunity afforded them in physical education, the program should aim at making this play a fruitful experience. Part of this preparation can be met by teaching a variety of skills well enough so that the child has the tools for leisure activities. In addition, the youngster should develop the knowledge, attitudes, and appreciation that will guide him in free play. Some of the ways physical education can contribute to the recreational ideal are:

1. Provide the child with a wide variety of activities that are of use in leisure or play activities. This should include active games and movement experiences suitable for the home and backyard.

2. Give the child experience in playing with and accepting other children in physical activities. Children should seek the company of other children of their ages and interests and not play alone.

3. Lay the basis for the child's enjoyment of physical activity, since children who have fun and can achieve success in movement experiences tend to participate more than those for whom physical challenges have been unhappy experiences.

4. Provide opportunity for each child to develop simple motor skills, particularly in throwing, catching, and propelling balls, so that children can participate successfully and competitively with their peers.

While one of the overall objectives of the school physical education program (K-12) is developing interest in what are called "lifetime sports," little actual exposure to these activities is inherent in movement activities for young children. The emphasis for this age level should be on play activities that have meaning *now*, with the establishment of favorable attitudes as a secondary goal.

DEVELOP CREATIVITY

Developing creativity is given status as an objective because of its vital importance in play and the educative process. Chapter 6 includes a discussion of creativity and how it relates to play and activity.

The Affective Domain

Program objectives in the affective domain include the acquisition of desirable social standards and ethical concepts, developing a positive self-concept, becoming secure in the environment, and developing positive approach behaviors toward physical education.

ACQUIRE DESIRABLE SOCIAL STANDARDS

A most important aspect of learning during early childhood is social learning, much of which can be developed through play and movement activities. Learning to live socially with other people is not something that is suddenly achieved. It is a slow process that takes much care and attention to develop. Learning to share, to take turns, to face up to the problems of hostility and animosity, and to discuss them in some reasonable fashion are by no means easy and take time.

The child needs to be able to play and get along with others, to take turns, to win and lose gracefully, to work for the common good, and to respect the personality of his or her fellows. These values will develop only if the teacher plans for their development and allots some time for their discussion. It is probably impossible and meaningless to attempt to decide precisely what social values a child should possess. What is probably more important is that the teacher deal with the process of valuing. Basically, this process involves discussing various situations and incidents that may arise and examing the pros and cons of the issue. All value judgments are made privately and tend to be long-lasting if they are self-selected. Too often, teachers attempt to impose values through indoctrination. When the child becomes old enough to be able to think as an individual, he or she questions these outside values and often rebels against them. More lasting effects are probable if students are given reasons why, and are allowed to participate in some of the important decisions that affect their school and personal environment.

Physical education should offer the student an opportunity to examine the reasons why rules are developed and why cooperation must occur if people are going to enjoy one another. As life is governed by social rules, customs, and traditions, so are games. Situations that involve fair play, honesty, and conforming to rules can be discussed when they arise in the setting of physical activity. The movement program can often be a miniature laboratory for dealing with situations that may arise in the bigger game of life. Children can be aided in establishing some long-term social values and will enter the later years of school life able to respect others, which involves accepting mistakes and weaknesses of others without ridicule.

DEVELOP A POSITIVE SELF-CONCEPT

The development of a positive self-concept is important for all children. The opportunity to learn motor skills encourages greater interest, more confidence for new adventures, and a more positive attitude toward oneself. It is the teacher's responsibility to help children develop a positive self-concept and to aid them in selecting experiences that will provide a challenge, yet at the same time will maximize opportunities for success. When this is accomplished, one can be relatively sure that a positive self-concept is developing. The self-concept a child possesses is vital in the learning process. It can make it possible for him or her to learn, or it may prevent or block the ability to learn. If a child can feel a sense of belonging and of being needed and respected, and can learn that successes outweigh failures, he or she will be on the way to establishing a positive self-concept.

The fact that each child can see and usually assess his or her own performance level makes physical activity an excellent medium for developing sound concepts of self. The proud look on a child's face when he or she first climbs a rope or catches a ball successfully reflects what is going on in the child's mind. One must be careful not to place undue emphasis on successful experiences, as failure is evident not only to the child, but to the peer group. Skillful teaching will usually dictate that the teacher seek and acknowledge success and ignore or soften the blow of failure. The self-concept is modifiable because it is learned. If it is learned, it can be changed. Physical education can do much to bring out the child and give him or her an opportunity for self-expression, creativity, and the achievement of success. Comfortable physical experiences, well within the emotional, physical, and intellectual limits of the child, are crucial.

Achieving success in physical education can be especially valuable to the child who performs at a lower level academically, but achieves a measure of success in physical activity. It is postulated that the child's experiences in using the body effectively, in developing a favorable self-image, and in achieving success will relate in a positive way to the challenges he or she meets in the classroom.

It is essential to understand the learner, but it is important for the learner to understand himself. Each child brings into the work his or her own basic characteristics, limits of intelligence, body structure, energy drive, and sensitivity to external stimuli. One goal of the movement program is to aid the child in fulfilling the old adage, "Know thyself."

DEVELOP SECURITY

When the young child leaves the security of the home, he or she is often jolted by being thrust into an unfamiliar and often an apparently hostile environment. Often there is little prior preparation to ease the shock of this transition.

It is not the intention of these discussions to center the solution of this problem on one single area of the curriculum. Making a child feel secure is the total responsibility of everyone and every facet of the school. While the feeling of security should permeate the atmosphere of the school, however, it should be fostered especially strongly in the movement education program.

While helping the child to accommodate to the school is an individual process, with strategies formulated as the situation dictates, the importance of interesting activity in disseminating a child's anxiety brings the role of play into the picture. A child who is happy in play and is accepted by other children in their play usually finds school a happy and interesting place.

SUMMARY

Movement is an important ingredient for healthy growth and development. Physical stress brings about an increase in strength, which causes the body to develop a stronger skeletal system.

Cardiovascular exercise is also important in the prevention of heart disease in youngsters at an early age. Heart disease risk factors have been identified in children as young as seven. One of the risk factors is obesity, which must be dealt with in elementary school youngsters. Not

dealt with in elementary school youngsters. Not only is obesity linked to heart disease, but it has a negative psychological impact on children and hinders their efficient learning of motor skills. Children are rewarded for physical attractiveness, and physical fitness helps to enhance this trait.

It is important that the program help children develop confidence and competency. Children will not perform skills in their adult years if they lack confidence in their abilities and feel that they are incompetent in skilled activities.

Basic drives of children influence the goals and achievements they choose to seek. Along the same lines, characteristics of children of different ages must be understood in order to develop a curriculum that is in line with their capabilities. Implications for curriculum development based on these characteristics are offered to aid the teacher in developing a meaningful program. Finally, when the drives, characteristics, and implications have been considered, objectives for a balanced program are listed and explained in detail. The objectives are developed for the three domains of learning: psychomotor, affective, and cognitive.

ADDITIONAL REFERENCES

American Association for Health, Physical Education, Recreation, and Dance. Proceedings. *California Association for Physical Education, Health and Recreation Journal* (May/June 1973).

Cowell, Charles C. "The Contribution of Physical Activity to Social Development." *Research Quarterly* 31(2) (1960).

Mayer, Jean. *Overweight—Causes, Cost and Control.* Englewood Cliffs, N.J.: Prentice-Hall, 1968.

Rarick, Lawrence G. *Physical Activity, Human Growth and Activity.* New York: Academic Press, 1973.

Chapter 3

Guiding the Learning Process

A good teacher makes the children glad it is Monday!
John Holt

To teach is to facilitate learning. Children learn when teachers teach. Teaching forms the bridge between what the students are now and what they may become.

The traditional view of the teacher as an imparter of learning, who concentrates on attitudes, skills, and knowledge, has been replaced with the view of a teacher as a facilitator of learning. The criterion for success in teaching is the degree to which each child has been given the opportunity to reach his or her potential as a functioning individual.

In their movement experiences, children need the opportunity to experiment and explore, not only to find out what they can do, but also to assess their personal limitations. A wide variety of learning experiences is needed, from which they can derive ideas and directions. Youngsters need a chance to make mistakes, learn from them, and renew their attack. While youngsters can teach themselves, they need perceptive guidance from the teacher to consolidate educational gains.

Since children rarely perform in a vacuum in a physical education class, they learn much unconsciously from others. A judicious blend of learning from within and learning from peers gives breadth and depth to movement awareness.

The learner can also derive value from planned observational experiences. Children can be encouraged to observe how other children respond to a movement problem, with their attention being focused on various aspects by means of pertinent comments. This should be a positive approach, never negative, and can be guided by the teacher commenting on what to observe. "Watch how Fred places his hands. What do you notice about the position of his fingers?" "Follow the motion of Emily's arm. What is she doing that makes the motion so smooth?"

The amount of direction the teacher gives to the learning process is critical. Too little direction can lead to the student's simply going through the motions without learning. Too much direction leads to conformity based upon the teacher's pattern and ideas, leaving little margin for the children to achieve in their own manner.

If the teacher can reach the important conclusion that the main thrust in working with children is to create an effective learning atmosphere, then other things will fall into place. For the child, it means literally "learning to learn" and having that learning guided into meaningful channels.

THE PROCESS OF LEARNING

The learning process can be made more productive if pertinent tenets from educational doctrine and motor learning principles can be applied. These vary according to the stage of learning, the activities, and maturity of the children.

Educational Considerations

Several areas need consideration: capability, motivation, and readiness to learn; maintaining and reinforcing the pace of learning; and transfer of learning.

CAPABILITY TO LEARN

The learning task should be within the capacity of the child; he or she must be able to do what is expected. A number of factors affect capability, among them maturational level, previous experience, physique, and state of physical fitness. It is obviously a waste of time to try to get children to perform a movement action or response before they are capable.

Maturational level involves gross physical and neural body management competencies necessary for the child to have a basis for success. These competencies can be challenged by the selected movement pattern. For example, a child must have the ability to track a flying object before he can become proficient in catching objects.

Capability can be modified by appropriate experience in movement. This tenet is the basis of progression in teaching skills. If a child cannot catch a ball, the ball can be rolled to her first. Later, she can receive the ball on an easily handled first bounce. The child might stand in place and toss the ball to herself. Yarn or fleece balls can be used. She must have the maturational level to accomplish the suggested substitute activities, or else the experience will be one of frustration.

Some physical capabilities also play a part, although young children rarely attempt challenges beyond their ability. To ask children to participate in lifting and carrying activities beyond their strength is an illustration of the limitations of physical capability. A child must have enough grip strength to support the body if he is to engage in climbing activities such as the horizontal ladder. Along the same lines, for a young child to enjoy propelling kiddie cars, he will need enough vitality for sustained activity.

MOTIVATION AND READINESS TO LEARN

Although a child may be capable of learning, he must also be motivated, that is, psychologically ready, to learn. Capability has both a physical and a neural basis, while motivation centers on psychological drives. The learner must have a need, a drive to act, or little learning will take place. Children must want to learn.

In working with young children, motivation should be strongly emphasized. Since their attention span varies and is generally shorter than that of older children, basing instruction on a high initial interest level will stimulate the children to better concentration and involvement. The intrinsic attraction of the act or object keys motivation here.

"Something new," "something different," "something challenging," "a new approach" are the antithesis of "the same old thing." Children delight in losing themselves in a new experience or approach. The novelty of the object or act stimulates the child to interact with it and learn about it. Mastery occurs when the child has explored and defined its characteristics so that there is little more for him or her to do or to attend to.

Children associate the physical education period with play, and play to them is fun. This feeling must never be lost. Pleasure as the activity unfolds then becomes self-reinforcing.

Knowledge of results is a strong motivator. Children can set their target behaviors, which may be specific or relative (improvement). The teacher can challenge with such statements as: "Show me four different ways you can . . . ." Or: "Do you remember how many times you were able to turn the rope yesterday? See if you can improve on that today."

Include in instruction the reason for doing things; teach not only the "how" but also the "why." Children learn more readily when they know the "why" of an activity. This attaches significance to the procedure and gives it a personal value for the learner.

A critical factor often overlooked by administrators is the image that the teacher presents to the children. A large part of this image derives from nonverbal communication. If children receive the impression that the teacher is prepared, enthusiastic, and positive in his approach, some of these feelings are bound to rub off on the children. Children identify with chosen models, and the teacher is a natural one with whom to identify. The teacher needs to demonstrate in behavior the characteristics he or she would like to see in the children.

A similar consideration, also involving the teacher, is that the teacher must leave with children the feeling that the movement experiences they undertake are important. After all, if the experiences are not regarded as important in contribution to overall development, why waste the children's valuable learning time with them? The children can sense the value that the teacher puts on the activities being presented.

As another factor to achieve motivation, activities must be of sufficient complexity to stimulate experimentation and exploration. If the challenge is such that the outcome is invariable and predictable, interest will diminish rapidly. Take the example of the child with a tennis ball who has the challenge to toss the ball into a wastebasket. If he holds the ball a foot above the wastebasket and drops it, success will be assured every time, but how long will the child want to keep doing this on his own volition? However, if the child is asked to bounce it in from different distances using different styles, this gives him some basis (uncertainty) to attempt to solve the problem. There must be something to be overcome, something for the child to master. Children need some kind of impetus leading to movement behavior that will be worth developing from their point of view.

MAINTAINING RECEPTIVENESS TO LEARN—FEEDBACK AND REINFORCEMENT

Feedback and reinforcement can be quite effective in modifying the learning process and maintaining the child's receptiveness to learning. Feedback refers to the impressions, feelings, or concepts that a child derives from a learning experience. Reinforcement implies a strengthening, a consolidation, an enhancement of learning as a result of feedback. Unfortunately, reinforcement can be negative and can cause detrimental effects in the form of blocks to learning. Therefore, it is important that children derive the proper feedback from learning experiences so that reinforcement can be positive.

Children should experience the consequences of their actions; that is, they should accomplish something according to their own standards. The learner builds confidence when he or she meets with success and is ready to reach toward higher achievement. The learning situation must be structured so that each child can reach a measure of success. One approach is to break down the total movement pattern into intermediate steps, each of which can be successfully completed. Each child can at least achieve something, although some children will achieve more.

As a corollary, reasonable goals should be set for each child which are within the child's own power to reach. Children are stimulated when they have a target goal that is both challenging and attainable. The child needs to have the feeling of "I did it." Conversely, fear of failure, which can be a serious block to learning, can be eliminated.

For young children, success is often equated with the praise and encouragement they receive from the teacher. Recognition of progress should be honest in its application, as children can readily detect false praise. Children with difficulties should be helped and encouraged toward successful responses. The child also seeks status through approval, which is reflected in the comments of the teacher. Young children are great attention seekers with their "watch me" approach. Recognition can be in both verbal and nonverbal terms.

Rewarding the skilled and the successful is relatively less difficult than providing the cor-

rect feedback for learners who do not get good results. Incorrect repetition of a skill will not change movement patterns that need adjustment. The student should be given a cue to correcting the performance, so that additional feedback may carry the stamp of success. A child who has been working diligently deserves praise for the effort, even if the resultant performance is somewhat below expectations. The main consideration is not to discourage the child by concentrating too hard on his errors (the negative approach). Approximations should be reinforced as steps in the right direction.

The ideal motivation for children rests in the satisfaction that children can derive from doing well in a reasonably complex or novel situation.

TRANSFER OF LEARNING

Transfer of learning in physical education can be defined as the ability of the child to apply previously learned concepts (cognitive elements) and skills (psychomotor factors) from one movement situation to another. A concept from an old response is used in the execution of a new movement pattern. The degree to which the new task is related to the old and the similarity of the new task to the old will govern the degree of transfer. Transfer can be planned or it can be incidental. One can shift students from throwing and catching yarn balls to handling rubber playground balls. Skill develops first with the yarn balls and then is transferred to the playground balls. Such concepts as tracking, giving with the catch, arm-leg opposition, and follow-through, important in successful throwing and catching, *if understood and applied*, facilitate transfer. To secure maximum transfer, one must teach for that goal.

Desirable transfer in the affective domain would include such general behavioral responses as concentrating on the task at hand, giving one's best, and working cooperatively with a partner. The development of application, self-directed learning, and self-control are matured to the point at which these become purposively directed behavior modifications, which transfer from one learning environment to one of similar nature. Little transfer will occur unless the teacher brings to the learner's attention, consciously and with forethought, the critical elements to be transferred.

MOTOR LEARNING PRINCIPLES

It is fruitless to attempt to set norms for young children establishing the age at which they should exhibit various behaviors. The development of gross motor skills is affected by so many different factors that it becomes a difficult task to establish an age at which children should be capable of certain performances. What is probably more useful and in line with the development patterns of youngsters is an attempt to arrange the environment so that each child has an opportunity to learn the various motor skills at a somewhat similar age. This will keep children from falling far behind their peers at an early age and avoids the "failure syndrome," which can be so traumatic that children never again feel comfortable in physical activities with peers. The discussion that follows will serve to remind the teacher that children should be aided in developing the patterns somewhat near the stated ages, but that variability of performance is a "normal" expectation.

It is important to examine some principles of motor learning that affect a youngster's developmental patterns. Knowledge of these principles will give teachers a better sense of what to expect for the child and allow for patterns of teaching to function at a higher level.

1. Evidence continues to pile up, showing that the earliest years of a child's life are the most important to the development of future movement and activity patterns. A child who is active at an early age will probably be an active person in adult life. If we are going to educate a person physically so that he or she may possess the necessary skills, knowledge, and values for a life of continued activity, the exposure must be started at an early age.

2. Educators have consistently underestimated the capacity of young children to perform skills or achieve movement tasks. Too often the "little games and little dances for little children" philosophy has prevailed. Given a chance, preschool children show the capacity to absorb successfully a wide variety of fundamental motor patterns and combinations, even those usually reserved for older children. Centering attention on custodial care and a happy environment, to the exclusion of physical achievement, is not in keeping with the best interests of the children.

3. The focus on cognitive learning through movement for preschool children may lead some educators to regulate movement competency to a secondary role. Children need to learn to move, learn through movement, and learn about movement equally. If undue emphasis is placed on cognitive learning, the experience is no longer physical education, but becomes an extension of classroom learning in a movement environment. In the case of symbol recognition (letters, numerals, forms, etc.) and such learning activities as word formation and

simple arithmetic skills, movement can be a valuable adjunct. Both psychomotor and cognitive learning hold important places in the hierarchy of development. Appropriate attention should be given to each, and neither should suffer because of emphasis on the other.

4. A first step in learning fundamental skills and acquiring concepts is for the child to be able to concentrate on the task at hand. Admittedly, this seems difficult to achieve with the emphasis on creativity and exploration in many of the movement experiences. If the child is in a play-learning experience, he or she should be motivated to become absorbed in what he or she is doing, so that the experience may be of value.

Exploration of itself accomplishes little in terms of specific goals in movement proficiency unless it becomes guided exploration, pointed toward certain target movement behaviors. At times, the teaching process must stimulate children to zero in on certain traits or goals. By whatever means possible, the children must be brought to the realization that they are participating in a learning experience for themselves and that this merits their concentration.

5. Repetition and the opportunity to experiment with various movement patterns are crucial in motor learning. Single experiences and one-time exposure have little effect on motor learning. A child needs to be reared in an environment filled with wide varieties of sense experiences and almost continuous activity. The child must be given opportunity to repeat the same activity many times in varying situations. The young child appears to have a natural desire to repeat, rework, and reiterate, which seems to be a vital drive toward the development of new motor patterns.

6. Motor skills have a tendency to develop in a progression from simple to complex. The complex skills are more difficult, if not impossible, to develop if the underlying skills have not been learned. The fundamental motor skills are learned during the "skill learning era" which falls between the ages of two and six. These natural skills take considerable time and practice for the necessary refinement to take place. Fundamental motor skills must be *overlearned* so that they will be performed automatically without conscious effort. This overlearning will allow the child to direct attention to new movements to be learned and integrated with those learned previously.

7. The development of motor skills is an individual matter, and wide variation among individual children of similar chronological age is apparent. However, the sequence and direction of growth is much the same in all young children, and it progresses in an orderly fashion.

Motor learning theorists have accepted three general principles that identify typical development in the young child.

a. Development is generally cephalocaudal; that is, it proceeds from head to foot. Thus coordination and management of body parts are seen in the upper body before they appear in the lower body. As a result, the child can usually throw before he can kick.

b. Development occurs proximodistally, i.e., from the part of the body closest to the center to those parts farther away. For example, the child can control the arm before the hand; therefore, he can reach for objects before he can throw them.

c. Development proceeds from the gross to the specific. Gross motor movements occur before fine motor coordination appears and refined patterns of movement develop. As the child becomes more adept at motor skills, there will be a gradual elimination of nonproductive movement.

8. The "start them young" approach, as promoted by misguided parents, and by some athletic coaches, is to be deplored. This approach is reflected in the many organized sports programs that attempt to teach sport skills to children at an increasingly early age. Little evidence is available to show that teaching skills as early as possible produces a more proficient athlete later in life. Because there are so many factors that affect the child's readiness, including heredity, environment, and parental pressure, teachers may find that the best key to readiness is the individual child's interest in the activity. Certainly, many emotional blocks have occurred because children have been frustrated by being forced into activities in which they possess little interest and do not show great ability. An environment that offers many opportunities for children to explore and practice various skills is a necessity rather than a luxury.

9. Much emphasis has been placed on play and exploration in a rich environment that provides children with the opportunity to learn and refine motor skills. There is also a need for specific, planned instruction in new motor skills for children. Studies have revealed that throwing and jumping skills can be enhanced in youngsters through proper instruction. Instruction in fundamental motor skills (which are often thought of as naturally acquired and developed) also has a positive effect on the development of such skills. Instructors must keep in mind that incorrect patterns in skills will also be well learned through repetition and practice during the skill-learning era, and that such incorrect practices will become difficult to change in later years.

10. Mental review during skill practice has an effect, although a minor one, on learning motor skills. Mental review can be taught simply by saying to a first or second grade child, for example, "Go over in your mind how this skill is to be done before you actually do it." Pertinent research supports the premise that the practice of mental review can have measurable effects on motor development.

11. Most psychomotor learning is specific. To secure a generalized motor pattern, a variety of related experiences, some in depth, should be implemented. For example, to aid the child in acquiring the generalized motor competency known as locomotor movement (walk, run, jump, hop, etc.), experiences in a wide variety of these skills should be planned. Not only should the child learn the separate movements, but he should also combine them in sequence through experimentation and exploration.

12. The majority of fundamental motor skills for young children should be taught by the whole method. There are times when a few simpler skills may be broken into components to utilize the part method, but the usual approach is to teach the movement pattern in its entirety.

13. Many motor skills, particularly complex skills involving sequencing in their execution, should be practiced in the sequential and timing patterns of the natural act. Some skills can be slowed down a trifle, but to slow them down to the point at which timing is lost inserts a negative factor that must be corrected later. A fundamental skill that can be slowed down effectively is skipping. The movement can be learned by using a slow step-hop, with alternating feet. Conversely, if a run is slowed up too much, it becomes an awkward movement that has little meaning for the child.

14. The addition of rhythm to a skill-learning situation not only enhances the quality of movement, but also adds breadth and motivation, capitalizing on the child's inherent love of rhythm. The rhythm must be appropriate for the movement pattern and approximate to the tempo of the movement. For fundamental skill patterns, deft use of the drum beat adds much to the instruction. In the presentation of suggested movement themes, challenges, and sequences suggested for development of particular skills, rhythmic movement ideas are included and integrated in the movement approaches.

15. For young children, early emphasis should be on exploration and experimentation with skills. The teaching process is not one of trial and error, but rather one of approximation and correction. Success can be determined when the approximation begins to bear a reasonable resemblance to the desired act. The key

to the level of performance lies in the child performing as well as possible in the framework of the situation.

16. The more skillful the child, the more flexible the presentation can be. When dealing with inept children, children with motor problems, and mentally retarded youngsters with motor problems, the learning approach should be more defined, concentrating on learning experiences designed to obviate selected motor deficiencies or problems as revealed by diagnosis.

17. The question of massed practice versus distributed practice in the development of motor skills needs clarification. Although psychologists are united in preferring distributed practice, all the evidence is not in, especially with regard to movement activities for young children. Some research study findings indicate that massing practice time during early experiences with a skill, followed by subsequent practice periods on a distributed basis, provides a more effective learning environment. After the movement experience has been adequately introduced, it can be followed up during the year with distributed practice sessions, planned for in the curriculum. Also implied is the sound pedagogical practice of providing a short review of the important concepts and background skills learned, before introducing progressively more challenging activities.

18. What length of time should be devoted to practice sessions for a particular activity or approach? As long as motivation and desire to continue are in evidence, the activity may be of value to the children. It is usually wise to cut off a presentation while interest is still high, leaving children with a good memory of the activity. Lesson plans should be flexible enough so that adjustments can be made to the duration of practice on a particular activity. Combining two or three different movement activity approaches into most lesson plans would seem a more sound approach for young children, rather than devoting an entire class session to one type of activity.

19. Children should be provided with pertinent information about the skill they are expected to learn or improve. If this skill involves previously learned and/or related information (transfer), this should be pointed out. Cognitive elements of a skill not only provide direction for better performance, but also give the child an evaluative foundation with which to judge his response.

20. In striving for quality of movement, two categories of information are important. The first includes those elements of the skill that are peculiar to the skill and pinpoints the various techniques necessary for its successful and efficient execution. The second category of information includes the principles governing better quality in movement competency, discussed in the following section.

21. If optimum retention is desired, overlearning is the key. The pattern must become an ingrained part of the child's coordinated movement competency. The greater the proficiency attained in a skill, the greater the retention. Skipping may be taken as an example. Once the child has acquired graceful movement in skipping, practicing the pattern—while it may not help to increase efficiency—will serve to "set" the pattern in the child's hierarchy of skills, so that he will not be apt to forget this skill pattern learned during childhood.

22. Performance of well-learned skills is generally improved by competition; the performance of poorly mastered skills or skills that are still being learned is diminished when competition enters the picture. Since many of the skills of young children are still being learned, it is evident that competition should be employed with caution, if at all.

23. One of the critical instructional techniques, which should be applied in all physical education programs, is the expansion and diversification of the movement potential of any activity by using the Laban-oriented movement principles of space, time, force, and flow. Judicious application of these factors can provide breadth, depth, and variety to any movement pattern.

24. Observation and consequent adjustment of the learning sequence is another needed instructional skill. In this technique, sometimes called prescriptive teaching, the teacher observes the children's reactions and responses to the movement patterns and then adjusts (prescribes) what should follow next, so as to counter or include the observed responses.

Observation is based on a knowledge of what to look for and observe. The teacher must be conversant with the crucial points of the activity when best performed. General factors of smoothness, rhythm, and continuity of movement, as well as specific skill points, will make for better performance. The teacher must first make a quick assessment of whether the child is making more or less progress than is appropriate for that child. He can then make changes in the learning process on the basis of this observation.

BASIC PRINCIPLES GOVERNING BETTER QUALITY IN MOVEMENT COMPETENCY

To provide the child with a cognitive basis for a better level of movement competence, certain principles should be taught. These principles are general in nature and can pertain to a variety of movement patterns. The child must first be made aware that there are such principles; he should then learn how to utilize them for more proficient movement. It is important that the teacher recognize the significant nature of these principles in coaching and helping youngsters with their movement patterns. The following principles are pertinent to movement patterns for preschool and primary children.

Visual Fixation or Concentration

The eyes should be focused on some point. This point can be either fixed or moving, depending on the response expected. In catching, the child should track the ball and "see" it into the hands. In throwing or bowling, the fixation is on the target. On the balance beam, the child should look ahead and not at the feet. When he is kicking the ball or contacting it with the hand, the eye should be focused on the ball.

Follow-through

Follow-through is the smooth conclusion or projection of the already initiated movement. It is the opposite of arrested motion. It is seen in such manipulative skills as throwing, striking, batting, and kicking. In throwing, even after the object is released, the arm continues the motion to a smooth completion. Follow-through is more important in skills in which accuracy enters the picture.

Relaxation

The child's body should be relaxed when executing movement patterns. To be relaxed means to employ only enough muscular effort to perform the skill. The antithesis of relaxation is "tightening up" or even rigidity. Relaxation is especially important in catching skills, for example, as the hands must "give" as they receive the object.

Social and emotional pressures can interfere with relaxation. The performer who executes a pattern easily by himself can have trouble when he is asked to demonstrate his pattern before peers. The learning atmosphere must favor the relief of tension during performance.

Opposition

The term "opposition" in physical education refers to the coordinated use of the arms and legs. In perceptual-motor terms, it refers to cross-lateral coordination. In throwing patterns, a step with the left foot coordinates with right-

handed throwing. In walking or running, the movement of the leg on one side is coordinated with the arm thrust on the other side of the body.

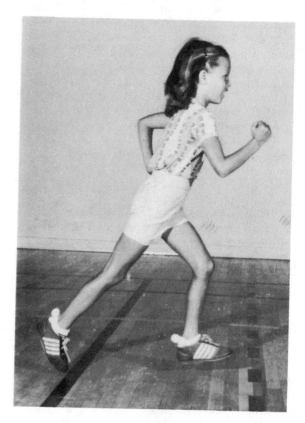

Opposition

Control with the Pads of the Fingers

The pads of the fingers are the controlling elements in many manipulative skills, particularly in ball-handling skills. While the palms of the hands may assist the fingers in control, an error in technique occurs when the palms, rather than the finger pads, become the controlling elements. Young children, who have small hands, do rely on the palms for control; as soon as it is practical, however, attention should be drawn to more efficient control by means of the finger pads.

Weight Transfer

A transfer of weight from the back to the front foot is a critical movement in throwing, batting, striking, and rolling skills. Most of the weight is initially on the back foot, but a transfer of weight to the front foot occurs during the execution of the skill, creating a rocking motion.

Development of Force

At times—although perhaps not often—young children wish to increase the force of a particular response. In pulling and pushing skills, more effective force can be applied after a stable base for the movement has been established. The feet should be spread apart laterally (widening the base), the knees bent, and the center of gravity lowered. The body should be lowered to coordinate muscular force in as straight a line as possible, with the big muscles in the lower part of the body (hips and legs) providing the primary force.

Force is also related to the number of body segments involved. The more the segments, the greater the force produced. A combination of body forces provides a more forceful movement than any single segment.

In throwing, striking, and kicking skills, if the initial preparatory movement is increased to allow a greater range of movement of the limb, the force is increased. This means that the foot kicks harder if it is drawn back a greater distance. The arm can throw farther (with more force) if it is extended back farther in the preparatory movement. While increasing the speed of the movement has the effect of increasing the force, however, increased speed may also have an adverse effect on accuracy.

SUMMARY

Many areas of motor learning need to be examined if a productive environment is to be developed for the child. Those areas that are important are capability, motivation, and readiness to learn. In order to maintain the pace of learning, it is necessary to consider feedback and reinforcement schedules used with students. Transfer of learning from one situation to another is important and is enhanced if the concepts are understood and applied on a regular basis. Transfer of learning can take place in the psychomotor, affective, and cognitive domains of learning.

When the teacher understands motor learning principles, the learning environment will be enhanced for the student. The teacher should understand that skills develop in a somewhat orderly fashion and require repetition and practice to become overlearned to the point of habit.

When teaching motor skills to children, there are certain basic principles that are important in establishing quality and proper patterns. For example, children need to track an object, regardless of the type of projectile, if they are going to catch it successfully. Opposition, follow-through, and transfer of weight are important skill principles to practice whether one is throwing, kicking, or striking an object.

Chapter 4

Curriculum and Planning

What a student prizes, he does. What a teacher values, he teaches.

While curriculum development can be exciting and stimulating, it also demands a great deal of hard work. Curriculum and lessons should be written up when teachers have a sufficient time to sit, think, and ponder. Too often, curriculum is written under a time deadline and the stress of day-to-day teaching, with the result that little creative thinking is applied to the project. The desired curriculum should be developed during the summer vacation, when the teacher has had time to relax after the school year and is in the proper frame of mind for creative endeavor.

The written curriculum should be a guide for the coming year. It should remind the teacher to avoid falling into old and boring patterns; to deter him or her from teaching a lesson that may be easy, but not very beneficial for students; and to steer the instructor through those hard-to-teach activities and units.

The curriculum should reflect the individual teacher's philosophy and feelings about children and physical education. It should be a compilation of the very best ideas and up-to-date activities that one desires to share with youngsters. Too often, in trying to write a guide that will be "different" and unique, instructors lose sight of the fact that such a guide must also be useful and practical and must fulfill the needs of students. Every curriculum guide is unique because it was developed by a unique individual. Do not neglect the best ideas that have been discovered in physical education just for the sake of being "different." For example, to avoid teaching a unit with playground balls because everyone else has taught it would deprive students of the opportunity to learn necessary

skills. It is not necessary to reinvent the wheel each time we build a new car!

CONSIDERATIONS FOR CURRICULUM CONSTRUCTION

The following guidelines are important in establishing an educationally sound physical education program.

1. The basic purpose of developing a curriculum is to give direction to the program. The curriculum should provide for the teaching of important activities on a year-to-year basis and the deletion of ineffective activities. It should be written in sufficient detail to provide necessary direction, yet retain a degree of flexibility.

2. The curriculum should contain material that is based on the needs, characteristics, abilities, and motivating drives of the youngsters. An activity should not be chosen solely because the teacher thinks it will be "fun." Directing child learning is a serious business, and the choice of activities should be based on sound reasoning.

3. The activities should aid children in reaching the basic goals of physical education. Selection should consider: (a) vigorous physical activity, which promotes growth and physical fitness; (b) instructional sequences leading to a broad range of movement competence and skill development; and (c) a variety of activities useful in leisure.

4. The curriculum should be broad and balanced. A wide variety of activities and experiences should be taught, using many different approaches. Early childhood is time for experi-

mentation, practice, and decision-making about activities that are personally enjoyable. The more activities a child can experience, the greater chance there is that he will experience success in some area. Teachers would do well to remember that the program should offer "something for everybody."

5. The program should be enjoyable for all children regardless of their skill level. Activities that require a high level of skill are often inappropriate for a large percentage of the class and will only serve to discourage many students. In addition, appropriate consideration for exceptional children and children with other special needs must be included in program planning.

6. Program activities should be selected to make possible the achievement of desirable behavioral changes, associated educational values, and personal benefits. Although it is true that behavioral changes in children and the values developed from participation are determined more by instructional procedures than by the program per se, the selection of activities should be made so that the desired change and growth can occur when the appropriate methodology is applied. For example, a program relying chiefly on exercises, games, sports, and relays will do little for the individual child in terms of self-direction, creativity, self-reliance, and individual level of progress.

7. Activities in the program should be taught in a sequential fashion. They should be organized into a meaningful progression, beginning with easy experiences and proceeding to more difficult ones. The program should also reflect progression from grade to grade, within each grade, and within each activity.

8. Special interests can affect the development of curriculum. For example, certain popular recreational activities (such as tennis or ice-skating) might be included if adults in the area perform them on a regular basis.

9. Climate can be an important consideration. Winter games would be inappropriate in the South and Southwest, for example, while year-round swimming programs might be impossible in the northern states. Activities normally taught outdoors in warmer parts of the country might have to be adapted to indoor performance. In parts of the South, periods of extremely hot weather make it impossible to carry out any vigorous physical activity at certain times of the year.

10. Curriculum should not be regarded as something that restricts the creativity and spontaneity of the teacher. Rather, it is to be considered a useful tool that will aid teachers in their work. Without a written curriculum, there can be little direction to the program. Without di-

rection, there is little assurance that the purposes of the program will be achieved.

CURRICULUM PLANNING

The following steps will aid teachers in developing a curriculum that is educationally sound. Regardless of the specific activities selected, the basis on which different curricula rest should be somewhat similar.

Understanding Motivating Drives

Teachers should have a good understanding of the drives that motivate children to action. A program that runs contrary to these drives is doomed to immediate failure. These drives are listed in Chapter 2 along with a discussion of how each drive will be manifested through various behaviors.

Identifying Characteristics, Interests, and Needs

The next step is to identify the characteristics, interests, and needs of children at various ages. While motivating drives are typical of all children, needs and characteristics are much more specific as to age. They may be affected by the geographical location or sociological background of the child as well. For example, children who live in poverty areas may have different needs than those living in an upper-middle-class area. Through careful consideration of research done by child development personnel and keen observation of children in the program, a meaningful and useful list of characteristics, interests, and needs can be developed. See Tables 1–3 (pp. 13–16) for a list compiled by the authors.

Developing Meaningful Objectives

Objectives for the physical education program should be based on the motivating drives of children and on their needs and characteristics. The objectives should be an overall statement of what the instructor would like to accomplish. Stated in another way, what will the program contribute to its participants? These statements of direction are sometimes called goals, or objectives; sometimes they are known as major instructional elements. The objectives for this text are listed in terms of what the program should contribute to the child and can be found in Chapter 2, pp. 13–22.

This step should not be taken lightly, since the objectives developed serve as the evaluative criteria for the activities and ideas that are included in the total curriculum. The objectives in the psychomotor domain can be accomplished through quality performance of the physical activities. In the cognitive and affective domains, on the other hand, mere accomplishment of physical deeds does not ensure that these related learnings will take place. It is apparent that one can participate in a physical education program and still learn the wrong values—i.e., cheating to win, or showing a lack of tolerance for those of less ability. The teacher is the crucial variable in developing strong cognitive and affective learning, and the teacher should deal with these areas on a regular and systematic basis.

Selecting Activities

Activities should be selected that will enhance and aid accomplishment of the objectives of the program. It should be emphasized that the activities must be selected on the basis of what they can do for children rather than on the basis that they are "fun" or that "kids will enjoy them." In many cases, "fun" is an adult judgment based on the adult's feelings toward an activity. Children enjoy activities because teachers help to make them enjoyable and because they meet the children's needs.

An example is in order at this point. If one of the objectives of the program is to develop a personalized level of physical fitness, then activities should be selected that will do so. The larger the number of activities gathered, the more novelty and variation there will be in the approach to developing physical fitness.

Organizing Activities into Units

After many and varied activities have been compiled, some scheme for organization should be carried out. A good approach is to organize the ideas and activities into instructional units. The activities in these units should be arranged in a continuum of the easiest to the most difficult (according to the judgment of the teacher). As the ideas are taught and field-tested by chil-

dren, the order may be changed according to demonstrated abilities of students. Organizing the collected activities in this manner will: (1) make it easy to assure that children will meet success rather than failure at the start of the unit; (2) ensure that safety and liability factors will be considered, since the activities will be presented in proper sequence; and (3) aid teachers in finding a starting point for sound instruction by allowing them to proceed through the activities until a significant number of children find difficulty performing adequately.

Another idea often valuable is to develop pertinent instructional procedures that will remind oneself as well as others using the unit to remember various points, such as safety hints, how to teach for quality rather than quantity, initial organization of equipment, ways to expand the activity for variety, and crucial factors to emphasize for proper motor skill development.

Determining Broad Program Areas

At this point, broad program areas can be established. Organizing the activities into units makes it easier to arrange them into categories that allow sufficient emphasis to be placed on all developmental areas of the child. These areas can then be allotted a percentage of program time based upon the drives and needs of the students. This procedure also simplifies answering questions of parents and administrators with respect to program emphasis.

The suggested percentages are to be regarded as approximate and subject to some adjustment. However, each area must have its proportional share of instructional time, and too much shifting will destroy a balanced program.

Allocating Activities to Age Levels

After the broad categories have been determined, the activities within each should be designated. Age level placement of specific activities within the broad categories is

TABLE 4. MOVEMENT PROGRAM
(AGE LEVEL EMPHASIS AND SUGGESTED YEARLY PERCENTAGES OF TIME)

	Preschool	Age 5 (Kindergarten)	Age 6 (First Grade)	Age 7 (Second Grade)
Movement experiences and play activities	35	30	30	30
Fitness development activities	5	5	10	10
Rhythmic activities	30	30	25	25
Apparatus, stunts, tumbling	25	25	20	20
Simple game activities	5	10	15	15
Swimming and water safety	(a)	(a)	(a)	(a)

[a]Swimming and water safety is a recommended area of instruction for young children. The amount of time allocated to this area would depend upon the facilities and instruction available. If swimming is included in the school program, it should proportionately reduce the percentage of time allowed to other activities.

regulated by arbitrary selection to some extent. Adjustment upward or downward with respect to age level should be made on an empirical basis after a period of class trial.

Another factor now enters the picture. A skilled specialist usually has more success in achieving higher skill levels with youngsters than someone who is not trained in the area and who has a more limited background. Table 5 is presented as an aid for program planning. Basically, it states that a certain activity should be part of a particular age level program. The activities to be included, the approaches to be utilized, and the instructional procedures to be followed are discussed later in the text.

On examining the table, you will notice that activities using jump ropes are included under *Educational Movement—Manipulative* and that reference is made to rope-jumping to music under *Rhythmics*. Varied activities with jump ropes, including rope-jumping without music, are recommended for children of preschool age through age seven. In contrast, rope-jumping to music is reserved for six- and seven-year-olds. Furthermore, rope-jumping to music should be

a considered inclusion in the rhythmic program, hence its placement there to emphasize this necessity.

An explanation of all aspects of the rhythmic program would demand too much space at this point and be out of context. The program breakdown for rhythmic activities is included in Chapter 11.

PHYSICAL EDUCATION PROGRAMS FOR EACH GRADE LEVEL

The section that follows gives a description of the type of program recommended for each grade level. It is evident that there is a correlation between the recommended programs and (1) the needs of children, (2) program guidelines, (3) broad category percentages, and (4) grade placement of specific activities.

The Preschool–Nursery School Movement Program

Several guidelines are of particular relevance to the movement program for young children.

TABLE 5.   SUGGESTED ALLOCATION OF SPECIFIC ACTIVITIES ACCORDING TO AGE LEVEL

Activity	Age Level			
Movement experiences and body mechanics	P[a]	5	6	7
Educational movement—locomotor, nonlocomotor	P	5	6	7
Stretch ropes			6	7
Educational movement—manipulative	P	5	6	7
Balloons and beach balls	P	5	6	7
Beanbags	P	5	6	7
Yarn or fleece balls	P	5	6	7
Playground balls (8½")	P	5	6	7
Small balls (sponge, softball size)				7
Paddles and balls		5	6	7
Hoops		5	6	7
Jump ropes	P	5	6	7
Parachutes		5	6	7
Rhythmics	P	5	6	7
Rope-jumping to music			6	7
Apparatus experiences	P	5	6	7
Bounding boards	P	5	6	7
Balance boards		5	6	7
Balance beams	P	5	6	7
Benches			6	7
Climbing ropes	P	5	6	7
Climbing frames	P	5	6	7
Floor apparatus	P	5	6	7
Individual mats	P	5	6	7
Jumping boxes	P	5	6	7
Ladders and bars	P	5	6	7
Stunts and tumbling		5	6	7
Simple games	P	5	6	7
Relays				7
Story games, poems, quiet play	P	5	6	7

[a]Preschool.

1. The program should be staged in an environment that includes sufficient space to allow for freedom of movement and that possesses the amount and type of equipment and supplies needed for movement.

2. The program should provide for exploring, experimenting, and practicing all types of movement skills in a variety of movement situations.

3. Although rhythmic movement is important, the program must not be restricted to this type.

4. Perceptual-motor elements should be included in the regular program of activities. Special help and remedial program activities should be provided as adjuncts to the general movement experiences.

5. The emphasis should be on the whole child and his or her responses, rather than on achievement of various isolated skill movements.

6. While it does give some consideration to the academic, cognitive aspects of learning, the program should focus most closely on the learning of movement. The program should strive for an unstructured approach in which cognitive goals are of secondary importance.

The program should include activities from the following categories:

1. *Gross movement experiences and play experiences.* The child learns to manage the body efficiently and to acquire fundamental skills when he can participate in a wide variety of movement experiences, performing them either freely or to rhythm. The capability of each child must be challenged but not overtaxed, and consideration for the child's readiness is very important.

2. *Manipulative skills.* The child should be given the opportunity to handle various play objects suitable for his age, such as balls, beanbags, and similar articles. He should also have access to put-together toys, block or construction sets, rhythm sets, "ride-em" toys, and toss games.

3. *Floor apparatus experiences.* Climbing, balancing, sliding down or jumping down, going through openings, and bouncing are the kinds of experience toward which apparatus play is directed. Any combination of boxes, planks, boards, ladders, and barrels can be utilized. Children should go over, under, through, and around various pieces of apparatus. Gym sets with combined climber-slide units are recommended. Old tires, both bicycle and automobile, enhance the opportunities for movement. Things to tunnel through hold the children's interest. Mats to receive the weight from jumping and to be used for simple stunts are needed. A play approach should dominate.

The Kindergarten Program

Educators are becoming aware of the characteristics of the learner at the kindergarten level, which is resulting in a stronger focus on the learning process and the child.

For many children, the time spent in kindergarten is a period of adjustment. At home, the child is the center of attention; in the classroom, however, he is just one of a group of children. Kindergarten attempts to ease what for many children is a difficult transition, from the security of the home to the uncertainty of the educational world.

Since young children are naturally active and learn best when they enjoy what they are doing, play-type activities are highly important in the kindergarten program. Most of the suggested activities for kindergarten children center around individual movement experiences and rhythmics. Some emphasis is given to simple stunts and apparatus activities and to simple games. While cooperation with others is encouraged, there is little emphasis on group or team play in the kindergarten program. The types of activities are chosen so as to give the child a good opportunity to explore, try out, and create. He learns to express himself through movement and continues to develop the skills of verbal communication—speaking and listening.

In movement, the child begins to lay the foundation of body management and other fundamental skills, with attention to laterality, directionality, balance, and coordination. Eye-hand coordination is developed by means of simple manipulative activities. Fitness needs are met within movement experiences. Perceptual-motor competency theory has strong application to methodology on the kindergarten level.

The First Grade Program

The first grade program includes many of the same activities as the kindergarten program, with some additional emphasis on apparatus experience, stunts, and tumbling. The largest portion of the first grade program is devoted to movement experiences, with attention to physical development through selected movement. As in kindergarten, there is emphasis on fundamental skills and efficient management of the body, stimulated through challenges to elicit a wide variety of movement. Locomotor skills are of prime importance, with some attention to nonlocomotor movements as well. Manipulative skills are stressed, with a foundation being laid for the important play skills of throwing and catching. Beanbags, yarn balls, and playground balls (8½-inch) are important tools for experimentation, as are hoops and jump ropes.

Activities to develop good body mechanics and posture are important, with attention to specific movements designed to strengthen the arm-shoulder girdle and the abdominal region. Both the "how" and the "why" of an activity should be emphasized. Perceptual-motor factors are an important consideration in selecting activities for the first grade child.

The rhythmic program should provide an extension of the movement-to-rhythm activities introduced in kindergarten, reinforcing the experiences and relating them to educational movement experiences. The creative aspects of rhythmic activities find a prominent place in the first grade. In more structured activities, action songs are stressed more than folk dance, although both may be included.

The apparatus, tumbling, and stunts program is important. The school should have sufficient apparatus to provide a rounded program in this area, including climbing ropes, climbing frames, fixed or movable ladders, balance beams, bounding boards, benches, and individual mats. Floor and mat stunts give the children an opportunity to react to directions and achieve a specific movement pattern. Methodology in apparatus experiences, stunts, and tumbling should be based on educational principles, so as to ensure a wide and flexible response to the tasks.

While games are included in the program, they have yielded their traditional importance to movement experiences. In addition to the usual gymnasium and playground games, story games, poems, and dramatic play have a place in the first grade program.

The Second Grade Program

In essence, the second grade program follows the pattern of the first grade, except that simple relays are introduced. Children are still encouraged to move in their own way, to experiment, and to explore, but specific patterns of coordination, such as throwing and catching, begin to mature at this age level. Continued practice in the fundamental locomotor, nonlocomotor, and manipulative skills is provided. Children should also be made aware of and be encouraged to develop good posture. A few simple forms of systematic exercise may be introduced, not yet including the more formal fitness routines.

In the rhythmic area, more emphasis is placed on folk dances; action songs, creative

rhythms, and fundamental rhythms continue to be important. Ball bouncing and dribbling skills to rhythm should be included at this age level, as the children begin to improve their manipulative competency.

Apparatus experiences, stunts, and tumbling receive continued attention. Youngsters begin to take pride in their achievements at this age.

Although unstructured, simple play activities are retained, the emphasis in play shifts to include some group activity in the form of low-organized games. In these activities, the fundamental locomotor and ball-handling skills are combined with group movement along a line, in a circle, and in other patterns to provide group experiences and an introduction to team play.

PLANNING THE YEAR'S PROGRAM

When planning the year's program for youngsters, the teacher should first consider the age level of the group. Preschool and kindergarten children should have a flexible program that allows for additions and changes based upon the play needs of the youngsters. Table 4, which lists broad program areas, can be used as a guide to ensure that all areas are covered. The plan for six- and seven-year-olds might consist of a weekly schedule that outlines the activities to be taught.

The reason for developing a yearly program plan is to make sure that all desired movement activities will be taught during the year. Without such a plan, the teacher runs the risk of finding that many activities were not presented or that the activities were covered too rapidly, so that students had nothing new to do toward the end of the year.

When laying out the yearly plan, it may also be wise to consider seasonal preferences for some activities, climatic factors, and special interests in various parts of the country.

PLANNING THE WEEKLY PRESCHOOL AND KINDERGARTEN PROGRAM

Since most learning experiences for preschool and kindergarten children are motor in nature, the play period provides an extension of the overall school program, but pointed more toward physical and motor goals. The program must be simple, flexible, and challenging, with the emphasis on body management competencies, selected fundamental skills, and hand-eye manipulative experiences. Relevant cognitive goals can be included as part of the movement experiences.

The teacher should draw up a list of appropriate and recommended learning experiences and then use a check list for recording those activities in which the children have participated. Each activity should be carried on long enough to have educational value, with changes or variations being introduced to provide the children with a wide range of movement experiences, including those which are new and exciting for them. The exploratory approach should dominate when activities are first introduced, with later emphasis given to broadening the experiences and developing quality in movement.

Activities are general in nature, and the program is not complicated by the need to schedule special fitness development activities. In the plans shown in Tables 6 and 7, the overall allot-

ments of time for the broad categories are maintained in the weekly schedule. Various units of activity that fall into the broad categories can then be selected to be taught. The teacher can vary the time schedule on any one day, according to the children's response to the material.

To make sure that all activities will be covered, the teacher should draw up a list of units of activity that are required material. This list is not meant to provide a rigid format, of course, but to give direction to the teacher. Some teachers find it helpful to have a second list, which includes units that are elective and can be covered as time permits.

TABLE 6.   SUGGESTED WEEKLY PLAN FOR THE PRESCHOOL PROGRAM

Monday	Tuesday	Wednesday	Thursday	Friday
Movement experiences and play activities (18 min)	Fitness development activities (4 min)	Movement experiences and play activities (18 min)	Fitness development activities (4 min)	Movement experiences and play activities (18 min)
Rhythmic activities (7 min)	Apparatus experiences (12 min)	Rhythmic activities (12 min)	Apparatus experiences (12 min)	Apparatus experiences (12 min)
Games (5 min)	Rhythmic activities (14 min)		Games (4 min)	
			Rhythmic activities (10 min)	

TABLE 7.   SUGGESTED WEEKLY PLAN FOR THE KINDERGARTEN PROGRAM

Monday	Tuesday	Wednesday	Thursday	Friday
Movement experiences and play activities (15 min)	Fitness development activities (4 min)	Movement experiences and play activities (15 min)	Fitness development activities (4 min)	Movement experiences and play activities (15 min)
Rhythmic activities (7 min)	Apparatus experiences (11 min)	Rhythmic activities (15 min)	Apparatus experiences (16 min)	Apparatus experiences (7 min)
Games (5 min)	Rhythmic activities (15 min)		Games (10 min)	Rhythmic activities (8 min)

PLANNING THE WEEKLY LESSON FOR FIRST AND SECOND GRADE

The physical education lesson should grow out of a unit of instruction or should be based on activity progressions as presented under the various activities. It is most important for each lesson to follow a written plan, especially for a beginning teacher. A written lesson plan will vary in form and length depending upon the material and the background of the teacher. A written lesson plan ensures that thought has been given to the lesson before the children enter the activity area. It helps prevent spur-of-

the-moment decisions, which interrupt the flow of the material to be taught. The teacher can always modify the lesson as needed, but the written plan does help him or her keep the central focus and purpose of the lesson intact.

Progression is more likely to occur in the following lesson if the teacher has the plan of the previous lesson for a guide. The teacher can also refer back to his collection of lesson plans for suggestion and improvement in future years.

A lesson can be divided into the following parts, each of which is discussed in the pages that follow.

1. Cardiovascular introductory activities (one to three minutes)
2. Fitness development activities (four to eight minutes)
3. The lesson focus
   a. Review of previously presented material
   b. New learning experiences
4. Closing activity (two to five minutes)

Except for the lesson focus, any of the parts can be omitted as needed in a particular lesson.

Cardiovascular Introductory Activity

The cardiovascular activity accomplishes just what the designation implies. Children come to the physical education class eager for movement, and the first part of the lesson is designed to meet this need. Once this has been accomplished, the lesson can proceed toward the achievement of its specific objectives. A secondary purpose of cardiovascular introductory activity is to serve as warm-up activity, preparing the body for the movements that are to follow. While serving as introductory activity, the movement patterns also have fitness implications and should be related to and coordinated with fitness development activities. In some cases, fitness development activities can serve as cardiovascular introductory activity.

Generally, some type of gross, unstructured movement, usually based on locomotor movements, is used for cardiovascular introductory activity. An enterprising teacher can employ many different activities and variations effectively as introductory activity. Examples are found in Chapter 5.

Correction, coaching, and at times direct instruction can help children achieve movement of reasonable quality during these introductory activities, but quality of movement should not be an overriding consideration.

Fitness Development Activities

The second part of the lesson devotes time to fitness development activities, defined as movement challenges that have as a major objective the physical development of the body and the various qualities of physical fitness—strength, power, endurance, and flexibility. Physical fitness activities and movement challenges, as they are to be included in the physical education lesson, are discussed in Chapter 5.

Lesson Focus

The lesson focus, which is the heart of the lesson, presents the learning experiences growing out of the overall instructional unit. The first consideration is to review and work with the activities of the previous lesson, until a satisfactory level of learning has been reached. In some instances, the entire lesson focus will be taken up with a repeat of the work of the previous lesson.

After sufficient time has been given to the review, the new learning experiences are presented. Skill instruction, participation in a rhythmic activity, or a progression of stunts and tumbling are the kinds of experiences that make up the lesson focus.

The amount of time to be devoted to the lesson focus is determined by the time demands of the other three parts of the lesson. After introductory and fitness development activities have been done, the remainder of the time, less that needed for the closing activity, can be devoted to the lesson focus.

Closing Activity

Closing activity can take many different forms. The lesson may be completed with a focal game that utilizes the skills under development in the lesson; or it may finish up with a game or other activity performed simply for enjoyment, which is perhaps unrelated to the lesson focus. In either case, children should gain a pleasurable feeling from the day's experiences.

Another important use for the closing activity is to offer relaxation activities. It is sometimes important that children be allowed an opportunity to unwind after a particularly exciting and stimulating activity. Children are seldom given time in school purely to relax with the aid of the teacher. Suggested ideas and activities for relaxation are offered in Chapter 17.

Closing activity can also include an evaluation of the lesson accomplishments, stressing and reinforcing important points about technique. Suggestions for activities to try at forthcoming lessons can be entertained at this time.

A consideration in closing the lesson is returning equipment, apparatus, and supplies to their proper storage places. The students, perhaps formed into squads under the direction of leaders, should assume this responsibility.

In some lessons, the closing activity may be minimal or deleted entirely. This might be the case when other activity as the focus of the lesson demands as much time as possible.

A sample lesson plan follows (on pp. 40–42). The first column, *Movement Experience—Content*, lists the sequences that will be taught in the lesson. These are not described in detail (since they are covered in the text), but do give the instructor guidance regarding the sequences to be presented during the week.

The second column is labeled *Organization and Teaching Hints* and provides the teacher with suggestions for efficient organization of the class as well as important points to be stressed and teaching cues. The instructor is encouraged to center on quality of movement as well as quantity.

The column headed *Expected Student Objectives and Outcomes* lists objectives that students should be expected to reach. The objectives are separated into the cognitive *(Cog.)*, psychomotor *(PM)*, and affective *(Aff.)* domains. Their major purpose should be to remind the teacher of the goals toward which the movement experiences are directed, or to encourage discussion of various cognitive or affective areas of learning. The goals represent an attempt to give the teacher some idea of what to expect from students; they should not serve as examples of concise behavioral objectives.

Finally, the *Notes and References* column should serve two purposes: (1) additional material can be referenced into this column for easy referral and an in-depth look at some activities; (2) for the purposes of evaluation of a lesson later on, notes can be made about progress, activities that worked well, activities in which difficulty occurred, and additional organizational points.

SUMMARY

A curriculum guide should be a valuable teaching aid to assist the instructor in planning and preparation of lessons. A number of considerations are offered that are important when the teacher decides to write a curriculum guide. Examples are: considering climate, including activities for special interests, and offering a broad range of activities and teaching approaches.

When planning a curriculum, several steps should be followed. The teacher should understand and have a working knowledge of the motivating drives of children. The instructor should be able to understand specific characteristics of children and base curricular offerings on these drives, characteristics, and needs. Objectives are the foundation of the curriculum because they give direction and goals for selecting activities that enhance the objectives. Activities are then selected based on the objectives and organized into units with sequence based on level of difficulty of the activity. Finally, broad programs areas are developed so that teachers can decide how much program time they want to spend on areas such as movement experiences, play activities, fitness activities, and rhythmic activities.

A description of the type of program that should be developed for the various age levels is discussed, based on these planning steps. For example, the preschool program should place more emphasis on play experiences than the second grade program, which becomes concerned about specific skill development.

The program for the school year should be developed so that it is a balanced program that includes all the desired activities to be taught systematically. After the yearly plan is developed, weekly lesson plans can be developed. In grades K–2, these plans contain four parts: cardiovascular introductory activity for immediate physical activity and warm-up (two to three minutes); fitness development activity (seven to eight minutes); lesson focus to teach activities directed toward the objectives dealing with various skills and body management competencies (fifteen minutes); and the closing activity, which is a game activity and lasts about five minutes.

SAMPLE LESSON PLAN

Educational Movement: Fundamental Skill—Running
Themes: Exploring Flight—Leaping; Use of Force
Manipulative Activity: Yarn Balls

Grades 1-2

Supplies and Equipment Needed:
One yarn ball for each child

MOVEMENT EXPERIENCE—CONTENT	ORGANIZATION AND TEACHING HINTS	EXPECTED STUDENT OBJECTIVES AND OUTCOMES	NOTES AND REFERENCES
Introductory Activity (2-3 minutes)			
Movement Combinations	Scatter formation.	PM—The student will be able to perform the various combinations and demonstrate an understanding of the movement terms.	*Movement in Early Childhood and Primary Education,* p. 47.
1. Hop, turn around, and shake.			
2. Jump, make a shape in the air, balance.	Stress consideration for others in general space.		
3. Skip, collapse, and roll.			
4. Curl, roll, jump with a half turn.			
Fitness Developmental Activities (7-8 minutes)			
Movement Challenges	Go rapidly from one shape to the other.	PM—The student will be able to perform all the movement challenges.	*Movement in Early Childhood and Primary Education,* pp. 49-53.
1. Make different shapes on the floor: Stretch, curl, twist, crooked.			
2. Animal movements—Puppy Dog, Crab Walk, Rabbit Jump.	Use formation.	Cog.—The student will be able to verbalize what body part each of the challenges develops.	
3. Challenge them to lie on back (supine) and bring up a foot to the opposite hand (right to left and left to right); bring up both feet to touch the hands.	Encourage good form while performing the challenges.		
4. Push-up position, lower the body an inch at a time until the chest touches the floor.	Increase the distance the animal movements are performed.		
5. Sway the body back and forth in different directions. Change the position of the arms.			
Lesson Focus (15-20 minutes)			
A. *Fundamental Skill: Running*	Scatter formation.	PM—The student will improve in running form—lightness, and the rhythmic pattern.	*Movement in Early Childhood and Primary Education,* pp. 123-25.
Run on balls of the feet.			
Head is up, eyes forward.	Use formation.		
Body lean depends on the speed.		Cog.—The student will be able to express the mechanics of good running form.	
In sprinting, use good arm action.	Cue by saying: "Run on the balls of the feet."		
1. In scattered formation, run lightly around the area, stop on signal			
2. Run lightly and change direction on signal.			

SAMPLE LESSON PLAN (Continued)

MOVEMENT EXPERIENCE—CONTENT	ORGANIZATION AND TEACHING HINTS	EXPECTED STUDENT OBJECTIVES AND OUTCOMES	NOTES AND REFERENCES
Lesson Focus (15–20 minutes) (cont.)			
3. Run zigzag throughout the area.	"Head up, eyes forward."		
4. Using a crossover formation, 20 yards or so apart, run low, touching the ground on either side alternately.	"Lift your knees." "Relax upper body." "Breathe naturally."		
5. Run forward, turn around in 4 steps, continue forward.			
6. Run with a high knee lift.	Items #4–11, use crossover formation.		
7. Run as lightly as possible. As heavily.			
8. Run to center, stop, and continue.			
9. Mix in giant leaps with your run.			
10. Clap your hands as you run.			
11. Try slapping your knees as you run.			
B. *Theme: Exploring Flight—Leaping*			
1. Run in different directions and practice your leaping. Alternate the leading foot.	Scatter formation.	PM—The student will be able to secure good height in leaping.	*Movement in Early Childhood and Primary Education*, p. 96.
2. As you run, try a leap for good height; for distance; for both.	Stress "soft" landing.	PM—The student will be able to land lightly.	
3. Explore the different arm positions which you can use in leaping. Which is best? Try sailing through the air like an airplane.	Cues: "Up and over." "Push off and reach." "Use your arms to help."	Cog.—The student will be able to explain how force is applied to result in an effective leap.	
4. Leap with a quarter or half turn.			
5. If there are benches or other obstacles present, leap over these. Put several in succession for consecutive leaps.			
6. Put one half the children down scattered in curled position, face to the floor. The others leap over as many as possible.			
7. Run and leap from an inclined bench.	Use a mat for landing.		
C. *Theme: Use of Force*			
1. Show us how you do some forceful movements, such as chopping, batting, hitting with a sledge, punching the punchbag.	Scatter formation.	PM—The student will be able to develop the ability to create more forceful movement.	*Movement in Early Childhood and Primary Education*, p. 97.
2. How does one bring in force to these: a. Total body coordination b. Developing torque c. Achieving a stable position d. Follow-through e. Preparatory movements	Practice these movements. Use brief discussion of factors.	Cog.—The student will be able to understand and apply the terms defining light and forceful movement.	
3. Show us a light movement you can make with the arm. Repeat the same movement more forcefully.			

SAMPLE LESSON PLAN (Continued)

MOVEMENT EXPERIENCE—CONTENT	ORGANIZATION AND TEACHING HINTS	EXPECTED STUDENT OBJECTIVES AND OUTCOMES	NOTES AND REFERENCES
C. *Theme: Use of Force* (cont.)			
4. Make some movements that are light and sustained, heavy and sudden, heavy and sustained, light and sudden.			
5. Make one part of the body move lightly, while another moves heavily.			
D. *Manipulative Activity—Yarn Balls* *Individual Activity*—Each child has a ball.	Scatter formation.	Aff.—The student will appreciate that to become skilled, one must practice.	*Movement in Early Childhood and Primary Education,* pp. 166-68.
1. Toss and catch to self.	Keep eyes on ball, stress "give."	PM—The student will be able to improve in the ability to track and catch objects.	
a. Increase height gradually.			
b. Side to side.			
c. Front to back.			
d. Toss underneath the legs, around the body, etc.			
e. Toss and clap hands. Clap around the body, underneath the legs.			
f. Toss and make turns—quarter and half.			
g. Toss, perform the following, catch: Heel click. Touch both elbows, knees, shoulders and heels.			
2. Bat the ball upward as in volleyball, catch. Bat the ball, run forward and catch.	Watch out for others.		
3. Toss forward, run and catch. Toss sideward and catch. Toss overhead, turn around, run and catch.	Use these with caution. Be sure of readiness.		
Partner Activity—One ball for two children.	Keep distances close.		
1. Roll the ball back and forth.			
2. Toss the ball back and forth, various ways.	Will take some force.		
3. Throw the ball back and forth.			
4. Exploratory activity—batting, kicking, etc.	Seek ideas.		
Game (5-7 minutes)			*Movement in Early Childhood and Primary Education,* pp. 265, 261, 266.
1. Four Out			
2. Animal Tag			
3. Leap the Brook			

Chapter 5

Fitness Development

The principle of a sound mind in a sound body is still the basis of excellence in living.

Thomas B. Quigley, M.D.
Boston, Massachusetts

Physical fitness as related to young children is often a matter for controversy. One argument against physical fitness development goes something like this: "Oh, you mean giving the children a lot of exercises—push-ups, pull-ups, and things like that—and they all move like robots to a count of four." A second mistaken notion is that any fitness program must be pointed toward the goals of bulging muscles, great strength, and the development of superathletes, who are disdainfully referred to as "jocks." Such ideas can convince planners to avoid any activities connected with fitness.

The authors are in complete agreement with the viewpoint that the aforementioned approach to developing fitness is totally out of place for young children, and that the goals are unrealistic, if not downright silly. But the authors also believe that no child should be deprived of the opportunity to develop the potential of his body, which can be achieved when a proper approach is made to fitness development.

To help the planner integrate fitness goals and procedures into the learning atmosphere, several points can be stressed.

WHAT IS PHYSICAL FITNESS?

Physical fitness is that quality of physical conditioning that enables children to meet the challenges of their environment, live fully, achieve, and have a sense of physical well-being. It implies that they are able to resist the stresses of their environment without undue fa-

tigue and have enough energy left over for play. The definition can be broken down into a number of concepts.

1. Youngsters should possess enough strength, power, endurance, and flexibility to meet easily and readily the maximum challenges they will need to meet during the day.

2. Children should start to develop a sturdy physique, which includes proper proportions of bone, muscle, and fatty tissue. An obese child fails to meet this standard.

3. Children should be more than just free from disease and removable handicapping disorders. Vitality, vigor, and vibrant living are qualities to seek in children.

4. Children's posture should be acceptable, as defined by commonly recognized body alignment standards. In a negative sense, this means the absence of characteristics of faulty posture in the anterio-posterior plane, such as round shoulders and hollow back, or an "S" or "C" curve in the lateral plane.

A personalized level of physical fitness can make a significant contribution to the overall development of children, and thus merits attention as an important part of the total school curriculum.

GUIDELINES FOR ACHIEVING PHYSICAL FITNESS IN YOUNG CHILDREN

Some general guidelines for physical fitness have been developed, pertaining to children from preschool through second grade. Specific suggestions related to structuring the learning environment are presented in the discussions that follow.

1. To develop optimum fitness, a generous amount of large-muscle activity must be offered regularly at progressive levels. Motivation is important, so that children will extend themselves within their movement challenges.

2. The type of activity should be selected so that it meets two requirements. The first is that the experiences be geared to the maturity level and physical condition of the learner. Flexibility must be built in to the program, so that it offers youngsters a wide variety of approaches for fitness development. The second requirement is that the activities have the potential to develop fitness.

3. Most, if not all, of the challenges should be incorporated into a play atmosphere. This means that there must be sufficient indoor and outdoor equipment to encourage large-muscle play and that activity challenges must be presented in such a way as to capitalize on the spirit of play. Many activities will not appear to the children as being related to fitness, but will seem to be rugged play.

4. Physical fitness activities should be planned to develop various physical qualities. The development of strength, power, endurance, and flexibility are discussed in turn in the following sections. While some physical educators include agility, speed, balance, and coordination in the list of qualities, these are not physical fitness components, but rather motor attributes, the development of which is centered in the movement program.

Strength. Strength may be defined as the ability of a muscle or muscle group to exert force. Among the child's learning experiences in physical education, there must be sufficient large-muscle activity in a wide range of activities done regularly and with enough intensity to develop strength. The improvement of strength is necessary for the development of physical fitness. Muscles can be developed only through the stress and tension exerted during activity demands. We need to make our children work progressively harder if their strength is to be developed.

Strength is necessary in skill performance, since without strength a low standard of performance can be expected, as muscles give out before they can reach their skill potential.

Power. Power implies the use of strength to apply force for effective movement. Teaching youngsters how to move effectively in situations demanding an application of force will develop their ability to apply powerful movements when needed.

Endurance. Endurance refers to the ability to carry on muscular effort over a period of time. It has its basis in strength, but also involves the cardiorespiratory system and internal body mechanisms. Endurance is seen in the child who can play and participate in learning activities for a longer period than the child who gets tired easily. To stimulate the development of endurance, the teacher should encourage participation in activities that increase the pulse and step up the breathing rate. (Note that young children will often pull back for a moment, rest, and then go on again at full steam.)

Experiences that include chasing and running games, in which most, if not all, children are active, and climbing activities can help to develop endurance. Active rhythms, action songs, and fundamental skill instruction also have endurance implications. No attempt should be made to force-feed endurance. Instead, the teacher should make sure that each lesson includes sufficient activity challenge.

Flexibility. Flexibility refers to the range of movement possible at the joints. A flexible child can stretch farther, touch his toes, bend over farther, and so on. He has more freedom of movement and can adjust his body to various movement challenges more readily. Youngsters need movement experiences in which they can stretch, reach, bend, hang, and otherwise force the joints into maximum ranges of movement.

Flexibility can be furthered by stimulating children to extend the limits of joint movement in twisting, bending, and rotational movements, particularly in the stunts and tumbling program. Children need to be urged to perform these joint movements by such directives as, "See how far you can stretch!" or "How far can you bend?"

PROGRAM ACTIVITIES AND PHYSICAL FITNESS

Integrating physical fitness values into the program does not involve a wholesale restructuring of activity patterns. It does involve taking a critical look at what is to be presented, and deciding how it can be adjusted to secure increased value. It means discarding activities in which only a few children are active, unless these activities are meant to be recovery- or relaxation-oriented. It means having sufficient equipment to keep all busy in active play. When it is necessary for children to take turns, for example, only two or three children should be sharing the equipment.

Many physical education activities devote attention primarily to the legs, lower body, arms, and hands. Activities which make demands on the arm-shoulder girdle area, such as hanging, climbing, crawling, and other arm-support activity are also necessary inclusions.

In another approach to upper body development, the teacher should select activities during which the children perform the movements on the floor and positions in which the body is partially supported by the arms. Care must be taken to include a variety of positions, including the crab position, in which the body is supported by the hands and feet, but faces the ceiling.

Stunts and tumbling activities in the program will pay off in total body development. These activities also provide ample opportunity for the exercise of balance control.

Pulling and pushing activities build muscles because of imposed resistance. Riding toys demand good leg action. Steps to climb and a place to jump from help develop strength.

To achieve endurance, the program must make demands on the individual in the form of muscular effort, which causes accelerated breathing. Generally, this involves activities including running or other sustained movement. While no activity should be carried on to the point at which the participants are breathless, the children do need to learn to push themselves beyond their first inclination to cease.

Creative activities (stories and songs) should be subtly guided so that children will respond with large-muscle movement, thus increasing endurance demands. Rope-jumping is another endurance activity that children should learn to enjoy, including individual rope-jumping to music.

Fitness for Preschool Children

Since much of the preschool learning atmosphere is centered around play, activities for physical development and fitness in young children should be integrated into their play experiences. To stimulate large-muscle play, apparatus allowing for a variety of movement—climbing, crawling, hanging, stepping, suspending the body—is a must. There must be enough equipment so that the child is moving, not waiting. By judicious direction, the child can be guided from one piece of equipment to another, so that the experiences will have variety. With some careful planning, an indoor facility can be designed for ages three to seven, with some special equipment needed for each level. Suggestions for equipment appear in Chapters 4, 6, and 23.

Each daily lesson should put some emphasis on cardiovascular and strength development. In the following pages, these activities are separated into two categories: cardiovascular introductory activities and strength development activities. The cardiovascular introductory activities are not highly organized and require little teacher instruction. They involve a great deal of large-muscle movement and will tire youngsters quickly. These activities should be alternated with strength development activities to allow students to undergo cardiovascular recovery. The cycle can be repeated as often as the children can manage.

Moving and stopping is a pattern that is often used with preschool children. For example, children can move to the beat of a tom-tom and then freeze. Different kinds of movements can be specified to increase the breadth of the lesson and enhance its novelty. As children begin to tire, they can perform strength development activities, such as swinging and circling activities, arm support activities, and abdominal activities. As soon as the children have recovered, the cardiovascular introductory activity of moving to the tom-tom can be continued.

This approach can also be used with kindergarten through second grade children. An alternate approach, that of devoting a specific part of the lesson plan to cardiovascular introductory activity and a part to fitness development, can be utilized as well. This approach was discussed earlier in Chapter 4.

The physical fitness activities should assure that the four areas of fitness (cardiovascular, trunk, arm-shoulder girdle, and leg) are covered, and that all body segments are exercised. A period at the beginning of each lesson should be reserved for movement activities that have the potential to develop fitness. This presentation should be started off with a cardiovascular introductory activity, as such activities satisfy youngsters' appetite for movement.

Progression from day to day should be built into the sequence. The teacher can state the challenge as follows: "Remember what we did yesterday? We are going to do a little more of that." Then, building on the prior experience: "Now, here is something a little different. See if you can follow the cues." Increased load can be achieved by having the children move faster or farther, changing direction more often, putting movements into more strenuous combinations, or increasing the duration of particular portions of the activity. Movement to a rhythmic beat has high utility in cardiovascular introductory activity. Changes in speed, direction, and type of movement are easily possible when performed to the drumbeat.

CARDIOVASCULAR INTRODUCTORY ACTIVITIES

Gross Locomotor Movements and Challenges

If an activity can be done quickly, requires gross locomotor movements, and has the element of interest and challenge, it will serve well as an introductory activity. Most of the activities use general space, with some combining movement in personal space. When the children move, they should move under good control and avoid contact with other children. Bumping and collisions should be quickly eliminated from the patterns.

RUNNING

Running is used as the basis for most movement sequences. Changes can be signaled with a word, drumbeat, or whistle or other sharp sound. Auditory perception and listening habits can be given practice in the sequences. The suggested movement patterns are quite flexible and can be changed as the situation indicates or the teacher wishes. Movement factors of space, time, force, and flow have strong application to these activities. Variety can be achieved by using different types of locomotion and involvement of various body parts. Above all, what is wanted is action.

Free Running. Children run in any direction, changing directions at will.

Run and Change Direction and/or Level. Children run in any direction, changing direction abruptly on signal. Instruct them to change level on signal. Combine these movements.

Run and Change the Type of Run. Children change the type of running to a soundless, very light run. Tell the children that, on signal, they are to run so lightly that you cannot hear them. Change in direction can also be incorporated.

Run and Stop (Freeze). Youngsters stop abruptly on signal. As an extension, they can freeze, which means that they must not move when they have stopped. Right and left directional concepts can be added by making the new start signal either "Right" or "Left." (The child moves right or left in relation to the direction he is facing.) Running and falling is also interesting, but with young children this movement needs some control. Teach them how to fall.

Run and Assume a Specified Position, Balance, or Pose. When the signal to stop occurs, the child assumes a pose either designated or by choice. This can be a balance position on a designated part of the body. The teacher can interject poses that represent feelings—happy, sad, funny, stern, etc.

Run, Stop, and Perform a Task. After stopping, the child can shake his body, twist, swing body parts, or do jumping or hopping patterns while in personal space. Body awareness can be furthered by specifying tasks that involve touching or identifying body parts. A few simple exercise movements may be specified, such as the jumping jack, curl-up, or push-up. The children can even carry jump ropes, so that they can do individual jumping when they stop. Hoop activity can be employed in a similar manner.

Move to Various Drumbeats. Most of the sequences listed above can be guided with a drumbeat, both to set a rhythmic pattern for movement and to signal changes. As another approach the teacher might say, "When you hear this drumbeat, move like a . . . and when the drumbeat changes to *this*, change your movement to that of a . . . ."

Moving to a drumbeat

Change the Type of Locomotion. Children begin with one type of locomotion and then change the movement. For example, they could begin with locomotor movement on the feet and switch to a movement that uses the hands.

Beanbag Routines. Each child carries a beanbag while running. When she stops, she balances on one leg and passes the beanbag around a leg, around the body, and in other ways that the child may think of. Another way to use a beanbag is to place it on the floor in the child's personal space. The child runs around the beanbag twice and then moves away in a straight line, taking a designated number of running strides. He then returns to the beanbag. In another informal activity that does not need signals, the child tosses or slides his beanbag to another spot and performs some kind of movement as he goes to the new spot.

Tortoise and Hare. Children run in place slowly (Tortoises), and on signal they change to a very rapid run (Hares), still moving in place.

Combinations of Movements. A combination of several movements can be specified, such as run, skip, and roll, or jump, twist, and shake. Many other combinations can be devised.

Ponies in the Stable. Each child has a "stable" (a spot or hoop on the floor). On the first signal, children gallop lightly (Ponies) or heavily (Horses) in general space. The next signal directs them to return to their stables and trot lightly in place.

Milk Carton Fun. Each child has a milk carton when he comes into class. Children are allowed to kick, throw, or run with the milk cartons for one minute. Patterns can be designated, such as figure 8, circle, square, etc.

Free Movement with a Ball. Children run, dribbling a ball. When a change is signaled, a child stops, balances on one leg with the other knee up, and passes the ball under the leg, around the back, and overhead, keeping his balance. He then resumes running and dribbling. Other challenges can be provided both for movement with the ball and manipulative movements in place.

Jumping and Hopping Patterns. Many combinations can be devised: jumping in all directions and back to place; or taking three jumps forward and a half twist, then three jumps back to place and again a half twist. The combinations should be worked out so that children return to the starting place.

Flying Objects. Each child has a "hangar" at the perimeter of the "air space." The Airplane (or glider, helicopter, or flying saucer) is in the hangar. On signal, the airplane flies, swoops, and banks around the air space, being careful not to intrude on others' air space. On signal, it returns to its hangar. The idea could be changed to feature birds flying away from and returning to their nests.

Partner or Group Activities

Partner or group activities offer excellent opportunities for introductory work.

Marking. Children can do what the British call "marking." Each child has a partner, who should be his equal in ability. One partner runs, dodges, and tries to lose the other partner, who must stay within one yard of him. On signal, both stop. The chaser must be able to touch his partner to say that he has "marked" him.

Follow Activity. One partner leads, performing various kinds of movements. The other partner must move in the same fashion.

Buckaroo. Children are organized into groups of three, with each group having a jump rope. Two children (the Horses) stand side by side with inside hands joined, and the third child (the Buckaroo) stands directly in back, about four feet behind them. All are facing the same direction. The horses hold the two ends of the rope, which is extended back to the Buckaroo as reins. The Buckaroo drives the Horses at different speeds about the area. The Horses can trot lightly, run hard, gallop, and pull heavily like draft horses. Rotate assignments.

Group Over and Under. Half the children find positions here and there around the play area, then each assumes a curled position. The other children leap or jump over the down children. On signal, the groups quickly change places. The down children now form arches or bridges, and the moving children go under

Ponies in their "stable"

these. As an extension of this activity, the children on the floor can alternate between curled and bridge positions. If a moving child goes over the curled position, the floor child immediately changes to a bridge. The moving child reacts accordingly.

Group Over and Under

Shrinking Space. This activity works best in areas having definite boundaries to limit movement. The movement area can be outlined with cones to give it better definition. The objective is to move in space without touching anyone. Children run at a moderate speed in a large space. After a short period, the space is made smaller. This is repeated several times. At the completion of the activity, the children who have touched no one are the winners. A drumbeat can guide the movement patterns.

Bridges by Threes. Three children in a group can set up an interesting movement sequence using bridges. Two of the children make bridges, and the third child goes under both bridges and then sets up his own bridge. Each child in turn goes under the two bridges made by the others. Different kinds of bridges can be specified, and the bridges can be arranged so that the child going under must make a change in direction. An over-and-under sequence is also of interest. The child vaults or jumps over the first bridge, and then goes under the next bridge, before setting up his own bridge.

New Leader. Groups of four to five children run around the area, following a leader. When the change is signaled, the last person goes to the head of the line and becomes the leader. The children must now imitate the movements of the new leader.

Manipulative Activity. Each child has a beanbag. As he moves around the area, he tosses the bag upward and catches it. On signal, the child drops the bag to the floor and jumps, hops, or leaps over as many nearby bags as possible. On the next signal, he picks up any convenient bag and resumes tossing it up and catching it. Using one less beanbag than there are children

adds to the fun. Hoops can also be used in this manner. Children begin by using hoops in a rope-jumping movement or by hula-hooping. On signal, the hoops are placed on the floor, and the children jump in and out of as many hoops as they can. Next, each child picks up a nearby hoop and resumes the movement pattern. The activity can also be done with jump ropes or can make use of different kinds of equipment.

Tambourine-Directed Activities

The tambourine can signal changes of movement because of its ability to produce two different kinds of sounds. The first sound is a tinny noise made by vigorous shaking. The second is a percussion sound made by striking the tambourine like a drum, with either the knuckles or the elbow. Movement changes are signaled by changing from one tambourine sound to the other. Suggestions for directives are listed according to the types of sound:

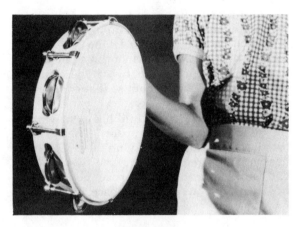

Holding the tambourine

SHAKING SOUND

"Remain in one place, but shake your body all over."

"Remain in one place, shaking your body all over, and slowly drop down to the floor."

"Run in any direction."

"Run very lightly, taking tiny steps."

DRUM SOUND

"Make jerky movements when you hear the drumbeat."

"Jump up and down in one spot."

"Jump in different directions, moving around the room."

"When you hear the drumbeat, start to run [walk, hop, etc.]."

"On the first beat, fall down. On the second beat, roll. On the third beat, form the shape of a . . . ."

To form a combination of movements, select one from each category. When the shaking sound is heard, the children perform that movement. When they hear the change to the drum sound, the children react accordingly.

Games

Selected games are quite suitable for introductory activity, as long as they keep all children active, are simple, and require little teaching. Usually a familiar game should be used, so that little organization time will be needed. Some appropriate games are: Animal Tag (p. 261), Back-to-Back (p. 261), Circus Master (p. 260), and One, Two, Button My Shoe (p. 262).

Miscellaneous Approaches

Children can run laps around the field or the gymnasium for warm-up activity.

Certain pieces of manipulative equipment, such as jump ropes, balls, hoops, and wands can be put out. Children can be directed to practice as they wish for a few minutes.

Climbing ropes, climbing structures, mats, boxes, balance beams, and/or benches can be arranged to allow the children to practice on a selected piece of equipment.

European Rhythmic Running

After observing its effectiveness in Continental programs, the authors are strongly biased in favor of including European rhythmic running among the introductory activities. Since it is based on the competence of running to rhythm, the activity should probably be limited to the first and second grades.

In many European countries, some kind of rhythmic running opens the daily lesson. This light, rhythmic running is done to the accompaniment of some type of percussion instrument, usually a drum or tom-tom. Much of the running follows a circular path, but it can follow other patterns.

To introduce a group of children to rhythmic running, have them stand in circular formation and clap to the beat of the drum. Next, as they clap, they can shuffle their feet in place, keeping time. Following this, have them stop clapping and run in place. The children should now be ready to move in a prescribed path, using the run. It is essential that the run be light, bouncy, and rhythmic, keeping strict time with the beat. Proper spacing between children is needed.

A number of movement ideas can be combined with the rhythmic running pattern.

1. On signal (whistle or double beat on the drum), runners freeze in place. They resume running when the regular beat begins again.

2. On signal, runners make a running full turn in four running steps, lifting their knees high while they turn.

3. As the children run normally in a circle, a signal can be given, and the children run in diverse directions, breaking up the circle. On a second signal, they form the circle again and continue as before.

European running to the beat of a drum

STRENGTH DEVELOPMENT ACTIVITIES

Development activities are those geared primarily to developing strength, with secondary consideration given to movement competency. Demands on different body segments is a goal. To achieve this, a classification of activities is devised around three major body areas—trunk, arm-shoulder girdle, and legs. Although many movements will put demands on more than one body area, and in some will apply to all three areas, the gross movement fitness work during any one daily lesson must be designed in such a way that all three body areas receive appropriate attention.

In all three categories, movements can be locomotor, or they can be done in place. If the movement is locomotor, the children must be directed to move in such a fashion that the desired area of the body will be exercised. The formations for educational movement (pp. 89–90) can be employed for locomotor movements. Nonlocomotor movements are generally done with the children scattered around the area.

The amount of physical effort that the children are to undergo probably becomes a question of instructor judgment. The children must be challenged and stimulated to exert sufficient effort so that development can occur.

A further point should be considered. Activities, by themselves, do not develop fitness. How they are taught and performed governs the value in terms of child development.

To round out the section on strength development, several individual group activities are suggested.

Trunk Development Activities

Movements include bending, stretching, swaying and twisting, forming shapes, and movements to exercise the abdomen. They have not been arranged in any order of difficulty, but the movements themselves should show progressive development. Since the challenge to abdominal muscles should be included, at least two activities should be selected from those specified for trunk development, with one of them taken from the group designed for the abdominal muscles.

BENDING

"Bend in different ways."

"Bend as many parts of your body as you can."

"Make different shapes by bending two, three, and four parts of your body."

"Bend your arms and then your knees in different ways and on different levels."

"Try different ways of bending the fingers and wrist of one hand with the other. Use some resistance."

STRETCHING

"Keeping one foot in place, stretch your arms in different directions, stepping forward or backward with the free foot. Stretch in different levels."

"On the floor, stretch one leg in space in various directions. Stretch one leg in one direction and the other leg in another direction."

"Stretch slowly in any way you wish and then snap back to the original position."

"Stretch with different arm [leg] combinations in various directions."

"See how much space on the floor you can cover by stretching. Show us how big your space is."

Have them combine bending and stretching movements.

SWAYING AND TWISTING

"Sway your body back and forth in different directions. Change the position of your arms."

"Sway your body while you bend over."

"Sway your head from side to side."

"Choose a part of the body and twist it as far as you can in one direction, then in the opposite direction."

"Twist your body at different levels."

"Twist two or more parts of your body at the same time."

"Twist one part of your body while untwisting another."

"Twist your head as far back as you can."

"Twist like a spring; twist like a screwdriver."

"Stand on one foot and twist your body. Untwist."

"From a seated position, make different shapes by twisting."

FORMING SHAPES

Children love to form different shapes with their bodies, and this interest should be utilized to aid in trunk development. Shapes can be formed in almost any position—standing, sitting, lying, balancing on parts of the body—and while moving. Shapes can be curled or stretched, narrow or wide, big or little, symmetrical or asymmetrical, twisted or straight.

ABDOMINAL EMPHASIS

Abdominal mucles are exercised most efficiently with the body in the supine position. The child starts by lying supine on the floor or mat. Challenges should direct him to lift the upper and lower portions of the body from the floor.

The following directives might be given to a child lying on his back on the floor:

"Sit up and touch your toes with your hands."

"Sit up and touch your right toe with your left hand. Do it the other way."

"Bring up your toes so that they touch behind your head."

"With your arms outstretched to the sides, bring the right leg up straight and then swing it over to touch your left hand on the floor. Reverse the movement. Now bring both legs up straight and swing them over to touch the right hand. Then the left hand. Return to a relaxed position, with your legs on the floor."

"Lift your heels about six inches from the floor and swing them from side to side without bending your knees. Cross your ankles and twist them, while keeping them off the floor."

"Lift your head from the floor and look at your toes. Wink with your right eye and wiggle your left foot. Reverse."

"Make your stomach go in and out like a bouncing ball."

Arm-Shoulder Girdle Development Activities

Movement experiences contributing to arm-shoulder development can be divided roughly into two groups of activities. The first includes movements in which the arms are free of any body support function. In the second, the arms support the body weight either wholly or in part.

In the first group, where the arms are free, movements such as swinging, pulling, pushing, lifting, and reaching can be exploited for development.

SWINGING AND CIRCLING

"Swing one arm [leg] at a time, in different directions and at different levels."

"Swing two limbs at one time (arm-arm, leg-leg, arm-leg) in the same direction and in opposite directions. Vary the levels."

"Swing your arms [legs] back and forth and form giant circles."

"Bend over. Now swing your arms as if you were swimming. Try a backstroke. A breaststroke. What does a sidestroke look like?"

"Make your arms go like a windmill. Go in different directions."

"How else can you circle your arms?"

"Pretend that a swarm of bees is around your head. Brush them off and keep them away."

REACHING AND PULLING

"Reach high into the sky and pull stars toward you."

"Using both hands, pull something high toward you. Pull something low toward you. Pull from different directions."

"Reach out and grab snowflakes. Did you get one?"

"Pull from different positions—kneeling, sitting, lying down."

"Reach out in one direction as far as you can and then reach out with the same hand in the opposite direction. Reach out high in one direction and low in another."

"With your hands clasped behind your head, pull your head forward. See if you can make wind by waving your elbows back and forth."

"From a sitting position, lift your knees and legs off the floor, while balancing on your seat. Cross and uncross your legs without letting them touch the floor. Can you pull your big toe up to your nose? Try it with the other foot."

"Reach up and climb a ladder to the sky. See how high you can reach."

PUSHING

"Pretend that you are pushing something heavy with both hands. Push it at a high level. Push it at a low level."

"Push up the sky slowly. Stand on tiptoes to hold it up."

"Push with one hand, then the other. Change hands back and forth."

"From a kneeling position, push yourself up to a stand."

"Lie on your tummy. Push yourself backward with your hands. Push yourself right and left."

"Sit on the floor with your legs outstretched. Place your hands alongside your seat and lift your seat off the floor."

LIFTING

"Lift your arms as high as you can. Extend them out wide. Bring them in close to your body."

"Kneel down. Start your arms low and lift them high. See how many different ways you can lift them."

"Pretend that you are lifting and throwing logs. Throw them in different directions. How high can you lift your log?"

Arm Support Activities

Arm support activities include movements in which the arms and legs act as support. These might be moving activities, employing the different kinds of crawls and animal walks, such as the Puppy Dog Run, the Cat Walk, the Alligator, the Rabbit Jump, the Lame Dog Walk, the Crab Walk, the Frog Jump, the Measuring Worm, the Turtle, and the Seal Crawl. These activities are discussed on pp. 185–89.

A convenient formation is the double line arrangement, in which children are positioned on opposite sides of the gym or playroom. As they perform movements, they simply exchange places, using care when they pass one another in the center. The walks can also be performed in free direction, with children moving as they wish.

In fixed arm/leg support positions, the children are directed to take a position, such as crab, push-up, side leaning, or bridge. Different challenges can be given to the children to stimulate movement:

"Lift one foot high. Now lift the other foot."

"Bounce both feet up and down. Move your feet apart while you bounce them."

"Do a push-up. Then inch your feet up to your hands and inch them back again. Inch your feet up to your hands and inch your hands out to get back into a push-up."

"Reach up and back with one hand and touch the other shoulder behind your back."

"Lift both hands from the floor. Try clapping your hands."

"Bounce from the floor, with both hands and feet off the floor at the same time."

"Lower the body an inch at a time until some part of your body (chin, nose, or chest) touches the floor. Return to the starting position. Lower the body again so that a different part touches the floor first."

"Inch your right hand out to the side. Return to the starting position. Now try it with your left hand. Try moving both hands out to the side."

There is value in maintaining each position for a length of time.

The various tasks to be done in these activities provide interest and challenge to the youngsters, and an informal and individual approach will stimulate the children to good effort in muscular work.

Leg Development Activities

Much leg development will be accomplished through the cardiovascular introductory activity, which often includes running. If further work is needed, a range of leg movement challenges can be added. Use of a drumbeat or appropriate music will be well received during these activities.

RUNNING PATTERNS

Running in different directions.
Running in place.
Tortoise and Hare (p. 46).
Rhythmic running (p. 49).
Running and stopping.
Running laps.

JUMPING AND HOPPING PATTERNS

Jumping/hopping in different directions back and forth over a spot.

Jumping/hopping in, out, over, and around hoops, individual mats, or jumping ropes laid on the floor.

Jumping/hopping back and forth over lines or down the lines.

ROPE-JUMPING

Individual rope-jumping.

COMBINATIONS

Many combinations of locomotor movements can be put together, such as run, leap, and roll; or run, jump-turn, and shake.

INTEGRATED MOVEMENT ACTIVITIES

Integrated movement activities are more demanding, since they combine both cardiovascular introductory activities and strength development activities. Children are kept moving in these routines, and thus will find success after they have developed some degree of fitness. Many different cardiovascular introductory and strength development activities can be substituted into these routines to maintain novelty, progression, and motivation level.

Mini-Obstacle Courses

A mini-obstacle course can be set up either indoors (across the floor sideways) or outdoors. The distance between the start and finish lines will depend upon the type of activity. A starting distance of about 30 feet is suggested; this can be adjusted. Cones can mark the course boundaries. The course should be wide enough so that two children at a time can move down the course.

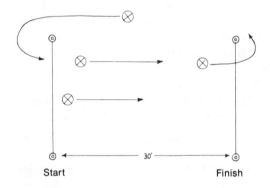

Each child does the stipulated locomotor movement from the start to the finish line, turns left, and jogs back to the start. The movement is continuous, and directions should be given so that there is little delay.

The following movements can be stipulated:

All types of locomotor movements—running, jumping, hopping, sliding, etc.
Movements on the floor—crawling, Bear Walk, Seal Crawl, etc.
Movements over and under obstacles, through tires or hoops

The number of children on each course should be limited to normal squad size or less.

Circular and Figure 8 Movements

Each child selects a spot on which he keeps his hands. Keeping the body straight, he walks the feet in a full circle back to place. Change direction. Try the movement with the back to the floor.

The child keeps the feet in place and walks the hands in a full circle. Vary as in the previous movement.

Four cones or beanbags are set down to form a figure 8 hopping circuit.

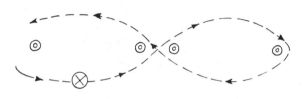

Figure 8 circuit

Have him change feet at the end of each full circuit. Skipping, jumping, galloping, and sliding can be used.

Four Corners Movement Formation

A rectangle is formed with four cones. The student moves around the rectangle, and each time she goes around a corner she changes her movement. Running, skipping, or sliding should be designated. When moving along the short sides, the student can hop or jump.

Using the four-corner idea as a basis, other combinations can be devised. For example, in one pattern, running is required along one of the long sides, and sliding is done along the other. In another pattern, one of the short sides has mats and requires three forward rolls. An animal walk on all fours is required on the other side.

Measurements can vary according to the level of the children and the movement tasks included. Outdoors, four rectangles can be laid out. Indoors, at least two should be established.

Station Activities

Station activities are defined as a number of activities arranged in the form of a circuit, around which the children move from one station to the next. Enough equipment or opportunity should be present so that children have a chance to move without unnecessary waiting. The total circuit should be varied and should include some tasks that are fun. In a six-station circuit, in a class of normal size, three, four, or five children should be allotted to a station.

Station 1. Beanbag target toss—waste baskets or target faces

Station 2. Individual rope-jumping

Station 3. Practicing various kinds of rolls on mats

Station 4. A piece of climbing apparatus or climbing ropes

Station 5. Hula hoops

Station 6. Moving over, under, or through equipment

Allow from forty-five seconds to one minute at each station. Children should understand that they must keep within the limitations as set by the teacher for each station. Play cards that youngsters comprehend can be placed at each of the stations to furnish direction. Rotation should probably be done on signal, as this causes less confusion than individual changing.

THE CIRCUS TENT

A station activity can be arranged in the form of a "circus tent," in which the stations are "cages" or circus acts. Pictures of circus animals and circus acts can be placed at each of the stations. The response is expected to be creative as it interprets the picture. Animal stations can be lions, elephants, ponies, monkeys, and the like. Circus acts can feature jugglers, tight and slack wire artists, Wild West, and trapeze artists. Stations can vary in number, as equipment needs are few. The time for rotating should be related to how long interest seems to continue.

POSTURAL CONSIDERATIONS

Good posture is an important part of physical fitness, since posture is dependent upon the strength of the muscles that hold the body against the force of gravity. Postural muscles work continually and require sufficient strength and energy to hold the body in correct alignment. Thus, the posture assumed by an individual can be an indication of his physical condition.

First of all, posture refers to the overall appearance of the body.[1] It is the habitual or assumed alignment and balance of the body segments while standing, sitting, walking, or lying down. In good posture, body segments are in good relation to one another, reflecting ease, gracefulness, poise, and efficiency of the body.

The transformation of the postural condition of a young child to that of an adult is a slow process. Except for orthopedic limitations, the posture of a young child is quite adaptable. It is only later in life, when connective tissue and muscle position is relatively fixed, that changing posture becomes difficult. The long-term

[1]Evelyn A. Davies, *The Elementary School Child and His Posture Patterns* (New York: Appleton-Century-Crofts, 1958).

target is a satisfactory adult posture, with intermediate steps of acceptable posture along the way.

Lateral curvature (scoliosis) merits serious attention. It can be caused by either structural defects or faulty habits of posture. Obvious signs are uneven shoulders and, in extreme cases, a head tilt to the side. This condition must be referred for treatment, with the responsibility centered on the parents to secure professional help. Some school systems are screening all young children to detect cases of lateral curvature that merit medical attention. The physical education and classroom teachers must then cooperate with the remedial measures instituted.

Anterior-posterior postural problems are easier to correct, since the cause may be a simple lack of knowledge about posture or faulty habits.

How do faulty posture habits cause posture problems? Improper positioning brings about adaptive shortening or stretching of the muscles, which in turn makes it difficult to return to good posture position.

A three-year-old child will have a protruding abdomen, a sway back (lordosis), and rounded shoulders (kyphosis). With the advent of demanding movement, the postural position flattens out somewhat in a gradual shift toward the adult model. First and second grade children can conform reasonably to more critical standards of posture.

What the Teacher Can Do

Most school age children are capable of assuming good posture. Whether they maintain it or not depends upon motivation, proper muscular balance, and the development of good posture habits. These are areas in which the teacher can function. Here are some points for the teacher to consider:

Know the reasons for good posture and be able to describe the elements of good posture in terms that can be understood by the children.

Be an example of good posture practice.

Provide a program of vigorous activity to strengthen the muscles used in maintaining posture.

Provide motivation through the use of posters, drawings, and other aids.

Develop a diagnostic sense with relation to posture in order to separate out for referral children whose conditions are beyond easy correction.

Be happy with a little progress in posture, since improvement comes slowly.

Seek help from the nurse, physical educator, and school physician as needed, while also working with the parents.

What Is Good Posture?

Posture varies with the individual's sex, age, and body type, and what is proper posture for one individual may not be suitable for another. The basic components of posture are much the same for all children, however. These elements are illustrated in the chart on p. 55.

DIRECTIONS FOR ASSUMING GOOD POSTURE IN STANDING POSITION

Feet. Toes are pointed straight ahead; weight is evenly distributed on the balls of the feet and the heels. Cue by saying, "Feet forward! Point your feet straight ahead! Feet parallel! Weight off your heels!" The feet should be parallel and from two to four inches apart.

Knees. Knees should be relaxed and easy. Avoid the back-kneed position in which the knee joint is held forcibly back as far as it can go. Remind the children: "Knees easy! Knees relaxed!"

Lower Back and Abdomen. The abdominal wall should be flattened but relaxed. The lower back curve should be natural and not exaggerated. Children can be told: "Tuck your seat under! Flatten your tummy! Push the body up, tummy in! Flatten your lower back! Hips under!"

Upper Body. The shoulders should be back and relaxed, and the shoulder blades should be flat. The chest should be up and raised. Give the children directions like: "Shoulders easy! Shoulder blades flat! Lift the chest! Chest high!"

Neck and Head. The head should be up and the chin in. The neck should be back. The ear should be directly over the point of the shoulder. Say: "Chin in! Head high! Stand tall! Stretch tall! Chin easy!"

LATERAL DEVIATIONS IN POSTURE

The discussion of posture to this point has been concerned mostly with the forward-backward plane of movement. The body must also be in balance in the lateral plane. From a structural standpoint, when viewed from the front or rear, a perpendicular line should divide the body into two symmetrical or equal halves. If parts of one of the halves cross over this line, there is an unnatural curvature. Again, habit plays a part. The position may result from faulty practices. A shift of the head may be caused by a visual or hearing problem, or both. Uneven shape or size of the bones, particularly the leg bones, will cause the pelvis to tilt laterally, with a compensating curvature of the spinal column.

The presence of lateral curvature can be determined by a check on the level of the pelvis or by noting whether or not the shoulders are even or if the head has a tilt to either side. It is estimated that about 50 percent of the population have some degree of lateral tilt.

Faulty habits contributing to this condition include standing on one leg, leaning against a support, and sitting improperly.

Lateral deviations that need attention are generally beyond the scope of the teacher, even the physical education specialist. Referral to proper medical attention is the recommended procedure.

GOOD WALKING POSTURE

Good walking posture begins with proper use of the feet. It is vitally important that the feet point forward and stay nearly parallel for best functional use. A person who walks with toes pointed out is subject to considerable strain in the arch and lower ankle, leading to a breakdown of the arch and lower leg structure. When he takes a step, the heel should touch first, with

the weight transferred quickly to the balls of the feet and to the toes for a push-off.

The legs should swing freely from the hips, with the knees bending enough to let the feet clear the floor.

The arms should swing in opposition to the legs, the body should retain the properties of good standing posture, and the eyes should be focused on a point on the floor 50 to 60 feet ahead.

PROPER SITTING POSTURE

The knee joint should form a right angle; the feet should be flat on the floor and pointed generally forward. The hips should be back against the chair, and the body should be erect. Forward movement of the body, as when the person is working at a desk, should occur mostly from the hip joint, with the head, upper body, and pelvis remaining in good balance.

OBESITY AND THE YOUNG CHILD

Obesity is a common problem that hampers optimum growth and development patterns of youngsters. It is a difficult and sensitive area to

POSTURE TYPES—PRIMARY LEVEL

Good Posture	Fair Posture	Poor Posture
Head up, chin in, head balanced above the shoulders with the tip of the ear directly above the point of the shoulders	Head forward slightly	Head noticeably forward, eyes generally down
Shoulders back and easy with the chest up	Chest lowered slightly	Chest flat or depressed Shoulder blades like "wings"
Lower abdomen in and flat	Lower abdomen in but not flat	Abdomen relaxed and prominent
Slight normal curves in the upper and lower back	Back curves increased slightly over normal	Back curves exaggerated beyond normal
Knees easy	Knees back slightly	Knees forced back in back-kneed position Pelvis noticeably tilted down
Weight properly placed with toes pointed forward	Weight a little too far back on heels	Weight improperly distributed

deal with, yet is one that requires attention. The obese child is a special case with his unique problems, and he needs special treatment. Since each case is different, the approach for each child must be individual in nature.

Obesity can be related to many factors, including genetics, emotional stability, organism malfunction, and diet-activity problems. Any attempt at solving the problem must take into consideration all the predisposing factors.

Obesity can be defined roughly in terms of overweight percentages. A child who is between 10 and 20 percent over the weight designations for his or her age and height can be classified as overweight. An obese child then becomes one who is more than 20 percent overweight. These percentages are neither fixed nor sacred, as they vary somewhat from one source to another. The advantage of a percentage definition is that it provides a mathematical definition for obesity, which is understandable to parents. However, skin-fold measurement is a more scientific means of identifying the obese individual.

Unfortunately, the odds are overwhelming that a fat child will stay that way as he or she grows up. About 85 percent of fat children have to fight fat for the rest of their lives.[2] The conception that the child will "grow out of it" normally is a mistaken one. Unless remedial action is taken early, the chances of solving the problem are slim.

Heredity and environment may be difficult to separate as causes for obesity. Fat runs in families. About one-half of the children with one obese parent end up as fat adults themselves. This jumps to 80 percent when both parents are obese. Many obesity problems are caused by parents who overfeed their children. Trying to remedy the problem in such an environment is extremely difficult.

Youngsters who are obese often see physical activity in a different light than do chidren of normal weight. Many of them have never experienced even moderate success in activity and find it an area that offers them little personal reward. The driving and enthusiastic attitude that many instructors exhibit toward physical activity is often resented by the obese child. Instructors should try to keep in mind that, in most cases, physical activity is not self-reinforcing for the overweight child.

Obesity is found in children of all ages. It is a serious problem, due to the fact that it is a contributing factor in heart disease. It also impedes the development of motor skills and limits the child's success in such activities. The most common factor found to create obesity is an imbalance between caloric intake and energy expenditure. Most obese children eat too much and fail to involve themselves in enough physical activity. The dietary problem is further complicated by between-meal snacking, eating junk food, and addiction to sweets and other high-calorie foods.

Measuring the triceps fold

Identification of the Obese Child

The most practical and common method of evaluating children to see if they are obese is to use skin calipers to measure skin folds. The triceps skin fold is the most representative area for measurement. Calipers are relatively inexpensive, and the measurement can be made quickly. To measure the triceps skin fold, pinch up the skin on the back of the upper arm, midway between the shoulder and the elbow. The calipers will then measure the thickness of the fold of skin and adipose tissue and will give a reading in millimeters. Table 8 (p. 57) can then be consulted to see if the child is obese.

[2]Alvin Eden, "How to Fat-proof Your Child," *Readers Digest* (December 1975).

Holding the skin calipers

TABLE 8.   OBESITY STANDARDS

Age (years)	Minimum Triceps Skin-fold Thickness Indicating Obesity (millimeters)	
	Males	**Females**
5	12	14
6	12	15
7	13	16
8	14	17

Source: C. C. Seltzer and J. Mayer, "A Simple Criterion of Obesity," *Postgraduate Medicine* 38(2) (1965): A101. Reprinted with permission.

Another method, which is less scientific, but can offer a reasonable estimate, is called the pinch test. Pinch up the skin fold with the thumb and forefinger. If more than an inch is pinched up, the child can be considered obese. Generally, the skin fold should be between one-half and one inch thick to be in the acceptable range. Various other sites can be used to measure, such as the back of the upper arm, the side of the lower chest, the abdomen, and/or the back, just below the shoulder blade. Perhaps a few situations do not require formal assessment. If a child looks fat, he is fat.

Establishing an Advisory Council

A council can be organized to aid the development of programs for these children with special needs. There are many phases to a sound program, and the addition of the following people to the council will facilitate development of the program.

1. *Elementary physical education specialist.* If there is a specialist on the faculty, he can be of great help in suggesting physical activities that will offer the obese child increased activity. He is often the key person in the program, since he will administer the program and be responsible for evaluation.

2. *School nurse.* The nurse is often the best person to make contact with the parents of the obese child. The matter of diet will enter the picture, and the nurse has more knowledge about these matters than anyone else in the school setting. Also, if a physician is needed, the nurse can recommend one.

3. *Principal.* The principal is in a position to offer support to the program and can also see the total school picture. He is a good person for parents to meet and can give them the feeling that the school totally supports the program.

4. *School psychologist.* Since many eating and activity patterns are related to personal adjustment problems, the school psychologist may be of aid in this area. This member can offer information about how the child should be handled and give special insight into personal development.

5. *Parents.* Parents should be on the council to offer insight into family problems that could make it difficult to implement the program. They can deliver information about the program from a layperson's viewpoint to other interested parents.

The council should meet regularly and discuss each case on an individual basis. Through these meetings, insight and direction can be offered to the elementary specialist or administering teacher.

Administration of the Program

The following items are not offered in any particular order, but will serve as a checklist of items to be considered in administering a program.

1. When a child has been identified as a candidate for the obesity program, his parents should be informed by a letter requesting parental approval allowing the child to participate in an individualized program. The letter should also ask the parents to attend a meeting in which the program will be discussed in detail. Parents should be involved to the extent that they are willing to participate, as the success of the program depends a great deal on their support.

2. The program should meet the personal goals of the child. For example, physical fitness may be more motivating to boys as an outcome of the program, whereas some girls might respond more to the promise of physical attractiveness. It is most important, and sometimes

difficult with young children, to secure a positive commitment from the child to the program.

3. Activities that the child is to carry out during the evenings can be detailed on a checklist and sent home with the child. The parents should look at the list each day. If the parent can take a special interest in the child's progress, the chance for good results will be increased.

4. The instructor should meet with the child once a week. He can see children individually or can meet with small groups of two or three children. The meeting time can be used for evaluating progress, checking the child's activity sheet and assigning new activities.

5. If feasible, it is motivating to youngsters to send home a piece of equipment for their use. For example, a jump rope might go home one week, and a playground ball the next. This equipment would be part of their assigned activity and would be returned at the next meeting.

6. The program should be designed for the individual child. He or she should not be expected to adapt to a rigid program. Start children at a level where they can find immediate success in performing the tasks. This will start to break their "I can't do this" failure cycle.

7. As the child becomes more involved in the program, let him or her help you plan the activity assignments. The long-range goal of the program would be that children learn to diagnose and prescribe activities for themselves throughout life.

8. Every time the child is evaluated during the course of the program, make sure the parents receive the results. The parents can then aid in reinforcing the child for his or her efforts.

The program for the obese child will need the cooperation of many people. It is a difficult problem to solve, and instructors should not be discouraged when only minor results are achieved. One must take the point of view that even if only one child is helped to overcome obesity, the effort was worthwhile.

Motivating the Obese Child

One of the more difficult areas to deal with in the program for the obese child is that of motivation. For most obese children, activity is not self-reinforcing and generates little desire for continued participation. The following guidelines may give the instructor some direction in this matter:

1. Show a sincere interest in the youngsters. They have to feel as though you have a special regard for them. They should be able to communicate to you their feelings about the program and their progress.

2. Exhibit enthusiasm for activity. Students learn that activity is fun by seeing important others enjoying it. Let them know that activity is an important part of your life and that you would miss it if it were taken away.

3. Use exciting activities and equipment to stimulate them to movement. For example, equipment should be brightly colored and easy to handle. Jump-rope activities may be much more exciting than running in place.

4. Discuss openly with the child the reasons for his obesity. The child should know that you understand his problem fully and are interested in helping him find a solution.

5. Help the child to understand that the program is for his own benefit. It should not be seen as a punishment, but as an opportunity for personal development.

6. Evaluate often and involve the child in the process of evaluation. It is reinforcing to follow one's progress, and evaluation can be a valuable motivating instrument for the child.

7. Above all, don't nag. Encouragement is the key to action.

SUMMARY

Physical fitness implies the ability to resist the stresses of the environment without undue fatigue and to have enough energy left over for leisure activity. Fitness activities for young children should include a good deal of large-muscle activity and should be geared to the maturity level of the student. The activities should be presented so that a balanced program is offered covering the following components: strength, power, endurance, and flexibility.

Much of the fitness experience for the preschool child should be integrated into the play experience. Emphasis should be placed on strength and cardiovascular introductory activities. Cardiovascular introductory activity warms children up and prepares them for the activity that is to follow. This type of activity is low-organized and requires little teacher instruction time. A wide variety of cardiovascular introductory activities is offered so that teachers can maintain the enthusiasm of the youngsters for movement.

Strength development activities are geared to develop the body with demands placed on different body parts to emphasize total fitness. Integrated movement activities combine both cardiovascular introductory activity and strength development activity and are used when children have developed some degree of fitness.

As posture patterns are beginning to stabilize in the preschool years, the teacher should be aware of what good posture is and how to help children improve their posture. Children can practice good walking, standing, and sitting posture.

Obesity is a severe problem that faces children at an early age. It is important to give attention to this area, since most obese youngsters grow into obese adults. The percentage of body fat can be measured to give teachers and parents an indication of when a child is becoming obese. Establishing an advisory council to help solve obesity problems is an important step in offering aid to youngsters with special needs.

ADDITIONAL REFERENCES

Hockey, Robert V. *Physical Fitness, The Pathway to Healthful Living.* St. Louis, Mo.: C. V. Mosby Co., 1973.

Johnson, Mary L., Burke, Bertha S., and Mayer, Jean. "The Prevalence and Incidence of Obesity in a Cross Section of Elementary and Secondary School Children." *American Journal of Clinical Nutrition* 4(6) (1956): 231.

Mayer, Jean. *Overweight: Causes, Cost and Control.* Englewood Cliffs, N.J.: Prentice-Hall, 1968.

Seltzer, Carl C., and Mayer, Jean. "An Effective Weight Control Program in a Public School Program." *American Journal of Public Health* 60(4) (1970): 679–89.

Chapter 6

Play and Creativity in Learning

Play is the way a child learns what no one else can teach him.

Lawrence Frank

A play atmosphere is important in preschool and kindergarten programs and has diminishing importance in the primary grades. A play atmosphere can be superimposed over most movement methodology for younger children. For this purpose, an understanding of play and its purpose in the growth and development of children is essential in developing a proper approach in movement programs for preschool and kindergarten children.

Children's play is a beginning step in the process of acculturation. As the child explores the environment, he experiments and begins to develop an understanding of the world. While playing with others, children must learn to operate with common agreement and to function within some social order. Through play, the child learns to make decisions, produce proper responses, find new techniques to solve problems, and discover behavior that is necessary for his own protection and well-being. The play instinct appears to be a strong motivator and is necessary for optimum development and maturity. To a child, play is not wasting time or exhibiting unproductive behavior. Rather, it is a method used to research the world and to achieve a peaceful living arrangement with the universe.

Children must play. If they are not given a healthy and safe environment in which to play, they will play where it is unhealthy and unsafe, such as the city streets. Adults should learn that play, for a child, is work, and that his play is hard and intense activity. The typical adult belief that play is a waste of time is manifested in poorly planned and uncreative play areas or the lack of any play areas at all.

As the world becomes more complex, there is a growing need for people who can solve problems creatively. A child can be encouraged in this direction through his play. Through play, a child can explore and experiment without fear of being wrong. He can let his natural curiosity guide him to new and exciting alternatives, without being restricted by others who already know that "it won't work." In the course of play, the child can become totally involved and absorbed in thought.

The playing process is a learning laboratory in miniature. The child becomes intensely focused on what he is doing and allows little to disrupt this concentration. Youngsters can brainstorm, think of many and varying alternatives, and venture far into the world of fantasy. Because the child can focus strongly on the task at hand and think in an unrestricted environment, his learning is easily and rapidly enhanced. Also, while he is playing, the child naturally repeats and practices an activity many times. One of the key factors in motor learning is repetition, and the play environment is conducive to this. To take advantage of Mother Nature's Learning Laboratory, teachers must learn to provide materials, equipment, ideas, and experiences for the child and then allow the child to play. The child will provide the energy and initiative necessary to discover new and meaningful answers as he follows his motivating drive to know and create.

TYPES OF PLAY

It may be of value to look at play as being of two types. The first type is free play, in which the direction and focus of activity comes from the child. This contrasts with guided play, in which the teacher guides the student through various systematic experiences that are designed to lead to conceptual learning. Both types are necessary in childhood learning, but each yields different results.

Free Play

Free play is spontaneous and directed by the child. It is a better choice for very young children. Learning in the cognitive and psychomotor domains can be developed, but it is difficult for the instructor to predict the outcome. Free play involves much imagination and fantasy. It aids in the development of some of the following areas:

1. *Individuality and uniqueness.* The child can deal with situations in his own way and at his own rate. He can begin to realize that his ideas are of worth, are different from others', and take varying amounts of time to develop.
2. *Insightfulness.* The child can become a keen observer in the play environment that allows one to analyze and make comparisons for development of meaningful insights. The ability to sense a change in the environment is vital for understanding the world.
3. *Imagination.* Nowhere can a child invent, imagine, fantasize, and make believe as he can in the unstructured play situation. The realm of a child's mind is expanded when he can find solutions for problems.
4. *Task persistence.* Through sustained periods of play, the child can learn to concentrate for long periods of time and maintain a high level of task persistence.

In essence, to play freely is to think, to feel, to move, and to enjoy. It can provide total integration of the affective, cognitive, and psychomotor domains of the child's being.

Guided Play

Guided play occurs when the teacher is interested in developing specific learning in cognitive, affective, and/or psychomotor domains. The teacher structures a situation and attempts to involve the child in the learning process. The goal or outcome is predetermined by the instructor, and the students are guided toward that solution or outcome. The crucial factor pertaining to whether guided play is actually play has to do with the way the child enters into the activity and continues voluntarily. As children become older, they gain more and can learn rapidly from guided play situations. Basically, guided play should be selected over unstructured play when more advanced and conceptual learning is desired.

Play for Psychomotor Development

Children love to see what they are capable of performing physically. The play situation allows them to test themselves, to compare themselves with others, and to meet the challenge of new situations. Through physical play, children can measure their strength, check their coordination skills, and develop an overall understanding of their strength and limitations. The area in which children play must offer challenges that the child desires to undertake. If not, play will occur in a physical environment that may be less than optimum. Adults must not underestimate the child's discretion in understanding his limits. Too often, adults remove equipment and apparatus that is challenging and offers some degree of risk. Children rarely extend themselves beyond their capabilities, however, if they are not directed to do so by adults. Physical play offers great opportunity to undertake the unknown, live with the risk involved, and conquer one's fear. Since physical accomplishments can be seen by all, they can be a source of visible personal accomplishment.

Physical play is an excellent medium for repetitive practice for developing motor skills. While children are at play, they will practice various motor patterns over and over without becoming bored. They will try new ways of swinging and crawling, will see how far or high they can jump and to what height they can climb. Other physical limits will be expanded throughout this constant and repetitive play cycle. Never again will the child have the time and opportunity to learn physically and be virtually unhindered by the demands of the world. Finally, during this period, children can learn a great deal through trial and error. Mistakes can be eliminated, and patterns improved, based upon the results of their performance. Through experimentation within this play area, children will learn to live comfortably within their physical environment.

Play for Affective Development

During play situations, children have many opportunities for interaction with others. According to Arnaud, "Play permits the child to experiment with possible options and solutions and to get others' reactions to these, without committing himself to the consequences of having tried out these alternatives in real life."[1] Simple games with rules and boundaries provide many occasions for children to learn to respect others, to respect property, and to play in a socially acceptable fashion.

Through play, children can learn to express feelings and see how the world will respond. Often they learn that it is not safe to tell others openly about feelings, and thus the play opportunity allows an emotional release. Youngsters live in a world surrounded by giants, who tell them what to do, how to do it, and when to do it. Sometimes, children find their motivations thwarted by these adults and/or peers. Through play, children can safely release inner tensions and express themselves.

Play is a time when children can push beyond the limits of their present environment through role-playing. Children love to play doctor, fireman, policeman, cowboy, nurse, dancer, and other roles that are within their area of awareness. Through role-playing, they can develop a feeling about their own personal nature and act out a role they might some day desire to emulate. They can organize situations with friends, and work and play with them in this context. The need for cooperation among peers to make this type of play successful soon becomes apparent, and bargaining and skills are learned as children select various roles. Give-and-take starts to become a way of life.

Through play, children can develop some positive attitudes and feelings toward physical activity. As many educators believe, attitudes toward life are formed at an early age. It would seem vital to aid the child in developing a set of values directed toward the need for physical activity. It is the task of the instructor to establish a climate for play that will allow children to feel that what they are doing is important. If teachers view play as important, children will soon learn that it is important to play and will learn to take an active part in their own lives.

Children need to learn to live with themselves. To do so, they need to become aware of their motives, desires, and abilities. In the play environment, they can come to grips with their capabilities without undue shock and surprise. Along the same line, the child needs to learn to play alone and to entertain himself. Children who have not learned the skill of solitary play often complain of boredom and having "nothing to do." As the child's self-knowledge grows, he will grow in self-confidence and self-reliance as well.

Play for Cognitive Development

Play offers children the opportunity to make decisions and then test their effectiveness in a controlled situation. Play is a learning activity and is often itself a nonverbal mode of communication. Practice in problem-solving is crucial to the development of fully functioning individuals. For children to be good problem-solvers, they must have good questioning ability. Guessing and trying out novel solutions are the beginning of the scientific method. One must ask questions to find answers. Through play, children can develop the ability to put in order, classify, label, and discover differences, as they solve relevant puzzles and problems.

Play allows children to follow the natural urge of curiosity. They can explore with their hands, eyes and tongues in an attempt to find out the hows and whys of living. A great deal of language development will occur due to observing models of importance. They can increase conceptual learning by associating various experiences that have occurred in play. Play, both free and guided, offers children a multitude of chances to develop cognitive skills without the fear of failure and rejection. Play can often be a superior medium for cognitive development when it is carried out in a suitable environment.

PLAY AND LEISURE ACTIVITY

Play should also be undertaken for the sheer enjoyment of playing. When play is seen as valuable and necessary to healthful living, it becomes an integral part of life. Although leisure is increasing, it appears that our knowledge of how to utilize it is not keeping pace. Will leisure be spent productively or will it contribute to a gradual deterioration of society? Too many people do not know how to play, since they were not allowed the opportunity to do so as youngsters. Some people merely become observers of others who are involved in play activity. Teachers must be alerted to the fact that playing during childhood is really the basis for the ability to play and enjoy oneself during adulthood. As the late Dr. Menninger put it, "Good mental health is directly related to the capacity and willingness of an individual to play. Regardless of his objections, resistances or past practice, any individual will make a wise investment for himself if he does plan time for his play and take it seriously."[2] We must begin to see the need for active play, not as an orna-

---

[1] Sara H. Arnaud, "Some Functions of Play in the Educative Process," *Childhood Education* 51(2) (1974): 72–78.

[2] Edward Greenwood, "The Importance of Play," *Menninger Quarterly* (Summer 1968).

ment, but as an integral part of the total education of children.

PLAY AND CREATIVITY

Children's play is a medium for expressing their creative drives. In play, youngsters can analyze situations and find new ways of reorganizing them. They might assign a different use to some implement, or create a new relationship with someone. Play is an outlet for fantasy and imagination that helps children put newfound ideas into action.

All children can be creative; all have a strong motivating drive to share their new ideas and productions. Playtime should develop confidence and a willingness to express and share. Creativity is the key to conflict resolution. In the complexity of modern-day living, new and undiscovered ways of resolving conflicts need to be developed. Children may be able to find new ways of communicating through play with peers. When youngsters are stimulated to question and probe, using creative thought and expression, problem-solving and progress will occur. The question, "How can we do this a better way?" is the cornerstone of creative thought.

Enhancing Creativity

A teacher must be highly sensitive to the fragility of the creative process. Students are often strongly rewarded for doing what they are told to do and discouraged from trying something different or unique. The teacher must know when to let learning flow and how to keep thoughts and ideas flowing. A few guidelines are offered for teacher behavior that will aid in increasing creative behavior.

1. The teacher should respect and even welcome a child's unusual questions. Finding answers to questions is self-rewarding to children and will perpetuate their knowledge-seeking strategies.

2. Opportunities for self-initiated activity should be allowed and teacher approval given to such activity. Employers constantly seek out individuals who are self-starters and can initiate new ideas. The teacher should reward self-direction as a step in establishing this pattern for adulthood.

3. Children should be shown that their ideas are desired and valued. This can be accomplished through careful listening to all serious suggestions, followed by thoughtful consideration. Ideas can also be tested and used, with youngsters given verbal or nonverbal credit for their contributions.

4. The teacher must learn not to show surprise when unorthodox solutions are offered. Too often, children are laughed at when their ideas seem unrealistic and unexpected. A teacher who displays an unassuming and accepting manner soon establishes an environment in which it becomes commonplace to look beyond simple and easily seen solutions.

5. Students must be able to do their creative thinking in a nonjudgmental atmosphere. The young child is not ready to have his ideas or thoughts rejected. Constant evaluation and categorization destroys the drive to create. Particularly during practice and the early stages of learning a new skill, children should not have to fear that others are going to measure and question their performance.

6. Bear in mind that the creative process is more important than the activity itself. A teacher should be a catalyst both to encourage and to protect children from outside ridicule. Teachers should not see themselves as authorities with the right to impose their ideas on others.

7. Creativity is not limited to the artist or performer. Every human being has a capacity for being creative, and it is the responsibility of the teacher to deal creatively with children in a way that will facilitate their creative development. Especially creative individuals may be unlike other students in that they are often positive thinkers with a great deal of faith in their abilities. They will possess needed knowledge in many areas and have the insight and confidence to try thinking of new ideas and behaving in nonconforming ways. Finally, they sometimes refuse to allow authority to limit their thoughts and actions. They will try new notions over and over and over.

8. Sometimes, certain directives will stimulate children to look beyond accepted practices and ideas. Some of the following might be useful: Rearrange, add, eliminate, turn upside down, reverse, combine, substitute, look for different ways, make smaller, make bigger.

9. The following principles may be helpful in sharing the creative process with children:

a. Judgment of new ideas must be deferred. To judge a new idea good or bad, wrong or right, immediately, will destroy the desire to create. Right or wrong is better judged by the glow in the child's eyes and his commitment to the task of the moment.

b. Quantity produces quality in that often many areas and avenues must be explored to discover one quality concept. Encourage brainstorming, in which ideas are shared as rapidly as possible without fear of rebuttal.

c. New ideas produce more new ideas. Improvements are made as people strive to better the status quo. New and better alternatives are often found when the *process* of looking for new ideas is valued.

SUPERVISING PLAY EXPERIENCES

Teachers can have a great influence on the effectiveness of play experiences for youngsters. The behavior the teacher exhibits toward play will tell children quickly whether play is seen as important. Some of the following considerations should be of value in establishing an optimum situation for play.

1. Children must be able to control the play situation. It is not play to a child when a teacher dominates the experience. Children need the power and the opportunity to control their own destinies, and play can offer this if it is student-controlled.

2. Motivation for play must be intrinsic. It doesn't work to tell children to "go and play." Children will decide when they are going to play and how they want to play. The teacher must allow time for play, but only the children can decide that they want to become deeply involved in the situation.

3. Teachers must become less involved educationally when it is time to play. There does not have to be a golden lesson learned from every situation. It is meaningless to speak of teaching children how to play. They are experts at it and only need a rich environment for maximum results.

4. Provision must be made in the school setting for play to occur. Extended play is necessary so that children can become engrossed in the activity and carry out more detailed and complex activities. Task persistence can never be learned if youngsters are only allowed to play for a short time. Too often, play is doled out in short segments as a reward for good behavior rather than as a required activity. Play must continue from day to day and be of some duration to render an important role in the development of children.

5. It is natural for children to talk a great deal during play, and they should not be expected to remain silent. A great deal of verbal behavior can be experienced during play sessions.

6. Teachers should not interfere with the playing process unless they are willing to participate on the child's terms. Children enjoy someone listening in and observing, but do not appreciate it when adults try to organize and arrange for something productive to occur from the situation.

7. A good understanding of child development is necessary if a teacher expects to be able to analyze a play environment and know when children need aid and understanding. The instructor should have a good feeling for which materials and equipment are necessary and exciting for youngsters. A great deal can be learned through keen observation about supplies and equipment that motivate youngsters.

EQUIPMENT AND PLAY AREAS

Equipment and materials for youngsters should be gathered and evaluated on the basis of what contribution they can make to the total development of students. At times, teachers or parents will buy toys for children only to find that the children themselves do not find them attractive and stimulating. If possible, one of best ways to evaluate equipment is to allow the children to play with it for an extended period of time. Organic and natural materials are usually attractive to children. Sand, water, clay, and wood are materials that should be available to children every day. These materials have different properties, and children need to be able to find out what they are capable of doing with the various media. This early exploratory stage may seem messy and unproductive to the teacher, but its value should not be underestimated.

The indoor play area should be carpeted and have sufficient storage areas for the equipment. Children love to play on the floor and will find the carpet comfortable, and teachers will enjoy the comparative quiet of such a floor. Storage areas are important if youngsters are to learn to share in the process of acquiring and putting away their play objects. On the other hand, there should be areas where children can leave ongoing projects from day to day without suffering the trauma of finding that someone has destroyed their accomplishments. Equipment that is purchased should be scaled down to a size that is easily handled by young children. If children are expected to get out their own equipment and help in moving it to various areas, it is necessary that the items not be too heavy or bulky for them to carry.

Criteria for Equipment Selection

Certain criteria can be useful in deciding what equipment should be purchased for enhancing the play environment of the young child. The ideal kinds of toys and equipment to purchase are those that satisfy the following criteria:

1. Do the toys and equipment meet the needs of the children? Are they interesting and stimu-

lating? Adult criteria such as expense, novelty, and popularity should be minor considerations and usually represent adult evaluations. Those toys or materials that are often most enticing to children can be found anywhere, are simple, and are often free (cardboard, dirt, paper, water, etc.).

2. Is the equipment flexible enough to be used in many ways? The more ways a child can find to use a certain piece of equipment, the more apt he is to play with it for a long period of time.

3. Is the toy durable and sturdy? Some toys may be too complex and will break easily. Children lack fine motor coordination and do not treat their play objects gently.

4. Can the object be manipulated? Does it allow for automatic self-correction so that children can learn as they play? For example, some of the Montessori materials offer the children immediate feedback as to whether they made the right decision. ("Put a square peg in the square hole.")

5. Is it safe? The following guidelines should be examined when one is deciding on the safety of equipment.

a. The toy should be appropriate for the developmental age of the child. Injuries occur when these two do not coincide.

b. The toy or equipment should be examined for sharp points and corners that might harm the child.

c. The toy should not break or come apart into small pieces that the youngster will be tempted to swallow.

d. The play object should be examined to see if it might pinch, crush, or cut body parts. Many objects have slots and holes in which tiny fingers may get caught.

6. Is the equipment necessary? Some play situations require a minimum of toys and/or equipment. For example, creative, finger, and dramatic play require little but the enthusiasm and inventiveness of the teacher. These activities offer children opportunity for expression and interpretation as well as physical involvement.

Suggested Equipment and Supplies

Materials listed are presented in two groups, those needed for children three to five years old and those that are used by children five to seven. Obviously, many of the toys can be used by children in both groups, and the lists are not meant to be all-inclusive.

PRESCHOOL CHILDREN (AGES THREE TO FIVE)

Cognitive development
Picture books
Tape recorders
Magnetic letters and numbers
Chalkboards
Simple board games
Card games
Finger plays
Songs and listening games

Affective development
Dress-up clothes and costumes
Dolls
Play animals
Dollhouses
Farm sets and garages
Material for playing fire station and policeman
Model airport sets and planes
Doctor and nurse materials
Telephones

Psychomotor development: Gross motor skills
Tricycles
Wagons
Climbing bars
Sandbox
Scooters
Balance beams
Benches
Jumping boxes
Bounding boards
Ladders
Climbing ropes
Individual mats

Psychomotor development: Fine motor skills
Blocks
Puzzles
Beads (large, snap-type)
Plā-Dōh
Rhythm instruments, e.g., wood blocks and triangles
Finger paints
Crayons
Beanbags
Yarn balls
Jump ropes
Magic stretch ropes
Stilts
Playground balls
Ping Pong paddles
Woodworking equipment
Painting materials

PRIMARY CHILDREN (AGES FIVE TO SEVEN)

Cognitive development
Reading books
Tape-recorded stories
Dramatic plays
Displays of collections, e.g., rocks, butterflies, and plants
Charts with number concepts
Materials to measure height and weight
Flash cards

Affective development
Materials for show-and-tell activities
Games that require sharing
Creative play materials
Toys that require cooperation, e.g., wagons, rocking boats
Equipment for simple skits and plays

Psychomotor development
Stilts
Wands
Tunnels and crawling tubes
Balls of all sizes, shapes, and colors
Bats and batting tees
Tires
Sawhorses
Parachute
Tumbling mats
Scoops
Roller skates

SUMMARY

Play is important in the natural development of children. It is a learning laboratory for children where they can explore, invent, succeed, and fail in a nonthreatening atmosphere. Two contrasting types of play are guided play and free play. Free play is spontaneous and directed by the child. Guided play occurs when the teacher is interested in developing specific learning outcomes through the play experience.

Play is an important part of learning how to use leisure productively. Play can enhance the creative drive in children. Various steps are offered the teacher to aid in increasing creative behavior among students. When teachers supervise play experiences it is important that they allow students to control and manipulate their environment. The play situation can be an excellent laboratory for teachers to see what materials, toys, and ideas motivate different students.

Equipment and play areas should be evaluated on the basis of the contribution made to the total development of the youngsters. Apparatus and equipment should be flexible, attractive, durable, and safe for the students to utilize during free time activity. Suggested equipment and supplies are offered for children of different age groups.

ADDITIONAL REFERENCES

Ellis, M. J., and Scholtz, G. J. L. *Activity and Play of Children.* Englewood Cliffs, N.J.: Prentice-Hall, 1978.
Frost, J. L., and Klein, B. L. *Children's Play and Playgrounds.* Boston: Allyn and Bacon, 1979.
Matterson, E. M. *Play and Playthings for the Pre-School Child.* Baltimore, Md.: Penguin Books, 1965.
Piers, Maria, ed. *Play and Development.* New York: W. W. Norton and Co., 1972.

Chapter 7

The Teacher in the Learning Environment

People seldom improve when they have no other model but themselves to copy after.

Oliver Goldsmith

We have often observed a teaching demonstration, purportedly of a particular style or method, and come away stimulated to better efforts. After reflection and pondering, we gradually arrived at the conclusion that the most critical component of the demonstration was not the methodology presented, but the personality of the teacher.

According to basic organizational theory, all learning activities in the schools are by nature teacher-guided. Student control of learning exists only to the extent that it is permitted, and students may have considerable influence, but never total control. The teacher always retains some degree of responsibility for maintaining a beneficial learning environment for students.

THE ROLE OF THE TEACHER

If teachers can abide by the dictum that, "If teachers will teach, children will learn," a big step in the direction of child development will have been taken. The responsibility of the teacher is to set the stage and create a suitable environment in which progress in learning can be attained. The teacher is no longer a director of child activity, but a facilitator of learning.

Mahatma Gandhi once said, "What does it matter that we take different roads, so long as we reach the same goal!" Teachers so often get bogged down in discussions about proper methods and approaches and lose sight of the goal of optimum development for each child. Given ten different teachers, one will find ten different approaches or variations in approach. The teacher has the right to select the methodology

and approach for a particular presentation so long as the anticipated target goals are accomplished.

In planning movement activities to achieve stated goals, a teacher needs adequate background to make a meaningful selection of the particular movements and skills the child should experience. Once movement patterns have been experienced by children, critical observation of their level of performance precedes prescription of activities to reinforce positive elements. Further diagnosis would govern the allotment of sufficient practice time to reinforce the correct patterns, including consideration for overlearning. In this process the teacher's actions may be defined as encouraging, challenging, and reinforcing.

A teacher must respect children if he expects to earn their respect. This is a two-way street, but demonstrating respect for students undoubtedly precedes receiving respect in turn. Knowing and being able to call each youngster by name is an important step in developing the children's respect.

Some teachers consciously or unconsciously emphasize areas of learning that they value, which is not educationally sound if these areas do not satisfy pertinent student needs. For example, a teacher who is an avid square dancer emphasizes the activity at the first grade level, when most curriculum specialists deem the fifth or sixth grade as most suitable for this activity. Another may like a particular sport and will stress its skills too heavily, because she feels secure in teaching these fundamentals.

If the teacher places too high a value on perfection or outstanding achievement, he can effectively prevent students from succeeding. A few children may meet these high standards, but the remainder are lost in a sea of frustration. This practice is observable in the areas of gymnastics and swimming when students are started at a very young age.

Managing children is a learned skill, and teachers must work at it constantly. Keeping up to date, acquiring new ideas, completing refresher courses, and delving into literature and critical research are essential for growth as a teacher.

All children should be expected and encouraged to work at or near their potential. It is the teacher's role to stimulate youngsters to this level of effort. Children should learn that success can be achieved only through good effort, and that the person who doesn't put forth this effort is selling himself short. Since children usually live up to teacher expectations, it is important to stress good traits in one's students.

The ability to listen is a great asset to the teacher. A teacher who does not or cannot listen to children has little business teaching. Listening also implies respect for what is said, no matter how irrelevant or trivial it may sound to the teacher. Remember that it may be a meaningful expression to the child. Eyeballing is important. Look at children when they talk to you.

Another trait of significance for teachers is the ability to observe critically. Watching children in action should stimulate the teacher to think: what is the next step to institute? What is the challenge? Finally, there is no substitute for a warm, friendly personality and a genuine liking for children. Without these, teaching can become a dehumanizing process.

INSTRUCTIONAL STRATEGIES

In the preceding section, we refer to certain broad instructional skills that should be developed to create a warm and enriching environment. How to work with children, directing their activities, and communicate with children in the learning environment are covered in the section that follows. Attention is also given to areas such as guiding student behavior, safety considerations, and health excuses and screening. The procedures discussed are general in nature, with more specific instructional considerations treated in the sections on the respective activities.

Working with Children

1. Seeking to understand all children as unique individuals begins with understanding the characteristics and needs of children of that age and maturity level. Information pertaining to the background of all children is also important. The teacher then has a better chance to appreciate the uniqueness of each student and can match the learning experiences with the children's specific needs.

2. Stress the youngsters' potential, not their limitations. Avoid pigeonholing children, placing them in a slot from which they will have difficulty escaping.

3. See that every student has an opportunity to be active in the learning situation. Self-directed activity is the basis of physical learning—and, for that matter, all learning. Equipment for individual work should be provided on a one-to-one basis, so that children do not have to wait for a turn. In group work, the groups should be kept small so that all children can make a contribution, and so that standing, watching, and waiting are kept to a minimum.

4. One of the functions of the teacher is to discover the talents of children, so that these may be developed to allow each child to make a significant contribution to group living. This helps children recognize themselves as persons of worth, capable of making a contribution to their peer group.

5. Somewhere in each skill presentation, children should have an opportunity to be creative and explore. Children need time to try out their ideas, solve some of their own problems, and "do their own thing." Lesson plans should reflect time for this opportunity.

6. Occasionally, the teacher can issue equipment and let children try it out on their own for a while. Such exploration is particularly beneficial if the piece of equipment is new to the children and/or is intrinsically attractive. This approach is especially beneficial for preschool children. It is essential that children be cautioned beforehand about any rules of safety that they must observe when they are trying out the new equipment.

7. Some considerations are important when children handle equipment:

a. Respect for equipment should be taught. Children should learn to take care of equipment as if it were their own.

b. Establish an efficient system for issuing and returning equipment. Children should handle this chore themselves whenever possible. If children can secure or return the pieces of equipment in one step, little instructional time will be lost. For example, instead of having one child get a sack of balls and issue them one at a time, place the balls against the wall and have each child get his own ball. Balls can be returned by following the same procedure.

c. When young children are handling larger pieces of equipment, such as benches or mats, specify the number of children needed to move the piece and identify the positions they are to take and the procedures they are to follow when doing so. Obviously, there will be some pieces of equipment that young children should not handle.

8. Group movement of children can create difficulty unless anticipated problems are planned for in the instructional process.

a. Some kind of entry behavior should be specified. When children move from the classroom into a play area, explain where and how they are to assemble. If the children are asked to sit down, aimless running, pushing, and shoving may be kept to a minimum. Some teachers like to have children assume a long-legged sitting position with the hands and arms in back, bracing the upper body. They theorize that in this position the hands are less likely to be on other children. The instructor can also specify that some type of introductory activity is to take place immediately upon entrance. They may be more inclined to listen after they have had an opportunity to move.

b. An important technique to acquire is the ability to disperse children quickly and easily, without fuss. Having approximate preassigned places is a solution. Painting spots, numbers, or even form symbols (triangles, squares) on the floor makes dispersal easy. The teacher merely says, "Go to your spot and wait for instructions."

c. Children should practice forming circles and other shapes. This is a skill that children need to learn and one that will improve with practice. Where circles are painted on the floor, the formation becomes easy. To make the circle smaller or larger, ask the children to take a step in or out—a tiny, average, or giant step as needed.

9. Use simple ways to divide the class into two groups or teams for games or group activities. The teacher can ask children to pair off and stand facing in pairs. The extra child pairs off with the teacher. One child in a pair is seated or stoops down. The standing children move to one side to become one group, and the others form the second. In another method, the children form a circle and divide it into two halves. Avoid asking children to count off or choose sides.

10. When a child is needed for a key role or leadership position, as in some games, it is best for the teacher to avoid selecting the child. Chil-

dren with birthdays during the week or on that day may be assigned these "honors." Asking for volunteers is futile, since the majority of the class will probably volunteer. Rotating key roles is important, and some effort should be made to see that all have a chance. Another approach is to post in the classroom the name of the "Citizen of the Week." The position can rotate, and every child can have a chance to be featured.

11. Assigning partners before an activity is to begin saves considerable time. Partners can be assigned for a period of time, a week or two. This also gives children an excellent opportunity to make new friends among their classmates.

12. Overstimulation should be avoided, but it will occur occasionally during demanding movement or game activities involving young children. The cause of overstimulation should be determined, and the situation corrected for the future. The high degree of excitement should be toned down before children return to class. Chapter 17 presents various relaxation techniques and activities.

13. Have respect for the dignity of children. Avoid grabbing them and pushing them physically from one spot to another. Remember that the child may not have understood your directions. The problem of communication manifests itself particularly clearly when you are dealing with hearing-impaired or mentally retarded children. Be patient. Allow some time to make sure that they have a chance to understand what is wanted.

14. When a substitute teacher takes over, make sure to familiarize him or her with the procedures and arrangements by which the children enter and leave the physical education lesson area. Children should be notified when a substitute teacher is coming, and prior discussions can be held with them on the ways in which they can help.

15. Never force children to do something that they feel incapable of doing. If you can help them build confidence in small increments, the necessary capability and courage to do the task will develop.

16. Some effort should be made to encourage students to work at a steady pace, which is a behavior that can be taught. Too often children plunge in, work hard for a while, and then slack off. Working at a steady pace is a behavioral skill that will be of value during the child's school career and throughout his life.

17. Stress and keep on stressing that children should keep their hands off one another. When children are moving in general space, they should be told not to bump, collide with, or interfere with other children.

Directing Activities

1. The teacher should use the daily lesson plan as the basis for instruction. Proper coverage of material is assured only through planned lessons.

2. In some manipulative activities, when movement stops on signal, it is wise to designate a neutral position where the object should remain while the teacher is speaking. For a playground ball, the neutral positon might be on the floor, between the legs of the player who was handling it at the signal. This will prevent the children from bouncing or tossing it while instructions are being given, which can be distracting to both teacher and students.

3. Teachers should plan learning experiences so that there is progression in small steps, to assure that success can be achieved along the way.

4. The "start-and-expand" technique should be the basis for skill-learning. The skill is presented in such a way that all children attempting it may meet with success. The skill can be expanded later on to offer more challenge.

5. A major technique to be acquired is the ability to change and vary an activity so that the most value can be secured from the experience. There are many ways of securing variety in movement experiences. Educational movement itself provides many ideas for extending the potential of activity. Teachers should be alert for changes and modifications that can increase interest and make more physical demands on the children. The children themselves are a source of suggestions for changes and variations. Teachers should be able to coax as much activity as possible from each presentation.

6. While desirable learning can come about in a proper learning atmosphere, such learning is not an automatic result of activities, but is the result of planning. In a good learning atmosphere, a child can learn to cooperate, to observe rules, and to respect the capacities of his teammates. On the other hand, in a poorly conducted class, he or she can learn to cheat, to become intolerant of the shortcomings of others, and to put winning over all other goals.

The development of courtesy, fair play, and honesty are important goals to be achieved by children. In discussions, children need to bring out what constitutes proper conduct in various situations.

Teachers should note in their lesson plans where opportunities exist for introduction of these social concepts. Their development must not be left to chance.

7. Beware of activities during which children are eliminated as a penalty for getting tagged or not accomplishing something. Usually these children are the inept or unskilled, who need the activity the most. Modify this practice by getting the eliminated children back into activity quickly. One solution is letting those eliminated sit out one turn or having them re-enter when another child goes out. Some kind of "re-admission price" can also be imposed, in the form of a movement task the child has to perform. He or she might, for example, be required to make 20 turns with a jump rope, or to bounce and catch a ball five times. The child returns to the activity after the required task has been completed.

8. Young children often become afraid to handle certain play objects, such as hard balls. Use a fleece ball, beach ball, balloon, or beanbag in introductory phases of a ball-handling skill. When children work as partners, begin by positioning them a short distance apart and introduce the simplest activity first. Have them begin in a stationary position before progressing to moving skills.

9. Know the activity, its component parts, and in particular the key points to be stressed for optimum execution and proficiency.

10. Try not to bluff. If a youngster asks a question that you cannot really answer, tell him honestly that you don't know or you are not sure, and that you will look it up. Be sure to follow up on this.

11. Children's movement patterns should follow sound mechanical principles consistent with their maturity level, but to expect all children to perform skills in an identical manner is an error.

12. Skills should be practiced in groups that are as small as possible, depending on the skill and the equipment available. Whenever practical, each child should have his own piece of equipment.

13. Remember that repetition is the soul of learning. If skills are to be acquired, see that sufficient practice occurs through a variety of approaches. In some complex motor skills, overlearning may be advisable.

14. When teaching young children how to do something, teacher demonstration should be used sparingly, as it leads to imitative behavior. Providing an immediate answer rules out guided discovery, problem-solving, and exploratory approaches.

15. Allow for choice of activity at times. Since letting the group make the choice sometimes results in disagreements, however, the teacher may wish to designate one child to select the activity for the group. The child may be picked because he has just had a birthday or because of some special achievement.

16. Use the more structured methods of organization only when needed. Stunts and tumbling are examples of activities in which some control is necessary for safety and good teaching.

17. Constantly be on guard against using too rigid an approach for preschool children. One needs a great deal of flexibility in working with these children.

18. A physical education class needs to provide a happy medium between quiet and boisterousness. Youngsters should be able to let off steam, but they should also be under control. There are two types of noise. The first is the noise growing out of purposeful activity, interest, and enjoyment. The second is noise that springs from disorder, lack of interest, rowdyism, and lack of control. Some children will yell just for the sake of yelling.

19. Use the whistle sparingly. Give one sharp blast and insist on the courtesy of attention. The whistle should be used only to halt activity. Starting commands for activities can be given by means of verbal signals. The whistle should mean, "Stop, look (at the teacher), and listen." In movement work, when a conversational tone is sufficient, hand signals should be substituted for the whistle.

Initially, it may be well to spend a little time making sure that the children have learned the signals, and that they have learned to observe the stop signal in particular. Early attention to establishing this habit will pay off in time saved later. To stop doing an exciting activity is not easy for young children.

Communicating in the Learning Environment

1. Recognize that communication is both verbal and nonverbal. Both modes have a place in communicating with children, and both merit teacher attention. Remember that actions sometimes speak louder than words.

2. Speak from a position in which you can see all the children. Avoid standing in the center of the circle. Position yourself so that you, the teacher, are facing the light source. Be sure that you have their attention before speaking; that is, establish eye contact with all the youngsters. When the children are seated, sit or kneel down with them so that you can communicate at eye level.

3. Use words that are appropriate for the children's age level. Make sure that they understand the action words in particular. When giving directions that contain a simile, be sure that they understand the term used. A child will comprehend "Bounce like a rubber ball," for

example. But he may not know how to "move like a little elf," if he has no idea what an elf is, or how to "be a puffing locomotive," when trains no longer "puff."

4. The teacher's speech should consistently reflect good grammar. Some teachers, for example, commonly direct children to "lay down" on the floor. This does not contribute to an effective learning atmosphere, as it helps perpetuate the error. Using baby talk with preschool children is another practice to be avoided. Refer to your class members as students, pupils, children, or young people, not as kids.

5. The teacher's voice should carry well enough to reach everyone in the group. Do not shout, however. Remember that you are not a drill sergeant. Use a conversational tone whenever possible.

6. Learn to listen. Listening is a lubricant for good communication, which helps to ensure that learning is taking place. Good listening implies caring and respect for what the child is about to say.

7. Develop a variety of phrases for encouraging, reinforcing, and approving pupil response. Nonverbal signals signifying approval should also be developed. Give attention to particular points when expressing approval: "I like the way you are holding the ball" is more helpful than "Fine!"

8. Keep your speech free of mannerisms, excessive repetition, and overreliance on certain words and phrases (such as "OK," "All right," and that irritating "and-uh").

9. Avoid rhetorical questions that are really commands and can invite an unwelcomed negative answer. Questions like, "Shall we go in now?" or "Would you like to . . . ?" represent poor communication.

10. Use appropriate methodology for phrasing questions and seeking answers. Construct questions in such a manner that they will stimulate a child to make a thoughtful reply and not just a "yes" or "no" response. Use probing questions to stimulate a flow of ideas. "What are other points?" "Let's have another reason." "Who has a different idea?"

11. If a child does not respond to your directions, first ask yourself whether the difficulty lies in the communication between you. Only then should you start to look for other causes.

12. Try asking students to express in words the joy and satisfaction they receive from an experience. Asking the right question may produce an answer such as: "I had a lot of fun with the hoops today." Or: "I did some things today that I never thought I could do." If the child can learn to put his feelings into words, he may develop a better self-image.

13. Students learn vicariously from directions given to others. If the teacher says, "Johnny, I think it might help you if you try . . . ," other students who are listening may benefit as well.

14. As a teacher goes with her class from the play area, another teacher asks, "How did it go?" Contrast these two answers: "I was proud of my class. They worked hard." And: "My kids were wild and noisy. It was nerve-racking." The difference in impact on the children is obvious. This technique, which has been called "ear-shotting," can be effective when it is used imaginatively and in the right way.

15. Sarcasm, ridicule, and flippant and cutting language are destructive behaviors that do not enhance the learning process.

16. Children do not like to be interrupted or not listened to. It sometimes surprises them when they are reminded they should exercise the same courtesy to the teacher.

17. Teachers must guard against too much verbalizing. Beginning teachers have a tendency to overexplain. The teacher who tries to make a "teachable moment" out of nearly any incident will end up by preaching or moralizing, and the pupils will react with a sinking feeling: "There he goes again."

18. For young children, it is good practice to center instructions on one or two points. Too many points only confuse the children and dilute the directions.

GUIDING STUDENT BEHAVIOR—DISCIPLINE

If children are to learn, the learning climate must be conducive to this goal. To maintain a good instructional atmosphere, several points are important. If disciplinary trouble develops, one must look first at the teacher and at the program; that is, is the deviant behavior being caused by some teacher behavior or by the content of the curriculum? After this question has been answered, attention can be turned to the children.

Youngsters are more comfortable in an atmosphere in which they know what they may and may not do. Too much permissiveness can lead to a chaotic situation. Too stringent controls, on the other hand, lead only to stifling conformity, not to effective learning.

Some aggression is normal in children, but it must be channeled into proper outlets. In establishing effective behavioral patterns, the key is to "accentuate the positive," reinforcing desirable directions. Negative behavior can sometimes be overlooked, unless it is disruptive.

One target behavior to inculcate in children is that of self-control. The teacher must identify the traits that make up the total behavior known as self-control in the learning situation. When these traits or approximations of these traits appear, they should be reinforced. Whether students work as individuals or in a rotating station plan, acceptance of responsibility for their own behavior is essential.

Teachers need to use care not to label students unconsciously or put them in niches according to expected behavior. Labeling, whether it be done privately or in front of students, certainly has no place in the educational picture. The labels applied to students are many and insidious—"dopy," "lazy," "trouble-maker," "dirty," "stupid," "bonehead," "moron." People who resort to name-calling do not deserve to be in the teaching profession. Studies show that students react to name-calling by behaving in just about the way they are expected to behave, living up to their labels.

The manner in which children react to stressful school pressures is individual in nature. Children should not be labeled as "normal" or "abnormal," but rather as those who can handle stressful situations in a socially sound manner, and those who have problems that interfere with their learning.

Since behavior variations are to be expected, it follows that an individual approach to problems is indicated. This makes it quite difficult to come up with "canned" solutions to specific behavior problems. Introspection by the teacher is in order to ascertain whether the problem lies with the child or with the teaching. If multiple student problems appear, the teacher's approach should be seriously questioned.

The best way to handle pupil behavior problems is to anticipate their occurrence and try to channel them into desirable directions. If problems appear, a decision needs to be made as to whether they are serious enough to be faced. Viciousness, disruptive behavior that interferes with the learning process of other children, and confrontation of the teacher by a rebellious student are signals that some action must be taken. The teacher must deal with the *causes* of misbehavior, not just the symptoms. When the causes of the problem are alleviated, the goal of establishing a climate in which misbehavior is not likely to occur becomes more realistic.

Problems of discipline usually should be dealt with promptly, individually, and privately. Furthermore, the group should not suffer penalties because of the action of one or two students.

It is necessary to set limits for behavior; be sure that these limits are consistent, reasonable, and enforceable. The practice of letting students "get away with" a problem behavior for a while and then suddenly tightening up on them has little merit. Students are quite sensitive to fairness in enforcing rules and dealing impartially with individuals. The reasons behind the rules should be made clear to the children.

The teacher should show warmth, friendship, and concern for all children. Children are sensitive to favoritism shown to certain students, especially those termed "teacher's pets." See that valued chores and responsibilities are shared among all.

Arguments between children will sometimes move the teacher into action as a referee. The best course is to avoid taking sides. Listen to the children and advise them to try to work out their differences without outside aid. Even if the teacher knows that one child is in error or lying, settling the matter in favor of the other individual will only look like taking sides. Only in cases of dire necessity should the teacher provide a settlement; rather, an effort should be made to negotiate an agreement between the antagonists. When one child is abusing another, of course, the teacher may need to step in and pass judgment on the seriousness and validity of the complaint. Remember, in such a situation, that nothing is to be gained by the teacher arguing with the children.

Teachers need to be alerted that a conflict can arise with parents over the often-held opinion that the school environment is too permissive and that children are not under enough discipline. Schools generally seek to develop the ability of students to manage their own affairs and find rational solutions to their own problems. Parents interpret this approach as giving children too much freedom or not keeping them under control. No apparent easy solution exists to resolve this difference of opinion.

Because of the attractiveness of physical participation, classroom teachers on occasion use exclusion from physical education as a disciplinary measure for breaches of conduct not related to physical education. This cannot be regarded as a sound educational practice, as the child has a right to take part in the learning experience.

Within the framework of the physical education class, temporary exclusion may be practiced effectively. A child who has misbehaved is told, "You go over to the sidelines and sit down. You tell us when you are ready to come back and play according to the rules."

Remember: the best antidote for discipline problems is a teaching climate of warmth, understanding, friendliness, firmness, and fairness.

SAFETY CONSIDERATIONS FOR THE INSTRUCTIONAL PROGRAM

The goal for any safety program in the schools is that children accept responsibility for their own safety and the safety of others. For young children, this goal is obviously a bit idealistic. Commendable progress can be made toward the overall goal, so that it may be well on the way to achievement in the primary grades.

The frame of reference for safety in the schools rests on two basic premises. The first is that the teacher has an educational and moral responsibility to provide a safe environment for children and conduct the program so that safety goals may be achieved. The second premise is even stronger: the law states that teachers must provide a safe environment. This responsibility is one that cannot be disregarded.

The following sections discuss safety considerations for the physical education program.

A Safe Environment

The area that the children use for activity must be a basically safe environment. There must be no safety hazards, there must be enough room, and appropriate equipment must be present. Appropriate equipment is defined as that within the scope and maturity level of the child with respect to safety factors. Since falls from equipment are potentially disabling, impact-absorbing materials are mandatory. Indoors, there must be enough mats, strategically placed. For outdoor installations, some type of approved, permanent, impact-absorbing material is a necessity.

Place mats under climbing apparatus

Two other safety elements need to be mentioned. The area, including the equipment, must be periodically inspected; and *all* play, recreation, and instruction must be supervised.

Separation of outdoor play space is advisable. Some teachers like to separate preschool and kindergarten pupils. Older children's play spaces should be set apart in such a way that balls and other objects do not come into the area designated for younger children.

An excellent practice is to give all children a tour by classes of the physical education facilities, both indoor and out, during the first week of the school year. As the children gather at a piece of equipment or enter an area, the guide explains any pertinent conduct and safety rules that should be followed. These rules should be posted in the gymnasium and on the general bulletin board. Not only is this procedure an excellent safety technique, but it also meets the legal requirement that the children have had appropriate safety instruction.

Safety in Instruction

Safety considerations in instruction begin with the selection of appropriate movement experiences, chosen within the maturity and developmental level of the children. The activity itself must not be beyond the capability of the child and therefore potentially hazardous. Every activity has its normal hazards, and these can be accepted.

Next, the teacher must consider the forthcoming activity and what is needed for safe participation. The children should have had basic lead-up activities for the accomplishment of instruction in the new experience. If safety factors are a consideration, these must be made known to the children and observed throughout the lesson.

Skill progression itself is considered a safety factor. The instructional steps used in teaching skills should be progressive. The child learns skills in logical order, so that each stage of learning meets a legal criterion of safety in presentation.

Rules governing different activities and pieces of apparatus should be developed by teachers and students. These should be made known to and observed by the children. It is wise to post the rules for the children, when they can read well enough to understand them.

Where children are in two or more groups, space the groups far enough apart so that collisions will not occur. Balls from one group going into other areas are a nuisance.

The children should learn to keep an eye on the ball and should not throw it to another person unless that person is watching. Set up rules about balls that leave the area. Only one child should go after the ball. Three or four children racing after a ball produces only disorder and danger in the heat of the competitive instinct. Stringent rules should be laid down for balls that go into the street or into other game areas, apparatus areas, etc. A stop-and-look pause should precede any attempt at recovery.

Some traffic rules are needed, particularly when one child follows another on an activity challenge. When children are to follow each other, have them keep a certain distance apart. One-way patterns should be established in some sequences.

Children should be cautioned against bringing sharp objects to the physical education class. Pencils and pens can cause physical harm. Watch for youngsters carrying glasses. Have a safe place for them. Children should not chew gum or munch on suckers while at play.

Shoelaces should remain tied. As soon as possible, this chore should be entrusted to the child. Children should either wear shoes or go barefoot. Skating around in stocking feet creates a hazardous situation. Stockings are slippery, and floor contact ruins them rapidly. Primary children can give attention to being properly dressed, including changing to gym shoes. Wearing long dresses or heavy boots shows evidence of lack of forethought.

In their movement experiences, children should have some practice in falling or collapsing to the floor under controlled conditions. It seems reasonable to think that this practice will take some of the surprise out of an accidental fall.

Avoiding nasty collisions is a goal of value to be sought in the safety program. During movement in general space, particularly when children are in rapid movement, emphasis should be placed on not touching or bumping anyone.

HEALTH EXCUSES AND SCREENING

One of the most vexing problems for the teacher is the handling of excuses for nonparticipation. If a nurse is present, excuses should be routed through her and recorded on the student's health record. With doctor's excuses, there is little problem, as they must be accepted on face value. With regard to excuses from parents, however, no easy solution exists. The nurse needs to accept the excuse with judgment and call the parent if further information is needed. A nice cliché reads this way: "If the child is well enough to come to school, he or she is well enough to take part in some activities." In practice, it doesn't work out that neatly. While most parents are sincere, they sometimes tend to be overly protective and resent any change in their recommendation as it appears on the excuse. When the child comes to school with only a verbal excuse, the nurse or teacher should get in touch with the parents. Another inconsistency is seen when a child who is excused from physical education plays vigorously and without limitation during recess. On the other side of the coin, a child may come with an excuse and then decide to play anyway.

If a nurse is not available, it is usually best to let the classroom teacher be responsible for excuses. The teacher knows the children and can make the best judgment in each situation. This becomes an indicated direction especially when a specialist teacher handles the movement activities. As the specialist works with the children, he will have little time to stop and engage in discussions about a student's participation. If certain children are only to observe, and others are to have limited participation, this information should be given to him by the classroom teacher.

Permanent excuses should come from physicians and should outline restrictions, which almost entirely concern limitations. In addition, when there are exceptional students in the class, the special education consultant should usually be involved. In such cases, limitations are not stressed. Designated children with physical or motor deficiencies should work on certain prescribed movements or challenges in their play.

Recording pertinent information in the child's anecdotal health record gives the succeeding teacher a basis to anticipate and meet the child's needs as he or she moves from one grade to the next.

Screening by the Teacher

When children play, the teacher is afforded an excellent opportunity to make observations in relation to their health status. Such observation involves discriminating teacher judgment. It is not enough just to look at a child and then say that he or she looks well or looks sick. When children play and exercise, certain observable signs often appear, which may be of importance. These signs may not appear when the child is quiet, but will show up when the child starts to move.

The instructor needs to be sensitive to these possible reactions and make note of them, while taking them in stride. The teacher should remember that all children have individual characteristics, and that some of these may even be classified as individual peculiarities. The instructor is further cautioned that *unusual* reactions are not necessarily *abnormal* reactions. He

or she should also be aware that preschool children are quite volatile and have their ups and downs. They tire at times, but are off and gone to more activity after a short period.

The task of screening children who respond poorly to exercise is not difficult, as it involves noting certain observable conditions that do indicate the presence of an abnormality. The Committee on Exercise and Fitness of the American Medical Association lists these observable signs, which may accompany or follow exercise, that are indications for referral and further investigation:

Excessive Breathlessness. Some breathlessness is normal with exercise, but breathlessness that persists long after exercise is cause for medical referral.

Blueing of the Lips. Except in a cold, wet environment, blueing of the lips or nail beds is an unnatural reaction to exercise. Its occurrence in the ordinary exercise setting is cause for medical referral.

Pale or Clammy Skin. Pale or clammy skin or cold sweating following or during exercise is not a normal reaction to physical activity within the usual temperature ranges of the gymnasium or playing field. Medical referral is recommended.

Unusual Fatigue. Excessive fatigue, as evidenced by unusual lack of endurance or early failure to maintain moderate activity, suggests the need for medical referral. It is dangerous to attribute such reactions to malingering until possible organic causes have been ruled out.

Persistent Shakiness. Unusual weakness or shakiness that continues for more than ten minutes following vigorous exercise is cause for medical referral. Normally, recovery will be reasonably prompt.

Muscle Twitching or Tetany. Muscular contractions, such as twitching or tetany, whether localized or generalized, sometimes occur as an unusual reaction to exercise. Such reactions may be abnormal and warrant medical investigation.

Other Symptoms. In addition, such symptoms as headache, dizziness, fainting, broken sleep at night, digestive upset, pain not associated with injury, undue pounding of the heart or uneven heartbeat, disorientation, or personality changes may be indications of abnormal functioning.

The Committee cautions that an occasional episode need not alarm the instructor, but recurring or persisting patterns of any of these symptoms, particularly when related to activity, indicate the need for medical review.

SUMMARY

Teachers must continue to develop qualities to enhance interpersonal relationships if they are going to stimulate youngsters to a high level of achievement. Traits such as listening, observing, and communicating meaningfully are an integral part of the teaching process.

In working with children, teachers must be able to manage the situation easily and efficiently if activity time is to be maximized in the gymnasium or on the playground. The "start and expand" technique is useful for maintaining motivation in children through reinforcement from successful experiences. Communication with the learner will be enhanced if the teacher will listen carefully, accept the student's feelings, and offer meaningful feedback.

Discipline is best handled when a student knows what the teacher's expectations are. Em-phasis should be on self-control and responsibility for one's own behavior. Many behavior problems can be anticipated if the teacher is alert to the various situations. Often, the teacher does not observe the class carefully or puts students in situations that encourage misbehavior, such as standing in line or performing and failing in front of others.

Teachers have an educational and moral responsibility to provide a safe environment for youngsters. This responsibility, coupled with the legal necessities, requires that the instructor monitor the situation on a regular basis to ensure that all important phases of safety are evaluated. Not only should a safe environment be offered, but instruction about safety should be part of a total lesson plan. Teachers should be aware of observable signs that may occur in children after exercise and that indicate possible health problems.

Chapter 8

Guiding Child Learning

A pedagogical method is of value only in terms of what it does for productive learning.

In the past two decades, physical education has been swept by many movements and fads. Some of these, considered panaceas for the educational and physical ills of children, were adopted wholesale without valid testing. Unfortunately, such uncritical acceptance tends to overlook two essential elements in the learning process—the child and the teacher.

Value is not automatically achieved by the use of any method. The necessary ingredients of selection and direction must be added, selection appropriate to the learner and direction toward target behaviors.

One other point merits discussion. Some educators are riding an inconsistency when they attempt to personalize the learning environment so that each child can achieve. They stress a particular kind of approach, believing that this approach is appropriate for *all* children because it helps them *individually*. Rather, the child and the situation of the moment should determine their approach. It may be in the best interests of the child, in some movement experiences and according to his capability, that the task approach be quite flexible, creative, and exploratory. At other times, for the same child, the task approach may be quite traditional and practical, as he is shown how to "do it this way." Observation and diagnosis become the critical steps in determining what approach is to follow. The teacher who has a grasp of many approaches holds the key to the situation. Educational movement methodology and its associated styles of teaching will give a teacher a framework in which he or she can function.

PROCESSES IN EDUCATIONAL MOVEMENT

The goals of educational movement, with respect to movement competency for younger children, lie in achieving good body management as well as developing skills, mostly fundamental skills, with some consideration given to special skills. (See "Continuum of Skill Development and Goals," p. 18.)

Movement analysis divides movement patterns into two broad categories governed by the type of movement behavior desired. If a wide variety of movement patterns is sought in an attempt to develop body management skills, the activity is categorized as *divergent* movement. On the other hand, if a specific outcome is expected in an attempt to develop a fundamental or specialized skill, the movement is identified as *convergent*.

Divergent Movement

Divergent movement seeks to develop body awareness and efficient management of the body in a variety of situations. The emphasis is on exploration, repetition, and creation. Movement tasks of this nature specify that certain elements of movement be included in the problem, but they do not specify a precise skill or movement. For example, the child may be asked to move about the room using a quick, low movement in alternation with a slow, high movement. Or the directive might be: "Find a way to make your ball travel around the floor." There is no right or wrong answer as long as the child solves the problem. The choice is the child's, and the teacher should accept the solution. Divergent movement activities will elicit a wider response of movement than problems for convergent movement. The instructional emphasis focuses on versatility and breadth of response.

Another approach, which is occasionally used in divergent movement, is expressive and imitative movement. Expressive movement involves showing feelings, such as being happy, gay, sad, angry, contrite, etc. Imitative movement mimics animals, personalities, and other elements. Expressive and imitative movement add breadth to the movement possibilities, but should not receive all the emphasis.

Divergent movement can be based on broad themes that give meaning to the movement patterns. An entire lesson can be based on a theme that provides the central idea for movement, or two or more themes can be combined in a day's lesson. Many themes can be used. Here are some examples:

1. Learning to receive and transfer the weight
2. Learning to take the weight on the hands (or another part of the body)
3. Making shapes in the air
4. Curling and stretching
5. Moving with the legs
6. Moving over and under things
7. Flight
8. Lifting and lowering
9. Moving symmetrically and asymmetrically
10. Leading with different parts of the body

Curling

Many other themes, some broad and some narrow, can be used. Additional themes can be established using equipment and apparatus.

Chapter 9 presents the development of themes with progressions and suggested instructional approaches.

Convergent Movement

Convergent movement involves a specific skill that can be named and identified, as opposed to general movement of a wide variety under divergent movement. Children may practice such convergent movements as walking, batting, bouncing, jumping, and pitching. A convergent movement can be identified by the fact that its name usually ends in the suffix *-ing.* Included in convergent movement are fundamental skills, specialized skills, and the more precise skills on apparatus. Convergent activity

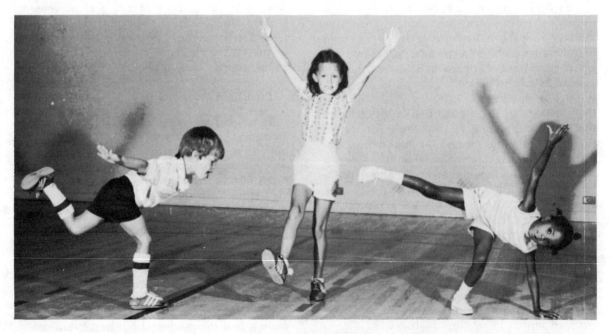

Stretching and balancing

implies a limitation; the child must conform to the specified activity, but the activity can be accomplished or interpreted by various responses. While the emphasis is on the development of a particular skill, which includes a concept of right and wrong with respect to technique, the child should be allowed to arrive at or discover for himself the best way or ways to do the skill, within reasonable limits.

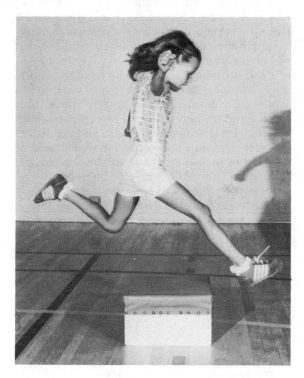

Flight over a jumping box

The more precise the skill, the more critical the need to establish good techniques. Good techniques should prevail even if the child feels more comfortable with a known departure from accepted form. The guided-discovery learning technique should be used here to guide the child away from an obvious error in skill execution.

Let us take as an example a violation of the principle of opposition as it applies to throwing. A child who throws with the right hand and steps with the right foot in throwing should be induced to step with the left foot, as the right-hand, right-foot throwing technique will establish an undesirable habit pattern that would need to be changed later on. The child should be encouraged to change this pattern even if, after exploration and experimentation, he or she feels more comfortable in the right-hand, right-foot throw.

When dealing with convergent movement, a different instructional approach is necessary than when using divergent movement. For convergent movement, the range of acceptable technique needs to be known and adhered to. In some cases this range can be broad; in others, it can be quite narrow.

Basically, the method of attack is to zero in on those approximations of acceptable technique as they appear and attempt to unify them into an integrated whole. Thus, the instruction converges on a particular target skill, which becomes the point of focus—hence "convergent" movement.

PROGRESSIVE DEVELOPMENT OF MOVEMENT COMPETENCY

Even within the framework of divergent and convergent movement, a progression of skill competency can be outlined, which flows from the natural appearance of skills in the human being. The first two elements of the progression come under divergent movement; the latter two are convergent elements.

DIVERGENT MOVEMENT

1. Children's play that stresses exploration and creativity. This is the diversive play approach, with focus on developing familiarity with an object, piece of apparatus, or situation. It should answer the question, "What can I do with or in this situation?"

2. An exploratory approach that emphasizes variety. The goal is body management, i.e., to determine through exploration if the body can move this way or that. With an object it answers the question, "What can the object do?"

CONVERGENT MOVEMENT

3. Performing a particular movement. This stage focuses on a particular movement pattern and challenges the student to experiment with a particular movement. While quality receives some emphasis, attention is focused mainly on fractional approximations of the movement as they appear.

4. Development of proficiency in a particular movement. Attention is directed toward how to perfect a movement, which requires more delineation and application of technique, together with planned practice and repetition.

The four stages range from free play to learning a defined skill. All four stages may and should employ exploration, but the allowable leeway in application would depend upon the goal. Experimentation and specific instruction are characteristic of the latter two stages.

INSTRUCTIONAL STEPS IN EDUCATIONAL MOVEMENT

The task approach, the guided-discovery technique, and the problem-solving technique are the basis for the development of many learning progressions in educational movement. The premise is that the child reaches conclusions through reactions to challenges and experiences in movement. In the command approach, on the other hand, the child is told what to do and how to do it. While the following steps represent a progression, the goals of the lesson will determine the final sequence of the steps and the relative importance of each step. Obviously, the first step cannot be varied, as it sets initial activity. The second step, to establish breadth and variation of movement, is usually stabilized in that position. The order of the other three steps is flexible.

Step One. Setting the Problem

This step is setting the stage, providing children with initial directions so that they understand what is expected and can practice a given type of movement. Information needs to be supplied for the following questions (not always in this order):

1. *What is the body to do? What is its focus?* The general movement task is specified, together with the goals that the children need to know.

2. *With what or with whom are the youngsters to move?* If different equipment is involved or is to be handled, this should be specified. Furthermore, relationships of the students to one another should be clarified. Are the children to work alone, with partners, or as members of a group?

3. *Where are the students to move?* The concern here is whether the movement is in personal or general space.

4. *How is the movement to be accomplished?* To be imposed in this step are the initial challenges, stress points, and any limitations that outline the problem.

As an example of how this step functions, consider the following directives. "Today we are going to work with beanbag movements to help our catching skills. You are to practice by yourself in your own space. Remember to keep your eye on the beanbag as you toss and that, in catching, your hands should create a soft home. Now, get a beanbag, move to your place, and find out what you can do with the beanbag while tossing and catching it." Note that the admonition about eye concentration and softness in catching could have been inserted

shortly after the children had started practicing. Or these could have been brought out through apt questioning. "Rex, I see you are catching well. Where do you focus your eyes when you toss the bag?" "Sally, what do we have to think about in using our hands in catching?" These are the kinds of skill principles that should be related to throwing and catching skills so that transfer may become more likely in various situations.

A different consideration occurs when the lesson is a part of a series. If this day's lesson were the second or third on a particular movement pattern, setting the problem could consist of beginning the present lesson where the last one left off. The teacher might issue the equipment and say, "You remember how we finished yesterday's lesson. Let's give a little time to . . . and see how much we remember of what we did." Observation and diagnosis take over to assess the amount of lesson time that should be devoted to review and to what should logically follow. Considerable time may be needed to reinforce the patterns of the previous day.

The "how" portion may impose limitations of movement by employing the following verbs that define certain actions.

LOCOMOTOR ACTIONS

climb	prance
collapse	roll
crawl	run
creep	skip
dart	slide
fall	start
freeze	step
gallop	stop
glide	tiptoe
hop	trace
jog	vault
jump	walk
leap	whirl
pivot	

NONLOCOMOTOR ACTIONS

balance	rise
bend	shake
bow	shiver
curl	sit
flutter	stretch
kneel	sway
lie	twist
lift	wiggle
lower	

MANIPULATIVE MOVEMENTS

bat	catch
bounce	dribble

hit   roll
hurl   throw
kick   toss
propel   volley
rebound

WORDS THAT EXPRESS RELATIONSHIPS

Words can be used to express the relationship of the body to objects, other individuals, or groups. There are words to explore meaning, words to contrast, words to give direction to movement in relation to other persons or things. The words can also provide cues as to how one part of the body can relate to another. Some examples follow.

above   inside
across   off
alongside   on
before   on top of
behind   out of
below   over
beneath   through
between   under
down   underneath
in   to the right of
in and out of   to the left of
in front of

Children should be able to develop their understanding of vocabulary so that they can make an appropriate movement response.

Step Two. Increasing Variety and Depth of Movement

Observation, diagnosis, and prescription enter the picture at this point and are employed throughout the process. In Step One, the students are given a task. On the basis of the observed responses, the teacher determines the pace of the increments that should be inserted into the lesson sequence.

The versatility of the child is challenged through judicious use of factors for securing variety of response. A thorough understanding of the factors and their potential to maximize movement possibilities is essential. The factors can be imposed singly or in combination.

FACTORS TO STIMULATE VARIETY AND DEVELOP BREADTH OF MOVEMENT

Space. Space factors include level, direction, size and place of movement, and patterns.

Level—low, high or in between
Direction—straight, zigzag, circular, curved, forward, backward, sideward, upward, and downward
Size—large or small movements

Place of movement—horizontal, vertical, or diagonal
Patterns—forming squares, diamonds, triangles, circles, figure eights, and other patterns
Ranges—wide, in the vicinity, nearby

Time. The time factor may be varied as follows:

Different speeds—slow, moderate, or fast
Acceleration or deceleration—increasing or decreasing the speed of movement
Even or uneven time—sudden, jerky, smooth, or even movement; variation in rhythm

Flow. The term "flow" has to do with continuity of movement.

Interrupted flow (bound flow)—stopping at the end of a movement or part of a movement
Sustained flow (free flow)—linking together smoothly different movements or parts of a movement
Sequential order (free flow)—linking together smoothly movements in a prescribed order

Force. Force will affect movement patterns by its extent and means of application.

Force factors—heavy or light, weak or strong, sudden or sustained, explosive or smooth
Varying the force—absorb, apply, diminish, or develop

Body Factors. A number of considerations about the use of the body can add variety to movement.

Shape—long or short, wide or narrow, straight or twisted, stretched or curled, symmetrical or asymmetrical
Weight bearing—different parts of the body supporting the weight or receiving the weight; different number of body parts involved in a movement
Execution—the movement may be done unilaterally (one-sidedly), bilaterally (both sides together), or cross-laterally (each side independently); it can be performed with a different part of the body or with a different number of parts
Body center-oriented—leading with different parts of the body, movements away from and toward the center of the body
Patches and points—some instructors have had success in referring to body parts in terms of patches and points: a patch refers

to any flat body surface, and a point to any angular or projecting part of the body

VARIATIONS WHEN WORKING ON APPARATUS

In addition to the variations just presented, variety in movement as the children work on large apparatus can be stimulated in the following ways:

1. Apparatus can be arranged in different sequences, combinations, and numbers. Benches and balance beams, for example, can be placed on an incline, suspended higher than normal, or placed in combination with other equipment.

2. Variety can be promoted by viewing apparatus as a three-step process, and each step can be varied. Various ways to get on or mount the apparatus can be stipulated. Things to do on or with apparatus can be outlined. Different means of dismounting or getting down from apparatus can be specified.

3. Things to do on apparatus can be varied. The child can be challenged to go over, under, around, or through apparatus. He can support himself in different fashions, bringing a variety of body factors into play.

4. Pathways can be set up that lead through a series of apparatus. The child is given a prescribed route to follow and certain actions to perform when covering the route. The challenges should begin with two points or challenges to be accomplished and then expanded by adding one to three more as capability indicates. Some examples follow.

    a. A three-station pathway is set, in which a roll is added between the second and third points. At stations 1 and 2 are two 12-inch cones supporting a wand. A mat lies between stations 2 and 3. Station 3 is a tire set upright in a holder. The child is directed to go under the first wand, over the second, roll on the mat, and go through the tire in any fashion so long as the tire remains in place.

    b. The pathway can employ or include symbol forms, such as starting through the red triangle, going around the green square, and coming back through the yellow circle.

Step Three. Developing Quality in Movement

After the children have exhausted the possibilities of variety, attention should be turned toward developing quality in movement. Have the children select and practice a movement with quality as the objective; encourage them to do it as well as it can be done under the circumstances. They may work on several movements, emphasizing good form and techniques, and such qualities as smoothness, lightness, coordination, and rhythm.

For convergent movement and proper development of skills, this step should include stress on critical points of technique that are important for the skill being practiced. This can be accomplished by demonstration, discussion, or a question-and-answer period.

The emphasis should be placed on doing it a little better, doing what is preferred, or doing it the most efficient or the easiest way. Observation of other children might be coupled with controlled demonstration. In convergent movement, the lesson development should bring out different acceptable techniques.

A pathway of challenges

Step Four. Sequencing and Combining Movement Patterns

A series of linked movements are combined so that they flow smoothly from one pattern to another.

The number of movement patterns to be linked together can be stated in the challenge. Attention to both the movements and the flow is necessary. The sequence can be self-selected or given as part of the problem.

Children can select movements from those that have been practiced and put them together in sequence, with good transition from one movement pattern to the other. For example, they may be instructed to "put together a light run, a heavy run, and a body turn."

For children in first and second grade, practice can be extended to include different types of movement that demand from youngsters the ability to think how they might put them together most effectively. A problem that emphasizes different movements could be: "As you bounce the ball, move with different locomotor movements in various directions. Select some definite combinations, and repeat them several times before changing to a new combination."

Step Five. Culminating Activity—Partner and Small Group Work

In the program for young children, partner work should be instituted slowly and with patience. The individual characteristics of the young child are given less attention when he is learning to work with a partner. Working with others is an important social goal, however, and one to be sought.

How many children should work together? Some suggestions follow.

1. In executing the desired movement theme, a child can serve as a stationary obstacle as his partner uses him to extend the possibilities of the theme.
2. There can be a critique of movement, with one child watching the other move and providing suggestions. Observation can be centered on one or two points, as young children will have difficulty in making an overall judgment about skill proficiency.
3. There can be imitative movement of the sort that was practiced. One child performs a movement pattern, and the other reproduces it. This can be a single pattern or movements in sequence.
4. In another approach, children move in parallel fashion to develop a series of movements. Begin with a series of two movements and add others, as seems practical.

5. Children can work cooperatively in forming different shapes, forms, letters, or figures. They can form the symbols while in an upright fashion or on the floor. Partners could form simple two-letter words, such as "he," "it," "to," "an," etc.

Group participation can extend some of the ideas listed above, but the groups should not be larger than three or four children.

Occasionally, an entire lesson might be devoted to partner activity. Partner and group work may be somewhat limited at the preschool and kindergarten level due to the individualistic nature of these children.

Partners can also work together in target activities for determining achievement. Balls can be rolled at different targets. Other tasks, such as seeing how far one can jump, add challenge and interest. Teachers are reminded that competition can enhance skills well learned, but is detrimental when skills are not sufficiently acquired.

LEARNING STYLES

Several learning styles most suitable for educational movement can be incorporated into the five steps. The teacher must keep in mind that all this methodology is quite flexible in application, dependent upon the situation at the moment, the child, and the target goals. These goals may be teacher-directed or self-directed. No matter what the approach, however, the style should be personalized for the child to the greatest extent possible within the scope of the style.

Table 9 (p. 84) illustrates the flow of instruction for three of these learning styles.

Task Style

In the task style, a certain action is to be accomplished. The teacher sets the task, and the child's movements are directed toward the stipulated action. Criteria for evaluating the movement pattern include (1) whether or not the child completed the movement according to the limitations specified, and (2) the degree of quality in the movement.

While setting the task can be expressed in unvarnished terms as a directive to do something, in practice it generally takes the form of a challenge to the student. The challenge employs such phraseology as: "Can you move . . ." or "Show me how you can move . . . ."

Here is an illustration. "Can you move across the room on three parts of the body?" The child has latitude to move in any way she wishes so

TABLE 9. FLOW OF INSTRUCTION—EDUCATIONAL MOVEMENT AND LEARNING STYLES

	Learning Styles		
	Task	**Guided-Discovery**	**Problem-Solving**
Step 1	Teacher sets the task.	Outline problem—directions, limitations, and initial challenge. Allow opening, flexible response.	
Step 2	Initial response. Repeat—apply space, time, force, body factors.	Experiment with teacher-selected options. Apply space, time, force factors. Teacher guides the discovery process.	*Self-directed* response. Probe and experiment. Try different approaches. Utilize space, time, force, body factors.
Step 3	Repeat and refine. Give attention to quality—stress points.	Select best option with aid of teacher. Continue to experiment and refine.	Choose one way. Work on improving quality, until it is smooth and efficient. Emphasis on self-improvement.
Step 4	Link task with other movements. Additional practice. Flow factors.	Add critical points of technique. Refine. Link in combinations. Using the established pattern, extend movement with space, time, force factors. Continue experimentation.	
Step 5	Alone or with a partner, refine and practice task patterns.	With a partner or group, refine patterns, provide repetition, extend movement horizons. Unify and integrate patterns.	

long as the movement involves three body parts and takes her across the room. The teacher may stimulate more movement (repetition) by judicious application of concepts of space, time, or force. He might say, "Repeat the same movement, but come back very lightly." This involves a change of force. After a period of experimentation, the teacher can direct the child to select a sequence (three parts) and practice it to smooth out the movement pattern. More repetition can be included, with emphasis on good techniques that affect this movement pattern. Later, children can be given tasks of a similar nature to develop more fully with a partner.

The task style is effective in developing and/ or improving skills. In the illustration just presented, one might substitute the skill of walking. The instructional sequences follow about the same pattern. Task style has a place in the schema if a particular movement pattern or a skill is the target goal.

Guided-Discovery Style

In the guided-discovery style, children are furnished a set of teacher-selected sequential cues, options, facts, or questions, all of which are intended to lead them to discover a predetermined answer or action. The child is given opportunity to experiment with different options and to determine what is good, what is best, and what is most feasible.

There is considerable teacher involvement in the guided-discovery approach. The teacher asks appropriate and guiding questions based on the learner's background. Students learn by

asking the teacher for clarification or direction. They can also learn through active participation, weighing the effects of experimenting with different options, and through observation of peers.

An illustration can help clarify the way in which this style is employed. It begins with a fact or concept that is already established and accepted, which the teacher knows and the children are to "discover."

Concept. In positioning the feet for throwing a ball (right-handed thrower), the forward-backward position of the feet with the left foot forward is the most efficient and effective. The teacher might set up the following options of feet placement for experimentation in throwing or rolling:

1. Legs crossed
2. Feet and legs together
3. Feet apart a short distance in straddle stance
4. Feet apart to full range of movement in straddle stance
5. Forward-backward foot placement, right foot leading
6. Forward-backward foot placement, left foot leading

The learning process depends upon securing feedback from each of the options, which are experienced in such a way that a rational selection can be made. The teacher may then amplify upon or clarify the option the youngsters have discovered.

Problem-Solving Style

The problem-solving style uses self-directed learning to provide a solution to a stated problem, for which no preconceived answer can be expected. The emphasis is to show different ways one can perform or what one can do with an object or on apparatus. Children direct their responses, and right and wrong responses are only judged in terms of problem solution.

The teacher asks the children to show ways or a definite number of ways to do something. The challenge might be: "How many different ways can you move across the floor dragging one foot?" Or: "What ways can you move in a triangular pattern, always leading with the head?" Or: "Can you find three different ways to . . . ?" If the child shows ways, or finds three ways, then his movement response is a correct solution to the problem.

Critical to this style is the use of the movement factors of space, time, and force. The goal is to extract as much movement and variety from the experiences as possible. The problem solution must amplify the child's level of knowledge, since it is not problem-solving if the child already knows the answer.

A successful application of the problem-solving method is seen in the use of themes. A theme might be the concept of up and down. The child explores upward and downward movement and develops responses to solve the problem of movement within the limitation of the theme.

It is obvious that problems can offer many possibilities for the movements that are expected as solutions. After the children have experienced many different solutions for the movement problem, they can select one movement answer and work on it to develop quality. Attention is given to doing as well as possible. Stress points that relate to the movement should be introduced. Partner and group actions can follow, provided the pattern lends itself to this kind of approach.

Problem-solving for younger children should be kept to a simple level. The problem must involve some thought for the solution, but not to the point that breeds frustration.

IMPLEMENTING THE STYLES OF LEARNING

Personalizing Instruction

To personalize instruction is to adjust what is to be learned to the capacity and needs of the learner, so that it will better fit some particular need of a particular child. Such instruction considers the respective roles of the teacher and the student.

It is difficult to talk about learning for young children without inserting elements of personalizing. The guidelines that follow contain such elements.

Repetition. Repetition is the basis for learning, and sufficient repetition in particular patterns is necessary. The teacher must develop the sensitivity to be able to determine when sufficient exploration and repetition have occurred at a particular stage so that children may move to the next level.

Experimentation. All children must be permitted free expression of movement within the limitations of the problem. Children should be directed toward the solution of the problem, and they must be allowed sufficient time to accomplish this goal, working at their own rate according to their ability.

Creative Opportunity. Youngsters should have the opportunity to come up with their own movement patterns based on experimentation and exploration. Creativity should show that movement patterns and concepts introduced in the lesson have been absorbed, and that the relevant points of the movement experiences have been applied by the students. In this context, creativity means coming up with something appropriate and worth continuing.

Focus on Potential. To help all students reach their full potential, high standards and a full effort should be demanded of each.

Challenging Quality. As soon as children have responded and succeeded in meeting the demands of the problem in the introductory stage, they should be stimulated toward more efficient movement. Inept or sloppy performance should not be tolerated beyond the initial stages.

Perceptive Guidance. For the teacher, the lesson period is one of observation, analysis, and perceptive guidance. This is a crucial part of the learning process and cannot be overemphasized. The teacher should circulate among the students, helping and assisting. Teachers who remain anchored to a spot in front of the class reduce coaching effectiveness. By moving among students, teachers can encourage them both verbally and nonverbally.

Demonstration

Demonstration may be defined as the process of showing another (or a class) how a movement is done. Demonstration in the learning environment can have two aspects, teacher demonstration and pupil demonstration.

Teacher demonstration leads to imitative behavior. As such, it is a restricting factor in divergent movement. The teacher might show youngsters certain points of technique more for the sake of motivating the children to try things than to induce them to "do it this way." Teacher demonstration must be kept to an absolute minimum, if it is used at all.

Pupil demonstration has its place, but it must serve a clear purpose in terms of learning. Demonstrations should be used infrequently at the beginning of a lesson, since children should be given opportunity to develop individual approaches rather than imitating the style of another. A few basics indicating the problem limits might be presented by demonstration early in the lesson, or even in the introductory phases, however, to give direction to the activity.

The demonstration should be directed toward increasing children's understanding and movement potential. Children need to observe and analyze, not just to be entertained by, the movements presented. In order that they may profit, the demonstration can be followed by a period of practice.

Sometimes the teacher can ask for volunteers, but it is probably more effective to pinpoint children who can illustrate particular technique points. Demonstration by more than one may prevent embarrassment in the timid child and motivate him or her to get involved. The teacher should rarely show a negative demonstration, a picture of "how not to do it." The choice of children to demonstrate should be varied so that all may have a chance if they desire. Questions and answers on what is good and why may be a part of the process. Generally, the demonstration should illustrate a particular point. If the demonstration proves unsatisfactory, the teacher should choose to ignore the difficulty, perhaps simply thanking the child for his help before redirecting attention to something else.

Sometimes half the class can observe what the other half has been doing or accomplishing. This gets everyone into the act. Such achievement demonstration has a place in the learning process. Children can be told that after a period of practice they can share their results with one another. Remember that young children are quite averse to showing ineptness; they should not be forced to demonstrate.

Stimulating Effort

While asking for variations in movement will sometimes stimulate the children to better effort, it is important that children also extend themselves within the movement itself. When presenting a movement problem, the teacher should include incentives; he may ask the child to carry out a task "as far as possible" or to move "with quick changes." Although competition between individuals is not an accepted practice in movement education, some questions like: "How far can you reach?" or: "How far can you jump?" lend themselves to measurement and encourage effort. Count the number of floorboards covered or reached, for example. Use beanbags or other markers and ask the children to place them "as far as you can." The device of having children stretch or reach until they pull themselves from their base will encourage them to extend their limits.

Observing an achievement demonstration

Phrasing the Challenge or Question

Stimulating an effective movement response from the children depends upon the manner in which the problem is phrased. Problems can be presented in the form of questions or statements, which should elicit and encourage variety, depth, and extent of movement. Teachers can secure ideas from the following directives, but every teacher will develop his or her own style and approach. In each example, the form is given first, and a specific application of the form follows.

PRESENTING A PROBLEM

Show me how a _____ moves. Show me _____.
"Show me how an alligator moves along the ground."
Have you seen a _____?
"Have you seen a kangaroo jump?"
What ways can you _____?
"What ways can you hop over the jump rope?"
How would you _____? How can you _____?
"How would you dribble a ball, changing hands often?"
See how many different ways you can _____.
"See how many different ways you can hang from a ladder."
What can you do with a _____? What kinds of things can you _____?
"What can you do with a hoop?"
Can you portray a _____?
"Can you portray an automobile with a flat tire?"
Discover different ways you can _____.
"Discover different ways you can volley a ball against a wall."
Can you _____?
"Can you keep one foot up when you bounce the ball?"
Who can _____ a _____ in such a way that _____?
"Who can bounce a ball in such a way that it keeps time with the tom-tom?"
What does a _____?
"What does a cat do when he is wet?"

PRODUCING VARIETY OR SETTING A LIMITATION

Try it again another way. Try to _____.
"Try to jump higher."
See how far [many times, high, close, low] you can _____.
"See how far you can reach with your arms."
Find a way to _____. Find a new way to _____.
"Find a new way to jump over the bench."
Apply _____ to _____.
"Apply a heavy movement to your run."
How else can you _____?

"How else can you roll your hoop?"
Make up a sequence _____.
"Make up a sequence of previous movements, changing smoothly from one movement to the other."
Now, try to combine a _____ with _____.
"Now, try to combine a locomotor movement with your catching."
Alternate _____ and _____.
"Alternate walking and hopping."
Repeat the last movement, but add _____.
"Repeat the last movement, but add a body twist as you move."
See if you can _____.
"See if you can do the movement with a partner."
Trace [draw] a _____ with _____.
"Trace a circle with your hopping pattern."
Find another part of the body to _____. Find other ways to _____.
"Find another part of the body to take the weight."
Combine _____ with _____.
"Combine the hopping with a body movement."
In how many different positions can you _____?
"In how many different positions can you carry your arms while walking the balance beam?"
How do you think the _____ would change if _____?
"How do you think the balance we are doing would change if our eyes were closed?"
On signal, _____.
"On signal, speed up your movements."

Stressing Quality in Movement

Establishing quality is a vital part of movement education. Without this aspect, movement is mere activity. If the educational process can be viewed as experimentation, selection, modification, clarification, and repetition, guidance and direction fall into their proper perspective. If desirable learning is to occur, children must be supplied with a framework to aid them in selecting the experiences that they wish to retain and develop. Thus retained and repeated, the movement pattern becomes a part of their being.

Guidance in movement occurs in two areas. It is important that students receive guidance in their attempt to achieve quality of movement and to apply the various principles governing movement and skill performance. (These principles, which are applicable to fundamental movement patterns as well as to skills, are discussed in Chapter 3.)

In divergent movement, there is no "right" way to perform a movement pattern, and guidance can be centered on general qualities of movement, such as lightness, smoothness, and coordination.

The second area in which guidance occurs is that of convergent movement. In many cases, there is a desirable way to perform the skill, and there are certain elements that should be avoided. For example, in a lesson emphasizing or including walking, stress should be placed on the feet being pointed reasonably forward. Teachers must know the basic element of skills so that proper techniques can be inculcated and undesirable habits avoided in the learning process.

Systematic progression is needed if skill performance is to improve. Increasingly difficult challenges must be presented, and effective repetition must be introduced. Experimentation and exploration continue to have a place in learning experiences for establishing skills, however. Often a performer will come to select the pattern he wishes to adopt after experimenting with a number of good or accepted patterns.

To what extent should form be stressed? Few younger children will reach perfection in form in any activity. On the other hand, children should not be permitted to acquire poor habits that will cause them difficulty later. While the emphasis should be on doing things as well as possible, this must not become an overriding consideration.

Proper postural habits must be emphasized throughout movement education, since these are related in many cases to quality of performance. Within the framework of achieving the child's maximum growth and development, there should be stress on possessing reasonable body alignment and establishing good postural habits.

ORGANIZING THE CLASS

Several ways to organize the class for instruction are presented in the following section. The single-activity organization should predominate, but station organization has value, and the choice period can be an enjoyable event.

Single-Activity Organization

In this design, all children are reacting to the same challenges and following similar steps throughout the lesson. The suggested format of instructional steps in educational movement is based on this arrangement. It is quite difficult, perhaps impossible, to institute progressive steps in the learning process if the children are scattered around, either individually or in groups, doing different activities.

In single-activity organization, the teacher conducts the class by following a lesson plan and provides guidance (coaching), demonstrations, and evaluation as segments of the lesson. In this arrangement, there must be enough equipment to ensure that each child may have his own piece. Waiting for a turn produces dead learning time and inefficient education.

Station Organization

In station organization, the class is divided into small groups of children, with each group being assigned to a station in the play area. Each station is a mini-learning center, featuring a particular movement experience. Each station designates the activity to be performed and provides the needed space.

For effective use of the station design, the children should have had some experience with the activities making up the station circuit. It is felt that young children need some basis upon which to superimpose their movement patterns, if their experience at each station is to be educational and not just random play.

How many stations? This depends to some extent on the time to be spent at each station. If the class has 30 minutes in total, six stations would allow four minutes at each station, with the remainder of the time devoted to explanation and follow-up.

It is imperative that goals be established beforehand and that directions be posted at each station. When the children come to a station, they should know what direction their efforts are supposed to take. This will help to prevent unprofitable activity.

The teacher can spend a few minutes at the beginning of the class going over the potential of the activites at each of the stations. This explanation should be broad enough in scope so that self-directed activity is possible. The basis for activity at each station can be designated by means of illustrated cards. The illustrations should leave much latitude for varied activity.

The teacher should circulate among the stations, encouraging, guiding, and observing. The presence of assistants makes the arrangement a better learning situation. It is the ideal situation if an adult or cross-age aide can be at each station.

The authors have had good success with this format of organization on a free play day for children. As much equipment as possible can be placed at various stations. If children are familiar with the equipment, they will need little guidance for their free play.

Depending on the age level of the youngsters, a set time to rotate is a desirable procedure. In many cases, children are not mature enough to rotate or change stations as they feel motivated.

A tape can be made that plays soothing music and also incorporates a time-change signal. This will relieve the teacher of the chore of watching the time and frees her to become more involved with the children. Some teachers have used automatic timers successfully for signaling changes.

Choice Periods

Choice periods, when children have a choice of different activities, can occasionally be observed. Equipment should be on hand for these activities, and should be returned when the child finishes with it.

FORMATIONS FOR MOVEMENT

Instruction involving nonlocomotor movement involves little planning, since children can undergo the movement experiences in personal space. When locomotor movement is taught, however, a different situation presents itself with regard to the manner in which the children can be organized for movement. The number of children, the space available, and the type of activity are factors that influence the choice of formation for effective teaching. The following formations can be considered for locomotor movement:

1. Children move individually in every direction. The children must be cautioned about collisions and the need to be courteous. Children should be directed to use all the available space to move in various directions.
2. Children move around the area in a circular fashion. Some teachers feel that this formation creates competition and tends to bring about conformity. On the other hand, collisions do not often occur, and the teacher can observe

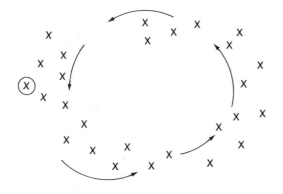

the children effectively when they move in a circle.

3. Children are in two lines on opposite sides of the room and move toward one another. On

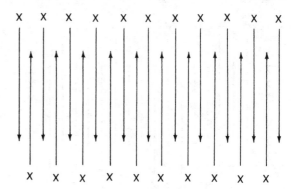

signal, the children cross to the opposite side of the area, exchanging positions with those across from them.

4. Children are in two lines opposite one another. Movement is to the center and back. A

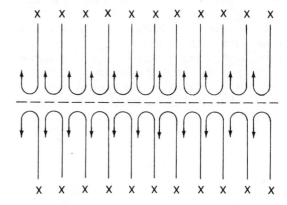

line can be formed with ropes, wands, or cones to mark the center limit. Children move to the center of the area and then return to place.

5. Children are on opposite sides of the room. One line, then the other, moves across and back. The line of children from one side crosses to a point near the other line and then makes a turn, returning to place. After these children have completed the movement, the other group takes a turn.

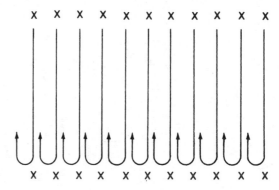

6. Children are on four sides of the area, exchanging position. The children along one pair of opposite sides exchange first, and then the others exchange. They alternate back and forth.

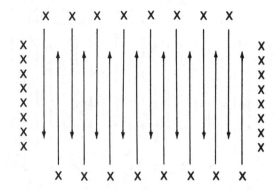

SUMMARY

In analyzing movement, movement patterns can be divided into two categories, divergent and convergent movement. Divergent movement aims toward the development of body awareness and management in a variety of situations. Emphasis is placed on exploration, repetition, and creation. Convergent movement involves a specific skill that can be named and identified. Included in convergent movement are fundamental skills, specialized skills, and the more precise skills on apparatus.

To enhance learning progressions in educational movement, five steps are presented: (1) setting the problem, (2) increasing variety and depth of movement, (3) developing quality in movement, (4) sequencing and combining movement patterns, and (5) culminating activity through partner and small group work. The first two steps need to be taught in that order, but the last three can be interchanged.

Different learning styles offer different modes of instruction for students. The task, guided-discovery, and problem-solving styles of learning place an increasing amount of responsibility on the learner to arrange his or her learning environment. The styles also offer an increased amount of time for creating and finding new movement patterns.

Teachers can personalize the learning opportunity for children by allowing them to experiment and create, through focusing on their potential, and by challenging them to quality performance after they have mastered movement patterns. To augment the different learning styles, teacher and student demonstration should be used following presented guidelines.

Different methods of organizing the class can be used in educational movement lessons. Single-activity organization or the use of stations are excellent choices. Finally, many formations for physical movement and organization of students are offered.

Educational Movement Themes for Divergent Movement

Our bodies are apt to be our autobiographies.
Frank Galett Burgess

The element of self-selection is paramount in educational movement. An opportunity for experimentation, exploration, and self-discovery must be included in the program. This ranges from the opportunity for children to explore within precise and narrow limitations to the opportunity for them to make choices about the activity they are to perform and the approach they wish to follow. It is the responsibility of the teacher to set the stage and create situations that challenge the child to develop his or her resources of movement. The teacher no longer dominates the lesson, but stimulates the children to use their ideas to plan different ways to carry out the movement experiences. Each child is encouraged to make what contributions he or she can to the whole. Since children have a desire to express themselves physically, as well as in other ways, satisfaction of this desire can only be obtained if the children have a measure of choice and an opportunity to exercise individuality.

Because the child expresses himself individually in movement, he can achieve a satisfactory measure of success *for himself*, rather than according to the teacher's or the group's standards. The child progresses according to her innate abilities, stimulated by the teacher and the learning situation. No child need feel awkward or self-conscious because she does not measure up to predetermined standards. The fact that a child may differ from other children in size, shape, maturity, or motor ability should not prevent him from achieving success and satisfaction. The child makes progress at his own rate and to his own satisfaction.

The deeper aim of educational movement is that it seeks to develop the child's awareness not only of what he is doing, but also of how he is moving to do it. It is hoped that children may come to appreciate their own ability and make better interpretation of their own movement patterns. The process then becomes an acquisition of movement experiences, rather than an accumulation of knowledge or subject matter. Each child should be given the opportunity to succeed in his own way according to innate capacity. There is value not only in the accomplishment of the child, but also in the manner by which this accomplishment is reached. The teacher attempts to establish a learning experience that will stimulate the child to think. Interestingly, although John Dewey said the same thing at the turn of the century, physical educators have just gotten around to achieving this goal.

The educational viewpoint that centers responsibility on the individual for self-direction in his learning also requires an adequate foundation of movement theory for good results. The impetus and raison d'être for educational movement lies in the analysis of movement, based on the Laban approach. The concepts composing the analysis of movement become the parameters of educational movement. Not only does the child learn to move and move to learn, he must also learn about movement.

CONTRIBUTIONS OF EDUCATIONAL MOVEMENT TO THE OBJECTIVES OF PHYSICAL EDUCATION

Educational movement must be guided. The teacher must be prepared to introduce originality and something of his own personality into the teaching process. Invention is the key to movement experiences. The problems are set up with instruction and demonstration kept to a minimum, to be used only as needed.

The emphasis in educational movement is on activity and movement of a *purposeful* nature. The teacher must be interested in promoting within the child both quantity and quality of movement. Only then does movement become an educational experience. Too often, children undergo movement experiences without guidance, without being instructed to do things as well as possible. Learning takes place primarily when a desirable motor pattern or concept is reinforced, or when a new pattern or concept is acquired.

If movement programs are conducted in the spirit we have outlined, there is little doubt that they can make a significant contribution to the lives of children. Most educators are convinced that important values can be achieved with such programs in both the cognitive and the affective domains, as well as in anticipated movement competency. It must be remembered that activity by itself will not achieve the objectives. The learning environment must be structured in such a way that achievement of the objectives becomes a predictable outcome.

EDUCATIONAL MOVEMENT THEMES

A movement theme refers to a specific perception about a movement, or the quality of a movement, which children are to experience so that it may become a part of their movement vocabulary and contribute to effective body management competency. It is postulated that if youngsters achieve well in incorporating all the movement themes into their world of movement, they will have achieved good body management. The process is regarded as part of divergent movement, since no special skills (fundamental or specialized) are specific goals. These skills may, however, be developed incidentally while the student explores and experiments with the suggested movement patterns for theme development.

The themes could be classified according to space, time, force, flow, and body factors. Such a procedure seems to cloud the issue, however, since theme development cannot be fully isolated from other movement factors. Whenever children move, they move in space, they move at a certain speed, they must apply force, and they employ various body parts. Flow from one movement to another is found in most theme developments.

In structuring a lesson focusing on themes, the teacher may wish to center the entire lesson on one theme. A more meaningful approach would be to include two or three different themes in a lesson. Each of the themes could undergo continuing development in successive class sessions.

One can imagine the positive effects in terms of public relations when a child reports to his parents, for example, "Today we had fun! We worked on 'taking the weight on the hands.'" The practice of theme development can also lead to better understanding and appreciation of the program on the part of parents, who are pleased that their children are participating in a program that is educational and enjoyable.

In the following section, some attempt has been made to couch the directives in the form of challenges to students. The teacher should also refer to the section on formulating challenges (p. 87). Care must be taken to express ideas and movement directions in correct terminology, appropriate for the children in the class. When terminology is new or unfamiliar, a basis for understanding must be established.

If each child is operating in personal space, movement formations are not a needed consideration. For movement in general space, the teacher is referred to suggested formations (pp. 89–90) for effective arrangements. In the discussion of some of the themes, an appropriate formation has been suggested. For locomotor movements, the express purpose of the suggested formation is to establish pathways of movement that are time-saving and do not restrict children in their responses.

The teacher must get out of the habit of believing that moving in a formation automatically means taking turns. Children in these formations are all active and are all participating at the same time, but are moving in stipulated pathways.

The themes are grouped into three classifications, based on the following rationale.

During the early stages of movement development, attention should be paid to establishing the *basic themes* of body awareness and of the different concepts of personal and general space. These themes are considered fundamental, and provide a framework upon which other themes can be superimposed. The bulk of the themes are *themes designed to develop understanding of elements of movement.* The teacher should review them and make choices in keeping with the maturity of the children. *Themes for expanded movement combinations* include flow-sequencing and cooperative partner activities. Many varied movement combinations are included in the flow-sequencing theme. Cooperative partner activities, which can be used with first and second grade children, present ideas about how other themes may be expanded through partner work. Since both these themes have wide application, they are placed in this category so that the teacher may use the information to supplement and expand the experiences found in any of the other themes.

BASIC THEMES

Body Awareness

These are the body parts to be learned:

Head—forehead, face, eyes, cheeks, eyebrows, nose, mouth, ears, jaw, chin

Upper body—neck, shoulders, chest, back, stomach, arms, forearms, elbows, wrists, hands, fingers, thumbs

Lower body—waist, hips, seat, thighs, knees, ankles, feet, arches, toes, heels

"We are going to see whether you can touch the body part I name [kindergarten]. I will say, 'Touch your hips.' As soon as you do this, you reply back to me, 'I am touching my hips.'" Note that this approach works well when the teacher alternates from the head and upper body to the lower body regions so that the children need to make gross motor changes.

Body part challenges

"When I name a body part, let's see whether you can make this the highest part of your body while you are standing still. [Or in some other stationary position.] Now, the next task will be a little more difficult. Move in a straight line for a short distance, with the body part named kept above all other body parts. What body part would be difficult to keep above all others?" [Eyes, both ears, both hips.]

"Now, move around the room, traveling any way you wish. [This directive could be limited.] The signal to stop will be a word describing a body part. Can you stop and immediately put both hands on that part or parts?"

"Toss your beanbag into the air. When I call out a body part, sit down quickly and put the beanbag on that part."

"This time, when I call out a body part, you are to move around the room as you wish, while holding with one hand a named body part. When I call out another name, you are to change the type of movement and hold the part with the other hand as you move."

Exploring Personal Space

There are several good ways to let the child experience his personal space. Have him take an individual jump rope and double it. From a kneeling position, he should swing it in a full arc along the floor. It should not touch another child or rope. "Show us how big your space is. Keeping one foot in place, outline how much space you can occupy. Sit Indian fashion and outline your space. Support your weight on your hands [or another part of the body] and outline your space."

"Make yourself as wide as you can. [Narrow, small, large, low, high, etc.] Try these variations from different positions—kneeling, balancing on seat, etc. Show us what kinds of body positions you can take while standing on one foot. Lying on your stomach. On your seat. Try the same with one foot and one hand touching the floor."

"Move from a lying-down position to a standing position without using your arms or hands. Return to lying down."

"Can you stay in one place and move your whole self—except for your feet? Sway back and forth first with your feet together and then with your feet apart. Which is better?"

"While lying on your back, move your arms and legs from one position slowly and then move them back to where you started." Explore other positions.

"Keeping one part of your body in place, make just as big a circle as you can with the rest of your body."

Explore different positions in which one leg or one foot is higher than the rest of the body. Work out a smooth sequence of three different positions.

"Pump yourself up like a balloon, getting bigger and bigger. Hold until I say, 'Bang.' "

"In your personal space, show me how a top spins. Keep your feet together in place. With your arms wide to the sides, twist and make your feet turn."

Note. Children should adjust their personal space so that they will not intrude on the space of others.

Moving in General Space

"Run lightly around the area, changing direction as you wish, without bumping or touching anyone, until I call 'Stop.' How many were able to do this without bumping into anyone?"

Have children run zigzag fashion in the area without touching one another. At a signal, they are to make an abrupt change of direction and also change to another type of locomotor movement.

"Run lightly in general space and pretend you are dodging someone. Can you run toward another runner and change direction to dodge out of his way?"

"Get a beanbag and drop it to mark your personal space. See how lightly you can run throughout the area. When the signal is given, run to your spot, pick up your beanbag, put it on your head, and sit down." [Or some other challenge.] "Try this skipping."

"We are going to practice orienteering. [Explain.] Find a spot on the wall and see whether you can run directly to the spot in a straight line. You may have to stop and wait for others so as not to bump into anyone, but you cannot change direction. When you get to your selected spot, pick another spot, and repeat."

"What happens when the general space is smaller? You had no problem running without touching anyone in the large space. Now, let's divide the area in half with these cones. Run lightly within this area so as not to touch or bump anyone. Now it's going to get more difficult. I'm going to divide the space in half once more, but first let's try walking in the new area. Now, run lightly." Decrease the area as it is feasible.

"Get a beanbag and again mark your personal space. Run around the beanbag until you hear 'Bang,' and then 'explode' in a straight-ahead direction until the call, 'Stop.' Return to your personal space."

"From your beanbag, take five jumps and stop. [There can be more than five; they can be hops, skips, gallops, or slides.] Turn to face 'home' and return with the same number of jumps. Take the longest steps you can and return with tiny steps."

"Show me how well you can move with these combinations in general space: run-jump-roll. Skip-spin-collapse. You devise a series of three movements and practice them."

"Today our magic number is five. Can you move in any direction, using five repetitions of a movement? Change direction and pick another movement to do five times."

"Blow yourself up just like a soap bubble. Can you huff and puff? Think of yourself as a big bubble that is floating around. When I touch you, the bubble breaks, and you collapse to the ground. This time, blow up your bubble again, float around, and when you are ready, say, 'Pop,' so that the bubble bursts."

"I am going to challenge you on right and left movements. Show me how you can change to the correct direction when I say either 'Right' or 'Left.' Now begin running lightly."

"This time, run rapidly toward another child. Both of you stop and bow to each other. Instead of bowing, shake hands and say, 'How do you do?' "

"From your personal space, pick a spot on a wall. See whether you can run to the spot, touch it, and return without bumping anyone. This time, it's more difficult. You are asked to pick spots on two different walls, touch these in turn, and return."

Note. Target goals in these movement experiences, in addition to developing movement competency, should be: (1) being able to share space with other children, (2) being able to move through space without bumping anyone, and (3) developing consideration for the safety of others.

THEMES LEADING TO AN UNDERSTANDING OF MOVEMENT ELEMENTS

Acceleration and Deceleration

"Staying in your own personal space, begin with some kind of movement and accelerate until you are moving as fast as you can. Reverse by beginning with a fast movement and slowing down until you are barely moving." For a sequence of two movements, have the children begin with one and accelerate, then change to another movement and decelerate. Try having them do two different body movements at the same time, one that accelerates and one that decelerates. Concepts can be stressed by relating this sequence to a car with its accelerator and the brakes, which decelerate. The prefixes for the two words should be explained.

Acceleration and deceleration can be combined into an endless number of movements, even when another theme dominates. The teacher should use ingenuity and imagination in working this theme into other movement sequences.

Balancing (Supporting the Body Weight)

"What are the ways you can balance on different surfaces of the body? Can you balance on three parts of the body, all different? Two? One?" Put together sequences of three or four balance positions, using different parts or different numbers of body parts. "Balance on your heels. On one heel."

"When I name a body part, balance on that part. This time, I will name a body part and say either 'curled' or 'stretched'. You balance on the part the way I call it."

"Balance on one foot with your arms and the lifted leg in different positions. Try some of the balances with your eyes closed. Bend over while balancing on one foot. Bend backward. Bend sideways."

"Support yourself with your hands and feet as wide apart as possible. Support the weight on both knees. One knee. On one foot and one hand. On the same side. On the opposite sides."

"Balance on your seat, moving your arms and legs to different positions without touching the floor. Balance on your tummy. Spin around on your tummy. On your seat."

"Stand with one foot forward and the toe of your back foot touching the heel of your forward foot. Stand with your legs crossed. Twist your body to wind up the crossed legs even farther."

Have children balance on patches and/or points. Set up challenges to go from one patch to another or to combinations of patches and/or points.

Balance movements should be done deliberately, since fast movement does not sufficiently challenge the balance recovery controls. Balance positions should be maintained from three to five seconds before changing.

Bending and Angular Motion

Have children practice a stooping position (about halfway down) and count the number of joints that are involved in the stooping movement. They should go down with a smooth, slow motion and rise in small increments.

"See if you can touch your shoulder with your hand, moving *only* the elbow joint. What other joints may need to bend?"

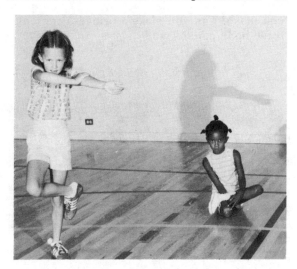

Balancing with a twist

"Show me a right angle [explanation needed] in a joint movement. Most joints can move more than a right angle. See if you can find some joints that can move only to a right angle or perhaps less."

With children seated on the floor with shoes off and legs extended, have them explore bending motions with the toes, feet, and ankles. "Can you bend the ankle and foot so that the heels are ahead of the toes? With the feet flat, can you bend the big toe so it points down, touching the floor? Try creeping with the toes to pull your heels forward. How about the reverse?"

"See how many different ways you can hook bent parts with another joint. Can you stoop down, put your arms *between* your legs, bring your hands around the *outside* of your ankles, and touch your fingers together? How close can you come?"

"Bend one part slowly and another part fast. Bend one part of the body while another joint is straightening."

"See if you can find five joints that will only bend—no rotating or circling." Have the children find partners to play One Behind. Partner shows a bending motion, which the second child observes. Partner changes to another bending motion (this can be on signal), and the second child performs the first bending movement. As further changes occur, the second child is always "one behind" in reproducing the patterns. Change roles.

Bridges

"Show me a bridge made by using your hands and feet. What other kinds of bridges can you make? Can you make a bridge using only three body parts? Two?"

Bridging on hands and feet

"Show me a wide bridge. A narrow one. A short bridge. A long one. How about a high bridge? A low one? Can you make a bridge that opens when a boat goes through? Get a partner to be the boat and you be the bridge."

Work up a sequence of bridge positions, going smoothly from one to the next.

"Move one end of the bridge while the other is still. Show how bridges can span various distances. What is the largest distance you can span? The smallest?"

Divide the class into four or five animal groups. Everyone makes some kind of bridge. When an animal group is named, all members go under bridges formed by the others and immediately form their own bridges again. Another way to stimulate uniqueness is for the teacher to say, "When I think you have made a really interesting bridge, I will tap you. You then go under two bridges and form another bridge."

Partners or groups of three can form bridges. More than this makes a complicated task.

Making a full back arch bridge individually can be facilitated by assistance from a partner. "Make a bridge over your partner."

Contrasting Movements (Opposites)

Be sure the teacher has established the understanding of contrasting movements (opposites). The first approach consists of having the children do a movement and then follow with an opposite movement. "Show me a wide shape. Now an opposite. Can you do a fast movement? Now its opposite."

"Let's see you do a big, fast movement. Now its opposite. I am thinking of a tiny movement done at a high level. Now, show me its opposite." Note that these are combination movements with two elements. The opposite movement must include opposites of both original limitations (tiny-high/large-low).

As another way of handling opposites, the teacher names a movement quality, and the child performs the opposite movement. "Show me a fast movement." The response is a slow movement. "When I say, 'Go,' show me three light jumps forward." The response will be three heavy jumps backward.

The teacher should provide the child with experiences to help him come up with the opposite himself. If the connections are continually made for him, the child will be deprived of the opportunity to think through the concept of opposite movements.

The following pairs of opposites are grouped under factors that stimulate variety of movement.

Use of space
Forward/backward, up/down, straight/curved or straight/crooked, left/right, high/low, near/far, rising/sinking

Time factors
Even/uneven, fast/slow, sudden/sustained, accelerate/decelerate

Force development
Heavy/light, sudden/smooth, strong/weak, tensed/relaxed

Flow
Sustained/interrupted, smooth/jerky

Body relationships
Up/down, forward/backward, over/under, above/beneath, in front of/behind, big/little, stretched/straight (or stretched/curled), large/tiny, long/short

Flight

"Show me how many different ways you can go through space." Have the children try again, using different levels. Have them lead with different parts of the body.

"See how high you can go as you go through space. What helps you get height?"

The use of equipment stimulates better effort and variety when propelling the body in flight. Five or six low jumping boxes, either one alone or two in combination, are recommended. Mats can be added, and the landing can be followed by rolls. Turning and making shapes in flight should be considered.

Two parallel lines two feet apart can represent a creek to be crossed. Other objects, such as small cones, individual mats, and masking tape, are useful. Avoid wands and jump ropes, which may cause falls.

Force—Heavy and Light, Strong and Weak, Sudden and Sustained

"Show me different kinds of heavy movements. Of light movements. Now, follow a heavy movement with a light movement."

"Walk lightly around your space. Walk heavily. Walk as though you want to make good footprints in wet sand at the beach. Walk as if you are barefooted and need to hurry over a section of hot pavement. Walk as if you are in glue and your feet are sticking to the floor."

"Jump heavily up and down. Jump lightly. Jump forward heavily three [or a different number] jumps. Jump backward the same way. Jump forward lightly and backward lightly." Mix light and heavy jumping sequences.

"Make your body as tight as possible. Relax. Hug yourself tightly, hold and relax. Hold your breath for ten counts, then breathe out. Hold your breath while hugging yourself and on signal say, 'Wah,' as you drop to the floor in a completely relaxed fall, like a rag doll. Take a deep breath, hold, and beat your chest with your fists."

Vary strong and light movements having sudden or sustained action. Put together three strong movements, changing from one to the other smoothly (sustained action). Try the same with sudden changes. Mix strong (or slow) movements with weak, slow, or sudden movements. "Show in your face the kind of movement you are doing." Form sequences.

Have the children take a wide, stretched position and pull in the various body segments, using strong motion, until they are standing straight. Have them try the same exercise lying on their backs, ending in a straight lying position.

"Pretend you are holding up the ceiling, which is beginning to fall. Show how to lift up a heavy log." Discuss proper positioning and angles of the body.

Partner activity with primary grade children often gives good results. Show the importance of base support in resisting movement. One partner pushes on the other's shoulder from the side to experiment with base support—feet together, slightly apart, apart the width of the shoulders, far apart, knees straight or bent.

One partner pushes the other backward; he provides moderate resistance. Try having him pull. "Show a fist to your partner and allow him to open it slowly. Now, show it again and prevent him from opening it. With your elbows out and your fists held together, let your partner pull your fists apart and then resist him."

Forming Letters, Numbers, and Shapes

"When I call out the letter [or number or shape], write it in the air as big as you can. Can you lie on your back and make the letter in the air with your foot? Now, the other foot. Perhaps some of you can write the letter with your head. Your knee. Draw it on the floor with your toe."

"Let's see if you can walk a pattern of your favorite letter in your personal space." Have children try other letters while hopping or skipping.

"I am going to show you some letters. [Have them on cards.] See if you can form these letters with your body in a standing position. On the floor. Find a partner and work on the letters together. Play a game where one partner walks a letter and the other guesses what it is."

The partners can put some simple words together, like "to," "so," "it," "in," "on," etc.

Forming a letter on the floor

The entire approach outlined above is equally useful for numbers and shapes. The following shapes are some that should be recognized by children—triangle, circle, oval, square, rectangle, diamond. Large flash cards are good props. Another effective idea is to use the overhead projector. Various shapes can be illustrated both by the teacher and by students. Colors can also be used to stimulate combinations of movements and shapes.

Leading with Different Body Parts

"As you move between the different markers [lines, beanbags], show how many ways you can travel on different body parts. Now, travel while two, three, or four parts of the body are in contact. Move across at different levels."

"Show me a way to travel, leading with your elbow. With one foot. With your head. Your seat. Your knee. Vary your travel with slow movements. With quick movements."

"In your own space, show me different kinds of body movements in which the elbow leads." Have them show movements in which corresponding parts of the body, such as the knees, the ankles, or the elbows, can touch each other and move apart.

Have children work with partners. One partner holds a hoop. The other shows different ways of going through the hoop, leading with different body parts. With children in a small group, and using cones and wands (four cones and two wands), set up a challenge course. Children go over and under the wands, leading with different body parts.

The formations suggested for movement (pp. 89–90) are useful for this type of activity.

Levels and Speed

Designate a portion of a line or a board in the floor. "Begin at the far end. Show me a slow, low-level movement down and back. What other ways can you go down and back slowly and at a low level? Change to a high level and fast movement. In what other levels can you move?"

Have children combine a low, fast movement down with a high, slow movement on the way back. Explore other ways and combinations. Vary the exercise by having them lead with different parts of the body.

"Move your arms at as high a level as you can. At as low a level as you can. In between. Show me a movement in which your body is at a high level and your arms are at a low level. Reverse."

"Using your hands and feet, travel at high, middle, and low levels." Have them lead with different parts of the body.

Have the children skip in general space. When the teacher says, "High!" the children each make a statue at a high level. Do this for low and in between as well. Have them skip around in groups of three. When the signal to stop is given, the three children freeze, with one in a high, one in a low, and one in a medium position. The children travel around the room and, when the signal to stop is sounded, they stop in a given level. Change the directive each time.

Alternate between two movement patterns: (1) running lightly at a very high level and stopping at a low level, (2) moving slowly at a low level and stopping at a high level.

"Travel around the room any way you wish and, at the drumbeat, change level but keep traveling." At the "stop" signal, they are to freeze on a specified number of body parts— two, three, or four. "Let's practice changing level by falling. Do this easily by breaking the fall with your hands. Now, try breaking the fall with your hands and rolling on a large part of the body. Now, let's run lightly and fall."

"Pretend you are a glider [or a bird]. Fly high. Fly low. Fly in between." Young children might like the bird to have a name.

The formations (pp. 89–90) are of value in developing pathways for movement in these activities.

Moving with the Weight Supported on the Hands and Feet

"Pick a spot outside your personal space and travel to and from that spot on your hands and feet. Try moving with your hands close to your feet. Far away from your feet." Have them show bilateral, unilateral, and cross-lateral movements. Build up a sequence.

Moving with the weight on the hands and feet

Have them move in different patterns. Have them turn in a circle, clockwise and counterclockwise. They can do this while looking at the floor and then while looking at the ceiling.

"Make one of your hands a foot and try moving on three feet. Move in different directions."

Have them turn the body over to the right until the face is looking toward the ceiling and continue in the same direction until the face is again toward the floor. Reverse direction.

"What kinds of animals can you imitate? Move with a springy kind of jump. What shapes can you make while you are moving?"

Note. When using terms such as bilateral, unilateral, and cross-lateral in directions to children, take care to explain them, including the significance of the prefixes.

Over and Under

Different ways of going over and under things can be explored. A wand across two cones, a jump rope suspended between two chairs, or a wand or baseball bat held by another child, provides a needed obstacle. Children on their hands and knees can provide a human bridge. A bench may be used if it is set on small jumping boxes.

Moving over and under obstacles

Jumping, hopping, or leaping can be combined with other ways of going over the obstacle. Different shapes can be specified. Turns in flight can be added.

In going under, the movement challenge could specify that the body is to face the floor, to face the side, or to face the ceiling. Leading with different parts of the body adds variety. The method of propulsion can be included in the challenge: no hands, no feet, one hand, one foot, etc.

Sequence patterning adds other challenges. The sequence could be: over and over; over and under; under and over; under, over, under; over, under, over.

Follow activity is excellent with a partner. The child can say to his partner, "I am going over and under," before beginning the sequence. This will help children learn the terminology.

Planes of Movement

"Show me a variety of movements in a horizontal plane. In a vertical plane. On a diagonal. Put together combinations so that we go in sequence from one type of movement to another." Explain the terms used.

"Here is a challenge. When I call out a plane of movement, you respond with a movement that is correct." Specify the plane of movement.

"With your arms outstretched, pretend you are a glider." Develop the concept of diagonal positioning when turning. Relate it to running when turning a corner.

Planes of movement is a theme that cannot be strongly developed on its own. It should be incorporated into other themes so that concepts may be reinforced.

Partial Rotative Motions—Swinging, Twisting, Shaking, Rocking, Swaying

"Show me some different ways you can swing parts of the body. Swing them high and smoothly. Twist your body as you swing. Let's try a leg swing. A knee swing. Let the arms move back and forth like windshield wipers—use both right and left arms. Make them move hard to get the snow and ice off the windshield."

"Twist one part of the body. Twist other parts. Twist one and, as you twist another, untwist the first. Twist the whole body around so hard it moves you in place. Twist your arms behind your back so that you can interlace your little fingers."

"Sit on the floor with your knees up. Twist your legs so that your knees move out and then in. March your feet right and left with twisting motions. Lie on your back, put one leg up, and pretend it is a submarine periscope. Move the periscope right and left, looking for ships. When you see a ship, send off a torpedo (the other foot)."

"As you sit on the floor, keep this position but twist to see directly behind you, right and left."

Have children shake different body parts—hands; hands and arms; hands, arms, and shoulders. "Pretend that someone has put a piece of ice down your back. Shake it out. Shake your seat like the hula dancers do."

"Try to shake one foot and one hand together—on the same side. On opposite sides. Now, each of you find a partner and get a beanbag. One partner gets on hand and knees, the other places the beanbag between the partner's shoulders. Try to shake the beanbag off. Try again with the beanbag on your seat."

"Shake 'water' from each hand. Shake your hands high and low. Shake them around your legs, behind your back."

"With your feet together, sway slowly from side to side. Sway so far over it makes you lose your balance. Sway forward and back. Now, try rocking—a faster motion—from side to side. Rock back and forth on your toes and heels."

"Rock back and forth in different directions on your seat. Make your body into a ball with your hands around your knees and see how many directions you can rock."

Rotative Motions—Circling, Rolling, Spinning

"Can you make full circles with your hands and arms at your wrists? At your elbows? Your shoulders? In the same way, what circles can you make with your legs and feet? Try this lying on your back. Can you make circles at any other joints of your body?"

"Can you keep two different circles going at the same time? Make a circle turning one way and another turning the other way."

"Hop [or jump or skip] in a small circle, keeping one or more of your body parts moving in a circle as you move. Reverse the direction of the circle."

With children in a seated position, have them explore different body areas to determine which joints allow circular motion. Approach the analysis systematically: fingers, hands, arms, shoulders, head, body, legs, feet, and toes. Target goals are knowing the names of the joints and understanding something about their functions.

With children in a standing position, experiment with making big arm circles with one arm, then both arms. "Can you make one arm circle forward and one circle backward? Show me four different ways you can make double circles, with both arms, in front of your body." This should result in double arm circles right and left, and circles inward and outward. Have the child lie on his back with the feet up and follow the same directions for the legs.

"Can you roll your body into a little ball? Now, slowly uncurl it. Roll it up again. Now, see if you can roll in different directions, while staying in your own space. Roll over like a log twice. Roll back."

"Can you roll over your shoulder? How about rolling over from a hands-and-knees position?"

"In a standing position, show me how you can spin to the right. Spin to the left. Try spinning on one foot, getting some help from the other foot as a pusher. Spin two or three times and then balance on one foot."

"From a low level, spin toward the ceiling to as high as you can go. Come back down slowly. Now start high and spin low."

"Show me how many different ways you can spin on different parts of your body. Be sure to spin right and left."

No attempt should be made to prolong spinning until the children become dizzy.

Shapes

"Let's try making shapes and see if we can name them. Make any shape you wish and hold it. What is the name of your shape, John?"

"Try to make different kinds of wide shapes. Show me other shapes you can make. What is the name of your shape, Susie?" [Susie replies, "Crooked."] "Show me different kinds of shapes that are crooked. I'll name some things, and you

make your body into that shape: ball, snake, hoop, square, bird, ..."

Shapes that can be interpreted are: wide/narrow, straight/crooked, straight/round or straight/curved, stretched/curled, symmetrical/asymmetrical, big/little, twisted/untwisted, and inverted/upright.

Forming shapes is used in many other themes. The emphasis here should be on understanding, recognizing, and experiencing as many kinds of shapes as possible.

"Select three different kinds of shapes and move smoothly from one to another. This time I will clap my hands as a signal to change to a different shape."

Have the children suggest other kinds of shapes, reinforcing the concept by having the children practice each kind of shape. This exercise could be divided into shapes while erect and shapes on the floor.

Taking the Weight on the Hands

"Put your hands on the floor and see if you can take your weight on your hands for a short time. How do you get your body into the air? What is the importance of the center of gravity? [This concept should be explained beforehand.] What different things can you do with your feet while your weight is on your hands?"

"Begin from a standing position and take your weight on your hands. Take care not to tip over. How should the fingers be placed to support yourself the best way? Can you take the weight on your hands and return the feet to the floor in a different place?"

"See how high you can send your seat up to the ceiling. Is it possible to take the weight on your hands for a moment and click your heels?"

"Put down a jump rope, making a straight line. Make a bridge face down over the rope so that the rope is just in front of your toes. What movements can you do with your feet back and forth over the rope? Get alongside the rope in a crouched position on all fours. Your hands and feet should be on the same side of the rope. Can you place your hands on the *other* side of the rope and by moving your seat toward the ceiling, bring your feet to that side [crouch jump]?"

"How many can send one foot up toward the ceiling? Hold the foot up there as long as you can. Try sending one foot up first and bringing the other up to it. Is it better with the arms straight or bent?"

"See if you can place one hand to the side, then put the other beyond it and move your seat toward the ceiling so that your feet land behind the second hand." Note that this activity is preliminary to the cartwheel. The immediate goal is to transfer the weight onto the hands *one at a time*. Practice with the concept of spread fingers for better support as well. Care must be taken that children do not overbalance.

Time Patterns

"Show me the different ways you can move through the area, using quick movements. Using slow movements. Using in-between movements. Do some very quick movements in place and then do a slow, traveling movement to another place. Repeat. Travel with quick turns and jumps, then sink to the floor, using a very slow action."

"See if you can start a movement slowly and increase it to a fast pace. Now, reverse—start moving rapidly and slow down. Select a spot some distance from you. Try to move slowly toward the spot. Gradually increase your speed of movement to the spot, and collapse to the floor when you reach the spot. Go back to your home spot, beginning fast and then slowing down to the point where you stop still as a statue at your original spot."

"See if you can make up a series of movements in which fast, slow, accelerating, and decelerating movements are linked together."

"See if you can repeat this beat when I clap my hands [even beat]. What is it, even or uneven? Listen to this one and repeat it [uneven beat.] What is it? Show me some movements to even time and some to uneven time. Put together a sequence of both types."

Traveling in Different Ways

An excellent procedure for this theme is to use the basic movement formation (p. 89) in which the children are located on the two long sides of the gymnasium and a row of cones, beanbags, or other markers is placed down the center lengthwise dividing the space in half. Each child follows a pathway to travel to the center from the side and then returns to his spot along his pathway.

"Can you move along the floor, using only your hands? This time, lie down, and use only your feet. Try moving on your seat, using your feet. Can you move with your feet in the air? Lead with your feet. Your head. Your side."

"Move on three [four] parts of your body. Do a movement on a high level and come back with a low-level movement."

"Who can go toward the center with a slow movement and come back with a fast movement of the same kind?"

"Can you move like a happy puppy? A slow cat? How about a frog? A rabbit? I wonder if anyone can move like an alligator. A turtle."

"Today is backwards day. Show me all kinds of movements in which you go backwards."

"How does a mechanical robot move? A giant?"

"Show me some movements in which your face is toward the ceiling. Toward the side. Toward the floor."

"Start with a slow movement and increase its speed. Now, do the opposite."

"Do a movement pattern that includes a roll. Try a crouch jump. Reach out with both hands and then bring your feet up to your hands."

"See how many jumps [hops, skips, steps] it takes to get to the center. Go back, using the same number of movements."

Receiving and Transferring Weight

Have the children project themselves into the air and practice receiving their weight in different fashions with the feet in various positions. "Try landing without making any noise. What do you have to do? See how high you can jump and still land lightly. Crouch with your hands touching, jump into the air, and land in a low position. Try a moderate-length standing long jump so that you can get height. Land lightly. Jump up and down with the body at different levels."

"From a kneeling position, fall and break the fall with your hands. Try breaking the fall with one hand. From a standing position, fall in a very relaxed way, like a rag doll. Fall like a melting snowman. Fall to the side and let your body roll. Fall with a twist. Try the fall from a kneeling position. From a sitting position."

"See how many different ways you can transfer the weight of your body from one part to another smoothly. [Explain "transfer."] Try some sudden transfers. Work up a sequence of three or four smooth transfers. Work up a sequence of a slow transfer, a sudden transfer, and another slow transfer."

Stretching and Curling

"In your own space, stretch out your body. Now, curl it up. How many different ways can you do this? Let's go slowly from a stretch to a curl. Go from a stretch to a straight body position and then curl. Can you do this with sudden movements?"

Have the children stretch and return to different balanced body positions. Add curling where you can. Have them unstretch body parts separately, first in a standing position and then while lying down.

"While you are sitting, can you touch your toe to your chin? With your legs straight out, can you touch your chin to your knee?"

"Let's see how high you can stretch—stretch to the ceiling. Take a deep breath, let it out, and drop to a low position. Now, stand on your toes and try stretching and holding the stretch."

Have them stretch by degrees in various movements, unstretching the same way.

Suggest different points of support to use while in a curled position—knees, back, side. "What kinds of rolling movements can you do in a curled position and still stay in your space?"

Have them play Rubber Band, in which you stretch slowly and then snap back into place. "Make a big soap bubble out of your body. When the soap bubble breaks, it becomes a puddle of water on the floor."

"Stretch to one side until it pulls you over. Keep one foot in place and see how far you can stretch in different directions."

Have them stretch in different planes—horizontal, vertical, and diagonal.

"Jump high and land in a stretched position. Jump again and return to your original position. Jump high to a stretched position, then jump low to a curled position, and roll in the curled position."

Stretching movements should be done slowly, with controlled movement to the limits. The curled position should form a little, tight ball.

THEMES FOR EXPANDED MOVEMENT COMBINATIONS

Flow—Sequencing Combinations of Movement

The emphasis in sequencing should be on sustained (bound) flow. The sequences can be experienced individually or in partner activities.

The illustrations given are in series of at least three challenges. If only two are pertinent to the situation, the teacher can select the first two movement patterns of a series. In introducing combinations, it may be well to start with the first two movements and add the third later on.

This is an area in which the children can often make fruitful suggestions. Be sure to let them arrange some of their own sequences.

Locomotor and nonlocomotor movements can be put together in various combinations, such as the following:

1. Run, leap, and roll
2. Shake (all over), gallop, and freeze
3. Stop, collapse, explode
4. Whirl, skip, sink slowly
5. Creep, pounce, curl

6. Lift, grin, and roll
7. Kneel, sway, jump to feet
8. Run, stop-look, explode
9. All fours run, roll, jump
10. Jumping jack, slide, jump turn
11. Hop, collapse, creep
12. Jump forward, shake, whirl
13. Rock on heels, jump high, sit down
14. Sink slowly, roll, jump turn.
15. Click heels right and left, jump half turn, run backwards
16. Twist, skip, sit down and smile
17. Turn around three times, clap hands twice behind the back, run, balance on one foot
18. Take fast, tiny steps in place; fall forward onto the hands; move forward on all fours
19. Take a deep breath; expel the air, saying, "Ah-h-h"; jump forward; spin and sink
20. Spin on the seat, roll forward, take five jumps in the direction of the roll

Partner Cooperative Activities

Partner activity should be included into most lessons for first and second graders, so that children come to regard partner work as normal and accepted. A lesson format can also feature partner cooperative activity. The following partner combinations should be considered:

Working Alternately, Taking Turns. "One partner does a movement pattern, and then the other partner tries something a little different. Take turns. Help your partner with suggestions."

Matching Movements. "You will need to watch carefully on this one. If one partner makes a series of slow, deliberate movements, can the other partner match these movements?"

Follow or Copying Movements. "See if you can watch carefully what your partner is doing so that when he finishes you can copy his movement pattern [can be a series of movements]. This time we are going to add movements. The first person will do a movement. The partner will repeat that movement and add one of his own. Next, the original partner will copy both previous movements and add another. Finally, the second partner will try to reproduce all three movements."

Partner as an Obstacle. "Let's have one partner make a shape on three [or four] points. See how many different ways the other partner can go through, over, under, and around the shape without touching the partner."

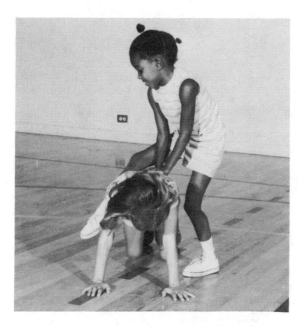

Moving over a partner

Resisting Movements. "Which group can show me some ways that one partner can pull the other along, while the one being pulled offers a little resistance? Can you work out some pushing sequences? Combine a series of pushing and pulling movements."

Forming Shapes. "I am going to call out a letter [or number or shape]. When you hear the letter, you and your partner use your bodies together to form that letter in a lying-down [or standing] position." Note that the children can form letters in series to make up simple words of two letters. Large flash cards are also excellent for this activity. Each card shows a letter, number, or form, which the partners form with their bodies. An overhead projector with appropriate transparencies can also be used.

Listening and Moving. Have one partner clap out a rhythmic pattern. The other partner is to repeat the clapping just as it was done, and then do a series of movements in keeping with the pattern.

Magic Number. "Today's magic number is nine. With your partner standing alongside you and holding hands, move around the room using the same kind of movement [walk, run, skip, tiny steps], so that each one is done nine times. Stop and decide on another movement. Now, since you have done so well with that, put together a series of either two or three different movements, changing smoothly from one to the other." Try the same activities with the partners in different positions, e.g., side by side but facing in opposite directions, or facing each other.

Note that for some movements the partners may drop hands.

Leading and Following. "You are going to have to observe carefully on this one. Your partner will travel around in general space, using different locomotor movements. You are to try to follow a little ways behind him and do the same kinds of movements, while maintaining your distance."

Contrasting Sequences. "You will have to think of opposites this time. Your partner will say, 'I am going to do a *fast* movement,' and then he does it. You will then reply, 'I will do a *slow* movement,' and you do so. Your partner will need to think of things to do so that you can reply to him with an opposite."

Taking the Partner's Weight. "Can you and your partner show me some interesting forms or statues in which one partner holds up part of the weight of the other? Both of you must be touching the ground, but one must be helping the other. When you think you have a really nice form, turn it completely around slowly in a small circle, keeping on the same spot and not changing your statue."

A Show-and-Tell Sequence. "You and your partner work up a sequence of three [two, four, five] movements in which both of you are moving in a similar fashion. Practice this for a while until it becomes smooth, and then we will have a demonstration." Note that when the time comes for achievement demonstration, it is well to have three or four pairs demonstrate at the same time. This prevents embarrassment, particularly when a demonstration has poor quality.

SUMMARY

Educational movement themes are offered for stimulating divergent movement. The themes discussed in this chapter are written in terms of a specific movement quality and/or understanding that children should experience to make it a part of their movement concepts and contribute to new body management competency.

Themes may be taught as a single lesson or can be combined to cover a related movement concept. Themes are offered in three categories. Basic themes provide basic understanding and are the foundation for more complex lessons. Themes for understanding elements of movement make up the bulk of the chapter and emphasize conceptual learning. Finally, themes for expanded movement combinations combine many of the concepts and movements learned to offer the child an opportunity to apply and practice new ideas.

Chapter 10

Creative Play Ideas

You cannot teach a man anything: you can only help him find it in himself.

Galileo

Creative play can be enriched through the use of story games, movement based on poems, finger plays, role-situation play, and creative rhythms. Children love to interpret and express feelings using gross body movement and imaginative actions. As a secondary benefit of creative play, children become aware of the cultural heritage from centuries of creative play ideas and activities.

What is presented in this chapter is meant to be illustrative of the kinds of creative play ideas that can be implemented. The teacher should and will collect many other fruitful ideas. Those who work in different geographical areas and with children of selected ethnic groups or nationalities will find different interpretations. For example, a poem about the wind and the waves is bound to be more meaningful to a child in New Jersey than to one in Kansas. Having a child "build" a snowman in Louisiana will certainly strain the child's imagination a bit. A poem or story about the desert has obvious meaning to children in the Southwest. In planning creative play appropriate to the composition of the class, the teacher should also be open to including activities touching on the heritage of Native Americans, Spanish-surnamed children, black children, and youngsters of other nationalities.

There are several guidelines for creative play. An experience should provide creative opportunity, be satisfying, and allow freedom of response. All should be encouraged to participate at their level of capability, regardless of the quality of response. The activity should be con-

ducted informally, in such a way that it will allow children to investigate their range of body movement and permit free response within the limits of the play activity sketch. There need be no fear of failure.

The skillful leader must have a creative approach as well. Remember that much can be done with simple materials. Children love to make props and "set the stage" for the forthcoming action. The teacher must not overlook the old, familiar stories and should capitalize on things the children already know. An idea need not be complicated or involved; children's play often centers around relatively simple things or ideas. The teacher should be able to draw out ideas and actions from students, building from the base of the original idea.

Grouping should be informal, with children in personal space or in a loose half circle. It is important to create a good physical setting for the idea, making sure that all are positioned so as to be able to see and hear the teacher or leader. Since it is important that a good story basis be set, the teacher will probably need to do the storytelling. Effective development of an idea can be guided by questioning that stimulates thought. "What do you think should come next?" "Where do we go from here?" "How can we show that in movement?" Effective or unique interpretation should be reinforced both verbally and nonverbally. "Johnny, I like that!" "That's good [fine, nice, dandy, etc.]!" "I like your idea!"

Note. Creative rhythms are both creative activities and rhythmic activities, and they could have been located in either section. Since the authors feel that a more coordinated creative play environment can be structured with the help of creative rhythms, however, we have included them in this section.

STORY PLAY

In story play, the children match their play-acting to the words of the story, which results in a sequence of fitting movement actions. The story should be examined carefully to determine what roles need casting and to decide how the students should be grouped for best results: do students within the class respond individually, with a partner, in small groups, or as an entire class?

Children love to act out and dramatize many of the old, familiar stories. Both the children and the teacher will have their favorites. Some of them may be in the following list, which illustrates the kinds of stories that have possibilities.

The Three Bears
The Three Little Pigs
Black Beauty
Cinderella
Rumpelstiltskin
The Shoemaker and the Elves
The Pied Piper
Mother Goose stories
Henny Penny
The Sleeping Beauty
The Town Musicians
Peter Pan

Stories may need to be adapted and rewritten, with only the main points of the story being used to direct the movement.

As an illustration, "Jack the Giant Killer" is given below. The story appears in the left-hand column, and the suggested actions are on the right. It should be emphasized that the actions grow out of discussions with the children about how *they feel* the story should best be interpreted.

Jack the Giant Killer

Once upon a time a giant, called Caramaran, lived on top of a mountain in a cave. He was a very wicked giant, and so the king of the country offered a large reward to the person who would kill the giant. So Jack, a country boy, decided he would try his luck.

Words	Suggested Action
One morning, Jack took a shovel and pick and started toward the mountain. He hurried, as he wished to climb the mountain before dark.	Picking up pick and shovel and running around in a circle.
Jack finally reached the foot of the mountain and started to climb up.	Walking around in a circle with high knee movements.
He came to a place where he had to use his hands to help him climb.	Making climbing movements, using hands and arms.
Just as it grew dark, Jack reached the top of the mountain. When he was sure the giant was asleep in his bed, he took his pick and began to dig a hole outside the cave entrance.	Vigorous digging, with trunk twisting, standing with feet apart.
After he had loosened the dirt with his pick, Jack took the shovel and threw the dirt up on all sides of the hole.	Vigorous shoveling, first right, then left, throwing the dirt in various directions.
Then Jack covered up the hole with some long straws and sticks he picked up.	Forward, downward bending, picking up straws, twisting alternately left and right.
After this was done, Jack waited until morning, when he called loudly and wakened the giant, who strode angrily out of the cave. Because he was very tall, he took big steps.	With arms overhead, stretching up tall, walking around in a circle on tiptoes.
The giant was so very angry that he didn't look where he was going and walked right into the hole Jack had made. Down he fell and was killed.	Stooping quickly as if falling.

Then Jack filled up the hole with the dirt he had taken out.

Jack went into the cave, got the giant's treasure, and ran home to tell his mother about it.

When he got home he was so excited and tired that he was all out of breath. Ever after this, Jack was called Giant Killer.

Making forward, downward movements, pushing dirt into the hole, moving around in a circle, and doing the same thing over again.

Running around in a circle in the opposite direction, carrying the treasure.

Deep breathing.

The teacher should consider putting stories on tape. This allows inclusion of time lapses so that the story can unfold along with the action. Recordings are another source of stories.

Action Poems

The field of poetry can be exploited to its fullest for source material for dramatic play. Mother Goose rhymes are particularly suited for such activity, and there are many others. Poetry has some advantages over stories because of its use of alliteration and rhythmic language, as well as its feeling content. Poems appeal strongly to young children.

Some examples of poems, together with suggested actions, follow. These actions are to be regarded as a guide to the kinds of things that might be done.

Next, a group of poems is presented for which no suggested actions are included. These poems are short and catchy, and their language provides good clues for actions. Some are from Mother Goose, some are from sources unknown, and a few are by well-known poets.

The Elephant

The elephant's walk is careful and slow;
His trunk like a pendulum swings to and fro.
But when there are children with peanuts around
He swings it up and swings it down.

The teacher reads the poem line by line, pausing between lines so that the children can react. Some prior discussion should be held to explain elephant actions and what is meant by a pendulum. Action can vary. Later, when they have learned the words, the children can recite as they move.

Row, Row, Row Your Boat

The verse to "Row, Row, Row Your Boat" is easily learned and can supply the basis for many interesting creative activities. The verse is:

Row, row, row your boat
Gently down the stream.
Merrily, merrily, merrily, merrily,
Life is but a dream.

Let the children make up verses substituting other movements for "row." They can then act out the verses that they have created. One child came up with this verse:

Run, run, run around
All around the room.
Merrily, merrily, merrily, merrily,
Zoom, zoom, zoom.

Other actions around which verses could be built include: walk, march, hop, jump, fly, swim, ride.

Wallaby Kangaroo

Words	**Suggested Action**
Wallaby, wallaby, kangaroo,	Holding the hands in front of the shoulders, to represent the paws of the kangaroo.
How do you jump the way you do?	Looking around from right to left, but not moving.
I'm sure if I tried for a year and a day,	Jumping around like a kangaroo.
I'd never be able to jump that way.	Continuing to jump like a kangaroo.

Three Blind Mice

Words	**Suggested Action**
Three blind mice, three blind mice.	Walking around with the hands over the eyes.
See how they run, see how they run.	Running lightly in different directions.
They all ran after the farmer's wife,	Pretending to chase one another or the teacher.
She cut off their tails with a carving knife,	Making cutting motions.
Did you ever see such a sight in your life	Standing up on tiptoes and looking around.
As three blind mice?	Putting the hands over the eyes.

How to Make a Happy Day

Two eyes to see nice things to do,
Two lips to smile the whole day through,
Two ears to hear what others say,
Two hands to put the toys away,
A tongue to speak sweet words each day,
A loving heart for work or play,
Two feet that errands gladly run—
Make happy days for everyone.

Talk with the children about happiness and how we can help everyone to be happy. As the verse is read or recited, the children point to the various parts of the body as they are mentioned. On the last line, everyone smiles!

Jack, Be Nimble

Words	Suggested Action
Jack, be nimble,	Moving around in various ways.
Jack, be quick,	Speeding up action; changing direction.
Jack, jump over the candlestick!	Jumping high into the air or leaping over a "candlestick."

Pat-a-Cake

Each child has a partner. Partners face each other.

Words	Suggested Action
Pat-a-cake, pat-a-cake, baker's man,	Clapping hands, clapping hands to the partner. Repeat. Shaking forefinger at partner three times.
Bake me a cake as fast as you can.	Stirring the cake fast and vigorously.
Pat it, and mold it, and mark it with a "T,"	Following words with movements of patting, molding, and putting a "T" on top of the cake.
And bring it safely home to baby and me.	Walking around in good balance, taking care not to drop the cake.

Children find another partner during the walking, and the poem is repeated.

Ripe Apples

Words	Suggested Action
Lovely ripe apples on branches so high,	Swaying back and forth with arms stretched upward.
I cannot reach them, 'way up in the sky.	Reaching up high with one arm at a time.
I stretch up so tall, and I jump this way.	Stretching upward on tiptoes. Jumping upward to pick an apple.
I know when I've picked them, I'll eat them today.	Pretending to eat apples, raising the hands alternately to the mouth.
I'll sit down and rest, and eat them some more.	Sitting down cross-legged and continuing to eat.
"Um-m-m. Aren't they good?"	Shaking head, rubbing tummy while repeating the last line in unison.

The Giant

Words	Suggested Action
Once a giant came a-wandering	Wandering around the room, taking "giant's" steps, with swaggering movements.
Late at night when the world was still.	Becoming quiet and putting a finger up to the lips to indicate silence.
Seeking a stool to sit on,	Swaggering around, looking for a place to sit.
He climbed up a little green hill.	Performing climbing movements to get to the top of the hill.
"Giant, giant! I am under you!	Crouching down and pretending that they are being stepped upon.
Move, or this is the last of me."	Trying to push the giant away.
But the giant answered, "Thank you,	Walking around, surveying the countryside.
I like it here, don't you see."	Swaggering with thumbs under armpits.

Giants and Dwarfs

Words	Suggested Action
Let us all be little men,	Walking around like dwarfs, with body in a hunched position and arms and legs bent.
Dwarfs so gay and tiny; then,	Continuing to walk, gaily.
Let us stand up straight and tall.	Walking on tiptoes, arms stretched upward.
We'll be giants, one and all.	Continuing to walk on tiptoes, occasionally turning around.

Hippity Hop

Each child has a partner; inside hands are joined.

Words	Suggested Action
Hippity hop to the barber shop,	Skipping around the room with partner.
To buy a stick of candy.	Stopping and facing partner. Reaching in pocket for money, holding up one finger.
One for you and one for me,	Pointing to partner, pointing to self.
And one for cousin Andy.	Joining inside hands again and skipping around the room.

Little Jack Horner

Words	Suggested Action
Little Jack Horner sat in a corner	Crouching down in a sitting position.
Eating his Christmas pie.	Eating out of the left hand.
He put in his thumb and pulled out a plum	Moving as indicated.
And said, "What a good boy am I!"	Putting thumbs in the armpits and strutting.

Ding Dong Bell

Ding dong bell.
Pussy's at the well.
Who took her there?
Little Johnny Hare.
Who'll bring her in?
Little Tommy Thin.
What a jolly boy was that
To get some milk for pussy cat,
Who never did any harm
But played with the mice in Daddy's barn.

I Love Little Pussy

I love little pussy, her coat is so warm.
And if I don't hurt her, she'll do me no harm.
I'll not pull her tail nor drive her away,
But pussy and I very gently will play.
She shall sit by my side, and I'll give her some food,
And pussy will love me because I am good.

The Scarecrow

The scarecrow stands
With hand in hand.
Walking isn't his style.
He scares the jay
And crow away
With just a painted smile.

Jack and Jill

Jack and Jill went up the hill
To fetch a pail of water.
Jack fell down and broke his crown,
And Jill came tumbling after.

Then up Jack got and off did trot
As fast as he could caper,
To old Dame Bob, who patched his nob,
With vinegar and brown paper.

When Jill came in, how she did grin,
To see Jack's paper plaster.
Dame Bob, vexed, did whip her next
For causing Jack's disaster.

There Was a Crooked Man

There was a crooked man, and he walked a crooked mile,
He found a crooked quarter against a crooked stile;
He bought a crooked cat, which caught a crooked mouse,
And they all lived together in a little crooked house.

The Duke of York

Oh, the brave old Duke of York
He had ten thousand men;
He marched them up to the top of the hill
And then he marched them down again.

And when they were up, they were up,
And when they were down, they were down.
And when they were only halfway up,
They were neither up nor down.

The Wrens

There were two wrens upon a tree.
Whistle and I'll come to thee.
Another came, and there were three.
Whistle and I'll come to thee.

Another came, and there were four.
You needn't whistle any more.
For, being frightened, off they flew,
And there are none to show to you.

The Wind

When the wind is in the East,
   It is good for neither man nor beast;
When the wind is in the North,
   The skillful fisherman goes not forth;
When the wind is in the South,
   It blows the bait in the fishes' mouth;
When the wind is in the West,
   Then 'tis at the very best.

The North Wind

The north wind doth blow,
And we shall have snow,
And what will poor Robin do then, poor thing?
He'll sit in a barn,
And keep himself warm,
And hide his head under his wing, poor thing!

Fishes Swim

Fishes swim in the water clear,
Birds fly high in the air,
Serpents creep along the ground,
Boys and girls spin 'round and 'round.

The Cuckoo's Nest

Last night and the night before,
   A lemon and a pickle came a-knockin' at my door.
I went upstairs to get my gun,
   And you shoulda seen a lemon and a pickle run.
One ran east and one ran west,
   And one flew over the cuckoo's nest.

Wee Willie Winkie

Wee Willie Winkie runs through the town,
Up stairs and down stairs, in his nightgown.
Rapping at the window, crying through the lock,
"Are the children in their beds, for it's past eight o'clock?"

Flying-Man

Flying-man, Flying-man,
   Up in the sky.
Where are you goin' to,
   Flying so high?
Over the mountains
   An' over the sea!
Flying-man, Flying-man,
   Can't you take me?

Barney Bodkin and Janie Jumpty

Barney Bodkin broke his nose,
Stubbed his foot and hurt his toes.
Hit his knee against a tree,
Bumped an eye and now can't see.
Barney Bodkin is always mad,
The whole thing makes me very sad.

Janie Jumpty bumped her chin,
Hurt her feet when she fell in.
Scratched her ankle on a log,
Hurt her ears in the fog.
Janie Jumpty is also mad,
Which makes me very, very sad.

Note. This bit of nonsense can provide help in identification of body parts.

Robert Louis Stevenson wrote beautiful poetry for children. Three of his poems are presented here.

Time to Rise

A birdie with a yellow bill
Hopped upon the window sill,
Cocked his shining eye and said,
"Ain't you 'shamed, you sleepyhead?"

Rain

The rain is raining all around.
It falls on field and tree.
It rains on the umbrellas here,
And on the ships at sea.

The Swing

How would you like to go up in a swing,
Up in the air so blue?
Oh, I do think it's the pleasantest thing
Ever a child can do.

James Whitcomb Riley has written many poems about children. Here is one favorite. (It might be mentioned to the children that this poem is written in rural Hoosier dialect.)

Naughty Claude

When Little Claude was naughty wunst
At dinner-time, an' said
He won't say "*Thank you*" to his Ma,
She maked him go to bed
An' stay two hours an' not git up,—
So when the clock struck Two,
Nen Claude says,—"Thank you, Mr. Clock,
I'm much obleeged to you!"

FINGER PLAYS

Finger plays are numerous and of a wide variety. None are long, and some are quite short. Many have been handed down over many years and are drawn from many cultures. They have long been used to interest and amuse children. Finger plays are usually appropriate for preschool and kindergarten children, but some may be used in the first grade.

Grandmother's Glasses

Words	Suggested Action
Here are grandmother's glasses,	Making the shape of glasses with the thumbs and forefingers.
Here is grandmother's cap,	Bringing the hands together to form a peak over the head.
And this is the way she folds her hands,	Folding the hands.
And lays them in her lap.	Laying the folded hands in the lap.

Hickory, Dickory, Dock

Words	Suggested Action
Hickory, dickory, dock,	Raising the left arm over the head and moving it back and forth like a pendulum.
The mouse ran up the clock.	Running the right hand up the left arm with fast finger action.
The clock struck one, the mouse ran down,	Clapping the hands overhead and running the right hand down the left arm with fast finger action.
Hickory, dickory, dock.	Moving the left arm back and forth like a pendulum.

Jack and Jill

Words	Suggested Action
Jack and Jill went up the hill	Putting the hands together with thumbs up and raising the hands in stages.
To fetch a pail of water.	Turning the hands over, thumbs down, and making a pouring movement.
Jack fell down and broke his crown,	Dropping the right hand down to the lap and tapping the head with the left hand.
And Jill came tumbling after.	Bringing the left hand down in circular movements.

My Fingers

Words	Suggested Action
I have ten little fingers,	Holding up the hands and waving the fingers back and forth.
And they all belong to me.	
I can make them do things.	Continuing to open and close fingers.
Would you like to see?	Holding hands up with fingers spread wide.
I can shut them tight	Moving as indicated.
Or open them wide;	
I can put them together	
Or make them hide.	

I can make them jump high;
I can make them jump low;
I can fold them up quietly,
And hold them just so.

Performing actions as indicated.

Little Miss Muffet

Words	Suggested Action
Little Miss Muffet sat on a tuffet,	Holding up the left hand with the thumb up to be Miss Muffet.
Eating her curds and whey.	Moving the thumb (Miss Muffet) back and forth.
Along came a spider,	Bringing the right hand forward toward Miss Muffet.
And sat down beside her,	Moving as indicated.
And frightened Miss Muffet away!	Putting the left hand quickly behind the back.

Two Little Duckybirds

Words	Suggested Action
Two little duckybirds	Resting the index fingers on the desk or the knees.
Sitting on a wall.	Lifting both index fingers up and replacing them.
One named Alice,	Lifting the right finger, replacing it.
One named Paul.	Lifting the left finger, replacing it.
Fly away, Alice,	Lifting the right hand and making a flying motion.
Fly away, Paul.	Lifting the left hand and making a flying motion.
That's too bad,	Raising the hands, making a sad face.
But that's not all.	Looking surprised.
Here comes Alice,	Replacing the right index finger on the desk or the knee.
Here comes Paul.	Replacing the left index finger.

Five Little Babies

Words	Suggested Action
One little baby—	Lifting and moving one finger.
Rocking in a tree.	Making a rocking motion with cradled arms.
Two little babies—	Moving two fingers.
Splashing in the sea.	Making splashing motions.
Three little babies—	Moving three fingers.
Crawling on the floor.	Making crawling motions with the fingers.
Four little babies—	Moving four fingers.
Knocking on the door.	Knocking on the desk or pounding fists together.
Five little babies—	Moving five fingers.
Playing hide-and-seek.	Covering the eyes.
Keep your eyes closed tight—	Keeping the eyes closed.
Now, peek!	Peeking.

Two Little Parrots

Words	Suggested Action
Two little parrots,	Holding two fingers up in each hand.
One in each hand.	Lowering and raising each hand in turn.
Isn't she pretty?	Looking toward the right hand, waving the fingers.
Isn't he grand?	Doing the same, looking to the left.
Her name is Susie.	Waving the fingers, right hand.
His name is Joe.	Waving the fingers, left hand.
Hear her say, "Good morning."	Moving Susie's "lip" and saying the words in parrot fashion.
Hear him say, "Hello."	Performing a bow with the left hand. Saying "hello" in parrot fashion.

The word *puppet* could be substituted for *parrot*, and the children could make simple hand puppets.

The Rain

This might help the children endure the rain on a day when they would like to go outside.

Words	Suggested Action
"Pitter, patter, pitter, patter,"	Drumming the fingers on the desk or table.
Hear the raindrops say,	Continuing to drum.
But if a sunbeam should peep out,	Bringing the hands to the eyes and peeping through the fingers.
They'd make a rainbow gay.	Outlining a rainbow with the arms.
"Rumble, rumble, rumble, rumble,"	Rolling the knuckles on the desk.
Hear the thunder say,	Continuing to roll them.
But soon the clouds will all be gone,	Forming clouds with the hands overhead.
And we'll go out to play.	Pulling the clouds apart and dropping the arms.

ROLE-SITUATION PLAY

Many everyday experiences from the childhood and adult world can form the basis for much dramatic play. The children can help the teacher plan the story to guide the play. A simple idea like Railroad Train can be a good basis. It could be developed in the following fashion.

Railroad Train. Each child is given the name of one part of a freight train. Several trains can be formed. The teacher tells a story in which the various parts of the train are mentioned. Several children are the engines, and the story usually begins with this portion of the train. As the story unfolds, the children form in line, one behind the other in the order named. After the trains have been assembled and all cars are on the train, the story continues by describing a train trip. The route is described in detail, with the train going slowly up and down grades, around curves, stopping at stations, and finishing up with a wreck. It is also possible to assemble the trains by having each of the parts of the train on side tracks and the train backing up to hook on the cars.

Some attention should be given to the story, as the imagination of the teller is very important. Also, children can make suggestions for the train ride.

For another illustration of how an idea can be expanded, let us take the children on an imaginary hike.

The Hike

Words	Suggested Action
Today we are going on a hike. What are some of the things we should take along?	Suggesting various articles that should be included.

We are going to roll our packs into a nice, neat bundle. Put down your tarp first, next arrange your blankets, and put in the rest of your things. Now let's roll the pack and tie it up.

Laying out the packs, rolling, and tying.

Off we go.

Marching two by two around the room, carrying packs.

Time to rest.

Removing packs and sitting down.

Off again.

Marching again.

Make blazes so we can find our way back. Make trail markers.

Making blazes in various manners. Arranging stones for markers.

Here we are. Pick out a good spot for the tent and put it up.

Cutting stakes and poles. Driving stakes and putting up tents. Arranging beds.

We need lots of wood for the campfire. Will you see what you can find?

Looking for wood; dragging in logs and carrying wood. Some cutting may be needed.

Build the fire and broil the steaks.

Moving as directed.

That's the bugle call for "turning in."

Going to one side, brushing teeth, washing up, and then crawling into tents, getting into bedrolls, and going to sleep.

It should be noted that integration with other subject fields is possible. Conservation practices can be stressed, and safety in the woods can be emphasized.

Other ideas for role-situation play can be borrowed from the lists under *Creative Rhythms— Dramatic Play*. Rhythm adds much to these experiences and should be a priority.

CREATIVE RHYTHMS—DRAMATIC PLAY

A program of creative rhythms is an essential inclusion in movement experiences for young children. A well-chosen rhythmic background, competently produced, is crucial to creativity in rhythms. Much of the rhythmic background can be produced with the drum and other percussion instruments. There are also many suitable recordings from which selections can be chosen. A teacher should have his own personal set with which he is familiar. The instructor can then sense which music will be relevant to a particular pattern. As a supplement to the recordings, a drum can add much to the delight the children take in rhythmic movement.

There are several subdivisions under which we can consider the total area of creative rhythms. These are (1) free rhythms, (2) identification rhythms, and (3) dramatic rhythms. While they are fairly well defined, there is some overlap, since all of them contain the necessary ingredients of creativity and movement to rhythm.

Free and Expressive Rhythms

A free rhythm allows the child to respond in movement according to the motivation he receives from the rhythm presented. The movements should be free and uninhibited, unencumbered by too many directions or limitations. Naturally, some stipulations are needed, but these should not stifle free movement.

One way to begin a free rhythm is to play a lively, challenging record and let the children move as they feel. If youngsters have not moved freely in the past, they may need some direction and guidance until they have developed a good backlog of movement experiences. Children can be stimulated to attempt different patterns of movement by asking them to "look around and see how others are moving."

At times, certain limitations can be put on movement, utilizing educational movement factors (space, time, force, flow, body factors); selected skills (hopping, skipping, etc.); or expressive qualities (emotions). Free movement should be permitted and encouraged within the limitations specified.

The following list presents some possibilities for free movement to rhythm with limitations emphasizing movement contrasts.

Space factors
Level: High/low
Size: Big/little
Direction: Forward/backward, straight/curved, straight/zigzag, up/down, right/left, in front of you/behind you

Time factors
Even/uneven, fast/slow, short/long (duration), acceleration/deceleration, equal in-

terval/unequal interval, variation in time or rhythm

Force factors

Cessation: Still/moving, moving/stopping, moving/freezing

Degree: Much/little, heavy/weak, strong/light

Application: Explosive/smooth, increasing/decreasing, sudden/sustained

Body factors

Shapes: Long/short, wide/narrow, straight/twisted, stretched/curled, symmetrical/asymmetrical

Execution: Unilateral, bilateral, cross-lateral

Body parts: Different parts, different number of parts, different parts weight-bearing, leading with different body parts

Expressive factors

Angry/sad, joyous/gloomy, stately/silly, bold/afraid, serious/frivolous, courageous/scared, energetic/lazy, healthy/sick, robust/weak, vigorous/tired, satisfied/disappointed

Other ideas that can be utilized are colors and children's names. A rhythmic beat will spell out Susan Peterson; a different beat will spell out Johnny Smith. Children can come up with a rhythmic pattern for one name and see how many names in the class fit this pattern.

Colors are less definite, since the children will interpret the colors differently. The color red, for example, will stimulate different and, at times, contrasting movement patterns.

INSTRUCTIONAL PROCEDURES

Children in free creative rhythmics should be allowed to move in their own way, rather than moving like "something." Free rhythms can be based on movement elements of space, time, and force, with the addition of expressive movement depicting emotions or feelings.

For younger children, contrasts are quite appropriate, such as "big/little" or "fast/slow." For children in the primary grades, middleground positions between the extremes can be employed. A level, for example, may be high or low, but it can also be in-between.

Judicious direction by the teacher is needed to stimulate exploration, invention, improvisation, and logical rhythmic sequences. Movements should be big and free (large-muscle movements). Spatial challenges should stimulate the children to move in many and diverse directions. Body factors—shape, size, and different parts—should help reinforce body aware-

ness and knowledge about body parts and their function.

The sound background should stimulate changes in movement factors by changes in the beat or tempo of sound or by special signals. Improvement in listening skills can occur when youngsters must react to changes in the rhythmic background. The progression should begin with individual movement, go on to movement with a partner, and then to small group patterns. Some caution must be observed with preschool children, as some children this age may not be comfortable working with partners.

Identification Rhythms—Imagery

The persons or things with which a child can identify are almost without limit. The child should know something about the characterization of the identity he is assuming, however. It is fruitless to ask a child to move "like a dwarf," when he has no idea what a dwarf is. The child should be given some background information about his identity, how it exists in the environment, and how it might be expected to move. He then has the tools to solve the movement problem.

There are many sources from which subjects for interpretation can be taken. The following are suggested movement themes:

1. *Animals*—elephants, ducks, seals, chickens, dogs, rabbits, lions, goats, other zoo animals
2. *Insects*—flies, spiders, dragonflies, snails, centipedes
3. *Sea denizens*—fishes (different kinds), alligators, sharks, whales, dolphins, crabs
4. *People*—soldiers, firemen, Eskimos, sailors, various kinds of workers, forest rangers
5. *Western life*—cowboys, Indians, Texas Rangers, rodeo participants, broncos, Brahma bulls
6. *Play objects*—seesaws, swings, rowboats, balls, and many common toys with which children play
7. *Make-believe world*—giants, elves, dwarfs, midgets, gnomes, witches, trolls, dragons, pixies, fairies
8. *Machines*—trains, planes, jet planes, rockets, automobiles, trucks, bicycles, motorcycles, construction machines, elevators
9. *Circus*—clowns, various trained animals, trapeze artists, tight- and slack-wire artists, jugglers, acrobats, musicians in the band

10. *Nature*—fluttering leaves, rain, snow, hail, winds of various forces, clouds, flowers (opening), growing plants
11. *Seasons*—autumn, winter, spring, summer; let the children suggest appropriate movements
12. *Holidays and special days*—Election Day, any of the holidays; the children can help

INSTRUCTIONAL PROCEDURES

An atmosphere of creative freedom must be a part of each presentation. Encourage children to explore, interpret, and express themselves with ideas and imagery relevant to the identity assumed. As mentioned, the children must understand and have a mental image of what they are trying to become.

The rhythm for the identity to be assumed is of considerable importance. Appropriate rhythm will make more meaningful such questions as: "What does the music [or rhythm] make you think of?" "How is the music telling you to move?" The children must listen well, so that they can coordinate their movement with the rhythm.

Several approaches can be utilized, each of which can be varied according to teacher preference.

1. Begin with a rhythm and let children decide what they would like to be, based on the character of the rhythm. The approach is, "What does this rhythm make you think of?" This is an open-ended approach, leading to diverse interpretations.
2. Select one of the themes from the list and develop in the same fashion as in 1, above.
3. Have children listen to a selected piece of music and then make a selection of what they wish to imitate. All children would be imitating the same character, object, or thing, but each child would have the privilege of creating its identity as he wished.
4. Have the children select a character or object with which they wish to be identified and then produce a suitable rhythm for this interpretation. If the teacher is familiar with the selections on the record, little time will be lost. Providing a suitable rhythm with a drum or tambourine is another solution.

Dramatic Rhythms

In an activity using dramatic rhythms, the children act out an idea, a story, a familiar event, or a procedure. This can be based on a story, a description, an idea, a poem, or a song. While it can take almost any form, some kind of action plan is necessary, with the children helping to develop the script. The teacher aids in setting the stage, but should avoid thrusting preconceived standards on the children. The idea may be expanded and can take many directions. Success may be judged by the degree to which children respond and interpret freely and creatively the roles they assume in the action.

Children are quite receptive to acting out in rhythm a story they know and like. When they have prior knowledge of the story, the children will offer more suggestions, and their movement interpretations will show more depth. Some children can even have speaking parts. Where possible, there should be several key roles. For example, if a witch is sweeping around with her broom, two or more witches will involve more children and add to the fun.

Ideas and sources for dramatic rhythms are found everywhere in the environment. Some ideas that have proved successful are:

1. *Construction projects*—building a house, laying concrete, digging a ditch, building a garage
2. *Winter fun*—making a snowman, going sledding, going skiing, throwing snowballs, ice-skating, playing hockey
3. *Sports activities*—playing football, basketball, or baseball; track and field; swimming; tennis; golf; boxing
4. *Celebrating holidays*—Halloween, Fourth of July, Thanksgiving, Veterans Day, Christmas
5. *Household tasks*—mowing the lawn, running the vacuum sweeper, chopping and bringing in the wood, picking and boxing fruit, cleaning the yard
6. *Summer activities*—camping, swimming, water skiing, hunting, fishing, canoeing, hiking
7. *Acting out stories* including firemen, policemen, cowboys, Indians, the Pony Express, the Oregon Trail
8. *Interpreting familiar stories*—Sleeping Beauty, The Three Bears, Little Red Riding Hood, Jack and Jill
9. *Interpreting selected action or story poems*
10. *Ideas using the seasons*—spring, summer, fall, winter

INSTRUCTIONAL PROCEDURES

No matter what idea has been selected, some prior preparation will be necessary to let the children absorb the content of the action and make some decisions about how action sequences should unfold. Some approaches that might be followed by the instructor are:

1. Select a story or idea, familiarize the children with it, and determine how the action will unfold. A variety of musical accompaniments can be chosen, including recordings, a piano selection, and the use of percussion instruments, rhythm band devices, or even vocal sounds. A tape recording can be made, following the adopted plan of action with an appropriate rhythmic accompaniment.

Several children could help with the rhythmic background. The teacher should probably be the one to read stories or verbal descriptions of action. Some ideas can proceed without verbal directions, however.

2. Select a record with good quality reproduction, a strong rhythmic beat, variations in tempo and patterns, and definite change points in the music. An idea or procedure can be chosen to fit the selection. The next approach is to work out with the children the rhythmic development of the idea to fit the music.

In some cases it might be feasible for all children to move sequentially to develop the idea. In other cases, a rotation system might be established, with different groups of children acting out designated interpretations. In addition, any children with special roles are assigned.

3. Use music designed expecially for dramatic sequences. Some of these may be selections from an album; sometimes an entire record is given over to a single story. Some of these records providing a story have both music and verbal keys developed on one side, with only music on the other side.

DEVELOPING AN IDEA OR STORY FOR DRAMATIZATION

An example of how an idea can be exploited for a lesson of rhythmic creativity is seen in "The Wind and the Leaves." One or more children are chosen to be the Wind, and the remainder of the children are the Leaves. Two kinds of rhythm will be needed. The first indicates the blowing of the Wind. The second rhythm is quieter and suggests the Leaves fluttering to the ground after the Wind has stopped. Thus, the story has two distinct elements, each of which offers many possibilities for creativity:

Rhythm 1—Fast, high, shrill, indicating the blowing of the Wind; the intensity and the tempo would illustrate the speed and force of the Wind

Rhythm 2—Slow, measured, light beat to match the Leaves fluttering in the still air and finally coming to rest at various positions on the ground

During the first rhythm, the children representing the Wind can show how they would portray a heavy blow. While this is going on, the Leaves show what they feel it means to be blown about.

During the second rhythm, the Wind is still, and the Leaves are fluttering to the ground. When the music stops, the Leaves are still and curled on the floor.

Additional sequences could be added with appropriate rhythmic background. For example, street sweepers could sweep up the Leaves and load them into a truck.

If a piano is available, accompaniment could be devised on it, using the black keys only. For Rhythm 1, pick two adjacent high treble *black* keys, alternating them rapidly. Then move slowly down the black keys to simulate leaves dropping to the ground. Rolling the fist on the piano would provide sweeping noise; a heavily struck key would indicate shoveling into the truck. Almost any rhythm that increases in tempo while it decreases in intensity would suffice for trucks driving away.

One teacher had success with a game called Guess What. The class was divided into groups of four or five students, and each was given the task to act out an idea, using percussion accompaniment. Each group put on its performance before the others; at the completion of each dramatization, the other groups guessed what the idea was. Be sure that the interpretations are not too long.

A number of excellent records are available, which combine a story with well-suited rhythm. On some of these, only the rhythm appears on one side, allowing the teacher to tell the story. A story format is usually included. The "Dance-a-Story" series of records by the Ginn Company are excellent story sources for young children.

The ideas under story play (pp. 105–12) should be scanned for possible utilization. It would be necessary to devise a rhythmic background for these stories.

SUMMARY

The ideas presented in this chapter offer many ideas that can stimulate creativity in young children. Creative experiences should provide for freedom of response, should be a satisfying experience, and should allow all to participate at a level of capability satisfying to each.

Story plays encourage children to match their play with the words of the story; this results in a wide variety of movement patterns. Action poems are similar to stories except that the prose is sometimes catchy and motivating to children, prompting them to remember the verses and use them during leisure.

Role situation play experiences are based on situations that children see in their everyday experiences. Stories can be created based on situations such as riding on trains, hiking, going to the airport or fire station, and visiting the zoo.

Creative rhythms are classified into three categories: free and expressive rhythms; identification rhythms—imagery; and dramatization.

Free and expressive rhythms allow the child to respond with movement according to the motivation received from the presented rhythm. Identification rhythms and imagery are based on persons, animals, machines, etc., and allow children to identify with these and move according to their interpretation of the situation. In a dramatization, children act out an idea, a story or familiar event, or a procedure. Children help organize the script of movement and then act it out with rhythmic movement.

Chapter 11

Fundamental Motor Skills and Development

Where we cannot invent, we may at least improve.
Charles Caleb Coltan

In a previous chapter, we have discussed body management competencies and appropriate themes that can be employed for their development. We will now examine the next hierarchy of movement competencies, the fundamental skills. While attention is still given to body management competencies, the teacher also stresses the fundamental skills needed as a basis for more specialized skills later on.

Early in the program, concentration will be focused on the skill or its reasonable approximation; later, emphasis can be placed on expansion, versatility, utility, and sequencing. The success of the program depends much on the teacher, who initiates and guides the simple skill patterns. Analytical observation will provide the key to sequential development of the patterns.

While it is difficult to identify all the skills that children should be able to perform adequately, certain fundamental skills involved in locomotion, body movement, and in the propelling and catching of objects can be identified as necessary for success in various movement experiences and will provide the foundation for further motor learning. The following skills are covered in the discussions in this chapter:

Locomotor skills
Skills with even rhythm—walking, running, hopping, jumping
Skills with uneven rhythm—skipping, sliding, galloping, leaping

Nonlocomotor skills
Bending, rocking, swinging, turning, twisting, stretching, pushing, pulling

Manipulative skills—sports-related skills
Throwing, catching, kicking, rebounding, striking

A brief motor analysis plus related diagrams are provided for each of the skills, followed by stress points and suggested movement experiences. Music and rhythmic accompaniment should be integrated into the development of skills. Most of these movement patterns are rhythmic in nature, and the accompaniment of suitable rhythmic stimulation enhances the learning process. The movements can be experienced with or without rhythmic accompaniment, however.

Some general instructional procedures follow in two groupings. The first set includes suggestions for development without rhythm, and the second discussion presents the means by which rhythm can help facilitate learning.

GENERAL INSTRUCTIONAL PROCEDURES

Instructional steps for educational movement should be followed, including strong application of the movement concepts of space, time, force, flow, and body awareness. A wide range of movement approaches should be employed.

Cognitive learning is important, so that the child may acquire understanding about the skills that are necessary for him to achieve well.

A child should experiment as an individual first and later with a partner or as a member of a small group. The approach should be flexible, and no attempt should be made to make this a formal drill session. Repetition is important—but it must be *correct* repetition.

One way to encourage repetition is to employ the "Magic Number" concept. The teacher sets a magic number, which defines the number of repetitions or skill movements in combination that should be experienced. The teacher might say, "Our magic number is seven. Put together walking steps and hopping so that they total seven." Or, "Every time you take seven running steps [skips, slides, etc.], change direction and level."

INSTRUCTIONAL PROCEDURES— FUNDAMENTAL RHYTHMS

Applying music or rhythmic accompaniment to direct the development of fundamental skills is usually termed *fundamental rhythms*. The concept of integrating rhythm into the general pattern of instruction is an excellent one. It is critical that the accompaniment be suitable for the intended fundamental skill. This means that the children should first internalize the rhythm so that they may apply it to the skill. The following steps provide a guide for this progression:

1. With children in a comfortable arrangement, introduce the rhythm. If you are using a record, discuss briefly the elements of tempo, rhythmic beat, and accent. Have the children listen for phrases and changes in the music.
2. Provide some kind of hand response so that they can beat the time. They can use their hands to beat against the tops or sides of the thighs. Add a foot response.
3. Provide information about the skill as needed. If this is not an initial presentation, several stress points may be enough.
4. Embark upon the activity experiences with the rhythm.

Early practice and experiences can be presented to a somewhat slower tempo, which can be increased to normal speed as the children learn the movement pattern.

Stops and starts can be based on pauses in the music or can be signaled by a drumbeat. Effective use of the drum or tom-tom is an important factor. Most skills have their own peculiar elements of timing, and the drumbeat must occur at the proper time.

An effective and interesting method of stimulating variation is to have the children change movement patterns or combinations with the completion of a phrase of music (eight counts or beats). The music provides the cue for changes, and the children must think ahead to plan the new patterns.

Another way to use changes in music is to employ records that make a definite change between the verse and the chorus, thus cueing a change in the movement pattern. Duration of the music can be specified by designating to the students the number of times a piece will be played through—i.e., once, twice, or three times.

Variations in patterns of movement can be accomplished by changing the type of locomotor skill or by alternating locomotor and nonlocomotor movements. Most manipulative movements to rhythm include ball-handling skills, but hoops, wands, and Indian clubs are also excellent tools for motivation. A valuable manipulative activity involving the application of rhythm is individual rope-jumping (pp. 178–81).

LOCOMOTOR MOVEMENTS

Walking

In walking, one is always in contact with the ground or the floor, and the feet move alternately. This means that the stepping foot must be placed on the ground before the other foot is lifted for its step. Marching is a more precise type of walk, accompanied by lifted knees and swinging arms.

Many different ways of walking should be experienced, but the underlying goal should be that children learn to walk gracefully and efficiently with good posture in normal walking patterns. Experiencing different walking patterns offers an excellent opportunity to stress postural factors.

SKILL ANALYSIS

The weight of the body is transferred from the heel to the ball of the foot and then to the toes for the push-off for the next step. The toes are pointing straight ahead with the arms swinging freely from the shoulder in opposition to the feet. The body is erect, and the eyes are focused straight ahead at slightly below eye level. Legs are swung smoothly from the hips with the knees bent only enough to clear the feet from the ground.

STRESS POINTS

1. The toes should be pointed reasonably straight ahead.
2. The arm movement should feel natural. Do not overswing the arms.
3. The head should be held up, and the eyes should be focused ahead.

4. The stride length should not be excessive; unnecessary up-and-down motion is to be avoided.

5. Walking should be done in good posture, with the head up, shoulders back, and tummy flat.

TEACHING CUES

"Head up—eyes forward."
"Point the toes straight ahead."
"Nice, easy, relaxed arm swing."
"Walk quietly."
"Hold tummy in, chest up."

SUGGESTED MOVEMENT EXPERIENCES

"Walk around in different directions, changing direction at will. On signal. On a count."

"While walking, bring up your knee and slap it with your hand on each step. Lift your knees as if you are walking in heavy snow."

"Walk on your heels. Your toes. The side of your feet."

"Gradually lower your body while you walk, as if you are going downstairs. Then raise your body again slowly, as if you are going upstairs."

"Walk silently, with a gliding step." Other variations may be introduced.

"Walk on tiptoes with your legs wide apart, rocking from side to side. Walk as high as you can on tiptoes."

"Clap your hands alternately in front of you and behind you. Clap your hands under your thighs as you walk."

"Walk slowly and then gradually increase your speed. Now, reverse the process."

"Take long strides. Tiny steps."

"On signal, change levels. How low can you walk? How high?"

"Walk quickly and quietly. Heavily and slowly. How slowly can you walk?"

"Change direction on signal, but keep facing the same way."

"Walk gaily, angrily, and happily. Show some other moods as you walk."

"Hold your arms in different positions. Make an abrupt arm movement each time you take a step. Walk as if you are on stilts."

"Walk different patterns—circle, triangle, figure eight [etc.]. Walk on the straight painted lines. The curved painted lines."

"Walk through heavy, sticky mud. On ice. On a rainy day. Through snow. Walk in shallow water and splash the water."

"Walk like a soldier on parade. A giant. A dwarf. Walk as if you are in church."

"Duck under trees or railings while you walk."

"Point your toes in different positions—in, forward, and out."

"Walk with high knees. Stiff knees. One stiff knee. A sore ankle. Walk as if you are a clown with big shoes."

"Walk to a spot, turn in place while stepping, and take off in another direction. Walk to the spot, using as few steps as possible, and walk back to your personal space, using as many steps as possible."

"Practice changing steps while walking."

"Walk in the goose step. [Explain.]"

"Walk backwards, looking back. Walk backwards with your eyes looking forward."

"Walk letters. Your name."

"Have your partner close his eyes. Sneak up on your partner from 15 or 20 yards away, so that he doesn't hear your approach."

"Walk, making yourself tall, then smile. Wide, then narrow. Round, then crooked." Have them use combinations such as wide-small, round-tall, etc.

"Walk like a floppy rag doll. Like a robot."

"Do side steps, crossing one foot in front of and then behind the other."

"Walk so that one foot always stays in back. Walk so that the heel of the leading foot touches the toe of the back foot."

"Walk as if the wind were coming briskly from the front. From either side. From behind you."

SPECIAL RHYTHMIC CONSIDERATIONS

1. Walking forward during one phrase (eight counts) and changing direction on the next.

2. Performing any of the prior movements, letting the drum signal a change or a stop.

3. Using high steps during one phrase, low steps during the next.

4. Walking forward on one phrase and walking in place on the next, with high knee action. Adding a turn-around while walking in place.

5. Walking forward on one phrase; continuing in the same direction, but walking backward on the next phrase.

6. Walking forward on the first phrase and sideways on the next. Walking a square in 16 counts (two phrases), with four counts to a side.

7. Walking forward on one phrase and, during the next phrase, doing any kind of movement in place. Changing direction and repeating.

8. Making up walking patterns to music, changing either every four or every eight steps.

Running

To run is to move rapidly in such a manner that, for a brief moment, both feet are off the ground. Running varies in speed from trotting or jogging, a slow run, to sprinting, a fast run for speed.

Running should be done lightly on the balls of the feet when speed is desired. Heels absorb the impact of body weight in distance running and jogging. Children may cover some ground on the run, or they can run in place. Running should be done with a slight body lean. The knees are bent and lifted. The arms swing back and forth from the shoulders with a bend at the elbows.

Since running uses the most rapid movement of the locomotor skills, some attention should be given to changing direction (dodging) and stopping in connection with the running patterns. In addition, a child should learn a few basics about initiating (starting) the run.

SKILL ANALYSIS

1. As the child grows older and matures, his running form will improve, and his speed will increase. Greater speed is attributed to a longer stride and an increased period of time during which the feet are not in contact with the running surface.

2. A decrease in upward body movement occurs as the running pattern matures. The mature pattern is characterized by smooth, level running, as contrasted with the bobbing-up-and-down form commonly seen in two- to four-year-olds.

3. The knees are lifted higher during the forward leg swing, and the heels are lifted closer to the buttocks on the forward swing of the recovery leg, as the running pattern matures. This provides the runner with some increase in speed.

4. When the running pattern is refined, upper body rotation decreases, and the hands move a shorter distance toward the middle of the body as they swing forward. More of a right-angle bend appears in the arms as the child matures.

STRESS POINTS

1. The heels of the feet should absorb the impact during jogging and distance running. This allows for shock absorption, which is important for comfort in running. When sprinting, children will naturally run on the balls of their feet rather than coming down on their heels.

2. The faster one desires to run, the more he must bend the knees and the higher he must lift them. To stimulate speed, tell children to push off the ground with greater force.

3. For greatest efficiency, the movement of the legs should be in a forward-backward plane. Avoid sideward motion.

4. In distance running, less arm swing is used than in sprinting for speed, in which arms move through a wide range of motion. Also, less body lean is used in distance running, although some body lean is used at any speed. Allow the child to use the arm movement pattern that is most comfortable and natural, but without excess motion.

5. In stopping, the knees should bend to absorb the force, and the center of gravity should be lowered and kept over the feet. A common fault is too much forward lean, which overbalances the child. The same elements have bearing on change of direction.

6. In the "get ready" position to begin running, feet are slightly apart with one foot ahead of the other, toes are forward with the weight on both feet, the body lean is slightly forward, and arms are in a ready position, slightly bent.

TEACHING CUES

"Run on the balls of the feet."

"Head up—eyes forward."

"Lift your knees. Push off hard with the trailing foot."

"Relax your upper body."

"Breathe naturally."

"For stopping, bend your knees, drop your weight, and keep the weight over the feet."

SUGGESTED MOVEMENT EXPERIENCES

"Run lightly around the area, changing directions as you wish, and avoid bumping anyone. Run zigzag through the area. Change directions on signal."

"Run and stop on signal. Run, change direction, and stop. Run, stop on signal, and jump backward [or sideward] with one jump or two [as directed]."

"Run. Turn around with running steps on signal, and continue in a new direction. On the next signal, turn around the other way."

"Vary trotting lightly with a faster run. Accelerate and decelerate your running patterns. Add force elements—light and heavy running."

"Select a spot on the floor [personal space]. Run and touch spots on the floor or walls and return to your spot."

"Run lightly in your personal space. On signal, run in general space. On signal, return to your personal spot and run in place lightly."

"Run forward. Backward. To the side. Run around a square, always facing the same direction."

"Free running, concentrating on good knee lift. Slap your knees as you run."

"Run at a low level, gradually increasing height. Reverse."

Have the children explore different leg actions—crisscross, toes in and out, kick up toes in front, kick up heels behind, legs in wide straddle position.

Have them run in different patterns in space—triangle, figure eight, circle, oval, etc.

Have them run using various steps—tiny, long, high on the toes, on the heels.

Have them run with arms in different positions—exaggerated arm movements, arms circling, arms overhead or stiff at the sides, etc.

"Touch the ground at times with either hand as you run."

"Select a partner and run with your inside hands joined. Run with right [left] hands joined so that one is running forward and one backward. Run this way in a circular fashion [on a spot]. Repeat with your other hands joined."

Add a magic number to running patterns.

"Run as lightly as you can. Run heavily."

"Can you run without bending your knees? Lean backward and run forward with your toes pointed."

Have the children run in general space. On signal, each greets many of the others with the two-handed hand slap while continuing to run. On the next signal, they resume running in general space.

"Select two lines. See how many times you can run back and forth between them."

The teacher or leader has three placards on sticks—green, yellow, and white. Green means "Run rapidly with good speed in general space." Yellow means "Run more slowly, emphasizing form." Red means "Stop."

Try "Countdown." The leader calls, "Ten, nine, eight, seven, six, five, four, three, two, one—blast off!" On the countdown, each child on each count makes abrupt movements in place. On "blast off," children run in general space until the signal is given to stop. The countdown begins anew.

"Try making yourself as tall as possible while running. As wide as possible."

SPECIAL RHYTHMIC CONSIDERATIONS

1. In running patterns as in walking, the use of the phrase of eight counts is excellent. Running can proceed for one phrase, and then a change of direction or movement can be inserted.

2. European Rhythmic Running (p. 49) should be experienced after the children have acquired some skill in running to a beat.

3. The drum or tom-tom can provide an effective beat for running, including changes in the run pattern. The children run in time to the beat. A louder beat calls for a change of direction. Two rapid beats signal a stop.

4. In response to a drumbeat, the children can run lightly when the beat is light and heavily when the beat is strong.

Hopping

In hopping, the body is moved up by one foot and lands on the same foot. The body lean (slight), the other foot (lifted), and the arms serve to balance the movement. Hopping can be done in place or as a locomotor movement. Hopping can also be done over an obstacle. Hopping should not be sustained on one foot too long. Children should change to the other foot after a period of time or when direction is changed. See that there is a similar amount of activity for both feet.

Shifting the postural pattern from one leg to the other (changing the hopping foot) should be given practice. Hopping on one foot, alternating feet, is the basis for skipping.

STRESS POINTS

1. To increase the height of the hop, the arms must be swung upward rapidly.

2. Hopping should be performed on the ball of the foot. Normally, the heel does not touch during the hop.

3. Start with small hops and gradually increase the height and distance of the hop.

4. A little "give" in the knee of the landing leg helps cushion the contact.

TEACHING CUES

"Hop with good upward motion."
"Stay on your toes."
"Use your arms for balance."
"Reach for the sky when you hop."
"Land lightly."

SUGGESTED MOVEMENT EXPERIENCES

Have children hop on one foot and then on the other, using numbered sequences such as 1-1, 2-2, 3-3, 4-4, 5-5, 2-1, 1-2, 3-2, 2-3. The first figure of a series indicates the number of hops on the right foot, and the second specifies the hops for the left foot. Combinations should be done for ten to twenty seconds.

"Hop, increasing the height. Begin high like a bouncing ball and gradually get lower."

"See how much space you can cover in two hops. In three. In four."

"Hop on one foot and do a heel-and-toe pattern with the other. Change to the other foot. See if you can set up a consistent pattern."

"Combine hopping in place with hopping ahead."

"Hop forward. Backward. Sideways."

Have children hop different patterns on the floor—numbers, letters, forms.

Have them hop while holding the foot of the free leg, using various hand positions.

Have them alternate little and big hops, either in place or traveling. Use various combinations.

"Hop quickly and slow down little by little."

"Try using different arm positions while you hop. Clap your hands in different positions as you hop."

Have them hop with different positions of the raised leg—high knee, stiff leg in front, forward lean with stiff leg backward, leg to the side, circle lifted foot, kick lifted leg forward and back, etc.

Have them add turns to hopping patterns, either in place or moving.

Have them hop with different body positions—forward, backward, sideward leans.

"Hop lightly. Heavily."

"While hopping, touch the floor with either hand and then with both hands."

"Select a line or board on the floor. Hop back and forth over the line, moving forward [backward or sideward] along the line."

Lay a jump rope on the floor in a straight line or other patterns. Have them hop over and along, in and out.

Do the same with a hoop. Children hop around the hoop, in and out.

With partners in side-by-side position, children explore different ways to hop forward, backward, sideward, or in merry-go-round fashion.

Use various patterns for hopping, such as hopscotch, squares, over the creek (two lines), etc.

A magic number can be employed successfully in combination with hopping patterns.

Use a beanbag to stimulate hopping patterns. Lay the bag on the floor and have children practice various ways to hop over it. Toss the beanbag a ways forward. Have them move to the beanbag while hopping and pick up the beanbag, continuing the hopping. The noninvolved foot should not touch the floor.

SPECIAL RHYTHMIC CONSIDERATIONS

1. As in walking, running, and other patterns, a phrase of music can be used to add interest to hopping.

2. Most hopping patterns can be directed by the drumbeat. Fundamental rhythm music especially designed for hopping is also useful.

Jumping

In fundamental movement, to jump means to take off (usually with both feet) and land on *both feet*. The arms aid in the jump by swinging upward, and the movement of the body, along with the force generated by the feet, lifts the weight. A jumper lands lightly on the balls of his feet with bent knees.

The standing long jump is often used as a test of motor coordination, but it is a difficult movement for a young child to perform. Because a successful long jump requires a high degree of total-body coordination, this jump can give the teacher a rough estimation of the child's ability.

SKILL ANALYSIS

1. Early jumping does not move forward, but tends to be in place. The child stands upright with the arms in front of the body.

2. As he matures, the child shows similar form in the upper body, but jumps in a forward direction and usually lands on one foot first rather than on both feet simultaneously.

3. As the child's ability develops, he performs the jump for distance. Often, takeoff will occur from one foot in an attempt to increase distance. The child lands with the arms alongside the body and bent at the elbow.

4. Improvement in jumping form occurs in the upper body as the arms are coordinated with the jump. In an attempt to maintain balance, the child places the arms behind her back on landing, and she will progress to the point of rotating them from front to back.

5. In the final and mature stage of jumping, the child thrusts his arms forward and upward as he leaves the floor. In preparing for landing, the arms are moved downward and the legs are thrust forward. At the moment of contact, the knees are bent and the arms are thrust forward to keep the body from falling backward.

STRESS POINTS

1. The knees and ankles should be bent before takeoff to achieve more force through muscle extension.

2. The jumper should land on the toes and bend the knees to absorb the impact.

3. The arms should be swung forward and upward, in rhythm with the takeoff, to add momentum to the jump and thus gain distance and height.

4. The jumper should keep the legs bent after jumping so that the feet will not touch the ground prematurely.

5. Some body lean at the completion of the jump is desirable, but not to the extent that the body overbalances and falls.

TEACHING CUES

"Swing your arms forward as fast as you can."
"Bend your knees."
"On your toes."
"Land lightly with bent knees."
"Jump up and 'touch the ceiling'."

To encourage children to throw their arms forward upon landing, the teacher stands in front of the child with palms up. He tells the child, "Jump forward and slap my hands." This will encourage the child to reach out with the arms, increasing the distance of the jump.

SUGGESTED MOVEMENT EXPERIENCES

"Jump up and down, trying to go as high as you can. Try small jumps. High jumps. Jump with your feet held tightly together."

Over a spot on the floor or a beanbag, have the children jump forward, backward, and to the side.

"Jump with your body stiff and your arms held at your sides. Jump like a pogo stick."

Have children practice jump turns in place—quarter-, half-, three-quarter-, and full turns.

Have them increase and decrease the speed of jumping, and increase and decrease the height.

Have them land with the feet apart and together. Alternate with the feet spread forward and backward.

"Jump and land quietly. How is this done?"
"Jump with your body at different levels."
"See how far you can go in two, three, and four jumps."
"Pretend you are a bouncing ball."
"Clap your hands [slap thighs] while in the air. Try holding your arms in different positions. Jump up and reach for a peach in a tree."
"Jump so that your hands can touch the floor."

Have children jump according to various patterns on the floor.

Work out sequences of small and big jumps, as well as sequences for in-place jumping and jumping on the move.

Have children jump and land with the feet in different positions—forward and backward, changing strides in place, straddle and close, straddle and crisscross, heavy on one foot and light on the other.

"Pretend to jump rope."

Let them try a Bleking step. The timing is slow-slow, fast-fast-fast. (See p. 247.)

Have them make four quarter-turns, first clockwise and then counterclockwise, using either two, three, or four jumps to a turn. These can be light jumps in place and heavier jumps to turn.

"Show me a shape while you jump. Show how different animals jump—a frog, a rabbit, a kangaroo."

Develop jumping patterns using a rope or hoop on the floor. (See p. 176 for more rope suggestions and p. 174 for more hoop ideas.)

Have the children find partners and explore different jumping patterns or sequences.

Add a magic number where feasible.

"While you are jumping, touch different parts of your body—nose, ears, shoulders, head, hips, heels. Jump and touch both toes."

Two children roll a ball between them, with a third child in the center jumping over the ball as it goes back and forth.

Jumping patterns should be supplemented with both individual and long rope-jumping.

"Pick out a line or spot away from you. Using a series of jumps, move to the spot and then jog back to where you started."

"Mark your spot well. Take a series of two jumps [or more] away from the spot. Return to your spot with the same number of jumps but with your eyes closed. How close did you come?"

SPECIAL RHYTHMIC CONSIDERATIONS

1. As in the case of hopping, not too many recordings are appropriate for jumping except those especially structured for the pattern. The teacher should rely on the drumbeat for most of the rhythmic background.

2. The Bleking step and record (p. 247) are excellent to use for jumping patterns.

3. Individual rope-jumping to music should be included when appropriate for the children's ability.

Skipping

Skipping is actually a series of step-hops done with alternate feet. To teach a child to skip, ask him to take a step with one foot and then take a small hop on the same foot. (If a child can't hop, he will not be able to skip.) He now takes a step and a hop with the other foot. Skipping should be done on the balls of the feet with the arms swinging to shoulder height in opposition to the feet.

STRESS POINTS

1. Smoothness and rhythm are target goals in skipping. Speed and distance are not.
2. The weight must be transferred from one foot to the other on the hop.
3. Arms are swung in opposition to the legs.
4. If a child is having trouble skipping, it may help to slow the step-hop sequence and call out, "Step-hop," in slow rhythm.

TEACHING CUES

"Skip high."
"Swing your arms."
"Skip smoothly."
"On your toes."

SUGGESTED MOVEMENT EXPERIENCES

Many of the suggested movement patterns under walking and running can be applied to skipping, particularly those that include changing direction, stooping, forming different floor patterns, moving at different speeds, and taking steps of different sizes. Others that may be considered are listed here.

Have children skip with exaggerated arm action and lifted knees.

Have them skip backward. Change from forward movement to backward and return.

"Clap hands as you skip—above your head, to the sides, and behind your back."

"Skip silently. Skip heavily."

Have them skip with a side-to-side motion. Add turns.

"Skip twice on one side [double skip]."

"Explore different skipping patterns with your partner."

"Skip in place, move forward, and again skip in place."

SPECIAL RHYTHMIC CONSIDERATIONS

Music is almost indispensable to skipping, since skipping should be done joyously and freely. Music with a good swinging beat does much to stimulate this goal. With a record, changing the direction or type of movement at the end of the music phrase is particularly effective for skipping patterns.

Sliding

The slide is really a gallop to the side. It is a one-count movement in uneven rhythm, employing about the same tempo and timing as the skip. The movement is always to the side, with the leading foot stepping to the side and the other foot following quickly. The movement should also be practiced to the other side so that the lead foot can be changed.

The movement should be done on the balls of the feet, and the weight shifted from the lead foot to the trailing foot. Body bounce during the slide should be minimal.

The slide has a sports-related function, in that it constitutes an important movement in basketball and football for guarding an opponent. It also has good utility in rhythmics for children, since many action songs and dances employ this movement. Show the children that they can slide through a space that is not wide enough to walk through.

STRESS POINTS

1. Emphasis should be placed on moving to the side. Often students will try to move forward and backward in the slide, which is actually galloping.
2. Practice sliding in either direction so that the lead foot changes and each leg gets a chance to lead as well as to trail.
3. The slide should be a smooth, graceful, and controlled movement.

TEACHING CUES

"Move sideways."
"Move smoothly; don't bounce."
"Slide your feet close to the floor."

SUGGESTED MOVEMENT EXPERIENCES

Have the children begin with short slides and increase their length. Reverse.

Have them slide in a direction, changing lead foot and direction at will. On signal, they change direction and/or lead foot.

Have them change levels while sliding. "Slide so that your hands can touch the floor with each slide. Slide with your hands reaching for the ceiling."

"Slide as quietly as you can. Slide noisily."

"Pretend you are a basketball defensive player and slide with a good basketball position."

An interesting way to slide is to lead in one direction and then, after a definite number of slides, do a half-turn in the air and continue the slide with the other leg leading, while retaining the original direction of movement.

"Slide in a circle with your face toward the center. With your back toward the center. Slide in a figure eight."

Have them slide a definite number of slides in one direction and use the same number of slides to return to the original spot.

"Work out sliding sequences with your partner, face-to-face, with joined hands. Circle like a merry-go-round."

Add more children to the circle and have them slide around the circle, left and right.

SPECIAL RHYTHMIC CONSIDERATIONS

Sliding is done to the same music and rhythmic beat as skipping. Sliding is enhanced by good music with an uneven beat.

1. The phrase-of-music approach works excellently with sliding. The child can slide for eight counts in one direction, then either slide back or change direction for the next phrase.

2. In matching sliding patterns to an eight-count phrase, there should be seven slides with a pause on the eighth count to provide better control.

3. Partner sliding is good preliminary work for learning to cooperate with a peer.

4. Sliding patterns with children facing in and hands joined offers a good basis for sliding to music. Circle left (eight counts) and then right (eight counts).

Galloping

Galloping is similar to sliding, but the progress is in a forward direction. One foot leads, and the other is brought up to it. There is more upward motion of the body than in sliding.

STRESS POINTS

The same as for sliding.

TEACHING CUES

"Keep one foot in front of the other."
"Lead with the other foot."
"Make high gallops."

SUGGESTED MOVEMENT EXPERIENCES

A most helpful way to teach the gallop is to have children (holding hands) slide first in a circle, either to verbal cues or to a drumbeat. Then gradually turn them to face the turn of the circle. This takes them naturally from the slide into the gallop. Next, have them drop hands and move freely in general space.

After a series of eight gallops with the same foot leading, a change can be made to the other foot. The changes can be reduced to four gallops and finally to two gallops. Since the gallop is used to teach the polka later in the rhythmic program, it is important for the children to learn to change the leading foot.

Have them change the size of the gallops.

Have them gallop in a direction and stop or change direction on signal.

"Gallop quietly. Gallop heavily."

Have them gallop with exaggerated motions—high knees, lifted arms and shoulders.

"Gallop in a large circle, making it smaller and smaller."

Have them gallop forward and backward and in various floor patterns.

Let them explore different ways of galloping with a partner.

SPECIAL RHYTHMIC CONSIDERATIONS

The gallop has the same rhythmic beat and timing as the skip and the slide. Accompaniment can be a recording or a drumbeat.

1. Change lead foot at the end of eight counts and then four counts.

2. Reverse directions at the end of eight counts.

Leaping

The leap is an elongated step designed to cover distance or to go over a low obstacle. Since a series of leaps is difficult to execute, leaping is usually combined with running. Leaping should emphasize graceful flight through space.

STRESS POINTS

1. Strive for height and graceful flight.
2. Landing should be light and relaxed.

TEACHING CUES

"Push off and reach."
"Up and over. Land lightly."
"Leap over the creek."
"Use your arms to help you leap."

SUGGESTED MOVEMENT EXPERIENCES

Leaping is usually combined with a short preliminary run or used during the course of a run.

"Practice leaping in different directions."
"See how high you can leap."
"Practice soft landings."
"Vary your arm position when you leap. Clap your hands as you leap."
"Leap with the same arm and leg forward. Try it the other way."
"Show a leap in slow motion."

Have them alternate the lead foot in leaping patterns.

Have them leap over objects. Use beanbags, carpet squares, or other children.

To act as obstacles for leaping, children should lie face down, flat on the floor, or be in a curled position.

Have them practice Leaping the Brook. (See p. 266.)

SPECIAL RHYTHMIC CONSIDERATIONS

It is difficult to apply rhythm to leaping patterns. There are a few specialized records that provide accompaniment to running and leaping patterns.

EXPANDING LOCOMOTOR SKILLS WITH COMBINATIONS, SEQUENCING, AND OTHER IDEAS

While our discussions of the respective skills have approached the development of each skill independently, good movement competency is characterized by the ability to shift from one movement pattern to another with ease and smoothness. Several approaches can be examined to provide experiences pointed toward this competency goal.

The problem-solving approach merits consideration. The student puts together combinations of his or her own choice within the limitations of the problem. The problem might be stated: "Put together a sequence that includes running, skipping, hopping, and leaping." The solution of the problem is valued in terms of how it meets the stated conditions. The movements can be in any order.

The task approach is more defined. The teacher might provide the following sequence to be followed: "Can you do five jumps forward, change to a light run, put in a leap for height, collapse to the floor, and relax?"

Some attention has been given to patterned movements, such as the forming of letters, numerals, and shapes. Stepping patterns and various configurations painted on the floor, hardtop, or movable bases can be used to stimulate this type of movement.

Small tiles about 12 inches square are excellent for foot patterns. These can be in two colors, one for the right foot and the other for the left. Permanent step patterns can be painted on rubber matting of the type used in halls, providing a quick and ready piece of equipment. (When the matting is rolled up, the footprints should be toward the floor. Otherwise, the matting may not lie flat, because the ends will curl up.)

Another procedure using tiles is to number them consecutively from one to ten or one to twelve. The tiles are scattered in near proximity to one another. The child can be challenged with a number sequence, such as one, five, three, eight. He then must follow this sequence with hopping, jumping, or stepping. Another approach is to have the child contact only the odd or the even tiles. Some simple addition could be used, such as one plus four equals five, or three plus four equals seven.

Painted geometrical forms on the floor or blacktop stimulate children during free play. These can range from a simple square or rectangle to more complex configurations, such as a map of the United States or an obstacle course painted on the surface. The most obvious forms of this type are the many and diverse hopscotch patterns. Configurations of this nature are found on pp. 330–31.

The last approach to be examined involves combinations guided by rhythm. This approach is worthy of special elaboration.

Rhythmic Guidance for Combinations

Putting together interesting and unique combinations to rhythm takes either special music or skilled use of the drum. Many of the commercial fundamental movement records include unique and stimulating music to guide the movements. The directions can vary from, "Walk—walk, hop—hop," to the more complex, "Run, twirl, and collapse."

An excellent approach for the teacher is to establish a rhythm on the drum and let the children follow with patterns of their choice. Three beat patterns are shown on p. 131 to suggest this approach. Others can be devised.

Beat patterns should be repeated often enough so that all possible interpretations can be forthcoming from the children. Many movement combinations, even alternating locomotor and nonlocomotor sequences, are possible.

With the creative approach, follow activity is excellent. Children can be in pairs or in small groups, but working in pairs is much less complex and should be employed before small group activity. First, the teacher gives the rhythm on the drum, then pauses for a moment. When the rhythm is given again, one child shows a movement sequence. On the next repetition of the rhythm, the other child of the pair reproduces or duplicates the movement sequence. The same pattern can be repeated several times, or a different pattern can be established on each repetition. After a number of opportunities, reverse the roles of the students.

Perhaps more effective are records that have special music for combinations and sequencing. There are generally three or more short cuts to a side, and they provide the kind of rhythmic background that is difficult for the teacher to improvise.

Phrases can also direct changes. Skipping, sliding, and galloping require about the same music. The children can be directed to change from one movement pattern to another at the end of a pattern.

1. Possible interpretation: Walk, walk; hop, hop, hop

2. Possible interpretation: Seven running steps; four hops, jumps, or walking steps

3. Possible interpretation: Seven skips, gallops, or slides; four hops, jumps, or walking steps

NONLOCOMOTOR MOVEMENTS

Nonlocomotor movements include bending, rocking, swinging, turning, twisting, stretching, pushing, and pulling. Some attention has already been given to these in the discussion of movement themes. The directives here provide more definite methodology, based on the task approach, with opportunity for individual choice to be included.

Nonlocomotor movements are easier for young children to perform because of their general nature and lack of emphasis on precise response. The movements should be used often as challenges for children with the focus placed on variety of response. Some sample responses are offered, but it is obvious that the youngsters will think up and develop many ideas of their own. As the children become more skilled in nonlocomotor movements, combinations of movements can be developed and integrated with locomotor movements. Music or rhythmic accompaniment is also an essential element to be included.

Bending

Bending is a movement like that of a hinge, which occurs at a joint, where adjacent bones of the body are joined together. Emphasis should be placed on learning where the body bends, why it needs to bend, and how we combine many different bends to produce various movements.

SUGGESTED MOVEMENT EXPERIENCES

"Can you bend up and down?"
"Can you bend forward and backward? Left to right? North to south?"
"Bend as many ways as you can."

"How many body parts can you bend below your waist? Above your waist? Using your whole body?"
"Sit down and see if you can bend differently than you did in a standing position."
"Who can lie down and bend six body parts?"
"Is it possible to bend two parts quickly and two parts slowly at the same time?"
Have children make a familiar shape by bending two body parts. Add two more parts.
"Think of a toy you have that bends. See if you can bend the way it does."
"Can you find a partner and bend with him? Have your partner make big bends while you make tiny bends."
"Show me how you would bend to look funny. Happy. Sad. Slow. Fast."

Rocking and Swaying

Rocking is a movement that occurs when balance is fluidly moved from one spot to another. The body weight is transferred to an adjacent body part in a gradual fashion. In rocking, the body should be in a rounded position where it touches the floor. Swaying is a slower movement than rocking, and the sway is somewhat more controlled than the rock, because the support base remains fixed.

SUGGESTED MOVEMENT EXPERIENCES

"How many different ways can you rock?"
"Show me how you can rock slowly. Quickly. Smoothly."
"Can you be a rocking chair?"
"Lie on your back and rock. Point your arms and legs toward the ceiling."
"Lie on your tummy and rock. Can you hold your ankles and make giant rocks?"

"Can you rock in a standing position?"

"Can you rock and twist at the same time?"

"Who can lie on his back, with the knees up, and rock from side to side?"

"Show me two ways to rock with a partner."

"From a good, solid base with your feet a little way apart, sway forward. Backward. To the side. If you sway from a base with your feet together, what changes need to be made?"

Swinging

Swinging can be effectively described as an action of body parts that move like a rope swing. Another example is the pendulum of a clock. However, one must remember that many children have never seen a pendulum clock. The teacher can put a weight on the end of a string about a yard long and demonstrate swinging motions. Note that most swinging movements are confined to the arms or legs.

Swinging is a rhythmic, smooth motion that is fun to do to waltz music. It is also effective to combine swinging with stepping at the beginning of each measure of music. In experimenting with swinging movements, some of them can be carried to extremes so that a full circle results. With music background, swinging and circular movements can form sequences. Music is important, as it gives the child the feeling of the swing.

SUGGESTED MOVEMENT EXPERIENCES

Have children explore the different ways in which arms and legs can swing.

Have children work out swinging patterns with the arms. Combine them with a step pattern forward and back.

Have them swing the arms back and forth and go into full circles at times.

Have partners work out different swinging movements. Add circles to the movements.

Turning

Turning is here defined as a rotating movement around the long axis of the body. It involves the body as a whole. It is recognized that the terms *turning* and *twisting* are sometimes used interchangeably to designate movements of body parts rather than of the body as a whole. One can turn the head either way, or the movement can also be called twisting the head. In the suggested movement experiences, emphasis is on the movement of the entire body. Body part movements sometimes called "turning" are included under *Twisting*.

In turning, the body should be under good control so that the child can turn quickly and easily, finishing with good balance.

SUGGESTED MOVEMENT EXPERIENCES

"Turn your body to the left. Right. Clockwise. Counterclockwise."

Post correct directions on the wall and have the children turn to face north, east, south, and west. The teacher might even introduce some in-between directions such as northwest.

"Can you stand on one foot and turn around slowly? Quickly? With a series of small hops?"

"Show me how you can cross your legs with a turn and sit down. Can you get up again?"

"Every time you hear the signal, see if you can turn once around, moving slowly. Can you turn two, three, or four times?"

"Lie on the floor and turn your body in an arc slowly. Turn over so that you are on your back. Turn back again."

"Find a friend and see how many different ways he can turn you and you can turn him."

"Play follow-the-leader with your friend. You make a turn, and he follows."

Twisting

Twisting is a rotation of a body part or parts around their own long axis. The following joints can be used in twisting: spine, neck, shoulder, hip, and wrist. Twisting differs from turning in that twisting involves movement around the body part itself. In turning, attention is focused on the space in which the part is moving. Children should be encouraged to twist as far as possible and with good control of the body parts. Remember that the children are used to hearing some of these movements called "turning."

SUGGESTED MOVEMENT EXPERIENCES

"Glue your feet to the floor. Can you twist your body to the left and to the right? Can you twist it slowly and quickly? Can you bend and twist at the same time? How far can you turn your hands back and forth?"

Have children twist two or more parts of the body at the same time.

"Can you twist one body part in one direction and another in the opposite direction?"

"Is it possible to twist the lower half of your body without twisting the upper half?"

"What can you twist while sitting on the floor?"

"Can you twist one body part around another part? Is it possible to twist together even more parts?"

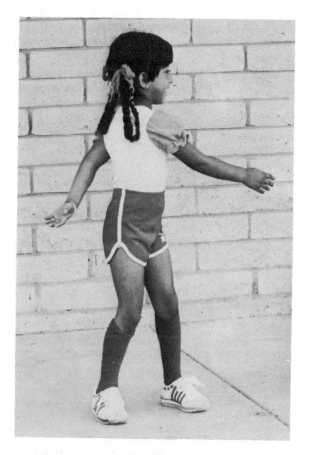

Twisting

"Balance on one foot and twist your body. Can you bend and twist at the same time?"

"Show me some different shapes you can make by twisting your body."

"Can you twist like a spring? Like a cord on a telephone?"

"Can you move and twist at the same time?"

Stretching

Stretching is a movement that extends the stretched part as far as possible. Stretching may involve moving a joint through its range of movement. Children can be told that stretching makes the body part stretched "as big as it can be." They should understand that stretching the muscles may cause some minor discomfort and that controlled movement is important. The muscle-stretching process is necessary to maintain and/or increase flexibility.

SUGGESTED MOVEMENT EXPERIENCES

"Stretch as many body parts as you can."

"Stretch your arms [legs, feet] in as many different directions as possible."

"Can you stretch a body part quickly? Slowly? Smoothly?"

"Can you bend a body part and show me which muscles are being stretched?"

"How many ways can you stretch while sitting on the floor?"

"Lie on the floor and see if you can stretch five body parts at once."

"Is it possible to stretch one body part quickly while two are being stretched slowly?"

"From a kneeling position, see if you can stretch to a mark on the floor without losing your balance."

"Stretch your right arm while your left arm curls."

"Find a friend and show me how many ways you can help each other stretch."

"Can you stretch and become as big as a giraffe?" Name other animals.

"Stretch and make a large bridge. Find a partner to go under, around, and over your bridge."

"Can you bend at the waist and touch your toes? See if you can keep your legs straight while you are stretching them."

"Can you stretch the muscles in your chest [back, tummy, ankles, wrist, fingers, etc.]?"

"Make a shape with your body. Now, stretch the shape so it gets bigger."

Pushing

Pushing is controlled and forceful movement used to propel the body away from an object or to move the object in a desired direction by applying force from behind it. The base of support should be broadened and the center of gravity lowered to increase stability. A line of force should be directed toward the object.

SUGGESTED MOVEMENT EXPERIENCES

"Stand near a wall and push against it while standing straight. Then push with your knees bent and one foot behind the other. In which position can you push with more force?"

"Push an imaginary object that is very light. Now imagine that you are pushing a very heavy object."

"Try to push a partner who is sitting on a jumping box. Now try to push a partner who is sitting on a scooter. What changes must you make in your body position?"

"Can you push an object with your feet without using your arms and hands?"

"Sit down and push a heavy object with your feet. Can you put your back against the object and push it?"

"How many different ways can you find to push your object?"

"Find a friend and try to push him or her over a line."

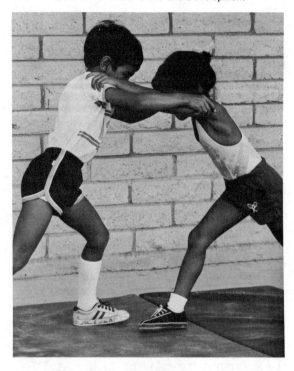

Pushing a partner

"Sit back to back with your partner and see if you can move him or her."

"Is it possible to lie on the floor and push?"

"Lie on the floor and push your body forward. Backward. Sideways."

"Lie on the floor and push yourself with one foot and one arm."

"Put a beanbag on the floor and push it with your elbow [shoulder, nose, etc.]."

"Can you move in crab position and push a beanbag?"

"Show me how you can push a ball to a friend."

"Push the ball toward the ceiling in a very smooth manner."

Pulling

Pulling is a controlled and forceful movement made in an attempt to move an object toward the body. When heavy objects are pulled, the base of support must be broadened and the center of gravity lowered. Pulling should be done in a controlled fashion. Jerking and tugging without coordinated effort should be discouraged. The vertical axis of the body should provide a line of force away from the object.

SUGGESTED MOVEMENT EXPERIENCES

"Reach for the ceiling and pull an imaginary object toward you quickly. Slowly and smoothly."

Have children use an individual tug-of-war rope and practice pulling at different levels with hands and arms.

"Pull something from a kneeling position."

"Can you pull with your feet while sitting on the floor?"

"Is it possible to pull a heavy object while lying on the floor?"

"Clasp your hands together and pull as hard as possible."

"Try pulling an object while standing on one foot only."

"Hold hands with a partner and gradually pull as hard as you can."

"Have your partner sit down and then see if you can pull him as slowly as possible."

"With your partner sitting on the floor, see if you can pull him to his feet."

"Can you pull with different body parts?"

Combinations of pulling and pushing movements should be arranged in sequence. Music phrases can signal changes from one to the other.

Rhythmic Accompaniment for Nonlocomotor Movements

Bending, swaying, twisting, swinging, and circling movements are done rhythmically to waltz music (three-quarter time). More abrupt movements can be stimulated by playing a piece with a good beat, or movement can be guided by a drumbeat. The movements should be large, free, and unhampered through the full range of motion.

When the music has definite phrases, one phrase can be used as a signal to make the movement to its full range, and another phrase allows the movement to return to its original position. Raising and lowering movements are appropriate for this approach, as are twisting and rotating various parts of the body.

To develop good body awareness, the children should understand the terms as they are used, which means that neither the movements nor the terms should be beyond their capacities.

Music with a staccato rhythm or a drumbeat can animate such forceful movements as striking, punching, or semaphore-like movements. Flexion and extension movements, either partial or full, are also suitable for this type of rhythm. Movements should be definite and sharp.

SPECIALIZED SPORTS-RELATED SKILLS

The specialized sports-related skills include catching, throwing, and kicking, among others.

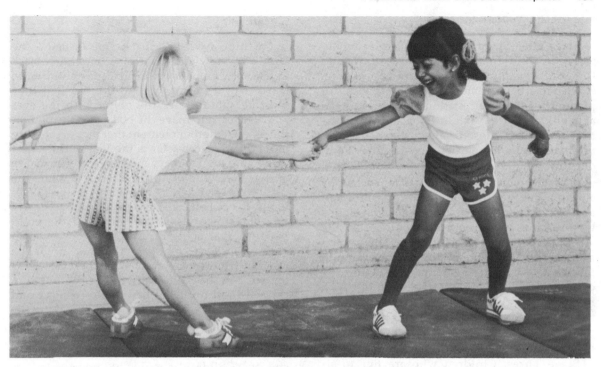

Pulling (note the incorrect base of support)

They are complex motor patterns, and children are not usually capable of exhibiting a mature pattern until the age of eight or nine. Since motor patterns are learned at an early age and are difficult to change thereafter, it is important to teach the pattern correctly. An example of incorrect learning appears to occur in the skill of throwing. Many students never mature in throwing patterns, whereas most youngsters in after-school sport programs learn to throw correctly. Many factors contribute to this situation. In many cases, very little emphasis is placed on correct form, and often children are not encouraged to learn properly. Once the incorrect pattern is practiced over and over for eight to ten years, it becomes next to impossible to change. Thus, if the skill-learning years do indeed occur between the ages of two and six, it is crucial to teach and encourage correctness of performance in the specialized sport skills if proper motor patterns are to be developed. Most complex skills must be practiced at near normal speed rather than in "slow motion." The analysis of the following skills should give the teacher an idea of the sequence of development, which is more important than the chronological age at which children learn.

Throwing

In throwing, an object is thrust into space and is accelerated by movement of the arm and total coordination of the body. Teachers should be aware of two early stages of tossing as practiced by young children. The patterns can often be seen in many youngsters and merits some mention. The first toss is a two-handed underhand throw that involves little foot movement. A large ball, such as a beach ball, will usually produce this type of throw, which begins with the ball held at waist level in front of the body. The child will usually complete the toss using only the arms, and he will sometimes have difficulty maintaining balance if he is encouraged to throw for distance.

The second kind of toss is the one-handed underhand toss. In this movement, which is similar to pitching a softball, the child will begin to develop body torque and to be able to shift the weight from the rear to the front foot. This toss requires a smaller object to throw, and beanbags, fleece balls, and small sponge balls work well for this toss.

Overhand throwing is not a natural act and, since it is an important play skill, it needs more definition and instruction. For this reason, the following skill analysis concentrates on overhand throwing. The teacher should be primarily concerned about children developing a proper form while throwing rather than throwing for accuracy. If one is interested in developing skillful patterns with full range of motion and speed of throw as the goals, accuracy should be a secondary consideration. As the pattern matures, accuracy can gradually be introduced.

OVERHAND THROWING

Stage One. Stage One can generally be observed in children between the ages of two and three. Movement at this stage is basically restricted to arm movement in the anteroposterior plane. The feet remain stationary and are spread at shoulder width, with little or no trunk rotation occurring. Most of the movement force originates from hip flexion, moving the shoulder forward, and extending the elbow.

Stage Two. Stage Two is usually reached by children between the ages of three and a half and five. Some rotary motion is now developed by the child in an attempt to increase the amount of force he can accumulate. This stage is characterized by a lateral fling of the arm with much rotation occurring in the trunk. Often the child will take a step in the direction in which he is throwing, although many children keep the feet stationary. This throwing style looks more like a discus throw than a baseball-style throw.

Stage Three. Children who are five to six years old are usually in this stage. The starting position is similar to the other stages in that the body is facing the target area, the feet are parallel, and the child is erect. In this stage, however, the child steps toward the target with the foot on the same side of his body as his throwing arm. This allows for some rotation of the body and shifting of the body weight forward as the step occurs. The arm action is nearer the overhand style of throwing than is the fling in Stage Two, and there is also an increase in hip flexion. Many students' throwing patterns never develop beyond this stage, and they continue to exhibit many of the behaviors described in this stage due to lack of instruction.

Stage Four. In this stage, the mature form of throwing is seen. It allows the child to apply the most force to the object being accelerated. The thrower uses the rule of opposition in this stage, which means that he takes a step with the leg opposite the throwing arm in the direction of the throw. This allows the thrower to develop maximum body torque. The child should address the target with the nonthrowing side of the body and stride toward the target to shift body weight. The sequence of movement is: step toward the target, rotate the upper body, and throw with the arm. The cue words often used are step, turn, and throw. The elbow should lead the way in the arm movement, followed by forearm extension and finally a snapping of the wrist. This pattern must be practiced many times in an attempt to develop total body coordination.

Catching

Catching is a skill that involves using the hands to stop and control a moving object. Catching is much more difficult for children to learn than throwing, due to the fact that they must be able to track the object with the eyes and also learn to move the body into the path of the object. Another element that makes catching more difficult to master is the fear of the object to be caught. Teachers must be careful to use objects that will not hurt the receiver while the early stages of catching are being mastered. Balloons, fleece balls, and beach balls move slowly and encourage visual tracking, and the child need not fear being hit in the face.

Stage One. In this stage, the child holds the arms in front of the body with the elbows extended and the palms up. The arms are held in this position until the ball makes contact and then are quickly bent at the elbows, making the catch a trapping movement as the arms press the ball against the chest. Often, the child will turn the head or close the eyes due to the fear response. Children should be encouraged to watch the object rather than the person throwing it.

Stage Two. In this stage, the child repeats much of the same behavior as in Stage One. Rather than waiting for the ball to contact his arms, however, the child makes an anticipatory movement. The child now cradles the ball to some extent.

Stage Three. As the catching pattern matures, the child prepares to catch by lifting the arms and bending them slightly. She still uses her chest as a backstop for the ball and cradles the ball with her arms and hands. As skill develops in this stage, an attempt is usually made to make contact with the hands first and then guide it to the chest.

Stage Four. In the fourth and final stage of catching, mature form is characterized by the child catching the ball with the hands. The child can be encouraged to catch with the hands by decreasing the size of the ball to be caught. As the child continues to improve in style, he will reach with the hands and then bring the object softly to the body; this is often termed "giving." The legs bend, and the feet are moved in anticipation of the catch.

Kicking

Kicking is a striking action carried out with the foot. There are different types of kicks: (1) the punt, in which the ball is dropped from the hands and kicked before it touches the ground; (2) the place kick, in which the ball is kicked off the ground; and (3) the soccer kick,

IMPORTANT TO EXPLAIN THE STAGES HERE INFO.

probably the most difficult of the foot-striking skills, due to the fact that the ball is moving before the kick.

Stage One. The body is stationary, and the kicking foot is flexed as the child prepares for the kick. The kicking motion is carried out primarily with a straight leg, showing little or no flexion at the knee. Very little movement occurs in the arms and trunk. The child concentrates on the ball.

Stage Two. In the second stage, the child lifts the kicking foot backward by flexing the leg at the knee. The child usually displays opposition of the limbs; in other words, when the kicking leg goes forward, the opposite arm moves forward. The kicking leg moves forward farther than in Stage One, with a follow-through motion.

Stage Three. The child now runs or walks toward the object to be kicked. There is an increase in the distance the leg is moved, coupled with an accompanying movement of the upper body to counterbalance the leg movement.

Stage Four. The mature stage of kicking involves a preparatory extension at the hip in order to increase the leg's range of motion. As the child runs to the ball and prepares to kick it, he takes a small leap to get the kicking foot into a ready position. As the kicking foot is carried forward, the trunk leans backward, and the child takes a small step forward on the support foot to regain balance.

Rhythm for Manipulative Activities

Manipulative activities to rhythm should be regarded as an opportunity to strengthen skills already experienced. If a child cannot do the skill well enough to meet the challenge of putting it to rhythm, the value of using rhythm is dubious.

The recordings designed for fundamental rhythms usually have cuts that are suitable for simple ball and balloon skills. When youngsters are ready, putting dribbling skills to music can be quite intriguing and rewarding. Polka music, or music of about that speed with a good beat, is suitable for dribbling to rhythm.

Many of these experiences will necessarily be limited to primary children, but selected younger children will be able to accomplish simple bouncing to rhythm. Suggested skill experiences are:

Have children bounce the ball and catch it.
Have them dribble a few times with both hands.
Have them dribble with one hand.
Have them volley balloons in time with the rhythm. This takes a light touch, since hard volleying will put the balloons out of reach and out of rhythm.
Have each child bounce to a partner, who catches the ball and returns the ball on the bounce. Rope-jumping to music is a manipulative activity, but is given special attention (p. 180) because of its unique contribution to that area.

SUMMARY

Fundamental motor skills are grouped into three categories: locomotor skills, nonlocomotor skills, and manipulative or specialized sports-related skills. Locomotor and nonlocomotor skills are described and the skills analyzed individually. Then stress points and teaching cues are offered to aid the teacher in proper instruction. Finally, movement experiences are listed that offer a wide range of activity yet still offer repetition and practice on the selected skill. This wide range of practice activities is important if the motivational level of children is to be maintained.

To offer further variation and variety while practicing on fundamental motor skills, rhythm can be introduced into the presentation. Locomotor skill practice sessions can be expanded through combining and sequencing movements.

Specialized sports-related skills should be learned at an early age so that children do not have to unlearn improper patterns. Even though most of the sports-related skill patterns do not mature until eight or nine years of age, children can begin to develop correct movements earlier.

Chapter 12

Gross Motor Activity on Apparatus

I have come to feel that the only learning which significantly influences behavior is self-discovered, self-appropriated learning.

Carl Rogers

Activities on apparatus play an important part in physical education programs for young children. There are many types of apparatus, some of which can be constructed.

There is little question that apparatus activities help meet the gross motor needs and interests of children. Young children are attracted to the challenge of apparatus, as it allows them to satisfy their normal inclinations to climb, balance, and hang. The chore of the teacher is to build a program based on these natural dispositions, so that a broad range of movement possibilities and capabilities may be realized.

Apparatus is extremely useful in physical education, particularly those types that encourage climbing and permit the body weight to be supported while hanging by the hands. Flexibility and stretching are enhanced, while grip and arm-shoulder girdle strength are developed. In addition, the child learns to manage the body while it is free of ground support.

Since research has shown that there are more hazards to be considered in using climbing equipment than in other physical activities, teaching youngsters respect for equipment and its proper usage are important goals of the apparatus program. It has been found that improper usage, climbing where not indicated, and roughhousing were contributing causes to playground equipment injuries. With the increased use of home playground sets, such emphasis on proper behavior seems warranted.

Pieces of equipment placed on the floor provide important extensions for educational movement. Exploratory and creative activity, as well as wide experience in body management, should characterize one approach to instructional procedures. Individual response in movement should be stressed, with the emphasis on doing but not on conformity. Variety in apparatus activity can be enhanced by the addition of hand apparatus, such as beanbags, balls, wands, hoops, blocks, and other items. Individual or partner manipulative activities, while the children perform and move on apparatus, add another dimension to the movement possibilities.

GENERAL INSTRUCTIONAL PROCEDURES FOR APPARATUS

The basic tenet of apparatus movement experiences is that, with guidance and direction from the teacher, each child will take responsibility for his or her progress at his or her own rate of development. In addition to taking part in creative and exploratory activities on apparatus, children should be challenged to accomplish certain movement patterns. Using the "Can you...?" or "Who can...?" approach, the teacher guides the child toward movement progress through limitations. The challenge should be general enough, but also subject to individual interpretation, testing the child's ability to put the coordinations and skills together in the manner described. Throughout the various suggested activity sequences for different pieces of apparatus are suggestions to challenge youngsters with movement patterns of this nature and move them to broader movement competency.

All children are to work purposefully, with safety, and under control. Three general rules contribute to achieving this goal. First, the arrangement of apparatus and the organization of children should be conducive to maximum involvement and activity on the part of the children. No one should be standing idly by, although, by its nature, apparatus work does necessitate some taking of turns and sharing.

The second point is that the teaching-learning situation must be a safe environment. Rules and regulations for safety need to be established and understood, and activities must be taught in a reasonable progression. Each teacher is responsible for checking equipment and adjusting it for safe use. Children are not to use apparatus or equipment without supervision.

The third point to be established is class control. The teacher should explain that working individually means working alone, without touching or interfering with others. The learning atmosphere should be quiet enough so that the teacher's voice can be heard above the activity sounds.

CLASS ORGANIZATION

Three formats are suggested for class organization. Choice of format will be influenced by the amount of equipment available, the target goals, the maturity level of the children, and the space available.

1. Single-Activity Format

In activities that use apparatus like balance beams, benches, individual mats, and magic ropes, the instructor can effectively follow a single-activity format, in which all children are reacting to the same challenge. There must be sufficient equipment so that good activity can be forthcoming, without waiting for turns.

In this type of class organization, activity progressions can be presented effectively, practice and repetition inserted as needed, and cognitive elements given proper attention.

2. Multiple-Station Format

When larger pieces of apparatus are involved, the station organization seems more applicable. Opportunity should be given for both exploratory and guided activity. Multiple-station organization is more productive if there has been preliminary instruction and orientation. Children at each station should have specified movement activities to perform or various challenges to overcome; otherwise the period

will satisfy only the play instinct. If there are safety considerations pertaining to a piece of apparatus, these should be made clear to children. Making them fearful of the apparatus is to be avoided.

Parents or cross-age tutors can make instruction more effective by supplying help at each of the stations. If they are utilized, then some simple written instructions about important student learning outcomes to be stressed at each station provide beneficial guidance for the activity emphasis.

Apparatus activities at stations can be effectively combined with manipulative activities to form interesting circuits and challenges.

Individuals, partners, and/or groups move from one station to another as directed by the teacher, or they may be given discretion to move as they choose. In choice activities, when a group of children move to a piece of equipment or a station where a crowd has already gathered, they should look for another place to go rather than try to force any of the present participants to leave. On the other hand, children already on the equipment need to be aware that they must share it and that, if they have been at a station for a period of time, they must move. It may not be feasible for children to visit all the stations during a class period. The balance of these experiences can be provided at the next lesson.

It is obvious that the type and number of equipment pieces will determine the character of the stations. One could follow this pattern in organizing stations:

Station 1
Large equipment: Climbing ropes, ladders, trestle tree- or sawhorse-supported items, parallel bars (low), step platform

Station 2
Large equipment: Wall-attached climbing frames, chinning or exercise bar, table, cutoff chairs and planks, benches

Station 3
Floor equipment: Floor ladder, balance beams, cutout boxes, jumping boxes, cones, wands, balance boards, tires

Station 4
Manipulative and other equipment: Scooters, hoops, various balls, cones, stilts, bounding boards, mats

Several comments are in order. The four stations are each of a multiple-use (choice) type. More stations could be utilized, with fewer opportunities at each. Not only should children be informed what they are to do at each station, but they should also know how they are to leave a station, in terms of the housekeeping procedures to be followed.

3. Challenge Circuit

A challenge circuit consists of equipment arranged in either single or multiple paths. When a single path is used, the number of children who can be active on the equipment is limited. The equipment is arranged in a prescribed order, and each child in turn follows that path. This kind of arrangement also works well with exceptional children, particularly the mentally retarded.

A multiple-path circuit gives the children a choice of several paths to follow, depending upon the equipment and the arrangement. The children might be challenged: "Let's see you move along the [specify piece of equipment] on two bases of support, go under the [piece], back up again, and jump off." Or: "Can you move across the beam with a follow step, crawl along the bench on your stomach, jump to the mat, and roll?"

A challenge circuit can serve effectively as a station in the multiple-station format, particularly when the number of children is too large for the circuit.

Return Activity

The use of return activity can increase the movement potential of mats, balance beams, benches, and other pieces of apparatus. In this technique, the child performs some kind of movement task on his way back (return) to his place in line. The return activity is usually something different, a change of pace, from the activity being emphasized. Since the instructional concentration is centered on the lesson activities, the return movements should demand little supervision. Choice and exploration should characterize return activities.

In return activity in combination with the balance beam–bench, the child performs on the bench, accomplishes the dismount, and does a forward roll on the way back to place. While one child is performing, another is dismounting, and a third child is rolling. While return activity procedures fit in well with the single-activity format, they can be used anywhere to provide a kind of mini-circuit.

Other Instructional Procedures

The start-and-expand technique reinforces the success approach by starting at a low point on the progression of skills. Achieving some measure of success is important. Serious enjoy-

ment and fun should be keynotes of the instructional climate in apparatus activities.

Some attention should be given to the dismount, as determined by the character of the apparatus. The dismount should be controlled by landing with the knees bent and the weight balanced over the balls of the feet. The child should land in good control and hold the position momentarily to show that he has control. Challenges, such as making shapes through the air, turns, stunts following the landing, and others, can be structured into dismounts.

While spotting is desirable in apparatus work, it is difficult for younger children to accomplish this readily and effectively. Children should not be afraid to ask the teacher to help them.

Traffic rules should be outlined, stipulating when the child next in turn is to start and specifying how many children should be on a particular piece of equipment at one time.

Children (with the possible exception of preschool children) should help set up and store the equipment. Apparatus equipment should be selected with this in mind. Mats should be placed where needed for safety and to cushion dismounts.

Program organizers should make sure that classes using similar equipment are conveniently scheduled, one following the other, to prevent having to spend too much time in setting up and dismantling equipment.

APPARATUS TYPES

The following types of apparatus are included in the instructional outlines in this chapter:

Climbing and body-support types
Climbing ropes, horizontal ladders, floor climbing sets, climbing frames, exercise bars, and apparatus sets of the German Stegel type

Apparatus used on the floor
Balance boards, balance beams, benches, bounding boards, gym scooters, individual mats, jumping boxes, magic ropes (stretch ropes), ladders (on the floor), stilts, used tires (automobile and bicycle), and a miscellany of other items

CLIMBING ROPES

Rope-climbing offers excellent developmental possibilities for the upper trunk and arms, as well as good training in coordination of the different parts of the body. Adequate grip and arm strength are necessary prerequisites to climbing. Becoming accustomed to the rope and gaining in confidence are important goals in early work on the ropes. Many children need to overcome a natural fear of height.

INSTRUCTIONAL PROCEDURES

1. Mats should be provided under all ropes.
2. The hand-over-hand method should be used for climbing, and the hand-under-hand method for descending.
3. Children should be cautioned not to slide, lest they get rope burns on their hands and skinned places on their legs.
4. If a climber becomes tired, he should stop and rest. Proper resting stops should be worked into the climbing activity.
5. Climbers should always have enough strength left to allow them to descend safely. No child should go higher than his strength will allow.
6. Spotters should be used initially in activities in which the body is inverted. The spotter can hold the rope steady while the child climbs.
7. Children swinging on the ropes should make sure that the other children are out of the way.
8. Marks to limit the climb can be put on the rope with adhesive tape. A mark eight to ten feet above the floor is the limit for all children until they can demonstrate sufficient proficiency to be allowed to climb higher.
9. As children develop adequate strength, tieing a knot at the end of the rope should be avoided. Youngsters have a tendency to sit and ride on such knots, which does not provide good arm-shoulder exercise.
10. Just being able to hang onto the rope is a good measure of success for some children. Increase the length of hanging time.

PRELIMINARY SEQUENCES

Progression is important in rope climbing, and the basic skill progressions should be followed.

Supported Pull-ups. In these activities, a part of the body remains in contact with the floor. Pull up hand-over-hand and return hand-under-hand.

1. Standing position: Grasp rope, rock back on heels and lower body to floor. Keep a straight body. Return to the standing position.
2. Kneeling position: Kneel directly under the rope. Pull up until on tiptoes.
3. Sitting position: Pull up; legs are supported on the heels.
4. Lying-down position: Lie on back with bent knees directly under the rope. Pull up to a crab position. Try moving the feet in a circle.

Hangs. In a hang, the child pulls himself up in one motion and holds the position for a length of time—five, ten, or twenty seconds. Stress progression.

1. From a seated position, reach up as high as possible and pull the body from the floor except for the heels. Hold.
2. Same as previous stunt, except: pull the body completely free of the floor and hold.
3. From a standing position, jump up, grasp, and hang. This should be a bent-arm hang with the hands about even with the mouth. Hold.
4. Repeat previous stunt, but add leg movements: one or both knees up; bicycling movement of the legs; half lever (bring one leg or both legs parallel to the floor); full lever (bring feet up to face).

Pull-ups. In the pull-up, the child raises and lowers his body repeatedly.

Repeat all activities under *Hangs,* except: substitute the pull-up for the hang. Pull up each time until the chin touches the hands.

Inverted Hang. Reach up high with both hands. Jump to a bent-arm position and at the same time bring the knees to the nose, inverting the body, which is in a curled position. In a continuation of the movement, bring the feet higher than the hands and lock the legs around

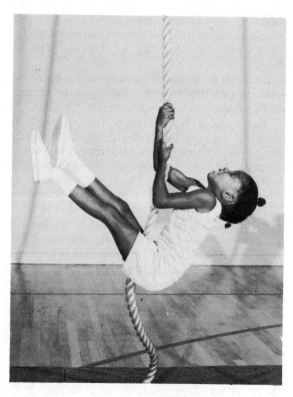

Jumping to an inverted hang

the rope. Body should now be straight and up-side down. In learning phases, the teacher should spot.

Swinging and Jumping. Use a bench, box, or stool for a takeoff point. To take off, the child should reach high and jump to a bent-arm position while swinging. Landing should be done in a bent-knee drop.

1. Swing and jump. Add half- and full turns.
2. Swing and return to perch. Add single and double knee bends.
3. Jump for distance, over a bar, or through a hoop.

CLIMBING THE ROPE

Scissors Grip. Approach the rope and reach as high as possible, standing with the right leg forward of the left. Raise the back leg, bend at the knee, and place the rope *inside* the knee and *outside* the foot. Cross the forward leg over the back leg and straighten the legs out with the toes pointed down. This should give a secure hold. The teacher should check the position.

Using the scissors grip to climb. From the scissors grip position, raise the knees up close to the chest, with the rope sliding between them, while supporting the body with the hand grip. Now, lock the rope between the legs and climb up with the hand-over-hand method as high as the hands can reach. Bring the knees up to the chest and repeat the process. Climbers should begin by climbing halfway. They can go on to climb three-fourths of the way and finish the progression by learning to climb to the top mark.

The top mark should establish the point beyond which the children should not be permitted to climb.

Leg-around Rest. Using the left leg and keeping the rope between the thighs, wrap the left leg completely around the rope. The bottom of the rope now crosses over the instep of the left foot *from the outside.* The right foot stands on the rope as it crosses over the instep, providing pressure to prevent slippage. To provide additional pressure, release the hands and wrap the arms around the rope, leaning away from the rope at the same time. If the right leg is used, the instructions should be reversed.

Using the leg-around rest to climb. Climbing with the leg-around rest is similar to climbing with the scissors grip, except that the leg-around rest grip needs to be loosened each time and reformed higher up on the rope.

DESCENDING

There are four methods of descending the rope. The only differences are in the use of the leg locks, since the hand-under-hand technique is used for all descents.

Reverse of the Scissors Climb. From an extended position, lock the legs and lower the body with the hands until the knees are against the chest. Hold with the hands and lower the legs to a new position.

Using the Leg-around Rest. From the leg-around rest, lower the body in the hand-under-hand method until the knees are against the chest. Lift the top foot and let the rope slide loosely to a lower position. Again secure with the top foot. Repeat until down.

Swinging on climbing ropes

Instep Squeeze. The climber keeps the heels together to squeeze the rope between the insteps. The hand-under-hand movement lowers the body, while the rope slides between the insteps.

Stirrup Descent. The rope is on the outside of the right foot and is carried under the instep of the foot and over the toe of the left foot. Pressure from the left foot holds the position. To get into position, let the rope trail along the right leg, reach under, and hook it with the left toe. When the force of the left leg is varied, the rope can slide smoothly while the descent is made with the hands.

STUNTS USING TWO ROPES

Two ropes, hanging close together, are needed for these activities.

Straight-Arm Hang. Jump up, grasp one rope with each hand, and hang with the arms straight.

Bent-Arm Hang. Same as above, except that the arms are bent at the elbows.

Arm Hangs with Different Leg Positions. These hangs include: single and double knee lifts; half lever (bring feet up parallel to floor, toes pointed); full lever (bring feet up to face and keep knees straight); bicycle (pedal like a bicycle).

Pull-ups. Same as a pull-up on a single rope.

Inverted Hangs. These hangs may be performed with the feet wrapped around the rope, with the feet against the inside of the ropes, or with the toes pointed and the feet not touching the ropes.

Skin the Cat. From a bent-arm position, kick feet overhead and continue the roll until the feet touch the mat. Return to the starting position. A more difficult stunt is to start from a higher position so that the feet do not touch the mat. Reverse to original position.

HORIZONTAL LADDERS, FLOOR CLIMBING SETS, AND WALL-ATTACHED CLIMBING FRAMES

Horizontal ladders, floor climbing sets, and wall-attached climbing frames are manufactured in a variety of models. The most practical equipment sets are the type that are attached to and can be stored against the wall. Some teachers like to have mini-sets of ladders and ropes in a corner of the classroom, sometimes called a fitness corner.

The climbing frame pictured here, manufactured by Centaur Athletics, affords children an exciting climbing experience. It can be stored against the wall and is easily moved into position. The frame can be purchased in two or three sections, and individual pieces of equipment can be bought to increase the flexibility and creative possibilities for children. Examples of the type of apparatus that can be acquired to enhance the frame are climbing ropes, horizontal ladders, balance beams and rope-climbing ladders. Climbing frames can be purchased in the United States from Centaur Athletics, Inc., Post Office Box 178, Custer, Washington 98240, or Robert Widen Co., Post Office Box 2075, Prescott, Arizona 86301.

Horizontal ladders and climbing frames provide excellent lead-in activities for young children prior to rope-climbing activities, because they are firm and afford a better surface for grasping. Children can learn to climb without worrying about the rope moving or having to use a leg grip.

Another type of climbing apparatus that is popular is the portable set, which can be placed on the floor. While these offer excellent movement possibilities, they also need to be set up and taken down. There is great variation in what these sets consist of and how they can be set up. They are valuable in exploratory and creative work.

Climbing frame

Benches should have hooks so that they can be attached to climbing sets to provide additional challenge and variation.

Apparatus sets for movement can be made from supports similar to sawhorses and longitudinal planks. In some schools, apparatus of the type called the Stegel is popular. In addition to sawhorse-type supports, the Stegel includes more beams or poles, a ladder, and sometimes a slide.

This piece of apparatus is manufactured in the United States in both wood and metal. Since the frames are bolted together, however, problems of handling and storage may arise. The tendency is simply to move them to one side of the activity area, as disassembly is laborious.

INSTRUCTIONAL PROCEDURES

1. The opposed-thumb grip, in which the thumb goes around the bar, is important. In most activities, the back of the hands should face the child (monkey grip). Vary the grip, however, using other holds, such as the lower grip (palms toward the face) and the mixed grip (one hand facing one way and one, the other).

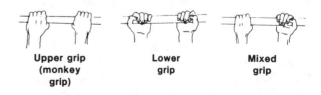

Upper grip   Lower   Mixed
(monkey   grip   grip
grip)

2. Whenever the child is learning an inverted hang, spotters should be present. The teacher or an older student should spot.

3. Speed is not the goal of this activity. In fact, the longer the child is hanging from the ladder, the more beneficial the activity can be. There is value in simply hanging.

4. In activities involving movement down the length of the ladder, all children should travel in the same direction. The child next in turn should start just when the child ahead is about to dismount.

5. Mats should always be placed under climbing apparatus when they are in use.

6. When dismounting from a ladder, the child should be instructed to land in a bent-leg position, on the balls of the feet.

7. Don't force children to climb the wall-attached climbing frames. Many children have a natural fear of height and need much reassurance before they will climb. If necessary, climb the frame with the child until he is confident of his ability.

8. Bars should not be used out of doors in wet weather, since they will become slippery.

Horizontal Ladder Activities

Hangs. The hangs should be performed with the opposed-thumb grip and with straight arms. Encourage the children to hang in a bent-arm position, however, to involve more muscles in the upper arms. The following hang variations are suggested:

1. Straight-leg hang. Keep legs straight and point toes toward ground.

2. Knees-up hang. Lift the knees as high as possible toward the chest.

3. Bicycle. Lift the knees and pedal the bicycle.

4. Half lever. Bring the legs up parallel to the ground with the knees straight and the toes pointed.

5. Inverted hang. Hang with the hands on a rung. Bring the feet up and over the next rung and hook the toes under a second rung. Release the hand grip, and hang in an inverted position.

Note. A spotter should be present during the child's first few attempts at inverted stunts.

6. Flexed-arm hang. Stand on a box if necessary to get in position. Hang as long as possible with the chin even with the hands.

7. Swinging. Hang from a rung with both hands and swing the body back and forth.

8. Swing back and forth and jump as far as possible. Vary with turns.

Moving Activities on the Horizontal Ladder. Travel the length of the ladder, using the rungs. Start by traveling one rung at a time and then skip one or more rungs to add challenge.

Travel the length of the ladder, using both side rails. Use just one rail to travel the ladder.

Climbing Frame Activities

It is obvious that the character of the climbing frame, together with all the arrangement possibilities, will determine the extent of its use and the activities most appropriate for it. However, some general guides for all frames are in order.

INSTRUCTIONAL PROCEDURES

1. Try to stimulate children to be versatile, clever, unique, and creative. Equipment purchased should allow children to arrange it in different ways.

2. In turn, the teacher should use imagination in arranging the apparatus in new and different combinations to extend the possibility of movement.

3. The teacher needs to make an assessment of the maximum number of children who should be on a particular set of climbing apparatus at one time and plan accordingly.

4. It is essential that children do not touch or interfere with others unless partner work is going on.

5. Challenges to children should consider sequence-building in three aspects: (a) how to mount (get on) the frame, (b) what to do on the frame, and (c) how to dismount (get off) the frame.

6. Challenges can be general or specific. A general challenge might be structured this way: "Each time you climb, find a new way to get on, different things you can do on the frame, and a new way to dismount." A more specific challenge or task would be worded like this: "Can you get on the frame with your legs held together, go in and out of openings on the same level, and swing off for a dismount?"

SEQUENCE OF ACTIVITIES

Suggestions for ways of mounting
"Enter the frame so that your hands are the last to leave the floor."

"Use a different part of the body to mount each time."

"Start in a lying-down position and pull yourself up with your hands."

"Mount so that only one foot touches the frame."

"Get on so that one hand and one foot are the last to leave the floor."

"Lead with different parts of the body [specify] as you get on."

Suggestions for movement patterns on climbing frames
"Move across the [apparatus] at the same level."

"Move so that your arms cross each other."

"Climb to the top of the frame on the outside [inside] and descend on the inside [outside]."

"Climb to the top of the frame and use only your arms and hands to come down."

"As you climb to the top, go in and out of as many openings as you can. Try it head first. Feet first."

"Make different kinds of stretched shapes as you support yourself on one arm."

"Balance on the central part of your body and release both your feet and hands."

"Suspend yourself in an upside-down position."

"Suspend yourself by your arms and swing your body from side to side."

"Using your legs to hold you, show a stretched shape with your arms held wide apart."

"With a partner, play follow-the-leader. Pass over [around and/or through] a shape made by your partner."

Suggestions for ways of dismounting

"Jump off. Jump off with a turn. Hop off. Jump off with different shapes."

"Swing off. Drop off [not too high at first]."

"Get on and off with the same part of your body."

"Get off so that your hands touch first." Select other body parts to touch first—seat, shoulder, knee, etc.

"Keep your feet together as you get off."

At times, allow the children to tell the teacher the sequence they are about to follow.

A "magic box" approach is also sound. The box contains small cards on which are directions for sequences. The child selects a card and performs as specified. Diagrams may also be included on the cards.

EXERCISE BARS

Low horizontal bars should be installed on the playground in a series of at least three, set at different heights. The program should be limited to simple hangs and climbs. To perform many of the more complicated stunts on the bar, it is necessary to have sufficient arm strength to pull the body up and over the bar. Although some of the youngsters will begin to have this capacity, the emphasis shold be on a more limited program.

A low turning bar constructed of four-inch pipe, 12 or more feet in length, has value in providing bar experiences for young children. The bar should be about 30 inches above the ground.

INSTRUCTIONAL PROCEDURES

1. Only one child should be on a bar at a time.
2. Do not use the bar when it is wet.
3. The basic grip is the opposed-thumb or monkey grip, upper style. The lower and mixed grips should also be used. (See p. 143 for description of grips.)
4. For young children, stress the value in simply hanging. Have them count to five or more seconds, to stimulate them to hang for longer periods. Give some attention to the flexed-arm hang, in which the chin is even with the hands.

SEQUENCE OF ACTIVITIES

Hangs. Feet pointed, one or both knees up.

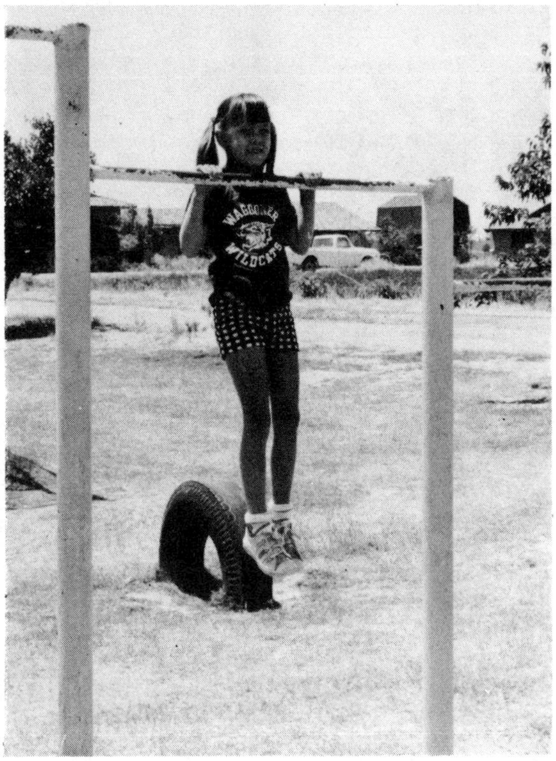

Hanging on a horizontal bar

Controlled Touching. Grasp the bar with hands slightly wider than shoulder width. Bring up knees to touch the bar between the hands. Touch the bar with the shoelaces. Touch the soles of the feet to the bar.

Swings. Swing back and forth, propelling the body forward to a stand.

Moving along the Bar. Begin at one side and move hand-against-hand to the other end of the bar. Move with crossed hands.

Sloth Travel. Face end of bar, standing underneath. Grasp bar with both hands and hook the legs over the bar at the knees. In this position, move along the bar to the other end. Return by reversing the movement.

Arm and Leg Hang. Grasp bar with upper grip. Bring one of the legs between the arms and hook the knee over the bar.

Double Leg Hang. Same as Sloth Travel, but bring both legs between the hands and hook the knees over the bar. Release the hands and hang in the inverted position. If the hands touch or are near the ground, a dismount can be made by releasing the legs and dropping to a crouched position on the ground.

Skin the Cat. Bring both knees up between the arms as in the previous stunt but continue the direction of the knees until the body is turned over backward. Release grip and drop to ground.

Skin the Cat

BALANCE BOARDS

Balance boards are small devices on which the child attempts to stand and keep balance while performing movement tasks. Balance boards can be of a single- or multiple-axis type. The amount of flat surface with which the base

contacts the floor will determine the degree of difficulty in balance. Boards can be rectangular, square, or circular. The types shown here are useful for young children.

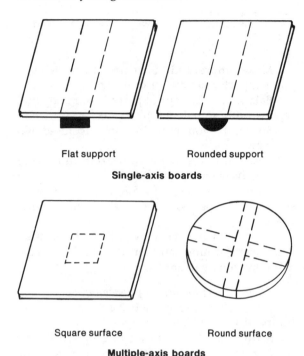

Flat support   Rounded support

Single-axis boards

Square surface   Round surface

Multiple-axis boards

INSTRUCTIONAL PROCEDURES

1. Rubber matting under a board gives it better stability and prevents floor damage.

2. The activity is of value for station teaching or choice activity. It is unlikely that there will be enough balance boards so that the entire class can participate in the activity at one time. Taking turns is also not feasible, as balance activities take time and waiting becomes exasperating.

3. A variety of balance boards should be available, including single-axis boards on which initial activities should be experienced. The width of the flat surface of the base determines the degree of difficulty in an inverse ratio; that is, the smaller the surface for the base, the greater the degree of difficulty.

4. Value comes through increasing the number and degree of difficulty of the challenges that are to be done in balance on the boards.

5. Initially, some children will direct their gaze downward. The teacher should help them learn to focus their gaze ahead.

6. Offer a sequence of activities that will assure initial success, so that the child will be comfortable in the balanced position on the board. The progression is usually from balancing on a flat surface to balancing on a rounded base, and

from using a single-axis board to using one with multiple axes.

7. Activities on the balance board are really not standardized. Much depends upon the teacher, who can vary the balanced positions with movement challenges.

8. Considerable time should be spent with younger children on simply maintaining balance. This competency is very important, since all other activities are based on it.

9. During the progressions described below, provide time for exploring and creative ideas.

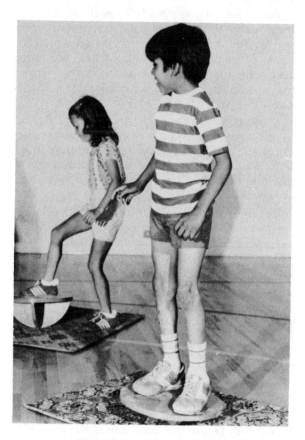

Balancing on balance boards

SEQUENCE OF ACTIVITIES

"Maintain your balance while you are standing on the board." Have children hold their hands in various positions and clap their hands in various ways. Add body awareness activities—touching both hands to designated parts of the body; touching right hand to left knee, left shoulder, left ear lobe, and other cross-combinations.

"Move your feet apart and back. Shift your balance to one foot and return to two. Balance on your toes. Your heels. On the sides of your foot."

"Maintain your balance while you go from tall to small and return. Touch your toes with your hands and return. Touch your heels and return. Touch the floor and return."

"Maintain your balance while you rock back and forth. Rock sideways. Make a quarter-turn and return. Turn all the way around on the board."

Have the children add kneeling, jumping, and hopping patterns.

"Raise one knee up as high as your thigh. Return. Repeat, standing on tiptoe. Kneel. Now, return to a standing position."

Have them work with manipulative items: balancing one or two beanbags on various parts of the body; tossing beanbags, yarn balls, and other balls to themselves; and bouncing a ball on the floor. Partners can toss beanbags or balls back and forth. Add hula hoop activity by having them turn hoops on selected body parts.

BALANCE BEAM

Balance beam activities are valuable in that they contribute to the control of balance in both static (stationary) and dynamic (moving) balance situations. The balance beam side of the balance beam–bench is ideal for this activity, with its two-inch-wide beam of approximately 12 feet in length. Balance beams come in many sizes, however, and they can be constructed from common lumber materials (see pp. 343–44). For preschool and kindergarten levels, a wider beam can be employed. The illustration on p. 343 shows a beam that can use either side of a two-by-four-inch board. Six-inch beams are sometimes used in special education programs. It is desirable to graduate to the narrower beam, however, as soon as the activities on the wider beam no longer challenge the children.

Learning good control of balance demands a considerable amount of practice and concentration. The teacher should not be discouraged by apparent slow progress. Proper practice will in time increase the child's proficiency in balance activities on the beam.

A rounded pole four to five inches in diameter provides additional challenge. The ends can be shaped to fit into the slots of the regular beam supports.

INSTRUCTIONAL PROCEDURES

1. Children should move with controlled, deliberate movements. Speedy movement is not a goal, as it tends to eliminate the need for good balance. Advise the performer to recover balance before taking another step or making another movement.

2. In keeping with the principle of control, children should move slowly on the beam, pause momentarily in good balance at the end of the movement, and dismount lightly with a small, controlled jump. Mats can be placed at the end of the beam where they are to dismount. Children must be reminded often until such control becomes established.

3. Visual fixation is important. Children should look ahead at eye level, rather than down at their feet, which is a natural inclination in early movements. This habit will prevent the child from moving smoothly in good posture, and it should be changed as soon as practical. Eye targets can be marked on the wall, and the child's gaze directed to them. Targets can be in different colors or can utilize different symbols.

4. If they lose balance, children should step off the beam, rather than teeter wildly and perhaps get off awkwardly. Allow the performer to step back on the beam and continue.

5. Success can be achieved on two levels. In early movements or in movement for young children, establish the rule that the child may step off once during a turn. Later, stipulate that he must not step off and he must pause in good balance at the end of the beam before dismounting.

6. Both laterality and directionality are important. Corresponding parts of the body (right and left sides) should be given equal attention. For example, if the child does follow-steps leading with one foot, the next time on the beam she should repeat the exercise, but lead with the other foot. Moving to the right and to the left should be given equal weight.

7. The child next in turn should begin when the performer ahead is about three-fourths of the way across the beam. The child should avoid making any abrupt movement that affects the beam, which might disturb the performer ahead.

8. In a class activity, when it is necessary to take turns, return activity should be a consideration. It increases the breadth of activity and extends the activity time, which in turn avoids unnecessary standing in line.

9. Some consideration can be given to using progressively smaller balance beams—four-inch, three-inch, and two-inch.

10. For younger children, early preliminary work for walking on the balance beam can be accomplished by using chalk lines drawn on the floor or the painted boundary lines of game courts.

11. Assistance should be requested at the discretion of the performer. When he feels the need for support, he will put out his hand to the spotter, who walks alongside the beam, ready to be of help as needed.

12. Offer much opportunity for exploratory and creative responses in each of the progressions.

13. Balance beams for young children should be positioned from about six inches to not over one foot above the floor. They should not be set at one foot until the children have acquired proficiency and confidence on lower beams.

SEQUENCE OF ACTIVITIES

For those who are ready to perform on balance beams, the following sequences will serve as a guide for activities. These are presented in terms of general movement themes. For children who are not quite ready for the activities, practice can be initiated on chalked or painted lines.

Moving across the Full Length of the Beam. In his early experiences of moving along the beam, the child can be assisted by another child who walks alongside the beam, providing a measure of help. Dispense with this assistance as soon as practical.

Types of steps—walk, follow steps, heel and toe, side (draw) steps, tiptoes, step behind, grapevine (step behind, step across).

Moving in different ways—forward, backward, sideward. Close one eye. Close both.

Different arm positions—on hips, on head, behind back, out to the sides, arms folded across the chest, forward-backward extended position, etc. Clap hands in front, behind, overhead, under the knee, and at other spots.

Balance objects (beanbags) on various parts of the body, using one or more bags.

With a partner—side by side (draw steps), facing each other, moving forward and backward, both facing the same way with partner in rear having hands on front person's shoulders, moving on parallel bars with hands joined. Try to have a "blind" person move on the beam, guided by the "seeing-eye dog."

Half-and-Half Movements. The performer moves to the center of the beam with one type of movement and continues across the second half of the beam, moving in a different way. A mark at the center of the beam may be of help. The activities specified in the previous section can be applied to this movement pattern.

Challenge Tasks at the Center. The performer moves along the beam to the center, using a selected movement, performs the movement challenge as specified, and finishes out the movement pattern on the second half of the beam. Some examples of the type of challenges that can be done at the center are:

Balances—any kind of static balance, such as the Stork Balance (p. 191), lifted leg, forward or backward lean; hold for five counts

Other challenges—full turn, touch the knee, touch the heel forward, pick up a beanbag at the center or from the floor, touch the nose to the knee

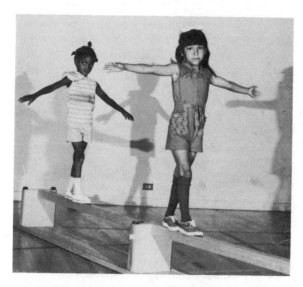

Balancing beanbags on different body parts

Using Wands and Hoops. Carry a wand or hoop. Step over the wand or through the hoop in various ways.

Step over or go under a wand (hoop) held by partner.

Use the hula hoop, twirling it on the arms or around the body while moving across the beam.

Moving through a hoop while walking the balance beam

Manipulative Activities to Self. Using a beanbag, toss it to self in various fashions—around the body, under the legs, etc.

Using a ball, toss to self. Circle the ball around the body, under the legs.

Bounce a ball on the floor and on the beam. Dribble it on the floor.

Roll a ball along the beam.

Jumping Patterns. Jumping sequences can be devised for going back and forth over the beam. Crouch jumps down the length of the beam offer more variety.

BENCHES

In addition to the balance beam activities, other valuable movement experiences are possible when the balance beam–bench is used with the bench side upward. Bench activities for preschool children should be chosen with care, but kindergarten and primary children can meet the challenges of most of the activities presented. A diagram for a bench that can be constructed is found on p. 344.

INSTRUCTIONAL PROCEDURES

1. All bench activities should be considered as having two parts in sequence, the activity on the bench and the dismount. Near the end of the bench activity, the youngster should be thinking about how he will dismount. Attention is usually focused on the body in flight and on appropriate body reaction when the body contacts the floor. The flight should be a relaxed, smooth movement, and meeting the floor should employ flexed foot and leg action. To reinforce these goals, the child can be instructed to go down far enough so that the fingers contact the floor.

2. Mats should be placed at the end of the benches to facilitate the dismount and allow for various rolls and stunts after the dismount.

3. Benches may be positioned horizontally, inclined, or in combination with other equipment for variation and greater challenge.

4. Four or five children should be the maximum number assigned to one bench.

5. The child next in turn begins when the performer ahead has reached about three-quarters of the way along the bench.

6. Return activities for the child to perform while returning to her place in line add to the activity potential.

7. Speed is *not* a goal in bench activities. Movements should be done deliberately and carefully, with attention given to good body control and management.

8. Attention should be given to use of corresponding parts of the body and to directional

movements. For example, if a child hops on the right foot, the next effort should be made on the left foot. In jump turns, both right and left movements should be utilized. A child naturally uses the stronger or preferred part of his body. The other side must be exercised as well.

SEQUENCE OF ACTIVITIES

Generally, children like to pull themselves along the top of the bench. A session of bench activities should include a good deal of this type of activity.

Pulls. Pull the body along the top of the bench in prone, supine, and side positions. Different leg positions can be specified. Also include movements with the feet forward.

Pulling the body along the top of the bench

Locomotor Movements. Walk, skip, slide, and hop along the top of the bench. Add various stunt walks such as the Rabbit Jump (p. 187), the Lame Dog Walk (p. 187), and others.

Seat Walk or Scooter Movements. Children try to move on the bench using a Seat Walk or Scooter Movements.

Seat Walk. With the feet forward, the weight on the heels, and the knees slightly bent, the child proceeds forward by "walking" on the buttocks. The legs are to be used only for balance and control.

Scooter Movements. From the same position as in the Seat Walk, the child moves the seat toward the heels, using heel pressure and lifting the seat slightly. He extends the legs again and repeats the Scooter Movements.

Pushes. A distinction must be made between pulling and pushing. Push the body along the bench top in prone, supine, or side positions with either the head or the feet leading.

Crouch Jumps. Primary children are generally able to accomplish these movements. Stand on either side of the bench, bend over and place both hands on the bench, gripping the sides. Take the weight on the hands and jump the feet to the other side of the bench by propelling the seat upward toward the ceiling. Each time a crouch jump is made, the hands are shifted slightly forward along the bench for the next jump, so that the performer makes progress toward the end of the bench.

Crouch-jumping over the bench

Passing on the Bench. Two children stand on the bench, one on each end. They explore the different ways that one can exchange places by passing each other on the bench without touching the floor.

Employing Manipulative Items. Wands and hoops can be used as obstacles to go over, under, or through. Beanbags can be balanced on various body parts. Beanbag or ball tossing to self while moving on the top of the bench challenges hand-eye coordination. A challenge of some difficulty is to pass a beanbag under the top of the bench while moving along the bench.

Dismounts. Dismounts give a definite finishing touch to the bench activities. The child performing an activity in a lying-down position can either rise to his feet at the end of the bench and dismount, or he can roll off the end in some fashion onto the mat.

Dismounts in a standing position generally involve jumping, which can be coupled with body turns in the air. The jump can be followed with a roll of some kind. Much latitude should be allowed the children in performing the dismount.

BOUNDING BOARDS

Bounding boards provide a unique type of movement similar to that of a trampoline. Such a board can be constructed easily from a piece of three-quarter-inch plywood, size two feet by six feet. The board is supported on pieces of four-by-four-inch lumber, which are padded with carpet to protect the floor. The plywood must be a quality product with few knots. Marine plywood, though expensive, is best (see p. 344).

INSTRUCTIONAL PROCEDURES

1. Two children can work on one board, with the performer moving forward to leave the board and return to place. Bounding should be done mainly in the center of the board. Emphasis should be on lightness, height, and relaxation during the bounding.

2. A chair back placed alongside the bounding board can serve as a support device for the performers, particularly those with low ability.

SEQUENCE OF ACTIVITIES

Bound in the center; both feet, one foot.

Bound in the center, using turns and different arm positions. Add hand-clapping.

Move across the board, using jumping and hopping. Return. Add turns and hand-clapping. Move sideward from edge to edge.

Bound with numbered foot combinations, alternating two, three, or four hops on one foot and then changing to the other. These are called twoseys, threeseys, and fourseys.

To the previous skills, add forward and backward leg extensions and leg changes sideward.

Bouncing on bounding boards

Use different numbers of hops when alternating; e.g., hopping once on the right foot,

twice on the left. Use other combinations—two-three, two-four, etc.

Selected skilled children may be able to jump rope or jump a hula hoop while on the board.

Exiting from the board is generally done forward, but can be to the side or backwards.

GYM SCOOTERS

If properly used, gym scooters make excellent devices for physical development for children. Since children love to ride on them, however, the activity will soon turn into free play unless some guidance is given. (Free play can, of course, be a legitimate goal at times.)

Scooters can be constructed (see p. 346). Use care in choosing the type of wheels, however, so that marking of the floor does not become a problem. If each scooter has a small hole in the center to fit over a carrier, the storage problem will be minimized.

Scooters have a wide range of utility. They can be used in creative and exploratory work, selected games and relays, and progressions, either individually or with partners.

A few special scooters designed for children with limb problems should be available. A ten-by-thirty-inch scooter is adequate to hold a handicapped child at full length. Some other child may have to provide the propulsion.

INSTRUCTIONAL PROCEDURES

1. Two safety rules are important in working with scooters. First, the children are not to stand on them as they would on skateboards. With the present popularity of skateboards, this rule is a necessary measure. The second rule is that scooters, with or without passengers, are not to be used as missiles.

2. Educational movement methodology is applicable to scooter work, but care should be taken to see that the session is a developmental period and not just fun.

3. Scooters may be used individually or with partners. This means that part of the time there should be one scooter for each child or at other times one for each two children.

4. In partner activity, one child is wholly or partially supported by the scooter, and the other child supplies the propulsion. Rotate positions frequently.

5. Individual work can provide good physical developmental values if the child will use diversity of propulsion means with the hands, placing demands on the arm-shoulder girdle.

6. Children should be cautioned to watch for possible contacts with other scooters to avoid bumping fingers as they grip the sides of the scooters.

SEQUENCE OF ACTIVITIES

The approach to activity with scooters should be flexible and allow for much latitude in student responses. Teacher direction should center on developing a variety of ways in which the scooter can be used. Controlled movements are the goal instead of unrestrained and inconsiderate travel. The following guides for movement will help bring out breadth in the movements.

Individual Movement Challenges (General). "What ways can you move on your scooter without standing on it?"

"Show how you can move forward in place. Backward. To the side. Turn around in place. Move yourself with the scooter in a triangle pattern without bumping into anyone. A square. A circle."

"What different ways can you position your body on the scooter and move? How can you move using hands alone? Your feet alone? Hands and feet together?"

Moving in different ways on the scooter

"Show me different ways to move with one particular part of your body in contact with the scooter—one hand, two hands, one knee, both knees, one heel, both heels." Note that all movements should involve one or both hands in contact with the scooter or the floor. This prevents the children from standing up on the scooters.

Individual Movement Challenges (Limitation). "Lie on your tummy on your scooter and move around. Now put your feet in the air and use your hands. Now, keep your hands out wide and use your feet to move yourself." Repeat the sequence with children lying on their backs. Have them spin in a circle.

"Sit on your scooter with your feet forward and push yourself with your hands. Try it as you sit cross-legged. Try to spin right. Left."

"Kneel on one knee and push yourself with your hands. Now, try kneeling on both knees. Keeping your toes on the scooter, walk your

hands in a big circle." Repeat with the heels on the scooter, body facing the ceiling.

Numbers and form concepts can be used in pattern travel. Scatter tiles or numbered markers around the room and challenge the children with sequence movements. A different type of movement may be specified as the child reaches each number in turn.

"Keep a balloon in the air as you move. Keep control of both the balloon and the scooter. Play balloon ball with your partner." A beach ball can also be used.

Keeping the scooter and beach ball under control

Partner Movement Challenges (General). "What ways can you move your partner without having your partner lose his position on the scooter?"

"Show how you can move your partner in a triangle pathway. A square. A circle. A figure eight."

Explore the different positions the partner on the scooter can take for movement.

Explore different ways one can pull the scooter with a rope.

Partner Movement Challenges (Limitation). "Push your partner while you hold his feet. His hands. One hand. One foot. One hand and one foot." Try the sequence with pulling.

Have children push and/or pull a partner who is on his stomach, on his back, seated, balanced on his seat, seated cross-legged style, kneeling, and in other positions.

"Can you move your partner like a wheelbarrow?"

Each partner has a scooter, and they cooperate to move in different positions—face to face holding wrists, back to back with elbows locked, and side to side with arms around each other's shoulders.

Explore different ways that a partner with two scooters can be propelled by the other.

Group Activity for Three to Five Children. One or more children are the engines (pullers), and others form a train of cars. Move the train with care around the room and drop off the cars at different stations.

Play follow-the-leader with two or three children.

INDIVIDUAL MATS

The use of individual mats, which originated in Great Britain, provides the basis for many exploratory and creative movements. Mats can vary in size, but the 20-by-40-inch or 24-by-48-inch sizes seem to be the most popular. In thickness, the three-quarter-inch type is standard, but this can also vary. The mat should have a rubber backing, which will prevent the mat from slipping on the floor. Foam-backed indoor-outdoor carpeting of good quality makes an excellent mat.

Mats are used to do things on and as obstacles to go over, across, or around. A mat can also act as a home base to which the child returns on signal. They are especially valuable in that they can act as a basis for early individual instruction in gymnastic activities.

INSTRUCTIONAL PROCEDURES

1. Educational movement techniques are most important in mat work, so that a wide variety of movement responses may be elicited.
2. Emphasize body management and fundamental skills of locomotor and nonlocomotor movement.
3. Mats should be far enough apart to allow for free movement around them without contact.
4. Each child should have a mat.
5. Children should learn to sit cross-legged on mats while awaiting directions.

SEQUENCE OF ACTIVITIES

Rigid adherence to the sequence presented below is not necessary, since the activities are quite flexible and demand mostly body management skills.

Task Movements. In these activities, the child changes movements on command. Commands used are:

"Stretch"—Stretch your body out in all directions, making it as wide as possible

"Curl"—Curl into a tight little ball

"Balance"—Take some kind of balance position

"Bridge"—Make a bridge over the mat

"Reach"—Keeping one toe on the mat, reach out as far as possible along the floor in a chosen direction

"Rock"—Rock on any part of the body

"Roll"—Do some kind of roll on the mat

"Twist"—Make a shape by twisting a part of the body

Stretching and curling on individual mats

"Relax"—Melt down to the mat and remain loose

"Shake"—In either a standing or a sitting position, shake all over, using gross motor movements

"Fall"—Fall to the mat, breaking the fall with the hands and arms

"Hot dog"—In a sitting position, pick up the short sides of the mat with the hands and raise the feet from the floor

"Ostrich"—Put the head on the mat and lift the arms wide so that the body is supported by the head and feet

To develop individual choice, use the command "Change," at which the child makes another kind of movement or shape. Balance can be developed by changing for balance on different parts of the body or a different number of parts—one, two, three, four, or five.

Balance activities on individual mats

Movements on and off the Mat. The children perform different locomotor movements on and off the mat in different directions. Turns and shapes can be added. Levels are another good challenge. Have them take the weight on the hands while going across the mat.

Movements over the Mat. The child goes completely over the mat each time.

Movements around the Mat. Locomotor movements around the mat are done both clockwise and counterclockwise. Have them do movements around the mat while keeping the hands on the mat or keeping the feet on the mat.

Using Mats as a Base. "Stretch and reach in different directions to show how big your space is." Have them do combination movements away from and back to the mat; e.g., two jumps and two hops, or six steps and two jumps.

Balloon Activity. Each child has a balloon. Challenge the child to keep the balloon in the air while his seat is in contact with the mat. Have him try this, keeping one foot in contact with the mat.

Mat Games or Fun Activity. Each child is seated on her mat. On signal, each child arises and jumps over as many different mats as she can. On the next signal, each child takes a seat on the nearest mat. The last child to get seated can be designated or pay a penalty. The game can also be played by eliminating one or two mats each time, leaving one or two children without a home base. To control roughness, make a rule that the first child to touch a mat gets to sit on it.

Another way to play is to base the activity on a magic number. If the magic number were ten, each child would jump over ten different mats and return to his home mat. As another variation, each child jumps over the first mat, touches the second, and so on until he reaches the magic number.

Using the same format of activity, several other related approaches can be implemented. Each child has a beanbag, which is placed on the edge of his mat. On signal, all children move as specified (walk, run, skip, hop, etc.) around the mats in different directions. On the next signal, each takes the nearest beanbag between her feet and jumps with it to home base, where she sits down. If the child is barefoot, he can pick up the beanbag with the toes of one foot while he hops on the other foot back to home base. After he sits down, he can put the beanbag on top of his head.

Another activity is based on ball skills. A ball is on each mat. On signal, children move over and around the various mats. On the second signal, each child picks up a ball and dribbles around the area. On the third signal, each child dribbles to home base and sits down with the ball in his lap.

Cardiovascular Introductory Activity. Each child on his mat reacts to the following directives:

Routine 1	*Routine 2*
"Run in place."	"Run in place."
"On your tummy."	"On your front, over to your back."
"Up and running."	"Up and running."
"On your back."	"Hands and knees, over to your back."
"Up and running."	"Up and running."
"On your side."	"Hands [front leaning rest], back, hands and knees."
"Up and running."	"Up and running."
"Hands and knees."	"Stomach, over on back, hands [front leaning rest]."
"Up and running."	"Up and running."
(Etc.)	(Etc.)

JUMPING BOXES

Jumping boxes will provide opportunities for children to carry out the natural activities of running, jumping, and propelling the body through the air. Boxes should be made in sets of two. They are usually square in shape, the larger one measuring about 18 by 18 inches (24 inches high), and the smaller box measuring about 16 by 16 inches (12 inches high), so that it will fit inside the larger box for storage. Tops should be padded and covered with durable leather or plastic cloth. A rubber floor pad can be placed under the box to offer good floor protection. Commercially constructed boxes have sloped sides for better stability.

INSTRUCTIONAL PROCEDURES

1. Attention should be given to "meeting the ground" in proper form, stressing lightness, bent-knee action, balance, and body control. Touching the floor with the fingertips, at times, will emphasize the bent-knee action.

2. When the 24-inch-high box is being used, mats should be placed to cushion the landing.

3. The exploratory and creative approach is important, since there are few "standard" stunts in jumping box activities.

4. A group of not more than four or five children should be assigned to each series of boxes.

5. Additional challenge can be incorporated into the activity by the use of hoops, wands, balls, etc. In addition, rolling stunts after the dismount extend the possibilities of movement.

6. Return activities work well with boxes.

7. Children should strive for height and learn to relax as they go through space.

8. The suggested activities that follow can be augmented with a little imagination. Let the children help expand the breadth of the activity.

SEQUENCE OF ACTIVITIES

Mounting the Box. Use combinations of the following locomotor movements to get on the box: step, jump, leap, or hop.

To develop balance control, step onto the box with one foot and take the full weight on the foot, holding the balance for three to five seconds.

Dismounting. The following dismounts can be used to develop body control:

Step, hop, jump, leap, or slide off the box to any side—forward, to the sides, back

Jump off with a quarter-, half-, or full turn

Jump off with different body shapes (stretch, curl up into a ball, jackknife, etc.)

Jump off and land at different levels

Jump over, under, or through various objects

Jump off and then perform a forward or backward roll

In any of these dismounts, substitute a hop or a leap for the jump.

Various Approaches to the Boxes. The approach to the box can be varied by performing combinations of movements, such as run, gallop, skip, hop, or animal walks (Bear Walk, Rabbit Jump, etc.).

Addition of Equipment. Use various pieces of equipment to enhance the box activities. Some suggestions follow.

Beanbags. Toss and catch while dismounting, or try to keep them on the head while mounting or dismounting from the box.

Hoops. Jump through a stationary hoop (held by a partner) while dismounting, or use the hoop as a jump rope and see how many times it is possible to jump it while dismounting.

Wands. Jump over or move under a wand.

Box Combinations. Boxes can be arranged in a straight line or other patterns. The child experiments with a different movement over each box as though running an obstacle course.

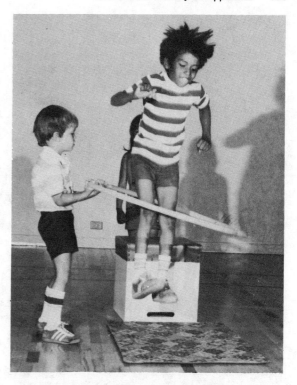

Dismounting through a hoop

MAGIC ROPES

Magic ropes originated in Germany. They resemble long rubber bands. Such ropes can be made by knitting wide rubber bands together, or they can be constructed from ordinary three-quarter-inch white elastic tape, available in most clothing stores. Loops on each end enable the child to thrust a hand through and grasp the rope. Ropes should be long enough to stretch to between 20 and 30 feet in length.

A major advantage of the magic rope is its flexibility; children have little fear of hitting it or tripping over it while they are performing. Ropes should be stretched tightly enough so that there is little sag.

INSTRUCTIONAL PROCEDURES

1. Two or more children must be rope holders while the others are jumping. Develop some type of rotation plan to allow all the children to participate. An alternate plan is to have one or both ends of the rope attached to something stable, thus eliminating one or both of the holders.

2. Many variations can be achieved with the magic ropes by varying their height and by raising and lowering opposite ends of the rope.

3. Since jumping activities are strenuous, alternate between jumping activities and activities that involve crawling under the ropes, etc.

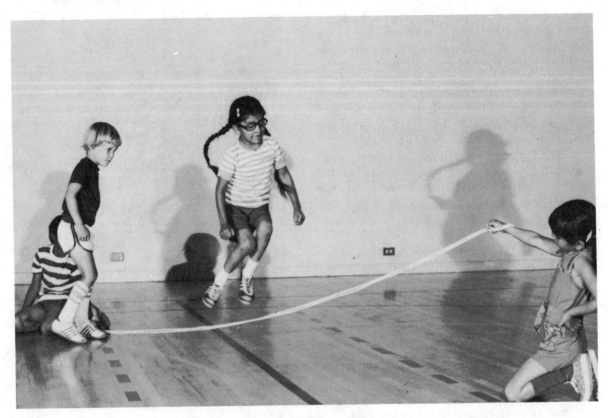

Jumping over a magic rope

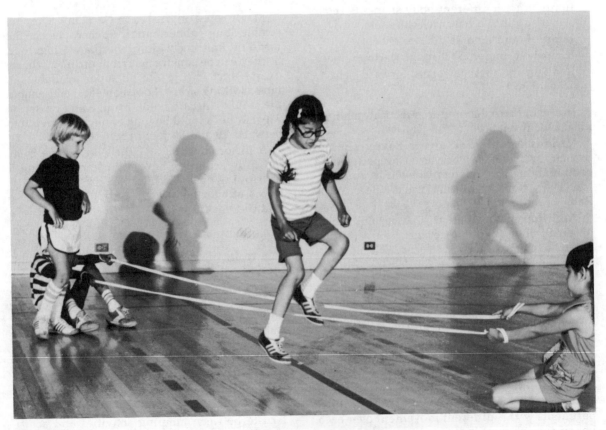

Following the leader through two magic ropes

4. Emphasize to the class that they should avoid touching the rope. The magic ropes can help develop the child's perception of the body in space if he regards the rope as an obstacle to be avoided.

5. To make better use of the rope, have children approach it at an angle, starting at one end of the rope and performing a sequence of jumping and hopping activities back and forth over the rope, finally reaching the other end. The straight-on approach allows the child to jump the rope only once.

6. At least eight ropes will be needed for a class.

7. The child next in turn should begin his movements when the child ahead is almost to the end of the rope.

8. Ropes can be used singly or in combinations of two or more. Begin activities with the single rope.

9. Try to develop a rhythmic response in the movement patterns, particularly in successive jumping or hopping patterns.

10. When working with young children, keep jumping heights low, gradually raising the height of the rope as their skill develops.

SEQUENCE OF ACTIVITIES

Single-Rope Activities. Begin with the rope parallel to the floor at a six-inch height. Children should begin at one end and progress down the line of the rope, performing the movement patterns.

Step over the rope and back, using a crossover step

Jump and/or hop over the rope

While jumping, add body turns

Go over and under the rope alternately

Crouch jump down the line of the rope

Try a straddle jump, alternating with the cross-legged jump

Repeat all movements with the rope slanted from six inches off the floor at the beginning end to 12 inches or more at the far end.

Raise the rope as the children's ability permits.

Double-Rope Activities. Vary the height and spread of the ropes. Begin at six inches for height.

Ropes parallel to each other

Jump or hop from one side into the center and out the other side

Crouch jump inside and out, from one side to the other

Work in straddle jump patterns, both straight and cross-legged

Go in over one rope and out under the other

Vary the height of the ropes so that one rope is higher than the other; if one is six inches high, the other can be twelve inches high.

Ropes crossed at right angles to each other

Perform various movements to get from one area to the other

Move in one direction the first time (clockwise or counterclockwise) and in the other direction the next time

Jump into one area and go underneath the next rope into the next area

MISCELLANEOUS PATTERNS

Use four or more ropes to create various floor patterns.

Use follow-the-leader activity to add variety.

Use two ropes. Have them close together at one end and far apart at the other, making a rough "V."

LADDERS

A ladder placed on the floor or on mats can provide good challenge for movement activities. Only two or three children at a time should work on this piece of equipment; otherwise, too much time is lost waiting for turns. Unless there are enough ladders, relegate this activity to station teaching or choice activity.

INSTRUCTIONAL PROCEDURES

1. The ladder should be placed in such a way as to minimize slippage and instability.

2. The ladder should have circular rungs of at least one inch in diameter, plus adequate side plates. The rungs may be rectangular.

3. Generally, movement should be down the length of the ladder. Return activity can use the areas alongside the ladder.

4. While exploration and creativity are of merit, the greatest value of ladder work probably comes from the child's ability to meet specific challenges.

5. Movement patterns should be rhythmic, deliberate, and accurate with respect to the challenges provided.

SEQUENCE OF ACTIVITIES

There is no established sequence of activities for ladder work. The teacher should use her own judgment when setting the range of activities from the simple to the more complex. The following movement patterns should be considered.

Walk, run lightly, jump, or hop down the center spaces without touching the ladder. Travel down the ladder with the body facing forward, backward, and sideward. Move at different levels.

Using straddle jumps, work out various patterns without touching the ladder. Use jumping and hopping patterns from the sides to the center and out again.

Walk on the rungs, the sides, both the rungs and the sides. Balance objects, such as beanbags, while moving.

Walk on all fours with the hands on the rungs and the feet on the sides or on the rungs. Walk with the hands on the sides of the ladder and the feet on the sides of the rungs. Walk facing backward or sideward on all fours. Explore other ways.

STILTS

Tin can stilts are generally considered in planning movement activities for young children. While it can be logically assumed that work with tin can stilts leads up to work with wooden stilts, to our knowledge, no one has offered research validation for this contention.

To make tin can stilts, choose cans with both ends intact and attach small ropes to the sides of the cans. The ropes should be long enough to reach the child's hands when he is standing upright. Using plastic can covers on the bottoms of the cans will help prevent floor damage.

INSTRUCTIONAL PROCEDURES

1. Children should walk as upright as possible and should look ahead, not down at the cans.
2. They should walk on hard surfaces (concrete or blacktop).
3. Have them work toward moving in short, even steps.

SEQUENCE OF ACTIVITIES

Mount on the cans, balance with the ropes held taut, and hold position.

Walk forward, backward, sideward on the cans. Turn around right and left.

Walk in patterns—circle, triangle, square, etc.

Step over a small obstacle, such as a board.

Walk down a line.

Walk up and down a stair platform.

OLD TIRES AS APPARATUS SUPPLEMENTS

Tires can be used as apparatus on which children can react to various movement challenges. They can be placed in different floor patterns to provide challenges for locomotor activities. In this way, they serve a similar purpose as hoops (see p. 174). They can also be imbedded in the ground or arranged in various fashions to serve as playground apparatus. This use of tires is discussed in Chapter 22. Tires also have value in manipulative activities (see pp. 175–76).

For young children, bicycle tires are more easily handled, but they limit the extent of movements that can be accomplished on or over floor patterns.

INSTRUCTIONAL PROCEDURES

1. Tires to be used indoors should be cleaned. Discard any tires that are so corroded that the hands become black when handling them.
2. For young children, the smaller sizes seem more appropriate, as they are more easily handled.
3. Tires laid flat on the floor need no support. If tires are to stand so that children can go through them, wooden stands should be constructed (see pp. 351–52).
4. Most, if not all, the activities are based on play elements, since children love to handle tires. Tires also have a quality of "give," which is intriguing to youngsters.
5. To keep rainwater out of tires used outside, bore at least four holes through the casings for drainage.
6. Tires may be used individually or in pattern groups.
7. With tires in pattern groups, return activity movements can be added.

SINGLE-TIRE ACTIVITIES

"Jump inside the tire and sink down slowly as far as you can. Rise as high as you can. Jump out. Run around your tire either way. Run backwards."

"Jump into the tire and jump out—forward, backward or to the side. Jump in and turn around. Can you make up a continuous jumping pattern?"

"Can you walk around the edge of the tire forward? Backward? Sideways?" Be sure to have them move both clockwise and counterclockwise.

"Stand in the tire and jump upward a number of times. Alternate light, high jumps with heavy, low jumps. Jump a number of times (you choose) and then jump out. Can you jump to the sides of the tire and back into the center?"

"Get down on all fours on the tire and make complete turns to the right and then to the left, without touching the floor. Try this with your body facing the ceiling."

"With one foot inside and one foot outside, can you straddle jump all around the tire without touching it? Try it the other way."

"Raise the tire to one edge and go through it before it falls to the floor."

"Stand astride the tire and see if you can make progress turning with small jumps. Can you make a quarter-turn? A half-turn? A full turn? Try it both to the right and to the left."

"Can you run through the tire with a step in the center?"

See how many of the previous challenges can be done with hopping patterns.

"Run, step on the tire with your leading foot, and jump over it."

While the body is supported by the hands and stretched out away from the tire, the child places the top of the insteps on the tire. This is like the push-up position. With cooperative movement of the hands and feet, keeping the body stretched out, he should move so that the hands make a big circle around the tire. Have him try this supported by the heels in crab position.

With a tire on a stand, explore the different ways a child can go through or over the tire.

MULTIPLE-TIRE ACTIVITIES

Place tires in some kind of pattern.

Some experimentation will be necessary with young children to determine how much they can do. Have them walk on the tire sides, run through the tires, jump in and out as they can, and perform similar movements. A tire placed in a stand situated at the end of the line of tires adds an obstacle through which the child must go. Be sure to specify some kind of return activity challenge in which the child can take part as he comes back to the beginning of the line of tires.

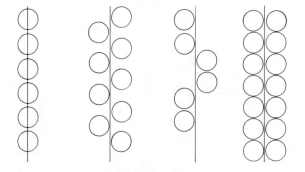

MISCELLANEOUS EQUIPMENT

The different pieces of apparatus previously discussed can and should be supplemented with other articles of choice. Some of these are commercially available, and others can be constructed at the school.

Drums or Barrels. Drums or barrels can be used as things to climb into and out of, or they can form tunnels to crawl through.

Tables and Chairs. Tables and similar platforms provide objects to climb onto and jump from. One side can have steps added to provide easier access. Sturdy chairs (not the folding type) with the backs cut off also serve for many movement challenges.

Paper Boxes. Large, sturdy paper boxes have good utility in play. Differently shaped holes can be cut in them, allowing the children to move through the holes, an activity that teaches form recognition. Cardboard sleds can be made so that one child can pull another around the playroom.

Rug Squares. Rug samples, which are available in squares or rectangles, are interesting play articles for children. Some of the movements explained in the section on individual mats may be performed on rug squares (see p. 153).

Mini-Climbing Sets. Sets made of planks and horses are readily constructed at school. The horses should have parallel slats to offer a variety of heights for the connecting planks or poles.

Riding Toys. A variety of kiddie cars, tricycles, and similar articles should be on hand to stimulate muscle effort and provide play outlets, especially for the preschool and kindergarten group. A number of bouncy, inflated riding toys are also on the market and are useful in movement programs.

Stepping and Jumping Patterns. A number of commercial sources offer floor cloths or mats on which are painted stepping, hopping, or jumping patterns. These are available in a wide variety and can be school constructed.

SUMMARY

Apparatus activities are an important part of the total program because they encourage large-muscle effort. Climbing ropes, horizontal ladders, exercise bars, and balance beams also require that the child conquer various fears in order to perform efficiently. When teaching activities requiring apparatus, it is important that the teacher organize the lesson so that activities are taught in proper progression and a safe atmosphere is maintained.

Classes can be organized and taught under three different formats. The single-activity format is the most structured and has the class performing the same activities at the same time. This progression is useful when introducing students to activities in which they have little previous experience. The multiple-station format establishes stations for activity organized around different pieces of apparatus. This format allows for more creativity and self-direction. Students move from station to station practicing activities they have experienced previously. The challenge circuit consists of equipment arranged in multiple or single paths. Youngsters are challenged to perform various tasks on various types of equipment and apparatus.

If the maximum amount of activity is to be gained from apparatus lessons, it is important to utilize return activities. During the trip back in line, the student is asked to perform a task that is usually unrelated to the instructional emphasis. Return activities should require little teacher supervision and should be activities that students have learned previously.

All apparatus activities listed in this chapter are prefaced with instructional procedures that offer teaching hints and procedures to aid in effective instruction. The activities are listed in progression to better facilitate the "start and expand" approach to instruction.

Chapter 13

Manipulative Activities to Develop Fundamental Skills

The good society is not one that ignores individual differences, but one that deals with them wisely and humanely.
John Gardner

Manipulative activities form a most important group of skills within the general area of movement competency for youngsters. It is important that they achieve some competence in these skills so that they may enjoy their own play and also meet success in play with their peers.

Early competency in handling objects provides a basis for the more specialized skills. Children with poor basic throwing and catching skills pose a problem for instructors in later grades.

Manipulative activities can strengthen both hand-eye and foot-eye coordination, as well as develop dexterity in handling a variety of play objects. Although much of the emphasis in this section will be on handling an object with the hands, the discussion will also include the feet and other parts of the body.

Because they are fundamental skills, manipulative activities invite pertinent application of educational movement methodology. In addition, the basic principles of skill performance have strong application in this area, particularly in throwing and catching skills.

Each unit of instruction begins by working with the children individually and then moves to partner or group activities. This necessitates that one manipulative item be on hand for each child. In partner participation, there should be one object for every two children. Be sure that the children have acquired enough skill competence individually so that partner activity will be productive.

In selecting a sequence of activities for a lesson, the teacher may take a suggested activity and develop it thoroughly with the children, or he may select activities from several themes. It is vital to the activities that the teacher employ perceptive teaching, carefully analyzing the resulting movement patterns so that he or she may guide the children toward acquisition of a degree of skill commensurate with their maturity level.

Good teaching technique also centers on *both* quantity and quality of movement. In the development of skills, children should be made aware of acceptable and unacceptable points of skill technique. This should not be an overriding condition, however. The teacher builds on approximations until some measure of success is reached, and then refinement can be sought from this base.

Beanbags, yarn balls, fleece balls, and paper balls should be used in teaching the first throwing and catching skills. Children are afraid of catching a ball that is too hard or has a quick rebound, and the softer balls eliminate this fear. After these introductory skills have been mastered, other types of balls are added, and more demanding skills are taught. The start-and-expand approach is a sound one for manipulative activities. Start the children at a low level of challenge so that all can achieve success, and expand the skills and experiences from this foundation.

BALLOON ACTIVITIES

Manipulative activities using balloons serve as fine introductory experiences for preschool children. In addition, balloons are excellent objects for handicapped children to handle.

A balloon can be closed with a rubber band or with one of the plastic-covered wire ties used for tieing garbage bags. Tieing a knot in the throat of the balloon can give permanence to the closure, but makes it very difficult to deflate the balloon. Blowing up round balloons a little less than full helps prevent them from breaking. As a variation, a BB shot or small washer can be placed inside the balloon to make it move faster and in a less predictable path.

The following challenges have been found to be successful in guiding this activity.

ACTIVITIES

"Keep the balloon up as long as you can. Work toward keeping it in your personal space. If the balloon goes to one side, where do you have to strike it to get it to return?"

Have children alternate hands while keeping the balloon airborne. Work out different number combinations with the right and left hands.

"See how long you can keep the balloon in the air without moving your feet. Touch the balloon at as high a level as you can. Let the balloon drop to a low level before you bat it."

"Try keeping the balloon up by touching it with just your fingers. Can you keep it up with one finger?"

Have the children contact the balloon with different parts of the body. Select a sequence of three or more body parts and have them see how many times they can complete that sequence before the balloon hits the floor. From the crab position, have them keep the balloon up by contacting it with only the feet. Have them tap the balloons in the air with the body part(s) named by the teacher. Have them call out the body part(s) with which they are hitting the balloons.

BEANBAG ACTIVITIES

Beanbags have been used in school programs for many years. Only recently, however, have these items been employed to stimulate movement experiences. The recent proliferation of activities using beanbags has been truly amazing.

Beanbag activities, which provide a good introduction to throwing and catching skills for children, should precede instruction with inflated balls. Because of their loose, flexible nature, the teacher need not be concerned that any possible rebound will interfere with immature catching skills. The physical character of the beanbag allows it to be handled by the small hands and bare feet of young children. In addition, it adapts itself to being balanced on different parts of the body. Since it will not roll when dropped, it can serve as a place marker; if mishandled, it can be recovered easily.

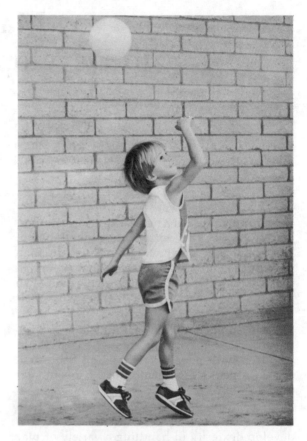

Keeping a balloon in the air

INSTRUCTIONAL PROCEDURES

1. Smaller beanbags (the four- or five-inch size) are suitable for preschool and kindergarten children. Primary children can use a slightly larger beanbag, five or six inches in width. The larger beanbag balances better and can be controlled more easily on various parts of the body, offering a greater measure of success for primary children.

2. Throwing and catching skills involve many intricate elements. Emphasize the skill performance principles of opposition, eye focus, weight transfer, and follow-through. It is important that children keep an eye on the object being caught and on the target when throwing.

3. Stress laterality and directionality, and work at different levels.

4. Give some attention to targets when throwing. The child should throw to a partner at about chest height, unless a different type of throw is specified. Teach all types of returns—low, medium, high, left, and right.

5. In early practice, stress a soft receipt of the beanbag when catching by "giving" with the hands, arms, and legs. Softness is created by holding the hands out toward the incoming beanbag and bringing it in for a soft landing.

6. In partner work, keep distances between partners short, especially in introductory phases. Six to eight feet or so seems to be a reasonable distance between partners for young children, and this can be increased about 50 percent for primary children.

7. Partners should take pride in skillful throwing, catching, and handling of the beanbag. Hard and difficult throwing, the purpose of which is to cause the partner to miss, should be discouraged.

RECOMMENDED ACTIVITIES WITH BEANBAGS

Activities are generally classified into individual and partner activities, while a few activities are appropriate for small groups. In addition, games using targets can round out the suggested activities.

INDIVIDUAL ACTIVITIES

In Place, Tossing to Self. "Toss and catch the beanbag with both hands. Right hand. Left hand. Catch it with the backs of your hands."

Have the children work out combinations—toss from side to side, right to left and reverse, front overhead to a catch behind the back, from the back to a catch in front, around different parts of the body. "Put the beanbag on top of your head and catch it as it drops forward. Catch it behind your back."

"Hold the beanbag over your shoulder with one hand, drop it down your back, and catch it with the other hand. Balance on one foot, drop the bag, and try to pick it up while balanced, without moving your foot."

Catching and tossing at different levels are important. Repeat activities as suitable while kneeling (one or both knees), seated, or lying on the floor.

"Catch as high and as low as you can."

In Place, with Challenge Movements. In these activities, many of the preceding movements are repeated, but a specified challenge movement is added between the toss and the catch. The following movement challenges add much interest to simple skills.

Half-turn. Toss bag overhead to the rear, turn around, and catch it.

Full turn.

Hand claps. In different positions, around the body, double claps.

Tossing and catching beanbags

Change position. Catch on one knee, squat-seated, balanced on one foot. Catch with feet off the floor.

Slap or touch body parts. With one hand or both, touch parts as named.

Others. Touch the floor. Do a heel click.

Adding Locomotor Movements. Locomotor movements are added. "Toss the bag forward, run, and catch it. Move to the side and catch it." Vary with different types of locomotor movements. Add ideas from the first two sections.

Balancing Beanbags on Body Parts. Begin with one bag and add another later. "Balance the bag on your head [shoulder, thigh, elbow, knee]. Sit down [turn around, walk up and down steps, over obstacles] while keeping control of the balanced bags. In crab position, keep the beanbag balanced on your stomach. Try shaking it off." With two bags, have the children balance on corresponding and/or different body parts.

Propelling and Handling Beanbags with Various Body Parts. Have them use various parts of the body to hold the bag and toss it to self—elbow, instep, between feet, between heels (hoist), knees, shoulders.

From a seated position, have them propel the bag with both feet so that it can be caught, then try this in a supine position. In a supine position, they pick up the beanbag between the toes, deposit it behind the head, using a leg lift and a full curl, and return to position. They go back the same way and pick up the bag with the toes.

Balancing beanbags on various body parts

"Try picking up the beanbag with your elbow. Carry it under your chin. Release and catch it."

Using Beanbags as Obstacles. Place the beanbag on the floor. Have children explore jumping and hopping patterns over the bag and make different kinds of bridges over the beanbag. Allow children to work out sequences.

Handling beanbags with various parts of the body

Manipulating with Bare Feet. "Pick up the bag by curling your toes. [This has value in strengthening the muscles that support the arch.] Pick up the beanbag with one foot and hop to an other spot. Turn around. Toss it to yourself with the right foot. The left. Toss it into the hoop."

PARTNER ACTIVITIES

Partner activity should not be undertaken until the children have demonstrated readiness with tossing skills. To assure success in catching, emphasis should be on easy, accurate throws and short distances.

Tossing Back and Forth. Have the children first slide the beanbag along the floor to the partner, then change to various kinds of throws—underhand, over the shoulder, overhead, side. The simple toss should be dominant in early practice.

Have them throw so that catches can be made at different levels. They should use right and left hands in turn for both throwing and catching. Early targets should be the partner's hands, held in front of his chest, the normal, "easy" position for catching. Later, add different targets—high, low, or to the side. Have them throw from different levels. Have them throw under the leg and around the body. Have them throw from between the legs, as the center does in football. Have them try imitating the shot put and the discus throw. Have them try the softball windmill (full arc) throw.

Have partners sit tailor fashion (cross-legged) about six feet apart. Have them throw and catch in various styles.

Use follow activities, in which one partner leads with a throw, and the other follows with the same kind of throw.

Have the thrower toss in various directions to make the partner move and catch.

With one partner standing still, have the other partner run around him in a circle as the bag is tossed back and forth.

Exchanging the Beanbag. "Stand back to back with your partner. Exchange a beanbag with him through your legs and then overhead. Stand back to back about six inches apart and exchange the beanbag around your sides. How far can you move apart and still exchange the bag?"

TARGETS AND GAMES

The use of targets adds a dimension of accuracy to beanbag practice. Youngsters can toss the beanbag at Indian clubs or blocks of wood in an attempt to knock them down. Informal target activities can be devised, such as: tossing into a hoop, tossing into a wastebasket, and using a target board with cutout holes. Holes can be triangles, circles, squares, and rectangles.

Beanbag Horseshoes. A toss game based on the principle of horseshoes can be organized as follows. A spot is put on the floor. Any beanbag tossed nearer the spot than the opponent's nearest bag scores a point. If the beanbag covers the spot completely, it scores two points. Games can be 10 to 15 points. Player scoring the point or points leads off with the next tosses. Each player can have two beanbags and toss both before the partner tosses; or the players can take turns tossing their bags.

FUNDAMENTAL BALL SKILLS

Ball skills are of vital importance to children in their play experiences. A good basis for these skills must be laid in the lower grades, with development continuing in the upper grades. Not only should the children acquire skill through varied experiences in handling balls, but they should also gain knowledge of skill principles essential to competency in ball-handling skills.

In handling an incoming ball, the child's success depends much upon his ability to track the incoming object and position his body in relation to the path of the ball. Included in the concept of handling an incoming ball are the situations in which the child provides rebound or propels the ball with the hand, bat, or paddle. In catching skills, the receiver must position his hands and arms precisely at the correct location.

All of this is based on the development of a complex perceptual-motor response, by which the child processes the incoming stimuli correctly and reacts accordingly. These critical skills demand much practice, and, the more critical the ball skill, the more precise and concentrated the practice must be. The experiences must be within the scope of the child's capability, as the potential in children from the preschool stage of development to the primary level varies widely.

Included in this section are the fundamental ball skills, in which the child handles the ball without the aid of other equipment, such as a bat or paddle. Ball skills are mostly of two types:

Hand-eye skills
Throwing, catching, bouncing, dribbling (as in basketball), batting (as in volleyball), and rolling (bowling)

Foot-eye skills
Kicking, trapping, and dribbling (as in soccer)

Other parts of the body are used on occasion, but the main emphasis centers on ball-handling with the hands and feet.

The Approach to Skill Development

Balls made of yarn, fleece, and paper are excellent for introductory skills on the preschool, kindergarten, and first grade level, as they help overcome children's fear of being hurt by the projectile. Some teachers have found good success with paper balls made from crumpled-up newspapers fastened with cellophane tape. One can also dip a paper ball in wallpaper sizing, which helps the ball retain its shape. Children can make the paper balls, which provides a mea-sure of motivation. These balls do not bounce, however, and children soon yearn to handle the kinds of balls used by older children.

Children should begin with yarn or fleece balls, and suggested activity progressions using these balls are presented first. Almost all of these activities can also be done with balls made of paper. Next, children should begin to play with rubber playground balls. The ball with an 8½-inch diameter, slightly deflated, seems to be preferred, since it is less lively than smaller sizes.

While yarn and rubber playground balls should provide the basic stock of balls, several other types have usefulness and provide additional challenges. A plastic ball with a hollow center and cutout sides is an interesting play object for children. Some firms are making a soft ball of sponge rubber, which serves somewhat the same purpose as the yarn ball. These are larger and softer than the old sponge ball, which is normally about two inches in diameter. Another type of ball that has value for primary children in introductory softball skills is the "soft" softball, a much softer version of the regular softball.

Large beach balls are excellent to use for beginning ball skills. Youngsters have difficulty tracking fast-moving projectiles, and a beach ball will move slowly and offer a larger object to catch. If possible, beach balls should be used prior to playground balls to eliminate the fear of being hurt by faster-moving objects. The stock of balls can be augmented from local stores, which usually carry a wide variety of rubber and plastic balls.

Instruction should begin with individual work and progress to partner and perhaps group work. After the children have acquired some skill in handling balls, a lesson should include both individual and partner activity.

In the suggested activity progressions that follow, a beginning is usually made with activities pointed toward developing the tactile sense. The child keeps contact with the ball and guides it with the hands in patterned rolling movements on the floor and around the body. Balancing on appropriate parts of the body helps the child in his tactile sensing of the object.

Scoops made from plastic bottles serve as an extension of the hand and provide another opportunity for movement experimentation for hand-eye activities. Tennis or sponge balls serve well with scoops, although small yarn balls are also good.

Primary children may also be ready for some bowling skills, since they love to knock down objects with the ball. Bowling must be differentiated from rolling, since it includes the concept of a ball directed at a specific target.

The large plastic bat, shaped like a bottle, because of its size and lightness, helps children achieve success with initial batting skills.

INSTRUCTIONAL PROCEDURES

1. Descriptions of throwing, catching, and kicking skills presented in Chapter 11, pp. 135–37, should be reviewed.

2. When children practice individually, it is essential that the experience be just that—individual. Each child should have a ball. Collect or borrow enough balls so that this is possible.

3. Balls should be moderately inflated. It is better to underinflate slightly than to overinflate. Overinflation causes a rapid rebound, which makes catching more difficult and also serves to distort the balls, sometimes permanently.

4. The principles of skill performance (pp. 28–30), particularly visual concentration, follow-through, arm-leg opposition, weight transfer, and total body coordination, have strong application to ball skills. These principles should be incorporated into the instructional sequences and should also be an important part of the coaching process.

5. In catching, a soft receipt of the ball should be created by making a "giving" movement with the hands and arms. The hands should reach out somewhat to receive the ball, and then cushion the impact by bringing the ball in toward the body with loose and relaxed hands. Balls should be handled with the pads of the fingers; they should not be "palmed."

6. In catching a throw above the waist, the hands should be positioned so that the thumbs are together. In receiving a throw below the waist, the catch is made by the hands with the little fingers toward each other and the thumbs out.

7. When throwing to a partner, unless otherwise specified, the thrower should position the ball at about the partner's chest height. A variety of target points should also be specified—high, low, right, left, knee-high, etc.

8. A lesson should begin with simple basic skills within the reach of all the children and progress to more challenging activities. The lesson must achieve something more than simply random manipulation. It must move from divergent to convergent movement.

9. Laterality is an important consideration. Right and left members of the body should be given practice in turn, in roughly equal time allotments.

10. Practice in split vision should be incorporated into bouncing and dribbling skills. Chil-

dren should learn to look somewhat forward, not at the ball, in bouncing and dribbling work.

11. The tactile sense can be brought into play by having children bounce or dribble the ball with their eyes closed, allowing them practice in getting the "feel" of the ball.

12. Rhythmic accompaniment, particularly for bouncing and dribbling activities, adds another dimension to ball skills.

13. Some guidelines for partner work merit consideration.

a. Distances between partners should be short at first and can be lengthened gradually.

b. In propelling the ball between partners, the children can progress from rolling the ball to throwing the ball on first bounce, then to throwing the ball on the fly.

c. Be sure that a disparity in skill between partners does not cause a problem for either partner. A skilled child can aid a less skilled performer, but the more skilled individual may resent being restricted in more complex skills by an inept partner.

d. The concept of throwing to a specific spot should be given attention. The natural target zone of ease for receiving is about chest height. Children can practice throwing to different levels and areas, with respect to the receiver.

14. When foot skills are being practiced on a hard surface, a partially deflated ball is more easily handled and will not roll wildly.

15. From a study of the best colors for balls, one might conclude that different ball colors should be used at different points during the program. When blue and yellow balls were used, catching scores were higher than when white balls were used. Good background contrast is also desirable.

Yarn Ball or Fleece Ball Activities

Yarn balls can be made in different sizes, but those ranging from four to six inches in diameter seem best for younger children. Instructions for making them are found on pp. 352–53. Fleece balls can be purchased in similar sizes.

Controlled Rolling, Manipulation, and Balance. The child assumes a wide straddle position, places the ball on the floor, and rolls it with constant hand guidance between and around the legs. He rolls the ball close to the body and also reaches out as far as possible. Have him try from a kneeling position on one knee. He continues the rolling from other positions: seated with legs outstretched, sitting cross-legged, and forming a bridge. Have him try from a forward stride position.

Utilizing the body positions in the previous discussion, have the child manipulate the ball around the waist and at shoulder level. This should be a rolling motion. Have him make large circles in the air with the ball, held either in one or two hands.

Have him bat the ball upward and catch it without moving from position.

Have him bat the ball lightly with the open hand from one hand to the other, maintaining control. He bats the ball upward with both hands, maintaining control.

"Balance the ball in your palm (not using your fingers) and go from a standing to a seated position without losing this balance. Return to standing position. On what other parts of the body can you balance the ball? With the ball balanced, walk in a triangle. A circle. Balance the ball on your head, drop it forward, and catch it. Backward."

"Roll the ball forward a short distance. When it stops, jump over it, and roll it back to your original place."

"Move in general space, guiding the ball with your hands. When you hear the signal, guide the ball back to your personal space." Have them use different body parts to guide the ball.

Toss and Catch to Self. Have the children toss the ball upward with both hands and catch it with both hands. Vary tossing and catching with right- and left-hand combinations. Toss it from side to side.

Tossing and catching fleece balls

"Move the ball under your leg. Around your body. Put the ball on your head and let it drop into your hands. Can you drop it behind you and catch it?"

"Toss the ball with both hands and catch it on the backs of your hands. Begin the toss with the backs of your hands and catch it on the backs of your hands. Begin the toss with the backs of your hands and catch with your palms. See if you can put both types of throws together into a pattern."

"Toss the ball under your leg. Around your body. Toss to the side with one hand and catch with the other hand. Toss overhead, rebound it with your head, and catch it."

Add challenges while tossing and catching: clap hands once or twice; clap hands in back or under leg; toss, turn (quarter- or half-) and catch; touch the floor; touch body parts; etc.

Have them try any of the above activities from a seated position. "With legs outstretched, hoist the ball with your feet and catch it."

"Toss and catch the ball high. Catch it at a low level."

Have them toss the ball into a wastebasket, box, or barrel target.

Bat the Ball. The movement is the batting used in volleyball. "Bat the ball upward; catch it with both hands. Bat it with both hands. With either hand. Bat the ball high and catch it while moving not more than one step." Alternate right- and left-hand batting, keeping the ball in the air.

"Toss the ball upward and see if you can rebound it with your head. Can you catch the ball after heading it?"

"With a small toss, bat the ball forward, chase it, and repeat by batting and chasing it back to place."

Repeat some of the above activities with the ball dropped from an uplifted hand.

"Pretend the ball is red hot and keep it in the air as long as you can by batting."

Foot and Leg Skills. "Using the side of the feet, move the ball in general space with small, easy kicks. This is called dribbling. Be sure to use both the inside and outside of the feet. Keep good control of the ball."

"Drop the ball and kick it with your knee. With your instep. Catch it after the kick."

"Kick the ball with very light kicks, alternating your right and left foot. On signal, move the ball back to your personal space and stand with it between your feet."

Working with a Partner. Have them roll the ball back and forth, beginning with a two-handed roll and moving to one-handed rolls.

"Toss the ball back and forth, first with two hands and then with one. Toss it under your leg to your partner. Toss as the center does in football."

"Bat the ball to your partner. Kick the ball back and forth, using the side of your foot both to kick and to stop or trap the ball."

Tossing into a wastebasket, box, or barrel can be done as partner activity. One partner tosses, and the other retrieves.

Have children roll the ball and knock down an Indian club or coffee can or bat the ball into a box.

"Plan a game in which you make the same kind of throw that your partner does. Then reverse your roles."

Playground Ball Activities

Activities with rubber playground balls fall into three categories: individual activities, partner activities, and target practice.

In considering individual activities, the teacher needs to think in terms of activities the child does while remaining in personal space, ball skills that can be performed against a wall, and activities in general space.

INDIVIDUAL ACTIVITIES IN PERSONAL SPACE

Controlled Rolling, Manipulation, and Balance. Have the children take a wide straddle position; place the ball on the floor; and roll it, with constant hand guidance, between and around the legs. Repeat, kneeling on one knee, and in seated position with the legs partially outstretched and the knees bent. "See how this works from a bridge position. Close your eyes and see if you can still keep control of the ball in this position."

Have them start in a standing position and manipulate the ball around the body at the waist, under the legs in turn, around the neck, etc., repeating the activity in other positions.

Rolling a ball without moving the feet

"Balance the ball on your hands. On one hand. On the backs of your hands. In the crook of your elbow. Sit down and balance it on your insteps; raise the ball slowly with your legs."

Discuss with the children why this kind of ball is more difficult to balance than a yarn ball or beanbag.

Have them control a rolling ball in different directions and patterns, while remaining in and near personal space. "Can you roll the ball while you lie on top of it?

"Put the ball on the floor and show the different kinds of bridges you can make over the ball."

Bounce and Catch. Have them bounce the ball and catch it with both hands, then with one hand. They should practice bouncing with different degrees of force so that the ball will come up to waist, chest, and nose height. Stress control. Have them bounce and catch with the body held at different levels—crouched, medium, and tall. Work out different combinations of bouncing and catching with one and two hands. Have them bounce and catch on the backs of the hands.

Have them bounce under the leg and catch—inside, outside, right, and left.

Have them bounce and catch to a drumbeat. Rhythm should alternate between heavy and light beats, with the ball bounced on the heavy beat.

"Close your eyes and bounce and catch. Remember to start with low bounces."

"Can you bounce the ball off your head and then catch it after it bounces on the floor? Before it bounces?"

Bat the Ball. "Bat the ball upward, using the flat of your hand. Your fist. The side of your hand. Catch it after the bounce. Catch it on the fly."

Have them bounce the ball off different body parts. Work for control. Try from the knee, foot, shoulder, head, elbow.

Foot Skills. "Put your toe on top of the ball and roll it in different directions. While pushing the ball with the inside of your foot, see if you can keep it near your space and under control."

Work on two-footed pick-ups, front and back.

Dribbling Skills. "Dribble the ball first with both hands, and then taking turns with your right and left hands." Reinforce learning of number concepts by specifying a certain number of dribbles before catching.

Using the guided-discovery approach, have them practice the dribble by batting the ball, then hitting it with the fist, and then pushing the ball downward with light wrist action. In this manner, they will learn that the third way is most effective.

As dribbling skills improve, have them work on various number combinations with the right and left hands: dribble under the legs, back around the body; kneel on one knee and dribble; dribble in standing position, moving in a small circle.

Have them try easy dribbling with the eyes closed.

"Go from a standing to a kneeling position and return while dribbling."

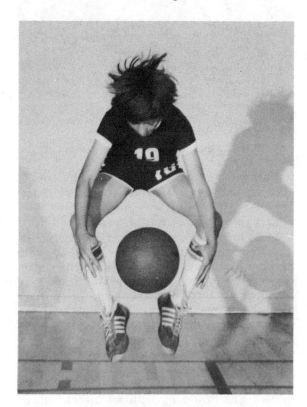

A two-footed pick-up

INDIVIDUAL ACTIVITIES AGAINST A WALL

The wall should be reasonably free of projections and irregular surfaces so that the ball will return to the thrower. Since wall space is usually limited, children may have to take turns or rotate as in station teaching. If the ball is to bounce after contact, the children stand back farther than if the catch is to be on the fly. When children are taking turns, the number of throws should be specified; after that number, the child relinquishes his turn to the next thrower.

Throwing and Catching. Have them begin by receiving the ball after the bounce and then progress to catching it on the fly. Have them practice various kinds of throws, emphasizing the need to use proper force to cause the rebound. They should practice different levels of throws, letting the ball return low, medium, and high. Add various challenges to be accomplished while the ball is in flight. Alternate between catching on the bounce and on the fly.

Batting and Handball Skills. "Drop the ball and bat it after it bounces." Have them keep the ball going, as in handball. They should practice different kinds of batting skills, working with the different hand positions—flat, fist, or side of the hand.

Kicking and Trapping. This must be a controlled activity, or it can become chaotic. Have them try to keep the ball along the floor while practicing the various kinds of kicking and trapping.

Throwing against the wall

INDIVIDUAL ACTIVITIES IN GENERAL SPACE

In individual activities using general space, an important consideration is sufficient control by children to avoid excessive contact and interference with others. Since spatial demands related to indoor activity may pose limitations, the activities may fit in more appropriately when performed outdoors.

Rolling and Manipulation. "Roll the ball, guiding it with your hands in different directions. Roll the ball forward, run beyond it, and stop it. Roll the ball forward, overtake it, jump over it, and turn and catch it."

"On all fours, move the ball with your head. Your nose. Your chin. In crab position, move the ball with your hands. Your feet."

Have them walk or jump to make progress with the ball held between the knees; between the ankles.

Have them lie in supine position with the ball held overhead in contact with the ground, bring the feet upward and beyond the head until the toes touch the ball, and return.

Toss and Catch. "Toss the ball upward and forward; run and catch it. Catch it after the first bounce. Toss it forward, let it bounce, run under the bounce, turn and catch it."

Have them toss the ball in various directions—forward, sideward, backward—run and catch it on the bounce and on the fly.

Batting the Ball. "Bat the ball upward in different directions, run and catch it on the bounce. On the fly. See how far you can bat the ball."

Foot Skills. Have them practice the soccer dribble, moving forward and in varying paths. Have them dribble around an imaginary point and return; making various patterns while dribbling.

Dribbling as in Basketball. "Dribble forward, using one hand; turn and dribble back to place, using the other hand." Have them dribble and change direction on signal and dribble so as to describe various pathways.

"Begin with a dribble in place and, on signal, change to a moving dribble. On the next signal, go back to a dribble in place. Can you skip or hop while dribbling?"

PARTNER ACTIVITIES

Before beginning to learn partner skills, the performer must show enough success in throwing and catching skills so that he does not become frustrated in the activity. Have them start by rolling the ball back and forth and proceed to catching it on the bounce and then on the fly. Keep distances appropriate to the capacity of the children.

Rolling. Have partners roll the ball back and forth, first with two-handed and then with one-handed rolls. Cones or Indian clubs placed between the children to provide a space through which the ball is to be rolled offer good stimulation for accuracy. Place cones or clubs far enough apart for success (four to five feet) and decrease the space between them as indicated.

A third child in the center can jump over the ball as it is rolled between the partners. This third person can make a bridge under which the partners roll the ball.

Jumping over a rolling ball

A bowling pin or club can be placed in the center as a target to be hit.

Throwing and Catching. "Toss the ball to your partner so that it arrives after one bounce. Try to have it come up waist high and then chest high. Use different kinds of tosses."

"Toss the ball to your partner on the fly; toss it softly so that he can catch it easily." Begin to develop a variety of throws. Concentrate on having the children throw the ball to the easy catching position at chest level. Later, have them throw the ball to different target points—high, medium, and low; right and left.

Have them try some odd throws, such as under the leg, backward and overhead, and a centering throw as in football.

First and second grade children should begin throwing and catching with soft fleece balls or softballs. Introduce regular throwing and catching skills as in softball.

Batting and Volleyball Skills. Some simple batting skills can be practiced. The experience is quite similar to the *underhand* volleyball serve.

Rolling the ball to a partner

Let the children explore different batting skills. Good teacher judgment is needed here to assure correct focus. Returning the ball back and forth, as in tennis, is similar to skills needed to play Four Square successfully.

Kicking and Trapping. Have children practice different types of *controlled* kicking between partners as well as different ways of stopping (trapping) the ball. A controlled punt can be attempted, preceded by a step with the nonkicking foot.

TARGET PRACTICE

Targets with concentric circles painted on the wall are good for developing throwing skills. Targets can also be mounted on the wall. Rolling hoops make challenging targets.

Wastebaskets can serve as targets for yarn balls. Smaller targets can be made from empty three-pound coffee cans. The principle of One-Step (p. 275) can be used with these cans. With the can upright, the child stands with the toes touching the can. He takes one step backward. Holding the arm out straight, shoulder-high, he drops the yarn ball into the can. He backs up one step and throws underhanded. Repeat using several steps. A second child may need to hold the can to keep it from tipping.

An old oil drum or barrel-type container can provide a target similar to a basketball hoop. Place a sloping bottom inside with a large hole cut out for the rubber ball to exit back to the thrower. The child tosses the ball into the drum, and the sloping bottom automatically causes it to roll back to him. This is an excellent device for children with limited mobility.

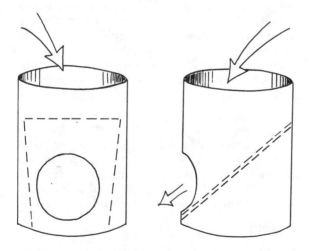

Ball return

For basketball shooting, provide baskets that are three, four, or five feet above the floor. Like

their older peers, the younger ones are motivated by getting the ball into the basket.

SCOOP ACTIVITIES

Scoops for catching can be made from plastic Clorox containers or similar bottles. Small balls (sponge or old tennis balls), beanbags, fleece balls, yarn balls, or even paper balls can be caught with scoops.

Activities that can be done with balls and scoops are similar in many respects to the activities outlined for beanbags (pp. 162–64) or playground balls (pp. 168–71). Activities are first performed individually and then with partners. Throwing can be done by hand or with the scoop.

INDIVIDUAL ACTIVITIES

"Pick up the ball from the floor with the scoop. Toss and catch with the scoop. Practice different ways of tossing and catching with the scoop."

Catching with a scoop

"Toss the ball against a wall and catch it with the scoop."

Have them toss the ball at targets—wastebasket, box, etc.

PARTNER ACTIVITIES

One partner rolls, tosses, or throws the ball by hand to the other partner, who catches it with the scoop. Vary the type of throw and method of catching.

With both partners holding scoops, they propel the ball back and forth with the scoops.

Have them bowl at an Indian club with a scoop-propelled ball.

PADDLE AND BALL ACTIVITIES

Paddles can be made out of clothes hangers and discarded nylon stockings(pp.345–46). The ball to be batted can be a table tennis ball or one constructed from crumpled paper, fastened together with tape. Badminton birds can also be used.

These activities should be mostly exploratory and should be regarded as introductory hand-eye skills for later paddle-ball work with regular paddles and balls. Certain guidelines for the skills can be established. Some attention should be given to the proper handshake grip.

INDIVIDUAL ACTIVITIES

"Place the ball on the paddle and balance it as you walk [or skip] around. Toss it lightly upward and catch it on the other side of the paddle."

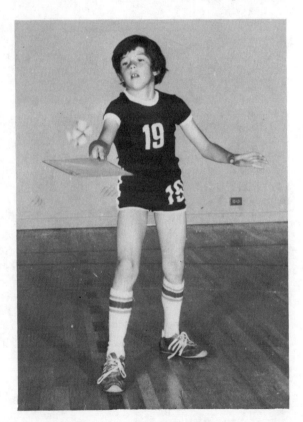

Using a homemade paddle and ball

"Bounce the ball upward with the paddle. See how many times you can bounce without a miss."

"Work with a partner and see if you can keep the ball going back and forth between you."

"Explore different things you can do with the paddle and ball."

Suspend a ball on a string four feet in length, so that it will swing back and forth. This will provide a chance for children to strike a moving object.

PARACHUTE ACTIVITIES

While parachute play can be enjoyed by all children, activities must be carefully selected for younger children, since some of the skills presented in the recommended list will be difficult for them. One parachute is sufficient for a class of 30 children.

Parachutes come in different sizes, depending upon whether their use was for personnel or cargo. Special parachutes (16 feet in diameter) can be purchased for use with preschool children.

Each parachute has an opening near the top to allow trapped air to escape and keep the parachute properly shaped. Modern parachutes are generally constructed of nylon.

VALUE OF PARACHUTE PLAY

Parachute play is a new and interesting technique for accomplishing physical fitness goals, which allows development of strength, agility, coordination, and endurance. Strength development is especially centered on the arms, hands, and shoulder girdle. At times, however, parachute activity makes strength demands on the entire body.

A wide variety of movement possibilities, some of which are rhythmic, can be employed in parachute play. Locomotor skills are much in evidence while the children manipulate the parachute. Rhythmic beats of the tom-tom or appropriate music can guide locomotor movements.

Parachute play provides many excellent group learning experiences, as youngsters must learn to cooperate in this type of play.

TERMINOLOGY

As the activities unfold, certain terms peculiar to the activity will have to be carefully explained. Terms such as "inflate," "deflate," "float," "dome," "mushroom," and others need to be clarified when they are introduced.

GRIPS

The grips used in handling the parachute are comparable to those employed in performing hanging activities on apparatus. Grips may use one or two hands; they may be overhand (palms facing away), underhand (palms facing), or mixed (a combination of underhand and over-hand grips).

INSTRUCTIONAL PROCEDURES

1. For preliminary explanations, the parachute can be stretched out on the ground in its circular pattern. Have the children seated back just far enough so that they cannot touch the parachute during the instructions. During later phases, when the children are holding the parachute, they should retain their hold lightly, letting the center of the parachute drop to the ground.

2. The teacher explains the forthcoming activity, demonstrating as needed. If there are no questions, the activity is initiated with a command such as: "Ready—begin!" Best success occurs when children start together on signal. At times, the teacher may wish to have the children lay the parachute down, back off a step or two, and sit down for further instructions or for a short rest.

ACTIVITIES

Activities are presented according to type, with variations and suggestions for supplementary activity included. Unless otherwise specified, activities begin and halt on signal. Pupil suggestions can broaden the scope of activity.

Adjusting to Different Levels. Two concepts can be stressed here: (a) adjust the parachute to be taut at high, low, and medium (in-between) levels; and (b) adjust the level to the height of specified parts of the body: nose, chin, neck, chest, waist, thighs, knees, shins, toes, overhead, ears, etc.

Exercise-Type Activities. Exercises should be done vigorously and with enough repetitions to challenge the children. In addition to the exercises presented, others can be adapted to parachute play.

Toe Toucher. Have children sit with feet extended under the parachute and the 'chute held taut with a two-handed grip and drawn up to the chin. They bend forward and touch the grip to the toes. Return to the original position, with the 'chute held taut.

Curl-ups. Have them extend the body under the parachute in curl-up position so that the stretched parachute comes up to the chin when held taut. Perform curl-ups, each time returning to the original position so that the parachute stays tight.

Backward pulls. Backward pulls are made by facing the parachute and pulling back, away from its center. Pulls can be made from a sitting, kneeling, or standing position.

Other pulls. Side pulls using a flexed-arm position can be structured. Other variations of pulling can be devised.

Hip Walk and Scooter. Begin with the parachute taut. Have them move forward with the Scooter (p. 198) and the Hip Walk (p. 198). They move back to place with the same movement until the 'chute is taut again.

Seesaw. From a sitting position, children pull the 'chute back and forth.

Tug-of-War. From a standing position, half the children pull one way, and the other half pull in the opposite direction.

Merry-Go-Round Movements. Merry-go-round movements, in which the center hole in the parachute remains above the same spot, offer many opportunities for locomotor movements, done freely or to the beat of a tom-tom. Rhythmic running, European style, is particularly appropriate (see p. 49). Holds can be one- or two-handed.

Many fundamental movements can be utilized while children move in a circular fashion, such as walking, running, hopping, skipping, galloping, sliding, draw steps, grapevine steps, and others. The parachute can be held at different levels.

Shaking the Rug and Making Waves. Shaking the Rug involves making rapid up-and-down movements with the parachute. In Making Waves, large movements send billows of cloth up and down like waves. Waves can be small, medium, or high. Children can take turns to see who can make the best waves.

Making a Dome. Begin with the parachute on the floor; the children are holding it with two hands and kneeling on one knee. To trap the air under the 'chute and make a dome shape, each child stands up quickly, thrusting arms above the head and returning to starting position. Have them try to throw the center of the parachute as high as possible to trap maximum air. Vary the activity by having all or some of the children move to the inside of the 'chute on the down movement, as if entering a cave. Domes can also be made while moving in a circle.

'Chute Crawl. Half the children, either standing or kneeling, stretch the 'chute out level with the floor. The remaining children crawl under the 'chute to the opposite side from their starting positions.

Mushroom Activities. With the 'chute on the floor and students on one knee holding it with two hands, they stand up quickly, thrusting their arms overhead. Keeping the arms overhead, each walks forward three or four steps toward the center. The arms are held overhead until the 'chute is deflated.

Making waves with the parachute

Mushroom Release. All children release at the peak of inflation and either run out from under the 'chute or move to the center and sit down, with the 'chute descending on top of them.

Full Moon. Place a basketball or cageball on the 'chute and let the children roll the ball in various directions by raising and lowering the edges of the 'chute.

Adapting the Parachute to Action Songs. The parachute gives new meaning to some of the old, familiar action songs. The following songs can be adapted to use with the parachute:

"Around We Go" (p. 214)
"Go Round and Round the Village" (p. 242)
"Guess What I Am Now" (p. 232)
"Ring Around the Rosie" (p. 221)

HOOP ACTIVITIES

Most American hoops are made of plastic, but wooden hoops are still used in Europe. The plastic variety is less durable, but more versatile. Extra hoops are needed, as there will be breakage. The standard hoop is 36 to 39 inches in diameter, but it is desirable to have smaller hoops for preschool children (30-inch).

INSTRUCTIONAL PROCEDURES

1. Hoop activities are noisy. The teacher might find it helpful to have the children lay the hoops on the floor when they are to stop and listen.

2. Hoops can inspire creativity in children. Allow them some free time to explore their own ideas.

3. Children will need an adequate amount of space in which to perform.

4. In activities that require children to jump through hoops, instruct the child holding the hoop to grasp it lightly so that if he hits the hoop it will not cause him to fall awkwardly.

5. A hoop laid on the floor can serve as a "home" in various activities. For instance, the children might leave their hoops to gallop in all directions and then quickly return to home base upon command.

6. Hoops make good targets. To make a hoop stand up, place an individual mat through the hoop and over its base.

7. A series of hoops placed on the floor can serve as a pattern for stepping, hopping, and jumping sequences. These sequences are presented first in the section that follows.

HOOP ACTIVITIES

Floor Targets. Place the hoop on the floor and use it as a guide for locomotor movements and other challenges.

"Jump [hop] in and out of the hoop. Clap hands as you jump. How many times can you jump in and out in 15 (20, 30) seconds?"

Have children do different locomotor movements clockwise and counterclockwise around the hoops.

Have them try the Bunny Jump. From a crouched position, outside the hoop, they reach inside with both hands and then jump to bring both feet inside. They go outside in the same manner, leading with the hands.

"Bend down, put both hands inside the hoop, and jump your feet completely across to the other side."

Have them take the weight on one hand first and then quickly add the other hand inside the circle, swinging the feet overhead to the other side. This is the beginning of the Cartwheel.

Have them stand on one foot in different balance positions, doing a forward lean, backward lean, and others.

"On all fours, keep only your feet inside the hoop and walk your hands around in a big circle. Try this with your hands inside the hoop and your feet outside." Repeat in crab position.

Have one partner hold a hoop six to eight inches from the ground. Have them practice hopping and jumping patterns in and out of the hoop.

"Make yourself as small as possible inside the hoop. As big as possible. Sit inside the circle. Do a seat spin, keeping your feet off the ground. Find a partner and put your hoops near each other. Work out different ways of moving in and out of the hoops, taking turns."

One partner holds the hoop horizontally about 12 inches above the floor. Have the other child crawl under the hoop without touching, stand up, and jump out.

Have them stand inside the hoop and do jump turns—quarter-, half-, three-quarter-, and full turns. "Jump and touch your heels with your hands. Touch your toes in this manner."

Have them do zig-zag jumping once around the hoop. They can go once around the hoop, alternating crossing and uncrossing the feet, with the hoop always between the feet.

Working out three-way sequences from a position inside the hoop: (1) jump, hop, and exit outside the hoop; (2) do a movement once around the outside of the hoop; and (3) return in some manner to the original position inside the hoop.

Most task movement explained under *Individual Mats* (pp. 153–54) can be employed with hoops.

Floor Patterns. Hoops can be placed in patterns on the floor as in the following illustrations. Have children try different kinds of movements, using the hoop patterns as follows:

Locomotor movement in upright position—walk, run, hop, jump, skip, slide

Locomotor movements with the hands in contact with the floor—on all fours, Bunny Jump, Frog Jump, Crab Walk; work out different combinations

Manipulating the Hoop. "Twirl the hoop on the floor like an egg beater to see how long it will spin by itself. Can you grasp it before it hits the floor? Give it a strong twirl this time and see how many times you can run [skip or hop] around the twirling hoop before it stops."

"Toss the hoop upward and catch it with one arm making a loop, then with both arms." Demonstrate the arm loops.

Have the children grasp the hoop with both hands and hold it horizontally overhead for five seconds, then vertically. Repeat while balancing on one foot.

Hula-Hooping. Have them twirl the hoop in hula hoop fashion around various body parts, such as a single arm, both arms, waist, legs, neck, and anywhere else that might work. "Change from one arm to the other without letting the hoop stop. Can you lie on your back and twirl it around your ankle?"

The Hoop as an Obstacle. "With your partner holding the hoop six inches from the floor, jump or hop in and out of the hoop. Jump in and go out under the hoop. Come up from below. Try not to touch the hoop."

"With your partner standing up and holding the hoop, do a Bunny Jump through. Come through backward. Lead with [specify different body parts] as you go through. Use the Crab Walk. Go through with your body in a twisted or curled shape."

Add another hoop held by a third person. Have the children jump in and out of the hoops in turn. They can jump into the first hoop and go out underneath, or go underneath the second hoop and come out with a jump. Work out other combinations.

Rolling Activities. "Roll the hoop and run alongside it. Keep it going. Roll it to the right and left. Try to guide the hoop to make a full turn and roll it back in the direction from which you came." Put some beanbags on the floor and have children roll the hoop in patterns around or between the beanbags.

The Hoop as a Jump Rope. "Use the hoop like a jump rope. Go forward, backward, and sideways."

Other Partner Stunts. "Toss the hoop back and forth with your partner. Hula-hoop on your arms and change from one partner to the other, exchanging the hoops. Can you find other ways to exchange the hoops?"

ACTIVITIES WITH OLD AUTOMOBILE TIRES

In the previous chapter, we discussed the use of tires as apparatus. Tires also can be used as objects to be manipulated.

Tires can be secured at no cost, but pose a difficult storage problem, since they tend to occupy considerable space. In spite of this, however, tires can be valuable tools in the movement program. A lesson with tires should include both manipulative activities and those in which the tire serves as a piece of apparatus to jump on, in, and over, and to move through and around. Tire activities for preschool and kindergarten children need to be selected with discretion, since the size and weight of the tires used will affect the children's performance.

INSTRUCTIONAL PROCEDURES

1. Tires with flat treads are more easily controlled than those with rounded treads.

2. Tires should be scrubbed thoroughly. Discard tires which cause the hands to become blackened. Painting the tires in bright colors will prevent this problem.

3. While laterality can be considered, children will probably continue to control the tire with the dominant side.

4. Motorcycle tires are smaller and lighter and can be used in place of automobile tires for young children.

MANIPULATING TIRES

Rolls. "Roll the tire in different directions. Roll the tire, run in front of it, and stop it. Roll the tire to your partner."

Children take partners; each has a tire. Use one tire as a target to which the other can be rolled. The target can be stationary or moving.

Spinning the Tire. "Spin the tire clockwise and counterclockwise. Which way can you spin it the longest? Spin the tire and run around it as many times as you can before it stops. Challenge one or more classmates to see who can make his or her spinning tire last the longest."

Balance Activities. "With the tire in an upright position, can you sit on it and balance? How about other positions?"

EXPLORATORY ACTIVITIES WITH JUMP ROPES

A jump rope placed on the floor can serve as a foundation for many individual exploratory activities built on educational movement patterns. The variety of movement possibilities are limited only by the imagination of the children and the teacher. The activities can be extended to partner and group work.

In the activities that follow, the rope is positioned on the floor. The movement factors of space, time, force, and flow (p. 81) have important application to these activities.

THE ROPE IN A STRAIGHT LINE

Most activities are done while the children progress down the line of the rope. When they reach the end of the rope, they should turn around, using a jump turn or other movement, and perform the same, a related, or a contrasting movement on the return trip. They should travel at different levels.

"Walk on the rope like a tightrope walker—forward. Backward. Sideways. Use follow steps or a heel-toe walk."

"Walk along the rope with one foot on each side. Walk with a crisscross walk."

"Hop back and forth along the rope. Hop twice on each side before changing. On the way back, change to hopping on the other foot."

"Jump back and forth down the rope with your body facing forward or moving sideways. Jump back and forth backward."

"Straddle jump down the rope. Change the feet back and forth (crisscross) while straddle jumping. Straddle jump down the line doing a heel click at each jump."

"Do crouch jumps from side to side." Have them try other movements on all fours.

Bring in the concept of time. "Do a slow movement down and a fast movement back."

Have them move at one level down the rope and at another level on the way back.

"Have the body form different shapes as you move down and back with [aforementioned] movements."

"Can you lie down alongside the rope and stretch out as long as the rope?"

"Can you lie down with one end of the rope under your waist and roll your body so that the rope is rolled around you? Stand up and shake the rope loose."

THE ROPE FORMING SHAPES

The rope can form many shapes on the floor, but the circle is the basis for the following activities. The suggested movement challenges can easily be adapted for other shapes (square, triangle, etc.).

"Make yourself as small as possible in the circle without touching the rope. Make yourself as big as possible, also without touching the rope."

Have children work out different kinds of jumping and hopping patterns in and around the circle.

Moving through jump rope shapes

"Jump from outside the circle and land in a crouched position inside. Spring out. Straddle the circle and jump around it that way. Jump crisscross fashion around the circle. Move both clockwise and counterclockwise."

"Put your feet inside the circle and have your hands make a big circle outside the rope. Repeat with your hands inside and your feet outside." They should do these challenges with the body facing the ceiling.

"Crouch outside the circle. Do a Bunny Jump inside and out again. Can you make your feet go completely across the circle by taking the weight on your hands? Try this by leading with one hand."

"Toss the rope upward and let it fall. Make a shape with your body as near as you can to the shape of the rope on the floor."

"Make the first letter of your first name with the rope. Make the first letter of your last name." Work out different jumping and hopping patterns in and out of these letters.

OTHER CHALLENGES WITH ROPES

Have them select partners and make two separate figures with the two ropes. Repeat challenges found in the previous section.

Have them tie two ropes together and make a larger figure. Work out different movements.

Moving through patterns made with jump ropes

Establish patterns with two or three ropes, such as a large plus sign or a six-spoked wheel pattern. Have children show what different movements they can do, using these patterns.

Arrange ropes in a line so that they are about 18 inches apart (see illustration). Work out movements in which performers walk, run, hop, or jump in the spaces between the ropes. Specify a return activity—moving on all fours, for example.

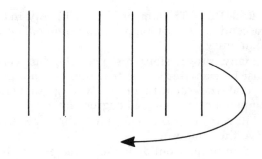

LONG ROPE–JUMPING ACTIVITIES

Groups of five make a convenient group for practicing long-rope skills. Two of the group are turners, and the others are jumpers. The children should rotate between turning and jumping. The rope should be 12 to 16 feet long. Specifying the number of jumps a child may take before exiting controls the jumping time in the center.

INTRODUCTORY SKILLS

Hold the rope six inches from the ground. Children jump over, back and forth. Raise the rope a little each time. Be sure to have them hold the rope loosely in the hands.

The Ocean Wave. Another stationary jumping activity is The Ocean Wave. The turners make waves in the rope by moving their arms up and down. The children try to time themselves so as to jump over a low part of the "wave."

Snake in the Grass. The holders stoop down and wiggle the rope back and forth on the floor. Children jump over the rope, trying not to touch it as it moves.

Rocking the Cradle. The holders swing the rope in pendulum fashion without turning it over. Children jump the rope as it passes under them.

Have the child stand in the center between the turners. Carefully turn the rope in a complete arc over the jumper's head. As the rope completes the turn, the jumper jumps over it. He immediately exits in the same direction as the rope is turned.

Children run through a turning rope without jumping by following a descending rope.

BASIC LONG ROPE–JUMPING SKILLS

Two basic concepts should be explained—*front door* and *back door*. These terms identify the direction from which the children are to enter the turning rope.

Front Door. When the rope on descent is approaching the jumper, this is front door. This position is so called because the rope is coming from the front toward the jumper as he runs into the jumping area.

Back Door. The jumper follows the rope in as it ascends and must jump the rope immediately upon entry.

Many progressions are possible, but care must be exercised to see that these do not get beyond the capacity of the young jumpers. Jumpers enter from a 45-degree angle.

"Run in the front door, jump the rope, and leave the same way."

"Run in the front door, jump, and go out the back door."

"Run in the back door; go out the front. Go out the back."

Have them run in front or back door, increase the number of jumps, and run out.

Have them run in front or back door, jump a specified number of times, and exit.

They run in front or back door, make quarter-turns while jumping so that a complete full turn is made after four jumps, and then exit.

Red Hot Pepper. Turners turn the rope with increased speed, and the jumper tries to keep up with the rope.

High Water. The rope is turned so that it is gradually higher and higher off the ground.

Two, three, or four children jump at a time. After some skill has been reached, children in combination can run in, jump a specified number of times, and run out keeping hands joined all the time.

Have them jump to the different routines described in the rhymes that follow. Some merely provide rhyme accompaniment while normal jumping goes on; others call for certain types of challenge movements.

RHYMES

As the jumpers become proficient, they can make use of many familiar rhymes that are used for long ropes. A few examples follow.

1. Teddy Bear, Teddy Bear, turn around.
   Teddy Bear, Teddy Bear, touch the
      ground.
   Teddy Bear, Teddy Bear, show your
      shoe.
   Teddy Bear, Teddy Bear, you better
      skidoo.

or

   Teddy Bear, Teddy Bear, say your
      prayers.
   Teddy Bear, Teddy Bear, go upstairs.
   Teddy Bear, Teddy Bear, turn out the
      light.
   Teddy Bear, Teddy Bear, say good
      night.

2. *For counting a definite number of turns*

   Bulldog, poodle, bow wow wow,
   How many doggies have we now?
   One, two, three, etc.

or

   Lady, lady, at the gate,
   Eating cherries from a plate.
   How many cherries did she eat?
   One, two, three, etc.

   The rope is turned a specified number of turns, after which the jumper exits.

3. *For "Red Hot Pepper"*

   Mabel, Mabel, set the table.
   Bring the plates if you are able.
   Don't forget the salt and—
      Red Hot Pepper!

   On the words "Red Hot Pepper," the rope is turned as fast as possible until the jumper misses.

4. *A more personalized rhyme*

   [Name of jumper] went to France
   To teach the boys [girls] how to
      dance.
   First a heel, and then a toe,
   Turn around, and out you go!

INDIVIDUAL ROPE-JUMPING ACTIVITIES

Individual rope-jumping is an activity that has lifelong use and can be started at the kindergarten or, in some cases, the preschool level. Rope-jumping is a rhythmic movement and is enhanced by the addition of suitable music. Some teachers like to add music to the jumping early in the program, but this is probably a matter of individual teacher preference.

Rope-jumping is an excellent complete body activity. It helps develop coordination, rhythm, and timing. It tones up the circulorespiratory system and increases both speed and endurance. It makes a contribution to weight control and total physical condition. It can contribute to good posture habits.

From an educational standpoint, rope-jumping has good value in the school program. It allows a maximum amount of student activity within a minimum amount of space and a short length of time. Since the activities are in progression, the teacher can begin at the student's level and develop from that point. It is inexpensive and easily taught.

It provides a creative activity that has unlimited possibilities for new material. The more proficient the youngsters become, the more they tend to invent steps and routines of their own. The activity is not seasonal in character.

Finally, for the teacher and administrator, rope-jumping provides excellent program material for school patron meetings and other demonstrations.

THE ROPE

To determine the proper length of rope for a particular individual, have him stand on the center of the rope. The ends, when drawn up on each side of the body, should terminate at approximately armpit height.

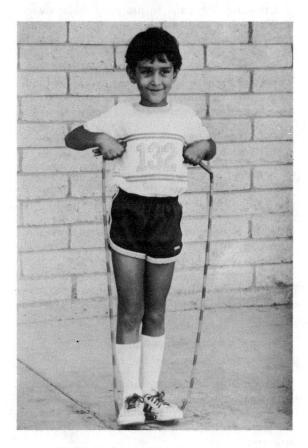

Adjusting the jump rope to the proper length

Preschool and kindergarten children can use six-foot and seven-foot ropes. For primary children, some eight-foot ropes will need to be added. The teacher may need a nine-foot rope. Enough ropes should be present so that each child can have a rope of suitable length.

Cotton sash cord and hard-weave synthetic rope serve well as jump ropes. Rope ends should be wrapped or fused to prevent unraveling. The authors have had excellent results with the newer jump ropes formed with plastic links. The ropes come in an assortment of attractive colors and can be color-coded for length. Handles help to provide good circular motion as the rope is turned.

THE TECHNIQUE OF ROPE-JUMPING

The rope should be turned with a quick, easy motion of the hands and wrists, not forcefully turned by the arms. The body should be erect, and the jumping done in a relaxed, easy motion. Stress good postural position by directing eye focus ahead and holding the head and shoulders up in erect position.

The rope should be held primarily with the thumb and the first two fingers, and the elbows should be kept near the sides. It is interesting to note that most European rope-jumping is done with the elbows out from the body.

The body should bounce lightly, usually on the toes, with just enough straightening of the knee joints to propel the body into the air. The clearance from the ground to where the rope goes under the feet should be minimal and easy.

TERMINOLOGY

The recommended steps in rope-jumping can be done in two rhythmic combinations: slow time and fast time.

Slow-Time Rhythm (Slow Rope, Slow Foot Motion with Rebound). In slow-time rhythm, the performer jumps over the rope, rebounds (jumps lightly in place) as the rope passes overhead, and then jumps again as the rope goes underneath. The rebound may be a simple bounce in place. Better jumpers, however, will merely bend the knees slightly and not leave the ground at all during the rebound. The rebound is found *only* in slow-time jumping.

The performer actually jumps over the rope to every other count or beat of the music. The odd beat occurs as the rope passes over the head, with the rhythm of the jumping carried with the rebound.

Fast-Time Rhythm (Fast Rope, Fast Foot Motion). In fast-time rhythm, the action is twice as fast as in slow time. The rope turns a full turn for each beat, and a jump pattern is made each time the rope goes underneath. This rhythm is more demanding than slow-time rhythm, as both the rope speed and the foot action are doubled.

INSTRUCTIONAL PROCEDURES

1. The skill of rope-jumping appears to be one that children learn at different rates and maturity levels. The teacher should not become discouraged with the activity if it appears that some children just do not seem to get it. Rope-jumping is a movement in which children sud-

denly find themselves capable of good performance.

2. Explain to the children that the activity is sometimes called rope-skipping (the old term), but that the basic movement is really a jump, hence *rope-jumping.*

3. To establish jumping rhythm and coordination with the rope, the rope can be folded in half and turned with one hand. Turn the rope forward, but at the side of the body. Another method is to have the children learn the jumping rhythm first and add a simulated rope turn.

4. Some teachers have had success in teaching long rope–jumping first. Begin with a simple jump over the held rope, progressing to jumping over a simple pendulum swing before moving to full jumping.

5. Begin first with the slow-time rhythm and limit movements to the standard two-footed jump and rebound. Some competency should be established before embarking on other aspects of rope-jumping.

6. A drumbeat is helpful in introductory work, with an accented beat for the jump and a lighter beat for the rebound.

7. The progression of activities can be taught without the addition of music, but is is preferable to introduce music early to help the rhythm and provide stimulation. Children seem to continue rope-jumping longer when spirited music is combined with the activity. Music also helps the child establish the basic jumping pattern while he is not using the rope.

8. Progression in rope-jumping for young children includes two basic rhythms, recommended progression of three step patterns (there are also others), crossing and uncrossing arms while turning the rope, and going from forward to backward turning without interrupting the rhythm.

9. While the instructional sequences are based on in-place jumping, children can move forward, backward, and sideward while jumping, provided that they do not interfere with others.

BASIC STEPS

The three basic steps, explained below, should be reasonably well mastered. Concentration should be focused on keeping in good rhythm and on efficient handling of the rope. The two-foot basic step serves to introduce rope-jumping and to emphasize the concepts of slow time and fast time. The alternate-foot basic step and the swing step forward can be used with either of the rhythms, but they have particular value in illustrating the change from slow time to fast time.

Two-Foot Basic Step. With feet together, the child jumps over the rope as it passes under the feet and takes a preparatory rebound while the rope is over his head.

Alternate-Foot Basic Step. As the rope passes under the feet, the weight is shifted alternately from one foot to the other, raising the unweighted foot in a running position.

Swing Step Forward. Same as alternate-foot basic step, except that the free leg swings forward. Keep knee loose and let foot swing naturally.

CROSSING ARMS FORWARD

Crossing the arms in jumping adds variety and supplies additional challenge. When the rope is overhead, starting the downward swing, the arms cross so that the hands exchange positions. Jumping can be continued in this position, or a return to normal position can be made. Arms can cross and uncross on alternate turns or on a specified number of rotations of the rope.

GOING FROM FORWARD TO BACKWARD JUMPING WITHOUT STOPPING THE ROPE

Some of the more skilled young children should be able to accomplish this maneuver. As the rope starts downward in forward jumping, rather than guiding the rope to pass under the feet, the performer swings both arms to one side (left or right) and makes a half-turn in that direction. The jumper is now facing the rope on the upward movement. The rope is now carried over the head to the back, and the jump is made with a backward turn. The return can be made by reversing the process.

RECORDS FOR ROPE-JUMPING

Musical and rhythmic accompaniment for rope-jumping can come from many sources, provided the piece has a good, solid beat at a steady tempo of 120 to 150 beats per minute. Some recordings found suitable for rope-jumping are:

1. Recordings of marches and polkas
2. "Wheels" and "Orange Blossom Special," Billy Vaughn (Dot 45-161774)
3. "Pop Goes the Weasel" (Victor 45-6180, 20151; Folkraft 1329)
4. "Bleking" (Victor 45-6169, 20989; Folkraft 1188)
5. Special records for rope-jumping:
   a. *Rope Skipping—Rhythms, Rhymes, and Routines* (Educational Activities AR 536)
   b. *Rope Skipping* (Educational Activities HYP 12)

c. *Rhythmic Rope Jumping* (Educational Activities K 4001)

ROPE-JUMPING ROUTINES

After they have gained some expertise, children can work out routines to a piece of music. This can involve changes from slow time to fast time, incorporating crossed hands, and using different steps. Make the initial routines simple, with a single action change.

OTHER MANIPULATIVE ITEMS

The list of manipulative items presented in this chapter can be supplemented by the following items, which are useful in station teaching and for free play.

Yo-yos. Yo-yos are favorite toys in many parts of the country. In fact, children perform some incredible yo-yo movements in organized competitions. A full set of progressions can be established.

Stretch Ropes. Simple stretch ropes, made by weaving rubber bands together until a full circle is formed, offer good movement possibilities. Children can stretch the ropes with different body shapes.

Mexican Ball Cups. The ball cup consists of a ball on a string attached to a handle on which a cup or scoop is placed. The object is to catch the ball in the cup or scoop. Cups can be made from tin cans; scoops, from Clorox bottles.

Catching a beanbag off the launcher

Indoor Croquet Sets. Small croquet sets (they can be homemade) are useful indoors where there is carpeting on the floor. Wickets can be made from coathangers, using blocks for support.

Footsie Launchers. A footsie launcher consists of a board 30 to 36 inches in length under which a fulcrum is positioned. A ball or beanbag is placed in a niche on one end of the board. The performer steps sharply on the other end of the board, propelling the ball upward. The motion of the board is somewhat like that of a teeter-totter.

Foam Shapes. There are many types and sizes of foam shapes, easily adaptable for children's play activities. Broom hockey, for example, can use foam pucks propelled by brooms.

Ribbons. If six- to eight-foot-long lengths of ribbon are fastened to small dowels, these make excellent play objects for children. They can be whirled and guided into moving patterns.

SUMMARY

Manipulative activities are the heart of fundamental skill development lessons. Manipulative activities strengthen hand-eye and foot-eye coordination. Instruction in manipulative activity units places emphasis on the individualized approach in which each child has a piece of equipment and receives the maximum amount of practice time. A lesson can be developed around one piece of equipment, or a theme can be developed utilizing many pieces of manipulative equipment.

When teaching units in this area, emphasis should be on both quality and quantity of movement. Students should have ample opportunity to practice the activity, while receiving instruction on proper patterns of movement.

Instruction in catching objects should place emphasis on removing the element of fear. This can be accomplished by using objects such as fleece balls, beach balls, and beanbags. The child can learn to toss and catch individually before learning to receive an object from a partner.

Jump ropes can be used in many different ways. Many exploratory activities can be taught with the jump rope placed on the floor so that the child learns to control the body in space. Later the child can progress to long rope-jumping and finally to individual rope-jumping activities.

All manipulative activity units contain instructional procedures to minimize planning time and are organized in progression from the easiest activities to the most difficult.

Chapter 14

Stunts and Tumbling

Variety is the very spice of life that gives it all its flavor.
William Cowper

The stunts and tumbling program challenges the child to accomplish certain prescribed types of movement, while it incorporates into the overall program a welcome change from exploratory or creative activity. The older term, *self-testing activity*, well describes the stunts and tumbling program.

Such personality traits as dedication and perseverance in a task can be furthered, as stunts are seldom mastered quickly or in a few attempts. Since much of the work is individual, the child faces his or her own capabilities and is given the opportunity to develop resourcefulness, self-confidence, and courage. At the same time, he or she learns to avoid foolhardiness and to have respect for his own safety and that of others.

Important physical values are developed in the program of stunts and tumbling. Coordination, balance, flexibility, and agility can be enhanced, and body management skills can be improved.

Because of the recent widespread interest in gymnastic events, as covered on television, there will be little need to "sell" such a program to parents and students. Introducing these activities in a rational and logical manner can lead the child to take a serious interest in them later on. When a child masters a challenging stunt, his satisfaction, pride of achievement, and sense of accomplishment contribute to a gain in self-respect and improvement in his self-image.

GENERAL INSTRUCTIONAL PROCEDURES

In developing instructional procedures necessary to carry on an educationally sound program of stunts and tumbling, overall consideration can be given to a number of areas.

Presenting Activities

1. While not all stunts require mats, it is well to include rolling stunts requiring mats in every lesson, as these stunts are the core of the program for young children. Keep any shifting of mats during a lesson to a minimum.

2. No two children will perform stunts the same way. Respect individual differences and allow for different levels of success. Build on approximations of the stunt.

3. While some emphasis on form and control should be established, this should be within the capacity of the children.

4. While gym shoes are a help to children in these activities, children can tumble in bare feet. Children need to be made aware of the necessity to come to stunts and tumbling sessions in clothing that will not restrict movement.

5. When the stunt calls for a position to be held for a number of counts, use a counting system like, "monkey one, monkey two," or "one potato, two potato."

6. When children are asked to reach out or place objects a distance along the floor, distances can be specified by having the children count boards on the floor away from a line or base position. Generally, the start should be made at a modest distance so all can achieve success, with appropriate increases to follow. In Balance Touch (p. 191), for example, the teacher can specify that the beanbag should be placed a certain number of board widths away from a line.

Distances can then be varied by increasing the number of boards between the line and the object.

7. Laterality is a factor that must be emphasized. The motor portion of the body is bilateral and should be so regarded. The teacher will have to call the children's attention to using the other side or member of the body. Where appropriate, a directive is included in stunt descriptions. The concept of directionality should be established in children so that they approach performance of stunts with the principle of right and left usage without waiting to be so instructed. If a balancing stunt is done on one foot, then, the next time, it should be tried on the other. If a roll is made to the right, a comparable roll should be made to the left. A teacher may wish to develop the stunt thoroughly on one side before making the change to the other side, but the change should be made.

8. In rolling stunts down the length of a mat, consideration for return activities should be made.

9. Demonstrations should be kept to a minimum in order to stimulate thinking-doing activities. If demonstration seems necessary, it should be done only after some experimentation by the children. Demonstration can show a particular point of contention, a stunt well done, or a unique and different way to accomplish the stunt. It should be recognized that teacher demonstration is adult activity and not typical of movements of young children.

10. Most stunts do not require spotters, but, in the few that do, make sure that spotters understand their responsibilites.

11. Thick (soft) tumbling mats are intriguing to children and eliminate the fear factor.

12. When he is learning rolls, placing mats on an incline may help the youngster develop momentum.

Basic Mechanical Principles

Certain simple mechanical and kinesiological principles should be established as the foundation of an effective program. If children can build upon these basic principles, instruction will be facilitated.

1. Momentum needs to be developed and applied, particularly for rolls. Tucking, starting from a higher point, preliminary raising of the arms are examples of devices to increase momentum.

2. The center of weight must be positioned over the center of support in balance stunts, particularly in the inverted stands.

3. In stunts where the body is wholly or partially supported by the hands, proper position-ing of the hands is essential for better performance. Fingers should be spread and pointed forward. The pads of the fingers apply pressure for a good basis of support. This hand position should generally be employed unless there is a specific reason to depart from it.

Safety Considerations

Few stunts on the primary level involve safety hazards. However, where needed, the child is entitled legally to know the inherent dangers of the activity, the safety considerations to be followed, and the duties of the helper or spotter. In addition, the following rules should be observed:

1. Emphasis should be placed on how to fall. Children should be taught to roll out of a stunt when balance is lost. In the headstand, children should try to return to the floor in the direction from which they started. The return is facilitated by bending both at the waist and at the knees.

2. Pockets should be emptied, and lockets, glasses, watches, and other articles removed. A special depository for these articles should be provided, or, better yet, they should be left in the classroom.

3. Fatigue and overstrain in young children should be guarded against. Allow children to practice at the pace they select.

4. Children should be encouraged but not forced to try stunts. Care should be taken not to use peer pressure to stimulate participation.

5. Body control is a basic element of the stunts and tumbling program. Children should learn to use controlled movements. Speed is secondary and, in some cases, even undesirable.

Sequence in Instruction

Each lesson should review prior accomplishments, especially those that are regarded as lead-up activities to the present lesson. Relating present activities to past experience is most desirable.

In presenting a stunt, the following steps form a meaningful progression:

The Significance of the Name. Most of the stunts have a characteristic name, and this should be a consideration in teaching. Labels for movement experiences are important to children, and whatever is to be represented should be described and discussed. For example, if a child is asked to move like an alligator, he should have knowledge of what an alligator is.

The Stunt Description. Stunts can be analyzed from the following steps, which can form the basis for presentation.

The starting position. The child needs to know what position or movement is involved in starting the stunt. This may be verbalized or accomplished through minimal demonstration.

The execution. Next, children need to know what they are to do, just how they are to move, and in what manner. Little demonstration in this phase should be done until children have had an opportunity to try out their idea of meeting the basic challenge as presented. Early emphasis should be on increasing the variety of movement, with later attention centered on quality of movement.

The finishing position. A few stunts, particularly balance stunts, require a definite finish position. In balancing stunts, for example, it is important that the child return to the starting position without losing balance or moving the feet. In other stunts, the requirement may be a particular finishing movement, which should be introduced as the movements are "polished up." Generally, children should have undergone experimentation and practice before the finishing act is added to the stunt routine. In some cases, the finishing act is a part of the routine description and should be introduced as the stunt is explained.

The flow factor can be given emphasis in setting up sequences of two or more stunts. For example, the child may be challenged to put together a roll, a balance stunt, and some kind of animal walk.

Class Arrangements for Instruction

Instruction arrangements can follow several patterns. Tumbling mats can be positioned in several ways. Six mats are a basic minimum.

Semicircular Arrangement. This formation focuses attention on the center of the semicircle. Each group should have a leader; in the diagram, the leader is represented by a small circle. The lines of children are well separated, lessening the opportunity for contact problems.

U-Shaped Formation. The mats are laid out in the shape of a U. The formation has good visual control possibilities for the teacher, and

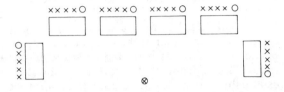

the children are able to see what their classmates are doing. Children can tumble across the mats in this formation.

Double Row Formation. In this formation three groups form a row on one side and three on the other. The teacher is never far from any group. Children can view one another.

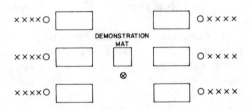

If sufficient mats are available, one mat may be placed in an appropriate central position in any of these formations, so that little movement of the children is necessary to view the demonstration. The mat should be exclusively for demonstration.

Individual Mats. Individual mats are excellent for many stunts, but are not as shock-absorbent for rolling stunts as are regular gym mats. However, two or three individual mats can be put together for multiple rolls.

Educational Movement Formations. For locomotor stunts like animal walks, some of the formations for educational movement are useful. See pp. 89–90 for selected formations.

SEQUENCE OF ACTIVITIES

The activities in the stunts and tumbling program are divided into five categories according to type.

Animal Movements. Stunts in this category specify imitative movement of selected animals, such as the alligator, puppy dog, kangaroo, bear, and others that have unique movements.

Balance Stunts. While it can be contended that many stunts have balance demands, the stunts in this category are those designed particularly to exercise balance controls. Many of the stunts specify that the balance is to be held for a specified number of counts.

Specialized Movement Stunts. This is a catch-all category that contains stunts designating a specialized kind of movement to be achieved. Most of the stunts in this category have a a critical achievement item by which the accomplishment of the stunt can be judged.

Tumbling and Inverted Balances. This category includes what might be termed the more standardized tumbling activities, such as the forward roll, the backward roll, the headstand, and lead-up activities and variations of the activities.

Partner and Group Stunts. Most of these stunts are partner activities, but some can be extended for small groups of three or four children.

LEVELS OF DIFFICULTY

Within each of the five categories, the activities have been given arbitrary ratings of difficulty, based on experience with children. The activities in the lists that follow are presented in these three classifications, based on degree of difficulty:

Level 1. Introductory challenge
Level 2. Moderate challenge
Level 3. Significant challenge

Structuring the Lesson

In a stunts and tumbling lesson for a particular day or for the weekly lesson plan, activities should be selected from all five categories. In addition, the lesson should include some rolling stunts from the tumbling category.

It is more logical educationally to allocate activities to levels of difficulty rather than to grade or age placement. Prior experience and training are factors in capability for stunts. A group of first grade children who have had no previous experience in stunts and tumbling certainly should not be assigned the same stunt activities as another group of the same grade level that has already achieved many of the introductory and moderate challenge activities.

Children with no previous experience, whether they are in kindergarten, first grade, or second grade, should begin with introductory challenge activities. Other children with some background should begin at the point of capability.

Another point in favor of the levels of challenge is that the teacher can use the activities of less challenge as review items before moving ahead to activities that need more concentrated effort and direction.

ANIMAL MOVEMENTS

Level 1. Introductory challenge
Rooster Walk
The Camel
The Robin
Puppy Dog Run
Cat Walk
Monkey Run
Kangaroo
Alligator

Level 2. Moderate challenge
Gorilla Walk
Bear Walk
Elephant Walk
Rabbit Jump
Lame Dog Walk
Crab Walk

Level 3. Significant challenge
Frog Jump
Double Lame Dog
The Turtle
Measuring Worm
Cricket Walk
Wicket Walk
Mule Kick
Seal Crawl
Reverse Seal Crawl
Elbow Crawl

Level 1. Introductory Challenge

ROOSTER WALK

"Bend forward just slightly, keeping your back straight and your head up. Bring your hands up so that the sides of your thumbs are in contact with your chest, and your arms form the wings. With your knees apart, walk on your toes with short steps. Stop occasionally and sound the crow of a rooster."

THE CAMEL

"The 'ship of the desert' is a slow, gangly animal. Bend forward at the waist and make a hump with your hands clasped behind your back. Because the camel moves *slowly*, your head and chest should come up with each step."

THE ROBIN

"Notice how a robin moves forward in little jumps, cocks his head, and listens for the sound of a worm. Place your hands flat on the back of your hips, but stand tall. Move forward with small jumps on your toes with feet and legs kept together. Combine three or four light jumps forward and cock your head and listen. When you hear a worm, bend over quickly and pull it out with your teeth."

PUPPY DOG RUN

"Place your hands on the floor, bending your arms and legs slightly. Walk and run like a happy puppy." The teacher should see that the youngsters look ahead. By keeping the head up in good position, the neck muscles are strengthened.

The Puppy Dog Run

Variations. In the Puppy Dog Run and the following two variations, have the children go sideward, go backward, and turn around in place.

Cat Walk. "Use the same position [as the Puppy Dog Run], but imitate a cat. Walk softly, stretch at times like a cat. Be smooth and deliberate. Say 'meow'."

Monkey Run. "Walk on all fours with your hands turned in so the fingers point toward each other."

KANGAROO

The arms are carried close to the chest with the palms facing forward. A beanbag is placed between the knees. Have the children move in different directions, employing small jumps, without losing the beanbag. Explain to the children about the pouch of the kangaroo.

ALLIGATOR

"Lie face down on the floor with your elbows bent. Move along the floor alligator fashion, keeping your hands close to your body and your feet pointed out." First, stress unilateral movements (i.e., right arm and leg moving together). Then, emphasize cross-lateral movements, in which the right arm moves with the left leg, and vice versa.

Moving like an alligator

Level 2. Moderate Challenge

GORILLA WALK

Have them bend the knees and carry the torso forward, with arms hanging at their sides. As the youngsters walk forward, they should touch their fingers to the ground and make appropriate facial expressions.

Variation. Let the children stop and beat on their chests like gorillas. Also, they can bounce up and down on all fours with hands and feet touching the floor simultaneously.

BEAR WALK

Have them bend forward and touch the ground with both hands. They travel forward slowly by moving the hand and foot *on the same side together*; i.e., the right hand and foot are moved together, and then the left hand and foot. Make deliberate movements. This movement is classified as unilateral.

Variation. Have them lift the free foot and arm high while the support is on the other side.

ELEPHANT WALK

The children bend well forward, clasping the hands together to form a trunk. The end of the trunk should swing close to the ground. They should walk in a slow, deliberate, dignified manner, keeping the legs straight and swinging the trunk from side to side. Stop and throw water over the back with the trunk. Follow the words with appropriate movements.

The elephant's walk is steady and slow.
His trunk like a pendulum swings to and fro.
But when there are children with peanuts around
He swings it up and he swings it down.

Swinging the trunk in the Elephant Walk

Variation. Arrange children in pairs, one as the mahout (elephant keeper) and the other as the elephant. The mahout walks to the side and slightly in front of the elephant, with one hand touching the elephant's shoulder. The mahout leads the elephant around during the first two lines of the poem, then during the last two lines releases the touch, walks to a spot in front of the elephant, and tosses him a peanut when the trunk is swept up. The mahout returns to the elephant's side, and the action is repeated.

RABBIT JUMP

The children crouch to the floor with the knees apart. The arms are between the knees, with the hands placed on the floor ahead of the feet. They should move forward by reaching out first with both hands and then bringing both feet up to the hands. Eyes should look ahead.

The Rabbit Jump

Emphasize to the children that this is called a jump rather than a hop because both feet move at once. Note that the jump is a bilateral movement.

Variations. Have them try this with the knees kept together and the arms on the outside. Have them alternate the knees together and apart on successive jumps. Have them go over a low hurdle or through a hoop.

Experiment with taking considerable weight on the hands before the feet move forward. This can be aided by raising the seat higher in the air when the hands move forward.

LAME DOG WALK

"Walk on both hands and one foot. Hold the other foot in the air as if it is injured." Have them walk for a distance and change feet. Eyes should be forward. Vary by moving backward and in other combinations. See if the children can move with an "injured" front leg.

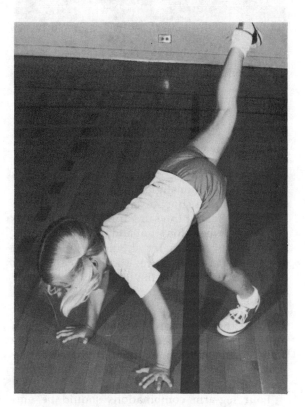

Moving like a dog with an injured foot

CRAB WALK

"Squat down and reach back, putting both hands on the floor without sitting down. With your head, neck, and body level and in a straight line, walk forward. Backward. Sideways."

Children have a tendency to lower the hips in this activity. See that the body is kept up in reasonable alignment.

Variations. As each step is taken with a hand, the other hand can slap the chest or seat.

Have them move the hand and foot on the same side simultaneously (unilateral movement).

Have them try balancing on one leg and the opposite hand. Hold for five seconds.

A Double Lame Dog Walk

In position for the Crab Walk

Level 3. Significant Challenge

FROG JUMP

"From a squatting position, with your hands placed on the floor slightly in front of your feet, jump forward a short distance, lighting on the hands and feet at the same time." Note the difference between this stunt and the Rabbit Jump.

Emphasis eventually should be placed on both height and distance. The hands and arms should absorb part of the landing impact.

DOUBLE LAME DOG

Have them support the body on one hand and one leg (same side). They then move forward in this position, maintaining balance. The distance should be short (five to ten feet), since this activity is strenuous.

Four leg-arm combinations should be employed. Cross-lateral movements of right arm-left leg and left arm-right leg should be varied with unilateral movements of right arm-right leg and left arm-left leg.

Variation. Keep the free arm on the hip.

THE TURTLE

With feet apart and hands widely spread, the body is in a wide push-up position about half-

A slow-moving Turtle Walk

way up from the floor (elbows somewhat bent). From this position, the children move in various directions, keeping the plane of the body always about the same distance from the floor. Movements of the hands and feet should occur only in small increments.

MEASURING WORM

Have them start in a front-leaning rest position. Keeping the knees stiff, they bring up the feet as close as possible to the hands by inching forward with the feet and regain the position by inching forward with the hands. Emphasize keeping the knees straight, with necessary bending occurring at the hips.

CRICKET WALK

"Squat. Spread your knees. Put your arms between your knees and grasp the outside of your ankles. In this position, walk forward or backward. Chirp like a cricket. Turn around right and left."

"See what happens if both feet move at once!"

WICKET WALK

The stunt gets its name because the child's position resembles the shape of a wicket in a croquet game. Children bend over and touch the floor with their weight *evenly* distributed on hands and feet. By keeping the knees straight, a wicket can be formed. Walk the wicket forward, backward, and sideward. Keep arms and legs as near vertical as possible.

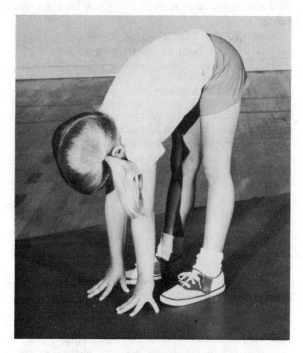

Starting the Wicket Walk

Be sure the knees are kept reasonably straight, since the stunt loses much of its flexibility values if the knees are bent too much. A common error in the execution of this stunt is to keep the hands positioned too far forward of the feet.

MULE KICK

"Stoop down and place your hands on the floor in front of your feet. Your arms are the front legs of the mule. Kick out with your hind legs while taking the weight on your front legs." Taking the weight on the hands is important.

The stunt can be taught in two stages. First, practice taking the weight on the hands momentarily. Next, add the kick.

Variation. Have them make two kicks before the feet return to the ground.

SEAL CRAWL

The child is in a front-leaning (push-up) position, the weight supported on straightened arms and toes. Keeping the body straight, he walks forward, using the hands for the propelling force and dragging the feet. Watch to see that the body is straight and the head is up.

Using the Seal Crawl to move

Variations. Let the children crawl forward a short distance and then roll over on their backs, clapping their hands like a seal, with appropriate seal grunts.

Crawl with the fingers pointed in different directions—out and in.

Reverse Seal Crawl. Turn over and attempt the crawl while dragging the heels.

Elbow Crawl. Assume the original position, but with the weight on the elbows. Crawl forward on the elbows.

The Seal Crawl can also be made more challenging by using the crossed-arm position.

BALANCE STUNTS

Level 1. Introductory challenge
One-Leg Balance
Double Knee Balance
Line Walking
Blind Person's Reach
Head Balance
Head Touch

Level 2. Moderate challenge
Tightrope Walk
Balance Touch
Hopping Balance
One-Legged Balance Stands
    Kimbo Stand
    Knee Lift Balance
    Stork Stand

Leg Balances—Leaning
   Backward
   Forward
   Sideward
Hand and Knee Balance

Level 3. Significant challenge
Tummy Balance
One-Leg Balance Reverse
Single Knee Balance

Level 1. Introductory Challenge

The child should begin to learn the underlying idea in balance stunts, i.e., that the position should be held for a specified length of time without undue movement or loss of balance and that a recovery must be made to the original position. Hold balances for three and five seconds. Also, have the child perform with the eyes closed.

ONE-LEG BALANCE

Begin by having children lift one leg from the floor. Later, they can bring the knee up. Arms should be free at first; then they can take specified positions, such as folded across the chest, on hips, on the head, or behind the back.

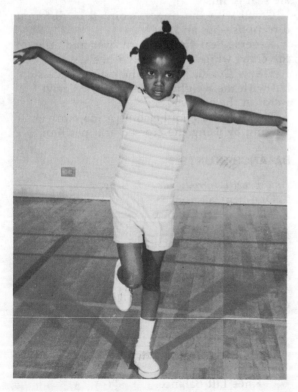

One-Leg Balance

DOUBLE KNEE BALANCE

Have them kneel on both knees, with the feet pointed to the rear; lift the feet from the ground, and balance on the knees. Vary the position of the arms.

Allow children to experiment with different positions for balance.

LINE WALKING

Use a line on the floor, a chalked line, or a board. Children walk forward and backward on the line, as follows, emphasizing good balance:
Regular steps.
Follow steps. The front foot moves forward, and the back foot moves up. One foot always leads.
Heel and toe. Take regular steps, but on each step bring the heel against the toe.
Hopping on the line. Change to the other foot.

BLIND PERSON'S REACH

Have them stand with the body straight, feet together. They extend the arms forward, palms down, then close the eyes and hold the position for ten seconds without moving the foot position or the arms noticeably from the horizontal position.

HEAD BALANCE

Place a beanbag, block, or book on the child's head. Have him walk, stoop, turn around, sit down, get up, etc.

The object should be balanced so that the upper body is in good posture. Use hand out to the side for balance. Later, have him vary the position of the arms—folded across the chest, placed behind the back, or down at the sides.

Structure problems by having children link together a series of movements.

Utilize painted lines on the floor or outdoor hardtop areas to provide directional challenges.

HEAD TOUCH

Have the children kneel on a mat on both knees, with feet pointed backward. Arms are outstretched backward for balance. They lean forward slowly and touch the forehead to the mat. Recover to position. Vary the arm position.

Level 2. Moderate Challenge

TIGHTROPE WALK

In the Tightrope Walk, children should give good play to their imagination. Set the stage by discussing what a circus performer on the wire might do. Have children select a board or chalked or painted line on the floor to be the

Head-balancing a beanbag

Balance Touch with a beanbag

wire. They can pretend to be on the high wire, doing various tasks with exaggerated loss and control of balance. Add such tasks as jumping rope, juggling balls, or riding a bicycle on the wire. Some may hold a parasol or a balancing pole while performing. Someone may be able to find a picture of a tightrope walker.

BALANCE TOUCH

An object (eraser, block, or beanbag) is placed a yard away from a line. Balancing on one foot, the child reaches out with the other foot, touches the object, and recovers to the starting position. He should not place weight on the object but merely touch it. He should try this reaching sideward and backward.

Variation. Have him try at various distances. On a gymnasium floor, count the number of boards to establish the distance for the touch.

HOPPING BALANCE

Have the children hop on one foot for a specified number of times (three, four, or five). At the completion of the number, they hold the balance without appreciable foot or body movement.

ONE-LEGGED BALANCE STANDS

Each balance stunt should be done with different arm positions. Have them begin with the arms out to the side and then try with the arms folded across the chest. Have the children devise other arm positions.

Each stunt can be held first for three seconds and then for five seconds. Later, the eyes should be closed during the count. The children should recover to original position without loss of balance or excessive movement. Stunts should be repeated, using the other leg.

Kimbo Stand. With the left foot kept flat on the ground, the child crosses the right leg over the left to a position in which the foot is pointed partially down and the toe is touching the ground. He holds this position for a specified count before returning to a standing position.

Knee Lift Balance. From a standing position, he lifts one knee up so that the thigh is parallel to the ground with toe pointed down. He holds, then returns to the starting position.

Stork Stand. From a standing position, he shifts all the weight to one foot. The other foot is placed so that the sole of the foot is against the calf of the standing leg. He holds, then returns to a standing position.

LEG BALANCES—LEANING

Backward. With the knee straight, the child extends one leg forward with the toe pointed so that the leg is level with the floor. He balances on the other leg for five seconds, with arms out to the side for balance. He should lean back as far as possible. The bend should be far enough back so that the eyes are looking at the ceiling.

Knee Lift Balance

Stork Stand

Forward. He extends the leg backward until it is parallel to the floor. Keeping eyes forward and arms out to the side, he bends forward, balancing on the other leg. He holds for five seconds without moving.

Sideward. He stands on the left foot with enough side bend to the left so that the right (top) side of the body is parallel to the floor. The right arm should be held alongside the head in a line with the rest of the body. Reverse, using the

Forward-leaning Leg Balance

right leg for support. (Support may be needed momentarily to get into position.)

HAND AND KNEE BALANCE

Have the children get down on all fours, with support on the hands and knees, supporting also on the feet with the toes pointed backward. They lift one hand and the opposite leg from the floor and balance on the other hand and knee. Have them keep the foot from touching during the hold. Reverse hand and knee positions.

Hand and Knee Balance

Level 3. Significant Challenge

TUMMY BALANCE

The children lie prone on the floor with arms outstretched to the sides, palms down. They raise arms, head, chest, and legs from the floor, balancing on the tummy. Knees should be kept straight.

Single Knee Balance

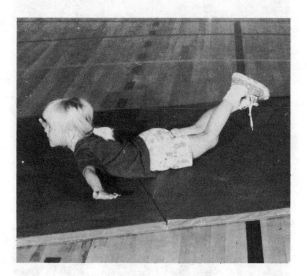

Tummy Balance

ONE-LEG BALANCE REVERSE

Children assume a forward balance position. In this, the body leans forward, the arms are out to the sides, and the weight is on one leg with the other leg extended behind. In a quick movement, the free leg swings down to give momentum to change to the same forward balance position facing in the opposite direction (180-degree turn). No unnecessary movement of the supporting foot should be made after the turn is complete. The swinging foot should not touch the floor.

SINGLE KNEE BALANCE

Balance is made on one knee (and leg), with the arms outstretched to the sides. Reverse position.

SPECIALIZED MOVEMENT STUNTS

Level 1. Introductory challenge
Gnome Walk
Toe Touch Walk
Goose Step
March in Place
Ladder Climbing
Directional Walk
Cross-legged Sit
Fluttering Leaf
Elevator
Rising Sun
Heel Click
Jump Turns
Jumping Jacks

Push-up Progressions
  Wall Push-up
  Wall Walk
  Knee Push-up

Level 2. Moderate challenge
Lowering the Boom
  Flat Tire
Turnover
Slippery Walk
Pogo Stick
Top
Spinning Top
Heel Stand
Turk Stand
Seat Circle
Thread the Needle
Crazy Walk
Reach Under
Push-up
The Treadmill

Level 3. Significant challenge
Curl-up
Squat Thrust
The Scooter
Hip Walk
Long Bridge
Heel Slap
Stiff Person Bend
The Rubber Person

Level 1. Introductory Challenge

When teaching the various walks, arrange the area so that the children can move far enough to get the feel of the experience. If the walk is done in personal space, one can have the children count steps to a definite number. The walking can be accompanied by a drumbeat. Challenge with different patterns and directions.

GNOME WALK

Have the children bend over and grasp their ankles. The knees can be bent. They walk in different directions. Remember to explain what a gnome is.

TOE TOUCH WALK

"Bend over and touch the opposite toe with your hand on each step."

GOOSE STEP

"As you walk, kick up your foot to touch your hand on each step. This is similar to the Goose Step used by some of the armies of the world in their parade formations."

MARCH IN PLACE

"March in place like a soldier, with your knees lifted high and your arms swinging vigorously." Add right and left full turns.

LADDER CLIMBING

Have them reach to grasp imaginary rungs and pretend to climb a ladder.

DIRECTIONAL WALK

Have them stand with their side facing the desired direction, arms at sides. They take a sidestep in the desired direction (right or left), simultaneously lifting the arm and pointing in the direction of movement. At the same time, they turn the head in the direction of movement and sound off the direction. They complete the sidestep by closing with the other foot, dropping the arm to the side, and turning the head back to normal position. The movements should be definite and forceful; the directional command should be called out crisply. After a number of sidesteps in one direction, reverse.

The walk serves to reinforce the concept of right and left.

CROSS-LEGGED SIT

Have them sit with legs crossed and body partially bent forward. Six commands are now given (in varying sequence):

"Touch the right foot with the right hand."
"Touch the left foot with the right hand."
"Touch the right foot with the left hand."

Directional Walk

"Touch the left foot with the left hand."
"Touch both feet with both hands."
"Touch the feet with crossed hands."

When the right foot is crossed over the left, it becomes the "left foot," and vice versa. If this seems too difficult, have the child start with the feet in normal position (uncrossed).

Variation. The stunt can be done as partner activity. One child gives the commands, and the other responds as directed.

FLUTTERING LEAF

"Keeping your feet in place and your body relaxed, flutter to the ground slowly just as a falling leaf would do in the fall." The arms can swing back and forth loosely to accentuate the fluttering movements.

ELEVATOR

"With your arms straight out at your sides, pretend to be an elevator going down. Lower your body a little at a time by bending your knees, keeping your upper body erect and eyes forward. Go into a deep-knee bend. Return to position." Add a body twist to the downward movement.

RISING SUN

"Lie on your back. Using your arms only for balance, rise to a standing position."

Variation. Have children fold the arms over the chest. Experiment with different positions of the feet. Feet can be crossed, spread wide, both to one side, etc.

HEEL CLICK

"Stand with your feet slightly apart. Jump up and click your heels, coming down with your feet apart." Have them try with a quarter-turn right and left.

Variations. Have the children clap hands overhead as they click the heels.

Have one or more children join hands. A signal is needed. The children can count, "One, two, *three*," jumping on the third count.

Some may be able to click the heels twice before landing. Landing should be with the feet apart.

Begin with a cross step to the side, and then a heel click. Try both right and left.

JUMP TURNS

Jump turns reinforce directional concepts. Use quarter- and half-turns, right and left. Arms should be kept along the sides of the body. Stress landing lightly without a second movement.

Number concepts can be worked in. The teacher calls out the number as a preparatory command and then says, "Jump." Number signals are: one—left quarter-turn, two—right quarter-turn, three—left half-turn, and four—right half-turn. After calling the number, pause a moment to give the children time to remember what it means.

Variation. Have the arms outstretched to the sides.

JUMPING JACKS

The object in this stunt is to do controlled jumps. Have students jump forward, backward, or sideward, two, three, or four times in succession, with emphasis on complete control at the end of the series. Add turns while jumping. For example, have the children jump forward three times with the last jump including a half-turn. The pathway can be a square or a rectangle.

PUSH-UP PROGRESSIONS

Since the child will be concerned with push-ups later on, some preliminary push-up movements can be included in the stunt program. Emphasis should be on doing and not on repetitive competition or on being tested. Emphasize movement with only the arms and keeping the body rigid.

Wall Push-up. Have children stand a foot or so from a wall, facing the wall, with the hands against the wall in push-up position. Keeping the feet in place, they move the body forward against the wall and push back to erect position. Increase the distance from the wall.

Wall Walk. In the position described for the Wall Push-up, have them walk along the wall for ten feet or so.

Knee Push-up. Mats should be used. Have them rest the body on the knees and hands with the arms straight. This is the modified push-up position. They lower the body to the mat by controlled movements of the arms. Challenge the students to return to original position. Once the students have acquired the skill, let them do a few knee push-ups.

Level 2. Moderate Challenge

LOWERING THE BOOM

"Start in a push-up position [front-leaning rest position]. Lower your body slowly to the floor." The movement should be controlled so that the body remains rigid.

Variations. Have children pause halfway down.

Have them come down in stages, inch by inch. Be sure they understand the concept of an inch as a measure of distance. Metric measurement can also be applied here. Have children lower themselves five to ten centimeters at a time.

Flat Tire. Children let themselves down slowly, to the accompaniment of noise simulating air escaping from a punctured tire. See how they react to a "blowout," initiated by an appropriate noise.

TURNOVER

From a front-leaning rest position (as in Lowering the Boom), children turn over so that the back is to the floor. The body should not touch the floor. Have them continue the turn until the original position is assumed. Reverse the direction. Have them turn back and forth several times. The body should be kept straight and rigid throughout the turn.

SLIPPERY WALK

The Slippery Walk takes some instruction, or the children will simply walk in place. Have them stand in stride position with one foot and the opposite hand forward. Now have them slide the feet (slippery) so that they exchange positions forward and backward. At the same time, the arms exchange position. Try to establish rhythmic movement. One can gain or lose ground with the movements.

POGO STICK

"Pretend to be a pogo stick by keeping your body stiff and jumping on your toes. Hold the hands in front of you as if you were holding the stick." Have them move in various directions, using jumps of varied height. Stress upward propelling action by the ankles and toes with the body kept stiff, particularly at the knee joint.

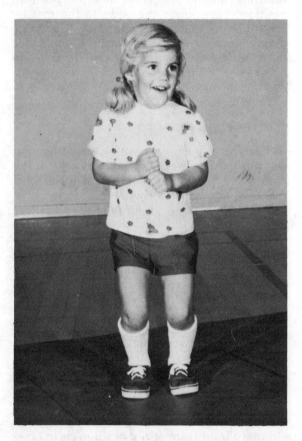

Ready to move like a pogo stick

TOP

From a standing position with arms at the sides, have children try jumping, turning to face the opposite direction, turning three-quarters of the way around, and making a full turn to face the original direction. Number concepts can be stressed by having children do half-, three-quarter-, and full turns.

Successful execution of the stunt should call for the child to land in good balance with hands near the sides. No movement of the feet should occur after landing.

Children should turn right and left.
Variation. Fold the arms across the chest.

SPINNING TOP

With the arms out to the sides, palms down, and with little quick movements of the feet, children spin around two or three times. Reverse directions. Avoid continual spinning, as some children can become quite dizzy.

HEEL STAND

Have the children begin in a full squat position with the arms dangling at the sides and jump upward to full leg extension with the weight on both heels, flinging the arms out diagonally. They hold momentarily and return to position. Several movements can be done rhythmically in succession.

TURK STAND

Have them stand with feet apart and arms folded in front or to the sides. They pivot on the balls of both feet and face the opposite direction. The legs are now crossed. They sit down in this position, then reverse the process. Have

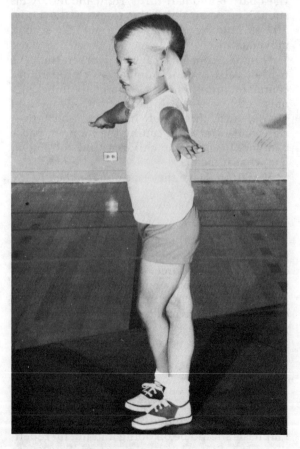

The Turk Stand after the pivot

them get up without using the hands for aid, and uncross the legs with a pivot to face the original direction. Very little change should occur in the position of the feet.

SEAT CIRCLE

"Sit on the floor, your knees bent and your hands braced behind you. Lift your feet off the floor and push with your hands so your body spins in a circle on your seat. Spin right and left."

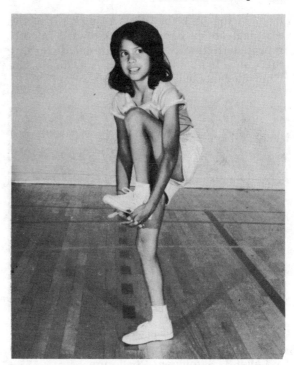

Threading the Needle

Seat Circle

THREAD THE NEEDLE

Have them touch fingertips together in front of the body and step through the arms, one foot at a time, with the tips still touching. They step back to original position. Have them lock the fingers in front of the body and repeat the stunt. Finally, see if children can step through the clasped hands without touching the hands.

CRAZY WALK

The child makes progress forward in an erect position by bringing one foot behind and around the other to gain a little ground each time. Set up a specified goal and challenge children to move this distance with the smallest number of steps.

Variation. Have them reverse the movements and go backward. This means bringing the foot in front and around to gain distance in back.

REACH UNDER

Have them take a position with the feet pointed ahead and spaced about two feet, or a little more than half a meter, apart, toes against

a line or board. They are to place a beanbag two boards (about four inches) in front of their feet and midway between them. Without changing the position of the feet, they reach with one hand behind and between the legs and pick up the beanbag. They pick it up with the other hand. Move the beanbag a board out at a time and repeat.

Variation. Allow the heels to be lifted from the floor.

PUSH-UP

From a front-leaning rest position, have them lower the body and push up back to original position. Be sure that the only movement is in the arms, with the body kept rigid and straight.

Variation. Children stop halfway down and halfway up. They go up and down by inches.

Note. Since the push-up is used in many exercises and testing programs, it is important that the children learn its proper execution early. At this point, interest should be directed to establishing the correct concept of the push-up rather than to competing.

THE TREADMILL

A wand or yardstick is needed. The children get into a sprinter's start position with one knee under the chest and the other leg extended backward. A wand is placed about six inches in front of the back toe. With a quick lift of the seat, legs are exchanged. Work toward smooth, repeated rhythmic motion without disturbing the wand. If no stick or wand is available, the children can exchange feet over a line.

Starting position for the Treadmill

Level 3. Significant Challenge

CURL-UP

Two children work together, with one child holding the other's feet. The performer lies on his back with the legs extended and feet one foot apart. The knees are up so that an angle of 90 degrees is formed at the knee joint. The feet are flat (soles down) on the floor. The hands, with the fingers interlaced, are behind the lower part of the head.

The Curl-up

The child curls up, touching the right and left elbows in turn to the opposite knees. One touch is made on each curl-up. Be sure the child returns the head completely to the floor each

time. No rest should be allowed, as the curl-ups must be continuous. The child may move at his own pace, however.

SQUAT THRUST

While the squat thrust is used as an exercise, the act of completing the cycle successfully is classified as a stunt. The stunt is done in four definite movements. The child starts from the position of attention. On count one, he squats down on the floor placing the hands flat on the floor (shoulder width apart) with the elbows inside the knees. On count two, he thrusts the feet and legs back so that the body is perfectly straight from head to toe in push-up position. On count three, the child returns to squat position: and on the last count, he returns to the position of attention.

Girls should do three in ten seconds, and boys should do four in the same amount of time.

First, teach proper positioning during each of the four phases. Then stress the rhythmic nature of the movements. Music may be added.

THE SCOOTER

The Scooter is an excellent movement for abdominal development. The child is on the floor in extended sitting position with arms folded in front of the chest but held chin high. To scoot, he or she pulls the seat toward the heels, using heel pressure and lifting the seat slightly. He then extends the legs forward again, and repeats the process.

The Scooter

HIP WALK

The child sits in the same position as in the Scooter, except that the arms are in thrust position, with the hand making a partial fist. The child makes forward progress by alternate leg movements. The arm-leg coordination should be unilateral.

LONG BRIDGE

Have the children begin in a crouched position with the hands on the floor, knees between the arms. They walk the hands forward a little at a time until the body is in an extended push-up position. Return to starting position.

Challenge children to extend out as far forward as they can and still retain the support.

Variations. Have them begin with a forward movement then change to sideward movement, establishing as wide a spread as possible. Another variation is to work from a crossed-hands position. Challenge them to lift one hand and/ or one foot from the ground momentarily.

HEEL SLAP

From an erect position with hands at the sides, have them jump into the air and slap both heels with the hands.

Variations. Use a one, two, three rhythm with small preliminary jumps on one and two. Have them make quarter- or half-turns in the air. During a jump, they slap the heels twice before landing.

STIFF PERSON BEND

Have them stand with the feet about shoulder width apart and toes pointed forward. They

Stiff Person Bend

place a beanbag six inches behind the left heel. They then grasp the right toe with the right hand, thumb on top. Without bending the

knees, they reach the left hand outside the left leg and pick up the beanbag without letting go of the toe with the right hand. Increase the distance slowly. Reverse positions.

THE RUBBER PERSON

This stunt is similar to the Stiff Person Bend. A beanbag is placed just outside the right heel. The child reaches the left arm back around the left leg and in front of his right leg to pick up the beanbag. The stunt can be done on two levels. Try it first, allowing him to lift the heels. Later, try to do the stunt with the heels kept on the floor.

TUMBLING AND INVERTED BALANCES

Level 1. Introductory challenge
Rolling Log
Side Roll
Forward Roll—first stage
Backward Roll—hand-clasped position

Level 2. Moderate challenge
Climb-up
Three-Point Tip-up
Forward Roll—second stage
Back Roller
Backward Curl
Backward Roll—regular

Level 3. Significant challenge
Forward Roll Variations
Backward Roll Practice
Frog Handstand (Tip-up)
Headstand
    Climb-up method
    Kick-up method

Level 1. Introductory Challenge

ROLLING LOG

"Lie on your back with your arms stretched overhead. Roll sideways the length of the mat. The next time, roll with your hands pointed toward the other side of the mat." To roll in a straight line, the feet should be kept slightly apart.

Variations. Have them alternate stretch and curl movements while rolling.

Have them start with a jump rope looped around the waist. When they roll, the rope will be rolled up around the waist. After the roll, they stand up and shake the rope so that it drops to the floor.

Another stunt is to have four to six children lying face down side by side. The child on the right (or left) does a log roll over the other chil-

Rolling Log

against the inside of the thighs, tucking the chin to the chest and making a rounded back. A push-off with the hands and feet provides the force for the roll. The child should carry the weight on his hands with the elbows bearing the weight of the thighs and assuming weight there. The force of the roll is then easily transferred to the rounded back. The child should try to roll forward to his feet. Later, have him try with the knees together and no weight on the elbows.

The instructor can help by kneeling alongside the child and placing one hand on the back of the child's head and the other under the thigh for a push, finishing the assist with an upward lift on the back of the neck.

dren and takes her place at the end of the line to be rolled over.

SIDE ROLL

Have the children start on hands and knees with the side selected for the roll toward the direction of the roll. By dropping the shoulder and tucking both the elbow and knee under, children roll over completely on the shoulders and hips, coming again to the hands-and-knees position. Momentum is needed to return to the original position. Children should practice rolling back and forth from one hand-and-knee position to another.

FORWARD ROLL—FIRST STAGE

Have the child stand facing forward with the feet apart. He squats and places his hands on the mat, shoulder width apart, with the elbows

Spotting the Forward Roll

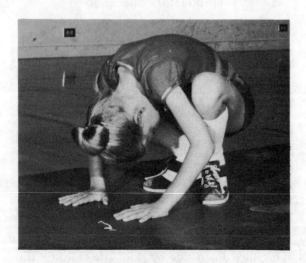

Beginning the Forward Roll

BACKWARD ROLL—HAND-CLASPED POSITION

Teachers can have good success teaching the backward roll by beginning with this approach. The child clasps the fingers behind the neck, with the elbows held out to the sides. From a crouched position he sits down rapidly, bringing the knees to the chest for a tuck to secure momentum. He rolls completely over backwards, taking much of the weight on the elbows. In this method, the neck is protected, and the pressure is taken by the elbows.

Remind children to keep their elbows well back and out to the sides to gain maximum support and ensure minimal neck strain.

Level 2. Moderate Challenge

CLIMB-UP

Have the child get down on a mat on hands and knees, with the hands placed about shoulder width apart and the fingers spread and pointed forward. Have him place the head forward of the hands so that the head and the hands form a triangle on the mat. He walks the body weight forward so that most of it rests on the hands and head and climbs the knees to the top of the elbows. This stunt is lead-up activity to the headstand.

Variation. Raise the knees off the elbows.

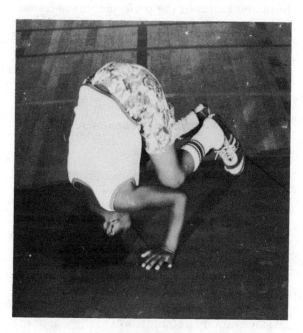

The Climb-up

THREE-POINT TIP-UP

The three-point tip-up ends up in the same general position as the climb-up, but with the elbows on the inside of the thighs. The child squats down on the mat, placing the hands flat, fingers pointing forward, with the elbows inside and pressed against the inner part of the lower thighs. He leans forward, slowly transferring the weight of the body to the bent elbows and hands until the forehead touches the mat. He returns to starting position.

This stunt also provides a background for the headstand and for the handstand, given in later grades.

Some children may have better success by turning the fingers in slightly, causing the elbows to point out more, offering better support to the thigh contact.

FORWARD ROLL—SECOND STAGE

Hands are on the mat, shoulder width apart, with the fingers pointed forward. The knees are *between* the arms. From this position, the child pushes off with the feet and rocks forward on the hands. "Just as you feel yourself falling off balance, tuck your head down between your arms with your chin on your chest." The back of the head touches the mat, and the weight is then borne by the rounded back. The child then grasps the shins and pulls himself to his feet. Those who have trouble should put the hands between the knees and the elbows against the thighs.

Variation. Have him do a forward roll with a ball held between the legs.

Teaching Suggestion. Remind children that no nose, no knees, no elbows are to be seen.

BACK ROLLER

This stunt is a lead-up to the regular backward roll. Begin in a crouched position, knees together, hands resting lightly on the floor. Have the child roll backward, securing momentum by bringing the knees to the chest and clasping them with the arms. He should roll back and forth rhythmically. On the backward movement, the roll should go well back on the neck and head. He should try to roll forward to the original position. Where children have difficulty in rolling back to the original position, have them cross the legs and roll to a crossed-leg standing position.

Back Roller

BACKWARD CURL

This stunt has three stages.

1. Have the child begin in a sitting position with the knees drawn up to the chest and the chin tucked down. The arms are placed out to the sides as the shoulders make contact with the mat. He rolls backward until the weight is on the shoulders and the feet and legs come back over the head so that the toes touch the mat. He then rolls back to starting position.

2. In this stage, the hands are placed alongside the head on the mat as the child rolls back. The fingers are pointed in the direction of the roll with the palms down on the mat. A good direction to the children is, "Point your thumbs toward your ears and keep your elbows reasonably close to your body."

3. The third stage is similar to the second, except that the child starts in a crouched position on his feet. In a deep-knee bend position, with the back toward the direction of the roll, the child secures momentum by sitting down quickly, bringing the knees to his chest.

The teacher has to recognize that this, like the back roller, is a lead-up to the backward roll. The hand pressure is an important item to be stressed. Teach children to push hard against the floor to take pressure off the back of the neck.

Variations. Have him touch the knees, instead of the toes, behind the head.

Another interesting challenge can be made using a beanbag. Have the child keep a beanbag between the feet and deposit it behind the head, returning to position. Next, he curls back and picks up the beanbag, returning it to original position.

A more difficult backward curl, which some children may be able to do, starts with the child sitting with legs crossed and the hands grasping the feet. He rolls backwards, touching the floor overhead with the feet. Return to position.

BACKWARD ROLL—REGULAR

The child should start with the back to the direction of the roll, in the same squat position as in the forward roll. He pushes off with the hands quickly, sits down, and starts rolling over on the back.

The knees should be brought to the chest, so that the body is tucked and momentum is increased. He quickly brings the hands up over the shoulders, palms up, fingers pointed backward. He continues rolling backward with the knees close to the chest. The hands will now touch the mat at about the same time as the head. It is vitally important at this point for him

to push hard with the hands. He continues to roll over the top of the head and pushes off the mat until ready to stand.

Proper hand position can be emphasized by telling the children to point their thumbs toward their ears and to spread their fingers for better push-off control.

Spotting. Care must be taken never to push a child from the hip, forcing him to roll over, as this puts undue pressure on the back of the neck.

The proper method of aiding the child who has difficulty with the stunt is as follows. The spotter stands in a straddle position with the near foot alongside at about the spot where the performer's hands and head will make contact with the mat. The other foot is one stride in the direction of the roll. The critical point is for the spotter to lift the performer's hips just as the head and hands of the performer make contact with the mat. This is accomplished by taking the near hand and reaching across to the far hip of the performer, getting under the near hip with the rear hand. The lift is applied on the front of the hips just below the beltline. The object is to relieve the pressure on the neck.

Level 3. Significant Challenge

FORWARD ROLL VARIATIONS

Continued practice to polish up the forward roll is recommended. Work toward getting the children to come to their feet at the end of the roll. Grasping the knees near the end of the roll is of help. Keep emphasizing "no nose, no knees, and no elbows."

Variations. Have the child roll with the ankles crossed, coming to the feet. He can turn around by uncrossing the ankles and roll back in the opposite direction.

Have him try a straddle roll to the seat or to a standing position. He can stand with the feet well apart and roll in that position.

Have him roll to a walk-out position. At the end of the roll, one leg is extended, and the child walks out off the mat.

Have him do a forward roll to the feet and jump into the air as a finishing act.

Have him combine two rolls.

BACKWARD ROLL PRACTICE

Continue practice with the backward roll. Work toward two successive backward rolls. Have children perform a forward roll with crossed legs, turn, and go into a backward roll.

A few children may be able to do a back extension. Just after the feet go overhead, the child pushes off and lands on the feet.

FROG HANDSTAND (TIP-UP)

The stunt follows the same directions as the three-point tip-up (p. 201). The child squats down on the mat, placing the hands flat, fingers pointing forward, with the elbows inside and pressed against the inner part of the knees. He leans forward, using the leverage of the elbows against the knees, and balances on the hands. The position is held for five seconds, then he returns to starting position.

The head does not touch the mat at any time. Hands may be turned in slightly, to help make better contact between the elbows and the insides of the thighs.

HEADSTAND

Two approaches are suggested for the headstand. The first is to relate the headstand to the climb-up. The second is to go directly into a headstand, using a kick-up to achieve the inverted position. With either method, it is essential that the triangle position of the hands and head be maintained.

In this position, the hands are placed about shoulder width apart, with the fingers pointed forward, spread, and slightly cupped. The head is positioned on the mat about ten to twelve inches forward of the hands, with the weight taken on the forward part of the head, near the hairline.

In the final inverted position, the feet should be together with the legs straight and toes pointed. The back is arched somewhat, with the weight evenly distributed among the hands and the forward part of the head.

The safest way to come down from the inverted position is to return to the mat in the direction that was used in going up. Recovery is helped by bending at both the waist and the knees. If the child overbalances and falls forward, he should tuck the head under and go into a forward roll.

Both methods of recovery from the inverted position should be included in the instructional sequences early in the presentation.

Climb-up Method. A spotter is stationed directly in front of the performer and steadies him or her as needed. If the spotter cannot control the performer, however, he must be alert to move out of the way if the latter goes into a forward roll when coming out of the inverted position.

The performer takes the inverted position of the climb-up and slowly moves his feet upward to the headstand position, steadied by the spotter only as needed. The spotter can first apply support to the hips and then transfer to the an-

kles as the climb-up position is lengthened into a headstand.

Kick-up Method. The goal of the kick-up method is to establish a pattern that can be applied to other inverted stunts, as well as serving for the headstand. Keeping the weight on the forward part of the head and maintaining the triangle base, the child walks the feet forward until the hips are high over the body; this resembles the climb-up position. He keeps one foot on the mat with the knee of that leg bent and the other leg somewhat extended backward. He kicks the back leg up to the inverted position, following quickly with a push by the other leg, thus bringing the two legs together in the inverted position. The timing is a quick one-two movement.

When learning, children should work in units of three students. One child attempts the stunt, while a spotter stands on either side. Positions are rotated. Each spotter kneels, placing his near hand under the shoulder of the performer. The performer now "walks" her weight above the head and kicks up to position. The spotter on each side supports by grasping the leg.

Teaching Points. The triangle formed by the hands and the head is important; the weight must be centered on the forward part of the head. Most of the troubles that occur while doing the headstand come from incorrect head-hand relationship. The correct placement can be ensured by making certain that the head is placed the length of the performer's forearm from the knees, and that the hands are placed at the knees.

Do not let children stay too long in the inverted position or hold contests to see who can stand on his head the longest.

Most of the responsibility for getting into the inverted position should rest on the performer. Spotters may help to some extent, but they should avoid pushing, pulling, and supporting the performer.

PARTNER AND GROUP STUNTS

Level 1. Introductory challenge
Seesaw

Level 2. Moderate challenge
Double Top
Toe Toucher
Bouncing Ball

Level 3. Significant challenge
Wring the Dishrag
Partner Pull-up
Chinese Get-up

Twister
Partner Hopping

Level 1. Introductory Challenge

SEESAW

Two children face each other and join hands. One child stoops down. The seesaw now moves up and down, with one child stooping while the other rises. The children can recite the words to this version of "Seesaw, Margery Daw" as they move:

Seesaw, Margery Daw,
Ma and Pa, like a saw,
Seesaw, Margery Daw.

Variation. Have the rising child jump into the air at the end of the rise.

Level 2. Moderate Challenge

DOUBLE TOP

Have partners face each other and join hands. Experiment to see which type of grip works best. With straight arms, they lean away from each other; at the same time, each moves the toes close to the partner's. They spin around slowly in either direction, taking tiny steps. Increase speed.

Double Top

Variation. Have them use a stooped position.

TOE TOUCHER

Partners lie on backs with heads near each other and feet in opposite directions. They grasp each other, using a hand-wrist grip; both partners bring up their legs so that the toes touch. Have them keep the weight high on the shoulders and touch the feet high.

Partners should be of about the same height. Strive to attain the high shoulder position, as this is the point of most difficulty in the stunt.

Variation. One partner carries a beanbag, ball, or other article between his feet. The article is transferred to the other partner, who lowers it to the floor.

BOUNCING BALL

Toss a lively utility ball into the air and let the children watch how it bounces, lower and lower, until it finally comes to rest on the floor. From a bent-knee position, with the upper body erect, each child imitates a ball by beginning with a high bounce and gradually lowering the height of the jump to simulate a ball coming to rest.

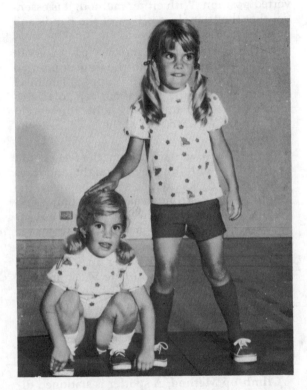

Ready for the Bouncing Ball

Variation. Have children do this as a partner stunt, with one partner serving as the bouncer and the other as the ball. Reverse roles. Try having one partner "dribble the ball" in various positions.

Toss the ball into the air and have the children move with the ball as it bounces lower and lower. As children go down, they should touch the hands to the floor to avoid the complete deep-knee bend position.

Level 3. Significant Challenge

WRING THE DISHRAG

Two children face each other and join hands. They raise one arm each (one raises the right; the other raises the left) and turn under that pair of arms, continuing in a full turn until they are back to original position. Care must be taken to avoid bumping heads.

Wringing the Dishrag

Variation. Try the stunt at a lower level using a crouched position.

PARTNER PULL-UP

Partners sit down facing each other in a bent-knee position with the heels on the floor and the toes touching. Pulling cooperatively, both come to a standing position. They return to the floor.

CHINESE GET-UP

This is a partner or group stunt. Two children sit back to back and lock arms. From this posi-tion, both try to stand by pushing against each other's back. They sit down again. If the feet are sliding, have them do the stunt on a mat.

Chinese Get-up

Variations. Try the stunt with three or four children.

From a halfway-down position, have children move like spiders.

TWISTER

Partners face and grasp right hands as if shaking hands. A swings the right leg over the head of B and turns around, taking a straddle position over his own arm. B swings the left leg over A who has bent over, and the partners are now back to back. A now continues with the left leg and faces in the original direction. B swings the right leg over, back to the original face-to-face position.

Halfway into the Twister

Partners must duck to avoid being kicked by each other's feet as the legs are swung over.

Variation. The stunt can be introduced by having them grasp a wand rather than hold hands.

PARTNER HOPPING

Children coordinate hopping movements for short distances and in different directions. Three combinations are suggested:

1. The partners stand facing each other. Each extends the left leg forward to be grasped at the ankle by the partner. Each then hops on the right leg.
2. Partners stand back to back. Each lifts the leg backward (bending the knee) and has the partner grasp the ankle. They hop as before.
3. Partners stand side by side with inside arms around each other's waist. They lift the inside foot from the floor and make progress by hopping on the outside foot.

If either partner begins to fall, the other should release the leg immediately. Vary by moving in different directions and patterns. Reverse foot positions.

SUMMARY

Stunts and tumbling are important in the development of coordination, balance, flexibility, and agility. Body management skills can be honed through the many different challenges offered in the stunts and tumbling unit. Affective domain outcomes are found in the areas of courage and perseverance as many of the tumbling and inverted balance activities are new to the young child.

Instructional procedures for this area offer keys to presenting activities and instructions for presenting basic mechanical principles to youngsters while teaching. Safety considerations are carefully discussed.

Many different class formations are offered depending on the needs and desires of the teacher. All formations should focus on ease of observing all students who are participating.

Activities are presented in five categories: animal movements, balance stunts, specialized movement stunts, tumbling and inverted balances, and partner and group stunts. Within each of the categories, the activities are evaluated and arranged in levels of difficulty. When organizing the lesson, the teacher should select activities from each category so that there will be a wide variety of challenges. The teacher should also select activities from the proper level of difficulty based on the experience and competency of the students.

Chapter 15

Rhythmic Movement—Children's Dance

Music is the universal language of mankind.
Henry Wadsworth Longfellow

Children love to move; in particular, they love to move rhythmically. Such movement is both a delight and a need. The need is apparent in the child's functional movement, since rhythmic movement is necessary for efficient performance of gross and fine motor skills. The rhythmic quality of good motion allows the child to move easily and gracefully and cope effectively with environmental challenges of space, time, and force. Through rhythmic patterns involving both gross body and locomotor movements, a child can gain better appreciation and understanding of the use of the body.

In contrast, the dysrhythmic child has difficulty maintaining order and sequencing to rhythmic patterns, making performance in sequential motor patterns difficult. A properly constituted rhythmic movement program can help these children to move more efficiently.

Fundamental movement represents only one aspect of the broad rhythmic approach, as it should be experienced by young children. Another important factor is the child's need for expressive and creative movement outlets. Through the medium of creative rhythmic movement, children can express their desires, feelings, and frustrations. Rhythmic movement as an important part of overall movement experiences can make important contributions to children's growth.

Dance for children should begin with natural movements that they already can do—walking, running, hopping, and perhaps skipping. Other, more structured movements can be added later.

CHARACTERISTICS OF RHYTHMIC BACKGROUND

Music has certain essential characteristics that children, no matter what their maturity level, should be able to recognize. At least some attempt should be made to familiarize children with basic musical terms, although the concept of meter may be confusing to younger children. It is necessary to exercise caution to see that these concepts do not stifle the child's spontaneity of approach to music.

Tempo. Tempo may be thought of as the speed of the music. Tempo can be constant, it can show a gradual increase (acceleration), or it can show a decrease (deceleration).

Beat. The beat is the underlying rhythmic quality of the music. The beat can be even or uneven. Music with a pronounced beat is easier for children to follow. It is sometimes referred to as *pulse* or *pulse beat*.

Meter. Meter may be defined as the manner in which beats are put together to form a measure of music. Common meters used in rhythmics are 2/4, 3/4, 4/4, and 6/8.

Accent. The notes or beats that carry the heavier emphasis are accented beats. Accent usually falls on the first beat of each measure. Accent is generally expressed by a heavier movement.

Intensity. The force or intensity of the music can be loud, soft, light, or heavy.

Mood. While mood is related to intensity, it extends the concept into the area of human feelings. Music can interpret many human moods, such as feeling cheerful, sad, happy, gay, warlike, fearful, stately, and others.

Phrase. A phrase is a natural grouping of measures. In most cases, the group of measures will total eight underlying beats or counts.

Patterns. Phrases of music are put together into rhythmic patterns. Children should recognize that the music pattern is being repeated or is changing to another pattern.

RECORDS FOR RHYTHMIC MOVEMENT

There are advantages and drawbacks to using either long-playing, standard, or 45-rpm records. Since long-play records offer more selections, fewer records will be needed. On the other hand, one rarely finds a record on which all the selections are of use. In addition, because the grooves are very close together, the teacher may find it difficult to start or restart a long-play record at a precise point. If a long-play record is damaged by being scratched, the entire record must be replaced. Finally, 45 rpm records are more easily stored.

Although the initial expense is higher, it is best for each teacher to have his or her own personal set of records. The teacher can eventually become familiar with all the records and know which selections can be used for specific activities.

Odd-lot used records, which can be secured at very little expense at rummage sales or at second-hand bookstores, will supplement the collection and add interest.

The record player should have a variable-speed control, so that it can be used for 33⅓, 45, or 78 rpm records. Since needle bounce can be a problem when vigorous activity is going on in the room, some protection against needle bounce will be needed. The machine should either have built-in protection or it should be cushioned on foam rubber pads. The volume must be sufficient to carry the music over the noise of the activity. It should also have an input for a microphone. Each classroom should have its own record player, as there are many times when teachable moments occur and music is desirable. The all-purpose room or gymnasium should also have its own record player.

PRODUCTION OF RHYTHMIC SOUNDS

Rhythmic sounds to stimulate children's rhythmic movement should be of good quality and appropriate for the movements they are designed to stimulate. Much of the success of rhythmic movement depends upon how effectively the sounds arouse and excite children. Some customary sources of rhythmic back-

ground suitable for movement are discussed below.

The first source is the dance drum or tom-tom. Good commercial suppliers have varieties of these instruments at a nominal cost. Different kinds of strikers, which produce sounds of varying timbres, are also available.

Effective use of a drum immensely increases the potential of a movement program. When you say to the children, "The drum is telling you something," this is literally true. It tells them what to do in terms of speed, force, sequence, and other movement qualities. It can signal starting and stopping of activities.

Some teachers prefer to use wooden strikers to perform the same tasks a drum might accomplish. These instruments give a sharp, resonant sound, providing a successful stimulus to movement. A percussion device of this nature can be made from two 12-inch lengths of round dowel, about the thickness of a broom handle.

A second important source of rhythm is the record player. Specialized record sets are on the market, designed for a variety of activities and purposes. Fundamental and other rhythm records, containing a number of short selections on both regular and long-play discs, are available from a variety of sources.[1] Each selection for fundamental skills is identified with the type of movement for which it was designed. This is also true for those selections specifically designed for creative activity. Combination activities, such as run, jump, and roll, are provided for on these records as well.

A third source of rhythmic accompaniment, the tape recorder, adds another dimension to the rhythmic program. Music can be recorded on tape in many different ways, the simplest of which is the straightforward recording of music. With a little practice, directions can be incorporated along with the music. Even primary children can help make recordings for the rhythmic program.

The piano is the fourth source of accompaniment. It offers excellent possibilities, but does demand a reasonable degree of skill, or the program will suffer. It has the further drawback that, if the teacher plays and follows the printed music, it is difficult for her to observe the children's progress. It is also difficult to provide demonstration and offer individual coaching help when one is playing the piano.

A fifth source is songs, poems, spoken phrases, and other vocal forms. The children can express themselves to a poem recited in a rhythmic manner. When an action song is used, the children can learn the music and the words,

[1]See Appendix A for list of record sources.

and the activity can proceed, using only the children's voices.

The guitar can also be useful both for stimulating movement and for accompanying movement songs. Children have become familiar with this instrument through watching television programs. Many teachers have skill with this instrument.

Rhythm band instruments and devices can at times be utilized in the program of rhythms. Children should experience playing in rhythm bands, as a parallel educational activity to the rhythmic movement program. Familiarity with these rhythmic devices, of which there are many kinds, will show them the potential for using them in the physical education program.

TYPES OF RHYTHMIC ACTIVITIES

While there is overlap and interchange of activities, for purposes of analysis and approach, certain rhythmic activity categories may be identified. Some of these have been presented in previous chapters, where they seemed to fit in more logically.

Creative Rhythms

Creative rhythms include free or expressive rhythms, identification rhythms, and those termed dramatization rhythms. In free rhythms, the children move as they feel motivated, producing a variety of unstructured responses. Identification rhythms are so called because a child assumes and acts out a particular identity when these rhythms are used.

Expression through movement and rhythm

In a dramatization rhythm, the children act out a story or a particular situation in sequential form. The activity goes beyond simply assuming an identity and acting out elementary movements. Some type of format or script is involved.

Since creative rhythms can be regarded as a form of creative expression, the area is already included among the discussions of developing overall creative expression in the child. Thus, creative rhythms can complement creative expression by being interwoven through stories, plays, and poems. Reference should be made to Chapter 10.

Fundamental Rhythms

Fundamental movement is centered on basic movement skills, mostly of the locomotor type, but including some nonlocomotor movements; a few skills involving manipulation of objects can be performed to rhythm. Since fundamental rhythms are an important means of developing movement skills, the concepts and activity approach have been included with the discussions of fundamental skill development in Chapter 11. Suggestions on the ways rhythm can be utilized in the development of various fundamental skills (walk, run, jump, etc.) are incorporated within the discussions of the separate skills.

Rhythmic Beat Repetition and Reproduction

If a child is to move rhythmically to a beat or pulse, this ability to perceive and mentally record the beat is fundamentally important for effective rhythmic movement. The goal in this area is to have children make accurate reproductions of the given beat, emphasizing better listening skills to develop their auditory perception. The teacher gives a particular beat

Clapping to the beat of the tom-tom

sequence, usually with a drum, and the children reproduce the beat by clapping their hands and/or tapping their feet. They learn to synchronize their responses to the presented beat sequence.

Singing Movement Songs

Movement songs are of infinite variety and number, and many of them are of Mother Goose origin. These range from songs with simple movements to those of a more traditional type. All, however, are based on the idea that, as children sing them, the words give direction to movements, which are generally subject to individual interpretation.

Folk Dances

Folk dances are traditional dances of either national or ethnic origin. Only a few dances are appropriate for young children, and these are usually modified for age level. Folk dances generally involve a patterned movement response based on either fundamental movements or dance steps. Dances for young children ordinarily employ only fundamental skills within the children's range of movement.

Musical Games

In musical games, a rhythmic factor is involved in the conduct of the game. Most people are familiar with Musical Chairs, which is an example of a game in this category.

APPROACH TO RHYTHMIC MOVEMENT

Preschool and Nursery School

For younger children, the approach to rhythmic activity should emphasize a flexible, creative methodology in which the process of moving and expressing themselves to rhythm is more important than the resulting movement patterns. Youngsters should find new ways of doing things and simply moving to rhythm, giving free rein to imagination and daring to enter new frontiers. Investigation, improvisation, invention, and exploration are the keys to developing movement patterns of a varied nature.

Children should begin to develop critical listening skills and react in keeping with the presented rhythmic pattern. Most of the emphasis in this section will be on simple creative dance and movement songs. Simple contrasting terms such as fast/slow, high/low, and up/down can help give direction to the movement responses. Emphasis on the movement factors of space, time, flow, and qualities in movement (force, expression, imitation) can make the patterns more productive in terms of growth potentialities.

Kindergarten

The same types of activity as in the preschool groups should be emphasized at the kindergarten level. In addition, children can be introduced to fundamental skill movement to rhythm. Movement songs become a little more challenging.

Rope-jumping ability, if acquired, can add the element of rhythm. Rhythmic games have good appeal. A few folk dances of a simple nature are introduced at this time; these are similar to singing movement songs.

First and Second Grades

Creative activities continue to play an important part in the program for first and second grades, with those activities employing rhythm becoming prominent. Stress on fundamental movement skills should be continued.

Action movement songs that require simple formations and movement changes beyond the capacity of younger children can be introduced. Rope-jumping skills should be expanded. Uncomplicated folk dances become a little more precise, anticipating the middle grades, when that emphasis on precision will become more pronounced.

GENERAL INSTRUCTIONAL PROCEDURES

Some general comments governing instructional procedures for all types of rhythmic activities are appropriate here. More specific procedures, related to different types of rhythmic activity, are included under the topical discussions that follow.

The area of content of rhythmic activities for young children lends itself readily and effectively to the creative-exploratory approach, except when teaching a specific dance. The teacher functions as a catalyst for action, focusing the children's attention on the problem to be solved.

It should be made clear to the children that they can respond spontaneously and freely within the limits of the challenge. It will give the children courage to persevere and venture into the unknown if they know that their efforts and individual responses are acceptable.

Much attention must be centered on developing breadth and depth of movement. Exploration should be invited by provocative and open-ended questioning. Deep involvement and variety of response should be encouraged. The object is to spur creativity and self-directed response.

Above all, nothing must interfere with the sheer joy and satisfaction that children find in rhythmic movement. The right response is one that feels good to them, and this feeling must not be denied.

After attention has been given to establishing breadth and variety of movement, efforts should be directed to refining the movement patterns, particularly when fundamental skills are involved. Attention can be focused on defining a given movement solution so that better control, more finesse, and better sequencing of movement are possible. If children are to improve in movement competency, this stage is important.

Where partners are required on the preschool level or in the primary grades, little emphasis should be placed on boy-girl partnerships. Any two children can become partners. One should avoid saying "boys" or "girls" when referring to specific groups in a dance pattern, except where necessary in some of the second grade dances.

An important technique in class control is to establish effective signals for starting and stopping activity. Generally, activity can be started at the spoken word or a rhythmic signal, such as "Ready and begin!" Stopping may be accomplished by cessation of the rhythmic background, a quick double beat on the drum, the raised hand of the teacher, or other (preferably consistent) means. Early attention to this facet of class procedure will pay dividends later in terms of more efficient use of class time.

If the teacher participates with the children, the teacher should use care in selection of movement patterns for himself. Some adults tend to react to "open" music by performing the more precise dance steps. The movements used by the teacher must be within the ability of the children.

When the teacher asks certain children to show their movements while others observe, she should exercise care to select the children who will not be embarrassed by performing in front of others. Perhaps two or three, or even more children could be chosen to give an achievement demonstration.

The teacher is freed for better instructional duty if someone else can handle the record player. If no parent or teacher's aide is available, older students in the school could serve as assistants. Establishing definite signals for starting and stopping the record player is important.

RHYTHMIC BEAT REPETITION AND REPRODUCTION

The introduction of practice in rhythmic beat repetition and reproduction, based on the theories of Kodaly and others, has provided an extension of movement experiences to rhythm. The experiences are valuable for all levels, including preschool through second grade.

A beat pattern of some kind is provided, generally by a drum. The children repeat or reproduce the pattern.

Several different approaches are possible. The enterprising teacher should be able to devise others.

1. Children clap in unison as directed by a drum. This rhythmic pattern should include the four basic meters—2/4, 3/4, 4/4, and 6/8. The patterns produced by the drum can be varied to include accents and different combinations of beats.

2. Children reproduce the beat pattern. A pattern generally covers two or three measures. Some ways this activity can be expanded are:

   a. Children substitute some gesture on the accented beat.

   b. While they reproduce the pattern, they step forward at the beginning of a pattern and backward at the next beginning.

   c. They reproduce first with clapping, then with a beat of the foot.

   d. Add two patterns together. The first pattern is given, and the children follow. The second pattern is provided, and the children reproduce the first pattern, followed by the second.

   e. Combine any of the above activities with locomotor movements.

Suggested Beat Patterns

The beat patterns for 2/4 and 4/4 are quite similar. Most of our illustrations of patterns for these two meters (see p. 212) are for 4/4 time, but a few 2/4 examples are also included. In the illustrations, a mark over a note indicates an accented note.

Each of the meters is presented in a separate diagram, with the basic beat structure shown first, followed by the accented basic structure. Accents are not provided for all the patterns, allowing the teacher flexibility in selecting accented patterns as desired. The teacher should regard these beat patterns only as a starting point, as many others can be devised.

SINGING MOVEMENT SONGS AND FOLK DANCES

A singing movement song is a song that has words, sometimes verses, that the children sing, usually in unison. Based on a fable, story, custom, or some kind of task, the words guide the children toward action that imitates the action in the song. There will be considerable variation among the resultant movement patterns as the

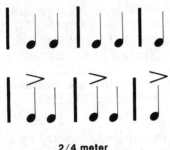

2/4 meter

6/8 meter

3/4 meter

4/4 meter

children follow and interpret the words in their own way. The only restriction is that the movements must be appropriate to the intent and format of the song. In many movement songs, the children move in similar roles; in some cases, there may be one or more key or special roles, which call for actions different from those done by the majority of the children.

A folk dance is a traditional dance of a given people and generally follows a definite pattern sequence as it unfolds. It may include words or verses, which help make the actions more realistic.

As practiced in the school setting, these folk dances incorporate many variations and departures from the original dance patterns. These are designed to simplify or eliminate some of the precise movements of adult-oriented folk dances. While there are a few exceptions, the folk dances in the kindergarten and primary grades require only fundamental locomotor movements within their patterns. The dances requiring specialized dance steps should be reserved for children at more advanced levels. In order to perform the simple dances with ease, the children must first become adept in using fundamental skills to move to rhythm.

Since the approach to teaching movement songs and teaching simple folk dances is quite similar on this level, the instructional procedures for the two are combined.

INSTRUCTIONAL PROCEDURES

1. If the activity is new, some background should be given to the children with regard to the nature of the song or dance and what it is supposed to represent. If known, something about its origin or source can be mentioned.

2. Children should listen to the music. They should then respond to the question, "How did the music make you want to move?" and can comment on its appropriateness for the nature of the song. Have youngsters clap the beat so they can get its feel.

3. Learning the words or verses can be facilitated by printing them in large letters on a poster or on the blackboard. A feasible approach is to have children learn a verse and add the action for just that much of the song or dance. One can then proceed a verse at a time.

4. Have the class walk through the pattern of the song or dance. In a song, be sure the key figure or figures know the necessary action. The tempo may be slowed down at first, but it should be moved up to regular speed as quickly as possible. Too slow a beat distorts some movements.

5. When children are singing, the source of the music should be loud enough for the children to hear over the voices; otherwise, the singing will soon be out of time with the music. Later, the music source may be dispensed with, as the children's singing can provide the accompaniment.

6. If difficulty occurs and frustration builds up, break off the instruction of the song or dance and shift to something the children know or like. One can return to the instruction at a later class session. Praise children for the progress they have made and inform them that the class will try the number again at a later time. Whether or not they are frustrated, however, it is always good practice to end up a rhythmic lesson with a number that the children like and enjoy. This will leave them feeling good about rhythmic activities.

7. The songs and dances that are presented in the following section represent the heritage of many lands and sources. The teacher is encouraged to add others to this basic collection, especially the more modern songs and dances.

8. The suggested list of songs and dances have been allocated according to approximate maturity level. This is not a sacred division, of course; songs for one grade may be used in another. The effective purposes served by such a division are that: (1) the songs are appropriate activities for the grade level, and (2) some adherence to the list will ensure that the children experience a variety of rhythmic numbers throughout their early schooling.

Preschool Activities

A vast fund of rhythmic materials exists for preschool children. It includes not only the old favorites, which have been handed down for centuries, but also the whole area of simple songs and music written especially for children. The presentation in this section will concentrate on the old, familiar favorites, to acquaint children with some of the songs that they can cherish.

These movement songs will not only help children discover rhythms, but will also provide a means for them to express themselves with their own movements based on the selected songs. In addition, each child should have the opportunity to sing easily and with expression in reasonable tune to the music. Youngsters can learn to sing with others and to match their singing with the accompaniment. Ultimately, it is hoped that they will like and enjoy music, building a foundation for future participation and appreciation of this important aspect of our culture.

The following section presents a number of songs suitable for preschool children.

Songs
Around We Go
Baa, Baa, Black Sheep
Bow-Wow-Wow
Brother John
The Cuckoo Clock
Diddle, Diddle, Dumpling
The Donkey
Eency Weency Spider
Good Morning
Humpty Dumpty
I'm a Little Teapot
Jack Be Nimble
Little Boy Blue
Mary Had a Little Lamb
Oh, Where, Oh, Where Has My Little Dog
    Gone?
Ring around the Rosie
Rock-a-Bye, Baby
Trot, My Pony, Trot
Who's That Knocking on My Door?
Yankee Doodle

Around We Go

Formation. Children are in a single circle facing the center, with hands joined.

Verse

1. Around we go, around we go, one big circle marching so.
2. Down we go, down we go, one big circle sinking so.
3. Up we go, up we go, one big circle rising so.
4. Around we go, around we go, one big circle marching so.
5. In we go, in we go, one big circle shrinking so.
6. Out we go, out we go, one big circle stretching so.

Directions

Line 1. All circle clockwise.
Line 2. All stop and slowly go down, bending the knees.
Line 3. All slowly rise.
Line 4. All circle clockwise.
Line 5. Children go toward the center.
Line 6. They walk backward to place and stretch.

Variation. Adapt the dance to a circle of children holding a parachute.

Baa, Baa, Black Sheep

Formation. Children are scattered. They can be seated.

Verse

1. Baa, baa, black sheep, have you any wool?
2. Yes sir, yes sir, three bags full.
3. One for my master, one for my dame,
4. And one for the little boy who lives in the lane.

Directions

Line 1. Children pretend to be sheep with horns.
Line 2. They nod head twice, hold up three fingers.
Line 3. They hold up a finger to emphasize "one," then repeat the action.
Line 4. Again they hold up one finger.

Bow-Wow-Wow

Formation. Children are seated in a circle. One child occupies a chair in the center.

Verse

Bow-wow-wow; whose dog art thou?
Little [Freddie Jones's] dog; bow-wow-wow.

Directions. One child is in the center and becomes the owner of the dog. During the first line, children clap three times and look in all directions as they ask the question. For the second line, they point four times at the center person, reciting his name, and then clap three times. Change the person in the center as the game is repeated.

Other animals could be named, such as:

Woof, woof, woof; whose bear art thou?
Meow, meow, meow; whose cat art thou?
Roar, roar, roar; whose lion art thou?

Brother John

Formation. Children are scattered.

Verse

1. Are you sleeping, are you sleeping?
2. Brother John, Brother John.
3. Morning bells are ringing, morning bells are ringing,
4. Ding, ding, dong; ding, ding, dong.

Directions

Line 1. Children walk around, asking the question of each other.
Line 2. They continue to walk and talk to each other.
Line 3. They hold their heads and sway back and forth.
Line 4. They pretend to ring bells.

The Cuckoo Clock

Formation. Children are scattered, seated.

Verse

Cuckoo, cuckoo, calls from the clock.
Let us be singing, when hours are ringing.
Fun time, fun time, soon will be here.

Directions. This is an adaptation of an old German folk song. The children can pretend to be cuckoo clocks and react accordingly.

Diddle, Diddle, Dumpling

Formation. Children are scattered.

Verse

1. Diddle, diddle, dumpling, my son John
2. Went to bed with his stockings on;
3. One shoe off, and one shoe on.
4. Diddle, diddle, dumpling, my son John.

Directions

Line 1. They do a jig in place, turning around.
Line 2. They pretend to sleep, with hands alongside face, and then point to stockings.
Line 3. They bounce on one foot, thrusting the other foot forward; reverse feet.
Line 4. They repeat action for line 1.

The Donkey

Formation. Children are seated in a circle.

Verse

Sweetly sings the donkey as he looks for hay.

If you do not feed him, this is what he'll say,

Hee-haw, hee-haw; hee-haw, hee-haw, hee-haw.

Directions. Children walk around during the first two lines. On the third line, they place both thumbs in the ears, and flap the "ears" on each "hee-haw."

Eency, Weency Spider

Formation. Children are scattered. They can be seated.

Verse

Eency weency spider went up the water spout.

Down came the rain and washed the spider out.

Out came the sun and dried up all the rain,

And the eency weency spider went up the spout again.

Directions. This can be done as a finger play or with gross movements, reacting to the words. Discuss with the children the kinds of things they should do with each line, stressing the concepts of up and down.

Good Morning

Formation. One child is designated as King or Queen for the day. The others are scattered around the room.

Verse

Good morning to you, good morning to you.
Good morning, dear [child's name], good morning to you.

Directions. During the first line, children walk about bowing to one another. During the second line, they face the King or Queen, bowing to him or her while repeating his or her name. They bow again on the last "good morning."

Humpty Dumpty

Formation. Children are scattered, in groups of three. One in each group is Humpty Dumpty. A chair can be used as a prop.

Verse

1. Humpty Dumpty sat on a wall.
2. Humpty Dumpty had a great fall.
3. All the king's horses and all the king's men
4. Couldn't put Humpty Dumpty together again.

Directions

Line 1. All walk around the chair, roly-poly fashion. Humpty Dumpty sits down.

Line 2. Humpty Dumpty falls off the chair; the others express surprise.

Line 3. Children scurry around the fallen Humpty Dumpty.

Line 4. They pretend to put Humpty Dumpty together again.

I'm a Little Teapot

Formation. Children are scattered.

Verse

1. I'm a little teapot, round and stout.
2. Here is my handle; here is my spout.
3. When I get all steamed up, then I
   shout:
4. Tip me over and pour me out!

Directions

Line 1. Children use their arms to show a round shape.

Line 2. One arm can form the handle; the other, the spout.

Line 3. Children shake hands overhead, fingers loose to indicate steam. Hands to mouth can indicate shouting.

Line 4. They lean to one side and pretend to pour out of the spout.

This is an old, traditional American rhyme. It can also be done as a finger play with the children seated.

Jack Be Nimble

Formation. Children are scattered.

Supplies. Each child can make his own candlestick.

Verse

1. Jack be nimble, Jack be quick,
   Jack jump over the candlestick.
2. Jack be nimble, Jack be quick,
   Jump back over the candlestick.

Directions. Each child has a candlestick (real or imaginary). He skips around to the words, but places himself in position to "jump over the candlestick." At the completion of the second verse, he jumps back over from the opposite direction.

Little Boy Blue

Formation. Children are scattered.

Verse

Little Boy Blue, come blow your horn.
The sheep's in the meadow, the cow's in
    the corn.

Where is the boy who looks after the
    sheep?
He's under the haystack fast asleep.

Directions. Children pantomime as desired
while singing the words.

Mary Had a Little Lamb

Formation. Children are organized in pairs,
one of whom is Mary, and the other, the Lamb.

Verse

1. Mary had a little lamb, little lamb,
    little lamb,
  Mary had a little lamb, its fleece was
    white as snow.

2. And everywhere that Mary went,
    Mary went, Mary went,
  Ev'rywhere that Mary went, the
    lamb was sure to go.

3. It followed her to school one day,
    school one day, school one day,
  It followed her to school one day,
    which teacher did not like.

Directions

  Verse 1. Mary pets the Lamb and pretends to
like it very much. The Lamb crouches down.

  Verse 2. The Lamb follows Mary around
wherever she goes.

  Verse 3. Mary brings the Lamb to school, and
teacher shakes her head.

Oh, Where, Oh, Where Has My Little Dog Gone?

Formation. Children are scattered.

Verse

Oh, where, oh, where has my little dog gone?
Oh, where, oh, where can he be?
With his ears cut short and his tail cut long,
Oh, where, oh, where can he be?

Directions. This is another song for which the teacher and the children can work out their own responses.

Ring around the Rosie

Record. Folkraft 1199.

Formation. Children are in a single circle, all facing the center, hands joined.

Verse

Ring around the rosie, a pocketful of posies.
One, two, three, and we'll all fall *DOWN!*

Directions. Children circle to the left as they sing. At the word *"down,"* children jump up-ward and land in a squat position in control. The game is repeated by circling in the opposite direction.

Children who fail to assume the squat position in control step back out of the circle for one game repetition. This will counteract the tendency of some children to take the words "fall" too literally.

Variation. The dance can be done with the children holding a parachute.

Rock-a-Bye, Baby

Formation. Children are scattered. They can be seated.

Verse

Rock-a-bye, baby, in the tree top.
When the wind blows, the cradle will
    rock.

When the bough breaks, the cradle will
    fall,
And down will come baby, cradle and
    all.

Directions. The children pantomime the action.

Trot, My Pony, Trot

Formation. Children are scattered.

Verse

Trot, trot, trot. Trot, my pony, trot.
Over fields and over gravel,
Oh, what fun it is to travel.
Trot, trot, trot. Trot, my pony, trot.

Directions. Children gallop informally around the area.

Variation. The first and last lines can be changed to: "Gallop, gallop, gallop. Gallop, pony, gallop." Other animals and actions can be chosen: "Jump . . . froggie"; "Hop . . . bunny."

Who's That Knocking on My Door?

Formation. Children are scattered.

Verse

Who's that knocking on my door?
Who's that knocking on my door?
Who's that knocking on my door?
It is [Susie Johnson].

Directions. This is an action song for which the children pantomime the action. All sing and act out the first three lines. Either by prior ar-rangement or by selection (pointing) each time, one child answers the last line, giving his or her name.

Other verses can be created, such as:

Who's that jumping up and down?
Who's that skipping to and fro?
Who's that turning 'round and 'round?

Actions follow the word directions. The children can come up with many more suggestions.

Yankee Doodle

Formation. Children take partners. One partner is the Pony, and the other is Yankee Doodle. Reins should be made so that Yankee Doodle can drive the Pony. Jump ropes can be used.

Verse

Yankee Doodle went to town, a-riding
    on a pony,
Stuck a feather in his cap and called it
    macaroni.

Yankee Doodle, doodle doo, Yankee Doo-dle dandy,
All the lassies are so smart, and sweet as
    sugar candy.

Directions. Children pretend to be high-stepping ponies during the first two lines. During the second line, Yankee Doodle "sticks a feather in his cap." All gallop around during the last two lines.

Kindergarten Activities

The kindergarten list is made up primarily of movement songs. The list of suggested activities is not extensive, as the kindergarten program can make use of the activities listed under both the preschool and first grade programs. Some of the dances are individual, and some require partners. The movements demand only the simplest kind of locomotor steps.

The following dances are suggested rhythms for kindergarten, for which the required skill is specified:

Dances	Skills
Farmer in the Dell	Walking
Baa, Baa, Black Sheep	Stamping, walking
Twinkle, Twinkle, Little Star	Tiptoe steps
Mulberry Bush	Walking or skipping
Bluebird	Walking
Let Your Feet Go Tap, Tap, Tap	Skipping

Ten Little Indians	Indian dancing	Snowball Touch Your	Walking Body
Pease Porridge Hot	Turning in a circle	Shoulders Ol' Texas	identification Mimetics

Farmer in the Dell

Records. Victor 21618 and 45-5066 (Album E 87). Folkraft 1182.

Formation. Children are in a single circle with hands joined, facing the center. One child is chosen to be the farmer and stands inside the circle.

Verses

1. The farmer in the dell,
   The farmer in the dell,
   Heigh-ho! the derry-o!
   The farmer in the dell.

2. The farmer takes a wife . . .

3. The wife takes a child . . .

4. The child takes a nurse . . .

5. The nurse takes a dog . . .

6. The dog takes a cat . . .

7. The cat takes a rat . . .

8. The rat takes the cheese . . .

9. The cheese stands alone . . .

Directions

Verse 1. The circle players walk to the left with hands joined while the Farmer is deciding on a child to be selected for his Wife.

Verse 2. The Farmer chooses another child, who is led to the center and becomes the Wife.

The child selected joins hands with him, and they walk around the inside of the circle in the opposite direction to that of the big circle.

Verses 3 to 8. Each child selected in turn joins the center group.

Verse 9. All children in the center, with the exception of the child who is the Cheese, return to the outside circle. The circle stops, and the children face the center, clapping hands during this verse.

Suggestion. The game should be repeated until all children have had an opportunity to be in the center.

Variations. Several Farmers may be chosen to start.

When the outer circle becomes too small, the children will no longer be able to hold hands.

Verse 8 can be: "The cat chases the rat." During this, the Cat does chase the Rat in and out of the circle, with the children raising and lowering their joined hands to help the Rat and hinder the Cat. If the Cat catches the Rat, he gets to be the Farmer for the next game. If not, the Rat becomes the Farmer. The Rat must be caught during the singing of the verse.

Baa, Baa, Black Sheep

Records. Folkraft 1191. Russell 700A. Victor E-83.

Formation. Children are in a single circle, all facing the center.

Verse

1. Baa, baa, black sheep, have you any wool?
2. Yes, sir, yes, sir, three bags full.
3. One for my master, and one for my dame,
4. And one for the little boy who lives down the lane.

Directions

Line 1. Children stamp three times, shake forefinger three times.

Line 2. They nod twice and hold up three fingers.

Line 3. Each bows to the person on the right and then to the person on the left.

Line 4. They hold one finger up high and walk around in a tiny circle, again facing the center.

Twinkle, Twinkle, Little Star

Record. Childcraft EP-C4.

Formation. Children are in a single circle, facing the center.

Verse

1. Twinkle, twinkle, little star.
2. How I wonder what you are.
3. Up above the world so high
4. Like a diamond in the sky.
5. Twinkle, twinkle, little star.
6. How I wonder what you are.

Directions. Children are in a large enough circle so that they can come forward seven short steps without crowding.

Line 1. Children have arms extended overhead and fingers extended and moving. Each child takes seven tiptoe steps toward the center of the circle.

Line 2. They continue with seven tiptoe steps in place, making a full turn around.

Line 3. Each child makes a circle with his arms and hands, rocking back and forth.

Line 4. Each forms a diamond with the fingers in front of the face.

Line 5. With the arms overhead and the fingers extended, they move backward to original place with seven tiptoe steps.

Line 6. They turn in place with seven tiptoe steps.

Mulberry Bush

Records. Victor 20806, 45-5065. Columbia 90037-V. Folkraft 1183.

Formation. Children are in a single circle, facing the center, hands joined.

Chorus

Here we go 'round the mulberry bush,
The mulberry bush, the mulberry bush,
Here we go 'round the mulberry bush,
So early in the morning.

Verses

1. This is the way we wash our clothes,
   Wash our clothes, wash our clothes.
   This is the way we wash our clothes,
   So early Monday morning.

2. This is the way we iron our clothes,
   . . . Tuesday morning.

3. This is the way we mend our clothes,
   . . . Wednesday morning.

4. This is the way we sweep our floor,
   . . . Thursday morning.

5. This is the way we scrub our floor,
   . . . Friday morning.

6. This is the way we make a cake,
   . . . Saturday morning.

7. This is the way we go to church,
   . . . Sunday morning.

Directions. The singing game begins with the chorus, which is also sung after each verse. As each chorus is sung, the children skip (or walk) to the right. At the words "so early in the morning," and at the same line in each verse, each child drops hands and makes a complete turn in place.

During the verses, the children pantomime the actions suggested by the words. Encourage the children to use large and vigorous movements.

If no record is used and the children are singing, the tempo can be slowed during the last verse (verse 7), so that the walk to church is stately and slow.

Bluebird

Record. Folkraft 1180.

Formation. Children are in a single circle, hands joined, facing the center. One child stands outside the circle and is the Bluebird.

Verse

Bluebird, bluebird, through my window,
Bluebird, bluebird, through my window,
Bluebird, bluebird, through my window,
Hi diddle diddle dum dee.

Chorus

Take a little boy [girl] and tap him [her]
    on the shoulder,
[Repeat twice more]
Hi diddle diddle dum dee.

Directions. During the verse, all circle children lift joined hands high, forming arches, under which the Bluebird weaves in and out. At the completion of the verse, the Bluebird should stand directly behind one of the circle players. During the chorus, the Bluebird taps the child in front of him lightly on the shoulders with both hands. This child then becomes the new Bluebird, with the old Bluebird keeping her hands on the new Bluebird's shoulders, forming a train. As the chorus is sung, the Bluebird train moves around the various directions in the center area of the circle. When the verse is sung again, the train moves in and out of the arches.

Continue the action until seven or eight children form the train.

Return the train children to the circle formation and begin anew with a new Bluebird. Two or three Bluebirds can be used.

Variation. The children should be able to make up additional verses, using other birds, such as: "Robin, robin, on my doorstep."

Let Your Feet Go Tap, Tap, Tap

Record. Folkraft 1184. This record uses the traditional music. The song can be sung to the tune of "Merrily We Roll Along," as illustrated.

Formation. Children are in a double circle, partners facing.

Verse

Let your feet go tap, tap, tap.
Let your hands go clap, clap, clap.
Let your finger beckon me.
Come, dear partner, dance with me.

Chorus

Tra, la, la, la, la, la, la, etc.

Directions

Line 1. Children tap foot three times.

Line 2. They clap hands three times.

Line 3. They beckon and bow to partners.

Line 4. They join inside hands and face counterclockwise.

Chorus. All sing and skip counterclockwise.

Variations. This can be done as a dance for two people. The first three lines are the same. On line 4, the partners hook right elbows; during the chorus, they skip in merry-go-round fashion.

Another variation is similar to the preceding one except that partners face one another, join hands, and circle clockwise in merry-go-round fashion. The movement is a light slide.

Ten Little Indians

Record. Folkraft 1197.

Formation. Children are in a circle. Ten children are selected and are numbered consecutively from one to ten, but they remain in the circle.

Verse

One little, two little, three little Indians,
Four little, five little, six little Indians,
Seven little, eight little, nine little Indians,
Ten little Indian braves [squaws].

Directions. The piece is played four times to allow a complete sequence of the dance.

As the verse is sung the first time, the Indians go from the circle to the center when their numbers are sung, while the rest of the children in the circle clap lightly.

During the second repetition of the music, the Indians in the center do an Indian dance, each in his or her own way.

The verse is sung again, but this time the Indians in the center return to the circle when their numbers are sung.

During the last rendition of the piece, all children dance as Indians, moving in any direction they wish, not retaining the circle formation.

The dance is repeated with another set of Indians.

Pease Porridge Hot

Record. Folkraft 1190.

Formation. Children are in a double circle, partners facing.

Verse

1. Pease porridge hot,
2. Pease porridge cold,
3. Pease porridge in a pot,
4. Nine days old!
5. Some like it hot,
6. Some like it cold,
7. Some like it in a pot,
8. Nine days old!

Directions. The music is repeated for the chorus. The dance is in two parts. The first is a patty-cake rhythm, done while the children sing the verse. During the second part, the children dance with a circular movement.

Part I

Line 1. Each claps own hands to thighs, claps own hands together, claps own hands to partner's hands.

Line 2. Repeat action of line 1.

Line 3. Each claps hands to thighs, claps own hands together, claps right hand against partner's right, claps own hands together.

Line 4. Each claps left hand to partner's left, claps own hands together, claps both hands against partner's hands.

Lines 5 to 8. Repeat lines 1 to 4.

Part II

Partners join both hands and skip around in a small circle, turning counterclockwise, for the first four lines, ending with the word "old!" They reverse direction and skip clockwise for the remainder of the verse. Each moves one step to the left for a new partner.

The change of partners should be added only after the dance has been mastered.

Variation. Partners can be seated and the patty-cake activity done with the feet. Children knock the heels to the floor for the first count. During Part II, they can move in some prescribed fashion to find another partner.

Snowball

Music. Lively music appropriate to walking or to whichever step is used.

Formation. Children are in a circle.

Directions. Tell children that this activity is like a snowball. "We roll a small snowball and as we roll, the snowball gets larger and larger." Two children are chosen to start, with the remainder seated in a circle. Appropriate music is needed.

The active children walk around the interior of the circle to music. When the music is stopped, each child goes to a circle player, bows and says, "Will you follow me?" The music is started again, and the two active players turn around and lead out, each followed by the chosen partner. They can weave out in different directions, using turns and various patterns, each followed by his partner. At this point, we have four children moving in the circle area.

The music stops, and all four active players move to the circle players, each choosing a partner. The actions and dialogue are repeated. When the music starts anew, we now have four couples moving. The sequence is repeated until all children have been chosen.

Variation. Different locomotor movements can be done as determined by the music.

Teaching Suggestions. The music should not play for too long a time, particularly during the early parts of the dance. Be sure the circle is large enough to accommodate the children in the center without crowding or jostling.

Touch Your Shoulders

Music. Verses are sung to the tune of "Mary Had a Little Lamb" (see p. 220).

Formation. No formation is needed; children can be in any arrangement.

Verses

1. Touch your shoulders and your knees.
   Touch your shoulders and your knees.
   Touch your shoulders and your knees.
   Make your feet go stamp, stamp, stamp.

2. Touch your elbows and your toes.
   [Repeat twice more.]
   Make your hands go clap, clap, clap.

3. Touch your ankles, reach up high.
   [Repeat twice more.]
   Shake yourself up in the sky.

4. Touch your hips and touch your heels.
   [Repeat twice more.]
   Jump up high. One, two, three.

Directions. The verses are self-explanatory in describing the action. Children use both hands in touching. Additional verses can be devised by the children, using body parts not previously mentioned and a different finishing line.

Variations. More movement can be brought in by making this a two-part dance. Alternate the verses with a chorus, during which the children sing the same tune, but with "La, la, la, la," etc. During the chorus, the children skip around the space. It will be a better social experience if, during the verse, each child faces another child.

Ol' Texas

Formation. Children are scattered.

Verse

1. I'm goin' to leave ol' Texas now,
   They've got no use for the long-horned cow;
   They've plowed and fenced my cattle range,
   And the people there are all so strange.

2. I'll take my horse, I'll take my rope,
   And hit the trail upon a lope;
   Say "Adios" to the Alamo,
   And turn my head to Mexico.

Directions. This is a popular Western song and will appeal to youngsters because of its cowboy flavor. A few explanations will make the action more meaningful. On a map of the United States, show where Texas is in relation to Mexico. Explain what a long-horned cow is, showing a picture of one if possible. Clarify the words "lope, " "Adios," and "the Alamo."

Let the children make up their own movement responses for each line. For example, the response to the first line could be to walk around, waving goodbye to everyone. During the second line, they could strut around like a long-horned cow.

First Grade Activities

The first grade movement songs and folk dances are introductory in nature and involve simple formations and uncomplicated changes. The movements are primarily walking, skipping, and running. Only a few of the dances are done with partners. Most of the activities are quite flexible in nature, and children can interpret the words and music in various ways.

The rhythmic activities listed under the kindergarten program should be added to the list of suggested dances below.

Dances	Skills
The Farmer in the Wheat	Skipping
Guess What I Am Now!	Interpretations
London Bridge	Walking
The Muffin Man	Skipping
Oats, Peas, Beans, and Barley Grow	Walking, skipping
Looby Loo	Skipping
Pussy Cat	Walking, draw step, jumping
The Thread Follows the Needle	Walking
I See You	Skipping, two-handed swing
Sing a Song of Sixpence	Walking
Dance of Greeting	Running, bowing
Hickory Dickory Dock	Running
Chimes of Dunkirk	Sliding

Farmer in the Wheat

Music. Verses are sung to the music of "Farmer in the Dell" (see p. 224).

Records. Victor 21618 and 45-5066. Folkraft 1182.

Formation. Children are in a single circle, facing the center. Three children—the Farmer, the Sun, and the Rain—stand in the center.

Verse

1. The farmer in the wheat.
   The farmer in the wheat.
   Heigh-ho the derry-o,
   The farmer in the wheat.

2. The farmer sows his wheat (etc.)

3. He covers them with dirt (etc.)

4. The sun begins to shine (etc.)

5. The rain begins to fall (etc.)

6. The wheat begins to grow (etc.)

7. The farmer cuts his grain (etc.)

8. The farmer stacks his grain (etc.)

9. They all begin to dance (etc.)

Directions

Verse 1. Children in the circle walk to the left with hands joined.

Verse 2. The Farmer skips around the inside of the circle counterclockwise and sows his wheat, while the other children continue to walk.

Verse 3. The children stop, drop hands, and face the center. The Farmer skips around the circle, tapping each child on the head; as he is touched, the child sinks down to the ground, becoming a wheat stalk.

Verse 4. The Sun skips around, spreading sunshine.

Verse 5. The Rain skips around, showering the wheat.

Verse 6. Children rise slowly and jerkily to a standing position with arms overhead to simulate the heads of wheat.

Verse 7. The Farmer skips around the inside of the circle and cuts the grain. Each child falls to the ground.

Verse 8. The Farmer skips around the group, arranging children by pairs to lean against each other to form stacks. (This verse may be repeated to take in all the children.)

Verse 9. Paired children, inside hands joined, skip counterclockwise around the circle. The Farmer, Sun, and Rain form a small circle and skip clockwise.

Guess What I Am Now!

Formation. Children are in a half-circle, facing the piano, with one child (the guesser) standing near the piano with back to the other children.

Verse

I'm very, very small; I'm very, very, tall.
Sometimes small, sometimes tall; guess
what I am now!

Guess What I Am Now

Directions. The guesser closes his eyes. Another child is designated to indicate the final pose—small or tall.

The children become small and tall, as the words direct, but on the completion of the final line they assume the same pose as the chosen child. The guesser then makes a choice of either small or tall. If the guesser is correct, he chooses another child to take his place. If wrong, he must try again. Allow only these two chances per child. If he fails the second time, the teacher picks the new guesser.

Variations. The formation can be a circle with the guesser in the center. In this case, the guesser can hold two pads over the eyes, as peeking would ruin the game.

Other selected contrasts add interest. The following can be considered big/little, narrow/wide, straight/crooked, stretched/curled, twisted/straight, forward/backward (bending).

Try the dance with the children holding a parachute. The guesser must stand to one side with back to the circle.

London Bridge

Record. Victor 20806.

Formation. Children are in a single circle, moving either clockwise or counterclockwise. Two children are chosen to form the Bridge. They face and join hands, holding them high in the air to represent a bridge ready to fall.

Verses

1. London Bridge is falling down,
   Falling down, falling down,
   London Bridge is falling down,
   My fair lady.

2. Build it up with iron bars (etc.)

3. Iron bars will rust away (etc.)

4. Build it up with gold and silver (etc.)

5. Gold and silver I have not (etc.)

6. Build it up with pins and needles (etc.)

7. Pins and needles rust and bend (etc.)

8. Build it up with penny loaves (etc.)

9. Penny loaves will tumble down (etc.)

10. Here's a prisoner I have got (etc.)

11. What's the prisoner done to you? (etc.)

12. Stole my watch and bracelet too (etc.)

13. What'll you take to set him free? (etc.)

14. One hundred pounds will set him free (etc.)

15. One hundred pounds we don't have (etc.)

16. Then off to prison he [she] must go (etc.)

Directions. All children pass under the Bridge in a single line. When the words "My fair lady" are sung, the Bridge falls, and the child caught is a prisoner. He or she must choose either gold or silver and must stand behind the side of the Bridge that represents his choice. No one must know which side is gold and which is silver until after he has made his choice as a prisoner. When all have been caught, the game ends with a tug-of-war.

Variation. Using more Bridges will speed up the game.

The Muffin Man

Record. Folkraft 1188.

Formation. Children are in a single circle, facing the center. One child, the Muffin Man, is in the center.

Verses

1. Oh, do you know the muffin man,
   The muffin man, the muffin man?
   Oh, do you know the muffin man,
   Who lives in Drury Lane?

2. Oh, yes, we know the muffin man
   (etc.)

3. Four of us know the muffin man
   (etc.)

4. Eight of us know the muffin man
   (etc.)

5. Sixteen of us know the muffin man
   (etc.)

6. All of us know the muffin man (etc.)

Directions

Verse 1. The children in the circle clap hands and sing, while the Muffin Man skips around, in and out of the circle. He chooses a partner by skipping in place in front of him. On the last line of the verse, "Who lives in Drury Lane?", the Muffin Man and his partner go to the center.

Verse 2. The action is the same, except that two children now skip, choosing two partners.

Verse 3. The action is repeated, with four children skipping and four partners being chosen.

The verses continue until all children have been chosen. When all have been chosen, the last verse is sung while the children skip around the room.

Oats, Peas, Beans, and Barley Grow

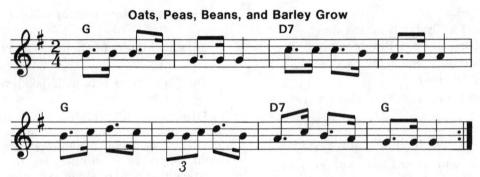

Records. Victor 20214. Folkraft 1182.

Formation. Children are in a single circle with a Farmer outside the circle.

Verses

1. Oats, peas, beans, and barley grow,
   Oats, peas, beans, and barley grow.
   Do you and I, or anyone, know how
   Oats, peas, beans and barley grow?

2. First, the farmer sows the seed,
   Then he stands and takes his ease.
   He stamps his foot and claps his
      hands
   And turns around to view his lands.

3. Waiting for a partner,
   Waiting for a partner,
   Open the ring and choose one in,
   While we all gaily dance and sing.

4. Now you're married, you must obey.
   You must be kind in all you say.
   You must be kind, you must be good

And keep your wife in kindling
   wood.

Directions

Verse 1. The children walk clockwise, while the Farmer walks counterclockwise around the outside of the circle.

Verse 2. Circle players stand in place and follow the actions suggested by the words. The Farmer also stops, outside the circle, and does the same.

Verse 3. Circle players again circle, with joined hands, and on the words, "Open the ring," arms are raised, and the Farmer comes inside to choose a partner. This should be done before the end of the verse.

Verse 4. Circle players now skip clockwise (hands are not joined), while the Farmer and his partner skip counterclockwise inside the circle.

This can be made progressive by having two and then four Farmers in action, but this is about as far as it should go.

Looby Loo

Records. Victor 20214. Russell 702. Folkraft 1102, 1184. Columbia 10008D.

Formation. Children are in a single circle, all facing the center, with hands joined.

Chorus. The chorus is repeated before each verse. During the chorus, all children skip around the circle to the left.

Here we dance looby loo,
Here we dance looby light,
Here we dance looby loo,
All on a Saturday night.

Verses

1. I put my right hand in,
   I take my right hand out,
   I give my right hand a shake, shake, shake,
   And turn myself about.

2. I put my left hand in (etc.)

3. I put my right foot in (etc.)

4. I put my left foot in (etc.)

5. I put my head 'way in (etc.)

6. I put my whole self in (etc.)

Directions. During the verse part of the dance, the children stand still facing the center and follow the directions of the words. On the words, "And turn myself about," they make a complete turn in place and get ready to skip around the circle.

The movements should be definite and vigorous. On the last verse, the child jumps forward and then backward, shakes himself vigorously, and then turns around.

Pussy Cat

Record. Russell 700B.

Formation. Children are in a single circle, all facing the center with hands joined. One player, the Pussy Cat, is in the center. If desired, more than one Pussy Cat can be in the center.

Verse

1. Pussy Cat, Pussy Cat, where have you been?
2. I've been to London to visit the Queen!
3. Pussy Cat, Pussy Cat, what did you there?
4. I frightened a mouse from under her chair!

Chorus. The chorus repeats the same music, but the children sing "Tra la, la, la," in place of the words.

Directions

Verse
Line 1. Sung by the circle children as they walk counterclockwise around the circle.
Line 2. Sung by the Cat as the children reverse the direction and walk around the other way.

Line 3. Sung by the children as they drop hands, walk toward the center, and shake a finger at the Cat.
Line 4. Sung by the Cat who, on the last word, "chair," jumps high into the air. The others pretend fright and run back to the circle.

Chorus
Line 1. Children take two draw steps (one to each measure) to the right, followed by four stamps.
Line 2. They repeat to the left.
Line 3. They take four steps (one to each measure) to the center.
Line 4. They take three steps backward in the same tempo as line 3, followed by a jump.

A draw step is made by stepping directly to the side and bringing the other foot toward it in a closing movement. It is a step with one foot and a close with the other, with one draw step made to a measure of music.

Variations. Have more than one Pussy Cat in the circle. Have a number of smaller circles, each with a Pussy Cat.

The Thread Follows the Needle

Records. RCA Victor 22760 (Album E87). Pioneer 3015.

Formation. A single line of about eight children is formed. Hands are joined, and each child is numbered consecutively.

Verse

The thread follows the needle,
The thread follows the needle.
In and out the needle goes
As Mother mends the children's clothes.

Directions. The first child (Number 1) is the Needle and leads the children, forming stitches, until the entire line has been sewn. When the music starts, the Needle leads the line under the raised arms of the last two children (Numbers 7 and 8). When the line has passed under their arms, they turn and face the opposite direction, letting their arms cross in front of them. This forms the stitch.

The Needle now repeats the movement and passes under the next pair of raised arms (Numbers 6 and 7). Number 6 is now added to the stitch when he reverses his direction. This is repeated until the entire line has been stitched, with the Needle turning under his or her own arm to complete the last stitch.

To "rip the stitch," children raise their arms overhead and turn back to original positions.

The game can be repeated with a new leader.

I See You

Records. Victor 20432. Russell 726. Folkraft 1197.

Formation. The boys and girls stand in two sets, as shown in the diagram (X = boys, O = girls):

(1) X X X X X X X
(2) O O O O O O O
(3) X X X X X X X
(4) O O O O O O O

Lines 1 and 2 are facing lines 3 and 4. The space between the two middle lines (2 and 3) should be from ten to twelve feet.

Lines 1 and 4 contain the active players. Each active player's partner is directly in front of him and stands with hands on hips.

Verse

I see you, I see you.
Tra, la, la, la, la, la.

I see you, I see you.
Tra, la, la, la, la, la.

Chorus

Tra, la, la (etc.)

Directions

Verse

Line 1. On the first "I see you," each active player looks over his partner's left shoulder in peekaboo fashion. On the second "I see you," each active player looks over the partner's right shoulder in the same peekaboo fashion.

Line 2. Tempo is doubled, and active players make three fast peekaboo movements—left, right, left.

Line 3. The action of line 1 is repeated, except that the first peekaboo is made to the right.

Line 4. The action of line 2 is repeated, except that the movements are right, left, right.

Chorus

Line 1. All children clap on the first note ("tra"), and the active players, passing to the left of their partners, meet in the center with a two-handed swing, skipping around once in a circle, clockwise.

Line 2. All children clap again ("tra") and each active player now faces his own partner, skipping around with him once in a circle, clockwise.

Partners have now changed places with the active players, and the entire pattern is repeated with a new set of players in the active roles.

Sing a Song of Sixpence

Records. Folkraft 1180. Victor 22760. Russell 700.

Formation. Players are in circle formation, facing the center. Six to eight players are crouched in the center as Blackbirds.

Verses

1. Sing a song of sixpence, a pocket full of rye,
   Four and twenty blackbirds, baked in a pie.
   When the pie was opened, the birds began to sing.
   Wasn't that a dainty dish to set before the king?

2. The king was in the countinghouse, counting out his money.

The queen was in the pantry, eating bread and honey.
The maid was in the garden, hanging out the clothes.
And down came a blackbird and snipped off ner nose!

Directions

Verse 1

Line 1. Players walk around in a circle.

Line 2. Circle players walk with shortened steps toward the center of the circle with arms outstretched forward.

Line 3. Players walk backward with arms now up. The Blackbirds in the center fly around.

Line 4. Circle players kneel as if presenting a dish (Blackbirds continue to fly around).

Verse 2

Lines 1, 2, and 3. Pantomime action of counting out money, eating, and hanging up clothes.

Line 4. Each Blackbird snips off the nose of a circle player, who now becomes a Blackbird for the next game.

Dance of Greeting
(A Danish Dance)

Records. Victor 45-6183, 20432. Folkraft 1187. Russell 726.

Formation. Children are in a single circle, all facing the center. Each child stands to the left of his partner.

Directions

Measure 1. All clap, clap, and bow to partner.
Measure 2. They repeat, but each turns back to partner and bows to neighbor.
Measure 3. They stamp right, stamp left.

Measure 4. Each player turns around in four running steps.
Measures 5 to 8. They repeat action of measures 1 to 4.
Measures 9 to 12. All join hands and run to the left for four measures (16 counts).
Measures 13 to 16. They repeat action of measures 9 to 12, with light running steps in the opposite direction.

Variation. Instead of using a light running step, use a light slide.

Hickory Dickory Dock

Record. Victor 22760.

Formation. Children are in a double circle, partners facing.

Verse

Hickory dickory dock, tick tock,
The mouse ran up the clock, tick tock.

The clock struck one, the mouse ran down.
Hickory, dickory dock, tick tock.

Directions

Line 1. Children stretch arms overhead and bend the body from side to side like a pendulum, finishing with two stamps on "tick, tock."
Line 2. They repeat action of line 1.

Line 3. They clap hands on "one." Children join hands with partners and run to the right in a little circle.

Line 4. They repeat the pendulum swing with the two stamps.

Chimes of Dunkirk

Records. Victor 45-6176, 17327. Folkraft 1188. Columbia A-3016.

Formation. Children are in a single circle with boys and girls alternating. Partners face each other. Hands are on own hips.

Directions

Measures 1 and 2. All stamp lightly left, right, left.

Measures 3 and 4. All clap hands overhead, swaying back and forth.

Measures 5 to 8. All join hands with partners and make one complete turn in place clockwise.

Measures 9 to 16. All join hands in a single circle, facing the center, and slide to the left (16 slides).

Second Grade Activities

The second grade program includes many activities similar to those taught in the first grade. In addition, there is more emphasis on partnered dances and on change of partners. The dance patterns tend to become more definite, and more folk dances are included. The movements are still confined primarily to the simple locomotor types, with additional and varied emphasis upon more complicated formations.

Some of the dances in the second grade, because of their nature, have boy and girl designations. This provides an introduction for later dances where boy-girl partners are necessary.

Dances	Skills
Down the Mississippi	Bending, scooter movements
Did You Ever See a Lassie?	Walking
Go 'Round and 'Round the Village	Walking
Shoemaker's Dance	Skipping
Jolly Is the Miller	Marching
Shoo Fly	Walking, skipping
Ach Ja	Walking, sliding
A-Hunting We Will Go	Sliding, skipping
How D'Ye Do, My Partner	Bowing, skipping
The Bleking Step	Bleking Step (step, step-hop)
Rig-a-Jig-Jig	Walking, skipping
Broom Dance	Marching, skipping
The Popcorn Man	Jumping, skipping
Hokey Pokey	Body actions, imitative movements

Down the Mississippi

Records. Victor 20806, 45-5065. Columbia 90037-V. Folkraft 1183.

Formation. None. Children can be scattered or in a circle as desired. Each child is seated on the floor with legs together and extended forward.

Verses

1. This is the way we row our boat,
   Row our boat, row our boat,
   This is the way we row our boat,
   Down the Mississippi!

2. This is the way we glide along (etc.)

3. This is the way we rock the boat
   (etc.)

4. This is the way we turn around (etc.)

5. This is the way we float for home
   (etc.)

6. This is the way we spell Mississippi,
   Spell Mississippi, spell Mississippi.

This is the way we spell Mississippi,
M-I-S-S-I-S-S-I-P-P-I. *Wow!*

Directions

Verse 1. Each child rows his boat in time to the music.

Verse 2. Each child folds his arms across his chest and bends forward and backward.

Verse 3. Each child, with arms outstretched to the side, bends from side to side.

Verse 4. Each child, by rowing with one "paddle" only, turns on his side completely around in stages.

Verse 5. Each child folds his arms across his chest and moves in any direction, as desired, using Scooter movements, reaching out with the heels and pulling the seat up to the heels.

Verse 6. Children sing the first three lines (no action) and then sound out (spell) Mississippi in staccato fashion. (May they never misspell *Mississippi!*)

Did You Ever See a Lassie [Laddie]?

Records. Victor 45-5066, 21618. Folkraft 1183. Columbia 10008D.

Formation. Children are in a single circle, facing half left, with hands joined. One child is in the center.

Verse

Did you ever see a lassie, a lassie, a
lassie?
Did you ever see a lassie do this way and
that?
Do this way and that way, and this way
and that way.
Did you ever see a lassie do this way and
that?

Directions

Measures 1 to 8. Children with hands joined walk to the left in a circle. Since this is fast waltz time, there should be one step to each measure. The child in the center gets ready to demonstrate some type of movement.

Measures 9 to 16. All stop and follow the movement suggested by the child in the center.

As the verse starts over, the center child selects another to do some action in the center and changes places with him.

Variations. It is fun to bring in other characterizations. Let the children come up with other impersonations; the child whose idea is accepted becomes the leader in the center. The teacher might suggest some ideas to start—butcher, blacksmith, soldier, etc.

Go 'Round and 'Round the Village

Record. Folkraft 1191.

Formation. Children are in a single circle, hands joined. Several extra players stand outside, scattered around the circle.

Verses

1. Go 'round and 'round the village,
   Go 'round and 'round the village,
   Go 'round and 'round the village,
   As we have done before.

2. Go in and out the windows (etc.)

3. Now stand and face your partner
   (etc.)

4. Now follow me to London (etc.)

Directions

Verse 1. Circle players move to the right, and the extra players on the outside go the other way. All skip.

Verse 2. Circle players stop and lift joined hands, forming the windows. Extra players go in and out the windows, finishing inside the circle.

Verse 3. Extra players select partners by standing in front of them.

Verse 4. The extra players and partners now skip around the inside of the circle, while the outside circle skips the opposite way.

Variations. All chosen players can continue and repeat the game until the entire circle has been chosen.

An excellent variation is to have the boys in the circle and the girls as extra players. In this way, everyone will select and be selected as a partner. Reverse the positions, putting the girls in the circle and leaving the boys as the extras.

The dance can be done holding a parachute. During verse 1, instead of holding hands, they hold the parachute with the left hand. During verse 2, they raise the parachute high. For verse 3, the player stands behind the circle player. During verse 4, extra players and partners skip around the outside of the circle.

Shoemaker's Dance

Records. Victor 20450, 45-6171. Russell 750. Folkraft 1187. Columbia A-3038.

Formation. Children are in a double circle, partners facing, boys on the inside.

Verse

See the cobbler wind his thread,
Snip, snap, tap, tap, tap.
That's the way he earns his bread,
Snip, snap, tap, tap, tap.

Chorus

So the cobbler, blithe and gay,
Works from morn to close of day.
At his shoes he pegs away,
Whistling cheerily his lay.

Directions

Verse

Measures 1 and 2. Hold clenched fists in front, about chest high. On "see the cobbler," roll one fist forward over the other three times. On "wind his thread," roll the fists over each other backward three times.

Measure 3. Fingers of the right hand form a scissors and make two cuts on "snip, snap."

Measure 4. Double up the fists and hammer one on top of the other three times.

Measures 5 to 8. Same action as in measures 1 to 4 except that three claps replace hammering the fists.

Chorus

Partners join inside hands, with outside hands on hips. All skip to the left around the room. Near the end of the chorus, all slow down, and partners face each other. All children take one step to the left to secure a new partner.

Variations. The words for the chorus can be omitted when the children skip with partners.

A more informal dance can be arranged with anywhere from two to five children forming a small circle, facing one another. During the verse part, the action is as described. During the chorus, children skip individually in diverse directions, forming small groups again. By forming small groups, and not just taking partners, the problem of pairing off is avoided.

Jolly Is the Miller

Records. Victor 45-5067 or 20214, E-87. Folkraft 1192. American Play Party 1185.

Formation. Children are in a double circle. Partners with inside hands joined face counterclockwise. Boys are on the inside. A Miller is in the center of the circle.

Verse

Jolly is the miller who lives by the mill.
The wheel goes 'round with a right
good will.
One hand on the hopper and the other
on the sack.
The right steps forward, and the left
steps back.

Directions. The children march counterclockwise with inside hands joined. During the second line, when the "wheel goes 'round," the dancers should make their outside arms go in a circle to form a wheel. Children change partners at the words "the right steps forward, and the left steps back." The Miller then has a chance to get a partner. The child left without a partner becomes the new Miller.

Shoo Fly

Records. Folkraft 1102, 1185. Decca 18222.

Formation. All are in a circle with hands joined, facing in. A boy stands with his girl on the right.

Verse

Shoo fly, don't bother me,
Shoo fly, don't bother me,
Shoo fly, don't bother me,
I belong to Company G.

I feel, I feel, I feel like a morning star.
I feel, I feel, I feel like a morning star.

Directions. The dance is in two parts and finishes with a change of partners.

Measures 1 and 2. All walk forward four steps toward the center of the circle, swinging arms back and forth.

Measures 3 and 4. All walk four steps backward to place with arms swinging.

Measures 5 to 8. All repeat the preceding steps (measures 1 to 4).

Measures 9 to 16. Each boy turns to the girl on his right, takes hold of both her hands, and

skips around in a small circle, finishing so that the girl will be on his left when the circle is reformed. His new partner is on his right. The dance is repeated with new partners.

Variation. For the second part of the dance, the following is an interesting substitute for the two-handed swing.

Designate one couple to form an arch by lifting joined hands. This couple now moves forward toward the center of the circle. The couple on the opposite side moves forward, under the arch, drawing the circle after it. When all have passed through the arch, the couple forming the arch turn under their own joined hands. The dancers now move forward to form a circle with everyone facing out. The dance is repeated with all facing out.

To return the circle to face in again, the same couple again makes an arch and the lead couple backs through the arch, drawing the circle after them. The arch couple turn under their own arms.

In this version, there is no change of partners.

Ach Ja

Record. Ruth Evans, *Childhood Rhythms*, Series VII.

Formation. Children are in a double circle, partners facing counterclockwise, boys on the inside.

Verse

When my father and my mother take the
     children to the fair,
Ach, ja! Ach, ja!
Oh, they have but little money, but it's
     little that they care,
Ach, ja! Ach, ja!
Tra la la, tra la la, tra la la la la la la,
Tra la la, tra la la, tra la la la la la la.
Ach, ja! Ach, ja!

Directions

Measures 1 and 2. Partners walk eight steps in the line of direction.

Measure 3. Partners drop hands and bow to each other.

Measure 4. Each boy now bows to the girl on his left, who returns the bow.

Measure 5 to 8. Measures 1 to 4 are repeated.

Measures 9 and 10. Partners face each other, join hands, and take four slides in line of direction (counterclockwise).

Measures 11 and 12. Four slides are taken clockwise.

Measures 13. Partners bow to each other.

Measure 14. Boy bows to girl on his left, who returns the bow. To start the next dance, the boy moves quickly toward this girl, who is his next partner.

A-Hunting We Will Go

Records. Folkraft 1191. Victor 45-5064, 22759.

Formation. Children are in a set with ten to twelve children in two lines facing each other, boys in one line and girls in the other.

○ ○ ○ ○ ○ ○
Head   Foot
× × × × × ×

Verse

Oh, a-hunting we will go,
A-hunting we will go,
We'll catch a fox and put him in a box
And then we'll let him go!

Chorus

Tra, la, la, la, la, la, la (etc.) (The music repeats.)

Directions. Everyone sings.

Lines 1 and 2. The head couple, with hands joined, slides between the two lines to the foot of the set (eight counts).

Lines 3 and 4. The head couple slides to original position (eight counts).

Chorus. Couples join hands and skip in a circle to the left following the head couple. When the head couple reaches the place formerly occupied by the last couple in the line (foot couple), they form an arch under which the other couples skip. A new couple is now the head couple, and the dance is repeated until each couple has had a chance to be at the head.

Variations. On the chorus, the head couple separates, and each leads his own line down the outside to the foot of the set. The head couple dancers meet at the foot and form an arch for the other couples. The other dancers meet two by two and skip under the arch back to place.

Head couple slides down the center of the line

In another variation, the first two couples slide down the center and back on lines 1, 2, 3, and 4. Otherwise the dance is the same.

How D'Ye Do, My Partner

Records. Victor 21685. Folkraft 1190.

Formation. Children are in a double circle, partners facing, boys on the inside.

Verse

How d'ye do, my partner?
How d'ye do today?
Will you dance in the circle?
I will show you the way.

Chorus

Tra, la, la, la (etc.) (The music repeats.)

Directions

Measures 1 and 2. Boys bow to their partners.

Measures 3 and 4. Girls curtsy.

Measures 5 and 6. Each boy offers his right hand to his girl, who takes it with her right hand. Both turn to face counterclockwise.

Measures 7 and 8. Couples join left hands and are now in a skater's position. They get ready to skip when the music changes.

Chorus. Partners skip counterclockwise in the circle, slowing down on the next-to-last measure (measure 7).

On the last measure of the chorus (measure 8), the girls stop, and the boys move ahead counterclockwise to secure a new partner. The dance is then repeated.

The Bleking Step

Records. Victor 45-6169, 20989. Folkraft 1188.

The music is in two parts. The first part has the rhythm of "Slow, slow; fast, fast, fast," which governs the pattern of the Bleking Step. The second portion of the music is designed for continual step-hops throughout. With this in mind, different dance sequences can be organized, of which one is presented here. First, the children should learn the Bleking Step.

Directions

Measure 1. Hop on the left foot and extend the right heel forward with the right leg straight. At the same time thrust the right hand forward. Hop on the right foot, reversing the arm action and extending the left foot to rest on the heel.

Measure 2. Repeat the action with three quick changes—left, right, left.

Measures 3 and 4. Beginning on the right foot, repeat the movements of measures 1 and 2.

Measures 5 to 8. Repeat measures 1 to 4.

Suggested Movement Patterns. Cue by: "Slow, slow; fast, fast, fast."

1. For Part I, children are scattered and do the Bleking Step in place individually. During Part II, children step-hop in different directions in general space. When the music returns to Part I, the dance is repeated.

2. Children are in pairs, with pairs scattered. The children of each pair face each other about three feet apart. It is important that both begin with a hop on the left foot, extending the right foot forward. When the music changes to Part II, children step-hop individually in general space, timing their movements to pair up once more

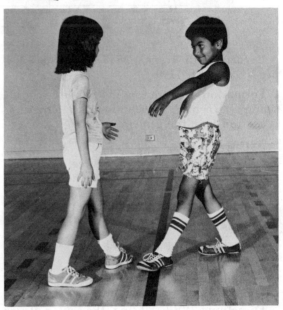

The Bleking Step

someplace with a different partner for the repetition of Part I.

3. Children are paired off, with partners facing and both hands joined. They do the Bleking Step (four sequences) in this position. On Part II, they step-hop individually until near the end of this portion, when they again secure partners.

Other movement sequences can be devised.

Variation. For Part II, use the basic schottische step, which is: Step, step, step, hop; step, step, step, hop. Using light running steps will work out with the rhythm of the piece quite well.

Rig-a-Jig-Jig

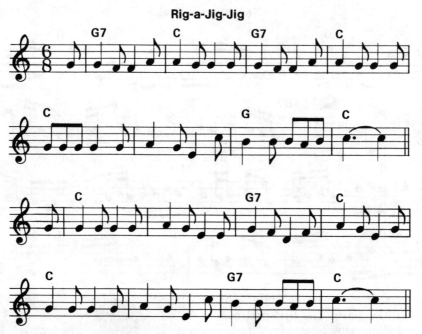

Record. Ruth Evans, *Childhood Rhythms,* Series VI, Folkraft 1199.

Formation. Children are in a single circle, all facing the center, boys and girls alternating. One child is in the center.

Verse

As I was walking down the street,
Heigh-ho, heigh-ho, heigh-ho, heigh-ho,
A pretty girl I chanced to meet,
Heigh-ho, heigh-ho, heigh-ho.

Chorus

Rig-a-jig-jig, and away we go,
Away we go, away we go.
Rig-a-jig-jig, and away we go,
Heigh-ho, heigh-ho, heigh-ho.

Directions. While all sing, the center player walks around the inside of the circle until the words "a pretty girl" and then stands in front of a partner. Girls choose boys and vice versa. He then bows to her on the last line of the verse.

He takes her hands in skater's position and on the chorus they skip around the inside of the circle while the circle players clap hands in time.

The dance is repeated with the partners separating and choosing new partners until all have been chosen.

The second time the verse is sung, the words "a nice young man" or "a handsome man" can be substituted for "a pretty girl."

Variation. The dance can be done by alternating boys and girls and using the appropriate verses. Select four or five boys to begin in the center. They choose partners and after the skip return to the circle. The girls continue the dance choosing five more boys, and so on.

Broom Dance

Record. Victor 20448.

Formation. Children are in a double circle, partners facing counterclockwise with boys on the inside. An extra boy with a broom is in the center.

Verse

One, two, three, four, five, six, seven,
Where's my partner, nine, ten, eleven?
In Berlin, in Stettin,
There's the place to find him [her] in.

Chorus

Tra, la, la (etc.) (The music repeats.)

Directions. The record has three changes of music and then a pause. The verse is sung during the first change and repeated during the second change. The chorus is the third change. During the verse, which is repeated, all march counterclockwise. The boy in the center hands the broom to another boy and takes his place in the inner line. The boy with the broom in turn hands the broom to another inner-line member and takes his place, and so on. The one who has the broom after the two verses are sung (on the word "in") takes the broom to the center. He then pretends to sweep while the others skip with inside hands joined. If there are extra girls, the dance can be done with the girls exchanging the broom by making the direction of the march clockwise.

Variation I. The first verse is sung during the first music change, and the children march as in the original dance. During the second music change, the following routine is done. Note that in this routine the broom may be exchanged only when the boys move to a new partner.

Measures 1 and 2. Beginning with the outside foot, take seven steps forward and pause on the eighth.

Measures 3 and 4. Beginning with the inside foot, take seven steps backward and pause as before.

Measure 5. Beginning on the outside foot, take three steps away and pause.

Measure 6. Beginning with the inside foot, take three steps in and pause.

Measures 7 and 8. Swing once around in place with a right elbow swing. As the boy comes back to place, he moves forward to the next girl. During the exchange of partners, the broom man gives the broom to another boy and takes his place.

Variation II. This routine is used during the first change of the music.

Boys and girls form separate lines, facing each other, about 20 feet apart. The broom man is in the center. The teacher holds the broom to one side.

Measures 1 and 2. The lines advance toward each other with seven steps.

Measures 3 and 4. The lines retreat with seven steps.

Measures 5 and 6. The lines again advance seven steps.

Measures 7 and 8. The lines retreat seven steps until the word "in." All, including the broom man, rush for a partner and get ready to march around the room. The player left goes to the center to become the new broom man. The new broom man now takes the broom from the teacher, and the dance proceeds in the second and third changes of the music as in the original dance. Note that the broom should not be given to the broom man until after the first music change.

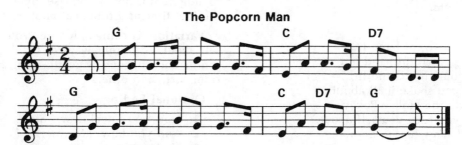

The Popcorn Man

Record. Folkraft 1180 ("The Muffin Man").

Formation. Children are in a single circle, facing the center with hands at sides. One child, the Popcorn Man, stands in front of another child of the opposite sex.

Verses

1. Oh, have you seen the Popcorn Man,
   The Popcorn Man, the Popcorn Man?
   Oh, have you seen the Popcorn Man,
   Who lives on [name of] Street?

2. Oh, yes, we've seen the Popcorn Man,
   The Popcorn Man, the Popcorn Man.
   Oh, yes, we've seen the Popcorn Man,
   Who lives on [name of] Street.

Directions

Verse 1. The children stand still and clap hands lightly, with the exception of the Popcorn Man and partner. These two join hands and jump lightly in place, keeping time to the music.

Verse 2. The Popcorn Man and partner now skip around the inside of the circle individually, and near the end of the verse each stands in front of a child, thus choosing new partners.

Verse 1 is now repeated with two sets of partners doing the jumping. During the repetition of Verse 2, four children skip around the inside of the circle and choose partners. This continues until all the children are chosen.

The children should choose the name of a street that they would like to put into the verses.

Hokey Pokey

Record. Capitol 6026.

Formation. Children are in a single circle, facing the center.

Verse

1. Put your right hand in,
2. Take your right hand out,
3. Put your right hand in,
4. And you shake it all about.
5. You do the Hokey Pokey,
6. And you turn yourself about,
7. For that's what it's all about.

Directions

Line 1. Step in slightly with the right foot and extend the right arm forward toward the center.

Line 2. Pull the arm back, step back.

Line 3. Same action as for line 1.

Line 4. Shake the hand vigorously.

Line 5. Raise the arms high overhead, shaking the arms and hips in time to the rhythm.

Line 6. Turn around in place, continuing the arm and hip actions.

Line 7. Face the center of the circle and clap hands three times, clapping on "that's," "all," and "-bout."

Additional Movements. Left hand, right foot, left foot, right elbow, left elbow, right hip, left hip, head, backside, whole self may be used. If all are used, the action becomes overly long, so judgment is necessary. Use some movements the first time and others at another time.

Variation. For line 6, where "you turn yourself about," different ways of turning in place can be chosen, such as gorilla turn, horse-and-rider turn, and others.

Optional Ending

1. Now you kneel down high,
2. And you bow, kowtow,
3. Now up again high,
4. And kowtow again.
5. You do the Hokey Pokey,
6. While you bow once more.
7. That's what it's all about.

Line 1. Kneel on both knees, arms overhead.

Line 2. Bow down and touch the floor.

Line 3. Up again to a kneeling position, arms overhead, as in line 1.

Line 4. Make another obeisance.

Line 5. Still kneeling, do Hokey Pokey motions.

Line 6. Bow once more, continuing motions.

Line 7. Slap the floor once for each word and syllable.

GAMES USING RHYTHMIC BACKGROUND

A number of interesting games can be played, using music as a part of the game. Most of them are simple in principle and are based on the idea of changing the movement when the music changes or stops. Some of them are similar to the old, old game of Musical Chairs.

Circle Stoop

Children are in a single circle facing counterclockwise. A march or similar music can be used, or the game can be played to the beat of a tom-tom. The children march in good posture until the music is stopped. As soon as the child no longer hears the music or beat of the tom-tom, he stoops and touches both hands to the ground without losing balance. The last child to touch both hands to the ground successfully pays a penalty by going into the mush-pot (center of the circle) or being eliminated. Children should march in good posture; anyone stooping, even partially, before the music is stopped should be penalized. The duration of the music should be varied, and the children should not be able to observe the stopping process if a record player is being used.

Variations. Employ different locomotor movements, such as skipping, hopping, or galloping, while using suitable music.

Use different positions for stopping instead of stooping. Positions like the push-up, crab, lame dog, balancing on one foot, or touching with one hand and one foot add to the interest and fun.

Partner Stoop

The game uses the same basic movement (stooping) as Circle Stoop, but it is done with partners. The group forms a double circle with partners facing counterclockwise. When the music starts, all march in line of direction. After a short period of marching, a signal (whistle) is given, and the inside circle turns around and marches the other way—clockwise. Partners are now separated. When the music is stopped, the outer circle stands still, and the inside circle players *walk* to rejoin their partners. As soon as a player reaches his or her partner, they join inside hands and stoop without losing balance. The last couple to stoop goes to the center of the circle and waits out the next round.

Variation. The game can be played by groups of three instead of partners. The game begins with the groups of three marching abreast, holding hands and facing counterclockwise. On the signal, the outside players of the threes con-

tinue marching in the same direction. The middle players of the threes stop and stand still. The inside players reverse direction and march clockwise. When the music stops, the groups of three attempt to reunite at the spot where the middle player stopped. The last three to join hands and stoop are put into the center for the next round.

Soap Bubbles

The teacher can show children how a soap bubble is made, how it floats, and what happens when it touches something or another bubble. The game is in three stages.

1. Each child in personal space pretends to blow himself or herself up like a soap bubble.

2. The Bubbles float around the space, making sure that they do not touch anyone or anything on penalty of breaking. Should this happen, the Soap Bubbles involved sink relaxed to the floor. During this stage, dreamy music is played.

3. When the music stops, Bubbles look around and bump each other, sinking to the floor like a puddle of water.

Variation. This could also be called Balloons. When the music stops, a Balloon Buster can go among the children and pop the balloons.

Follow Me

The game has its basis in the phrasing of the music. The children are in circle formation, facing in, with a leader in the center. The leader performs a series of movements of her choice, either locomotor or nonlocomotor, for the duration of one phrase of music (eight beats). The children imitate the movements during the next phrase. The leader takes over for another set of movements, and the children imitate during the next phrase following. After a few changes, the leader picks another child to take the place as leader.

Variations. A popular way to play this game is to have the children follow the leader as she performs. This means changing movement as the leader changes and performing as the leader does, with everyone keeping with the rhythm. A change is made as soon as the leader falters or loses her patterns or ideas.

The game can be done with partners. One partner performs during one phrase, and the other partner imitates the movements during the next phrase. The teacher can decide which couple is making the most vivid and imaginative movements and is doing the best job of following each other's movements.

Freeze

Children are scattered around the room. When the music is started, they move around the room guided by the character of the music. They walk, run, jump, or use other locomotor movements appropriate to the selected music or beat. When the music is stopped, they freeze and do not move. Any child caught moving after the cessation of the rhythm pays a penalty.

A tom-tom or piano provides a fine base for this game, as the rhythmic beat can be varied easily and the rhythm can be stopped at any time. In the absence of a tom-tom or drum, two sticks or Indian clubs can be knocked together to provide the beat.

Variations. Specify the level at which the child must freeze.

Have the child fall to the ground or go into a specified position, such as the push-up, crab, lame dog, a balance, or some other position.

Specify the kind of statue or pose to be assumed.

Right Angle

A tom-tom can be used to provide the rhythm for this activity. Some of the basic rhythm records also have suitable music. The children change direction at right angles on each heavy beat or change of music. The object of the game is to make the right angle changes on signal and not to bump into other children. Other angles could be specified.

Arches

The game is similar to London Bridge. Arches are placed around the playing area. To form an arch, two players stand facing one another with hands joined. When the music starts, the players move in a circle, passing under the arch. Suddenly, the music stops, and the arches come down by dropping the hands. All players caught in an arch immediately pair off together to form other arches, keeping in a general circle formation. If a "caught" player does not have a partner, he should wait in the center of the circle until one is available. The last players caught (or left) form arches for the next game.

The arches should be warned not to bring down their hands and arms too forcefully, so that the children passing under them will not be pummeled. Also, children with glasses need consideration in the process of catching, since glasses can be knocked to the floor when the arches close. Glasses should be removed, or children with glasses can begin by being the arches.

Variation. Different types of music can be used, and the children can move according to the pattern of the music.

Old Man, Old Lady

A definite line down the center of the play area is needed. The whole class can participate, with half the class on one side of the line and the other half occupying the area on the other side. To begin, each child holds hands with another child across the line. There must be an extra child on one side, or the teacher can play.

Music can be supplied by a record player, piano, or drum. When the music or the rhythm starts, all children move to the beat as they wish, staying in their half of the area. When the music stops, all children rush to the line to try to find a partner from the opposite group and hold hands across the line.

There will be one without a partner, who is the Old Man or Old Lady. The Old Man or Old Lady now moves to the other side, so that this group now has a uneven number. The game is continued.

The game becomes more fun when different kinds of movements can be specified, such as varied locomotor movements, animal imitations, moving on all fours, et cetera.

Whistle March

A record with a brisk march is needed. The children are scattered around the room, individually walking in various directions, keeping time to the music. A whistle is blown a number of times, at which signal lines are formed of that precise number, no more and no less. The lines are formed by having the children stand side by side with locked elbows. As soon as a line of the proper number is formed, it begins to march to the music counterclockwise around the room. Any children left over go to the center of the room and remain until the next signal. On the next whistle signal (single blast), the lines break up, and all walk individually around the room in various directions as before.

Teaching Hint. It may be well to make a rule that children may not lock elbows with the same children with whom they formed the previous line.

ROPE-JUMPING TO MUSIC

Rope-jumping is a rhythmic activity that can be enhanced by the addition of suitable rhythm. An appropriate rhythm adds much to the fun of the jumping activities. These activities were presented in Chapter 13, pp. 178–81, and for that reason they are not repeated here.

SUMMARY

Children should be able to identify certain characteristics of music through movement such as tempo, beat, meter, accent, intensity, and phrase. Tom-toms, records and tape recorder, piano, and guitar are excellent means of producing rhythmic sounds.

In this chapter, rhythmic activities are grouped into six categories. Creative rhythms include free or expressive rhythms, identification types, and dramatization rhythms. Creative rhythms ally closely with creative expression through stories, plays, and poems. Fundamental rhythms focus on movement skills, locomotor, nonlocomotor, and object-handling in nature. Rhythmic beat repetition and reproduction is a category in which youngsters make accurate reproductions of various beats, with an emphasis on developing auditory perception. Singing movement games require children to sing and interpret through movement the words of a song. Folk dances are traditional dances of national or ethnic origin. Folk dances involve a patterned movement response based on fundamental movements or dance steps. The last category, musical games, includes activities that incorporate music or rhythm into the game.

Rhythmic activities for young children emphasize the process of moving and expression through movement with little emphasis on desired movement patterns. As children mature, an emphasis is placed on simple folk dances, rope-jumping to music, and action movement songs, even though creative movement dominates a large share of the rhythmic program.

Chapter 16

Game Activities

Children can be helped to learn many things through play and games, but if they do not have fun in doing so, the game is over.

All children should have the opportunity to participate in a variety of games, which are the collective heritage of centuries of children. Games have good recreational value, provide opportunity for fitness development, and offer a necessary outlet for natural exuberance.

Games for young children feature a great deal of individual and creative play. Games with an emphasis on cognitive learning goals are included in the program. Games that require a great deal of teamwork or scorekeeping are usually not included in the program at this age level. The games must be simple and easily taught and must demand few specialized skills. A large number of the games require fundamental locomotor movements and provide an exciting medium in which to practice such movements.

Dramatic elements are present in many of the games, while others help establish number concepts and shape recognition. Games based on stories and poems are popular with children of this age.

CONTRIBUTIONS OF GAME ACTIVITIES TO THE CHILD'S TOTAL DEVELOPMENT

Games are an excellent medium for social and moral development, since certain rules must be followed if the game is to be enjoyed by all. As games become more organized and rules are strictly enforced, children learn to modify their behavior to comply with that of others and to remain within social boundaries. As they ma-

ture, they become more aware of the need for teamwork if all players are to reach their goals. Some of the more complex games require that youngsters work cognitively to develop simple strategies.

Games are not inherently fun. They must be taught in an atmosphere that makes children believe that their full participation is needed for a successful game. If a child is left out or eliminated because of his poor skill level, the game will be an unhappy experience for him. As a general rule, games are not fun for children if they are constantly unsuccessful. In a proper environment, however, some of the following goals for children can be reached:

PSYCHOMOTOR DOMAIN

1. Children will be provided vigorous large-muscle activity with developmental potential, resulting in good muscular development and control.

2. Children will develop the ability to run, maneuver, dodge, start, and stop under control.

3. Children will learn to manage and control the body while under the stress of competition.

COGNITIVE DOMAIN

4. Children will gain in mental alertness while they are reacting strategically to game situations.

5. Children will learn to understand and follow rules and be able to apply this knowledge to nonsupervised periods of play.

AFFECTIVE DOMAIN

6. Children will learn to play with others in a socially sound manner without bickering, quarreling, and fighting.

7. Children will understand and feel the need to play fairly and exhibit good sportsmanship.

8. Children will amplify their understanding of self and others.

Games that offer the most value for overall development of children are those in which most or all children are active simultaneously. These games should encourage the children to put out a maximal effort while participating. Games in which a majority of children are inactive can sometimes be effectively used to provide a period of lesser activity following a strenuous activity. Games of this type usually involve a runner and chaser, while the remainder of the children have little part in the play. Some games of this nature have been included later in the chapter, with more detailed explanations given.

Games should be analyzed from the standpoint of whether or not they require a skill that the children should practice before playing the game. Rarely should a game be used to develop a proper skill pattern, since the competitive aspect will usually undo a pattern that has been poorly learned. This caution is given here, not to discourage the use of games, but to emphasize that games should not be the major medium used for skill development and practice. If children need more practice on skills, the teacher should select appropriate movement activities to bring children to the minimum level of skill needed to play the game pleasurably. The acquisition of necessary skills through practice sessions becomes more meaningful when children see their purpose in a game situation.

Games should be taught in a general progression. In other words, children should first learn a simple game that requires few skills and can easily be mastered by all. As youngsters become more skilled, more skills can be added, and the difficulty of the games increased. Early emphasis (in preschool and kindergarten) should be on learning to play well together.

COMPETITION AND GAMES

The games for preschool children do not require a high degree of skill and thus provide an opportunity for all children to participate successfully. Games in which all children can do well are joyous situations. Children can become involved in a group and respond with energy, laughter, and excitement. Sometimes, however, children are eliminated because of lack of skill, and suddenly the joy is over. If certain children are unsuccessful in most game situations, they will become negative and antagonistic toward game activities. Competitive games can build barriers between people, since, in such activities, youngsters are asked to work against one another rather than together.

Some people advocate noncompetitive games for youngsters. In these "no-win" games, an environment can be developed in which youngsters are working and playing together to reach a common goal. Winning or losing does not and should not become the overriding reason for playing a game. The game experience becomes a situation in which a child can show off his newly acquired skills and learn to help a friend acquire skills of his own. Most children at this age will play games only if they are personally rewarding and provide activity for all. This is the reason why their free play is dominated by tag games, run-and-chase activities, and games that require no equipment save a healthy body.

Competition is not inherently bad or good. The important issue is how it is handled by the teacher. Some of the following points should be considered when the question of competition for young children is addressed:

1. Young children do not see competition as a group process in which seeking a common goal is the primary purpose of the game. They are individuals and enjoy playing for themselves. Rules are something that can be changed to make the game more enjoyable and that can be ignored if desired. Thus, their games should be simple and unstructured and should contain few rules.

2. Competitive situations may be rewarding only for those students capable of winning regularly. Highly skilled children usually enjoy competition, since they have a good chance of finding success. Thus, the teacher should use *low-achieving* youngsters as a guide in evaluating the effect of competition on a healthy environment for all the children.

3. If children are to compete against one another, the teacher should encourage all participants to enjoy the activity rather than emphasize the importance of winning. It would seem a worthwhile endeavor to point out that every child is valued and important regardless of his or her performance in the game situation. In some unfortunate cases, children receive attention and teacher approval only if they are winners. This practice obviously places a large premium on winning at all costs.

4. There is some evidence to support the thesis that rewarding a winner with extrinsic re-

wards may actually decrease a child's intrinsic motivation to participate in an activity.[1] When the extrinsic motivation is removed, the child loses the desire to participate for the fun of it. In some cases, this feeling may become generalized to include all physical activity. Emphasis should be placed on the joy of participation rather than the importance of receiving a reward, ribbon, or gold star. Some extrinsic motivations have been found desirable to stimulate retarded children, however.

5. Finally, all children should have a reasonable chance for success. This might be accomplished by grouping, pairing a child with someone near his or her own ability, and basing comparisons on improvement and effort rather than on sheer ability and skill. For example, competition might be varied by matching individuals against peers of somewhat equal ability, thus keeping the goals of competition within the students' level of aspiration. Another useful form is autocompetition, according to which students compete against themselves, trying to improve upon their own past performance.

In summary, competition, which is a part of the American way of life, can be a useful ingredient in balanced development and growth when used wisely by a caring teacher. An environment in which teachers are warm and friendly, firm but consistent in their judgment, and in which children are allowed to explore their environment without fear of failure will help each child reach a higher level of personal growth.

MODIFICATION OF GAMES

The primary purpose of modifying games is to make them more enjoyable and productive for youngsters. The game must provide the child with a successful experience if he is to participate willingly in such games in the future. A teacher should realize that when a number of children are having difficulty with the game, it is time to change it. It is exciting to see children respond enthusiastically to a new variation of a game. Introducing modifications can also revive interest when it lags and can help the teacher to expand the use of an activity.

The following are some suggested ideas for modifying games to suit the needs of all children better:

1. The distance that players are to run can be lengthened or shortened. For example, in Flying Dutchman, have the runners go twice around the circle instead of once. In Kick Soft-

ball, the distance between bases can be varied to make it easier or more difficult to get on base.

2. The runner's route can be varied. In circle games, for example, the runners can be challenged to weave in and out of the other players as they move. Some interesting variations can be offered by asking players to perform various challenges during their run, such as jumping, clicking the heels, or moving under an obstacle.

3. The method of locomotion can be changed. So many games for primary children require that all children run. Many of the fundamental locomotor movements can be practiced if children are restricted to move by skipping, hopping, galloping, sliding, etc., instead of running.

4. For primary grade children, the game might be played by partners or small groups instead of by individuals. For example, tag games can be played in groups of two or three players, who are required to hold hands while chasing and fleeing.

5. Vary the method and spot of tagging. Certain spots can be stipulated for a tag to be made, such as knee, shoulder, and elbow. Students could be required to tag with the right or left hand or with an elbow, or to make a toe-to-toe tag.

6. The basic formation of the game can be altered. Instead of playing the game of Fireman in a circle, it might be played with children in a rectangle, triangle, or diamond shape.

7. The boundaries for the game area can be manipulated to make it more or less challenging. For example, tagging becomes easier when the area is decreased in size. Depending on the skill of the players, the boundaries might be subtly changed to help individuals find success.

8. Some mild penalties might be added to the game to increase the risk and excitement of the game. For instance, in the game Midnight, the teacher might tell the youngsters that they will not be chased unless they are really running away. This will avoid the situation in which one child lags behind, trying to be caught in order to be It and become the center of attention. Too often, however, the penalties that are added to games appear to be a punishment rather than something one desires to do for the joy of it.

9. The number of key players can be increased. This might mean increasing the number of taggers, runners, or throwers in a game so that the amount of activity is increased for all participants.

10. Various aids or hindrances can be added to a game. In Cat and Rat, players can raise or lower their arms depending on whether the Cat

[1]David Greene and M. R. Lepper, "How to Turn Play into Work," *Psychology Today* 8 (September 1974): 49–54.

or the Rat is moving through the "windows." The teacher might regulate the modification in order to help less skilled players.

11. The height or size of goals can be changed. A hula hoop tied to a basket might be a much better target for children attempting to sink a basketball. If youngsters are playing some kicking games, the goals might be broadened to offer more success opportunities.

12. The projectiles used in a game can be varied. Beach balls or balloons would be much more appropriate to use than volleyballs, when young children are learning the skill of volleying. A large playground ball might be easier to kick than a regulation-size soccer ball. Certainly, smaller basketballs are easier for small children to handle with ease and confidence. Striking games might make use of a larger bat and ball to make contact easier. Fleece balls might be substituted for harder and heavier projectiles to remove the children's fear of being hurt.

13. In tag or chase games, call out "Reverse"; this signals the children to reverse roles. If they were chasing, they now become runners, and vice versa. This signal might also be used to change the direction of a ball passing around the circle.

Over the years, children and teachers have developed many other ideas for varying and modifying many traditional games. Pertinent and worthwhile suggestions of this nature are presented in the respective game descriptions.

SAFETY SUGGESTIONS FOR GAMES

Because they arouse the competitive spirit, games have some built-in hazards, which must be anticipated and for which safety precautions need to be established.

Slipping and Falling. Emphasis should be placed on the importance of running properly, and children should practice turning and changing direction properly. The playing area should be kept free of dangerous objects. The teacher should make certain that all players are aware of any hazardous conditions of the playing area, such as slickness, holes, or loose pebbles.

Collisions and Tripping. Stress the need for all players to be alert. Many collisions occur in goal games in which the children are divided into two groups and begin to run past one another toward opposite goals. The suggested list of games includes no games of this nature. If there is more than one chaser or catcher, the danger is multiplied. The group should be scattered to avoid collisions. If players are running in opposite directions, they should pass each

other to the right. Children should be taught to tag by touching, not shoving, and the teacher should insist that tagging be done properly.

Spatial Factors. Sufficient room for the games should be provided. Colliding with fences and walls during running and chase games is an ever-present danger. Establish boundaries far enough from these and other obstacles to ensure safety. If separate groups of children are playing games, keep them far enough apart so that they will not overrun one another.

INSTRUCTIONAL PROCEDURES FOR CONDUCTING GAMES

1. The principal ingredient of successful games leadership is a vigorous, snappy approach. Such an attitude, combined with a spirit of enthusiasm, will do much toward producing the desired results.

2. Know the game well before attempting to teach it. This means identifying the safety hazards, anticipating the difficulties, and adapting the game to the group and the situation.

3. Complete all preparations before starting to introduce the game. Draw lines and boundaries and have supplies ready for distribution.

4. When explaining the game, keep your discussion brief and to the point. Tell the children what is to be done and what is to be avoided. Demonstrate or diagram as needed. Students should be comfortable during explanations.

5. Sometimes it is a good idea to have a trial period so that children can understand the game before playing it "for real." Children, like adults, resent losing a point or getting caught if they think this results from their lack of understanding of a game.

6. Enforce the rules impartially once they have been established. Discuss with the children the reasons for the rules.

7. Where lines and limits are important, establish them definitely so that there will be no question when a child is out of bounds or beyond the limits. Make clear and enforce the penalty for an infraction.

8. Watch the players carefully for a decrease in interest in the game. Change the game before it dies a natural death. Occasionally, the teacher can stop a game even when children are showing the most interest, so that they will look forward with anticipation to the activity at a later time.

9. Be sure that everyone has had a turn, whenever this is practical. Have children identify themselves by raising their hands or by the use of some other device to show that they have not had a turn.

10. Avoid overemphasizing competition. Centering too much attention on winning causes the skilled to resent being on the same team with the less skilled.

11. Watch for fatigue, especially in a chaser who is unable to catch a runner. Make a change, picking another child to be the chaser.

12. Be careful of the situation in which some child is made the "goat" or butt of jokes. Not only is this poor citizenship, but the psychological hurt to the child may be deep and permanent. The possibility of physical hurt due to physical handicaps must not be ruled out. The slow, heavy child, who cannot move as well as others, is at a disadvantage in dodgeball games and other activities demanding mobility.

13. Although games that eliminate children in the course of play do have a place in the program, they should be used with caution. Elimination should not be carried down to the "bitter end." It is better to play the game so that a small number of the children are eliminated and then declare the remainder the winners.

EXPLORATION WITH GAMES

Children should have the opportunity to make up or design games of their own. The teacher can set the problem by specifying what is available to them in the nature of space, equipment, and number of participants. For example, the space could be designated as a 20-foot square or as two parallel lines 30 feet apart. A game could also be created that required no equipment, or the children could be given a ball (any size) to work with.

A second opportunity for children to design their own games generally follows a practice period with some manipulative object or on a fundamental skill. The teacher directs the children to organize an original game, either individually, with a partner, or as a member of a small group, that will include the just-learned skill in some fashion. The teacher might give the children this basis for a game: "In your game, include a striking skill with the paddle and ball in such a way that you and your partner keep score. If you like, use a hoop or jump rope to help you with your game."

CLASSIFICATION OF GAMES

The games in this chapter are grouped under four major headings, which describe the amount of activity they offer children as well as whether they require or do not require equipment or supplies. *Active games* are those in which most or all of the children participate simultaneously. In *moderately active games,* only some of the children are active, while the others are generally sitting or standing, providing game background or waiting a turn.

The teacher should base his selection of a game on the amount of activity that has gone before. If the lesson has been a demanding one, a moderately active game might be a judicious choice. Moderately active games should be played as resting activities, and they have a place in the curriculum as such. Although they are fun, they rate low in developmental value; in these games, therefore, it is important to keep the action going as rapidly as possible. For example, a rule can be made that runners may travel only partway around the circle before a change is made to another runner.

On the opposite side of the coin, if the lesson has placed little demand on the cardiovascular system, an active game should be played. The game should complement the lesson and be an integral part of the lesson rather than an afterthought. In this way, the game can be used to practice learned skills in a competitive situation and increase the amount of activity offered.

The four categories of games are as follows:

1. Active games that require no equipment or supplies
2. Active games that require equipment or supplies
3. Moderately active games that require no equipment or supplies
4. Moderately active games that require equipment or supplies

The games under each of the four categories are also grouped according to the *maturity level* at which the child can participate successfully in the activity: preschool, kindergarten, first grade, or second grade. This subdivision can serve as a guide for those teachers who are not familiar with the individual games. Instructors should understand that this classification is only approximate, since many of the games can be adapted to all maturity levels.

The instructor should be aware that many of the preschool games may be too difficult for three- and four-year-old children. If the games are to be used with children at this age level, the teacher should recognize that it may take some time and practice before the children develop adequate skill to enjoy the activity.

ACTIVE GAMES THAT REQUIRE NO EQUIPMENT OR SUPPLIES

Preschool games
Shadows and Moonlight
Kneeling Tag
Redwoods
Marching Ponies

Popcorn
Statues
Circus Master
Midnight

Kindergarten games
Animal Tag
Back-to-Back
Charlie over the Water
Old Man (Old Lady)
One, Two, Button My Shoe
Squirrel in the Trees
Tag Games
Where's My Partner?
Animal Chase

First grade games
Caged Lion
Flowers and Wind
Forest Ranger
What Is Your Job?
Hill Dill
I Can Do What You Can!
Four Out
In the Creek
Leap the Brook
May I Chase You?
Mousetrap
Three Person Tag
Red Light
Stop and Start

Second grade games
Bronco Tag
Busy Bee
Couple Tag
Hooked Elbows Tag
Crows and Cranes
Eagles and Sparrows
Fly Trap
Frog in the Sea
Monsters
Triple Change

Preschool Games

SHADOWS AND MOONLIGHT

Playing Area. Gymnasium or playground.
Players. 20 to 40.
Supplies. None.
Skills. Running, skipping, and dodging.
Maturity Level. Preschool.
Directions. One or more children are chosen to be chasers. They go to the corner of the room and hide their eyes. The rest of the children skip or run near the chasers, chanting, "Shadows and moonlight, Ghosty won't be out tonight." The chasers play the role of Ghosty and pretend they are asleep. When they awake, they shout, "Boo,"

and everyone races home, trying to avoid being caught by Ghosty.

Variations. Different locomotor movements can be substituted for both chasing and running, and combinations of different tasks can be added. A little realism can be injected by having the Ghosty put on a mask. The game would certainly be appropriate around Halloween!

KNEELING TAG

Playing Area. Playground or gymnasium.
Players. Entire class.
Supplies. None.
Skills. Running, right and left discrimination.
Maturity Level. Preschool.
Directions. Two or more children are It. They attempt to tag the other children, who can be "safe" by kneeling on one knee. The child tagged changes places with the child who is It.

The teacher should specify which knee is to be used and should change this designation partway through the game. The game can be played progressively, with the children tagged joining the taggers. Play until about half the children have been tagged.

Children need to be encouraged to dare a little, as no one will be caught if everyone kneels all the time. Players kneeling on the wrong knee are not "safe."

Variation. Color concepts can be stressed by selecting a color for safety. This can be done easily when playing in a gymnasium, where lines of different colors are already on the floor. Construction paper in different colors can also be taped to the floor to serve as "safe" bases. Markers of this type are not likely to survive very long, however. Children are instructed to kneel on red, green, or another color to be "safe."

REDWOODS

Playing Area. Gymnasium or playground.
Players. Entire class.
Supplies. None.
Skills. Body management competency.
Maturity Level. Preschool.
Directions. Divide the class into the Forest Rangers and the Redwoods. If the teacher can show the children a picture of redwoods, it will make the game more realistic. The Redwoods are scattered about the area, holding their arms up like the branches of the trees. The Rangers walk in and out and under the Redwoods, trying not to touch them or bump into any other Ranger. A poem is recited, perhaps two or three times, while the Rangers are walking through the forest.

The wind blows through the trees.
It makes you wiggle your knees.
The trees sway to and fro.
Back and forth you go.

The Redwoods react accordingly. Reverse the roles after a period of time, since the Trees will get tired of holding up their "branches."

MARCHING PONIES

Playing Area. Playground, gymnasium, or classroom.
Players. Entire class.
Supplies. None.
Skills. Marching, running.
Maturity Level. Preschool.
Directions. One child is the Ringmaster and crouches in the center of a circle of Ponies formed by the other children. Two goal lines on opposite sides of the circle are established as "safe" areas. The Ponies march around the circle in step, counting steps consecutively. At a predetermined number (which has been whispered to the Ringmaster by the teacher), the Ringmaster jumps from the crouched position and attemps to tag the others before they can reach the safety lines. Anyone tagged must join the Ringmaster in the center, helping him catch the next time.
The game should be reorganized after six to eight children have been caught. Those left in the circle are declared the winners.
Variations. Ponies must gallop to the "safe" area.

POPCORN

Playing Area. Playground, gymnasium, or classroom.
Players. Entire class, divided into two groups.
Supplies. None.
Skills. Curling, stretching, jumping.
Maturity Level. Preschool.
Directions. The children should be given a short preliminary explanation of how popcorn pops when heat is applied. Half the children are designated as Popcorn. They crouch down in the center of the circle (the "pan on the stove") formed by the rest of the children. The circle children act as indicators of the heat under the Popcorn. One of them should be designated the leader, whose actions will serve as a guide to the other children. The circle children, who are also crouched down, gradually rise to a standing position, extend their arms overhead, and shake them vigorously to indicate high heat. In the meantime, the Popcorn in the center begins to "pop," and the children who are Popcorn jump to their feet. This action should begin at a slow pace and increase in speed and height as the heat grows higher. In the final stages, the children are popping up rapidly.
Change groups and repeat.

STATUES

Playing Area. Playground or gymnasium.
Players. Entire class, organized into pairs.
Supplies. None.
Skills. Body management, balance.
Maturity Level. Preschool.
Directions. Children are paired off around the area. One child is the swinger, and the other is the Statue. The swinger takes the Statue by one or two hands and swings him around in a small circle. The teacher voices a directive, such as, "Pretty!", "Funny!", "Happy!", "Animal!", or some other evocative word. The swingers immediately release the Statues and sit down on the floor. The Statues take a pose in keeping with the directive. The teacher or a committee of children can determine which children are making the best statues. The object is to hold the position without moving.

Swinging the Statues

After the winners have been determined, the partners reverse positions. Children should be cautioned that the swinging helps to position the Statues, but that it must be controlled.
Variations. Some recommend that the directive be given *before* the swinging starts, so as to give the Statue more time to think about what pose to take. Some kind of signal must then be added to key the swing release.

CIRCUS MASTER

Playing Area. Playground, gymnasium, or classroom.

Players. Ten to forty.
Supplies. None.
Skills. Imagery, fundamental locomotor movements.
Maturity Level. Preschool.
Directions. One child, the Circus Master, is in the center of the circle formed by the other children. He stands in the center, pretends he has a whip, and gets ready to have the animals perform. He gives a direction like the following: "We are going to walk as elephants do, like this!" He then moves in a small circle, demonstrating how the children are to perform. He commands, "Elephants ready—*walk.*" The children imitate elephants walking around the large circle, while the Circus Master performs in a small circle in the center. When ready, the Circus Master calls, "Halt," takes a place in the circle, and another child comes forward to the center.

Several children can be chosen in advance to be Circus Masters. This is an excellent idea for young children, since it gives them time to be prepared with a particular animal imitation. If the group is large, however, interest would die long before all the children could take a turn in the center. Make arrangements for other children to be in the center when the game is played at a later date.

Variation. All children can stand on the end line, with the child who is It standing in the middle of the room. The child who is It says, "Everybody travel across the floor," and specifies the way they are to move. The class travels to the other side of the gym in the way the caller has suggested. Ways that can be specified are: running, hopping, galloping, skipping, jumping, moving like an animal, moving on two hands and one foot, etc.

MIDNIGHT

Playing Area. Playground.
Players. Six to fifteen.
Supplies. None.
Skills. Running, dodging.
Maturity Level. Preschool.
Directions. A safety line is established about 40 feet from a "den" in which one player (the Fox) is standing. The others (the Chickens) stand behind the safety line. They move forward slowly, asking, "Mr. Fox, what time is it?" The Fox answers in various fashions, such as, "Bedtime," "Pretty late," "Three-thirty," and so on. She continues to draw the players toward her. At some point, the Fox answers the question with "Midnight!" and chases the others back to the safety line. Any player caught joins the Fox in her "den" and helps catch others. No player in the "den" can chase until the Fox calls

out, "Midnight." As a variation, the words "dinner time" can be substituted for "midnight," meaning that it is time for the Fox to chase the Chickens so that he can have dinner.

Kindergarten Games

ANIMAL TAG

Playing Area. Playground or gymnasium. Two parallel lines are drawn about 40 feet apart.
Players. Entire class.
Supplies. None.
Skills. Running, dodging.
Maturity Level. Kindergarten.
Directions. The children are divided into two groups, each of which takes a position along one of the lines. The children of Group 1 get together with their leader and decide what animal they wish to imitate. Having selected the animal, they move over to within about five feet of the other line. Here they imitate the animal, and Group 2 tries to guess the animal correctly. If they guess correctly, they chase Group 1 back to its line, trying to tag as many as possible. Those caught must go over to the other team.

Group 2 now selects an animal, and the roles are reversed. However, if the guessing team cannot guess the animal, the performing team gets another try.

To avoid confusion, have the children raise hands to take turns naming the animal. Otherwise, there will be many false chases.

If the children have trouble guessing, then have the leader of the performing team give the first letter of its name or a characteristic of the animal.

BACK-TO-BACK

Playing Area. Playground, gymnasium, or classroom.
Players. Entire class.
Supplies. None.
Skills. Fundamental locomotor movements.
Maturity Level. Kindergarten.
Directions. There must be an uneven number of players. If the number of students is even, the teacher can play. On signal, each child stands back to back with another child. One child will be without a partner. This child then claps hands for the next signal, and all children change partners, with the extra player seeking a partner.

Variation. More activity can be brought in by adding an extra command. After the children are in partner formation back to back, the teacher can say, "Everybody—run!" (or skip, hop, jump, slide, etc.). Other commands can be given, such as, "Walk like an elephant." The children move around the room in the prescribed manner. When the whistle is blown, they immediately find a partner and stand back to back.

CHARLIE OVER THE WATER

Playing Area. Playground, gymnasium, or classroom.

Players. Ten to twenty.

Supplies. None.

Skills. Skipping, body management skills.

Maturity Level. Kindergarten.

Directions. The children are in circle formation with hands joined. One or more extra children are in the center, depending on the number of children in the circle. The one in the center is Charlie. The circle children skip around the circle to the following chant:

Charlie over the water,
Charlie over the sea,
Charlie caught a bluebird,
But he can't catch me!

On the word "me," all circle children drop hands, stoop, and touch the ground with both hands. The center players try to tag the circle players before they stoop. Any player tagged changes places with the center player. The game then continues.

Children should be cautioned to retain their balance while stooping. If they fall, they can be tagged.

The following chant can be used if a girl is in the center:

Sally over the river,
Sally over the sea (etc.)

Variations. One way to increase the possibility of being tagged is to have the players make a full turn in place before stooping. Other positions can be stipulated instead of stooping. Balancing on one foot, crab position, push-up position, and others can be used.

This game can also be played with a ball (see p. 273).

OLD MAN (OLD LADY)

Playing Area. Playground, gymnasium, or classroom.

Players. Entire class.

Supplies. None.

Skills. Fundamental locomotor movements.

Maturity Level. Kindergarten.

Directions. A line is drawn through the middle of the area. Any convenient line can be used. Half the children are on one side, half on the other. Children hold hands with a partner across the center line. There must be an extra person (the teacher or another child). The

teacher gives a signal for the children to move as directed on their side of the line. They can be directed to run, hop, skip, etc. At a whistle, the children run to the center line, and each reaches across to join hands with a child from the opposite group. The one left out is the Old Man or the Old Lady. Children may reach over, but not cross, the line. The odd person should alternate sides so that the Old Man can be on the other side at times.

Playing Old Man, Old Lady

The game can also be done to music, with the players rushing to the center line to find partners when the rhythm stops.

ONE, TWO, BUTTON MY SHOE

Playing Area. Playground or gymnasium. Two parallel lines are drawn about 50 feet apart.

Players. Entire class.

Supplies. None.

Skills. Running.

Maturity Level. Kindergarten.

Directions. One child is the leader and stands to one side. The remainder of the children are behind one of the lines. The leader says, "Ready." The following dialogue takes place between the leader and the children:

Children	Leader's response
"One, two."	"Button my shoe."
"Three, four."	"Close the door."
"Five, six."	"Pick up sticks."
"Seven, eight."	"Run, or you'll be late!"

As the children carry on this conversation with the leader, they are toeing the line, ready to run. When the word "late" is spoken by the leader, the children run to the other line and return. The first child across the original line is the winner and becomes the new leader.

The leader can give the last response in any rhythm, by pausing or dragging out the words. No child is to start running before the word "late."

Variation. The children pantomime the leader's directions.

SQUIRREL IN THE TREES

Playing Area. Playground or gymnasium.
Players. 15 to 35.
Supplies. None.
Skills. Fundamental locomotor movements.
Maturity Level. Kindergarten.
Directions. A "tree" is formed by two players facing each other and holding hands or putting their hands on each other's shoulders. A Squirrel is in the center of each "tree," and one or two extra Squirrels are outside. A signal to change is given. All Squirrels move out of their "trees" to another "tree," and the extra players try to find "trees." Only one Squirrel is allowed in a "tree."

To form a system of rotation: as each Squirrel moves into a "tree," he changes places with one of the two players forming the "tree."

Variations. A third person can be added to the "trees" to make "tepees" for the children to hide in safely.

To add more activity to the game, it can be stipulated that all children perform locomotor movements when the signal to change is given. The children forming the "trees" must hold hands as they move, while the Squirrels try to get into a "tree" that is on the move.

A simplified version of the game can be played by using hoops as "trees," eliminating the need to use two players to form each "tree."

TAG GAMES

Playing Area. Playground with established boundaries or gymnasium.
Players. Any number.
Supplies. None.
Skills. Fundamental locomotor movements.
Maturity Level. Kindergarten.
Directions. Tag is played in many different ways. Children are scattered about the area. One child is It and chases others to tag one of them. When he does, he says, "You're It." The new It chases other children. Different tag games are played as follows:

1. Being "safe" by touching an object of a specified color or material. Touching wood, iron, the floor, or a specified color can make a runner "safe."

2. Being "safe" by taking a particular pose or doing a specified movement. Some actions used to become safe are:

Stoop—touch both hands to the ground
Stork—stand on one foot (the other cannot touch the floor)
Turtle—be on one's back, feet pointed toward the ceiling
Hindu—make an obeisance with the forehead to the ground
Nose and toe—touch the nose to the toe
Back to back—stand back to back with any other child
Wood—touch wood
Metal—touch metal
Tree—touch a tree with one hand and one foot simultaneously

3. *Locomotor Tag.* The child who is It specifies how the players shall move (skip, hop, jump, etc.). He must also use the same kind of movement as he tries to catch them.

4. *Frozen Tag.* Two children are It. The rest are scattered over the area. When caught, they are "frozen" and must keep both feet in place. Any free player can tag a "frozen" player and release him. The object of the taggers is to "freeze" all the players.

WHERE'S MY PARTNER?

Playing Area. Playground, gymnasium, a classroom.
Players. Entire class.
Supplies. None.
Skills. Fundamental locomotor movements.
Maturity Level. Kindergarten.
Directions. Children are arranged in a double circle by couples, with partners facing. The inside circle has one more player than the outside circle. When the signal is given, the circles skip to the right. This means that they are skipping in opposite directions. At the command "Halt," the circles face each other to find partners. One player is left without a partner and must try to get one on the next turn or face elimination.

Reverse the direction of the circles.

Variations. Children can gallop, walk, run, or hop instead of skipping. The game can also be played to music. When the music stops, the players seek partners.

ANIMAL CHASE

Playing Area. Playground. Two goals are marked out 50 feet apart. Halfway between the lines and off to one side, a square represents the "zoo."
Players. Entire class.

Supplies. None.
Skills. Running, dodging.
Maturity Level. Kindergarten.
Directions. One child is the Animal Hunter and stands in the center of the area. All children are stationed on one of the two goal lines. Each player is secretly given the name of an animal, with several players having the same animal designation.

The Hunter calls out the name of an animal. If no one has this name, she continues calling different names until some players having an animal name are identified. Those players run to the opposite goal line and return. As soon as the runners start, the Hunter must return to the "zoo" (to "get her gun"), return to the center area, and try to tag a runner. Generally, the runners can get to the other goal line without difficulty. One the return trip, they must dodge the Hunter to return to the other animals.

Any animals caught are taken to the "zoo" and sit until all have run. If a number of children are playing the game, the teacher can limit the length of time the Hunter can chase before being replaced.

First Grade Games

CAGED LION

Playing Area. Classroom or gymnasium. A ten-foot square is drawn to represent the cage.
Players. Ten to twenty.
Supplies. None.
Skills. Running, dodging.
Maturity Level. First grade.
Directions. One child is selected to be the Lion and takes a position on hands and knees inside the ten-foot square ("cage"). Other players tantalize the Lion by standing in the "cage" or running through it. The Lion tries to tag any of the children. Any child who is tagged by the Lion trades places with him.
Variation. *The Queen's Land.* The forbidden area, consisting of a 20-foot square, is known as the Queen's Land. The Warden tries to catch (tag) anyone who is on the Queen's Land. If successful, he exchanges places with the tagged player, who becomes the new Warden.

FLOWERS AND WIND

Playing Area. Two parallel lines are drawn, long enough to accommodate all the children. The lines are about 30 feet apart.
Players. Ten to thirty.
Supplies. None.
Skills. Running.
Maturity Level. First grade.
Directions. The children are divided into two equal groups. One is the Wind, and the other is the Flowers. Each team takes a position on one of the lines, facing the other team. The Flowers secretly select the name of a common flower. When ready, they walk toward the other line and stand about three feet away from the Wind. The players on the Wind side begin to call out names of flowers. When the chosen flower has been guessed, the Flowers take off and run back to their goal line, chased by the players of the Wind team.

Any player caught must join the other side. The roles are reversed, and the other team chooses a flower name.

If one side has trouble guessing, then have the Flowers give the first letter of the name, the color, or the size of the flower.

Variation. An added feature, which makes the game more meaningful, is to have the game follow a study of flowers. The children can collect pictures of flowers and glue them onto stiffened paper, to be available during the game.

FOREST RANGER

Playing Area. Playground, gymnasium, or classroom.
Players. Entire class.
Supplies. None.
Skills. Running.
Maturity Level. First grade.
Directions. Half the children form a circle, facing in. These are the Trees. The rest of the children are the Forest Rangers and stand behind the Trees. An extra child, the Forest Lookout, is in the center. The Forest Lookout starts the game with the command, "Fire in the forest, run, run, run!" Immediately, the Forest Rangers run around the outside of the circle to the right (counterclockwise). After a few moments, the Lookout steps in *front* of one of the Trees. This is the signal for each of the Rangers to step in *front* of a Tree. One player is left out, and he now becomes the new Forest Lookout. The Trees become Rangers, and vice versa. Each time the game is played, the circle must be moved out somewhat, as the formation narrows when the Rangers step in front of the Trees.

Discuss with children the duties of a forest ranger and how important it is to preserve our heritage of trees from fire.

WHAT IS YOUR JOB?

Playing Area. Gymnasium or playground. Two parallel lines, 20 to 30 feet apart, are goals for the runners.
Players. Entire class.
Supplies. None.
Skills. Running.
Maturity Level. First grade.

Directions. The children are divided into two groups. Each has a leader and lines up on one of the goal lines. One group decides on a job. They then skip up to within five feet or so of the other team, saying, "Here we come!" The team on the line replies, "What is your job?" The advancing team says, "We'll show you!" They then proceed to act out the job. The team on the line attempts to guess the occupation, so that they can chase the acting team back to their goal. A point is scored for each player tagged prior to reaching his goal.

For young children, the teacher should have a number of suggestions of occupations from which a choice can be made. One approach is to give three suggestions and let the group choose one of them.

Variation. The game can be called, "What Am I Playing?" and can refer to a sport or game.

Teaching Hints. Children should raise hands and be recognized in order to guess what the job is. Otherwise, there will be many abortive runs as children shout out guesses.

HILL DILL

Playing Area. Playground. Two parallel lines are drawn about 50 feet apart.
Players. Ten to fifty.
Supplies. None.
Skills. Running, dodging.
Maturity Level. First grade.
Directions. A player is chosen to be It and stands in the center, between the lines. The other children stand along one of the lines. The center player calls, "Hill Dill! Come over the hill!" The children run across the open space to the other line, while the one in the center tries to tag them. Anyone caught helps It in the center. The last person caught remains in the center and is It for the next game.

Once the children cross over to the other line, they must await the next call.

Variation. More than one player can be It.

I CAN DO WHAT YOU CAN!

Playing Area. Playground, gymnasium, or classroom.
Players. Not more than six or seven in a group. Any number of groups can play.
Supplies. Usually none. The game can be played with each child using the same piece of equipment, such as a ball, a wand, or a beanbag.
Skills. Varied, depending on the leader's choices.
Maturity Level. First grade.
Directions. This is primarily a follow-the-leader type of game. Each group works independently of the others. Each group forms a semi-circle with the leader in front. The leader starts any type of activity he wishes, and the other children attempt to make the same moves. After a brief period, the teacher initiates a change, and another leader moves to the front of the group.

This works well with selected pieces of hand apparatus, provided each child in the group has the same type of equipment. Tossing, throwing, catching, bouncing, hoop stunts, and beanbag tricks are some activities that are easily adapted to the game. Caution children not to demand outlandish or silly performances of the others in the group.

FOUR OUT

Playing Area. Gymnasium or playground.
Players. Entire class.
Supplies. None.
Skills. Running, stopping, balances.
Maturity Level. First grade.
Directions. This is a challenge game in which there is movement and stopping ("freezing"). The signal for stopping is "Glue"—which fastens the feet to the floor. Other commands given are:

"Mud"—walk through mud
"Flypaper"—walk on something sticky
"Snow"—walk in deep snow
"Puddles"—tiptoe through the puddles
"Hot pavement"—move very rapidly on the toes
"Molasses"—you can barely lift your foot

The teacher calls the cues out in different order, coming up with "glue" occasionally. Any child who makes a mistake gets one dud. When a child makes four duds, he must sit out one turn.

Variations. This format could be used with any type of challenge activities, particularly manipulative acts, to increase the difficulty of the game. Children who drop a beanbag or ball would have that counted against them.

IN THE CREEK

Playing Area. Playground, gymnasium, or classroom.
Players. Entire class.
Supplies. None.
Skills. Jumping, leaping, hopping.
Maturity Level. First grade.
Directions. A "creek" is formed by drawing two parallel lines one to two feet apart, depending upon the ability of the children. The lines should be long enough to accommodate the children comfortably with enough room for

each to jump. If necessary, two or three sets of lines can be drawn.

The children line up on one of the "banks," all facing the "creek." The object of the game is to make the children commit an error in jumping.

The teacher or leader gives one of two directions: "In the creek" or "On the bank."

Children on the "bank" jump into the "creek" or over to the other "bank," depending upon the command. When they jump onto the "bank," they immediately turn around and get ready for the next command.

If children are in the "creek" and the command "In the creek" is repeated, they must not move.

An error is committed when a child steps on a line, makes a wrong jump, or moves when he should remain still.

Children who make a mistake are kept out for one turn.

After a period of time, the original directions may not challenge the children. Different combinations can be set up. "In the creek" might mean to jump and land with both feet. "On the bank" on one side would require a leap. "On the bank" on the other side would require a hop. False commands can also be given, such as, "In the ocean" or "In the lake." No one is to move on these commands under penalty of elimination.

It is a good plan to keep things moving fast with crisp commands. Children should be responsible for judging their own errors.

LEAP THE BROOK

Playing Area. Gymnasium or playground.
Players. Entire class.
Supplies. None.
Skills. Leaping, jumping, hopping, turning.
Maturity Level. First grade.
Directions. A "brook" is marked off on the floor for a distance of about 30 feet. For the first ten feet, it is two feet wide, for the second ten feet, three feet wide, and for the last ten feet the width becomes four feet.

The children form single files and jump over the narrowest part of the "brook." They should be encouraged to do this several times, using different styles of jumping and leaping.

Stress landing as lightly as possible on the balls of the feet in a bent-knee position.

After they have satisfactorily negotiated the narrow part, the children move up to the next width, and so on.

Teachers should remember that fitness values are derived only from repeated effort. Good form should be stressed throughout the game.

The selection of the distances is arbitrary, and they may be changed if they seem unsuitable for any particular group of children.

Variation. Use different means of crossing the "brook"—leaping, jumping, hopping. Also, specify the kinds of turns to be made—right or left; quarter-, half-, three-quarter- or full turns. Have the children use different body shapes, arm positions, etc.

MAY I CHASE YOU?

Playing Area. Playground.
Players. Ten to thirty.
Supplies. None.
Skills. Running, dodging.
Maturity Level. First grade.
Directions. The class stands behind a line long enough to accommodate all. The runner stands about five feet in front of the line. One child in the line asks, "May I chase you?" The runner replies, "Yes, if you are wearing _____." He can name a color, an article of clothing, or a combination of the two. All who qualify immediately chase the runner until one tags him. This person becomes It.

The children will think of other ways to identify those who may run. Boundaries may be necessary.

Variation. This game is sometimes called The Man From Mars. The line players say in unison, "Man from Mars, may we chase you to the stars?" The game then proceeds as described.

MOUSETRAP

Playing Area. Playground, gymnasium, or classroom.
Players. 20 to 40.
Supplies. None.
Skills. Skipping, running, dodging.
Maturity Level. First grade.
Directions. Half the children form a circle with hands joined, facing the center. The other children are on the outside of the circle. Three signals are given for the game. These can be given by word cues or by whistle.

The circle players form the "mousetraps," and the outer players are the Mice.

Signal 1. The Mice skip around the circle, playing happily.

Signal 2. The circle players raise their joined hands to form arches. These are the "mousetraps." The Mice run in and out of the "traps."

Signal 3. The "traps snap shut" (the arms come down). All Mice caught join the circle.

The game is repeated until all or most of the Mice are caught. The players exchange places, and the game begins anew.

Do not allow the children to run in and out of adjacent openings in the "traps."

Variation. The parachute can be used to provide a fine version of this game.

Signal 1. The parachute is on the ground. The Mice run around the 'chute holders.

Signal 2. The parachute is raised to chest height. Mice go in and out of the "trap," but not through adjacent openings.

Signal 3. The parachute comes down and traps the Mice inside.

THREE PERSON TAG

Playing Area. Playground or gymnasium.
Players. Entire class in groups of three students.
Supplies. None.
Skills. Running, dodging.
Maturity Level. First grade.
Directions. The three players in each group stand side by side in a line, holding outstretched hands. They drop hands so that they are about fingertip distance away, but remain in a line. On signal, the two outside players move forward and try to tag each other before the third person (the player in the middle) can tag either of them. Points can be awarded for tagging (to the inside player) and for avoiding the tag (to the players on the outside). A time limit of ten to fifteen seconds can be set before starting the process over.
Variations. The middle player can begin by sitting between two standing players. Players do not hold hands.

Various locomotor movements can be used for moving.

RED LIGHT

Playing Area. An area 60 to 100 feet across with a goal toward which the players move.
Players. Entire class.
Supplies. None.
Skills. Fundamental locomotor movements, stopping.
Maturity Level. First grade.
Directions. The object of the game is to move across the area successfully without getting caught. One player is the leader and stands on the goal line. She counts very rapidly from one to ten with her back to the players. She quickly adds the words "Red Light" and then turns around. In the meantime, the players have been moving across the area during the counting and must "freeze" on the words "Red Light." Any player caught moving after "Red Light" must return to the starting position. The first player across the area wins and is the leader for the next game.

After the leader has sent back all who were caught, she turns her back again to begin the count. Although the players may move when her back is turned, she may turn around quickly and catch any movement. Once the leader starts counting, however, she cannot turn around until she calls out "Red Light."

Variations. Instead of counting, the leader (with back turned) can clap hands five times, turning around to catch movement on the fifth clap.

In an excellent variation of the game, the leader faces the oncoming players. He calls out "Green Light" for them to move and "Red Light" for them to stop. If the leader calls any other color, the players should not move.

Different types of locomotion can be worked in. The leader names the type of movement (hop, crawl, etc.) before turning his back to the group.

STOP AND START

Playing Area. Playground.
Players. Any number.
Supplies. None.
Skills. Fundamental locomotor movements, stopping.
Maturity Level. First grade.
Directions. The children are in the center of the playground, scattered, far enough apart so that each has room to maneuver. The teacher or leader stands a little to one side and gives directions. He points in a direction and calls, "Gallop." Any other locomotor movement can be used. Suddenly, he calls, "Stop." All children must stop immediately and make no further movement. Anyone moving can be sent over to the side to another group.

Second Grade Games

BRONCO TAG

Playing Area. Playground or gymnasium.
Players. 15 to 30.
Supplies. None.
Skills. Running, dodging.
Maturity Level. Second grade.
Directions. One child is a runner, and another is the chaser. The remainder of the children are divided into groups of three. Each group of three forms a Bronco by standing one behind the other with the last two grasping the waist of the player in front. The front player is the "head," and the player on the end is the "tail." The runner tries to hook on to the "tail" of any Bronco. The "head" of that Bronco now becomes the runner.

The chaser pursues the runner, who tries to avoid being caught by hooking on to a Bronco.

The chaser now has to pursue the new runner. If tagged, the roles are reversed, and the runner becomes the chaser.

The game is more interesting if the children change places rapidly.

BUSY BEE

Playing Area. Playground, gymnasium, or classroom.
Players. Entire class.
Supplies. None.
Skills. Fundamental locomotor movements.
Maturity Level. Second grade.
Directions. Half the children form a large circle, facing in, and are designated as the stationary players. The other children seek partners from this group, and each stands in front of one of the stationary players. An extra child is in the center and is the Busy Bee.

The Busy Bee calls out directions, which are followed by the children. These can be called in any order; children will devise their own directions. These might include: "Back to back." "Face to face." "Shake hands." "Kneel on one knee." "Kneel on both knees." "Hop on one foot."

The center child then calls out, "Busy Bee." Stationary players stand still, and all inner-circle players seek another partner, while the center player also tries to get a partner. The child left without a partner becomes the Busy Bee.

Each child should be thinking of the different movements he might have the class do if he should become the Busy Bee. When changing partners, a child should not be allowed to select the stationary player next to him as his partner.

After a period of time, rotate the active and stationary players. Also, vary the game by using different methods of locomotion.

Variations. Select a definite number of changes—ten, for example. All children who have not had the same partner during the ten exchanges and who have not been "caught" and become the Busy Bee are declared the winners.

Instead of having the children stand back to back, have them lock elbows and sit down, as in the Chinese Get-up (p. 205). After they sit down and are declared "safe," they can get up, and the game proceeds as described above.

COUPLE TAG

Playing Area. Playground or gymnasium. Two goal lines are established about 50 feet apart.
Players. Any number.
Supplies. None.
Skills. Running, dodging.

Maturity Level. Second grade.
Directions. Children run by pairs with inside hands joined. All pairs, except one, line up on one of the goal lines. One pair is in the center and is It.

The pair in the center calls, "Come," and the children run to the other goal line, keeping hands joined. The pair in the center tries to tag any pair, using *only* their joined hands.

As soon as a couple is caught, it helps the center couple. The game continues until all are caught. The last couple caught is It for the next game.

Variation. If the tagging seems difficult, have the tagging pair use their free hands to tag.

HOOKED ELBOWS TAG

Playing Area. Gymnasium or playground.
Players. Entire class, in groups of two students.
Supplies. None.
Skills. Running, dodging.
Maturity Level. Second grade.
Directions. Players are paired and stand back to back with elbows hooked. One or more players are declared to be It. When the signal "Change!" is called, all players unlock elbows and perform some predetermined locomotor movement. The players who are It try to tag one of the loose players. A player is "safe" when he finds a partner and hooks elbows.

The teacher should not let any student be It for too long, as this position is tiring.

CROWS AND CRANES

Playing Area. Playground or gymnasium. Two goal lines are drawn about 50 feet apart.
Players. Any number.
Supplies. None.
Skills. Running, dodging.
Maturity Level. Second grade.
Directions. Children are divided into two groups, the Crows and the Cranes. The groups face each other at the center of the area, about five feet apart. The leader calls out either "Crows!" or "Cranes!", using a "kr-r-r-r" sound at the start of either word to heighten the suspense.

If "Crows!" is the call, the Crows chase the Cranes to the goal. If "Cranes!" is called, then the Cranes chase. Any child caught goes over to the other side. The team that has the most players when the game ends is the winner.

Variations. Have children stand back to back in the center about a foot apart.

The game can be played with the two sides designated Blue and White. Instead of having someone give calls, a piece of plywood painted blue on one side and white on the other can be thrown into the air between the teams. If blue comes up, the Blue team chases, and vice versa.

Another variation of the game is to have a leader tell a story, using as many words beginning with "cr-" as possible. The players run only when they hear the words "crows" or "cranes." Words that can be incorporated into a story are "crazy," "crunch," "crust," "crown," "crude," "crowd," "crouch," "cross," "croak," "critter," etc. Each time one of these words is spoken, the beginning of the word is lengthened with the "kr-r-r-r" sound. No one may move on any of the words except "crows" or "cranes."

EAGLES AND SPARROWS

Playing Area. Playground. Two parallel lines are drawn about 50 feet apart. A circle is drawn in the center, representing the Eagle's "nest."
Players. Entire class.
Supplies. None.
Skills. Running, hopping, dodging.
Maturity Level. Second grade.
Directions. One player is the Eagle. He is down on one knee in the "nest." The other players circle around, flying like sparrows, until the Eagle suddenly gets up and chases the Sparrows to either line. Any Sparrow caught joins the Eagle and helps catch others. However, no center player can chase until the Eagle starts.

If the group is large, begin with two or three Eagles in the center.
Variation. All Sparrows must take three hops or jumps before they can start running.

FLY TRAP

Playing Area. Playground or gymnasium.
Players. Entire class.
Supplies. None.
Skills. Fundamental locomotor movements.
Maturity Level. Second grade.
Directions. Half the class is scattered around the playing area, sitting on the floor in tailor fashion (cross-legged). These children form the "trap." The other children are the Flies, and they buzz around the seated children. When a whistle is blown, the Flies must "freeze" at the spot. If any of the Trappers can reach the Flies, that Fly is seated at his location and becomes a Trapper.

The game continues until all or most of the Flies have been caught. Some realism is given to the game if the Flies make buzzing sounds and move with their arms out like wings.

A little experience with the game will enable the teacher to determine how far apart to place the seated children. In tagging, the children must keep their seats on the ground.

After all the Flies have been caught, the children trade places.

Change the method of locomotion occasionally.

FROG IN THE SEA

Playing Area. Any small area indoors or outdoors.
Players. Six to eight in each game.
Supplies. None.
Skills. Fundamental locomotor movements.
Maturity Level. Second grade.
Directions. One player is the Frog and sits down tailor fashion (cross-legged). The others mill about, trying to touch him, but, at the same time, keeping out of reach. They can call, "Frog in the sea, can't catch me!" The Frog must stay in the sitting position and try to tag those tantalizing him. Anyone tagged exchanges places with the Frog.

Care should be taken that the children do not punish the Frog unnecessarily.
Variations. The Frog may not tag anyone until the teacher says, "Jump, Frog."

The game proceeds as originally described. When the teacher says, "Jump, Frog," the Frog can move in any direction with a jump. He is permitted to tag both during the original part of the game and at the jump.

MONSTERS

Playing Area. Gymnasium or playground, 35 feet by 70 feet.
Players. 20 to 40.
Supplies. None.
Skills. Running and dodging.
Maturity Level. Second grade.
Directions. All players are lined up at one end of the playing area. One or more players are designated as taggers. When the taggers declare, "Monsters," the rest of the players attempt to move from one end of the playing area to the other without being tagged. If one of the players is tagged, he now becomes a Monster and must "freeze" where he was tagged. The Monsters can also tag, but cannot chase, because their feet are "frozen" to the floor. Thus, the players must not only avoid the taggers, but must dodge and move around the Monsters. When all players have been tagged, new taggers are selected.

In some cases, when there are only a few players left in the game, they will hesitate to move to the opposite end. This may be a good time to start a new game. Decide whether the Monsters are required to keep both feet "frozen" to the floor, or whether they are allowed to move one foot and pivot on the other.

TRIPLE CHANGE

Playing Area. Playground or gymnasium.
Players. 15 to 30.
Supplies. None.
Skills. Running.
Maturity Level. Second grade.
Directions. Players form a large circle, facing in. Three children stand in the center. Those forming the circle and those in the center are numbered off by threes. The players in the center take turns, each calling out his or her number. When a number is called, all those with that number change places. The one in the center *with this number* tries to find a place. The child without a place goes to the center and waits until the other center players have had their turns.

Variation. The teacher could call out the numbers, not necessarily in order, to add an element of suspense to the game.

ACTIVE GAMES THAT REQUIRE EQUIPMENT OR SUPPLIES

Preschool games
Shapes
War Dance
Tommy Tucker's Land
Bowling Pin Knockdown
Who Am I?

Kindergarten games
Krug Hoop Search
Colson Goal Ball
Fleece Ball Follow
Lucky Seven
Automobiles

First grade games
Charlie over the Water (Ball Version)
Hot Potatoes
The Hunter
Kick Target Ball
Straddle Bowling

Second grade games
Follow Me
Jump the Shot
Buccaneer Ball
Balance Dodgeball
One-Step
Scooter Cageball Tag
Galloping Lizzie

Preschool Games

SHAPES

Playing Area. Indoors or outdoors.
Players. Entire class.
Supplies. Two sets of cardboard shapes are needed, one of each shape in the large size (say, 18 to 24 inches) and enough of the smaller size (about 12 inches) to supply at least one for each child. The shapes can be triangles, squares, rectangles, ovals, full circles, half-circles, diamonds, pentagons, and hexagons. The shapes can be made as a class project.
Skills. Fundamental locomotor movements, visual discrimination.
Maturity Level. Preschool.
Directions. The large shapes are placed around the outer borders of the playing area and are used only to provide a shape for identification. The smaller shapes are scattered around the playing area. There can be extra small shapes.

On signal, the children hop, jump, run, or leap over as many shapes as they can. On a second signal, each child selects a shape nearby and stands on it. After each child is standing on a shape, a third signal is given. Each child then picks up the shape and places it in front of the larger matching shape. The matching is then checked for accuracy.

A second approach is to have children signal according to the shape on which they are standing. The teacher can say, for example, "Triangles, raise your hands," or, "All standing on circles, hold up your hands."

WAR DANCE

Playing Area. Gymnasium.
Players. Entire class. Each child plays individually, but children could be in pairs or threes.
Supplies. Each child has a marker (a beanbag or Indian club) to be his or her "fire."
Skills. Body awareness, knowledge of body parts.
Maturity Level. Preschool.
Directions. Each child, in his personal space, puts down a "fire" marker. He dances around the "fire" with an Indian war dance. When the teacher calls out the name of a body part, the child pokes that part into the "fire." Since the "fire" is hot, the child pulls the part out quickly.

Two, three, or four children can be dancing around the "fire." Call out the names of body parts loudly enough for the children to hear.

Variation. The game can be played as Ice Water. Each child has a "tub of ice water" to dance around, and he pokes the named body part into the "water."

TOMMY TUCKER'S LAND

Playing Area. Playground, gymnasium, or classroom.

Players. Eight to ten.

Supplies. About ten beanbags for each game.

Skills. Dodging, running.

Maturity Level. Preschool.

Directions. One child is Tommy Tucker and stands in the center of a 15-foot square, within which the beanbags (the "treasure") are scattered. Tommy is guarding his "land" and the "treasure." The other children chant:

I'm on Tommy Tucker's land,
Picking up gold and silver.

The children attempt to pick up as much of the "treasure" as they can while avoiding being tagged by Tommy. Any child who is tagged must bring back the "treasure" and retire from the game. The game is over when there is only one child left or all the beanbags have been successfully filched. The teacher may wish to call a halt to the game earlier, if it has reached a stalemate. In this case, the child with the most "treasure" becomes the new Tommy.

BOWLING PIN KNOCKDOWN

Playing Area. Playground or gymnasium, an area approximately 30 feet by 70 feet, hard-surfaced, with two end lines and a center line.

Players. 20 to 40, divided into two teams.

Supplies. 20 to 30 Indian clubs or bowling pins. Eight to twelve playground balls (8½-inch diameter).

Skills. Bowling.

Maturity Level. Preschool.

Directions. Half the clubs or pins are set up three feet forward of each team's end line. The playground balls are distributed among the children on both teams. On signal, each player who has a ball runs to the center line and attempts to knock over one of the opposing team's pins by bowling (rolling) his ball. After a player has bowled a ball, he must retreat to the end line. No player may guard a club or protect it in any way; players must stay on their own end line to catch a ball. After a ball passes the pins, another player may pick it up and move to the center line to bowl again.

Any club knocked down during the course of the game (either on purpose or accidentally) stays down until a new game is started. The first team to knock over all the pins of the opposing team is declared the winner.

It is against the rules to pick up a ball before it passes the pins or to guard a club. Children who commit an infraction might be asked to stay out of the game for a minute or asked not to throw any balls for a specified time.

WHO AM I?

Playing Area. Indoors or outdoors. There must be sufficient room to move around.

Players. Entire class.

Supplies. Place markers, which can be hoops, individual mats, beanbags, or large pieces of cardboard.

Skills. Fundamental locomotor movements.

Maturity Level. Preschool.

Directions. This game stresses important knowledge that children should have at their fingertips. Markers, which serve as home bases, are scattered around the area—one marker less than the number of players. Children are challenged to use different locomotor movements to move around the room. At the signal (hand clap or drumbeat), each attempts to find a home base. The child left out (without a base) must give her full name. Later, home addresses and telephone numbers can be added. If the class is large, then two "empty" spots should be used. If a child is caught a second time, an exchange is made with a child who has not been caught and has not stated his name.

The teacher should have a list of the children's names, addresses, and telephone numbers, to check the accuracy of the answers.

Kindergarten Games

KRUG HOOP SEARCH

Playing Area. Playground or gymnasium.

Players. Entire class, divided into groups of three.

Supplies. Hula hoops of various colors, one for each group.

Skills. Various locomotor movements, perceptual-motor competency.

Maturity Level. Kindergarten.

Directions. Each group of children is assigned to a hula hoop. The color of the hoop in which they are standing determines the color assigned to each member of the group. The hoops should be spread out over a wide area in order to increase the amount of running each child is required to do.

To play the game, two or three "extra" children are selected who are not in any group. They will try to get into a hoop when the other children are asked to move. This, in turn, will leave some new children out. When a certain color is called, all children standing in a hoop of that color must move to another hoop quickly, in an attempt to avoid being left out.

Variations. The game is quite flexible and can be changed to meet the needs of the students.

More than one color can be called simultaneously, various locomotor movements can be stipulated for changing hoops, or various body parts can be placed in a hoop. As an example, the teacher might say, "Green and red, skip, and place your left hand and right foot in the hoop." Students can also be selected to give the directions to the rest of the class.

Teaching Hint. If a variety of colored hoops is not available, use crepe paper or other material to mark the hoops.

COLSON GOAL BALL

Playing Area. Playground or gymnasium. The area should be 30 feet by 60 feet and can be marked off with cones. The area may have to be longer for older and more skilled children.

Players. 20 to 30, divided into two teams of equal ability.

Supplies. Six to ten playground balls (8½-inch diameter).

Skills. Throwing, catching.

Maturity Level. Kindergarten.

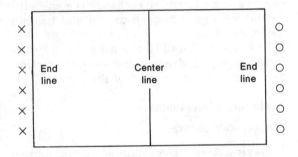

Directions. The playing area should be divided by a center line, which players cannot cross during the course of the game. Each team stands on its own end line and is given half the playground balls. At the starting signal, players scatter in their half of the playing area. Those who have a ball run to the center line and attempt to throw it across the opposing team's end line.

A point is scored each time a ball crosses the end line, whether on the ground or in the air. The first team to score ten points is declared the winner. The teacher can keep score by watching both ends of the field or can appoint two students to do the scoring. Players try to block and stop all throws and then toss them across their opponents' end line. In no case may a ball be kicked.

FLEECE BALL FOLLOW

Playing Area. Gymnasium or playground. The running area must be quite large, to prevent students from colliding with one another.

Players. Entire class, in groups of two students.

Supplies. One fleece ball or beanbag for each group of children.

Skills. Throwing, catching, running, and dodging.

Maturity Level. Kindergarten.

Directions. Partners play catch with the fleece ball or beanbag. On signal, the child with the ball runs, and his partner tries to catch him. A point can be scored if the ball-carrier avoided the tag. To eliminate arguments, make the rule that if the player has the ball in his hand at the signal, or if it is on its way toward him, he runs. It usually works best to set a time limit of five to fifteen seconds of running before starting a new game of catch.

LUCKY SEVEN

Playing Area. Gymnasium or playground.
Players. Two.
Supplies. Beanbag or ball.
Skills. Manipulative skills.
Maturity Level. Kindergarten.

Directions. The number seven is regarded as a lucky number and provides the theme of the game. One child is the performer, and the other is the observer. A challenge is set up, such as, "Catch the beanbag with one hand in seven different ways." The performer then attempts to find seven successful ways to catch. If he drops the beanbag or ball, or repeats any of the catches, the turn is forfeited. If he is successful, he is awarded another turn. After this turn, successful or not, he surrenders the object to his partner, and the roles are reversed. A score of one point can be awarded for each successful lucky seven.

AUTOMOBILES

Playing Area. Playground or gymnasium.
Players. Entire class.
Supplies. Each child has a "steering wheel."
Skills. Color concepts, running, stopping.
Maturity Level. Kindergarten.

Directions. The children pretend they are Automobiles, driving around the area. Each child will need a "steering wheel," which can be a small hoop, a deck tennis ring, or a shape that the child has made out of cardboard. The teacher has three flash cards, colored red, green, and yellow, respectively. These are the "traffic control" signals.

The children drive around the area, steering various paths, responding as the teacher holds up the cards one at a time. The children follow the traffic directions: Red—Stop, Green—Go, and Yellow—Caution.

An "ambulance station" and a "fire station" can be established and equipped with appropriate Automobiles. When one of these comes forward, making its characteristic siren noise, all other Automobiles pull over to the side of the "road" and wait until the Ambulance or Fire Engine has gone by.

Variation. This game can be played without equipment. Children are in pairs, facing each other, hands on each other's shoulders. One is the Driver and steers the Automobile around in different directions.

Teaching Hint. Have children use the proper hand signals for making turns, slowing down, and stopping.

First Grade Games

CHARLIE OVER THE WATER (BALL VERSION)

Playing Area. Playground or gymnasium.
Players. Eight to twelve.
Supplies. One volleyball or a playground ball.[2]
Skills. Skipping, running, stopping, bowling.
Maturity Level. First grade.
Directions. The children are in circle formation with hands joined. One child, Charlie, is in the center of the circle holding a ball in his hands. The children skip around the circle to the following chant:

> Charlie over the water,
> Charlie over the sea,
> Charlie caught a bluebird,
> But he can't catch me!

On the word "me," the children drop hands and scatter. On the same signal, Charlie tosses the ball into the air. He then catches it and shouts, "Stop!" All children stop immediately and must not move their feet. Charlie rolls the ball in an attempt to hit one of the children. If the child is hit, that child becomes Charlie; if Charlie misses, he must remain as Charlie, and the game is repeated. If he misses twice, however, he should pick another child to be Charlie.

If a girl is in the center, the chant should go:

> Sally over the water,
> Sally over the sea (etc.)

HOT POTATOES

Playing Area. Gymnasium, playground, or classroom.
Players. Eight to twelve in each group.
Supplies. Six balls and six beanbags.

Skills. Object-handling skills.
Maturity Level. First grade.
Directions. Children are seated in a small circle, close enough together so that objects can be handed from one to another around the circle. A few balls and/or beanbags are introduced and are passed around the circle, then a few more are introduced. The object of the game is to pass the balls or beanbags rapidly so that no one gets "stuck" with more than one object at a time. If someone does get "stuck," the game is stopped, and the player moves back out of the circle and waits. After three children are out of the circle, the game starts over.

Start the game with two or three objects and gradually add objects until someone is holding more than one at a time.

Variation. On signal, the players reverse the direction of passing.

THE HUNTER

Playing Area. Playground, gymnasium, or classroom.
Players. Entire class.
Supplies. Individual markers are needed to serve as home base for each child. If playing in the classroom, the children can use their seats for "home."
Skills. Imitation, running.
Maturity Level. First grade.
Directions. A leader, the Hunter, walks around the room in any manner he wishes. He begins the game with the question, "Who wants to hunt ducks [bears, lions, rabbits]?" The players volunteering fall in line behind him and start on the hunt. The Hunter can pantomime various hunting movements—creeping through "underbrush," taking aim, etc. When ready, he shouts, "Bang!" All run "home," including the Hunter. The first one back "home" is chosen as Hunter for the next game.

To make the game interesting, the Hunter should take quite a few children on the hunt. Be sure that all get a chance to hunt.

Variation. A novel method of making leader changes is to have one place (seat or marker) designated as the leader for the next time. This is chosen only after the Hunter takes the occupant out. The teacher can make this selection, the location of which is unknown to the runners.

KICK TARGET BALL

Playing Area. Gymnasium or playground.
Players. 12 to 15 (usually half the class).

---

[2]This game can also be played without a ball, as a kindergarten activity (see p. 262).

Supplies. Four to six empty quart or half-gallon milk cartons. Three playground balls.

Skills. Kicking, trapping.

Maturity Level. First grade.

Directions. Have children bring in empty milk cartons. The cartons are set up in the center of a circle of players. Start with two playground balls and add one more if the game seems slow. The object is to kick the ball across the circle to knock over one of the milk cartons. Players should handle the ball only with the feet. Each child has an immediate area of his own in the circle, and balls coming to that area belong to him, if they can be stopped with the foot.

If a ball is in the center area, a player can go forward and kick it to another player. The game can be aimed at knocking all the cartons over or at achieving a definite game score. In the latter case, anyone whose kicked ball knocks down a carton goes forward and sets it up again.

Teaching Hint. This is a good opportunity for children to learn to share. Watch for the player who attempts to "hog" the action.

STRADDLE BOWLING

Playing Area. Playground or gymnasium.

Players. Four to six.

Supplies. Volleyball or rubber playground ball.

Skills. Bowling for accuracy.

Maturity Level. First grade.

Directions. Children may compete within a group, or teams can compete against each other. One child is the bowling target and stands in straddle position with his feet wide enough apart so that the ball can pass through easily. Another child is the ball chaser and stands behind him.

A foul line is drawn 15 to 25 feet from the target, depending upon the ability of the children. The bowlers line up behind this line for turns.

Children can be given one chance or a number of tries. To score a point, the ball must go between the legs of the target. When the children on the throwing line have bowled, two of them relieve the target and the chaser.

Variations. Scoring can be changed to allow two points if the ball goes through the legs and one point if it hits a leg.

Other targets can be used. A box lying on its side with the open side facing the bowler forms a good target. Two or three Indian clubs at each station make excellent targets. Scoring could be varied to suit the target.

Bowling One-Step. For groups of squad size or smaller, each of the players in turn gets a chance to roll at an Indian club or bowling pin. A minimum distance is established, short enough so that most bowlers can hit the pin (ten to fifteen feet). The player keeps rolling until he misses. The player takes a step backward each time he knocks down a pin. The winner is the one who has moved the farthest back.

Children should be cautioned that accuracy, not speed, is the goal. The players should also experiment with different spin effects to cause the ball to curve.

Second Grade Games

FOLLOW ME

Playing Area. Playground or gymnasium.

Players. Eight to thirty.

Supplies. A marker for each child. Squares of cardboard or plywood can be used.

Skills. All locomotor movements, stopping.

Maturity Level. Second grade.

Directions. Children are arranged roughly in a circle, each standing or sitting with one foot on a marker. An extra player is the Guide and moves about the circle, pointing at different players and telling them, "Follow me." Each player chosen falls in behind the Guide. The Guide now takes the group on a "tour," with the members of the group imitating the movements made by the Guide. The Guide may hop, skip, do stunts, or perform other movements, and the children following must do likewise. At the signal "Home," all run for places at the markers. One child will be without a marker. This child chooses another Guide.

It is not a good idea to make the last child the new leader, as this will cause some children to lag behind and try to be last. In our version, that child gets to choose a new leader.

Variation. Another way to overcome the children's tendency to lag would be to make the first one back the new leader or to have a special leader marker. The first one to this marker becomes the new leader.

A penalty can be imposed on the one who does not find a marker.

JUMP THE SHOT

Playing Area. Playground or gymnasium.

Players. Ten to twenty.

Supplies. A jump-the-shot rope. (A soft object, such as an old, deflated ball, is tied to the free end of the rope to give it some weight.)

Skills. Jumping over a rope.

Maturity Level. Second grade.

Directions. The players stand in circle formation. One player stands in the center, holding a jump-the-shot rope.

The center player turns the rope under the feet of the circle players, who must jump over it. Anyone who touches the rope is eliminated and must stand back from the circle. Re-form the circle after three or four children are eliminated.

The center player should be cautioned to keep the rope close to the ground. The speed can be varied. A good way to turn the rope is to sit cross-legged and turn the rope over the head.

BUCCANEER BALL

Playing Area. Gymnasium or playground.
Players. 20 to 40.
Supplies. 20 to 25 playground balls (8½-inch diameter).
Skills. Controlled dribbling and bouncing.
Maturity Level. Second grade.
Directions. Two-thirds of the children are given a ball to bounce. The remaining children are the Buccaneers, who try to take the balls away from the other players. Once a Buccaneer gets a ball, he bounces it and tries to keep it away from the other Buccaneers. Players must get the ball away from one another *without* body contact. If body contact does occur, it is a foul, and the player who committed the foul must move to a different player and attempt to take away that player's ball.

Variations. Children may bounce the ball with both hands, then move to dribbling only with the dominant hand and finally to dribbling with the nondominant hand. For even more challenge, children can be asked to perform various locomotor movements while bouncing the ball.

BALANCE DODGEBALL

Playing Area. Playground or gymnasium.
Players. Entire class.
Supplies. A playground ball or fleece ball for each child who is It.
Skills. Throwing, dodging.
Maturity Level. Second grade.
Directions. Children are scattered over the area. One child has a ball and is It; or several players can be It. The players who are It try to hit other players, who dodge. Children are "safe" when they are balanced on one foot: that is, one foot must be off the ground, and the other foot, which supports the weight, must not be moved on penalty of being hit. Hits should be made below the shoulders. Anyone legally hit becomes It.

Teaching Hint. To discourage the player who is It from standing next to a player, waiting for him to lose balance or touch a foot to the ground, have the balancing child count rapidly to ten. The player who is It must then leave and seek another child.

ONE-STEP

Playing Area. Playground.
Players. Two. Any number of pairs can compete against one another, depending upon the space available.
Supplies. Ball or beanbag.
Skills. Throwing, catching.
Maturity Level. Second grade.
Directions. This game is excellent for practicing throwing and catching skills. Two children stand facing each other about three feet apart. One has a ball or beanbag. The object of the game is to throw or toss the ball in the stipulated manner so that the partner can catch it *without moving the feet* from their position on the floor. When the throw is completed successfully, the thrower takes one step backward. She awaits the throw from her partner. Limits can be established, back to which the partners step; or the two children who can move the greatest distance apart, as compared to other couples, are the winners. Variables to provide interest and challenge are (1) the type of throw, (2) the type of catching, and (3) the kind of step. Throwing can be underhand, overhand, two-handed, under one leg, around the back, etc. Catching can be two-handed, left-handed, right-handed, to the side, etc. The step can be a giant step, a tiny step, a hop, a jump, etc.

When either child misses, moves his feet, or fails to follow directions, the partners move forward and start over. Two lines of children facing each other make a satisfactory formation for having a number of pairs compete at the same time.

SCOOTER CAGEBALL TAG

Playing Area. Indoors.
Players. Half the class.
Supplies. A gym scooter for each child, a cageball.
Skills. Rolling the ball, handling the scooter.
Maturity Level. Second grade.
Directions. Each child is on a scooter. One of the children is It and also rolls a cageball. It must roll the cageball as he moves on his scooter in an attempt to roll the ball and hit (tag) any other player with the ball, who will then become It. If It misses, he must recover the ball and make another attempt.

Two games can go on simultaneously in separate halves of the indoor space.

GALLOPING LIZZIE

Playing Area. Playground.
Players. Ten to fifteen.
Supplies. Beanbag or yarn ball.
Skills. Throwing, dodging, running.

Maturity Level. Second grade.

Directions. This is a version of the game of Tag. One player is It and has a beanbag. The other players are scattered on the playground. The player with the beanbag runs after the others and attempts to hit one with the beanbag (below the shoulders). This person then becomes It, and the game continues. Be sure that It throws the bag and does not merely touch another person with it.

Variation. The game can be played by children in pairs. In such a case, both the children become It, but only one of the players handles the beanbag. A specific kind of toss can be specified—overhand, underhand, left-handed.

MODERATELY ACTIVE GAMES THAT REQUIRE NO EQUIPMENT OR SUPPLIES

Preschool games
Blind Man's Bluff
Fire Chief
Guess the Leader
I'm Very, Very Tall
Mother, May I?
The Scarecrow and the Crows

Kindergarten games
Cat and Rat
Gallop Tag

First grade games
Cat and Mice
Hound and Rabbit

Second grade games
Two Deep
Cross Over
Flying Dutchman
Weather Vane

Preschool Games

BLIND MAN'S BLUFF

Playing Area. Playground, gymnasium, or classroom.
Players. Eight to ten.
Supplies. One blindfold for each game.
Skills. Perceptual concepts.
Maturity Level. Preschool.
Directions. Blind Man's Bluff is one of the old, traditional games. One child is blindfolded and stands in the center of a small circle formed by the other children. Another child is chosen to be inside the circle, and the Blind Man tries to catch him. As his quarry dodges, the Blind Man calls out, "Where are you?" The other must respond immediately by making a sound of a baby chick: "Cheep, cheep!"

When the Blind Man has caught the other player, he tries to identify the player by feeling the face, arms, and clothes. Identification does not affect the outcome of the game, but simply adds to the fun. Two other children are chosen to replace the first two players.

Circles should be kept small, so that catching is not too difficult. Make sure the blindfold is adequate, since the game will be spoiled if the children can see under it.

Variation. The circle children can make a buzzing sound ("Z-z-z-z"), which becomes louder as the Blind Man nears his quarry.

FIRE CHIEF

Playing Area. Playground, gymnasium, or classroom.
Players. Entire class.
Supplies. None.
Skills. Running.
Maturity Level. Preschool.
Directions. A Fire Chief is appointed. He runs around the outside of a circle of children and taps a number of them on the back, saying, "Fireman" each time. After making his round of the circle, the Chief goes to the center. When he says, "Fire!" the Firemen run counterclockwise around the circle and back to place. The one who returns first and is able to stand in place motionless is declared the winner and the new Chief.

The Chief can use other words in an attempt to fool the Firemen, but they should run only on the word, "Fire." This merely increases the fun, since there is no penalty for a false start. To add to the gaiety, the circle children can make siren sounds as the Firemen run.

GUESS THE LEADER

Playing Area. Indoors or outdoors.
Players. Entire class.
Supplies. None.
Skills. Imagery, imitation.
Maturity Level. Preschool.
Directions. One or two children are designated as guessers. They turn their backs and hide their eyes. The remaining children are scattered around the area. The teacher points to one child, who becomes the leader. The object of the game is for the guessers to guess who the leader is.

While the guessers have their backs turned and their eyes hidden, the leader strikes a pose (makes a statue), which the children imitate. The guessers turn back and try to guess who the leader is. The leader changes the pose, which is again held by all the children, and the guessers try to tell who the leader is. The children should attempt not to give away the identity of the leader.

The guessers can consult with each other and point to one of the children who they think is the leader. If this is a correct guess, other children are selected to replace the guessers and the leader. If not, two more guesses are allowed, at which time the game is stopped, and new children are chosen even if no correct guess has appeared.

I'M VERY, VERY TALL

Playing Area. Classroom or gymnasium.
Players. Entire class.
Supplies. None.
Skills. Imagery.
Maturity Level. Preschool.
Directions. One child is in the center and hides her eyes. The remainder of the children form a circle, with one of them designated as leader. The leader directs the action. The action follows the verse, which is recited by the children. The leader pantomimes "tall" or "small" as the last line is repeated. The child in the center then guesses whether the children are "tall" or "small."

Sometimes I'm very, very tall.
Sometimes I'm very, very small.
Sometimes tall, sometimes small,
Guess what I am now.

Variation. Use other terms such as "thin"/ "wide," "crooked"/"straight," etc. Let the children come up with their own suggestions.

MOTHER, MAY I?

Playing Area. Playground or gymnasium.
Players. Six to eight.
Supplies. None.
Skills. Fundamental locomotor movements.
Maturity Level. Preschool.
Directions. Starting and finishing lines are established about 40 feet apart. In a gymnasium, the game can proceed across the floor. One child is It and stands between the two lines. The remainder of the children stand on the starting line. The object of the game is to reach the finish line first.

The player who is It tells one of the players how many steps he can take and what kind of steps they must be. The player then asks It, "Mother, may I?" He must await the reply before he moves. It may occasionally answer, "No." If a player moves without asking permission, or after It has refused permission, he must go back to the starting line.

The steps should be varied to provide different kinds of movements. Steps such as baby steps, scissors steps, giant steps, hopping steps, bunny steps (jumps), and others are appropriate for the game. The first to reach the finish line is It for the next game.

THE SCARECROW AND THE CROWS

Playing Area. Playground, gymnasium, or classroom.
Players. Entire class.
Supplies. None.
Skills. Dodging, running.
Maturity Level. Preschool.
Directions. The children form a large circle to represent the "garden," which the Scarecrow is guarding. Six Crows scatter on the outside of the circle. The Scarecrow assumes a characteristic scarecrow pose inside the circle. The circle children raise their joined hands and let the Crows run through into the "garden," where they pretend to eat. The Scarecrow tries to tag one of the Crows, and the circle children help the Crows by raising their joined hands, allowing them to leave the circle, but they try to hinder the Scarecrow. If the Scarecrow runs out of the circle, all the Crows immediately run into the "garden" and pretend to nibble at the vegetables, while the circle children hinder the Scarecrow's reentry.

When the Scarecrow has caught one or two Crows (the teacher can decide), a new group of children is selected to be Scarecrow and Crows. If the Scarecrow has failed to catch any Crows after a reasonable period of time, a change should be made.

Kindergarten Games

CAT AND RAT

Playing Area. Gymnasium or playground.
Players. Ten to twenty.
Supplies. None.
Skills. Running, dodging.
Maturity Level. Kindergarten.
Directions. All the children except two form a circle with hands joined. One of the extra players is the Cat, and the other is the Rat. The Rat is on the inside of the circle, and the Cat is outside. The following dialogue takes place:

"I am the Cat."
"I am the Rat."
"I can catch the Rat."
"Oh, no, you can't."

The Cat then chases the Rat in and out of the circle. The circle players raise their arms to help the Rat and lower them to hinder the Cat. When the Cat catches the Rat (or after a period of time, if the Rat is not caught), the two children can select two others to take their places.

Variation. Instead of having the children raise and lower their arms to aid or hinder the runners, the teacher can call out, "High windows," or "Low windows." The circle players raise and lower their hands only on these signals.

GALLOP TAG

Playing Area. Playground or gymnasium.
Players. 12 to 20.
Supplies. None.
Skills. Basic locomotor movements.
Maturity Level. Kindergarten.
Directions. Children are in circle formation, facing in. One child walks around the outside of the circle and tags another child on the back. Immediately, he gallops around the circle, in either direction, with the child who was tagged chasing him, also at a gallop. If the player in the lead gets around to the vacated spot before being tagged, he joins the circle. If he is tagged, a second try is made. If the runner fails this time, he joins the circle, and another child is chosen.
Variations. The children can run or skip.
Slap Jack. Have the child tagged run in the *opposite* direction. The child who gets back to the vacant place first gets to keep the place. The other child tags again for another run.
Run for Your Supper. The children stand with clasped hands. The runner tags a pair of clasped hands and says, "Run for your supper." The two children whose hands have been tagged run in opposite directions, with the one getting back first keeping the place. The original runner, after tagging the clasped hands, merely steps into the circle, leaving only one space for which the two runners compete. Having the two runners bow to each other or shake hands as they pass each other on the opposite side of the circle, before continuing the run back to place, makes the game more enjoyable.

First Grade Games

CAT AND MICE

Playing Area. Playground, gymnasium, or classroom.
Players. Ten to thirty.
Supplies. None.
Skills. Running, dodging.
Maturity Level. First grade.
Directions. All the children except four form a large circle. One of the four extra children is chosen to be the Cat, and the three others are the Mice. On signal, the Cat chases the Mice, who are inside the circle. The Mice cannot leave the circle. As they are caught, they join the circle. The last Mouse caught becomes the Cat for the next round. The teacher should start at one point and go around the circle selecting Mice, so that each child gets a chance to be in the center.

The teacher can adjust the size of the circle by asking the children to take a step forward or backward.

HOUND AND RABBIT

Playing Area. Playground or gymnasium.
Players. 15 to 30.
Supplies. None.
Skills. Running, dodging.
Maturity Level. First grade.
Directions. Players are scattered around the area in groups of three. Two of the three make a "tree" by facing each other and putting their hands on each other's shoulders. The third child, who is a Rabbit, stands between them. An extra Rabbit is outside the groups and is chased by a Hound. The Hound chases the Rabbit, who takes refuge in any "tree." Since no "tree" may hold more than one Rabbit, the other Rabbit must leave and look for another "tree." When the Hound catches the Rabbit, they exchange places, and the game continues.

A rotation system should be used whenever a Rabbit enters a "tree." The three children in the group should rotate so that the entering Rabbit becomes a part of the "tree," and one of the children making up the "tree" becomes the Rabbit.

Second Grade Games

TWO DEEP

Playing Area. Playground or gymnasium.
Players. 15 to 20.
Supplies. None.
Skills. Running, stopping.
Maturity Level. Second grade.
Directions. All children except two form a circle, standing about fingertip distance apart and facing the center. A runner and a chaser stand on the outside. The chaser tries to catch the runner, who can save himself by stopping in front of any player. This player now becomes the runner and must avoid being caught. When the chaser tags the runner, the positions change immediately, and the runner becomes the chaser.

Encourage the children to make changes often. If there seems to be too much running, make a rule that a child may travel only halfway around the circle before he must make a change.

CROSS OVER

Playing Area. Playground with two parallel goal lines about 40 feet apart.
Players. 15 to 20.

Supplies. None.
Skills. Running, dodging.
Maturity Level. Second grade.
Directions. Divide the players into two groups; each group stands on one of the goal lines. A catcher is in the center between the two lines. He faces one of the lines and calls out the name of one of the players. This player immediately calls out the name of a player in the other line. These two players try to exchange positions, while the catcher tries to tag one of them. Any player tagged becomes the catcher for the next call.

If there are more than 20 children, it is best to divide the group into two separate games. Since only two children are running at a time, the game can drag when played by a large group.

Variation. When the group is larger than 20, the game can be played by partners. When the catchers call out a name, the named child and his partner respond. The catchers hold hands on the inside and use only their free hands to tag. No tagging counts if the catchers separate, and a pair running across the area are counted as caught if they are unable to keep together.

FLYING DUTCHMAN

Playing Area. Playground or gymnasium.
Players. 20 to 30.
Supplies. None.
Skills. Running.
Maturity Level. Second grade.
Directions. The children are in a circle with hands joined. Two children outside the circle, with hands joined, are the runners. The runners go around the outside of the circle and tag a pair of joined hands. The runners continue around the circle, while the tagged pair runs around in the other direction. The first pair back to the vacated spot gets to keep the spot, and the other two become the runners. Be sure to establish rules for passing when the couples go by each other on the way around. Couples should keep to the right in passing. Change runners after two unsuccessful runs.

Variations. The runners can reverse their direction immediately after tagging.

The game can be played by groups of three instead of couples. The tag is made on the back of any one person, who joins the persons on either side of him to make up a group of three. Groups must keep hands clasped, or they will be disqualified.

WEATHER VANE

Playing Area. Playground, gymnasium, or classroom.
Players. Entire class.

Supplies. None.
Skills. Jumping, turning.
Maturity Level. Second grade.
Directions. Children stand alongside their desks or are scattered throughout the area. A leader stands at the front of the class and gives the directions. He calls out the names of the four main compass directions: "North," "South," "East," or "West." The children jump in place, making the necessary turn in the air to face the direction called. This may involve a quarter-, half-, or three-quarter turn. If the leader calls a direction in which the children are already facing, then the children jump in place without turning. All turns should be in the same direction (right or left) for a period of time to avoid confusion.

A child can sit down after a stipulated number of errors. An alternate method would be for each child to keep track of the number of errors he has made.

Variations. After the children become skillful in turning, several variations can be introduced. A full turn could be required when a direction is repeated. Turning to the right and to the left could be alternated.

MODERATELY ACTIVE GAMES THAT REQUIRE EQUIPMENT OR SUPPLIES

Preschool games
Colors
The Magic Fountain

Kindergarten games
The Mechanical Man (The Bionic Woman)
Ball Toss
Ball Passing
Call Ball

First grade games
Teacher Ball (Leader Ball)
Circle Straddle Ball
Exchange Dodgeball

Second grade games
Roll Dodgeball
Kick Softball
Beanbag Target Toss

Preschool Games

COLORS

Playing Area. Playground, gymnasium, or classroom.
Players. Entire class.
Supplies. Markers: circles, squares, or triangles cut out of colored construction paper.
Skills. Perceptual concepts, running.
Maturity Level. Preschool.

Directions. Markers of five or six different colors should be used. One is given to each child; a number of children should have the same color. The children are seated in a circle. Each child places his marker in front of him.

The teacher calls out one of the colors, and all players having that color run counterclockwise around the circle and back to place. The first one seated upright and motionless is declared the winner. Different kinds of locomotor movements can be specified, such as skipping, galloping, walking etc.

After a period of play, have the children move one place to the left, leaving the markers in place on the floor.

Variations. Use markers stressing shapes instead of colors. Use a circle, triangle, square, rectangle, star, or diamond.

Use numbers instead of colors.

Many other categories—animals, birds, sea creatures, etc.—can be used in place of colors.

THE MAGIC FOUNTAIN

Playing Area. Playground, gymnasium, or classroom.

Players. Entire class.

Supplies. Pictures of animals, a box, and a stool or table.

Skills. Imagery, imitation.

Maturity Level. Preschool.

Directions. About a dozen animal pictures are placed in a box on a stool or table to one side. This is the "magic fountain." The children are seated in a circle on the floor. Four or five children are selected by the teacher; one of them is designated to take one of the pictures out of the "magic fountain." She shows the picture to the rest of her group, but keeps it hidden from the remainder of the children in the circle.

As soon as all the chosen children have seen the picture, they return to the circle area and imitate the animal they saw in the picture. When the circle players have guessed the animal, the animal imitators return to the circle formation, and another group of players is chosen.

Children who wish to guess what animal is being imitated should raise hands for recognition.

Kindergarten Games

THE MECHANICAL MAN (THE BIONIC WOMAN)

Playing Area. Indoors. A small space is all that is needed.

Players. Small groups of three or four children.

Supplies. Different objects to identify—beanbag, small ball, rolled-up paper, etc.; blindfolds.

Skills. Ability to follow directions, tactile sense.

Maturity Level. Kindergarten.

Directions. One child is the Mechanical Man (or the Bionic Woman) and is blindfolded. An object is placed somewhere in the room. One child is the handler of the Mechanical Man. The object is for the handler to direct the Mechanical Man to the target object. He does this by specifying so many steps forward or to the side and reaching in this or that direction. The Mechanical Man can move only as the handler directs. When the Mechanical Man finds the object, he examines it with the hands and tries to identify it.

Variation. The game can also be called Robot, with the child moving like a robot.

Teaching Hints. While the game is fun for everyone to watch, it is better to have several games going on at the same time. Be sure the blindfold is effective, since the game will soon lose all interest if the child can peek.

BALL TOSS

Playing Area. Playground, gymnasium, or classroom.

Players. Groups of six to eight.

Supplies. A ball or beanbag for each group.

Skills. Throwing, catching.

Maturity Level. Kindergarten.

Directions. The children form a circle with one child in the center. The center player throws the ball to each child in turn around the circle. The ball is returned to the center player each time. The object of the game is for the children to make good throws and catches completely around the circle. After each child has had a turn in the center, the teacher can ask each circle to total the number of center players that were able to complete all their throws without any errors.

BALL PASSING

Playing Area. Playground, gymnasium, or classroom.

Players. Entire class, divided into two or more circles.

Supplies. Five or six different kinds of balls for each circle.

Skills. Object handling.

Maturity Level. Kindergarten.

Directions. The basis for this game is the child's love of handling objects. Two or more teams combine to form a circle, which should contain no more than 14 children. The children need not be in any particular order.

The teacher starts a ball around the circle; the ball is passed from player to player in the same direction. The teacher introduces more balls, until five or six are moving around in the circle at the same time and in the same direction. If a child drops a ball, he must retrieve it, and a point is scored against his team. After a period of time, a whistle is blown, and the points against each team are totaled. The team with the lowest score wins.

When sufficient balls are not available, beanbags, large blocks, or softballs can be substituted.

CALL BALL

Playing Area. Playground, gymnasium, or classroom.

Players. Six to eight in each circle.

Supplies. A large playground ball or volleyball.

Skills. Throwing, catching.

Maturity Level. Kindergarten.

Directions. The children form a circle with one child in the center. The center child has a ball. She throws the ball into the air, at the same time calling out the name of one of the circle children. This child runs forward and tries to catch the ball *before* it bounces. If successful, he becomes the center player. If not, the center player throws again.

Variations. Give the children numbers and let more than one child have the same number. This makes the catching competitive.

Use the names of colors or animals, with more than one child assigned to the same color or animal.

Move the children back and have them catch the ball on the first bounce.

Catch the Cane. Instead of tossing a ball into the air, the center player balances a wand on one end on the floor. The child whose number is called tries to catch the cane before it hits the ground. A little experimentation will determine how far back the circle should be from the cane.

Play with a balloon. The center player bats the balloon into the air. The child whose name is called then keeps it aloft.

First Grade Games

TEACHER BALL (LEADER BALL)

Playing Area. Playground or gymnasium.

Players. Six to eight.

Supplies. Volleyball or rubber playground ball.

Skills. Throwing, catching.

Maturity Level. First grade.

Directions. One child is the Teacher (or Leader) and stands about ten feet in front of the others, who are lined up facing her. The object of the game is to move up to the Teacher's spot by not making any bad throws or missing any catches.

The Teacher throws to each child in turn, beginning with the child on her left; the children must catch and return the ball. Any child making a throwing or catching error goes to the foot of the line, on the Teacher's right. Those in the line move up, filling the vacated space.

If the Teacher makes a mistake, she goes to the foot of the line, and the child at the head of the line becomes the new Teacher.

The Teacher scores a point for herself if she remains in position for three rounds (three throws to each child). She then takes a position at the foot of the line, and the child at the head of the line becomes the Teacher.

This game should be used only after the children have practiced throwing and catching skills. It can be worked in as a part of the skill-teaching program.

Playing Teacher Ball

Variation. Introduce specific methods of throwing and catching: "Catch with the right hand only," or "Catch with one hand; don't let the ball touch your body."

CIRCLE STRADDLE BALL

Playing Area. Playground, gymnasium, or classroom.

Players. Ten to fifteen.

Supplies. Two volleyballs or rubber playground balls.

Skills. Ball-rolling, catching.

Maturity Level. First grade.

Directions. Children are in circle formation, facing in. Each child stands in wide straddle step with the side of the foot against the neighbor's. The hands are on the knees.

Two balls are used. The object of the game is to roll one of the balls between the legs of any player before he can get his hands down and stop it. Each time the ball goes between the legs of an individual, a point is scored against him. The players having the fewest points against them are the winners.

Be sure the children catch and roll the ball rather than bat it. Children must keep their hands on their knees until a ball comes toward them.

After practice, the following variation should be played.

Variation. One child is in the center with a ball and is It. The other children are in the same formation as described above. One ball is used. The center player tries to roll the ball through the legs of any child he chooses. He should mask his intent, using feints and changes of direction. Any child allowing the ball to go through his legs becomes It. All players start with hands on knees until the ball is in play.

EXCHANGE DODGEBALL

Playing Area. Playground or gymnasium.
Players. 12 to 20.
Supplies. Volleyball or rubber playground ball.
Skills. Throwing, dodging.
Maturity Level. First grade.
Directions. Children form a circle with one child, It, in the center. The children are numbered off by fours or fives, in such a way that there are three or four children who have the same number. The center player also has a number, which she uses when she is not It.

The center player has a ball, which is placed at her feet. She calls a number, and all children with that number move out and begin to exchange places. The center player picks up the ball and tries to hit one of the moving players. The center player remains It until she can hit one of the children. Hits should be made only below the waist.

Variation. Use animal names instead of numbers.

Second Grade Games

ROLL DODGEBALL

Playing Area. Playground or gymnasium.
Players. 20 to 30, divided into two teams.
Supplies. Two volleyballs or rubber playground balls.
Skills. Ball-rolling, dodging.
Maturity Level. Second grade.
Directions. Half the children form a circle; the rest of the children are in the center. Two balls are given to the circle players. The circle players roll the balls at the feet and shoes of the center players, trying to hit them. The center players move around to dodge the balls. When a center player is hit, he leaves the circle.

After a period of time, or when all the children have been hit, the teams trade places. If a specified time limit is used, the winner is the team having the fewest hits. Alternatively, the team that has put out all the opponents in the shortest time is the winner.

Variation. Center players are down on their hands and feet. Only one ball is used. Do not let the children play too long in this position, as it is quite strenuous.

Teaching Hints. Be sure that the children have had practice in rolling a ball. Balls that stop in the center are "dead" and must be taken back to the circle before being put into play. It is best to have the player who recovers a ball roll it to a teammate rather than return to place with the ball.

KICK SOFTBALL

Playing Area. Small softball field with a home plate three feet square.
Players. Ten to fifteen players on each team.
Supplies. Soccer or playground ball (8½-inch).
Skills. Kicking a rolling ball, throwing, catching.
Maturity Level. Second grade.
Directions. The batter stands in the kicking area (home plate). He kicks the ball, which is rolled to him by the pitcher. The ball should be rolled at only moderate speed. An umpire calls balls and strikes. A strike is a ball that rolls over the three-foot square; a ball is one that rolls outside this area. Strikeouts and walks are called as in softball. The number of foul balls allowed should be limited to one. (A second foul ball is out.) No base-stealing is permitted. Otherwise, the game can be played like softball.

Variations. The batter kicks a stationary ball. This saves time and eliminates the need for a pitcher.

When small children are playing, a beach ball may be used. Small children find a beach ball exciting to handle and not as frightening as a playground ball.

BEANBAG TARGET TOSS

Playing Area. Classroom or gymnasium. The target is three concentric circles, drawn on the floor, with radii of ten inches, twenty inches, and thirty inches. A throwing line should be established ten to fifteen feet from the target; the distance can be increased as the children's skill develops.

Players. Two to six for each target.

Supplies. Five beanbags. Blocks of wood or round, smooth stones can be used in place of beanbags.

Skills. Throwing for accuracy.

Maturity Level. Second grade.

Directions. Each player stands at the throwing line and tosses the five beanbags (one at a time) toward the target.

Scoring

Center area—15 points
Middle area—10 points
Outer area—5 points
Any bag touching a line—3 points

To score the full number of points in an area, the bag must be completely inside that area, not touching a line. If the bag touches a line, it scores three points.

Each child is given five throws, and the child's score is determined from the final position of the five bags.

Variations. Two children can compete against each other, alternating single throws until each has taken the allotted five. The score of each is noted. For a second turn, the child who scored the highest during the first round throws first.

When playing the game outside, players can use flat stones on a hard surface.

SUMMARY

Games are an excellent medium for social and moral development since certain rules must be followed to make the games enjoyable for all. Games are enjoyable for young children if they allow them to feel successful and capable of making a contribution to the games. The most effective games for young children are those that keep all children active simultaneously. In most cases, games should not require that children possess a high level of skill to participate successfully, since the competitive pressure will encourage improper or poorly executed skill performance.

Competition is not inherently bad or good. How it is handled by the instructor of young children is the key issue. Youngsters enjoy playing for themselves rather than in a group and often find it difficult to follow set rules. All children should have the opportunity to find success at one time or another in the competititve setting. In many situations, competition will take care of itself if children are given the opportunity to explore games without teacher intervention.

Games can be modified to make them more enjoyable and in line with the physical limitations of young children. Distances can be shortened, boundaries modified, and the height and/or size of the goals changed to allow for the age and abilities of the participants. Safety is also an important consideration for game activities. Teachers should be aware of space limitations, should anticipate collisions and tripping situations, and should prepare the playing surface to minimize sliding and falling.

Games in this chapter have been classified into four categories: active games that require no equipment or supplies, active games that require equipment or supplies, moderately active games that require no equipment or supplies, and moderately active games that require equipment or supplies.

ADDITIONAL REFERENCES

American Association of Health, Physical Education, Recreation and Dance. *Desirable Athletic Competition for Children of Elementary School Age*. Reston, Va.: AAHPERD, 1970.

Orlick, Terry, and Botterill, Cal. *Every Kid Can Win*. Chicago: Nelson Hall, 1975.

Tutko, Thomas, and Bruns, William. *Winning Is Everything and Other American Myths*. New York: Macmillan Co., 1976.

Chapter 17

Relaxation

How much have cost us the evils that never happened!
Thomas Jefferson

Relaxation is a subject that many teachers talk about, while doing little to help themselves or their students to learn to relax. Some instructors believe in the "drainage" theory of relaxation, which states that demanding physical activity will drain off the child's excess energy and tension and leave him relaxed and ready to settle down to his schoolwork. This theory has not been substantiated, however, and classroom teachers often complain of youngsters coming from physical activity classes "all psyched up" or "hyper."

The desire to beat someone at a given task is not conducive to relaxation. When an activity is being offered specifically for the purpose of allowing children to relax, therefore, it should not have a competitive flavor. In fact, there is considerable evidence to show that the tremendous urge toward competition in our society is one of the reasons why excitability and irritability are so prevalent among Americans. The point is not to condemn all competition or activities that contain a competitive element, but to direct attention to the need for some type of activity that is specifically designed for the purpose of relaxing.

Most activities in movement programs are selected for what they can offer the child in terms of physical development. It would seem useful to offer children some additional activities that emphasize relaxation and harmony of movement. If children can be taught to relax through physiological means at an early age, they will reap the benefits of a happier and less stressful life style in later years.

It is interesting to note that we spend 12 to 16 years teaching youngsters how to discipline and sharpen their mental senses so that they may achieve academic success, yet we spend little time teaching them how to derive enjoyment from their physical self. Today many adults pay out large sums in an attempt to learn how to relax. Witness the growth of interest in hatha yoga, which teaches a technique of "complete relaxation." It is conceivable that time could be allowed in the curriculum to teach some of these practices to youngsters.

This approach should not be construed as an attempt to turn physical education classes into meditation or relaxation sessions. Rather, it is an effort to introduce alternate ideas into the total curriculum so that children may experience another facet of physical education.

The suggested relaxation techniques that follow are appropriate to use for short periods between activities or at the end of a lesson.

IMPLEMENTING RELAXATION ACTIVITIES

1. The teacher must see relaxation as an important part of the program. The teacher's attitude toward relaxation activities will determine whether students see them as important or as a waste of time.

2. It is unrealistic to expect good results the first few times relaxation skills are taught. Many children have never experienced a time during which they are asked to "do nothing but relax."

3. A quiet and uninterrupted environment is essential to ensure any degree of success in relaxation. Soft music in the background will sometimes aid children in learning to unwind.

Checking to see if the children are relaxed

4. If physical activity classes are taught indoors, it can be helpful to turn down the lights.

5. The teacher should speak in a soft and reassuring voice. Speaking at a low level while moving throughout the area seems to work well.

6. After children have had several opportunities to practice relaxing, they should be encouraged to close their eyes. Some youngsters will have a difficult time doing so if they are somewhat untrusting and feel uneasy in the environment.

7. Although the best position for relaxing is the supine position, many of the activities can be performed while sitting. The legs shoud be straight rather than flexed, and the arms should be at the sides.

8. Some words trigger thoughts that help the body relax. For example, "limp," "flabby," "soft," "loose," "gradually," and "melting" are words of this nature.

RELAXATION ACTIVITIES

1. Jacobson[1] has done a great deal of work with the technique of "progressive relaxation." In this technique, a muscle or muscle group is first tensed and then relaxed slowly and smoothly. All the major parts of the body can be relaxed as one works down from the head to the toes. An example would be: "Frown and squinch up your face, making many wrinkles, and then slowly relax your face and smooth it

out." Each time a muscle group is relaxed, a big breath of air can be exhaled.

2. While standing, children can slowly take a deep breath, and expel the air as completely as possible, while simultaneously dropping the head and collapsing the chest.

3. Directions can be given to stimulate the child's imagination. For example, children can be told to "float through the air like a feather," or to "be a snowman and gradually melt." They might curl into a tight ball, and be told to "let all the air out of the ball as slowly as possible."

4. Use soft, soothing music to stimulate relaxation.

5. "In a sitting position, see if you can relax by listening to the rhythm of your breathing." Many meditation techniques use breathing as a key to concentration and relaxation.

6. Students can lie supine on the floor, close their eyes, and relax all muscles while taking deep, regular breaths. The teacher can move among the children and check the limpness of their limbs.

7. Shaking can be a nice release from physical tension. Children can be directed to shake various parts of their bodies (arms, legs, hips, knees, ankles) loosely, either in sequence or in combinations. They can practice being as "loose" as possible. As a closing activity, they can be challenged to make the biggest smile possible—in all directions, at their friends.

---

[1]Edmund Jacobson, *Progressive Relaxation,* 2d ed. (Chicago: University of Chicago Press, 1968).

8. Sometimes a welcome change of pace can be offered at the end of the session, when children are putting away their equipment. They can be told, "When you hear a loud drumbeat, flop to the floor like a Raggedy Ann doll and relax."

9. Individual mat activities can lead in smoothly to a period of relaxation. Children can be directed to assume a certain position and then to "let it go" in order to relax. For example, they can curl, stretch, and relax; or reach, bridge, rock, and relax. In this practice, students can learn to differentiate between the tension necessary to generate various positions and the lack of tension necessary to relax.

10. Children can also relax in the classroom setting. They sit at their desks, place both hands on the desk top, and lay their head on one of their arms. They can then be asked to relax and melt like an ice cream cone.

Teachers should be aware that youngsters must *practice* relaxation in the same way as they practice any other skill. Repetition of the techniques and familiarity with the experience will bring about good results.

SUMMARY

Relaxation activities are offered for short periods between activities or at the end of a lesson to allow children a release after intense activity. Teachers' attitudes toward relaxation have a great effect on whether children see relaxing as an important part of a productive lifestyle.

Learning to relax takes practice, and teachers should expect improvement when emphasis is placed on this area. A soft, reassuring voice and soft background music can enhance the environment for successful relaxation. Many activities are offered to stimulate and aid children in the process of relaxation.

Chapter 18

Perceptual-Motor Programs

Children are our most valuable resource.
Herbert Hoover

PERCEPTUAL-MOTOR CONSIDERATIONS FOR THE REGULAR PROGRAM

In the 1960s, based on the work of Delacato, Kephart, Barsch, and others, perceptual-motor programs were introduced into the field of physical education, where they made a lasting impact. These programs grew out of the concern to find an efficient, simple, and effective means to help children with learning problems to do better academically, primarily in the area of reading readiness.

In the perceptual-motor process, stimuli are received by the various senses, and carried to various levels of the brain. The information received is then processed, and some behavior is evoked in response to the information. A child with a deficiency in the perceptual-motor process may fail to reach his potential in various academic areas, if the disability is severe or the child is immature developmentally.

The first section of this chapter will examine the implications of perceptual-motor theory that are of value to integrate into the regular program of movement experiences for children. A discussion of perceptual-motor programs designed for children with learning disabilities and children with motor problems is found in the latter part of the chapter.

What is a perceptual-motor response? A perceptual-motor response is an appropriate response to a perceived stimulus. The child receives the stimulus, makes sense out of it (integrates it), and makes the appropriate response. Since much of academic learning involves this goal of appropriate response, it behooves educators to give attention to the area of sensory-motor integration.

Perception in motor learning involves discrimination through certain sense mechanisms: auditory, kinesthetic, tactile, and visual, and the balance control mechanism. These sense channels receive cues from the environment; this evokes an appropriate motor response.

Auditory Discrimination

Children must learn to interpret sounds and respond correctly to auditory cues. The child must be able to listen, and listening goes beyond simply hearing. The child should be able to distinguish among various sounds, pick out specific tones, and discriminate rhythms. His understanding of words and terms becomes important, so that he may be able to interpret them, making the appropriate movement response.

Memory recall and sequencing require retrieval of correct information from either immediate or past experiences. For example, should the teacher designate the task as "run, jump, and roll," the child must record and retrieve this sequence and reach back into his past experience for what the terms "run," "jump," and "roll" mean. Reproductive rhythmic response also involves memory recall and sequencing. A challenge could be presented as follows: The teacher beats out a short rhythm on a drum. The children reproduce the rhythmic pattern first with hand-clapping, next with foot-tapping, then with a response more appropriate to the rhythm.

While there is good value in having children explore and participate in creative learning experiences, another kind of self-learning occurs when children develop the ability to react with the correct motor response to such action commands as "start," "stop," "change direction," "freeze," etc. These actions should be initiated by other auditory cues, such as the drumbeat, music sounds, or a whistle. Understanding, sequencing, and being challenged by such action terms as "over," "under," "around," "through," "in front of," "up," "down," and others broaden the learning experience and reinforce the idea that play can be educational.

The ability to listen, follow directions, and develop a successful response to those directions is a learning skill that may have positive effects on the child's approach in the classroom.

Visual Discrimination

Visual coordination has two important aspects. The first is concentration and convergence on near and far-off objects. Convergence describes a turning inward of the lines of sight of the two eyes to focus on an object. For objects at a distance, the lines of sight become practically parallel. The eyes should be able to accommodate and adjust to near and far-off objects. The ability to judge distance should also be present.

The second aspect of visual coordination is the ability to track objects in flight or objects moving in space from one point to another. This is an essential ingredient in many manipulative skills and games.

Some elements of form recognition can be experienced in play situations. Children should have experiences in symbol and form recognition, including adjectives such as "large" and "small" and colors. The child might be directed to hop three times on a large, red circle, move on his hands and feet to a small, blue triangle, and return to a black square. Other colored forms would be out on the floor, to provide variety and to permit choice.

Visual-motor learning includes three pertinent coordinations: hand-eye, foot-eye, and hand-foot-eye coordinations cover most throwing, catching, rebounding, striking, and kicking movements. Since most of these are self-explanatory, a simple illustration will suffice. Suppose you ask a youngster to close his eyes when throwing a ball to another child. For children with immature patterns of throwing, the result will illustrate the importance of vision in a target skill. On the other hand, a highly skilled basketball player might be able to shoot a free throw successfully with the eyes closed,

because the throw has become automatic for him. Looking at the basket first before closing the eyes would provide a mental picture, based on visual memory retention, which can aid success.

Kinesthetic Discrimination

Kinesthesis is a sense mediated by proprioceptors lying in the muscles, tendons, and joint mechanisms. These sensors provide information about the body position in relation to its environment, about relationships among different body segments in their various positions, and about precision of movement. Knowledge of body position and its parts contributes to body awareness. The development of body awareness is an important objective in the movement program.

In skill development it is important that the children get the "feel" of the action, an experience derived from the kinesthetic sense. The pattern must be repeated often enough so that the "feel" of the act is established. In a negative sense, this discrimination should also inform the child when the performance doesn't feel right.

The ability to relax while performing certain skills relies to some extent on kinesthetic sense information. In precision acts, the correct muscle groups must tense, the guiding muscles must perform their function, and those muscles that might impede the action must relax.

Tactile Discrimination

Tactile discrimination depends on the sense of touch. For motor activities, the important tactile sensors are located in the fingers and palms of the hands and the soles of the feet. The sense of touch is important in activities in which objects are handled. How to hold an object for the most productive result is learned through experimentation. For example, most balls should be controlled with the finger pads, particularly for target throws. Use of apparatus can develop tactile sense, because of the different hand holds it requires. In many cases, tactile discrimination is monitored by kinesthesis on an intersensory level.

Holding and controlling objects like balls, hoops, and beanbags has value in improving tactile discrimination.

Balance Control

Balance is achieved through postural adjustment to gravity. Two types of balance are recognized, and there are movement experiences for each type. The first is static balance, which is balance without locomotor movement on a fixed base. In static balance, the child raises one leg from the ground and balances on the other foot while standing in place.

The second type of balance is dynamic balance, which involves balance control while moving. Simple walking is a skill without much challenge that requires balance control. Walking on a balance beam puts more critical demands on balance mechanisms.

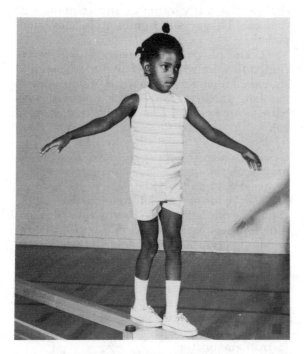

Balance control on the beam

Balance is required while the child is airborne. There must be control of the body and knowledge of its position as the body is in flight. For young children, the opportunity to jump from modest heights can help develop this ability.

Although balance is monitored to some extent by kinesthesis, balancing is mainly monitored by the vestibulary balance mechanism, located near the organs of hearing. This mechanism responds to changes in head velocity (acceleration and deceleration) and translates these movements into an awareness of the balance position.

Visual perception also plays a part in control of balance, providing external information about the position of the body in space. The relationship between visual perception and balance can be pinpointed by having the child stand on one leg for ten seconds in balance, then having her repeat the task with her eyes closed, noting the difference in ability to balance.

To enhance balance control, the child should return to his original position in good balance after completing a balance stunt or act and should land in good balance after being airborne.

Intersensory Functioning and Integration

The goal of the perceptual-motor approach is a well-coordinated child, who can function well not only in play and movement patterns, but also in the classroom learning environment. Attention should be directed to the mechanisms of coordination; more or less generalized coordinations, rather than specific activities, should be developed. The sense channels should be stimulated to result in a variety of movement experiences. Many of these are highly specific movements demanding a single correct response.

To make the most of movement experiences as productive activity for children, teachers can derive much from perceptual-motor theory that will be of value in the regular physical education program. Movement competency is a major objective of physical education, and perceptual-motor principles can help the child attain this goal. Rather than attempt to make a separate area of perceptual-motor programs *within* the school's movement experiences for all children, the authors believe that there should be only one program of physical education, which incorporates the best of all principles to serve the needs of all the children.

There is still a need for special perceptual-motor programs for children with learning disabilities or motor problems, of course, and for the use of these principles in special education programs.

A caution should be mentioned. In no sense does the physical education program pretend to teach reading or any of the other academic skills. The goal is the development of a well-coordinated child whose motor status will not interfere with his ability to learn.

Laterality

If a child develops laterality, it implies that he can move corresponding parts of the body separately, together, simultaneously, or in a cross-lateral pattern. In motor patterns, the term is applied mostly in relation to the limbs. If a child moves one limb or the limbs on the same side, this is a unilateral movement. If both arms and/or both legs are moved similarly at the same time, this is a bilateral movement. A cross-lateral movement occurs when an arm and the opposite leg are moved together. There are some nonlateral patterns as well. The two arms and/or legs can make movements of a different type, as when one arm is raised straight up and the other is extended forward.

Laterality is a learned movement pattern. An infant will reach out with both hands first and then learn to reach with one hand, thus changing from a bilateral to a unilateral movement. When he begins to crawl, he should move the right arm in coordination with the left leg and vice versa (a cross-lateral pattern).

The ability to use the different patterns of laterality with ease and versatility of movement is a valuable generalized coordination. The ability to make changes with effectiveness from one pattern to another is inherent in the concept of laterality. A good example may be seen in skipping, in which the child must make changes in postural and laterality patterns.

Directionality—Internal and External

With respect to internal directionality, the child should be able to identify the right and left sides of the body. He should be able to follow directions that tell him to move a right or left part, which also requires that he be able to identify body parts. The child's response movements should make sense when he is given a direction such as, "Kneel on your right knee." This right-left discrimination of internal directionality develops earlier than the sense of direction with respect to the environment. Instructions that we take for granted with older children may need to become learning challenges for their younger counterparts. Teachers should avoid demonstrating what their instructions describe, as this removes the challenge to think.

The other type of directionality is external, which refers to the child's orientation in external space. The standard directions of north, south, east, and west, representing compass points, are used only occasionally in movement activities.

The child must be able to extend the perception of internal directionality to movement in relation to his environment. That is, he must be able to move right or left, as desired. An understanding of directionality may be extended by using commands such as "forward and backward," "up and down," "in front of and behind," "around," "through," "over and under," "to the _____ side of," "outside and inside," among others. Contrasting terms (fast/slow, over/under, etc.) should receive special attention.

IMPLICATIONS FOR MOVEMENT METHODOLOGY AND ACTIVITIES

We have examined the perceptual-motor theory and seen how these needed coordinations can be developed. The following suggestions are offered to provide integration of the concepts into movement programs for children.

1. A wide range of movement challenges should be experienced by the child. The teacher needs imagination and ability to help children explore the many varieties and combinations that can be devised from simple movement patterns.

2. The concept of laterality should be included in all movement challenges. The child should counter a move to the right with one to the left. Throwing should be practiced with both arms, in turn. Change the lead foot, in galloping, for example. No effort need be made to determine or establish dominance. In patterns in which the children move on all fours, unilateral, bilateral, and cross-lateral movements should be practiced.

3. A wide range of manipulative skills should be offered to develop visual-tactile coordination. See that the children have a chance to handle many different objects, both on an exploratory level and with stipulated limitations. Build sequences and patterns of movement from both visual and auditory input.

4. Body awareness is an anticipated goal, which should be reflected in activities that allow the child to identify various body parts and learn their function.

5. Balance can be enhanced by the use of the balance beam and other pieces of balance apparatus. The teacher should make sure that balance activities are practiced at controlled speeds, stressing that the child must complete the activity in good balance. A variety of static and dynamic balance challenges should be provided.

6. Sequencing is important and should be prominent in the program. The challenge to put together three or more activities in sequence forces children to reach back into motor memory to devise combinations.

7. Reproductive activity provides interesting possibilities. The child can reproduce sounds made by a drum or musical instrument or he might reproduce a movement pattern demonstrated by another child.

8. Integrating form recognition into the program is another approach to be followed. The integration of such forms as the triangle, square, rectangle, circle, and diamond into movement experiences is thought to be helpful in learning to conceptualize forms and symbols.

9. The concept of directionality should be featured in all movement activities.

10. Because perceptual-motor competency develops in an ordered fashion, it is necessary to give good attention to fundamental skills before the more complex skills can be superimposed on them.

11. The program should serve as a diagnostic instrument to screen children with motor problems who can be referred for further evaluation. This is a matter of observation and teacher judgment.

In accomplishing the movement tasks that flow from perceptual-motor concepts, it appears that one must adhere to certain patterns of movement. Both exploratory and defined challenges should be a part of the child's overall movement learning experiences.

PERCEPTUAL-MOTOR PROGRAMS FOR CHILDREN WITH LEARNING DISABILITIES

The previous section has focused on the inclusion of perceptual-motor concepts in the curriculum of movement experiences in the regular program of activities. In this section, we will turn our attention to the values and implementation of a perceptual-motor program for children with learning disabilities.

The discussion is based on the following premises:

1. The program should include only those for whom some benefit is possible.

2. Perceptual-motor programs have value for underachievers and those with learning disabilities who have *related* motor dysfunctioning.

3. For normal children up to and including the first grade level, it appears that the effectiveness of the program is minimal. For normal children beyond that level, there is no value in involving them in the program.

4. The program must be on an individualized basis, pointed toward certain academic objectives.

5. Perceptual-motor programs are not a replacement or substitute for physical education.

6. Attention must be given not only to the execution of a perceptual-motor movement, but also to the quality of that movement. For example, if a child is given the challenge to hop in the pattern of a triangle, he must give thought not only to accomplishing the task, but also to how well he is able to hop.

7. Movement should be performed at a medium to a slow pace. Faster movement is often uncontrolled movement, and as such defeats the purpose of the lesson.

Historically, perceptual-motor programs have evolved from attempts to remedy learning disabilities, not to enhance normal learning rates. Much has been made of the relationship between motor dysfunctioning and low academic achievement, but studies have failed to substantiate a significant *direct* relationship. If the perceptual-motor dysfunction underlying the academic difficulty can be given attention, however, the child can make progress. It might be said that perceptual-motor programs improve little more than the motor qualities being practiced.

One point should be clarified. The cause-and-effect relationship between motor performance and intelligence has not been established. By improving skill performance of mentally retarded children, intelligence levels will not necessarily increase. On the other hand, one cannot say that brilliant children are always the most highly skilled.

Another debatable point is whether or not there is an "incubation" effect; that is, that a period of time, perhaps years, must pass before the effects of a perceptual-motor program can be determined in relation to academic performance. Controlled studies to support this hypothesis are most difficult to implement in such a way that the variable can be isolated and valid conclusions drawn.

There is no question about the premise that perceptual-motor programs of sufficient depth and intensity can develop movement competency, but the development of skills *per se* does not lead automatically to better academic performance.

Some educators hold that while academic performance in reading, writing, and spelling is not directly improved, certain concomitant values derived from such a program develop needed personal qualities. With the emphasis on success and the development of a positive self-concept, it is postulated that a more secure basis is laid for facing the problems of the academic challenges. In addition, such critical skills as listening to absorb direction, following directions, visual perception, and reproducing as directed can be enhanced by perceptual-motor programs, which may then have a positive effect on classroom performance.

As a child's competence in movement increases, a definitive effect on his personality may be seen. Since peer groups respect skill attainment and welcome into play those who can perform at a similar level with themselves, becoming adept in respected skills has an impact on personality. A child loves to be respected and accepted, and this acceptance can be triggered by a peer-linked skill attainment. It can be reasoned that acceptance by peers heightens an individual's general regard for school and can, in turn, have a desirable effect on overall school performance.

Another line of reasoning should be brought in. It is possible that some children react favorably to the individual attention given them in the program, together with the encouragement and relaxed atmosphere. This is called the "halo" effect, meaning that the child achieves well because achievement is expected of him. For some children in a remedial program, this may be the first time they have been singled out for special attention and individual work.

While value for increased academic performance is difficult to substantiate from a research viewpoint, most educators teaching perceptual-motor programs are strongly dedicated and convinced that there is good value in their execution. Some feeling is present among these educators that the program has good merit, in that it ensures that all students receive a sound foundation of perceptual-motor learning as a preventative measure. This, however, is also difficult to substantiate.

Characteristics of the Child with Learning Disabilities

The learning-disabled child is defined as one who possesses normal intelligence but, for some unexplained reason, fails to achieve on a level comparable to that of his fellow students of similar aptitude. Approximately 15 to 20 percent of children in the early elementary grades have been diagnosed as having learning problems to the extent that they may be regarded as learning-disabled. In a large proportion of these children, evidence of perceptual-motor deficiencies is present.

A caution must be observed in attaching labels to children with regard to learning problems. Simply to pigeonhole a child as "clumsy" solves no problems and relegates the child to a category from which he will find it difficult to escape. Some children thought to be disabled may simply be immature, while other children may be slow starters.

Children with learning disabilities may display, but do not always display, a number of the following characteristics:

1. The child fails to achieve; that is, he does not respond to learning tasks, does not follow directions, does not pay attention to the teacher, or fails to complete his tasks in responsible fashion. This may reflect incapability or willful choice.

2. The child may demonstrate undesirable behavior traits by not starting or trying, and he shows little desire or interest in class. This child may exhibit negative class behavior or may exceed behavior limits.

3. The child may be quiet and withdrawn. In addition, he may be rejected by the peer group and in need of security and success.

4. The slow learner is often below average in coordination and muscular development.

5. The child may show sensitivity about his failure to live up to parental expectations.

With respect to motor dysfunctioning, the following signs may appear:

1. The youngster may have trouble holding or maintaining balance. The lack of coordination is evidenced by a certain clumsiness and lack of fine motor control.

2. The child may show evidence of dysfunction in lateral dominance, which refers to the ability to do things well or better with the hand or limb on one side of the body. The youngster may not know right from left and may have to hesitate or think carefully before being able to come up with a definite movement or answer to a direction.

3. Spatial orientation is another area in which indications can appear. The child may have difficulty in gauging where he is in space with respect to his body, and may bump and collide with objects and other children. Hand-eye coordination may be poor, with the youngster finding little success in handling the simple tools of physical education, i.e., beanbags, balls, and other objects that involve a visual-motor-perceptual relationship.

How Can These Children Be Identified?

Two general means can be employed in discovering individuals with learning problems and related motor dysfunctions. The first way is through teacher observation, guided by the characteristics of the slow learner and his lack of coordination and movement competence. The teacher may note that the child exhibits problems in learning situations and decides that the child's coordination and movement patterns should be checked. On the other hand, the teacher may observe an inept and uncoordinated child and recommend that the child's academic performance be examined to see if related learning problems exist.

A second means of discovering such individuals is the use of a formulated test, which covers the important variables of perceptual-motor dysfunctioning. These variables can be roughly classified into four categories of test items, although not all tests include all four.

1. *Body image.* This category includes knowledge of the name and functions of the different parts of the body. It also covers internal awareness of right and left parts.

2. *Balance and postural control factors.* Balance and postural controls are inseparable; a person cannot develop one without affecting the other. A variety of both static and dynamic balance tasks are found in perceptual-motor evaluation instruments.

3. *Time-space relationships.* This category includes the ability to move to rhythm and move the body effectively in relation to the challenges of the environment. A child should be able to gauge body movement with ease and without error in going over, under, around, and through articles and following various pathways.

4. *Coordination.* Coordination involves moving the separate parts of the body with ease and control and integrating the movements of body parts. It implies good ability to change from one pattern to another and to produce unilateral, bilateral, and cross-lateral movements on demand.

Current tests generally include a variety of test items, so that broad discrimination is possible. The tests, however, vary a good deal in the selection of items; even the choice of a test for a particular perceptual factor may vary. In assessing balance control, for example, some sources test static balance by use of held balance positions, while others test dynamic balance by observing control with balance beam movements. Tests in general have few items of objective measurement, but rely on the element of subjective judgment.

Sensory Motor Awareness Survey

Sensorimotor training is an integral part of the curriculum of the Early Child Education Project of the Dayton, Ohio, public schools. The emphasis is on a preventative program for all children rather than a remedial program for a selected few. As a part of the program, the following survey is used to provide information about each child.

The test is used in the Dayton schools as a screening device. If a child does not score well in any of the areas, he or she is given special help. Total score is not used.

It should be noted that the test includes some cognitive items such as form recognition and identification.

DAYTON SENSORY MOTOR AWARENESS SURVEY FOR FOUR- AND FIVE-YEAR-OLDS

Date of Test _____

Name _____ Sex _____ Birth _____ Center _____

Body Image. One-half point for each correct part; nine points possible.

_____ 1. Ask the child to touch the following body parts:

Head_____ Ankles_____ Ears_____ Stomach_____ Elbows_____

Toes_____ Nose_____ Legs_____ Chin_____ Back_____

Eyes_____ Feet_____ Mouth_____ Waist_____

Wrists_____ Chest_____ Fingers_____ Shoulders_____

Space and Directions. One-half point for each correct direction; five points possible.

_____ 2. Ask the child to point to the following directions:

Front _____ Back _____ Up _____ Down _____ Beside you _____

Place two blocks on a table about 1 inch apart. Ask the child to point:

Under _____ Over _____ To the top _____ To the bottom _____ Between _____

Balance. Score two points if accomplished.

_____ 3. Have the child stand on tiptoes, on both feet, with eyes open for 8 seconds.

Balance and Laterality. Score two points for each foot; four points possible.

_____ 4. Have the child stand on one foot, eyes closed, for 5 seconds. Alternate feet.

Reprinted by permission of the Dayton, Ohio, public schools, W. T. Braley, consultant.

DAYTON SENSORY MOTOR AWARENESS SURVEY FOR FOUR- AND FIVE-YEAR-OLDS—Continued

Laterality.   Score two points if the child keeps his feet together and does not lead off with one foot.

_____ 5.   Have the child jump forward on two feet.

Rhythm and Neuromuscular Control.   Score two points for each foot if accomplished six times; four points possible.

_____ 6.   Have the child hop on one foot. Hop in place.

Rhythm and Neuromuscular Control.   Score two points.

_____ 7.   Have the child skip forward. Child must be able to sustain this motion around the room for approximately 30 feet.

Integration of Right and Left Sides of the Body.   Score two points if cross-patterning is evident for each.

_____ 8.   Have the child creep forward.

_____ 9.   Have the child creep backward.

Eye-Foot Coordination.   Score two points if done the length of tape or mark.

_____ 10.   Use an 8 foot tape or chalk mark on the floor. The child walks in a crossover step the length of the tape or mark.

Fine Muscle Control.   Score two points if paper is completely crumpled. Score one point if paper is partially crumpled. Score zero points if child needs assistance or changes hands.

_____ 11.   Using a half sheet of newspaper, the child picks up the paper with one hand and puts the other hand behind his back. He then attempts to crumple the paper in his hand. He may not use his other hand, the table, or his body for assistance.

Form Perception.   Score one point for each correct match.

_____ 12.   Using a piece of paper with 2 inch circles, squares, and triangles, ask the child to point to two objects that are the same.

Form Perception.   Score one point if circle is identified correctly. Score two points if the triangle and square are identified correctly.

_____ 13.   Ask the child to identify by saying, "Point to the circle." "Point to the square." "Point to the triangle."

Hearing Discrimination.   Score one point if the child taps correctly each time.

_____ 14.   Ask the child to turn his back to you. Tap the table with a stick three times. Ask the child to turn around and tap the sticks the same way. Ask the child to turn his back to you. Tap the table again with the sticks (two quick taps, pause, then two more quick taps). Have the child turn back to you and tap out the rhythm.

Eye-Hand Coordination.   Score one point for each successful completion.

_____ 15.   A board is used with three holes in it. The holes are ¾, ⅝, and ½ inch in diameter. The child is asked to put his finger through the holes without touching the sides.

SPECIALIZED PERCEPTUAL-MOTOR ACTIVITIES

The following activities have been included in special programs for children with movement problems.

Crawling and Creeping Patterns

1. Unilateral crawling—crawl forward on hands and knees, using the arm and leg on the same side together.

2. Bilateral movement—move forward, reaching out with both hands and then bringing the feet up to the hands (Bunny Jump).

3. Cross-lateral crawling—crawl forward, moving the right arm and the left leg at the same time, and vice versa.

Variations. Move forward, backward, sideward, make quarter-turns right and left.

Add turning the head first toward the leading hand and then opposite to it, coordinating with each movement.

Command Movements Involving Jumping, Hopping, and Turning

1. Jump forward, backward, sideward. Jump in patterns.

2. Hop forward, backward, and sideward, stressing right and left.

3. Hop in various combinations: R-1, L-1; L-1, R-1; R-2, L-2; L-2, R-2; R-2, L-1; L-2, R-1. (The notation R-1, L-1 means to hop once on the right and once on the left.) In addition to the combinations listed, others can be devised.

4. Jump with quarter-turns right and left; half-turns right and left.

5. Establish the directions (east, south, west, north) and call out directions with the children making jump turns.

Command Movements— Angels in the Snow

Children are on their backs with hands at the sides and feet together. On any command, the arms and legs, as designated, move out and then back along the floor. The directions are given as follows:

"Right arm, left leg—*move*" (pause) "*back*."

Then alternate the words "out" and "back," repeating each movement six to ten times.

Angels in the Snow

The following movements are suggested:

Bilateral—both arms, both legs, both arms and both legs together

Unilateral—right (or left) arm, right (or left) leg, right arm and right leg together, left arm and left leg together

Cross-lateral—right arm and left leg, left arm and right leg

Note. The Angels in the Snow exercises were originally designed to be given by the examiner pointing to an arm or leg and saying, "Move that arm [leg]." This, however, is individual activity and not generally suitable for group work. Children could work in pairs, however, and this movement challenge could be given.

Command Movements—Standing Position

These movements follow the same command pattern as Angels in the Snow, with the directive given first, followed by the execution command, "Move." The position is held until the leader says, "Back." Children should learn to exercise good control in waiting without preliminary movement until the command "Move" is given, at which time they make the prescribed movement. The initial movement is held until the teacher can check the accuracy of the response. Two approaches can be used. The first is to change from one pattern to another, without repetition of any pattern. The other is to repeat a pattern as when giving exercises. Repeat six to ten times.

Types of movements that are effective are:

Right arm, right leg forward (unilateral)
Left arm, right leg forward (cross-lateral)
Both arms forward (bilateral)
Both feet forward—a jump (bilateral)

Add the turn of the head to the movements. The head is usually turned toward the arm that is moved forward, but this can vary. Such a command would be, "Right arm and left foot forward, head right—*move*."

Side steps left and right can be used, with arms still moving forward and head turning as directed.

Imitation of Movements

The children stand facing the teacher so that all can see the teacher. Feet are apart enough for good balance (six to twelve inches), and arms are at the sides. The teacher makes various definite movements, starting with the arms. Arm and leg movements in combinations are also to be imitated. Children imitate the movements on the same side (right for the teacher, left for the children). There should be emphasis on all three types of movement—unilateral, bilateral, and cross-lateral. A mixture of movements are done to the side first. Later, forward movements of the arms can be added.

GAMES

Some games based on imitation of movements are useful and fun for the children. In Do This, Do That, the child imitates the movement as done when the leader says, "Do this!" When the leader says, "Do that!" no one is to move. Those caught can have points scored against them. The game Simon Says follows the same principles, with the children moving when the command is preceded by "Simon says."

In another, similar game, the leader attempts to confuse the children by giving directions, which they are to follow, and then making a different movement. For example, the leader can say, "Touch your shoulders," and at the same time put his hands on his hips. The children are to follow the verbal directions only.

Obstacles

Wands and chairs can be used as obstacles. A wand over the top of two chairs makes an obstacle under which the children move. They move underneath without touching, backward or sideward as well as forward. Another obstacle can be made by having a wand over the seats of two low chairs or over 12-inch hurdle blocks. The children step over this barrier without touching it. A hoop can be held by a partner, allowing the child to crawl through without touching.

An effective obstacle arrangement can be structured with traffic cones, blocks, wands, and a hoop or tire supported on a stand.

The child goes over the first wand, under the second, and through the hoop. Repeated efforts should employ variety in the different ways a child may meet the challenge of the obstacles.

Blast-off Launcher

A Blast-off Launcher, of which commercial varieties exist, can be used to provide challenge for hand-eye coordination. The child places a beanbag on the launch pad, propels the bag into the air with a forceful stamp of the foot on the end of the launcher, and catches the bag. Challenge with different combinations of catching and employ either foot in the launching process.

Baseball Rebound Net and Stand

A rebound net frame of the type used for baseball practice can be used with beanbags and balls to exercise hand-eye coordination. The child tosses or throws the object against the net, from which it is rebounded.

Balloon Keep-It-Up

The task for the child is to keep one or more balloons in the air by repeatedly striking them with a selected instrument, such as a small paddle, wand, small bat, or baton. This should give

exercise to ocular tracking and spatial estimation. Sufficient room is necessary, and extra balloons will be needed.

Identifying Body Parts

The purpose of this activity is for the child to learn and know the precise location of the named body parts and be able to touch them with both hands without looking at his body or securing cues from other children. Children stand and face the teacher, who says:

"Touch your shoulders."
"Touch your hips."
"Touch your head."
"Touch your ankles."
"Touch your ears."
"Touch your toes."
"Touch your eyes."
"Touch your elbows."
"Touch your knees."

Early in the activity, after each direction, children repeat the following, "I am touching my _____ ," inserting the correct term. The teacher may do the activity with the children during the initial phases, but should revert to verbal cues as soon as practical.

Stepping Stones

A number of red and black asphalt or vinyl tiles are needed. Twenty to thirty are sufficient to form interesting patterns. Involved in this activity are foot-eye coordination and right-left discrimination.

Arrange the tiles in a formation that varies from the straight line, so that children have a challenge of different stepping patterns. The object is for the child to step on red tiles with the right foot and black tiles with the left. Mark the child's feet with the appropriate color, using ribbons, garters, crepe paper, or something similar. Give the following instruction: "Your right foot is marked with a red ribbon, and your left with a black. You are to walk down the pathway of tiles, stepping on red tiles with your right foot and black tiles with your left. You must always step on the very next square and you are not to skip any tiles."

You can tell the child to say, "I will step on the red tiles with my right foot and the black tiles with my left."

The pace should be definite but not hurried. After some practice, more difficult patterns can be laid out. The child can also walk to the beat of a drum or to the rhythm of music appropriate for walking.

Many types of step patterns are available on the commercial market, some employing only stepping, and others providing challenge to movement memory.

Form Recognition and Sequence Building with Geometric Forms

Geometric forms of two sizes are needed in each of the following shapes: circle, triangle, square, and rectangle. Thus, a set of forms consists of eight shapes, four large and four small. Sets should be painted in two colors, with random selection from large and small shapes. A support for each shape is made from a piece of wood.

Two kinds of activities can be employed with the shapes:

Shapes Placed Flat on the Floor. Challenges can be structured as follows:

"Can you walk around the largest circle?"
"Jump three times inside the large circle, hop once inside the small triangle, and return."
"Take the weight on the hands inside the red rectangle, balance on one foot inside the blue circle, and return."

Shapes Standing Upright in Supports. The purpose is to go through the shapes without touching them. Various means of going through can be specified, such as head first, feet first, on your back, etc. Sequence building is also important. Some challenge illustrations follow:

"Go through the large circle and back through the small triangle."
"Go through the small circle head· first, through the large triangle feet first, and return through the large rectangle as you wish."
"Crawl to the large triangle, then to the small circle, and then to the big rectangle."

Floor Ladder Activities

A wooden ladder is placed on mats and used as a floor target for a number of activities. The child begins at one end of the ladder and performs while moving along its length. Activity challenges that are of value are:

"Walk, run, hop, or jump between the ladder rungs, moving forward and to the side."
"Walk on the rungs, balancing carefully on each. Do not touch the floor."
"Do different movements on hands and feet on the rungs and on the sides of the ladder."

Free choice of movements. The child creates his own patterns.

It is important that all movements be done under good control and that the child be given creative opportunity to come up with his own selection of movement.

Balance Boards

Balance boards are small devices on which the child tries to stand and keep the board in balance. Generally, a balance board has either a circular or square platform about 15 inches wide and a rounded bottom to provide the challenge for balance. A rubber pad should protect the floor. The activities are somewhat limited, consisting of maintaining balance with a variety of challenges. See p. 344 for a description of the various types of balance boards.

SEQUENCE OF ACTIVITIES

1. Secure a balanced position on the board. Change position of arms.
2. Secure balance and gradually lower the body to touch the board.
3. Change from a two-foot to a one-foot balance. Change from one foot to the other. Move the feet together and move them apart.
4. Tilt forward until the front edge of the board touches the floor and return to the starting position. Also try tilting backward, right, and left.
5. Hold and maintain balance while performing the following tasks:
    a. Bounce and catch a ball with two hands.
    b. Toss a ball into the air and catch it with both hands.
    c. Try both of the above stunts with one hand.
    d. Dribble a ball and keep track of the number of successful bounces made without losing balance.
    e. Twirl a hoop on various body parts and maintain balance.
    f. Jump rope on the board.
    g. Do some of the above activities with eyes closed.
6. Balance on various body parts such as knees, tummy, and seat.
7. Jump from the floor to the board and gain balance without touching the floor.
8. Pick up a beanbag from the board.
9. Balance on the board with a partner.
10. Start from a standing position on the board and move to a kneeling position. Reverse and move to standing position.
11. Toss and catch beanbags, balls, or hoops with a partner. Change a hoop from performer's

arm to partner, without stopping the twirling or losing balance.

Bounding Boards

Bounding boards provide a unique type of movement similar to that of bouncing on a trampoline. Such a board can be constructed easily from a piece of three-quarter-inch plywood, size two feet by six feet. The board is supported on pieces of four-by-four-inch lumber, which are padded with carpet to protect the floor. The plywood must be a quality product with few knots. Marine plywood, though expensive, is the best.

Two children can work on one board, with the performer moving forward to leave the board and return back to place. Emphasis should be on lightness, height, and relaxation during the bounding. For the most part, bounding should be done in the center of the board.

SEQUENCE OF ACTIVITIES

1. Bound in the center: two feet, one foot.
2. Bound in the center, using turns and different arm positions. Add hand-clapping.
3. Move across the board, using jumping and hopping. Return. Add turns and hand-clapping.
4. Bound with numbered foot combinations, alternating two, three, or four hops on one foot and then changing to the other. These are called twoseys, threeseys, and fourseys.
5. To the previous skills, add forward and backward leg extensions and leg changes sideward.
6. Use different numbers of hops when alternating, such as hopping once on the right foot and twice on the left. Use other combinations such as 2-3, 2-4, etc.
7. Add rope-jumping with slow time and fast time. Use hoops.

Bounding Devices

Mini-trampolines and tire tubes with platforms on them for rebounding provide experiences similar to those on the bounding board.

Ocular Pursuit

Several activities that seem outside the realm of physical education should be discussed. The first of these is ocular pursuit, which concerns practicing eye muscular control in tracking objects. This is accomplished in several ways, but essentially all the methods stress a fixed head position and having the eyes follow a moving object. One means is to have the eyes track a ball that swings back and forth on a three-foot string with movement similar to that of a pendulum.

Another method is to follow visually a ball rolled back and forth across the floor from a distance about ten yards away. A device employing a series of inclined troughs to guide the path of a ball or marble has some use. The ball drops down from one level to another in a regular path, and the eyes follow its movements.

There is some doubt whether the use of ocular pursuit for the specific development of eye musculature should be included in physical education programs. This seems to trespass on optometry and the province of the oculist.

Another area of emphasis is chalkboard work during which the child makes required patterns with chalk on a chalkboard. The usual patterns are large circles, which are made with each hand in turn and with both hands together. Repetition and comformity to a selected pattern govern this procedure. This kind of activity may better be carried on in the classroom.

THE PERCEPTUAL-MOTOR TEAM

The physical education instructor should be a member of the perceptual-motor team, since coordination and movement competence are major goals of that program. He can cooperate with special perceptual-motor programs and can also give encouragement and special help in the regular physical education program to individuals identified as needing such aid. The instructor can effectively encourage and support the efforts of other personnel in helping children solve their problems. In particular, he can make sure the child achieves, has a measure of success in his efforts, and does not become threatened by situations he perceives to be too difficult.

SUMMARY

Perception in motor learning involves discrimination through certain sense mechanisms: auditory, kinesthetic, tactile, visual, and balance. Activities used in the regular program to enhance perceptual-motor abilities are offered in the first half of the chapter. Auditory, visual, kinesthetic, and tactile discrimination skills are discussed, as are balance, laterality, and directionality skills necessary to develop a fully functioning person.

Perceptual-motor programs for children with learning disabilities should be offered in addition to the regular physical education program and should include those children for whom some benefit is possible. Perceptual-motor programs appear to be most beneficial for underachievers and those with learning disabilities who have related motor dysfunctioning. In most cases, the program is individualized and based on the child's diagnosed needs.

In diagnosing youngsters with perceptual-motor dysfunctions, four variables are usually evaluated: body image, balance and postural control factors, time-space relationships, and co-ordination of body parts, along with integration of body parts. The specialized perceptual-motor program offers many activities that deal with specific problem areas. Command movements, creeping and crawling patterns, imitation of movements, and activities on equipment such as balance boards, bounding boards, and various obstacles are examples of program content.

REFERENCES

Barsch, Ray H. *Achieving Perceptual-Motor Efficiency.* Seattle, Wash.: Special Child Publications, 1967.

Cratty, Bryant. *Perceptual and Motor Development in Infants and Children.* Los Angeles, Calif.: Macmillan Co., 1970.

Delacato, Carl H. *The Diagnosis and Treatment of Speech and Reading Problems.* Springfield, Ill.: Charles C. Thomas, 1963.

Frostig, Marianne, and Horne, David. "An Approach to the Treatment of Children with Learning Disorders." In *Learning Disorders,* edited by J. Hellmuth, vol. 1, pp. 293–305. Seattle, Wash.: Special Child Publications, 1965.

Kephart, Newell C. *The Slow Learner in the Classroom.* Columbus, Ohio: Charles E. Merrill Books, 1960.

Chapter 19

Children with Special Needs—Special Education

*We are all faced with a series of great opportunities—
brilliantly disguised as insoluble problems.*

John Gardner

The problem of providing a full range of learning experiences in the public schools for handicapped children in the United States is monumental, as there are more than eight million such children. Children with handicapping conditions include mentally retarded, hearing-impaired, visually impaired, speech-impaired, seriously emotionally disturbed, orthopedically impaired, and neurologically handicapped children, as well as those with other health-impairing conditions and specific learning disabilities. In addition, the teacher needs to consider children with postural problems that are not serious enough for them to be termed orthopedically handicapped, children with motor problems (poorly coordinated children), obese children, and those whose levels of physical fitness are abnormally low.

Much benefit can be derived through early recognition of problems followed by appropriate remedial measures at the preschool and primary levels, when many of the handicapping conditions can be markedly helped. Later, these conditions become more fixed for the individual and less responsive to helpful measures. Also, the earlier a child learns to live with a handicap, the more effective will the necessary adjustment be.

The terms "special children" and "exceptional children" are other ways of referring to handicapped children. In the discussions that follow, these terms will be used interchangeably. Programs for the handicapped are also termed Special Education. The main thrust of the discussions as they evolve will be on physi-cal education programs as they affect the handicapped.

PUBLIC LAW 94-142

With the advent of Public Law 94-142 (94th Congress, 1975), the Education for All Handicapped Children Act, a new day has dawned for the handicapped child. The basic purpose of the law is to: assure that all handicapped children have available to them a free and appropriate education that emphasizes special education and related services to meet their particular needs, assure that the rights of handicapped children and their parents or guardians are protected, provide assistance to states and local education associations to provide for the education of all handicapped children, and institute assessment practices to assure the effectiveness of efforts to educate handicapped children. The federal government, in addition to outlining the format by which handicapped children are to be educated, will provide funds to implement the provisions of the law.

PRESCHOOL EMPHASIS FOR THE SPECIAL CHILD

To prepare children for successful school experiences and to make mainstreaming a reality, professionals are advising and implementing programs to help preschool children with special problems. Public Law 94-142 has a component for providing special services to handicapped children aged three through five. The law is somewhat nebulous as to how these services are to be implemented and provided, however. Funds can be allotted separately and independently of school programs.

Since preschool education is usually not an area of emphasis in school districts, outside agencies, many organized especially for the purpose, have taken the lead in establishing programs to help preschool handicapped youngsters. Many of these programs, however, are a downward extension of what is already going on in the school and the community.

The goal of these programs, some of which admit children below the age of three, is to help children acquire the ability to learn effectively conceptual and cognitive skills and to reach levels of development (fine and gross motor skills) essential for subsequent learning and school adjustment. The key words are early intervention, which can prevent consequent school failure and emotional trauma. Emphasis should be on total development; the program should not single out cognition, physical qualities, preacademic skills, or sociability, or pay attention to the handicapping conditions alone. Many professionals are convinced that, to be maximally effective, such programs should begin just as soon as the handicapping condition has been identified, regardless of age. The programs are based on the concept that children acquire a significant proportion of their learning before the age of six, and that this period should be utilized for those who need special preparation to meet the future challenges of the school environment.

Two misconceptions should be rejected as not in the best interests of children. The first is that one must accept the inevitable, that "nothing can be done for the child; just take the child home and love him." All children can learn, but they learn at different rates. An outstanding elementary teacher provides this bit of pertinent, well-stated educational philosophy: "You don't ever, ever give up on a child." [1]

The second misconception is shared by those who advise the parents to wait until the child is older before attempting to remedy his condition. Such good advice usually goes: "It's too early for effective treatment; wait until the child is ready."

The process for working with handicapped children is essentially threefold:

1. Identifying children with needs and diagnosing those needs. Communication, auditory and visual functioning, preacademic learning skills, motor skills, social skills, and health qualities should be considered.

2. Doing something about the children's needs. This concerns both the items to be stressed as revealed by the pretesting and the approach necessary to gain the target objectives.

3. Record-keeping and establishing an ongoing program. When the child reaches kindergarten, the accumulated information should be made available to the teacher to provide the next logical step in a continuing program of special concern throughout the child's entire school career—elementary, junior high, senior high school. The child's needs at any subsequent level should be given attention based on his prior achievement as recorded in the child's dossier.

Teachers have no trouble identifying young children with severe or obvious handicaps, but they can overlook some of the mildly or moderately handicapped. Communities should look into establishing agencies that can accomplish valid diagnosis and provide a sound basis for the treatment that is to follow. Few such agencies exist now in the community, but their number is increasing.

In the area of remedial treatment, most preschool programs function as Parent Education Programs (PEP). A PEP agency center, staffed usually by a child development specialist, provides overall direction and supervision. The actual fieldwork is done mainly by volunteer paraprofessionals. The volunteer teaches the parent, and the parent, in turn, teaches the child. Volunteers need training in home visiting techniques so that they can use their remedial expertise effectively. The usual pattern is for the volunteer to visit the home once per week for about an hour. Paraprofessionals are usually given compensation on an hourly basis plus travel allowance.

Among the agencies, assigned home visit loads weekly ranged from ten to twenty per volunteer, with fifteen as a central figure. Some agencies reserve one day per week, usually Friday, for record-keeping, planning, and discussions with staff and other volunteers.

The volunteer-parent relationship should be one of trust, with information about the family kept confidential. The volunteer can suggest, but it is the parent who makes the decision regarding direction. Common sense is an absolute requirement for the volunteer. A sense of humor and the ability to laugh are needed quali-

---

[1]This statement is attributed to Mrs. Ella May Zuroske, an elementary school teacher in the Pullman, Washington, school system. Mrs. Zuroske, a friend of the authors, was named in 1980 Educator of the Year in the state of Washington.

ties, as is a genuine feeling of concern for the child and the attendant problems.

The PEP approach can help parents provide emotional security and a comfortable, non-threatening learning experience. They need to understand the importance of early identification of child problems and to establish an effective means of meeting youngsters' needs. The parent can take an interest in the process and has a part to play in the child's destiny. In comparison with teachers, parents have a stronger and more long-lasting influence on the preschool child. The goal is to guide this influence to function in the best interests of the child.

Mostly, there is a need to change parent behavior, as few parents have the necessary skills to facilitate commendable progress. Sometimes parents do only what they want to do, and the task becomes one of parent motivation. Parents derive motivation when they see change; but it is even more important for the child to see progress. The PEP system seeks to provide parents with management skills for organizing learning and developmental activities to take care of the special, identified needs.

Parents can be aided in a variety of ways, beginning with the establishment of good rapport, followed by liberal doses of encouragement from the volunteer. Breaking down target goals into smaller increments of steps along the way is of prime concern. Some programs furnish handouts (task cards), which provide guidance in the progressions. Concentrating on a few factors at a time is thought to be of value, although focus on the whole child must not be lost.

An area of concern in home programs is the lack of opportunity for the development of social skills, primarily among the severely retarded and handicapped. Children should have social contacts with peers; when this is lacking, scheduled group activity is indicated. Mainstreaming can begin on this modest basis.

For the children, certain goals can be proposed. Independence (learning to manage alone) and interdependence (working with others) should be stressed. The pace should be comfortable, challenging, appropriate to the cultural background of the child, and within his capacity. Communication and language goals should accompany physical and developmental goals. Learning deficiencies should be given parallel attention, and behavior may need to be modified. The key word in all programs is individualization, which connotes pretesting, ongoing testing, and posttesting. Record-keeping is most important, and progress charts are helpful.

Programs are based on the principle that all children can learn, albeit they learn at different and personalized rates, and that parents can function as important facilitators of learning. The more severe the handicap, perhaps, the more structured the learning sequences should be. The old adage that "nothing succeeds like success" is most relevant in PEP programs.

Overall progress can be seen as occurring in stages. In stage one, the key should be that the child responds to the learning environment with pleasure. In the second stage, he responds with success, learning individual skills and concepts. The third stage reflects values learned through group participation—cooperation, sharing, establishing friendships, and the like. In Parent Education Programs, this last stage may not be fully realized, but one can still develop some group skills that are important for successful entry into the kindergarten level.

The degree of retardation, delayed progress, and/or physical handicap will certainly govern the direction of treatment. Attention may be needed to teach the nonwalking child to stand and walk; help the handicapped child to adjust to a prosthetic device or wheelchair; and guide the efforts of the motor-deficient child to walk, run, jump, hop, and skip, as well as to walk up and down stairs. Self-help skills, such as toilet training, personal hygiene, dressing oneself, and feeding oneself may need development. Programs should concentrate first on maintaining and reinforcing gains and later on accelerating development, particularly in the case of severe retardates and developmentally delayed children.

From this underlying basis, programs can take many directions, depending upon results of pretesting. Further development of gross motor skills can be given attention. A variety of movement activities featuring balance, directionality, body awareness, laterality, right-left discrimination, hand-eye and foot-eye coordination, and other perceptually oriented challenges should be instituted.

Growth of fine motor skills can be enhanced by manipulative activities such as sorting, threading, cutting, matching, and other tactile challenges. Emphasis centers on using articles normally found in most homes.

Preacademic skills include listening (as opposed to simply hearing), following directions, completing tasks, form and letter recognition, understanding simple number concepts, color discrimination, and simple word recognition. Sequencing, combining, and reproducing are valuable experiences, which can be reinforced in selected movement challenges. The program should stress the development of a positive self-concept and a constructive attitude toward learning.

In conclusion, it should be emphasized that a remedial program should be inaugurated as early as possible for the child, and should be regarded as the beginning of a coordinated plan covering the child's entire school career.

KINDERGARTEN AND PRIMARY SCHOOL EMPHASIS FOR THE SPECIAL CHILD

For children in kindergarten and primary school, the principle of early intervention still holds. Some type of screening should be done, ideally before school begins, but, if necessary, early in the year. Screening serves to identify conditions not uncovered during the preschool years. Even when a preschool remedial program exists, some children with special needs may not have been in the preschool program.

Concerning those children who were in preschool remedial programs, the records should be made available to the kindergarten teacher. A teacher can work more effectively with a child if these are known: (1) the entry behaviors the child presently exhibits, (2) skills the child has yet to learn, (3) special developmental needs, and (4) related information pertaining to the background of the child.

Public Law 94-142 stipulates that every handicapped child be afforded the opportunity to participate in the regular program of education unless it has been determined by a due process that participation with peers in the regular classroom situation is not in the best interests of the child. To participate fully in public education becomes a fundamental right of handicapped children, and the handicapped must be educated in the least restrictive environment possible. This process is known as mainstreaming. Literally, this term means integrating the handicapped child into the mainstream of living.

What particular relevance does the law have for physical education? Under its provisions, physical education becomes a required content area and educational experience of all handicapped children's programs. It is worthy of note that physical education is the only educational discipline mentioned in the law. The provision of physical education services is regarded as an essential and integral part of the handicapped child's education and highly important in the physical development and well-being of such children. The term "physical education" has been defined in the law to include: (1) physical and motor fitness; (2) fundamental motor skills and patterns; and (3) skills in aquatics, dance, and individual and group games and sports. The term further includes special physical education, adapted physical education, movement ed-

ucation, and motor development. All handicapped children, then, must be given the opportunity to participate in the regular physical education program available to nonhandicapped children, unless it is prescribed that such participation is not in their best interests. In addition, this participation must meet the target goals of the child's individual education program.

The law requires that an individual education program (IEP) must be developed for every handicapped child. This program is to be developed by a designated committee including, but not limited to, the child's classroom teacher, a parent or guardian, special education personnel, a physical education representative, and a medical advisor as needed. The IEP is to specify target goals, educational content by which the goals can be implemented, support services, and evaluation procedures. Inclusion of a parent or guardian on the committee is considered vital, and, if necessary, arrangements are to be made for interpreters for parents who are deaf or do not speak English. The IEP will further state the extent to which the child will be able to participate in regular educational and physical education programs.

One aspect of the law that has caused some unfavorable comment is the necessity for children to be identified and labeled as handicapped individuals in order to come under its provisions, with funds being dispensed to school districts in proportion to the number of children so designated. To attach labels to children and pigeonhole them according to certain factors is contrary to educational principles.

MAINSTREAMING

Special students who are mainstreamed in public schools can be divided into three categories, according to how their needs are met educationally.

Regular Students. These students can function adequately in regular classes with or without the support of medical or counseling services.

Students with Supplementary Services. These students participate in regular classes on a full-time basis, but receive supplementary services either at school or in the home setting, usually under the guidance of a special education consultant.

Part-Time Students. These students' time is apportioned between regular and special classes, because the regular class experience will not meet their special needs entirely. Thus, they are under the guidance of both the regular classroom teacher and the special education instructor.

Students with more serious problems will be in special classes within a school, in a special school, or in home care. While the interests of the latter children are worthy of serious attention, the emphasis in these discussions will be on the integration of the exceptional student into the regular educational program as it affects physical education.

For younger children, the key to mainstreaming is the classroom teacher and/or physical education specialist. The teacher must be convinced that the handicapped child belongs in the regular classroom, and that he has or can acquire the special skills needed to serve this child. Mainstreaming is a radical change and one that must be faced. Some teachers may have handicapped children assigned to them without first having had the opportunity of dealing with their own feelings about these children. Until recently, teachers have been geared to identify special children and refer them for placement outside the regular classroom.

The problem is complicated when physical education enters the picture. Many a classroom teacher does not feel totally adequate to teach physical education; when one or more handicapped children, with their specialized IEP goals and implementation needs, are added to the class, the teacher may feel overburdened. Since most physical education for younger children is taught by the classroom teacher, this problem needs solution.

What about the effect of mainstreaming on both the regular students and the special child? Research and practice seem to provide good indication that the handicapped benefit markedly from being educated with children without handicaps, both in educational achievement and socially. As they observe increased participation by the handicapped in the regular classroom activities, educators are gradually being led to believe that mainstreaming helps normal children develop more positive attitudes toward special children. They are finding that the inclusion of special children does not hold back class progress and that behavior patterns of children without handicaps are not affected by the participation of special children.

A practice that has been of benefit to special education classes has been called "reverse mainstreaming." In this practice, groups of children without handicaps come into a special education physical education class and participate together with the special students. This participation should be a two-way street, with both groups deriving benefit. The emphasis is mostly social and recreation-oriented. Activities selected are those within the capacity of the handicapped group, but also fun and challenging for the visitors. The activities should be organized for small groups or the total group, so that handicapped and nonhandicapped children play together. For example, Wheelchair Dodgeball is an interesting, suitable game. A cageball (24-inch or 30-inch) is rolled by a wheelchair child so as to contact another child. This child then becomes It and rolls the ball to touch another child. Another game might be Guess Which Hand. Children take partners; one holds his hands behind his back. The other partner guesses which hand holds an object. If the guess is correct, the child loses the object to the guesser.

The session can be further glamorized by serving some kind of refreshments at the completion of the period.

DEVELOPING THE LEARNING ENVIRONMENT

A number of strategies and considerations are important in establishing the best possible learning environment for the exceptional child.

Acquiring Background on the Child and the Handicapping Condition

Through a perusal of literature, records, and the child's IEP, and consultation with pertinent supervisors and officials, the teacher should acquire a thorough understanding of the handicapping condition and its possible effect on the educational progress of the child. To understand what the child is faced with and must endure is the first step. This reinforces the need for the teacher to be involved early in the planning as a member of the child's guiding committee. For physical education, recommendations for movement and limitations for activity should be spelled out in the IEP.

The teacher must be aware that certain occurrences will negatively affect the child's self-concept and attempt to avert them. The ability to cope successfully with behaviors manifested by the handicapped individual is a needed strategy. An understanding of the complexities that affect the family structure of the child's home life can also be helpful. This background is essential if the child is to be integrated successfully into regular classroom living.

Cooperating with Support Services

Many children will be receiving special help provided by a variety of support services. Close cooperation by the teacher with the support services is certainly most desirable. The teacher needs to know and understand what the support groups are trying to accomplish, so that he may encourage and reinforce remedial measures in the classroom setting. Simply making the child available at prescribed times for special help is one direction of cooperation.

It becomes obvious that a team approach is needed. Frequent interchange of information concerning the child will be helpful to both the teacher and the special instructor. Cumulative records must be kept, to which each must contribute data. These data form a basis for planned meetings as well as providing a foundation for assessing progress.

The teacher should become knowledgeable with respect to where to turn for special help and which sources are of value to parents when they seek advice or help.

Preparing the Peer Group

Sooner or later, the peer group becomes aware of a child's limitations. Members of the child's class need guidance and direction in accepting the child fully as a person of worth. Guidance is necessary in helping children to learn how to judge when friendly assistance is in order and when it is unnecessary or unwanted. Genuine concern and respect for another child requires both dedication and guidance; few children come by these attributes naturally. Above all, the expression of pity is to be avoided.

To be accepted and, more than that, to be one of the gang are prime goals of the special child. If the association with the regular classroom accomplishes nothing more than that, it has accomplished much.

Providing a Climate of Success

Instructional strategies should be formulated individually for each exceptional child so that he or she is able not only to achieve and make progress, but to be conscious of making such progress. Establishing the appropriate learning environment predicates an individualized learning pattern based on the child's entry level and capacity to function. While generalized objectives of physical education apply to the exceptional student as they do to the regular student, the special student may not do as well. Personalized goals must be set and reviewed periodically.

When working with special children, teachers need to divide goals into subgoals, allowing children to make progress in small increments. To achieve and make progress is important, and children must be conscious of achieving.

Working Cooperatively with Parents

Now that special children are in school, parents have a legal right to be involved in the decision-making process regarding their children. The parent should be fully aware of the measures taken by the school to help the impaired child. In particular, approval should be secured from parents for procedures involving paramedical attention or unusual formats. No permission is required for those activities normally found in the regular curriculum.

Periodically, the parent should meet with the committee that is guiding the child's educational progress. Procedures for supplementing and continuing an effective learning environment in the home should be outlined. Information covering a basic explanation of the ailment, educational measures that the school is undertaking, and recommended home procedures to supplement the school approach are often helpful. Parents are entitled to know what the school is doing and what they can do to help at home.

INSTRUCTIONAL STRATEGIES

Instruction for the special learner must be individualized for the most part so that the objectives of the child's IEP can be realized. Since one of the child's needs (which could be an objective of the IEP) is contact with and acceptance by other children, integration with other children and group contacts need to be planned and monitored carefully. Ideally, other children should not only accept fully but also seek out the company of the handicapped child. The special child needs to be able to make a contribution to group effort and be respected for it. A variety of contacts with other children should be planned—with partners, by threes, or in small groups.

If much of the instruction for all students is personalized, then little problem will exist for the special learner. The program involves a continuum of diagnosing learning, social, and developmental needs, setting prescriptive procedures for meeting the needs, and periodically evaluating progress. The process becomes one of repetition of these steps.

Even though the law (P.L. 94-142) requires appropriate physical education experiences, the approach should be that the child can benefit materially from movement experiences designed to meet IEP goals. Socially, the experiences provide another bond with fellow students. Some special children undoubtedly have lived sheltered lives in their preschool years and have not been sufficiently challenged physically, a challenge that the physical education program should meet. The child should be included in the regular format of activities as much as feasible and have other activities altered or adapted as needed. The key for this child's success should be progress and not comparison with a possible norm.

Caution should be exercised whenever the competitive element enters the picture. All children, including the handicapped, might better be challenged to accomplish a stated number of movements ("Can you jump in three different ways?") than to perform more movements than anyone else ("How many times can you jump?"). In group work, the special child must be protected from those situations where his group suffers because of his inept performance. The rule of thumb is that the special child should make a contribution to the group and not be a detriment.

Another instructional approach is fragmentation of goals to provide intermediate steps toward stated goals. In this way, the child can see himself making progress, and this realization will stimulate him to further effort. A handicapped child may find difficulty in reaching the stated goal, but can make progress in increments toward that goal.

Attention to special physical elements can be important. A wheelchair child will need to develop grip and arm strength to the point where he can manipulate himself in and out of the chair without assistance. Partially sighted children who have a fear of running can substitute rope-jumping skills for this fundamental skill.

The start-and-expand approach for introducing activities is sound because this approach gives the handicapped a chance to succeed. The progressions are started at a low enough level to include the entry level of the handicapped. Progression then proceeds from that point. The learning rate for the special child should be one that is challenging but does not breed frustration and failure. The handicapped child, like others in the class, should be expected to put forth top effort in achieving progress. To allow the handicapped to get by with an indifferent performance because of lack of effort is certainly not sound methodology.

The handicapped child must be guided to an awareness that there may be activity challenges in class sessions that he cannot fully meet, or that there may be types of activities in which he cannot take part. In such a case, the movement challenge must be adapted for the special child without drawing attention to the change, if possible.

It may be appropriate for the child to take part in certain activities and movement patterns tailored to his special needs. Specialized help can be utilized here, with such assistance coming from teacher assistants, parent volunteers, older students (from middle, junior high, or senior high school), and cross-age help (peers). The child should be familiar with the expected levels of achievement so that he can help guide the efforts, thus becoming a partner in the developmental process.

The instructional method of approach for the special child may need to be more direct and less open-ended than for the normal child. Mentally retarded students need more explanation and demonstration, and movement patterns that are more limited and repetitive.

To what extent should class members be informed about the handicapped child's problems and condition? One guiding principle is that this be done without violating the child's privacy or personally embarrassing him. If the handicap is obvious and highly visible, then considerations become a matter of routine, probably handled mostly by incidental means. Common sense and good teacher judgment are the keys. In the case of a mentally retarded student, class members may not be keenly aware of this condition, except that they may recognize that the child is a little slower at accomplishing tasks.

Mentally Retarded Children

Children exhibiting retardation are classified in the learning situation according to the degree of disability in functioning. The classroom teacher will come in contact most often with children in the mildly retarded range (I.Q. from 50 to 75). Such a child has from one-half to three-quarters of the intelligence capacity and potential of a child with an I.Q. of 100. Children with an I.Q. below the level of 50 normally cannot function successfully in a regular classroom environment and need special classes. Normally, they are not mainstreamed successfully and are not a consideration in the discussions that follow.

A basic goal is to develop the capacity of the mildly retarded child to become integrated to function as a participating member of society. For such a child, mainstreaming becomes of prime importance.

The present level of achievement and performance of the child should dictate to the teacher what measures should be taken. Any approach must be based on accepting the child at his present level, while assuring the child that he is an individual of personal worth. No magic formula or panacea exists as a sure-fire solution to retardate problems. One must focus on the individual, not the activity.

The mildly retarded child derives great benefit from physical education, since the belief that these youngsters are also lacking in physical capacity is without foundation. They may have less resistance to fatigue, have less strength, and show more fatty tissue than normal children, but not necessarily. These conditions may be due to related causes, such as lack of attention and stimulation. Perhaps the youngster has not been sufficiently challenged to reach the levels of strength, coordination, and agility he may be capable of attaining. Perhaps the child has been pigeonholed as one who can't do this and can't do that, and he has reacted as expected.

For mildly retarded children, one should focus on success. Concentration on achieving and understanding simple skills can lead to better emotional stability and personality adjustment. But it does take patience, care, and individual attention. The approach must be personalized, even during group activity.

Attention should be centered on those ability traits that have the potential for progress. Developing these traits has value in terms of both self-regard and peer relationships. The positive approach, the positive emphasis, should be stressed.

Motivation is critical to helping mentally retarded children achieve. While praise judiciously given may have some effect, tangible awards may be the key to stimulate the child to try. Unless he tries, the handicapped child cannot achieve.

The pace of learning will be governed by the degree of retardation. Directions concerning how to proceed in a learning experience, which a normal child can digest, might not be clear to the retarded child. Before the child can achieve, he needs to know what is expected. Verbal directions should be kept short and simple. Demonstration may be needed to get the point across.

Progression increments in learning need to be made smaller and more definite. Simply exploring and finding out what can be done with a piece of equipment can become an unfruitful experience unless the child's efforts are directed.

The teacher may have mildly retarded students who are chronologically older and probably more skillful at some tasks than the other children. Some of these children will be grade repeaters. Assigning them responsibilities as helpers or equipment monitors, and giving them other tasks within their capacities, provides these children the recognition they need

Retarded children will benefit from participation in educational movement programs, where perceptual-motor skills are practiced.

Since many of these children show motor problems, it is hoped that increasing their competence and coordination in physical skills will have a positive effect on their performance in the classroom.

It should be remembered that educable mentally retarded children are more like normal children than they are different from them. Their basic needs for play and movement competence are not radically dissimilar from the needs of the nonretarded. Such children do not show as much deviation from normal movement competency and coordination as they exhibit in mental performance.

Visually Impaired Children

Visually impaired children range from partially sighted children to those without vision, the blind. Blind children and those with severe visual problems will probably remain in special education classes, on either a part-time or full-time basis. The teacher may have children with varying degrees of partial vision, however.

Such children need to develop confidence in their ability to move freely. Furthermore, they need to feel that movement can be fun and safe for them. Ordinarily, they can participate in most movement activities, with the exception of certain phases of manipulative activities and games or races in which collisions are a danger.

If corrective lenses are worn, attention to safety and proper fitting is requisite. Guards for glasses, elastic holder straps, and unbreakable features are effective directions that can be considered. If glasses are taken off for an activity, arrangements for their safety must be made. Responsibility should be centered on the child to put the glasses at a safe spot or into the designated container and to retrieve them later.

In catching and throwing activities, speed and direction need to be controlled. The capacity of the child to track an object through the air should be determined. Brightly colored (preferably yellow) balls are easier for the partially sighted child to catch. Having adequate lighting and a contrasting background helps increase the visibility of the object. Distances should be set according to skill, and progress should be unhurried.

In some tagging games, a skilled child can hold the hand of the partially sighted student, providing a necessary safety factor. The visually impaired child needs the confidence and experience of playing with children with normal sight.

Attention should be devoted to providing experiences in which children can work on apparatus, climb, and move and jump above ground level. Stair climbers, boxes, and balance beams are useful to promote variety in these movements.

Auditory-impaired Children

In general, auditory-impaired children are capable of performing most, if not all, activities that are within the range of children with normal hearing. Many of these children wear hearing aids, which prove to be only a minor limitation in movement activities.

When working with these children, the chief problem to be solved is that of communication. The child should be placed close to and facing the teacher, so that he can watch the teacher's lip movements. If there is music or another reproduced sound, the child should be stationed near the source. It is essential that the child understand the directions for any acitivity, so that he will know what is expected. Having another child help or show him what is to be done should be used only to supplement verbal directions.

Other children should learn how to speak to a child with a hearing problem. The key is to speak more slowly and enunciate clearly without shouting. This must be a positive act with the speaker facing directly toward the impaired child, so that the child can observe lip movement.

Some children with hearing problems speak in a strained and abnormal manner. The children in the class need to develop sensitivity to this condition and to understand that this is normal speech for a person with this handicap.

Children With Orthopedic Handicaps and Other Health-limiting Conditions

Since orthopedic handicaps include a wide range of conditions, it is quite difficult to make generalizations about suggested approaches. Such handicaps may be temporary, such as being on crutches or wearing a splint, or permanent. Teachers see fewer post-polio cases today than they did in the past, but such children are occasionally encountered.

Realistic goals need to be set with respect to the handicapping condition. The emphasis should be on what the child can do. There may be times, of course, when the child cannot participate in an activity. At such times, some modification can often be devised to include the child. Alternate activity is another direction.

Peer regard and consideration are developed as other children make a special effort to include the child and help with his movement patterns. In many cases, the handicap and its effect on resultant movement patterns are quite obvious

to other children. This is particularly true if the child has limited mobility, which affects the capacity to participate in activities requiring running.

If the condition is under medical guidance, the limitations and restrictions should be known and followed to the letter. This is particularly true of children with certain more permanent restrictive handicaps, such as asthma or cardiac problems.

Asthmatic problems usually indicate a certain amount of restriction in vigorous activities, which can cause breathing distress.

This caution is relevant for children with cardiac problems as well. A limitation on vigorous activity is usually the necessary restriction. Otherwise, children with cardiac and asthmatic problems can participate in most activities provided they do not lead to a stressful situation.

Children with Neurological Handicaps

Many of these children, especially the ones with cerebral palsy, have quite visible signs of their condition. In palsied children, the excitability threshold is critical and must not be exceeded. Peer interaction should have guidance, so as to avoid pity on the one hand and negative reactions on the other. The specified limitations on the child's activity must be closely followed. For some, the goal of movement may be to accomplish the simple fundamental movements that the other children do with ease. Most of these special children have intelligence that is within the normal range. Their chief problem is control of movement.

Epileptic children will show varying degrees of control of seizures, and most of them will be under control medication. Limitations on activity may be required. If the child detects the onset of a seizure during physical activity, he should go to the periphery of the area immediately and relax. Generally, a seizure must run its course, and little can be done other than to make the child comfortable and not let him injure himself. If special considerations or actions are necessary for a particular child during a seizure, specifics must be made known to the teacher. The severity of seizures varies greatly from those of quite short duration, which are difficult to detect, to the severe episodes of grand mal epilepsy.

ONGOING PROGRAMS OF SPECIAL EDUCATION

One problem for parents of preschool children seeking a way to meet special needs is locating an agency to help. The school district has a responsibility to meet these needs when the child enrolls in the schools, but help for preschoolers is more difficult to locate. Several sources can supply information.

Parents should turn to the state educational agency for referral to programs that may be of help. Most state agencies have a department concerned with special education, and information can be secured from that source. The county or city health officer should also have information about programs. A few programs are connected with institutions of higher education, drawing expertise from child development departments and utilizing interested students as helpers.

A number of federally funded experimental programs have been developed, known as Nationally Validated Developer Demonstration Projects. These are available for adoption by schools. Some of these programs concentrate on learning disabilities rather than on other handicaps, but all provide special help to meet special needs. Most of them involve parents as teachers or helpers, and most include a home-visit format.

The following list of programs will illustrate the kinds of programs that are available. Undoubtedly, many good programs exist that are not on this list. The listed programs have national approval and are available for adoption. Recommendation is not to be inferred from the listing.

Basic Adaptable Skills for the Individual Child
Montevideo Follow Through Resource Center
Sixth and Grove Avenue
Montevideo, MN 56265

Child Development Center
Ocean View School District
Huntington Beach, CA 92646

Curative Rehabilitation Center
Cerebral Palsy Project
9001 West Watertown Plank Road
Wauwatosa, WI 53226

Early Prevention of School Failure
114 North Second Street
Peotone, IL 60468

Follow Through—Parent Education Resource Center
Richmond Public Schools
Richmond, VA 23200

Games Children Play—Interdependent Learning Model
Atlanta Follow Through Resource Center
2960 Forrest Hill Drive, Southwest
Atlanta, GA 30315

Portland Follow Through Program
Parent Involvement in Early Childhood Centers
ECE Elliott School
2231 North Flint
Portland, OR 97200

Model Preschool Center for Handicapped Children
College of Education and Child Development and Mental Retardation Center
University of Washington
Seattle, WA 98195

The Portage Home Teaching Project
CESA 12
Box 564
Portage, WI 53901

Project Home Base
Yakima School District #7
104 North Fourth Avenue
Yakima, WA 98902

Teaching Research Infant and Child Center
Monmouth, OR 97231

SUMMARY

The terms "special children" and "exceptional children" are interchangeable designations for handicapped children. Public Law 94-142 assures that all handicapped children have available to them a free and appropriate education that emphasizes special education and related services to meet their particular needs. The law provides for special services to handicapped children three through five years of age. The process of remediation involves three steps. The first is to identify children with special needs and diagnose those needs. After diagnosis, objectives are established and emphasis placed on those activities that aid in reaching the stated goals. The final step is to establish a record-keeping system and to establish an ongoing program. Accumulated records should be passed on to future teachers in order to establish a continuous program of special concern throughout the child's school career.

Physical education is regarded as an important part of the total development and education of the handicapped child and is the only educational discipline mentioned in Public Law 94-142. The law requires that an individualized education program (IEP) be developed for every special child. The IEP is developed by the child's classroom teacher, parent or guardian, special education personnel, and physical education teacher.

Mainstreaming is the practice of placing handicapped students in regular classes. There are varying degrees of mainstreaming from complete participation within regular classes to varying amounts of time in special classes and regular classes. Reverse mainstreaming involves groups of children without handicaps coming into a special education class and participating with the special students.

In the final part of the chapter, instructional strategies are offered for dealing with specific handicaps such as mental retardation, visual impairment, and neurological handicaps. This section offers examples of ongoing programs that have received national attention and lists addresses for corresponding for information.

Chapter 20

Aquatic Activities

It is better to be safe than sorry.

Swimming and water safety form a most important area of instruction, which should be made available to every child. A child should know how to swim by the age of seven or eight. A community-wide approach is needed for such a program, in which the school may or may not have a part. If the responsibility falls to the schools, then a number of steps need to be taken.

The first step is to seek facilities. Cooperation can generally be secured from the municipal recreation department, the YMCA or the YWCA for the use of a pool. In some cases, the program can utilize recreation facilities during the month of May, before heavy summer use begins. If the pool is outdoors, there must be a means of maintaining the water temperature at a comfortable level.

A portable pool can also be used. Commercially built pools, which can be set up by a crew in one day, are now available. A great deal can be accomplished, as far as water skills are concerned, in a pool 24 feet square with a depth of three feet. The pool can be placed in one location for four to six weeks and then moved to another school. Some states, recognizing the usefulness of these pools, have authorized the installation of water valves and a drain hole connected to the sewage system in new school construction.

WHO SHOULD TEACH SWIMMING?

Parents can be excellent teachers for young children if they are confident in the water and can function in an instructional situation. If

they do not feel confident in the water, parents should take a swimming course themselves before attempting to teach children. A common approach is to have professional instructors work with volunteer parents who come to the school and become, in effect, paraprofessionals.

A professional instructor must see swimming as an educational endeavor. He is more concerned about the development of swimming ability in all children than with the encouragement of a few outstanding swimmers. He should be firm, yet possess a great deal of patience. Patience is discussed as a critical requisite due to the fact that most children are hesitant to enter a pool and need reassurance and guidance to progress adequately. Being knowledgeable about swimming, as well as child growth and development, is essential.

WHEN SHOULD SWIMMING BE TAUGHT?

In most aquatic programs, children are not given swimming instruction before the age of three. However, some programs are being developed around the country in which children as young as six months old are receiving instruction. Some specialized programs have achieved good results with this approach, but the authors feel that any group approach should not be taught before the age of three. Shaffer states: "Developmentally, there is no apparent advantage in teaching six-month-old infants to swim. The fact that they react in a reflex manner to hold their breath and rise to the top of the water does not indicate that it is possible to

311

teach infants to swim so as to insure their safety in the water."[1]

Certain considerations affecting a child's readiness to learn require a certain degree of motor development that is usually not attained prior to the age of three. Finally, some medical experts feel that children under the age of three are more subject to infection than those who are older. Shaffer feels that a child's immune systems are minimal and leave him susceptible to infection and disease.[2]

CONSIDERATIONS FOR THE PROGRAM

The pool should be clean and warm. Water temperature should be kept at about 85 to 90 degrees if children are expected to stay in for any length of time. A pool maintained strictly for young children should be purified every two hours, as compared with the six- to eight-hour period for adult pools. Many instructors prefer a pool that has a uniform water depth of two and one-half to three feet. If all the children can touch the bottom, teachers do not have to worry about someone being in the "deep end."

Lessons should be kept short, usually from 15 to 30 minutes of water time. Young children enjoy water, but they tire quickly when they are learning new skills. Children should be asked to leave the water before they become chilled. It is always a good idea to leave children with a fond memory of the activity by having them quit before they become fatigued.

Youngsters will exhibit wide variation in their ability to swim when they enter the class situation. The instructor must build new skills based upon each child's own level of performance. Sometimes the amount of ability displayed by a group of children may depend on their socioeconomic level, with youngsters in the higher income areas displaying more skill. This may reflect the fact that they have had the opportunity for private lessons.

Some youngsters may not be ready to participate in a swimming program even though adults deem it necessary. They will sit on the side of the pool and express a lack of interest in the activity. Through patience and gentle encouragement, the children will gradually become involved as they build confidence in adults. There need be no rush to force children into swimming; let them ease into the water at their own rate.

Children should master one skill before proceeding to the next. A most important consider-ation in teaching swimming is that children develop a positive attitude toward swimming and a respect for water. Positive attitudes are formed when children find success and are allowed to proceed at their own rate.

The swimming environment should be attractive and enticing to youngsters. Bright toys, such as animals, boats, beach balls, and sand pails should be available for children to use. The water should be a medium for play, through which the child becomes excited and ready to participate. Through exposure to water, while playing with toys and friends, the youngster can develop a relaxed attitude toward the instructional program.

If possible, there should be a play period at the end of the lesson. This will give children a chance to practice newly learned activities and leave them with a good feeling about the day's activities. The free activity at the end of the lesson may be as important as the lesson itself.

INSTRUCTIONAL ACTIVITIES

There are three phases in the aquatics program. In the first phase, children are primarily concerned with adjusting to the water. Children should be expected to overcome their fear of water and to become familiar with its potential for enjoyment. During the second phase, which introduces drownproofing skills, the child learns to enter the water from many different angles and learns how to float, bounce off the bottom, and recover equilibrium from various positions. In the final stage, instruction is primarily directed toward developing swimming skills and learning specific strokes. Students should be able to use many different methods to propel themselves and should feel comfortable in deep water.

Phase 1. Adapting to the Water

At this stage, the child should gradually become involved in the activity in the water and should be allowed to experiment with and explore his new environment. The experience should be unhurried and reassuring. During this stage of water adaptation, the child should learn: (1) how to get into the pool; (2) how to adjust to the temperature of the water; (3) new perceptions about buoyancy and loss of equilibrium; and (4) how the water affects the eyes, ears, nose, and mouth.

[1]Thomas E. Shaffer, "Swimming for Infants—Not Recommended," *JAMA* 214(13) (1970): 2343.
[2]*Ibid.*

Learning to Adjust to the Water. "How many parts of your body can you wet down with water?"

"Put water on your face. On your neck. Your tummy."

"Walk slowly into the water."

"See if you can gently slide into the water."

Learning to Move in the Water. "Bounce up and down. Clap your hands. Bend your knees."

"Can you bounce on one foot? Two feet? From one foot to the other?"

"Can you walk in a circle? A square? A triangle?"

"Can you run? Slowly? Quickly?"

"Can you jump forward? Backwards? To the side?"

"Walk on your toes. On your heels. On the sides of your feet."

"Can you take giant steps? Quick and small steps?"

"Play Follow-the-Leader with a friend."

"Play a tag game with some friends."

Learning to Put the Head Under Water. "Take a handful of water and splash it on your face."

"Can you wash your face with water? With both hands? With no hands?"

"How slowly can you place your face in the water? How long can you keep it in the water?"

"Can you hold hands with a partner and put your face in the water?"

"Try to put your head in the water and open your eyes."

"Can you put your head completely under water and open your eyes? Can you make a funny face?"

"Can you and your partner put your heads under water together and make a sad face at each other?"

"See if you can put your head under water and count the number of rocks on the bottom."

"Put your head under and see what color the toys on the bottom are."

"Put your head under the water and try to pick up one of the toys on the bottom."

GAMES TO ENCOURAGE ACTIVITY IN THE WATER

Many of the games that are played in the gymnasium or on the playground can be adapted to the water. Some of the following are especially useful.

Simple Tag Games. Many tag games can be used to stimulate youngsters to move through the water. For example, partner tag games will encourage use of the "buddy" system, in which one always stays with his partner. Children might play a tag game in which they have to tag body parts that are underwater. In another approach, they have to use various locomotor movements to propel themselves through the water.

Relays. In simple relays, the children are asked to move from one side of the pool to the other. A circle formation might be used, and students are asked to move around the group and back to their "home" when their name or number is called.

Secret Mission. A hidden object is given to one of two groups of youngsters. The goal is to take the object across the pool without being tagged by the team moving from the opposite side.

Magic Potion. Youngsters are lined up on one side of the pool. One child is chosen to be It. When the chosen player declares, "Magic potion, come through the ocean," the others try to move to the other side of the pool. Those caught become It and help in tagging the rest of the class.

GAMES TO ENCOURAGE OPENING THE EYES UNDERWATER

Stoop Tag. In this active tag game, one or more children are selected to chase the others. To be "safe," children must stoop and be completely underwater. They can also move without being tagged if they remain completely underwater.

Water Dodgeball. Beach balls should be used. A few students are selected to be throwers. They can move wherever they please to throw at other players. The dodging players must go underwater to avoid being hit. If a player is hit with the beach ball, she now becomes a thrower in place of the player who threw the ball.

Phase 2. Drownproofing Skills

In this phase, it is assumed that children are now comfortable and confident around a water environment. They have faith in the instructor and are ready to learn new skills. During this phase, they should learn good breath control and rhythmic breathing, learn to bob off the bottom, to float, and to recover from a buoyant position.

SUGGESTED ACTIVITIES

Developing Breath Control. "Take a big breath and blow it into the air slowly."

"Take a big breath in through your mouth and breathe out through your nose. Do it slowly."

"Take a big breath and blow water out of your cupped hands."

"Take a big breath, put your head under the water, and see how long you can hold your breath."

"Find a friend and see which of you can stay underwater the longest."

"Can you put your face in the water and blow bubbles? Can you hum a tune? Can you say a word or two?"

"Can you put your face in the water and blow bubbles and then lift your face out and take a big breath? Do it slowly at first and gradually speed up."

"Find a friend. When he is underwater blowing bubbles, you take a big breath. Then you go underwater and blow bubbles while he takes a big breath. This is like a seesaw."

"Beginning slowly, bob underwater and blow bubbles, then come up and take a breath. Continue to bob up and down, taking a breath each time you come up. Gradually speed up."

"Practice bobbing and breathing while moving in different directions. See how far you can travel while bobbing."

Learning to Float. "Can you make a shape in the water with your body?"

"Can you make a shape in the water with your body while your feet are off the bottom?"

"Can you make a shape with your body while you are completely underwater?"

"Can you do the jellyfish float?" (The arms and legs simply hang limp.)

"Can you float with your arms out to the side like an airplane?"

"See if you can float with your arms in front like a long fish."

"Try pushing down with your hands, lifting your head, and taking a breath." (This is an important skill, as a youngster could use it if trapped in deep water.)

"Is it possible to float in a different shape?"

"How many different ways of floating can you show me?"

"Can you float on your back?" (It may be necessary to hold the back of the child's head up until he is confident that he will not sink. The child should keep his head back and his chest up.)

"Can you scull your hands back and forth while floating on your back?"

"While floating on your back, can you change to a front float position? Can you change from front to back?" (This is an important skill, as the child could use it to rest in an emergency.)

Learning to Recover from a Floating Position. "From a front floating position, lift your head and your knees, push down with your arms and hands, and see if you can stand up."

"From a back floating position, lift your head, drop your seat, push up with your arms and hands, and see if you can stand up."

"Float, make a different shape, and see if you can stand up."

"See how many different ways you can float and recover."

Phase 3. Swimming Skills

This phase of aquatic instruction involves propelling the body through water. After buoyancy has been learned, the child should be able to move a reasonable distance in the water safely. Learning specific skills is a goal in this phase, as the child grows into a skilled and mature swimmer. It is not the purpose of this chapter to discuss stroke technique and refinement, as these are covered in better detail in other sources. This section will discuss the beginning skills necessary to propel the body through the water, using the arms and legs, as well as learning to jump into deep water and recovering to the side of the pool.

SUGGESTED ACTIVITIES

Gliding in the Water. "Can you push away from the side of the pool and glide in a front floating position?"

"How far can you glide? Can you kick while gliding?"

"Can you glide and move your arms?"

"Can you glide through the water in a back floating position?"

"While gliding in a back floating position, can you move your legs? Your arms? Your arms and legs together?"

Propelling Oneself in the Water. "How far can you propel yourself in the water?"

"While propelling yourself, can you change from a front floating position to a back floating position?"

"Can you do the dog paddle stroke?" (The face should be in the water.)

"Can you do the dog paddle stroke with a little leg action?" (Keep the knees somewhat straight and the legs under water.)

Jumping into Water of Moderate Depth. Contact with the bottom of the pool is a measure of security for the young child. Jumping into deep water should be preceded by jumping into shallower depths. Initially, the instructor can stand in the water and provide the comfort of nearness. In some cases, the instructor can cushion the jump, but this should be dispensed with quickly. The child can be encouraged to try, but should not be forced.

If the pool has a slanted bottom, jumping can be done in progressively deeper water. If the child takes a deep breath before the jump, he will be more likely to expel air as he contacts the water.

Jumping into Deep Water. The teacher should use a pole as a teaching aid and should work with children individually. Youngsters should not attempt to jump into deep water until they feel confident and desire to try the new venture.

"Hold onto the pole [held by the teacher] with both hands and jump into the water."

"Can you jump into the water without holding onto the pole?" (The instructor should immediately offer the child the pole as the child surfaces.)

"Can you jump into the water, surface, and swim to the side of the pool?" (To surface, the child should use the arms and legs.)

"Can you jump into the water, surface, and swim a longer distance than before?"

GAMES TO UTILIZE SWIMMING SKILLS

Rock Pile. Many small rocks can be spread out on the bottom of the pool. On signal, youngsters move quickly to see how many rocks they can retrieve.

Treasure Hunt. Pennies can be used to motivate the children to dive underwater and see how many they can gather. If the teacher desires, the pennies can be used to buy various rewards at the end of the lesson.

Follow-the-Leader. Leaders can create different challenges for the rest of their squad members. Leaders should be encouraged to use all the skills they have learned.

Keep Away. Children are divided into two groups. A beachball is used, and teams try to keep it from each other. A rule should be set that body contact is to be avoided, so that youngsters will not be fearful of being forced underwater.

OTHER CONSIDERATIONS

The portable pool is an excellent solution for a swimming orientation program, as the depth of the water can be varied. It may be placed in a vacant space or classroom. While a drain is convenient, the water can be pumped out with a separate pump. For an outside installation, some schools have success with an air-bubble dome.

The water level in a regular pool can be lowered to accommodate young children. However, lowering and raising the water level in these pools is both time-consuming and expensive.

In visiting other countries, the authors have noticed two innovations, which merit trial in this country. In Western Germany, pools of a constant depth are used, with an arrangement to adjust the depth for different age groups. The pool is constructed with a movable floor, which can be raised and lowered to change the depth. No water need be taken out. The entire floor is moved upward by a series of levers on the side or by an arrangement similar to a hydraulic lift.

In Sweden, Denmark, and Germany, some pools for young children have a series of steps at one end, which usually go across the width of the pool. The steps are about seven inches in height and ten inches in width. The children can go into the water literally step by step, entering as they wish. They can sit on a step and kick water. They can slide along a step on their tummies. This is planned in the original pool construction. Steps are lined with the same ceramic tiles as the pool. The accompanying diagram provides a top view and cross section of the steps.

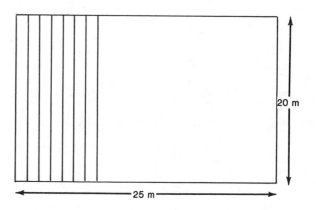

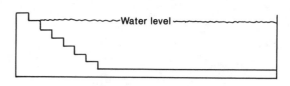

Learner pool with steps

SUMMARY

Swimming and water safety form an important part of the physical education program for young children. Children should be given instruction in swimming after the age of three to ensure that the child's immune systems are well developed. The water should be kept warm and clean, and a preferable teaching station in the pool would contain water at a depth of two and one-half feet.

Instruction in swimming should proceed slowly, with lessons built on a sound progres-

sion of skills. A positive attitude toward water
and respect for water are two important attitudi-
nal outcomes. The swimming environment
should be attractive to youngsters so that they
will be motivated to enter the water.

There are three phases to the aquatics program for young children. Adapting to the water
is the first phase and teaches children to move,
to place the head underwater, and to open the
eyes underwater. The second phase places an
emphasis on drownproofing through breath
control, learning to float, and recovering from
the float position. Finally, basic swimming
skills, such as gliding in the water and jumping
into moderate and deep water, are taught.

Chapter 21

Organizing for Effective Teaching

There is a great difference between knowing and understanding: You can know a lot about something and not really understand it.

Charles F. Kettering

It is gratifying to note a growing understanding among administrators of the potential of physical education as an educational tool for children. It is of cardinal importance that the administration recognize that physical education is a developmental and instructional program, an important part of the child's school experience, and that this teaching area merits planning and appropriate support. The following section lists important responsibilities that the administration should assume so that children may have profitable learning experiences in physical education.

ADMINISTRATIVE RESPONSIBILITIES

1. Determine the direction the program should take. This will require an ongoing curricular guide based on state guidelines and incorporating sound movement theory.

2. Provide for competent direction of the program by a qualified consultant or supervisor. Administrators should consider the establishment of a physical education committee to provide overall guidance for the qualified individual in charge of the program.

3. Arrange for facilities, equipment, and instructional supplies necessary to maintain a quality program. Administrators should have long-range plans for facility development and revolving equipment procurement and replacement, as well as provision for adequate storage, care, and repair of supplies.

4. Establish and maintain through the custodial force good standards of sanitation, cleanliness, and healthful physical education facilities.

5. Provide an emergency care system, including an emergency care station and appropriate procedures.

6. Provide in-service education as needed.

7. Provide enough teaching stations and sufficient instructional time to meet at least minimal statutory regulations.

THE ROLE OF PARENTS

Parents are usually concerned about the physical development of their children and are willing to cooperate with teachers, provided they understand the physical education program with respect to what it can accomplish and how they can help.

The school can employ dissemination techniques and demonstrations to provide parents with basic information about the program and what it can do for their children. If parents come to see the value of suitable attire for physical education, for example, they may not send children off to school wearing long dresses, knee-high boots, and other garments that inhibit full participation. In addition, they can encourage their children to be more physically active and enlist children's cooperation at home in the achievement of overall objectives of physical education.

If parents are sufficiently well informed about the philosophy of the program and what the program is attempting to achieve, they will be able to make more rational decisions concerning whether or not their children should be excused from an activity.

Parents can gain familiarity with the program by visiting the school, by helping as a parent volunteer, or by participating in PTA discussions and programs. Administrators as well as parents must recognize that, to serve effectively as a volunteer aide, a parent must undergo some preparation and must agree to conform to patterns set by the school.

PATTERNS OF TEACHING RESPONSIBILITY

The most prevalent pattern of teaching responsibility in physical education for young children calls for the classroom teacher to handle instructional chores. A few systems employ special teachers; but, by and large, the classroom teacher is assigned the responsibility of teaching physical education.

How can a quality program be implemented? The key person is the consultant or supervisor, without whom the learning experiences for children suffer. As mentioned, a curriculum guide is needed, upon which the program will be based. The supervisor helps the teacher to make the most out of the scheduled learning experiences.

The supervisor should have a regular schedule of service, keeping the teacher ahead of forthcoming lessons. If the supervisor can supply lesson plans of a flexible nature that the teacher can follow or adapt, better quality instruction can result. The supervisor also should be on call to help or even teach areas with which the teacher may have difficulty.

It is also helpful to designate one teacher in each school as the physical education representative; it is particularly helpful if the supervisor has several schools assigned. The representative is primarily responsible for equipment needs, including its storage. All requests for equipment and supplies are routed through this person.

If a specialist teacher handles the class, the cooperation of the classroom teacher is still needed. The specialist needs to be informed regarding which children are to be excused and which are to have restricted activity. If the specialist teaches only a portion of the classes, and the classroom teacher handles the remainder, coordination is needed. This can involve a division of activities; or the classroom teacher can build on the lesson structure devised by the specialist.

SCHEDULING

For young children, a daily period of physical education is the desirable goal. Periods can range from 20 to 30 minutes; the shorter period is more appropriate for preschool children. This standard pertains to instructional time and does not include time needed for moving to and from class, changing shoes, visiting the washroom, and cleaning up.

Class size should not exceed more than one classroom. The practice of sending two or more classes with one teacher for physical education results in little more than a supervised play period.

Rather than schedule a class for the same set period each day of the week, the schedule can be varied. This gives each classroom a chance at the more preferred times.

For preschool or kindergarten children, it may be desirable or necessary to hold part of each physical education lesson—or some entire lessons—in the classroom. Sufficient play space is needed, and the classroom area must be large enough for movement. A carpeted floor is of considerable help when physical education activities are going on.

The teacher should concentrate on activities that can be carried out successfully in the classroom space. Each classroom should be fairly self-sufficient with respect to equipment needs, but some things can be checked out from general physical education supplies. The classroom program must be an extension of the regular physical education program and should not simply be a recreation period.

The children should follow a plan for getting the room ready for physical education. Reversing the procedure, putting the room back into shape for classroom work, should be a part of the plan.

POLICIES FOR HEALTH AND SAFETY

The school has both a moral and a legal responsibility toward its students with respect to their health and safety. The moral responsibility is part of the school's broad educational purposes, namely, to provide a school setting in which each child may develop an optimum level of personal health. The legal responsibility arises out of the public's assumption that the school cannot escape the legal obligation to provide a healthful and safe environment for the child.

In today's society, the administration is justifiably concerned that the teacher conduct physical education classes in such a manner as to minimize the possibility of a lawsuit. Much emphasis centers on the rights of students in relation to school responsibility. If the child's rights are violated, he or she may attempt to recover.

The following section discusses some considerations for an effective school health and safety program.

Periodic Health Examination

Every student should undergo a periodic health examination. This examination should determine, among other factors, the extent of a child's participation in physical education. Ideally, this examination should be yearly and should include all health factors having a bearing on the child's educational experience. In practice, however, examinations should be scheduled on entrance into school.

The examination should classify students in one of three categories: (1) normal participation in physical education, (2) participation subject to certain adaptations or restrictions, and (3) severe limitations or nonparticipation. The teacher must have access to the results of the examination in order that each student may receive the consideration stipulated in the examination.

An examination form approved by the local medical society makes for more consistent information. Agreement can also be reached with the local medical society with respect to a standard fee for the examination.

Excuses and Readmittance

If a child is to be excused from physical education for a day or two for health reasons, the teacher can accept a note from the parent. If the excuse involves a significant length of time, it should be accepted only on the recommendation of a physician. Readmittance of children who have been out for a period of time should also be subject to a physician's recommendation. Excuses and readmittance cases should be routed through the school nurse's office, if one is available. In the absence of recommendations from both physician and nurse, consultation by the principal with the parent is probably the best solution.

Students who have been absent because of illness or some other condition should be observed closely for signs that might suggest that they are not ready to participate in unlimited physical activity.

Good rapport between the physician and the school is important in handling the health problems related to excuses and readmittance. One physician from the local medical society should be designated to provide liaison between those responsible for physical education and members of the medical profession.

Healthful Environment for Physical Education

A healthful environment for physical education requires attention to standards for school safety, hygiene, and sanitation. In addition, the physical education setting should emphasize good standards in cleanliness, ventilation, and heating. Ventilation should be sufficient to remove objectionable odors. Temperatures should range from 65 to 68 degrees, depending upon the extent of the activity. Generally, a temperature comfortable for an elderly teacher is too high for active youngsters.

A healthful environment also includes attention to mental hygiene. Proper student-teacher relationships in activity areas are important. Students should be able to relieve tensions through activity. Physical education should be a period during which students lose rather than acquire tensions.

Cleanliness of the gymnasium floor is particularly important in the present-day physical education program, as many of the movements require the children to place their hands or bodies on the floor. The floor should be swept in the morning just prior to the classes. In addition, it should be swept as often as needed between classes. A wide dust mop should be handy for this purpose.

Securing cooperation from the custodial force is the key to success in this area. It must be understood that the gymnasium floor must meet more critical standards than the average classroom floor. Certainly, children need to be made conscious of the need for their cooperation in helping maintain good standards of sanitation.

As a basic minimum, children should wear gym shoes during the physical education class. The practice of having children "skate" around in stocking feet limits children greatly in their responses to activity challenges. It would be better to have children move in bare feet, rather than in stocking feet. The teacher should also wear appropriate clothing and footwear.

Safety Considerations

It is often said that proper safety is no accident. Safety education should be positive in terms of what approaches and considerations are needed and should not be based on "scare" tactics. A school safety committee is desirable to set safety regulations, policies, and procedures. The committee should be composed of students, faculty, the school nurse, and perhaps representatives of the PTA. A school safety code should be established, and a written compilation of the code, including all policies, regulations, and procedures, should be in the hands of teachers. Regulations affecting the students should be posted. The committee should be open-minded and receptive to safety suggestions from students, faculty, and others. An important function of the committee would be to review accidents for the purpose of determining appropriate preventive measures to be taken.

The school safety program has three aspects: (1) a safe school environment, (2) safety education, and (3) safety services. Each is discussed in turn.

SAFE ENVIRONMENT

The school must be certain that the school environment meets all the criteria for safety. This involves a number of aspects.

Health Status. The health status of the children must be ascertained through a health examination so that no child may be placed in a physical environment beyond his capacity.

Provision for a Safe Teaching Place. There must be sufficient room for the activity, and the area must be suitable for the intended purpose. The character of the activity will determine the amount of space needed for safe play, including sufficient boundary clearance from walls, fences, and other obstructions. The area should be free of posts, wires, holes, and other hazards. Broken glass and other miscellaneous junk on the ground is a notorious safety hazard. Sprinkler heads and pools of water can also cause serious injury.

Safety in Equipment and Supplies. The equipment and supplies provided must be suitable for the level of the children and the selected activity. The equipment should be in good functioning condition.

Inspection of Facilities and Equipment. For each class, the teacher needs to make a quick assessment of the safety aspects of the equipment and instructional materials to be used. In addition, inspection of facilities and equipment should be made on a regular basis, perhaps monthly. This would include both the items for physical education and playground equipment used in recess or free play. The principal should implement this responsibility, but it also has ongoing implications. Whenever a teacher or child notices an item that needs repair or seems dangerous, this should be reported to the school office. A notation should be made of the needed correction, since equipment that can cause injury should be taken out of service until proper repair is made.

Supervision of Activities and Play Periods. All school-sponsored activities must be supervised, including recess, noon-hour recreation, and after-school play. Much of this supervision can be assigned to qualified teacher aides, releasing the teacher for instructional duties. Under law, a class may not be turned over to high school students or cadet teachers, as supervision must be supplied by a certified individual or designated school employee.

Proper Selection of Activities. The selected activity must stand up under scrutiny as a proper educational medium for the group involved. Teachers should avoid highly specialized or difficult games beyond the ability of children. A tendency by some citizens to establish and operate athletic programs for younger children is a direction that the school should take no part in or incorporate into the school program. These programs are of dubious merit and seem to satisfy adult preferences rather than children's needs.

SAFETY IN INSTRUCTION

The teacher has the responsibility of instructing children in skills needed in an activity so that they may take part in it safely. The instructional approach should cover the essential points in sequential order.

A second requirement is consideration of hazards inherent in the activity. The teacher must take proper safety precautions and also inform children about hazards and the means to avoid them.

One caution needs to be mentioned. A few teachers in movement theory like to give children objects to be handled or allow them to explore on apparatus with little preliminary instruction and few safety cautions. This approach has negative legal implications.

SAFETY SERVICES—EMERGENCY CARE

In spite of all precautions, accidents will occur in various phases of the school program. The school has a responsibility to arrange a system of emergency care, to ensure that prompt and appropriate measures will be taken to protect the child who has been injured. Emergency care procedures should follow this sequence:

1. The administration of first aid is the first step. The problem of proper care is solved if a school nurse is present. If there is no nurse, at least one person in the school should have first aid certification. Some principals like to have the school secretary receive such certification, because this individual is readily available. If one of the teachers is responsible for administering first aid, proper supervision must be supplied for the class when he is called to the scene

of the accident. The individual who is responsible for first aid procedures will determine whether the child can be moved and in what fashion he can be moved. A suitable place where children can be taken in case of accident or illness should be provided.

2. Unless the injury is such that the child needs to be taken to a doctor without delay, the parents should be notified. The school should have on hand sufficient information pertaining to each student to give direction in case of an emergency. This information would include telephone numbers of the parents, both at home and at place of employment. In addition, it is a good idea to have written permission from parents to refer the child to the family doctor for treatment in case of emergency. Sometimes the name of a neighbor or close friend to whom the child can be referred in case the parents cannot be contacted is helpful.

3. The third step is to release the child to the parents or other person designated by them. Policies for transportation should be established.

4. A report of the accident should be filled out promptly, generally on a form adopted by the school system. The teacher and the principal should each retain copies, the additional specified copies being forwarded to the administration. The report should contain all necessary details with respect to full names of the child and witnesses; details of the accident including place, time, activity, circumstances, and disposition of the child.

5. Follow-up procedures should be instituted to prevent future occurrences.

The Medicine Chest. Whether or not to have a medicine chest is a debatable point. The medical association for the area (local or county) should help make such a decision. Only those medications and materials approved by the association should be in the medicine chest, and approved directions for use of the contents should be prominently posted. If a child is to take medication during school time, the procedure should be under the direction of the school nurse and only on a physician's written prescription, which is also endorsed by the parents. The medicines should be kept by the school nurse and not left in the hands of the child.

STUDENT INSURANCE

The school should make available accident insurance providing compensation in case of accident to a child. If a parent rejects the option of school accident insurance, in case of an accident he will have little basis for objection to expenses that could have been partially or fully covered by insurance. Physical education insurance for young children is relatively inexpensive.

OTHER SAFETY CONSIDERATIONS

Dogs and other animals should be kept out of the schoolyards. Children can trip over the animals, and the possibility of being bitten is always present. Whenever the skin is broken from an animal bite, the possibility of rabies must *always* be considered. The animal must be caught and held for the authorities. Only by observing the animal for a period of two weeks or so can the possibility of rabies be rejected.

The rubbish-burning area should be barricaded from children. Children are naturally attracted to fire, and they love to handle burning materials.

Throwing stones and snowballs must be controlled. Other habits of rowdyism that might lead to injuries should be discouraged.

Special rules must be established for procedures in various areas, particularly in the use of various pieces of apparatus on the playground. These should be discussed with the children and posted.

LEGAL RESPONSIBILITY

Since children are subject to compulsory attendance laws, the school has the legal responsibility of providing a safe environment for them. Teachers, as individuals, share this responsibility. While the teacher cannot be held responsible for all accidental occurrences in activities under his supervision, he can be held legally responsible for the consequences of his negligence, which have proven injurious to one of the children.

Liability occurs when the teacher is held responsible for a given situation, and it is always determined by a court action. Negligence by the teacher must be established. A person is deemed negligent when he has failed to act as a reasonably prudent person would act under the circumstances. If the teacher could have foreseen the causes leading to the injury, and failed to take action as a prudent person would, then the ruling of negligence can result.

Each teacher needs to ascertain that the children's environment meets all the criteria of safety. In addition, teachers should consider taking out liability insurance, which is available quite reasonably in conjunction with memberships in some educational societies. The schools themselves should have liability insurance that covers adequately all teachers and other staff members.

OPERATIONAL POLICIES

The Supervised Play Period

Commonly called recess, the supervised play period gives youngsters a time for relaxation and relief from tensions. The teacher assigned to supervise the period should approach the duty with a positive attitude, recognizing the importance of play and helping children get the most out of this activity.

Children should be reminded that they need to exhibit self-discipline and follow certain playground rules. The playground time can also serve as an exploratory period for the skills learned in physical education.

The Noon-Hour Play Period

The lunch time provides another supervisory period of concern to the school. The first part should be devoted to a happy, restful lunch. After this, children can participate in free play, some of which can be in the classroom with quiet games. Each classroom should have a supply of suitable games to satisfy a variety of interests.

Schools should consider employing auxiliary personnel to supervise the noon-hour play period. It is unfair to expect teachers to give up their lunch time for supervisory chores. These should be paid personnel who have undergone orientation concerning their duties and responsibilities.

The noon hour is often an ideal time to offer special programs—for example, an intramural program in which participation is restricted to poorly skilled students. A low-fitness program might also be arranged at this time, or a physical activity performance might be presented to the rest of the school.

Playdays

Although interschool playdays usually do not represent a feasible activity for young children, holding a playday within a school can be enjoyable. The playday could be for the entire school or for a portion of the children—one grade level, for example.

An afternoon can be given over to the affair. Most of the emphasis should be on socializing and fun. Games, relays, and contests are appropriate activities. If teams are participating in different activities, these should be composed of a mixture from different classes.

The program can contain both familiar and new activities. Unique or unusual "fun" activities can make the day a memorable one for the children. If children are to be divided into groups, a color scheme using ribbons will work well. Volunteer help might be needed to make the day successful.

Paraprofessionals and Teacher Volunteer Aides

In the nursery, kindergarten, and primary school, volunteer teacher aides can be of assistance. Some recognized advantages of using teacher aides are that: (1) with the help of aides, teachers have more of a chance to carry out individualized instruction; (2) aides can provide direction at stations in a system of rotation station teaching; (3) aides can be of special help in working with one or more handicapped individuals; (4) they can help with equipment and other chores, allowing the teacher to have closer contact with the children; and (5) they can help with testing.

Some disadvantages of teacher aides are: (1) a high rate of turnover, (2) ineffective instructional and discipline procedures, (3) unprofessional behavior, (4) need for orientation, and (5) irregular attendance.

Should the teacher aide help with instruction? Some state regulations limit teacher aides to noninstructional duties, while others allow them to carry out some instruction under the direction of the teacher.

The paraprofessional is defined here as an individual with certain basic training, short of certification, who is employed by the school to assist the teacher.

Each school should set up guidelines for teacher aides and paraprofessionals based on a careful examination of state statutes. Some general guidelines follow:

If a teacher aide works with children, it should always be in the presence of the teacher. A paraprofessional should work under the supervision of, but not necessarily in the presence of, the teacher.

The teacher aide cannot be assigned, nor can the paraprofessional assume, the educational responsibilities of the teacher. Teacher aides and paraprofessionals should only be assigned duties that they are qualified by preparation, interest, and experience to fulfill effectively. This work should supplement the efforts of the teacher.

A written policy for teacher aides and paraprofessionals should be a functioning instrument. Basic to the entire program is a determination of need, particularly for paraprofessional services.

PROMOTIONAL IDEAS AND PUBLIC RELATIONS

Parents generally experienced a different kind of physical education when they were in school than the physical education being taught today. For this reason, it is important that parents develop a better understanding of current educational thought about physical education. There are a number of approaches by which this may be accomplished in the school.

A Quality Program

By far the most important asset to public relations is a quality program. Parents will discern the confidence and enjoyment that their youngsters secure from their movement experiences and will appreciate the apparent physical development of the children as they participate in a program of merit. Parents can take note of their children's progress and register their feelings about the impact of the program.

Involving the Parents

Parents can view firsthand demonstrations of program activities. This can take place at a festival or during a program for the Parent-Teacher Association. The PTA also can be a vehicle for discussions, panel presentations, and selected visual aids. Parents should have the opportunity to ask questions and resolve points of contention.

Parents' nights also have benefit. The parents attend an evening class arrangement and observe their children in action as they participate in selected learning experiences, including physical education.

Parents can also serve as volunteers. In this way they will gain better understanding and appreciation of what can be accomplished.

School Promotional Ideas

Progress reports to parents about school activities should include reference to physical education. In addition, public information media should be exploited. The impact of new equipment, new activities, or a new slant can be given publicity. Pictures are important and should include proper identification of the children.

Brochures covering the year's program, yearly summaries, and essential accomplishments lead toward better understanding. A file of pictures should be maintained for ready accessibility.

Service clubs can provide outlets for descriptive talks, films, and other informational ideas, often leading to material support in the way of enrichment supplies or equipment.

Exhibitions and Demonstrations

Parents like to see their children in demonstrations, and one way to assure a large audience is to involve many children in the program. Some other points follow:

1. Include children at all skill levels. Avoid concentrating on the "stars."
2. The selected activities should be typical of the program, rather than a collection of specialty events. It should show that the program is well rounded. Some numbers performed with music have a fine impact on the audience, as well as providing demonstrations of rhythmics.
3. Since the presentations are to be typical, they should not require too much practice time. The numbers should go off smoothly, of course, but perfection is not a goal.
4. Arrange to have someone give a running commentary during the numbers, using a microphone. This keeps the audience informed about points being stressed and necessary interpretations.
5. The children should be appropriately dressed for the activities, but elaborate or intricate costuming should be avoided. Simple costume items that the children can make themselves might be considered.
6. The demonstration can show both instructional approaches and accomplishments.
7. The principal should say a few words to welcome the guests. He can stress his confidence in the educational potential of physical education, which will reinforce in the minds of both children and parents the importance of physical education.
8. It is important to avoid embarrassing children by placing them in a competitive situation at which they may fail due to lack of strength or skill.

SUMMARY

Educational institutions have a moral and legal responsibility to establish a healthy and safe environment for children. Young children should have a periodic health examination to determine their capability to participate actively in the physical education program. An examination form for the medical exam should be consistent with forms used by other schools in the area. A healthful environment should emphasize high standards of cleanliness, ventilation, and heating or cooling.

Proper safety standards should be established by a school safety committee composed of students, faculty, the nurse or health representative, and an administrative officer of the school. The program for safety should consist of three phases: a safe environment, safety education, and safety services. Teachers and/or schools can be held legally responsible for the consequences of a child's accident if negligence on the part of the teacher or school can be established.

Promotion of a quality physical education program is important to the continued success of the program. Involving parents in a demonstration program with their children gives both teacher and parents a better feel for what takes place in the physical education program and at home. Progress reports that offer parents an insight into the performance and progress their children are making in physical education are important.

Chapter 22

Creative Play Environments

Play is the most educational process of the mind—Nature's ingenious device for insuring that each individual achieves knowledge and wisdom.

Neville V. Scarfe

Youngsters possess a great deal of physical vitality, which helps them in their constant quest to learn. The playground should be an environment in which children can explore and create. The typical playground lacks equipment, however; it is simply a wide open space. It is quite possible that such an environment may actually do more to hinder than to enhance the child's total development. If children learn to see the playground as an extension of their natural environment, they might become better adjusted to the outdoors. Instead, they often learn that the only sources of enjoyment lie within the constraints of a building, e.g., movie theatres, libraries, ice-skating rinks, etc. In the playground, children should gain an appreciation of their bodies as well as of their natural habitat. When youngsters come to appreciate the outdoors, they will desire to improve its quality. In essence, the playground can provide necessary opportunities and situations for balanced growth of the total child.

THE VALUE OF A CREATIVE PLAY ENVIRONMENT

The play environment can offer children a wide variety of benefits, some of which are listed in the following section.

Physical Development. The playground can offer children the opportunity to climb, jump, balance, swing, throw, skip, hop, and run. Through the medium of play, the child constantly moves physically, explores limitations and abilities, and tries new challenges. Amer-

ican children often lack shoulder girdle strength, and the playground can be a useful tool for developing this part of the body through varied climbing and hanging activities.

Excitement and Novelty. Children love to try something new and different. The play environment can provide an opportunity for the child to find new and rewarding activities and to discover new ways to be active. If the area is flexible and offers children a chance to mold it to their needs, they will find novel and exciting ways to enjoy it over a long period of time.

Imagination and Creativity. Children can pretend to be many different people—super-people who can fly, great climbers of mountains, soldiers who have to hide in a fort, etc. Many original games that provide hours of enjoyment can be devised by the youngsters. The play area should be a place where the youngsters can feel relaxed about trying out new ideas, where "anything goes" and may be enjoyed by peers.

Courage and Confidence. Calculated risks are a necessary part of healthy development for youngsters. When a child recognizes some activities as risky, yet overcomes the threat, he can develop courage and confidence in his ability.

Emotional and Physical Outlet. Children are under constant pressure to conform to teacher-desired outcomes. Their school days are filled with scheduled activities; often, little time is left for free activity. The playground can offer him a chance to relax or do something that he wants to do. In this manner, the playground can be a necessary outlet for emotions, as well as offering children some physical activity during the school day. It is interesting to note that the luxury children enjoy most is free time to enjoy in their own personal way.

Skill Practice. Children are sometimes hesitant to try new activities if they feel incompetent among their peers. The playground can offer them a chance to try new skills that they are unsure of and to practice those that have been taught in physical education classes. Most children, like most adults, would rather practice newly learned, but unmastered skills in a situation of relative privacy. In particular, the children should be provided with opportunities to practice the motor skills of climbing, hanging, and other movements while suspended on apparatus, and of jumping and returning to level ground.

Social Development. Children love to play together. Much of the equipment and apparatus demands that they take turns and share with others. Many of the games that children invent require that others play and cooperate. Another aspect of social development is learning to lead and to follow, as the situation demands.

Peer Learning. Children learn from one another as well as from the teacher. The play environment offers children a chance to share knowledge with one another and to show new ideas and challenges. Learning can take place at a rate that is acceptable to each child, based upon his individual needs.

CONSIDERATIONS IN PLANNING A PLAY ENVIRONMENT

Use of Natural Environment. If possible, much of the play area should be natural and unchanged. For example, trees, small streams, and mounds of dirt are often most attractive to children when they are playing. Children find great joy in climbing a hill, playing King of the Mountain, and then running as fast as possible down the other side. An encouraging trend today is that school and city officials often work together to build a larger and more effective community school park for youngsters. In the early stages of planning, school sites and city parks are planned adjacent to each other so that each can use the larger area when necessary, and both contribute funds to develop the area.

Exciting Features. The playground must be planned carefully so that the equipment selected is part of a total scheme. When children first see the play environment, it should be so attractive that they find it difficult to resist. Bright colors, exciting shapes, a wide variety of equipment, and various textures will make the area attractive and appealing to children.

Imaginative and Creative Play. The playground should invite children to invent new games and activities. Equipment and landscaping should approximate many things that children see in real life or read about, so that they can "pretend" and act out their fantasies. For example, trees can be forts, tunnels can be secret passageways, and a jumping platform might allow the "biggest jump in the world."

Courage and Challenge. Equipment used should challenge the courage of the child. In addition, it should allow children to succeed in mastering it. In this way, the child's self-image can be enhanced. As the child moves through the simpler tasks to the more difficult, a growth in self-confidence can be noted.

Safety. The play environment must encourage safe play. Rotating or swinging equipment is a common source of accidents for youngsters and in turn usually offers little to the total development of children. Large pieces of apparatus should be stable and immovable. Good examples of this are climbing apparatus, which develop strength and offer children a challenge.

Space Arrangement. It may be well to arrange the play environment so that certain areas are designated for age-group play and for specific types of activity. For example, due to differences in physical strength and vigor between preschool and primary children, it may be wise to have a play area for each or a time when each group is scheduled for the area. Open spaces should be left for game activities and other movements that demand a large area. A part of the play environment might be allotted for relaxing activities, such as rocking and swinging activities. Tunnels can be installed in one area, where children can "get away from it all." An area for growing plants and garden crops will allow children to learn to appreciate the wonders of nature. In this area, much vegetation could be grown to give children a place to hide, as well as to observe the natural growth of an area.

Equipment Arrangement. Pieces of play apparatus should be grouped fairly close to one another. This tends to give continuity to the child's play experiences. If pieces of equipment are widely spaced, children will have less opportunity to make total use of the area. Some feel that the pieces of equipment should be close enough together to prevent a great deal of running from one piece to another. Whether one finds this necessary or not, the equipment should be seen by the child as constituting a "whole" play environment, where all pieces are to be used in combination. Another factor to keep in mind when arranging equipment and apparatus is that the arrangement should help simplify supervision by teachers. For example, if the equipment were spread out around the border of the playground, it would be quite difficult to keep an eye on all the youngsters while they were playing.

Year-round Use. The play environment should be developed so that children can utilize it four seasons of the year. Children like to go outdoors all year round, and play areas should be planned to allow this. For example, in the Southwest, some metal equipment becomes so hot that it is impossible to use in the summer. In rainy areas, drains might need to be installed in tunnels and covered areas that are below ground level. Weather and seasons should add a further dimension to the play area and offer children more variety and novelty rather than force them away from the area.

EQUIPMENT AND APPARATUS SELECTION

Equipment should be selected with the needs and characteristics of children in mind. Some of the following guidelines may be of value to those who wish to select appropriate equipment to create a functional play environment.

The equipment should enhance physical development. It should stimulate youngsters to climb, swing, jump, and crawl. Of particular importance is the need to offer opportunity for upper body development, and equipment should be evaluated according to how much exercise it allows the upper body. In many cases, it is wise to avoid purchasing equipment that has moving parts, such as merry-go-rounds and swings, if muscular development is desired. Rather, the equipment should have many hand- and footholds to stimulate and challenge youngsters to climb.

Flexibility should be a key consideration in the selection process. Equipment that can be used in only one manner will lose its appeal for children after their initial exploration. Children should be able to change the area in some way, as well as trying different ways of playing on the equipment. All things being equal, the more a piece of equipment can stimulate creative interpretation and movement, the more valuable it is in the total playground theme.

Much equipment and apparatus can be made from inexpensive and even primitive materials. Sandboxes, walls and hills to climb, ropes to swing on, and cardboard boxes and barrels to hide in are often the pieces of equipment most attractive to youngsters. On the other hand, some of the commercial equipment included

later in this chapter may prove easier to acquire and is excellent if it meets the needs of children.

The equipment should be hazard-free and should allow children to move in relative safety. For example, moving parts that might pinch fingers should be avoided. Some wooden apparatus does not weather well in the hot sun or the cold of winter and starts to splinter, creating a hazard. Sharp edges and pointed protrusions in equipment should be avoided. Of equal importance is a periodic equipment checkup to discover possible hazardous situations.

The equipment and apparatus should be specifically designed for youngsters. Some playground structures appear to have been made for adults rather than for children. The equipment should be evaluated as to its ability to make youngsters feel comfortable while at play. If equipment is too tall, children will be afraid of falling off. If hand- and footholds are spaced too far apart, they will risk slipping and falling.

Meeting challenges and taking risks are integral parts of an exciting and productive childhood. Equipment should hold various challenges that induce youngsters to try skills that they are not sure they can master. It should offer the child an opportunity to discover that a new understanding cannot take place without a degree of risk. On the other side of the coin, if the equipment is too challenging or risky, children may experience failure, frustration, and possible injury.

In all likelihood, a combination of portable and permanent equipment in the play area is educationally sound. In early planning stages of playground development, a storage house for equipment should be included. Some of the more challenging equipment, which requires supervision, could be under lock and key, if supervision was not available at certain times. The use of portable equipment allows the playground to be used in many different ways. Various combinations of equipment can be developed and set up to stimulate students to increased participation. Along the same lines, there should be some equipment that can be moved and carried by the child; this lets him feel, at times, that he is the master of his environment. This consideration is of value when children are involved in taking out and putting away their equipment for their lessons.

FACILITIES

It should be an axiom in program-planning that the type of program desired should determine the facilities that need to be acquired. In too many cases, the facilities that are already available must be used; these areas, planned by individuals who are unaware of the needs of youngsters, become a restrictive factor in proper program development. Whenever possible, therefore, one should establish the type of program desired and necessary for optimum development of children and then plan facilities to meet these needs. The planned facilities should be large enough to meet any projected enrollment. Space is the element in facilities that is most often underestimated. A good criteria for quick evaluation of a preschool is the amount of space that is available for youngsters to run and frolic in.

Planning Indoor Areas

The indoor play area should be located where the noise and enthusiasm generated by youngsters will not bother those who are involved in less active situations. This might mean building it in a separate wing and connecting it to the main building with a covered walkway. Isolating the area from the remainder of the building also makes it accesssible for use by after-school and community groups.

Climate considerations are also important when planning facilities. When weather makes it necessary that children play indoors most of the time, a minimum of one indoor teaching station for each eight classrooms should be established. The facilities should permit that a minimum of three periods of physical activity per week for each child be scheduled.

When facilities are to be used by outside groups, a separate storage area or cabinet is essential. If outsiders have access to the regular supply room, sooner or later, some of the equipment will be found missing or broken. If they have a separate storage area, they can be responsible for stocking it with the equipment they desire to use.

The combination gymnasium-auditorium-cafeteria facility leaves much to be desired, creating more problems than it solves. Such an area has been called a "multipurpose room." A better term probably would be "multiproblem room." Using the cafeteria is particularly difficult. The gymnasium must be vacated prior to the lunch hour for setting up chairs and tables, and it is not available for activity until the facility has been cleaned, which usually involves mopping. This eliminates any noon-hour recreational use, leaving children with inadequate play space during inclement weather. In extreme cases, the gymnasium cannot be used until midafternoon, when the custodian has completed his cleaning chores.

Play and practice for special events is not compatible with the free atmosphere needed for physical education activities. Special programs, movies, and other events necessitating chairs can further complicate the situation.

One other problem frequently associated with a combination auditorium-gymnasium facility is the use of the physical education storeroom for the storage of such bulky auditorium equipment as portable chairs on chair trucks and portable stages, to say nothing of lighting fixtures and other paraphernalia for dramatic productions. Unless the storage area is large enough—and most of them are not—an unworkable and cluttered situation is the result. The best solution is to have two separate storerooms if the facility is for dual use, or one storeroom that is large enough.

Where multiple use of the facility is intended, floor markings and boundaries should be placed on the floor after the first or second sealer coat. Temporary lines needed during the year can be laid down with pressure-sensitive tape. These tapes are difficult to remove completely, however, and are also apt to take off some of the finish when they are removed.

The diagram on p. 329 shows how floor markings may be placed in order to maximize use of the facility.

A hardwood, preferably maple, floor is recommended. Other surfaces limit community use and create both safety and maintenance problems.

Walls should have a smooth surface extending eight to ten feet upward from the floor, both for safety and to aid rebound. Walls and ceilings should have acoustical treatment. When possible, plan to have a recess in the wall for each set of ropes on tracks.

Lights should be of sufficient intensity and should be recessed to prevent damage. The lights should be arranged so that they can be serviced from the floor. Beams may be exposed to allow apparatus to be attached.

Electrical outlets should be available on all walls. An overhead permanent public address system is desirable, permitting a permanent installation of the record player for easy and quick access. In original construction, this cabinet can be recessed.

Windows should be placed high on the long sides of the gymnasium. Skylights are not recommended. Protection from glare and direct sun rays should be provided.

Considerations for Outdoor Areas

Outdoor planning should include provision for sufficient field space, hard-surfaced areas, apparatus areas, and other needed space. Play area standards should meet the minimum size of ten acres, with one additional acre for each 100 pupils (according to maximum projected enrollment). Automobile and bicycle parking areas should be in addition to play areas.

Outdoor areas should be suitably turfed, surfaced, leveled, and drained. An automatic sprinkler system is desirable, but the sprinkler heads should not prove to be safety hazards.

Separate areas should be established where children of various age groups may play in safety without interference. A fence or hedge may be used to divide one area from another. The areas should have a covered section, so that children may play outdoors in inclement or extremely hot weather. It is helpful if the area can be protected from excessive wind and dust. Fencing in the area also aids in easing the burden of supervision, as well as discouraging stray dogs.

Another important consideration for the outdoor area is to develop hardtop areas that can be marked for various movement patterns and games. These markings can be especially useful for perceptual-motor development and for playing court games. Markings to enhance the area and increase its usefulness are shown on pp. 330–31.

RECOMMENDED EQUIPMENT AND APPARATUS FOR PLAY ENVIRONMENTS

Equipment and apparatus selection should be limited only by imagination and safety considerations. Many exciting pieces of apparatus were not developed for children's play, yet they provide opportunity for creative play and physical development. Also of note is the interest that commercial organizations are showing in

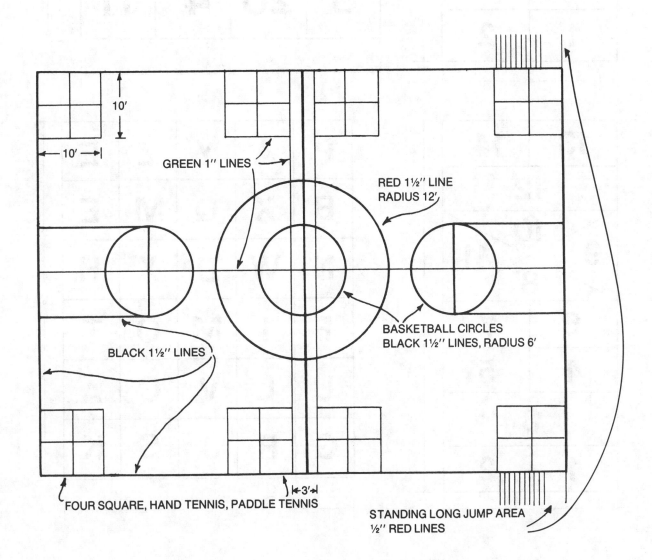

GREEN 1" LINES

RED 1½" LINE
RADIUS 12'

BASKETBALL CIRCLES
BLACK 1½" LINES, RADIUS 6'

BLACK 1½" LINES

FOUR SQUARE, HAND TENNIS, PADDLE TENNIS

STANDING LONG JUMP AREA
½" RED LINES

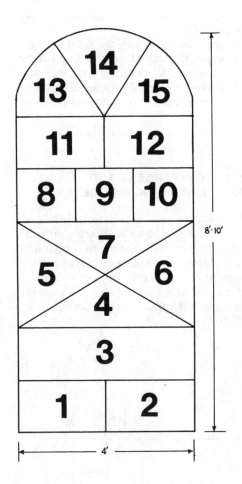

1	15	9	5
12	6	18	19
16	10	2	13
3	14	17	7
8	20	4	11

5'

4'

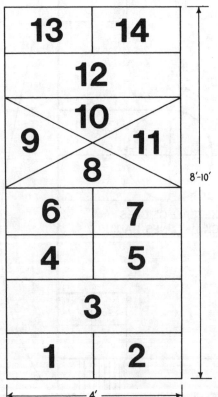

P	A	Y	Z	E
B	X	Q	M	E
N	W	D	X	H
F	I	M	O	T
U	L	V	C	A
G	R	J	S	K

6'

5'

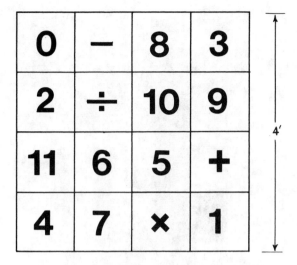

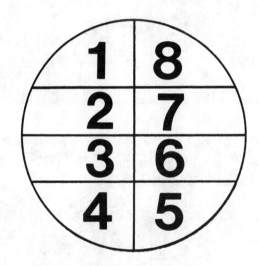

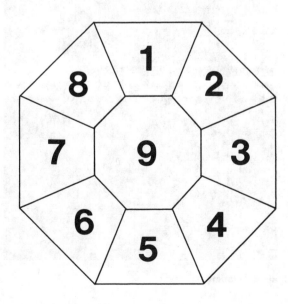

developing play area apparatus to meet the needs of youngsters. In this section (pp. 331–36), both school-constructed and commercial equipment and apparatus are illustrated. The photographs should serve to catalyze ideas that can be used in specific situations.

The equipment and apparatus are grouped according to the developmental values they offer children. If teachers are interested in developing upper body strength, they are referred to the section pertaining to this area. In developing a total play environment, equipment should be selected from each of the categories in order to offer children an opportunity for balanced and varied development. The categories of equipment can also be useful when one wishes to develop an obstacle course for physical development. Apparatus can be selected from each of the categories and installed in such a way that the same part of the body is not exercised twice in a row. Such a course offers children an area that can be used for fitness purposes as well as a creative and recreational play environment.

Upper Body Development

American children are traditionally weaker in the upper body and stronger in the legs than children from other countries. One of the reasons for this may be that play areas usually have a dearth of climbing structures. Climbing is important, not only from the standpoint of physical development, but because it offers children an opportunity to take a risk and learn to overcome the fear of new situations.

The following pieces of equipment are useful for activities that develop the upper body:

Large spools (of the type used for telephone cable or electric wire) set on end to climb on and jump from, solidly secured so that they will not tip over

Climbing poles placed next to platforms that children can reach by climbing the poles

Logs and clean railroad ties, positioned vertically, with handholds or handles placed in strategic locations for climbing

Climbing ropes attached to tracks (tracks can be locked up in a storage area when school is not in session)

Tires attached to telephone poles or logs for climbing through and around

Jungle gyms (five to six feet in height) that are anchored securely

Tree houses that allow different methods of entry, i.e., using a ladder, a climbing rope, a climbing pole, or a cargo net

Cargo nets stretched over poles so that a child can move from one side of the area to the other (the net should be positioned from four to five feet above the ground)

Long wooden ladders positioned horizontally at varying heights to offer differing degrees of challenge

Cable covered with garden hose for hand-over-hand climbing (the cable can be attached at a low end and stretched about 25 feet to a higher end of about six feet, so that children of different heights can climb and drop within their personal limits of safety)

Portable climbing equipment, which can be adjusted to create different challenges

Logs anchored vertically with handholds provided for climbing

The following photographs illustrate various types of climbing apparatus.

Lower Body Development

Equipment and apparatus for enhancing lower body development should encourage children to use various locomotor movements. It should stimulate youngsters to run, jump, hop, skip, chase, and flee. Allow enough space for this apparatus, since many of the activities that develop the lower body involve low-organization games that require plenty of room.

Equipment for upper body development

Equipment for upper body development

Suggestions about equipment for lower body development follow.

Free running space for children to race, play tag games, and practice fundamental loco-motor movements

Railroad ties anchored vertically at varying heights and distances, which encourage children to walk, run, hop, and jump from one to the other

Old automobile tires laid on the ground in various patterns so that children can move in and out, around and over the tires, using different movements

Stairways for climbing up, hopping down, and jumping off

Portable hurdles for jumping and leaping over without touching

Concrete stepping stones that are placed in patterns to encourage opposition patterns while moving, or placed certain distances apart for games of hopping and jumping, such as Hopscotch

Wagons and wheelbarrows for pushing and pulling loads that overload body muscles

Garden areas that allow children to dig, shovel, and rearrange the area are enjoyable and useful for leg development

Small hills and valleys landscaped into the play area offer good lower body opportunities

Miniature challenge circuits that contain tires for children to move in and out of, sand pits to run or jump through, and poles arranged in various fashions to move around as fast as possible

Pits for the running broad jump should be available to allow children to see how far they can jump

A running track is often highly motivating to youngsters who love to run and race against peers

Some of these ideas are illustrated in the accompanying photos.

Coordination and Rhythm

Coordination and rhythm are often best developed in small group or partner activity. Many court games require a partner, as do certain skills such as long rope–jumping or moving on a seesaw. If possible, pipe music outdoors so that it can be a part of the children's rhythmic activity. A wide variety of equipment must be available so that youngsters will not become

Equipment for lower body development

Equipment for lower body development

bored with the challenges that rhythm and co-ordination pose for them. Some suggestions follow:

Sand pits for digging and building tunnels and houses

Horizontal ladders to be used to travel across

Areas designated for rope-jumping and ball-bouncing (music piped outdoors enhances the rhythmic experience)

Large blocks for building forts, houses, etc.

Balls, jump ropes, hula hoops, and magic ropes, which can be stored outdoors for easy access

Large nets that children can throw into without need for great accuracy

Markings painted on the hardtop areas can increase body coordination and cognitive knowledge simultaneously

The following illustrations suggest other ideas that might be used.

Rocking or banana boats require that two or more persons coordinate movements for optimum performance

Seesaws are sometimes useful for developing rhythm and learning to work together

Hoops and tires for rolling require good body coordination

Tricycles and scooters are excellent for learning to coordinate upper and lower body movements

Some children enjoy a punching bag, which increases its speed of movement as it is hit harder

A ball on a tether is useful for developing striking skills, since the ball always returns (as children become more skillful, they can hit the ball in combinations, such as with the left, then the right hand)

Balance

Balance activities should be offered at varying degrees of difficulty. For example, balance beams of different widths can be placed on the playground at various heights. The level of difficulty of a balance board depends on the size of its base of support. Children should be encouraged to use controlled movements when practicing balance activities. The following ideas might be considered for enhancing balance skills:

Logs, anchored securely, and used as a balance beam

Boards that serve as a bridge across some obstacle or between two or more pieces of equipment

Coordinating movement on a banana boat

The seesaw is useful for developing coordination and rhythm

A bridge for balance

Old railroad tracks secured and used as balance beams

Wooden ladders secured six to twelve inches above the ground (children can use a ladder like a balance beam, moving along the edges, or they can walk the rungs; a similar challenge is to mount the ladder when it is in an inclined position)

Boards placed on old automobile tires will rock as they are mounted and thus provide a challenging balance activity

Platforms placed on three or four car springs that rock when children stand on them

Balance boards can be placed in different areas for independent work

Bounding boards provide opportunity to balance the body while it is in the air and regain balance upon landing

Dramatic and Creative Play

Dramatic play requires that children have many places to play alone as well as to use the environment in a creative way with friends. There must be opportunity to act out adult roles and to create new ideas and act them out in front of others. The equipment should be somewhat abstract so that children can use it for any purpose they desire rather than the single purpose for which it was designed. Places to hide, deliver mail, put out fires, be a nurse, or build a house are always in constant use by children.

The following ideas and pictures offer uses for apparatus and equipment that might be used for dramatic play:

Culverts, brightly painted with various shapes and designs and secured in various positions, can be mounted in combination with other pieces of equipment to enhance the creative possibilities

Culverts buried under mounds of dirt make exciting tunnels and hideouts

Using culverts for hideouts

Used automobile tires can be mounted in combination to make tunnels and other challenge pathways, and loose tires that can be moved can be used to build obstacles

Painted automobile tires can be used as obstacles

Large wooden boxes stacked and fastened together can become study and relaxation areas

Old cardboard cartons formerly housing refrigerators and washing machines provide unlimited ideas for acting out adult roles

Blankets and pieces of canvas are useful for building houses and holding secret meetings

Old automobiles, tractors, boats, railroad cars, etc., can provide excellent places for children to explore and act out various roles

An old boat for dramatic play

Barrels with the ends cut out can become tunnels (when anchored), horses to ride (when suspended), and climbing apparatus (when fastened together in a pyramid shape)

Tree houses and playhouses that simulate adult living enclosures are excellent apparatus for dramatic play

Discarded cable spools are good tables for doing art work, playing house, and serving dinner to others

SAFETY CONSIDERATIONS

Falls to the ground have been shown to be the largest single hazard with playground equipment. Head injuries are usually the result of a fall onto a surface not providing impact protection. This points out the need for some type of safe landing surface. This might be a sand pit which is regularly maintained, or some other shock-absorbing material placed under the apparatus. A newer product on the market is made from treated and pulverized automobile tires and offers excellent absorbent qualities.

Supervision by a competent adult is mandatory when any climbing equipment is being used. More often than not, injuries to children occur when the equipment is used in a manner for which it was not designed—climbing on top of horizontal ladders or hanging upside down on jungle bars, for example. The point is that adults must keep a watchful eye on the area of play. The equipment and apparatus should be located in one area so that it may be watched by a minimum number of teachers.

The equipment should be scaled to the proper size, depending on the age of the children using the area. There will probably be some degree of risk involved if the equipment is going to be attractive and worthwhile, but the risk factor must not be excessive. This will usually mean that the climbing equipment should

not exceed five to six feet in height for preschool children. If the equipment requires that children drop off when they become fatigued, as when using horizontal ladders, the drop should not be more than twelve inches. It seems necessary to remind children that at no time should they hang in an inverted position without being spotted by an adult.

The equipment and apparatus should be inspected regularly to ensure that all fasteners are secure and that no sharp, protruding objects are present. Protruding bolts and screws should be covered with protective caps. Wooden equipment should be refinished regularly and checked for splintering.

Finally, safety is an attitude that should be developed in children at an early age. Most children will not push themselves beyond their physical limits unless prodded by an adult. They should be praised when they act in a prudent and safe manner and reoriented when they fail to do so. It is the responsibility of the educational organization to provide a safe environment.

SUMMARY

A creative play environment is important for the optimum development of children. It can offer children the chance to develop courage and confidence in physical capacities, provide an area for developing the body physically through a play experience, and stimulate the sense of creativity in a relaxed setting. In the play environment the child can practice skills over and over without the fear of failing in front of others. On the other hand, the play area gives rise to many social opportunities and allows children to learn to cooperate without adult intervention.

When planning a play environment, several considerations should play a part. The area should have different sections for children of different ages, and the selection of equipment and apparatus should be based on the size and maturity of the children. Equipment selected for a play area should enhance physical development, should be flexible to allow for personal interpretation, and should offer children a degree of challenge and risk. Much equipment can be designed from inexpensive and primitive elements, since children universally enjoy dirt, water, and trees to climb.

Suggested pieces of equipment and apparatus are grouped according to the developmental values they offer children. Five categories are offered: upper body development, lower body development, coordination and rhythm, balance, and dramatic and creative play.

Safety is an important consideration when designing a play environment. There is a need for a shock-absorbing surface under apparatus where falls may occur. Supervision by an adult is important if climbing equipment is used. The equipment should be scaled to proper size depending on the age of the children. Equipment should be regularly inspected to assure that all fasteners are secure and no sharp objects are protruding.

Chapter 23

Equipment and Supplies

"Equipment" refers to those items of a more or less permanent nature. "Supplies" include those nondurable materials that have a limited lifetime. To illustrate the difference: playground balls are listed under Supplies, while the longer-lasting climbing ropes come under the category of Equipment. Equipment needs periodic replacement, and budgetary planning must consider the usable life span of each piece of equipment. Supplies are generally purchased on a yearly basis.

It is important not only to have adequate financing for equipment and supplies, but also to expend funds wisely.

If the objectives of physical education are to be fulfilled, there must be a good supply of instructional materials. Enough equipment should be present so that there is little waiting for turns. In handling manipulative items, the "one-for-one" principle should prevail. Each child should have an object of his own to work with. This is also true of individual mats. In partner work, there should be one object for every two children. Having a minimal operational list of instructional supplies stabilizes the teaching process.

Policies involving purchase, storage, issue, care and maintenance records, and inventory are necessary if maximum use and return from the allotted budget is to be realized. Program features should be established first; the purchasing plan will be based on this information.

Constructed or homemade equipment should receive serious consideration. Quality must not be sacrificed, however. Articles from home, such as empty plastic jugs, milk cartons, old tires, and the like should be regarded as supplementary and enrichment materials. Care must be taken that the administration does not look for the cheap, no-cost route for supplies, sacrificing

valuable learning experiences if an appreciable cost is indicated.

Some articles can be constructed sufficiently well and economically by the school or at home, and these merit consideration. Such items as yarn balls, hoops, balance beams, bounding boards, and others can be made locally.

In the case of other articles, such as nylon paddles and plastic bottle markers, the administration must be reminded that constructed equipment is usually a temporary solution. Such equipment can be used during the early phases of a program, since equipment costs are initially high and sometimes cannot be met immediately; but it should be replaced with better-quality equipment as soon as feasible.

PURCHASING POLICIES

The purchase of supplies and equipment involves careful study of needs, prevailing prices, quality of workmanship, and materials. Safety and protection of the participants are of vital concern.

Pooling the needs of the entire school system and buying in quantity generally results in better use of the tax dollar. However, there may need to be compromise about the type and brand of materials in order to satisfy different users within a school system. If bids are asked, there is need to make careful specifications for materials. Bids should be asked only on those items specified, and "just as good" merchandise should not be permitted as substitutes.

One individual within a school should be responsible for the physical education supply area, including keeping records of equipment and supplies and purchasing these items. Needs vary from school to school, and it is practical for school district authorities to deal with a single individual within a school. Prompt attention to repair and replacement of supplies is more likely under this system. This individual should also be responsible for testing various competitive products to determine which will give the best service over time. Some kind of labeling or marking of the materials is needed if this is to be accomplished.

An accurate inventory of equipment should be undertaken at the beginning and end of the school year. Through a sound system of inventorying, durability of equipment and supplies and the amount of supplies lost or misplaced can be established.

Equipment that is purchased should be of good quality. Such equipment will last from seven to ten years, and replacement costs will be held to a minimum. The policy of some school district purchasing agents of selecting items of low cost with little regard to quality, in order to stretch the budget dollar, is unsound.

Budgetary planners should consider the yearly procurement of instructional supplies, as well as major replacement and procurement of large items, usually staggered over a period of years. Once sufficient equipment and supplies have been procured, the budget problem becomes one of replacement and repair.

INDOOR EQUIPMENT

A shortcoming of many schools is the lack of suitable developmental equipment in the indoor physical education facility. As the basis for a good program, it is imperative that the gymnasium be equipped with overhead support equipment, climbing structures, climbing ropes, balance beams, and mats.

Boxes for jumping and vaulting should also receive strong consideration in planning. Overhead support equipment includes horizontal ladder sets, exercise (horizontal) bars, and chinning bars. Climbing sets may be fixed or portable. Climbing ropes are particularly valuable tools for physical education. Suggested items for consideration in equipping an indoor facility follow.

Balance Beams. A wide (four-inch) beam is recommended for the preschool, kindergarten, and early first grade. For older children, the usual two-inch beam should be used. Balance beams with alternate surfaces (two-inch or four-inch) can be constructed of normal building materials.

Balance Beam - Bench. The balance beam-bench can provide many interesting movement experiences. It can function as a bench and, when turned over, as a balance beam. When equipped with hooks, the bench can be added to other pieces of apparatus to expand the possibilities of movement.

Climbing Ropes. Climbing ropes are essential to the program. There should be at least eight ropes; having more ropes permits better group instruction. Climbing rope sets on tracks are most efficient. With little effort and loss of time, the ropes are ready for activity. Ropes are available in a variety of materials, but good quality manila hemp seems to be the most practical. Ropes should be an inch and a quarter to an inch and a half in diameter.

Portable Climbing Structures. These are portable sets usually based on wooden or metal horses, which include supported bars, ladders, and other equipment for climbing. A wide variety of common materials should be utilized for climbing. Wooden boxes, ladders, beams, and steps-slide devices represent possibilities to extend movement experiences.

Tumbling Mats. Mats are basic to any physical education program, and at least six should be on hand. Enough mats must be available to provide safety flooring for climbing apparatus. Mats should be four feet wide and six to eight feet long. Light folding mats, while not as soft as some of the others, have the advantage that the children can handle them with ease. Folded mats also stack more easily. Mats should have fasteners so that at least two may be coupled together. They should have plastic covers, as the old canvas mats are most difficult to keep clean.

Bounding Boards. These measure two feet by six feet and are generally made of three-quarter-inch marine plywood. Knots in poor plywood will cause the boards to break. Four boards should be constructed.

Balance Boards. Four to six balance boards of different types will provide a desirable extension of apparatus experiences.

Record Player. A good record player with a variable speed control is a must for the program. The physical education program should have its own record player, as it will be constantly needed for a good rhythmic program. It is also helpful to have a tape recorder for personalized routines.

Supply Cart. It is desirable to have a cart to hold supplies. Other carts can be utilized for the record player and for mats, both regular and individual.

Jumping Boxes. Small boxes used for jumping and allied locomotor movements have good value in extending the opportunities for fundamental movement skills. For preschool and kindergarten, boxes should be eight inches and sixteen inches in height. For older children, boxes 12 and 24 inches high offer sufficient challenge. The box with the lesser height can measure 16 by 16 inches, while the taller box can be 18 by 18 inches in size. The smaller box can be stored inside the larger box.

The tops of the boxes should be padded with carpet padding and covered with leather or durable plastic. Holes drilled through the sides will provide finger holds for ease of handling. Eight boxes, four of each size, are a minimum number for the average size class.

Horizontal Ladder Sets. Horizontal ladders that fold back against the wall make an excellent addition to indoor equipment. The ladder may be combined with other pieces of apparatus in a folding set.

Climbing Frames. Climbing frames are becoming increasingly popular and available in this country. A type of frame that has been well accepted in public and private schools is the Centaur Frame, which can be ordered from Centaur Athletics, Inc., Post Office Box 178, Custer, Washington 98240.

SUPPLIES FOR PHYSICAL EDUCATION

A basic list and an optional list of supplies should be established for each program. The basic list stipulates the instructional materials that should be available for teaching. In addition, there should be extra items held in storage for replacement during the year. Optional supplies will depend upon personal preferences and funds available.

Basic Supplies

Balloons (1 for each child)[1]
Balls
    Balls of various sizes
    Beach balls, 12-inch to 16-inch (15 to 20)
    Cageballs, 24-inch (2)
    Playground balls, rubber, 8½-inch (1 for each child)
    Small balls, 2¼-inch, sponge or old tennis balls, assorted colors (30 to 50)
    Yarn or fleece balls (1 for each child)
Ball inflator with gauge
Bats, plastic, and whiffle balls (10 bats and 30 balls)
Batting tees for striking skills (4 to 6)
Beanbags, 4-inch or 6-inch, assorted colors (2 for each child)
Cones, rubber, for boundary markers (24)
Gym scooters (1 per child)
Hoops, 30-inch or 36-inch (1 for each child)
Indian clubs (16 or more)
Mats, individual, 20 inches by 40 inches or 24 inches by 48 inches (1 for each child)

Paddles, wooden or clothes-hanger (1 for each child)
Parachute, 24-foot or 28-foot size (1)
Records (as needed)
Ropes
    Jump ropes, individual, 6, 7, or 8 feet long (1 for each child)
    Jump ropes, long, 14 to 16 feet long (12)
    Jump-the-shot ropes (3)
    Magic or stretch ropes (12)
Scoops, bottle (1 for each child)
Stopwatches (3)
Tambourine (1)
Tom-tom (1)
Tote bags for balls (12 or more)

Optional Supplies

Beanbag targets
Bongo boards
Deck tennis rings (16)
Frisbees (1 for each child)
Repair kits for balls
Stilts, tin can (1 set for each child)
Tape, colored—for temporary lining
Tires, old automobile or bicycle
Tool chest—saw, hammer, pliers, etc.
Tubes, auto, oversides, inflatable

The preceding list is meant to be only a representative list of optional items. Many other items can be purchased commercially or constructed and added to the list.

STORAGE PLANS

When a teacher takes a class into the gymnasium for physical education, he has the right to expect and be assured of having sufficient supplies to conduct the class. There should be a master list stipulating the kinds and quantities of supplies that should be in storage, and—most important—the supplies themselves should be on hand. The supplies in the storage facility are to be available for physical education classes and after-school activities. They should not be used for recess or free play periods, as each classroom should have its own supplies for this purpose.

A systematic procedure should be established for the storage of equipment and supplies. "A place for everything and everything in its place" is still the key to good housekeeping. Bins, shelves, and other places where supplies and equipment are to be kept should be labeled.

Some schools have found it helpful to use small supply carts. The cart holds the articles in more frequent use. It does take up space, but it is quite a time-saver. Carts can be built inexpen-

[1]Begin the year with a gross of balloons (144), as there will be considerable breakage.

sively to a personal plan, or an equipment carrier can be purchased. Other carts to hold the record player and to store and move mats are helpful.

An off-season storage area should be established to which articles not in present use can be moved. Reserve new equipment not yet placed in use should be kept in a separate area, perhaps under lock and key.

A few schools dispense with a central storage area and make each classroom responsible for its own supplies. Advantages of this approach are that (1) less time is wasted; (2) the teacher knows just what supplies are available; (3) definite responsibility may be fixed in case of loss or damage; (4) children feel a sense of responsibility for "their" materials; (5) there is no competition or overlap in demands for supplies by different classes.

Disadvantages given for this plan are that (1) it is initially expensive; (2) storage facilities are needed for each classroom; and (3) equipment must be marked carefully to ensure its being returned to the right classroom.

CARE, REPAIR, AND MARKING

A definite system should be established for repair of supplies and equipment. A quick decision needs to be made about whether a piece can be repaired locally or whether it must be sent out. If the repair process is lengthy and not efficient, children and teachers may prefer to use the article until it cannot be salvaged rather than be deprived of its use.

Balls must be inflated to their proper pressure. They should be checked periodically with an accurate gauge. (The needle should be moistened before it is inserted into the valve.) Children should not sit on balls and should kick only balls made specifically for kicking (soccer balls, footballs, and playground balls).

Softball bats and wooden paddles should not be used to hit rocks, stones, or other hard materials; they should not be knocked against fences, posts, or other objects that will damage them. Broken bats should be discarded, as they are unsafe even if taped around the break. Children should learn to keep the trademark up when batting. Bats should be taped to prevent slippage.

Cuts, abrasions, and breaks in rubber balls should be repaired immediately. In some cases, this repair can be handled by applying a vulcanizing patch of the type used for tire tube repairs. In others, a hard-setting rubber preparation may be used. Some repairs are beyond the scope of the school, however, and the ball should then be sent away for repair.

Mats are expensive, and care is needed if they are to last. A place where they can be stacked properly should be provided. A mat truck is another solution, provided there is space for storing the truck. The newer plastic or plastic-covered mats should be cleaned with a damp, soapy cloth.

For off-season storage, balls should be deflated to some extent, with enough air left in them so that they keep their shape.

For small items, clean ice-cream containers (two-gallon) make adequate storage receptacles. Most school cafeterias have these and other containers, which may be used in the storage room to provide order. Small wire baskets also make good containers for small physical education materials.

An area should be established for the equipment needing repair, so that articles out for repair are evident at a glance.

All equipment and supplies should be marked. This is particularly important for equipment issued to different classrooms. Marking can be done with indelible pencils, paint, or stencil ink. However, few marking systems are permanent, and re-marking at regular intervals is necessary. Sporting goods establishments have marking sets available for this purpose.

An electric burning pencil or stamp is also useful but must be used with caution so as not to damage the equipment being marked.

Rubber playground balls come in different colors, and an assignment to a classroom can be made on the basis of color. A code scheme can also be used, employing different colors of paint. It is possible to devise a color system by which the year of issue can be designated. This offers opportunities for research into equipment use.

RECOMMENDATIONS AND SPECIFICATIONS FOR CONSTRUCTING EQUIPMENT AND SUPPLIES

The following discussion is divided into two major sections. The first section offers recommendations for sources and materials needed to construct equipment and supplies, as well as recommended usage. The second part consists of diagrams and specifications for building equipment in an economical manner. Thus, if the recommended equipment can be described without an illustration, it will be found in the first section.

Constructed Equipment and Supplies

Some supplies are designed especially for children. Junior-size footballs and basketballs are available and should be used. Rubber-covered balls generally prove more satisfactory than the leather variety for use in the elementary school, particularly during wet weather.

Children can use light foam sponge balls for skills of the volleyball type. When playground balls are used for soccer skills, they work more satisfactorily when slightly deflated.

When children are working on simple bouncing skills, it is desirable for each child to have a ball. The supply of balls can be augmented by tennis or sponge balls. Discarded tennis balls from the high school tennis team are a good source. Holes can be poked in the tennis balls if they are too lively for the children to handle. Sponge balls are inexpensive, and, with care, they will last indefinitely.

For jump ropes, three-eighth-inch sash cord is suitable. The ends should be whipped or dipped in some type of hardening solution to prevent them from unraveling. Adhesive tape can also be used to bind the ends of the ropes. The new plastic link jumping ropes are particularly attractive and should be considered. With care, these will last indefinitely. Most jump ropes for preschool children should be six and seven feet in length. For kindergarten through second grade children, some ropes should be made eight feet in length. Instructors need a nine-foot rope. Rope ends should be marked or color-coded to identify length.

Beanbags can be made easily. Good quality, bright-colored muslin is suitable. Some teachers have had success in asking parents to save the lower pant legs of cut-off denim jeans and have the children bring them to school. This material wears extremely well. Some prefer a beanbag with an outer liner, which snaps in place to allow for washing. Another idea is to sew three sides of the beanbag permanently. The bag is filled through the fourth side, which is then whipstitched. The beans can be removed through the side when the bag is washed. Beanbags should be four or six inches square and can be filled with dried beans, peas, wheat, rice, or even building sand.

For games requiring boundary markers, pieces of rubber matting can be used. Small sticks or boards, painted white, are also excellent. A one-by-two-inch board, three or four feet in length, makes a satisfactory marker.

A jump-the-shot rope can be made by using an old, completely deflated volleyball tied to the end of a rope.

Old tires, even those from bicycles, can be used as throwing targets. See Chapter 12 for many ideas for activities utilizing tires.

Indian clubs can be turned in the school wood shops. Many substitutes can also be made, however. Two-by-two-inch lumber, cut off in short pieces (six to ten inches long) will stand satisfac-

torily. Lumber companies generally also have available round poles from one to one and a half inches in diameter. Sections of these make satisfactory Indian clubs. Broken bats also can be made into good substitute clubs.

White shoe polish can be used for marking lines and making designs. It will come off the floor with a little scrubbing.

Coffee cans (three-pound) can be used as targets.

Empty half-gallon milk cartons also have a variety of uses.

Old bowling pins can be obtained from most bowling alleys free of charge. Since they are too large for the children to handle easily, cut off the top six to eight inches. If a bowling pin is sliced horizontally, the resulting disc shapes can be used for hockey pucks and shuffle board discs. Another way to trim bowling pins is illustrated on p. 345.

Improvised balls can be made from crumpled newspaper bound with Scotch tape. Papier-mâché balls are also useful. Light foam rubber cubes can be trimmed to make interesting throwing and catching objects.

A better value for rubber traffic cones can be realized if these are purchased from a highway supply source. These are usually less expensive than those purchased from physical education equipment supply firms.

Plastic jugs can be utilized in place of traffic cones.

Diagrams and Specifications for Constructed Equipment

BALANCE BEAM

The balance beam is used for many types of activity. Two types of stands for a beam utilizing

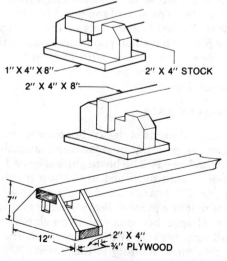

Balance beam

a two-by-four are shown. The beam can then be placed with the wide or the narrow side up, depending on the skill of the performer. If the beam is longer than eight feet, a third stand should be placed in the middle. Care must be taken to sand and apply multiple coats of finish to prevent splintering and cracking.

BALANCE BEAM–BENCH

The balance beam–bench is an extremely important piece of equipment in the elementary school and preschool program, due to its flexibility and many uses. When set on its feet, it serves as a bench for the many bench activities that develop shoulder girdle strength. When turned over, it can be used as a balance beam for many balance activities. One end can be set on a jumping box to make an incline for climbing and pulling oneself up.

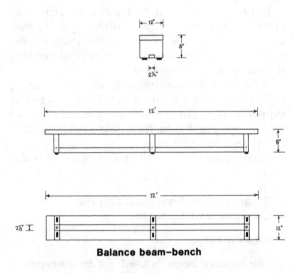

Balance beam–bench

The balance beam–bench can be set on two boxes and used as an obstacle to go over or to crawl under. The size of the beam can be varied to meet the needs and skills of the youngsters. Many people have had good success in building this piece of equipment with birch plywood. It can be made out of any good quality plywood, however.

BALANCE BOARDS

Many different styles of boards can be constructed, depending on available materials and individual needs. The board should have a piece of rubber matting glued to the top to prevent slipping. The board should be placed on an individual mat or a piece of heavy rubber matting. A square-shaped board is easier to balance than a round one, because the corners touch the floor and give more stability to the board.

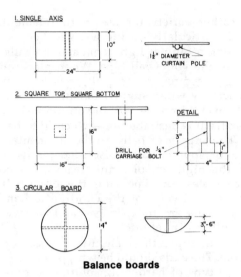

Balance boards

BLOCKS AND CONES

Blocks with grooves on the top and on one of the sides are excellent for forming hurdles with wands. A four-by-four-inch timber cut into various lengths—six, twelve, and eighteen inches—gives a variety of hurdle sizes. Cones can be notched on top and used in place of the blocks. Cut a half-inch notch on each side of the top lip of the cone.

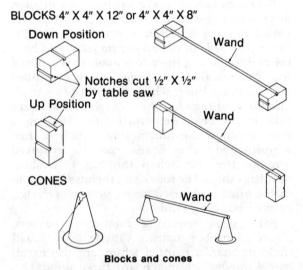

Blocks and cones

BOUNDING BOARD

Bounding boards should be made from good quality three-quarter-inch marine plywood, as this type of plywood is stronger and will hold up under repeated bounding. If the boards exhibit a tendency to break, a stop can be put under the middle of the board. A two-by-four-inch padded board the width of the bounding board usually works adequately.

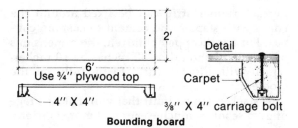

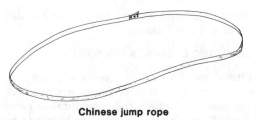

Bounding board

Chinese jump rope

It is not necessary to finish the boards. Glue the plywood to the supporting timbers. Different lengths of boards will give varying amounts of bounce and can be adapted to the size of the student. Heavier students should not bound on boards made for younger children.

Materials
1 piece ¾-inch marine plywood 2 feet by 6 feet
2 pieces 4-by-4-inch boards, 2 feet long, trimmed as shown
6 carriage bolts, ⅜-inch diameter, 4 inches long
2 pieces of carpet about 8 inches by 24 inches
Glue

BOWLING PINS

Bowling alleys will give away old reject tenpins, which can be used for many purposes. Suggested uses are for field and gymnasium markers, bowling games, and relays. Cut off the bottom two inches from the pin and sand it smooth. Pins can be numbered and decorated with decals, colored tape, or paint to enhance their attractiveness.

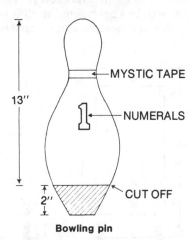

Bowling pin

CHINESE JUMP ROPE

Chinese jump ropes can be made by stringing together a number of rubber bands. A preferable method is to use common clothing elastic with a width of three-quarters of an inch and sew it

together at the ends. Another method is to use "shock cord," which can be purchased in a boating marina in different diameters. It can be fastened at the ends with a squeeze clamp. A piece of cord or elastic ten to fifteen feet long will make a good rope for young children.

CLOTHES-HANGER PADDLES

Clothes-hanger paddles can substitute quite effectively for manufactured paddles if they are used with a light foam rubber or newspaper ball. They are excellent for primary age children because of their light weight and the fact that they will not injure the children. A badminton bird can be used with the paddle for various activities such as hitting over a net and performing many individual stunts.

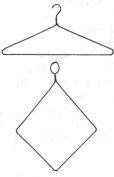

Clothes-hanger paddle

Materials
Old nylon stocking
Wire coat hanger
Masking or athletic tape
String or wire

Directions. Bend the hanger into a diamond shape. Bend the hook into a loop, which will become the handle of the paddle. Pull the stocking over the hanger, beginning away from the handle, until the toe of the nylon is as tight as possible against the point of the hanger. Hold the nylon at the neck of the hanger and stretch it as tight as possible. Tie the nylon tightly with a piece of heavy string or light wire. Wrap the rest of the nylon around the handle, making a smooth, contoured surface. Complete the paddle by wrapping tape around the entire handle to prevent it from loosening.

GEOMETRIC OBSTACLES AND TARGETS

Obstacles of various shapes and sizes can be made out of plywood or from large sheets of styrofoam if a lighter and less durable piece is desired. Bases for the targets can be made from short pieces of two-by-four lumber. The obstacles can be painted in different colors and designed in different shapes to encourage children to learn and improve their perceptual-motor abilities while at play. The targets and obstacles can be laid on the floor and used as equipment to move around and through and as part of a mini-obstacle course.

GYM SCOOTERS

Scooters are easily constructed from commonly available materials. The casters should be checked to see that they do not mark the floor.

Materials
1 piece 2-inch yellow pine board cut 12 inches by 12 inches (square)
4 ball-bearing casters with 2-inch hard rubber wheels
4 feet of protective rubber stripping and cement
Screws and paint

Directions. Actual dimensions of the board will probably be 1⅝ inches by 11⅝ inches by 11⅝ inches. Two pieces of three-quarter-inch plywood glued together can be substituted. Sand all the edges and apply two coats of paint or varnish. Fasten the four casters approximately 1½ inches in (diagonally) from the cor-

ners. A rubber strip can be fixed around the edges with staples and cement to cushion contact. For handicapped children, the dimensions of the board should be 30 inches by 10 inches, which will allow a child to lie fully on the scooter.

A stacker can be built that will make storage of gym scooters much easier and more efficient.

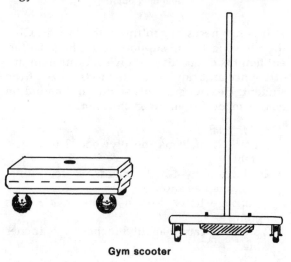

Gym scooter

If wheels are attached to the stacker, the scooters can then be easily moved where needed. The length of the center pole will depend on the number of scooters that need to be stored.

HOOPS

Hoops can be constructed at low cost from half-inch plastic water pipe, which unfortunately only comes in drab colors. Homemade hoops can also be constructed in different sizes. A short piece of doweling can be used to join the

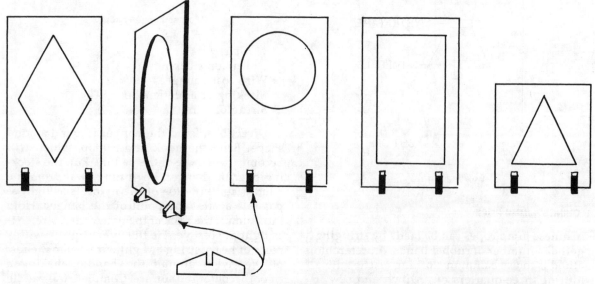

Geometric obstacles and targets

ends together, then fixed by means of a power stapler or tacks. An alternate method is to use special pipe connectors. Weatherstrip cement helps make a more permanent joint.

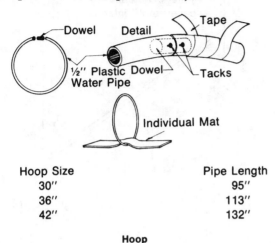

Hoop Size	Pipe Length
30″	95″
36″	113″
42″	132″

Hoop

HORIZONTAL LADDER (PORTABLE)

The horizontal ladder should be made of maple or some similar hardwood, if it will be subjected to heavy use. The height of the ladder should be five feet, and a mat should always be placed below the climber when it is in use. The width of the ladder should be eighteen inches,

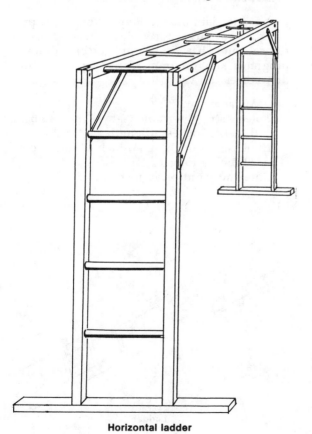

Horizontal ladder

and the rungs should be placed eight to twelve inches apart, depending on the ages of the children. The length can be varied, but should probably be from seven to nine feet. The board at the base of the ladder should be from four feet, six inches to five feet wide. If rubber feet are placed on the base, it will ensure that the ladder will not move or slide while children are playing on it.

INDIVIDUAL MATS

Individual mats can be made from indoor-outdoor carpeting that has a rubber backing. This will prevent the mat from sliding on the floor and offers some cushion. The mats can also be washed easily when they become soiled. If possible, mats of different colors are preferable, because they can be used for games, color tag, and for easy division of the class according to the color of mat. Carpet stores often have many small pieces and remnants that they will sell cheaply or give away.

20″ X 40″ or 24″ X 48″

Individual mat

JUMPING BOXES

Jumping boxes are used to develop a wide variety of body management skills. The dimensions can be varied to satisfy individual needs, but if the boxes are made that so they fit inside of each other, storage will be less of a problem. The boxes can also be used to transport equipment and supplies when not being used for their primary purpose.

Materials
¾-inch marine plywood
Wood screws, paint, and glue
Carpet pad remnants
Naugahyde or similar material to cover boxes
Upholstery tacks

Directions. The four sides should be cut to similar dimensions and then sanded together to make sure that they are exactly the same size. Use a countersink and drill the screw holes, apply glue to the joints, and screw them together. When the box is assembled, sand all edges to remove any sharpness. Paint the boxes, preferably with a latex base paint, as it will not chip as easily as enamel. If handholds are desired, drill a hole and then cut the hole with a sabre saw.

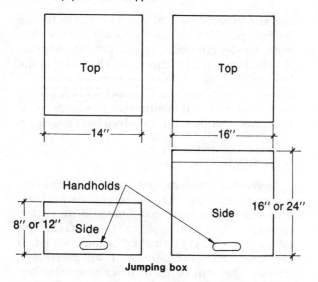

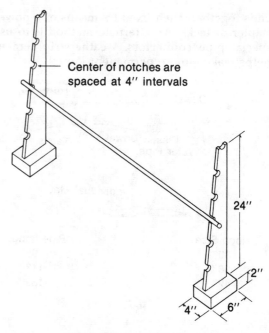

Center of notches are spaced at 4″ intervals

Jumping box

Finally, cut the carpet pad remnants to the size of the top of the box and cover with a piece of naugahyde. The naugahyde should overlap about four inches on each side of the box so that it can be folded under to double thickness and then tacked down.

Another variation with the boxes is to make two openings on the sides of the boxes that will allow a two-inch-by-eight-inch plank to fit into them. The boxes now can be used as obstacles to go over and under, to walk across, and to do animal walks across. A larger size box will make this apparatus more exciting to youngsters.

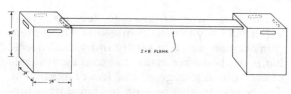

Jumping box (variation)

JUMPING STANDARDS

Jumping standards are useful for hurdling, jumping, and over-and-under activities. Many shapes and sizes are possible.

Materials
2 pieces ¾-inch plywood, cut as diagrammed, 25 inches long
2 pieces wood block, 2 inches by 4 inches by 6 inches
Glue and paint

Directions. The wood blocks should be morticed lengthwise about one-inch deep. After the uprights have been cut to form, set them with glue into the blocks, making sure that the uprights are plumb.

Jumping standard

Paint as desired. Various small colored circles can be placed at each of the corresponding notches of the uprights for better identification and also color identification and recognition.

LADDER

A ladder laid on the floor or on a mat provides a floor target for varied movement experiences and has value in perceptual-motor programs and programs for exceptional children. Sizes can vary.

Materials
2 pieces straight-grained 2-by-4-inch timbers, 9 feet, 6 inches in length
10 pieces 1¼-inch or 1½-inch circular poles, 20 inches long
Glue and paint or varnish

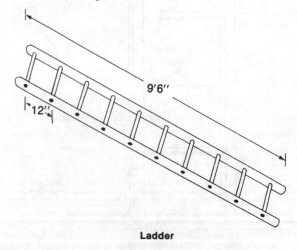

Ladder

Directions. Round ends and sand edges of the timbers. Center holes for the ladder rungs 12 inches apart, beginning 3 inches from one end. This should come out 3 inches from the other end. Cut the holes for the rungs one-sixteenth of an inch smaller than the diameter of the rungs. Drive all the rungs into one of the timbers first, gluing them. Assemble the other timber in place. Varnish or paint.

MAGIC (STRETCH) ROPES

Magic or stretch ropes can be made by stringing together 25 or 30 large rubber bands. Common clothing elastic can also be used to make excellent ropes. Some have had success with "shock cord," which can usually be purchased in a boating marina.

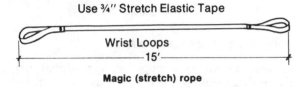

Use ¾" Stretch Elastic Tape

Wrist Loops
—15'—

Magic (stretch) rope

MAT-TUBE TRAMP

The mat-tube tramp is useful for learning balance skills as well as body control while in the air. The tubes should be tied together (or taped) so that they will not spread apart when the children are jumping on them. A tumbling mat can then be placed on the inflated tubes to create a safe jumping platform. Many of the activities that can be done on bounding boards can also be done on the mat-tramp.

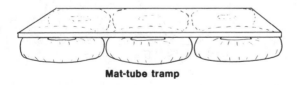

Mat-tube tramp

PADDLES

Paddles can be made in many sizes and with different thicknesses of plywood. Usually, quarter-inch plywood is best for kindergarten through second grade. Paddles can be painted or varnished; the handles can be taped to give a better grip. Holes can be drilled in the paddle area to make it lighter and decrease air resistance. Good quality plywood, perhaps marine plywood, is essential.

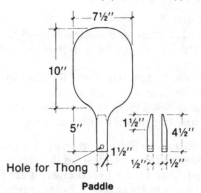

Paddle

PLASTIC MARKERS AND BALL CATCHERS (SCOOPS)

Half-gallon plastic jugs filled halfway with sand and recapped make fine boundary markers. The markers can be painted different colors to signify goal, out-of-bounds, and division lines. The jugs can also be numbered and used to designate different teaching stations or areas. Plastic bottles can also be cut down to make ball catchers.

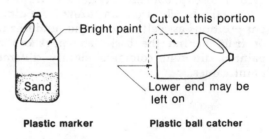

Plastic marker **Plastic ball catcher**

PULL BOARD

The pull board is an excellent piece of apparatus for building strength in the upper arm and shoulder girdle, particularly in those youngsters who are quite weak in this area. Children can pull themselves along the board with their arms while lying on their backs, sides, and fronts. To strengthen the leg areas, students can hook their toes or heels on one of the rungs and then pull their bodies toward their feet.

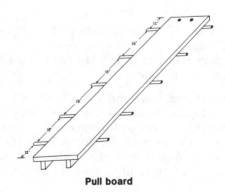

Pull board

Materials

1 board, 1 inch by 8 inches, 8 to 10 feet long
2 boards, 2 inches by 4 inches, 8 to 10 feet long
5 dowels, 1-inch diameter, 20 inches long (old broom handles work well)
8 round-head, ⅜-inch bolts, 5 inches long
10 finishing nails, 1½ inches long

Directions. Drill holes in the two-by-four on wide sides at intervals desired. Secure the two-by-four to the board two inches in from each side. Place dowels through holes, glue, secure with finishing nails so that they do not turn. Finish carefully after sanding so that children can easily slide on it. Hooks can be placed on the end so that the board could be put at an incline to create more of a challenge.

RING TOSS TARGET

Many ring toss targets can be made from one-by-four-inch lumber and old broom or mop handles. They can be made to hang on the wall or to lie flat on the ground. Quoits made from garden hose (p. 350) are excellent for throwing to the targets. Children can throw from different positions as well as overhand, underhand, or from behind the back. The pegs can be painted different colors to signify different point values.

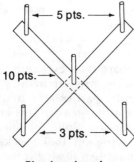

Ring toss target

Materials

2 pieces 1-by-4-inch boards, 18 to 20 inches long
5 pegs 6 inches long (old broom handles)
Screws and paint

Directions. Glue and screw the one-by-four boards together as shown. Bore the proper size holes in the boards with a brace and bit and glue or screw the pegs in the holes. Paint the base and sticks and, if desired, number each of the sticks according to their point value.

ROCKING BOAT

The rocking boat can be used as a boat and turned over to be used as a stairway. Children find this a favorite piece of equipment and can learn to cooperate together while rocking. It should be made out of three-quarter-inch stock and glued together. Screws should be used on the seats to make the boat more secure. Boards should be fastened for foot placement in front of the seats and near the bottom of the boat.

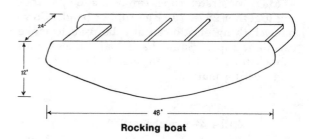

Rocking boat

QUOITS OR DECK TENNIS RINGS

Deck tennis is a popular recreational net game that requires only a ring as basic equipment. The rings are easily made by students and can also be used for playing catch and throwing at targets. The rings can be made from heavy rope by braiding the ends together, but usually the method shown is easiest. Weatherstrip cement helps strengthen the joints.

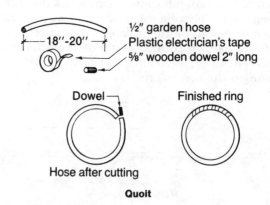

Quoit

SPONGE BALLS

Sponge balls are excellent for children when they are learning proper throwing, catching, and kicking patterns. They eliminate the child's fear of being hurt by the object and, if a heavier grade of sponge is used, they are heavy enough to throw easily. To make them, first cut a cube of sponge, and then round the corners with scissors. Different colors make the balls more enticing for the youngsters. Larger sizes should be made for those children who are in the early stages of catching and throwing. Smaller sizes seem to be easier for youngsters learning to throw one-handed.

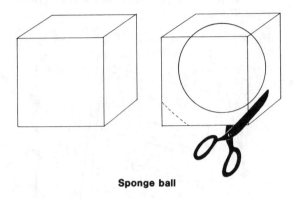

Sponge ball

STAIRS

Stairs can be used for many purposes by young children. They can be an obstacle to move over, a prop for many games and dramatic activities, and a jumping platform for them to learn to jump and land properly.

The stairs can be made out of three-quarter-inch plywood or half-inch pine. They should be securely fastened with screws and glued. The edges should be sanded, and three coats of durable varnish applied. It is important to build the steps high enough so that they are challenging and offer some element of risk to the young-sters. A tumbling mat can be placed alongside the stairs for youngsters to cushion their landing.

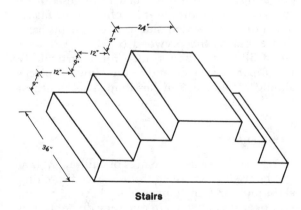

Stairs

TIN CAN STILTS

Tin can stilts are made out of clothesline and two-pound coffee cans. Punch two holes in the

sides of the cans (one on each side, near the bottoms). Turn the cans over and thread the rope through the holes. The line should be between five and seven feet in length. The plastic lids should be placed on the bottoms of the cans so that they will not mar the floors. Youngsters stand on top of the cans, hold onto the clothesline, and walk, jump, play tag games, etc.

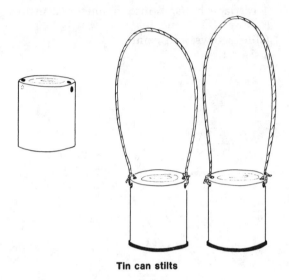

Tin can stilts

STRIKING TEE

Striking tees provide children many opportunities to strike a ball. A four- or five-foot-long piece of one-inch doweling is used, with holes drilled near the ends. Balls of various sorts can then be fastened to a piece of rope approximately ten feet in length. Nylon rope one-eighth-inch in diameter works well. The rope is then threaded through the holes, as illustrated in the diagram. The ball can be adjusted to various heights by pulling on the rope. If a number of these are made, the children can learn to hold them for one another. Doweling with a smaller diameter can be used for younger children.

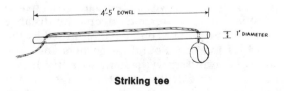

Striking tee

TIRE STANDS

Tire stands can be used to hold tires in an upright position. The tires can be used for movement problems, over-and-through relays, and vaulting activities, and as targets. Tires are much cleaner and more attractive if they are painted inside and out.

Materials
2 side pieces—boards 1 inch by 6 inches by 24 inches
2 end pieces—boards 1 inch by 6 inches by 13 inches
4 carriage bolts, ⅜-inch diameter, 2 inches long
Glue, screws, and paint
1 used tire

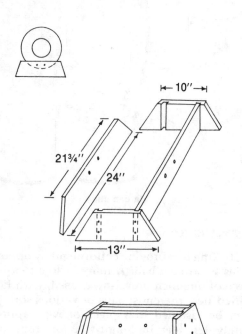

Tire stand

Directions. Cut the ends of the side boards at an angle of 70 degrees, as shown. Dado each end piece with two grooves three-quarters of an inch wide and one-quarter inch deep. The distance between the grooves will be determined by the width of the tire. Round off corners and sand edges. Glue and screw the stand together. Install tire to frame by drilling two three-eighths-inch holes in each side of the frame and tire. Secure the tire to the frame with the bolts. Paint both tire and frame a bright color.

Note. Dimensions of the frame will vary according to the size of the tire, making it necessary to adjust the frame dimensions to the tire.

TRIANGLE CLIMBER

The triangle climber is useful for climbing, and other pieces of equipment can be hooked to it. For example, the pull board or the balance beam–benches can be attached to it to create some inclined challenges.

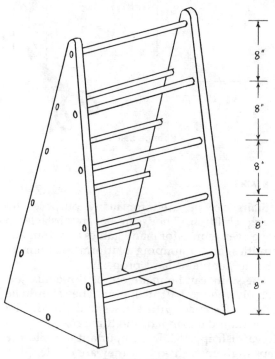

Triangle climber

It should be built from three-quarter-inch plywood, with the rungs made from one-inch doweling. Differently shaped triangles can be cut so that three different heights can be made, depending on which side is used as the base. The edges of the plywood can be filled with wood filler and then sanded for a particularly fine finish. The wide end of the plywood pieces should be about 36 inches long. The length of the dowels should be between 30 inches and 36 inches.

YARN BALLS

Yarn balls are useful pieces of equipment that can be used to enhance throwing and catching skills and for many games. They have an advantage over regular balls in that they do not hurt if one is hit by them and they can be used in the classroom or other limited areas. They can be made by older children or by the PTA. Two methods of making yarn balls are offered here; both work well, and choice is left up to the individual. When possible, wool or cotton yarns should be used, because they shrink when soaked in hot water or steamed and will make a tight, effective ball. Nylon and other synthetic yarns are impervious to water and will not shrink.

Materials (Method 1)
1 skein of yarn (wool) per ball
Piece of box cardboard 5 inches wide and
    about 10 inches long
Strong light cord for binding

Directions (Method 1). Wrap the yarn 20 to 25 times around the five-inch width of the cardboard. Slide the yarn off the cardboard and wrap it in the middle with the cord, forming a tied loop of yarn. Continue until all the yarn is used up.

Take two of the tied loops and connect (tie) them together at the centers, using several turns of the cord. This forms a bundle of two tied loops, as illustrated.

Next, tie bundles together until all bundles are used.

The final step is to cut and trim the formed ball. Cutting should be done carefully so that the lengths are reasonably even.

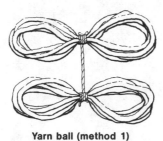

Yarn ball (method 1)

Materials (Method 2)
2 skeins of yarn (wool) per ball
2 cardboard doughnuts
Strong, lightweight cord for tieing

Directions (Method 2). Make a slit in the doughnuts so that the yarn can be wrapped around the cardboard. Holding strands from both skeins, wrap the yarn around the doughnut until the center hole is almost completely filled with yarn. Lay the doughnut of wrapped yarn on a flat surface, insert scissors between the two doughnuts, and cut around the entire outer edge. Carefully insert a double strand of the lightweight cord between the two doughnuts, catching all the individual strands around the middle. Tie as tightly as possible with a double knot. Remove the doughnuts and trim the ball if necessary.

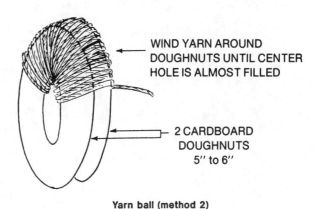

WIND YARN AROUND DOUGHNUTS UNTIL CENTER HOLE IS ALMOST FILLED

2 CARDBOARD DOUGHNUTS 5" to 6"

Yarn ball (method 2)

SUMMARY

Each child should have a piece of equipment to practice skills; this is an important guideline when deciding amounts of equipment to purchase. Equipment can be constructed by the school as long as the goal is to supplement the needed equipment and supplies rather than replace good equipment with a poor-quality, low-cost substitute. Good-quality equipment will last seven to ten years, if properly cared for, and thus on a per-year basis one is justified in buying good-quality materials.

Supplies for schools are listed, and descriptions and dimensions are offered. A systematic procedure should be established for the storage of equipment and supplies. An inventory of equipment should be taken on a regular basis and missing equipment replaced. The equipment should be marked so that it can be identified as belonging to the physical education supply room and can be returned to its proper area.

Equipment constructed by the school can serve a useful purpose. Diagrams and specifications for building such materials are offered in the last section of the chapter.

Record Sources

Bowmar Records
622 Rodier Drive
Glendale, CA 91201

Canadian F.D.S.
Educational Recordings
605 King Street
West Toronto, 2B, Canada

Children's Music Center
5373 West Pico Boulevard
Los Angeles, CA 90019

Dance Record Center
1161 Broad Street
Newark, NJ 07114

Educational Activities, Inc.
P.O. Box 392
Freeport, NY 11520

Educational Recordings of America, Inc.
P.O. Box 231
Monroe, CT 06468

Educational Record Sales
157 Chambers Street
New York, NY 10007

Folkraft Records
10 Fenwick
Newark, NJ 07714

Freda Miller Records for Dance
Department J, Box 383
Northport, Long Island, NY 11768

Hoctor Educational Records, Inc.
Waldwick, NJ 07463

Kimbo Educational Records
P.O. Box 246
Deal, NJ 07723

Mail Order Record Service
P.O. Box 7176
Phoenix, AZ 85011

Master Record Service
708 East Garfield
Phoenix, AZ 85006

Melody House Publishing Co.
819 NW 92d Street
Oklahoma City, OK 73114

Merrback Records Service
P.O. Box 7308
Houston, TX 77000

RCA Victor Education Dept. J
155 East 24th Street
New York, NY 10010

Record Center
2581 Piedmont Road NE
Atlanta, GA 30324

Rhythms Productions Records
Dept. J., Box 34485
Los Angeles, CA 90034

Rhythm Record Co.
9203 Nichols Road
Oklahoma City, OK 73120

Russell Records
P.O. Box 3318
Ventura, CA 93003

Standard Records & Hi Fi Co.
1028 NE 65th
Seattle, WA 98115

Windsor Records
5530 North Rosemead Boulevard
Temple City, CA 91780

Appendix B

Bibliography

The bibliography is organized into the following seven divisions:

1. Curriculum (Programs) in Elementary School Physical Education
2. Games and Sports
3. Rhythmic Activities—Children's Dance, Poems, and Rhymes
4. Play, Fundamental Skills, Rope Jumping, Fitness
5. Movement Theory—Educational Gymnastics
6. Special Education—Programs for the Handicapped
7. General and Miscellaneous Topics

1. CURRICULUM (PROGRAMS) IN ELEMENTARY SCHOOL PHYSICAL EDUCATION

Ackerman, Jeanne V. *Developmental Physical Activity: An Individual Approach.* Washington, D.C.: Hawkins and Associates, 1978.

American Association for Health, Physical Education, Recreation, and Dance. *Movement Activities for Places and Spaces.* Reston, Va.: AAHPERD, 1977.

Arnheim, Daniel D., and Pestolesi, Robert A. *Elementary Physical Education: A Developmental Approach.* 2d ed. St. Louis, Mo.: C. V. Mosby Co., 1978.

Block, Susan Dimond. *Me and I'm Great: Physical Education for Children Three through Eight.* Minneapolis: Burgess Publishing Co., 1977.

Brink, Edward F., and Rada, Roger L. *Experiences in Movement: Movement Activities for the Elementary School.* Dubuque, Iowa: Kendall/Hunt Publishing Co., 1975.

Bucher, Charles, and Thaxton, Nolan A. *Physical Education for Children: Movement Foundations and Experiences.* New York: Macmillan Co., 1979.

Burton, Elsie Carter. *Physical Activities for the Developing Child.* Springfield, Ill.: Charles C. Thomas, 1980.

———. *The New Physical Education for Elementary School Children.* Springfield, Ill.: Charles C. Thomas, 1977.

Caldwell, Learohn. *A Creative Approach to a Successful Elementary Physical Education Program.* Baton Rouge, La.: Legacy Publishing Co., 1977.

Cochran, Norman A., Wilkinson, Lloyd C., and Furlow, John J. *Learning on the Move: An Activity Guide for Preschool Parents and Teachers.* Dubuque, Iowa: Kendall/Hunt Publishing Co., 1975.

Corbin, Charles B. *Becoming Physically Educated in the Elementary School.* Philadelphia: Lea and Febiger, 1976.

Dauer, Victor P., and Pangrazi, Robert P. *Dynamic Physical Education for Elementary School Children.* Minneapolis: Burgess Publishing Co., 1979.

Davis, Robert G. *Elementary Physical Education: A Scientific Approach.* Winston-Salem, N.C.: Hunter Publishing Co., 1979.

Diem, Liselott. *Who Can?* Reston, Va.: AAHPERD, 1977.

Elliot, Margaret E., Anderson, Marian H., and LaBerge, Jeanne. *Play with a Purpose: A Movement Program for Children.* New York: Harper and Row, 1978.

Figley, Grace, Mitchell, Heidie C., and Wright, Barbara L. *Elementary School Physical Education: An Educational Experience.* Dubuque, Iowa: Kendall/Hunt Publishing Co., 1977.

Gallahue, David L., and Meadors, William J. *Let's Move: A Physical Curriculum for Primary, Intermediate, and Middle School Teachers.* Dubuque,

357

Iowa: Kendall/Hunt Publishing Co., 1979.

Gilbert, Anne Green. *Teaching the Three R's Through Movement Experiences.* Minneapolis: Burgess Publishing Co., 1977.

Graham, George, et al. *Children Moving: A Reflective Approach to Teaching Physical Education.* Palo Alto, Calif.: Mayfield Publishing Co., 1980.

Hall, J. Tillman, Sweeny, Nancy Hall, and Esser, Jody Hall. *Physical Education in the Elementary School.* Santa Monica, Calif.: Goodyear Publishing Co., 1980.

Hill, Katherine F., et al. *Movement Plus for the Elementary School.* Dubuque, Iowa: Kendall/Hunt Publishing Co., 1976.

Kirchner, Glenn. *Physical Education for Elementary School Children.* Dubuque, Iowa: William C. Brown Co., 1978.

Kruger, Hayes, and Kruger, Jane Myers. *Movement Education in Physical Education.* Dubuque, Iowa: William C. Brown Co., 1977.

Logsdon, Bette J., et al. *Physical Education for Children: A Focus on the Teaching Process.* Philadelphia: Lea and Febiger, 1977.

Marzollo, Jean, and Lloyd, Janice. *Learning through Play.* New York: Harper and Row, 1972.

Morris, G. S. Don. *Elementary Physical Education.* Salt Lake City: Brighton Publishing Co., 1980.

Pangrazi, Robert P., and Dauer, Victor P. *Lesson Plans for Dynamic Physical Education for Elementary School Children.* Minneapolis: Burgess Publishing Co., 1979.

Peck, Judith. *Leap to the Sun: Learning Through Dynamic Play.* Englewood Cliffs, N.J.: Prentice-Hall, 1979.

Robbins, Stuart G., chairman. *New Perspectives for Elementary School Physical Education Programs in Canada.* Ottawa, Ontario: Canadian Association for Health, Physical Education, Recreation and Dance, 1976.

Schurr, Evelyn L. *Motor Experiences for Children.* Englewood Cliffs, N.J.: Prentice-Hall, 1980.

Seagraves, Margaret C. *Lesson Plans for Elementary Physical Education.* Winston-Salem, N.C.: Hunter Publishing Co., 1979.

Stanley, Sheila. *Physical Education: A Movement Orientation.* Toronto, Ontario: McGraw-Hill Ryerson, 1977.

Torbert, Marianne. *Follow Me: A Handbook of Movement Activities for Children.* Englewood Cliffs, N.J.: Prentice-Hall, 1980.

Turner, Lowell F., and Turner, Susan Lilliman. *Elementary Physical Education: More Than Just Games.* Palo Alto, Calif.: Peek Publications, 1976.

Van Holst, Auke. *Physical Education Curriculum for Elementary Grades.* Volumes 1–4, Kindergarten through Grade 3. Dubuque, Iowa: Kendall/Hunt Publishing Co., 1980.

Vannier, Maryhelen, and Gallahue, David L. *Teaching Physical Education in Elementary Schools.* Philadelphia: W. B. Saunders Co., 1978.

2. GAMES AND SPORTS

American Association for Health, Physical Education, Recreation, and Dance. *Guidelines for Children's Sports.* Reston, Va.: AAHPERD, 1979.

Arnold, Arnold. *The World Book of Children's Games.* New York: World Publishing, 1972.

Heaton, Alma. *Double Fun: 100 Outdoor and Indoor Games.* Provo, Utah: Brigham Young University Press, 1974.

Milberg, Alan. *Street Games.* New York: McGraw-Hill, 1976.

Morris, G. S. Don. *How to Change The Games Children Play.* 2d ed. Minneapolis: Burgess Publishing Company, 1980.

Mulac, Margaret E. *Fun Games.* New York: Collier Books, 1963.

Nelson, Esther L. *Movement Games for Children of All Ages.* New York: Sterling Publishing Co., 1975.

New Games Foundation. *The New Games Book.* Garden City, N.Y.: Dolphin Books, Doubleday and Co., 1976.

Reader's Digest. *Book of 1000 Family Games.* Pleasantville, N.Y.: Reader's Digest Press, 1971.

Rockwell, Anne. *Games (and How to Play Them).* New York: Thomas Y. Crowell Co., 1973.

Spencer, Zane A. *150 Plus! Games and Activities for Early Childhood.* Belmont, Calif.: Fearon Publishers, 1976.

Thomas, Jerry R., ed. *Youth Sports Guide for Coaches and Parents.* Reston, Va.: AAHPERD, 1977.

Werner, Peter H. *A Movement Approach to Games for Children.* St. Louis, Mo.: C. V. Mosby Co., 1979.

3. RHYTHMIC ACTIVITIES—CHILDREN'S DANCE, POEMS, AND RHYMES

American Association for Health, Physical Education, Recreation, and Dance. *Children's Dance.* Reston, Va.: AAHPERD, 1973.

——. *Guidelines for Children's Dance.* Reston, Va.: AAHPERD, 1971.

Avenel Books. *177 Favorite Poems for Children.* New York: Crown Publishers, 1974.

——. *Treasury of Best-Loved Rhymes.* New York: Crown Publishers, 1967.

Bley, Edgar S. *The Best Singing Games for All Ages.* New York: Sterling Publishing Co., 1957.

Boorman, Joyce. *Creative Dance in the First Three Grades.* New York: David McKay Co., 1969.

Gelineau, R. Phyllis. *Songs in Action.* New York: McGraw-Hill, 1974.

Joyce, Mary. *First Steps in Teaching Creative Dance to Children.* Palo Alto, Calif.: Mayfield Publishing Co., 1980.

Nelson, Esther. *Dancing Games for Children of All Ages.* New York: Sterling Publishing Co., 1973.

———. *Musical Games for Children of All Ages.* New York: Sterling Publishing Co., 1976.

Vick, Marie, and Cox, Rosann McLaughlin. *A Collection of Dances for Children.* Minneapolis: Burgess Publishing Co., 1970.

4. PLAY, FUNDAMENTAL SKILLS, ROPE JUMPING, FITNESS

American Association for Health, Physical Education, Recreation, and Dance. *Play.* Reston, Va.: AAHPERD, 1980.

Diem, Liselott. *Children Learn Physical Skills.* Volume 1, *Birth to 3 years,* Volume 2, *Ages 3–5.* Reston, Va.: AAHPERD, 1978.

Fahey, Thomas D. *Fun and Fitness for Kids.* New York: Butterick Publishing Co., 1979.

Frost, Joe L., and Klein, Barry L. *Children's Play and Playgrounds.* Boston: Allyn and Bacon, 1979.

Jacobson, Phyllis C., and Valentine, Ann. *Fundamental Skills in Physical Education.* Provo, Utah: Brigham Young University Press, 1977.

Lorin, Martin I. *The Parents' Book of Physical Fitness for Children.* New York: Atheneum, 1978.

Markum, Patricia Maloney, editorial associate. *Play: Children's Business.* Washington, D.C.: Association for Childhood Education International, 1974.

Mather, June. *Learning Can Be Child's Play.* Nashville, Tenn.: Abingdon Press, 1976.

O'Quinn, Garland, Jr. *Developmental Gymnastics.* Austin: University of Texas Press, 1978.

Piers, Maria W., ed. *Play and Development: A Symposium.* New York: W. W. Norton and Co., 1972.

Skolnik, Peter L. *Jump Rope!* New York: Workman Publishing Co., 1974.

Smith, Paul. *Rope Skipping: Rhythms, Routines, Rhymes.* Freeport, N.Y.: Educational Activities, 1969.

Weininger, Otto. *Play and Education: The Basic Tool for Early Childhood Learning.* Springfield, Ill.: Charles C. Thomas, 1979.

Wickstrom, Ralph L. *Fundamental Motor sPatterns.* Philadelphia: Lea and Febiger, 1977.

5. MOVEMENT THEORY— EDUCATIONAL GYMNASTICS

American Association for Health, Physical Education, Recreation, and Dance. *Educational Gymnastics.* Reston, Va.: AAHPERD, 1978.

Cope, John. *Discovery Methods in Physical Education.* London: Thomas Nelson and Sons, 1967.

Gensemer, Robert E. *Movement Education.* Washington, D.C.: National Education Association, 1979.

Gerhardt, Lydia A. *Moving and Knowing: The Young Child Orients Himself in Space.* Englewood Cliffs, N.J.: Prentice-Hall, 1973.

Morison, Ruth. *A Movement Approach to Educational Gymnastics.* Boston: Plays, 1974.

Noble, Neal, consultant. *Learning Through Movement Education.* Chicago: The Athletic Institute, 1975.

Stirrat, Margaret H. *Introducing Educational Gymnastics in the Primary School.* Woll-

stonecraft, Australia: Physical Education Publications Co-operative, 1972.

Thornton, Samuel. *Laban's Theory of Movement: A New Perspective.* Boston: Plays, 1971.

Tillotson, Joan, et al. *A Program of Movement Education for the Plattsburgh Elementary Public Schools: The Final Report of a Title III Elementary and Secondary Program.* Plattsburgh (N.Y.) Public Schools, 1969.

Williams, Jean. *Themes for Educational Gymnastics.* London: Henry Kimpton, 1979.

6. SPECIAL EDUCATION— PROGRAMS FOR THE HANDICAPPED

American Association for Health, Physical Education, Recreation and Dance. *Get a Wiggle On.* Reston, Va.: AAHPERD, 1978. Helping the blind and visually impaired.

———. *Move It!!!* Reston, Va.: AAHPERD, 1978. Helping the blind and visually impaired.

———. *Physical Education and Recreation for Individuals with Multiple Handicapping Conditions.* Reston, Va.: AAHPERD, 1978.

Arnheim, Daniel D., and Sinclair, William A. *The Clumsy Child: A Program of Motor Therapy.* St. Louis, Mo.: C. V. Mosby Co., 1979.

Buell, Charles E. *Physical Education for Blind Children.* Springfield, Ill.: Charles C. Thomas, 1974.

Cadman, Louis A., Fullerton, H. M., and Wylie, Edward J. *Parents Handbook: A Handbook for Parents of Pre School Handicapped Children.* Wichita Falls, Tex.: Region IX Education Service Center, 1976.

Clarke, H. Harrison, and Clarke, David H. *Developmental and Adapted Physical Education.* Englewood Cliffs, N.J.: Prentice-Hall, 1977.

Cratty, Bryant J. *Motor Activity and the Education of Retardates.*

Philadelphia: Lea and Febiger, 1974.

———. *Remedial Motor Activity for Children*. Philadelphia: Lea and Febiger, 1975.

Drowatzky, John N. *Physical Education for the Mentally Retarded*. Philadelphia: Lea and Febiger, 1971.

Gliedman, John, and Roth, William. *The Unexpected Minority: Handicapped Children in America*. New York: Harcourt Brace Jovanovich, 1980.

National Education Association. *Education for All Handicapped Children: A Study Report*. Washington, D.C.: National Education Association, 1978.

Pohl, Rudolph. *The Handbook of Special Education*. Old Saybrook, Conn.: Institute for Learning, 1975.

Sherrill, Claudine. *Creative Arts for the Severely Handicapped*. Springfield, Ill.: Charles C. Thomas, 1979.

Vodola, Thomas M. *An Individualized P. E. Program for the Handicapped Child*. Neptune City, N.J.: V.E.E., 1973.

———. *Diagnostic-Prescriptive Motor and Physical Tasks for the Normal and Atypical Individual*. Neptune City, N.J.: V.E.E., 1978.

———. *Individualized Motor Programming: Normal, Mentally Retarded, and Learning Disabled*. Neptune City, N.J.: V.E.E., 1979.

Watson, Marjorie. *Mainstreaming, with Special Emphasis on the Educable Mentally Retarded*. Washington, D.C.: National Education Association, 1977.

Werner, Peter H. *Learning Through Movement: Teaching Cognitive Content Through Physical Education*. St. Louis, Mo.: C. V. Mosby Co., 1979.

7. GENERAL AND MISCELLANEOUS TOPICS

Aitken, Margaret H. *Play Environment for Children: Play Space, Improvised Equipment, and Facilities*. Bellingham, Wash.: Educational Designs and Consultants, 1972.

American Association for Health, Physical Education, Recreation and Dance. *Echoes of Influence for Elementary School Physical Education*. Reston, Va.: AAHPERD, 1977.

———. *Essentials of a Quality Elementary School Physical Education Program*. Reston, Va.: AAHPERD, 1970.

———. *Foundations and Practices in Perceptual Motor Learning: A Quest for Understanding*. Reston, Va.: AAHPERD, 1971.

———. *Personalized Learning in Physical Education*. Reston, Va.: AAHPERD, 1976.

———. *Teaching Safety in the Elementary School*. Reston, Va.: AAHPERD, 1972.

American Association for Health, Physical Education, Recreation and Dance and The Athletic Institute. *Planning Facilities for Athletics, Physical Education and Recreation*. Reston, Va.: AAHPERD, 1979.

Appenzeller, Herb. *Physical Education and the Law*. Charlottesville, Va.: The Michie Co., 1978.

Baldwin, Alfred L. *Theories of Child Development*. New York: John Wiley and Sons, 1967.

Bruya, Lawrence D., ed. *Proceedings: Early Development of Motor Patterns in Young Children*. Denton, Tex.: North Texas State University, 1980.

Cratty, Bryant J. *Movement Behavior and Motor Learning*. Philadelphia: Lea and Febiger, 1973.

Felker, Donald. *Helping Children to Like Themselves*. Minneapolis: Burgess Publishing Co., 1974.

Flinchum, Betty M. *Motor Development in Early Childhood*. St. Louis, Mo.: C. V. Mosby Co., 1975.

Furth, Hans, and Wachs, Harry. *Thinking Goes to School: Piaget's Theory in Practice*. New York: Oxford University Press, 1974.

Gallahue, David L. *Developmental Play Equipment for Home and School*. New York: John Wiley and Sons, 1975.

Hafen, Brent Q., ed. *Weight and Obesity*. Provo, Utah: Brigham Young University Press, 1975.

Humphrey, James H. *Improving Learning Ability through Compensatory Physical Education*. Springfield, Ill.: Charles C. Thomas, 1976.

Gesell, Arnold, Ilg, Frances L., and Ames, Louise Bates. *The Child from Five to Ten*. New York: Harper and Row, 1976.

Jacobson, Edmund. *Teaching and Learning*. Chicago: National Foundation for Progressive Education, 1973.

McClenaghan, Bruce A., and Gallahue, David L. *Fundamental Movement: A Developmental and Remedial Approach*. Philadelphia: W. B. Saunders Co., 1978.

———. *Fundamental Movement: Observation and Evaluation*. Philadelphia: W. B. Saunders Co., 1978.

Malina, Robert M. *Growth and Development*. Minneapolis: Burgess Publishing Co., 1975.

Sage, George. *Introduction to Motor Behavior: A Neuropsychological Approach*. Reading, Mass.: Addison-Wesley Publishing Co., 1971.

Siedentop, Daryl. *Developing Teaching Skills in Physical Education*. Boston: Houghton Mifflin Co., 1976.

Skinner, Louise. *Motor Development in the Preschool Years*. Springfield, Ill.: Charles C. Thomas, 1979.

Werner, Peter H., and Simmons, Richard A. *Inexpensive Physical Education Equipment for Children*. Minneapolis: Burgess Publishing Co., 1976.

U.S. Consumer Product Safety Commission. *Hazard Analysis of Injuries Relating to Playground Equipment.* Washington, D.C.: U.S. Consumer Product Safety Commission, 1975.

Zaichkowsky, Leonard D., Zaichkowsky, Linda B., and Martinek, Thomas J. *Growth and Development: The Child and Physical Activity.* St. Louis, Mo.: C. V. Mosby Co., 1980.

Index

F

M